Wireless Radio–Frequency Standards and System Design:

Advanced Techniques

Gianluca Cornetta
Universidad San Pablo-CEU, Spain

David J. Santos
Universidad San Pablo-CEU, Spain

Jose Manuel Vazquez
Universidad San Pablo-CEU, Spain

A volume in the Advances in Wireless
Technologies and Telecommunication
(AWTT) Book Series

An Imprint of IGI Global

Managing Director:	Lindsay Johnston
Senior Editorial Director:	Heather Probst
Book Production Manager:	Sean Woznicki
Development Manager:	Joel Gamon
Development Editor:	Myla Harty
Acquisitions Editor:	Erika Gallagher
Typesetters:	Milan Vracarich, Jr.
Print Coordinator:	Jamie Snavely
Cover Design:	Nick Newcomer, Greg Snader

Published in the United States of America by
Engineering Science Reference (an imprint of IGI Global)
701 E. Chocolate Avenue
Hershey PA 17033
Tel: 717-533-8845
Fax: 717-533-8661
E-mail: cust@igi-global.com
Web site: http://www.igi-global.com

Library of Congress Cataloging-in-Publication Data

Wireless radio-frequency standards and system design : advanced techniques / Gianluca Cornetta, David J. Santos, and Jose Manuel Vazquez, editors.
    p. cm.
  Includes bibliographical references and index.
  ISBN 978-1-4666-0083-6 (hardcover) -- ISBN 978-1-4666-0084-3 (ebook) -- ISBN 978-1-4666-0085-0 (print & perpetual access) 1. Radio frequency integrated circuits--Design and construction. 2. Systems on a chip. 3. Metal oxide semiconductors, Complementary. I. Cornetta, Gianluca, 1969- II. Santos, David J., 1967- III. Vazquez, Jose Manuel, 1954-
  TK7874.78.W57 2012
  621.384'12--dc23
                        2011048062

This book is published in the IGI Global book series Advances in Wireless Technologies and Telecommunication (AWTT) (ISSN: 2327-3305; eISSN: 2327-3313)

British Cataloguing in Publication Data
A Cataloguing in Publication record for this book is available from the British Library.

All work contributed to this book is new, previously-unpublished material. The views expressed in this book are those of the authors, but not necessarily of the publisher.

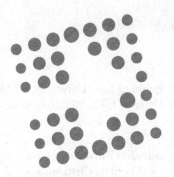

Advances in Wireless Technologies and Telecommunication (AWTT) Book Series

Xiaoge Xu
The University of Nottingham Ningbo China

ISSN: 2327-3305
EISSN: 2327-3313

MISSION

The wireless computing industry is constantly evolving, redesigning the ways in which individuals share information. Wireless technology and telecommunication remain one of the most important technologies in business organizations. The utilization of these technologies has enhanced business efficiency by enabling dynamic resources in all aspects of society.

The **Advances in Wireless Technologies and Telecommunication Book Series (AWTT)** aims to provide researchers and academic communities with quality research on the concepts and developments in the wireless technology fields. Developers, engineers, students, research strategists, and IT managers will find this series useful to gain insight into next generation wireless technologies and telecommunication.

COVERAGE

- Cellular Networks
- Digital Communication
- Global Telecommunications
- Grid Communications
- Mobile Technology
- Mobile Web Services
- Network Management
- Virtual Network Operations
- Wireless Broadband
- Wireless Sensor Networks

IGI Global is currently accepting manuscripts for publication within this series. To submit a proposal for a volume in this series, please contact our Acquisition Editors at Acquisitions@igi-global.com or visit: http://www.igi-global.com/publish/.

Titles in this Series

For a list of additional titles in this series, please visit: www.igi-global.com

Cognitive Radio Technology Applications for Wireless and Mobile Ad Hoc Networks
Natarajan Meghanathan (Jackson State University, USA) and Yenumula B. Reddy (Grambling State University, USA)
Information Science Reference • copyright 2013 • 370pp • H/C (ISBN: 9781466642218) • US $190.00 (our price)

Evolution of Cognitive Networks and Self-Adaptive Communication Systems
Thomas D. Lagkas (University of Western Macedonia, Greece) Panagiotis Sarigiannidis (University of Western Macedonia, Greece) Malamati Louta (University of Western Macedonia, Greece) and Periklis Chatzimisios (Alexander TEI of Thessaloniki, Greece)
Information Science Reference • copyright 2013 • 438pp • H/C (ISBN: 9781466641891) • US $195.00 (our price)

Tools for Mobile Multimedia Programming and Development
D. Tjondronegoro (Queensland University of Technology, Australia)
Information Science Reference • copyright 2013 • 357pp • H/C (ISBN: 9781466640542) • US $190.00 (our price)

Cognitive Radio and Interference Management: Technology and Strategy
Meng-Lin Ku (National Central University, Taiwan, R.O.C.) and Jia-Chin Lin (National Central University, Taiwan, R.O.C.)
Information Science Reference • copyright 2013 • 354pp • H/C (ISBN: 9781466620056) • US $190.00 (our price)

Wireless Radio-Frequency Standards and System Design Advanced Techniques
Gianluca Cornetta (Universidad San Pablo-CEU, Spain) David J. Santos (Universidad San Pablo-CEU, Spain) and Jose Manuel Vazquez (Universidad San Pablo-CEU, Spain)
Engineering Science Reference • copyright 2012 • 422pp • H/C (ISBN: 9781466600836) • US $195.00 (our price)

Femtocell Communications and Technologies Business Opportunities and Deployment Challenges
Rashid A. Saeed (UIA, Malaysia) Bharat S. Chaudhari (International Institute of Information Technology, India) and Rania A. Mokhtar (Sudan University of Science and Technology, Sudan)
Information Science Reference • copyright 2012 • 295pp • H/C (ISBN: 9781466600928) • US $190.00 (our price)

Advanced Communication Protocol Technologies Solutions, Methods, and Applications
Katalin Tarnay (University of Pannonia, Hungary) Gusztáv Adamis (Budapest University of Technology and Economics, Hungary) and Tibor Dulai (University of Pannonia, Hungary)
Information Science Reference • copyright 2011 • 592pp • H/C (ISBN: 9781609607326) • US $195.00 (our price)

www.igi-global.com

701 E. Chocolate Ave., Hershey, PA 17033
Order online at www.igi-global.com or call 717-533-8845 x100
To place a standing order for titles released in this series, contact: cust@igi-global.com
Mon-Fri 8:00 am - 5:00 pm (est) or fax 24 hours a day 717-533-8661

Table of Contents

Section 1
Novel Techniques, Design and Simulation

Section 2
RF-MEMS and Passive Devices

Section 3
Baseband Processing and Wireless Standards

Detailed Table of Contents

Section 1
Novel Techniques, Design and Simulation

    Thierry Taris, University Bordeaux I, France
    Aya Mabrouki, University Bordeaux I, France

In this chapter the authors evaluate a new and promising solution to the problem of power consumption based on "optimum gate biasing." This technique consists in tracking the MOS operating region wherein the third derivation of drain current is zero. The method leads to a significant IIP3 improvement; however, the sensitivity to process drifts requires the use of a specific bias circuit to track the optimum biasing condition.

    Rafaella Fiorelli, University of Seville, Spain & Instituto de Microelectrónica de Sevilla, Spain
    Eduardo Peralías, Instituto de Microelectrónica de Sevilla, Spain
    Fernando Silveira, Universidad de la República, Uruguay

This chapter presents a design optimization methodology for analog radiofrequency (RF) blocks based on the gm/ID technique and on the exploration of all-inversion regions (from weak inversion or subthreshold to strong inversion or above threshold) of the MOS transistor in nanometer technologies. The use of semi-empirical models of MOS transistors and passive components, as inductors or capacitors, assure accurate designs, reducing time and efforts for transferring the initial block specifications to a compliant design. This methodology permits the generation of graphical maps to visualize the evolution of the circuit characteristics when sweeping both the inversion zone and the bias current, allowing reaching very good compromises between performance aspects of the circuit (e.g. noise and power consumption) for a set of initial specifications. In order to demonstrate the effectiveness of this methodology, it is applied in the design of two basic blocks of RF transceivers: low noise amplifiers (LNAs) and voltage controlled oscillators (VCOs), implemented in two different nanometer technologies and specified to be part of a 2.4 GHz transceiver. A possible design flow of each block is provided; resulting designs are implemented and verified both with simulations and measurements.

J. P. Carmo, University of Minho, Portugal
J. H. Correia, University of Minho, Portugal

This chapter presents a wireless interface for intra vehicle communications (data acquisition from sensors, control and multimedia) at 5.7 GHz. As part of the wireless interface, a RF transceiver was fabricated in the UMC 0.18 μm RF CMOS process and when activated, it presents a total power consumption is 23 mW with the voltage supply of 1.5 V. This allows the use of only a coin sized battery for supplying the interface. The carrier frequency can be digitally selectable and take one of 16 possible frequencies in the range 5.42 5.83 GHz, adjusted in steps of 27.12 MHz. These multiple carriers allow a better spectrum allocation and at the same time will improve the channel capacity due to the possibility to allow multiple accesses with multiple frequencies.

Amparo Herrera, University of Cantabria, Spain

One of the industry sectors with the largest revenue in the telecommunication field is the wireless communications field. Wireless operators compete for being the first to place their products in the market to obtain the highest revenues. Moreover, they try to offer products that fulfill the user demands in terms of price, battery life, and product quality. All these requirements must be also fulfilled by the designer of the MMIC (Microwave Monolithic Integrated Circuits) circuits that will be used in those wireless terminals, achieving a reliable design with high performance, low cost, and if possible, in one or two foundry iterations, to bring the product out to the market as soon as possible.

Ahmed El Oualkadi, Abdelmalek Essaadi University, Morocco

This chapter presents a systematic design of a Σ-Δ fractional-N Phase-Locked Loop based on hardware description language behavioral modeling. The proposed design consists of describing the mixed behavior of this PLL architecture starting from the specifications of each building block. The description language models of critical PLL blocks have been described in VHDL-AMS, which is an IEEE standard, to predict the different specifications of the PLL. The effect of different noise sources has been efficiently introduced to study the overall system performances. The obtained results are compared with transistor-level simulations to validate the effectiveness of the proposed models in the frequency range around 2.45 GHz for wireless applications.

Section 2
RF-MEMS and Passive Devices

Chapter 6

Anis Nurashikin Nordin, International Islamic University Malaysia, Malaysia

Today's high-tech consumer market demands complex, portable personal wireless consumer devices that are low-cost and have small sizes. Creative methods of combining mature integrated circuit (IC) fabrication techniques with innovative radio-frequency micro-electro-mechanical systems (RF-MEMS) devices have given birth to wireless transceiver components operated at higher frequencies but manufactured at the low-cost of standard ICs. Oscillators, RF bandpass filters, and low noise amplifiers are the most critical and important modules of any wireless transceiver. Their individual characteristics determine the overall performance of a transceiver. This chapter illustrates RF-oscillators, which utilize MEMS devices such as resonators, varactors, and inductors for frequency generation. Emphasis will be given on state of the art RF-MEMS components such as film bulk acoustic wave, surface acoustic wave, flexural mode resonators, lateral and vertical varactors, and solenoid and planar inductors. The advantages and disadvantages of each device structure are described, with reference to the most recent work published in the field.

Chapter 7

Masoud Baghelani, Sahand University of Technology, Iran
Habib Badri Ghavifekr, Sahand University of Technology, Iran
Afshin Ebrahimi, Sahand University of Technology, Iran

The aim of this chapter is to provide the reader with deep information in the field of RF MEMS, covering their current and possible applications, design, modeling, and simulation. Also, their problems, such as power handling, packaging, frequency extension, etcetera, are discussed. In addition, this chapter will introduce case studies in RF MEMS area for researchers.

Chapter 8

Gianluca Cornetta, Universidad San Pablo-CEU, Spain & Vrije Universiteit Brussel, Belgium
David J. Santos, Universidad San Pablo-CEU, Spain
José Manuel Vázquez, Universidad San Pablo-CEU, Spain

The modern wireless communication industry is demanding transceivers with a high integration level operating in the gigahertz frequency range. This, in turn, has prompted an intense research in the area of monolithic passive devices. Modern fabrication processes provide now the capability to integrate onto a silicon substrate inductors and capacitors, enabling a broad range of new applications. Inductors and capacitors are the core elements of many circuits, including low-noise amplifiers, power amplifiers, baluns, mixers, and oscillators, as well as fully-integrated matching networks. While the behavior and the modeling of integrated capacitors are well understood, the design of an integrated inductor is still a challenging task since its magnetic behavior is hard to predict accurately. As the operating frequency approaches the gigahertz range, device nonlinearities, coupling effects, and skin effect dominate, making difficult the design of critical parameters such as the self-resonant frequency, the quality factor, and self and mutual inductances. However, despite the parasitic effects and the low quality-factor, the integrated inductors still allow the implementation of integrated circuits with improved performances under low supply voltage. In this chapter, the authors review the technology behind monolithic capacitors and inductors on silicon substrate for high-frequency applications, with major emphasis on physical implementation and modeling.

Section 3
Baseband Processing and Wireless Standards

Chapter 9

Javier González Bayón, Universidad Politécnica de Madrid, Spain
Carlos Carreras Vaquer, Universidad Politécnica de Madrid, Spain
Angel Fernández Herrero, Universidad Politécnica de Madrid, Spain

Orthogonal frequency division multiplexing (OFDM) has been the focus of many studies in wireless communications because of its high transmission capability and its robustness to the effects of frequency-selective multipath channels. However, it is well known that OFDM systems are much more sensitive to a carrier frequency offset (CFO) than single carrier schemes with the same bit rate. Therefore, a frequency synchronization process is necessary to overcome this sensitivity to frequency offset. Synchronization is performed in two stages: acquisition and tracking. After a first estimation and correction of the CFO performed in the acquisition stage, there still remains a residual frequency offset (RFO) due to real system conditions. Therefore, the RFO tracking has to be performed for all the receiving data.

Chapter 10

Gianluca Cornetta, Universidad San Pablo-CEU, Spain & Vrije Universiteit Brussel, Belgium
David J. Santos, Universidad San Pablo-CEU, Spain
José Manuel Vázquez, Universidad San Pablo-CEU, Spain

Multi-mode and multi-band transceivers, i.e. transceivers with the capability to operate in different frequency bands and to support different waveforms and signaling schemes, are objects of intense study. In fact, hardware reuse among different standards would help to reduce production costs, power consumption, and to increase the integration level of a given implementation. The design of such transceivers is indeed very complex, because it not only implies the choice of the architecture more suitable for the target application, but also the choice and the design of reconfigurable building blocks to perform tuning among the different standards and signaling schemes. In addition, different standards may have considerably different requirements in terms of receiver sensitivity, linearity, input dynamic range, error vector magnitude (EVM), signal bandwidth, and data rate, which in turn make the design of a multi-mode reconfigurable transceiver a very challenging task. In this chapter, the authors present the most common techniques and architecture schemes used in modern wireless communication systems supporting standards for cellular, wireless local area networks (WLAN), and wireless personal area networks (WPAN), i.e. GSM, WCDMA, IEEE 802.11 (Wi-Fi), IEEE 802.15.1 (Bluetooth), IEEE 802.15.4 (Zigbee), and IEEE 802.15.3 (UWB). State-of-the-art techniques for multi-standard cellular, WLAN, and WPAN transceivers are thoroughly analyzed and reviewed, with special emphasis on those relying on bandpass sampling and multi-rate signal processing schemes.

Chapter 11

    Angel Fernández Herrero, Universidad Politécnica de Madrid, Spain
    Gabriel Caffarena Fernández, Universidad San Pablo-CEU, Spain
    Alberto Jiménez Pacheco, École Polytechnique Fédérale de Lausanne, Switzerland
    Juan Antonio López Martín, Universidad Politécnica de Madrid, Spain
    Carlos Carreras Vaquer, Universidad Politécnica de Madrid, Spain
    Francisco Javier Casajús Quirós, Universidad Politécnica de Madrid, Spain

In this chapter, the main aspects of the design of baseband hardware modules are addressed. Special attention is given to word-length optimization, implementation, and validation tasks. As a case study, the design of an equalizer for a 4G MIMO receiver is addressed. The equalizer is part of a communication system able to handle up to 32 users and provide transmission bit-rates up to 125 Mbps. The word-length optimization process are explained first, as well as techniques to reduce computation times. Then, the case study are presented and analyzed, and the different tasks and tools required for its implementation are explained. FPGAs are selected as the target implementation technology due to its interest for the DSP community.

Chapter 12

    Hrishikesh Venkataraman, Dublin City University (DCU), Ireland
    Bogdan Ciubotaru, Dublin City University (DCU), Ireland
    Gabriel-Miro Muntean, Dublin City University (DCU), Ireland

The next generation of cellular networks has evolved from voice-based to data-centric communication. The recent focus has been mainly on high data-rate services like mobile gaming, high quality music, Internet browsing, video streaming, etc. which consumes lots of bandwidth. This puts a severe constraint on the available radio resource. In this chapter, the IEEE 802.16 based multihop WiMAX networks (802.16j) is introduced, and the system design is explained in detail. The chapter outlines the background and the importance of multihop wireless networks, especially in the cellular domain. Different types of multihop design for WiMAX is explained, along with a detailed analysis of the effect of the number of hops in the WiMAX networks. Further, in order to support next generation rich media services, the system design requirements and challenges for real-time video transmission are explained.

Preface

The amazing progress experienced by CMOS VLSI technology in the last decade, in the pursuit of an ever increasing scaling of the feature size, has led to extremely tiny devices. The scaling of transistor size has improved not only the achievable level of integration, but also the transistor switching speed. This, in turn, has disclosed new potential applications for CMOS technology in high-performance RF communication systems and devices.

In state-of-the-art CMOS processes it is quite common to have transistors with a unity current gain frequency (f_T) larger than 100 GHz, which makes these devices suitable for very high-frequency applications that were once dominated by bipolar, BiCMOS, and GaAs technologies. Fully-CMOS radio transceivers and systems-on-chip are rapidly gaining popularity and increasing their share into the wireless market. Moreover, RF CMOS technologies bring with them new architectures and astonishing levels of integration that cannot be achieved with other technologies. CMOS technology brought with it new transceiver topologies and circuit techniques. The traditional super-heterodyne receiver was soon replaced by homodyne architectures with direct conversion to baseband, much more suitable for a fully monolithic implementation in CMOS. On the other hand, monolithic planar inductors with decent quality factors were soon available, allowing the design of tunable amplifiers, on-chip matching networks, source-degenerated amplifiers, et cetera. Consequently, RF CMOS technology has become the dominant technology for applications such as GPS receivers, GSM cellular transceivers, wireless LAN, and wireless short-range personal area networks based on IEEE 802.15.1 (Bluetooth) or IEEE 802.15.4 (ZigBee) standards. In many cases, such transceivers must meet very aggressive design goals such as low cost, low-power dissipation, and light weight. CMOS integrated circuits for RF applications are being intensely studied due to their potential for low cost, high scalability, and integration, which makes them suitable for Systems on Chip (SoC) implementations.

Mastering good design practices in the CMOS RF area has become a necessity for current RF Engineers. Traditional design practices are now undergoing a process of deep changes that will leave behind the now mature analog-based techniques, and will gradually move into software-controlled, mainly digital architectures (the so-called, Software Defined Radio paradigm). In addition, the introduction of deep-submicron processes (90 nm and below) poses new severe design problems and challenges.

This book introduces the RF designer to this brave new world. The RF designer in mind is a graduate or PhD student in the RF area, or a practicing professional who needs a better insight on radio frequency circuit and systems design. In both cases, the objective is to present in a single volume most of the hottest topics and latest developments in the RF area.

The book is divided into three sections:

1. Novel techniques, Design and Simulation
2. RF-MEMS and Passive Devices
3. Baseband Processing and Wireless Standards

Section 1 (Chapters 1 to 5) explores new design practices, simulation techniques, and applications. It comprises five chapters dealing with topics such as LNA linearization, low power design based on the g_m/I_D technique, and behavioral modeling and co-simulation of analog and mixed-signal complex blocks for RF applications.

Section 2 (Chapters 6 to 8) deals with integrated passive devices for RF-ICs; both standard planar monolithic devices (capacitor and inductors) and MEMS (Micro-electromechanical Systems) are thoroughly treated. SAW (Surface Acoustic Waves) and BAW (Bulk Acoustic Waves) design and implementation issues are presented and analyzed, as well as all the issues related with their integration with bulk CMOS processes.

Finally, Section 3 (Chapters 9 to 12) covers baseband design techniques and wireless standards. Also, hardware techniques for the implementation of multi-mode multi-standard, OFDM, and MIMO transceivers, as well as emerging standards like mobile WiMax, are presented and comprehensively discussed.

Enjoy the reading!

Gianluca Cornetta
Universidad San Pablo-CEU, Spain & Vrije Universiteit Brussel, Belgium

David J. Santos
Universidad San Pablo-CEU, Spain

José Manuel Vázquez
Universidad San Pablo-CEU, Spain

July 2011

Acknowledgment

We hope the reader will find this book useful. We apologize in advance for any possible mistake we could have made during the writing and editing process. We also want to express our gratitude to all the authors for accepting our invitation and particularly to Myla Harty of IGI Global for her patience and support in all the stages of the book production.

Gianluca Cornetta
Universidad San Pablo-CEU, Spain & Vrije Universiteit Brussel, Belgium

David J. Santos
Universidad San Pablo-CEU, Spain

José Manuel Vázquez
Universidad San Pablo-CEU, Spain

Section 1
Novel Techniques, Design and Simulation

Chapter 1
Optimization of Linearity in CMOS Low Noise Amplifier

Thierry Taris
University Bordeaux I, France

Aya Mabrouki
University Bordeaux I, France

ABSTRACT

In this chapter the authors evaluate a new and promising solution to the problem of power consumption based on "optimum gate biasing." This technique consists in tracking the MOS operating region wherein the third derivation of drain current is zero. The method leads to a significant IIP3 improvement; however, the sensitivity to process drifts requires the use of a specific bias circuit to track the optimum biasing condition.

INTRODUCTION

The growing demand for wireless services has prompted the proliferation of many wireless standards. However, the wireless spectrum is a scarce resource and circuit designers have to put a particular effort in developing solutions that guarantee the various wireless standards to coexist. Spectrum crowding increases the number of interferers and this, in turn, degrades the overall performance of a wireless transceiver and put severe constraints on system linearity require-

DOI: 10.4018/978-1-4666-0083-6.ch001

ments. This chapter is specifically concerned with linearity issues in low-noise amplifiers (LNA's). There are basically two sources of non-linearties: device non-linearties (characterized by the input compression point ICP1), and non-linearties due to interferers (characterized by the input-referred third-order intercept point IIP3). The linearity of a transistor is directly connected to its current consumption: the larger the current the more linear the transistor. However, increasing the device bias current is not a practical solution in handheld or portable devices where low power consumption heavily constrains system's specifications. Consequently, most of the state-of-the-art linearization techniques aim at mitigating the effects of the intermodulation products, thus improving the IIP3. Two ways to improve LNA's linearity are reported in the literature. One relies on a parallel feedback or feed forward path to compensate the non-linearties of the amplifier, the other uses ad-hoc compensation networks that require an thorough study of the amplifier topology in order to understand the mechanism that generates such non linearties. Nonetheless the major shortcoming of such techniques is their high power consumption that makes them unsuitable for low-power applications. The growing demand for more connectivity and service in *wireless communication* systems has brought out new challenges for circuit and system architectures. Among them is the management of a large number of communication standards in the radio part which requires frequency agility and *high linearity*. Indeed the various standards coexisting in the front-ends increase the number of interferers which degrade the overall system performances. Two building blocks are particularly concerned by such linearity purpose: the Power Amplifier (PA), in the transmitter, and the *Low Noise Amplifier (LNA)*, in the receiver. However the linearity cannot be investigated with the same approach in these two kinds of amplifier. First, the PA is typically a large signal circuit where as the LNA is a small signal one. Furthermore the PA is the last stage of the transmitter, it is expected to provide a powerful output signal with good efficiency. The LNA, which is the first stage of a receiver, amplifies a weak signal collected by the antenna with the lowest noise as possible. In this chapter we focus on this last block.

The linearity is usually characterized by the input compression point (ICP1) and the *input-referred third-order intercept point (IIP3)*. The first is the maximum input power for which a circuit behaves linearly at its fundamental frequency. The second estimates the cross modulations occurring in the circuit because of its non linear response. This last specification is directly concerned by the increasing number of standards in modern receivers. Led by low cost production and high yielding the development of wireless devices is supported by silicon technologies among them *CMOS* and BiCMOS are the most popular nowadays. The ultimate goal, pursued over a couple of decade, is the System On Chip implementation (SOC) which would definitely tackle the problems of multi chip integration. To address it pure CMOS solution is expected since digital makes the decision for the technology choice. As a matter of consequences RF CMOS concentrates many research efforts (Jussila et al., 2001) (Zargari et al., 2002) and especially the linearization of CMOS front-end.

The linearity of a transistor is directly connected to its current consumption: the larger it is the most linear it is. With such mere approach the addressing of some IIP3 specifications, in CDMA as instance, leads to a prohibiting power consumption of the receiver, linearization techniques are so mandated to address it. Low and very low power applications like wireless sensor networks first aim at extending battery life of their nodes. To do so communication protocol, network organization, deployment and circuit design are optimized to allow power saving. For these applications the overall RF performances are relaxed but they need dedicated techniques to be completed under the lowest power consumption.

Two types of solutions aiming the improvement of the linearity in LNA are identified in the state of art. The first compensates for the non linearity occurring in the amplifier by a parallel feedback or feed forward path. It is rather a system approach performing high blocker rejection well suited for cellular phone applications. The feed forward principle is presented in the Figure 1(a), the time delay/multiplier chain generates a replica copy of the non linear term generated in the LNA that is cancelled at the output. The circuit is presented in the Figure 1(b), it is implemented in a 0.25μm CMOS technology and operates at 5GHz under 2V/22mW (Lin et al., 2006). In the Figure 2(b), a feedback solution is depicted (Werth, Schmits, & Heinen, 2009). The active cancellation filter

Figure 1. (a) Feed forward linearization principle; (b) circuit schematic (Lin, Wang, & Chang, 2006)

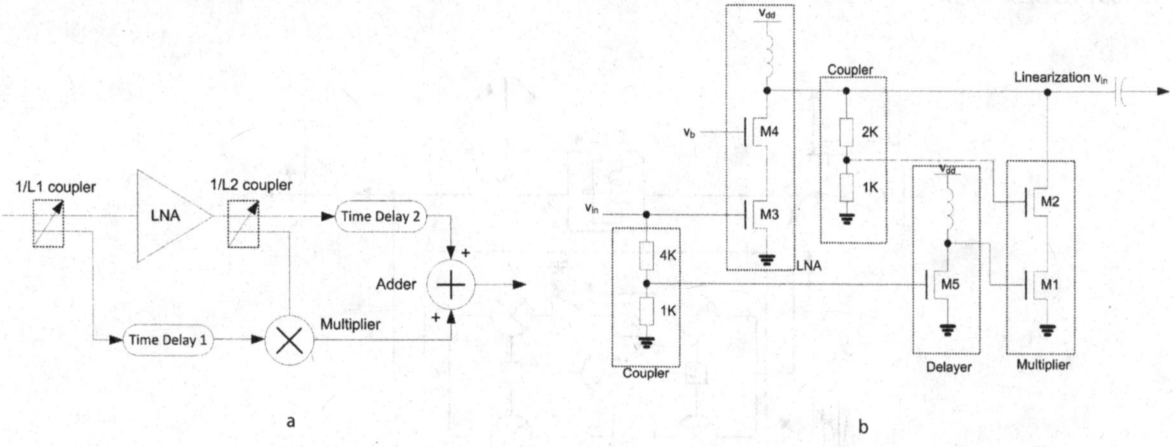

a

b

core only collects and processes the blocker that is (re)injected in the LNA for a global cancellation. The circuit schematic is showed in the Figure 2(b), it achieves a 23dB gain at 1.9GHz with 150mW power consumption under 2.5V. In a desensitization scenario, gain drops by more than 12 dB for a -15dBm blocker at 20MHz offset without feedback interference cancellation while a gain degradation of merely 3 dB is measured with feedback interference cancellation enabled. It consumes a 60mA under 2.5V and it is implemented in a 65nm CMOS technology.

The linearity can be also increased by a dedicated design of the LNA. This circuit approach requires to investigate the topology of the amplifier and to accurately analyze the mechanism providing such non linearities. The derivative superposition method, Figure 3(a), is based on superimposing different regions of the FET DC transfer characteristics with opposite signs of the 3rd order derivation (Werth, Schmits, & Heinen, 2009), (Aparin & Larson, 2005), (Ganesan, Sanchez-Sinencio, & Silva-Martinez, 2006), and (Kim, Ko, & Lee, 2000). It requires a precise manual bias control of parallel FET, MB in Figure 3, and an accurate scaling to achieve the distortion cancellation. The post distortion method, Figure 4 (Kim et al., 2006) and (Kim & Kim, 2008), compensates the IM3 generated in the master

cascode LNA (M1, M2) by a scaled parallel cascade (M3, M4). The measurement results of these circuits are reported in Figure 3(b) and 4(b). Dedicated to cellular band CDMA they exhibit high IIP3, 22dBm and 8dBm respectively, and outstanding RF performances, a more than 15 dB gain and a noise figure lower than 2dB. But the set up of parallel compensation makes them power expensive, 25 and 31 mW respectively, and so unsuited for modern low power applications.

A more promising solution is based on *"optimum gate biasing"*. It consists in tracking the MOS operating region wherein the third derivation of drain current is zero. It occurs in the moderate inversion (MI) (Toole, Plett, & Cloutier, 2004) mode where the transistor provides limited analog performances. The work presented in the Figure 5(a) achieves an IIP3 of 10.5 dBm for a 2mA/2.7V supply. The gain and NF are 14.6 dB and 1.8dB respectively at 880MHz. However the narrow range of VG1 ensuring a significant improvement of IIP3 is very sensitive to process drifts. Hence it requires a specific bias circuit, Figure 5(b), which tracks the optimum biasing condition.

*Figure 2. (a) Feedback linearization principle; (b) circuit schematic (Werth, Schmits, & Heinen, 2009.
©2009, IEEE)*

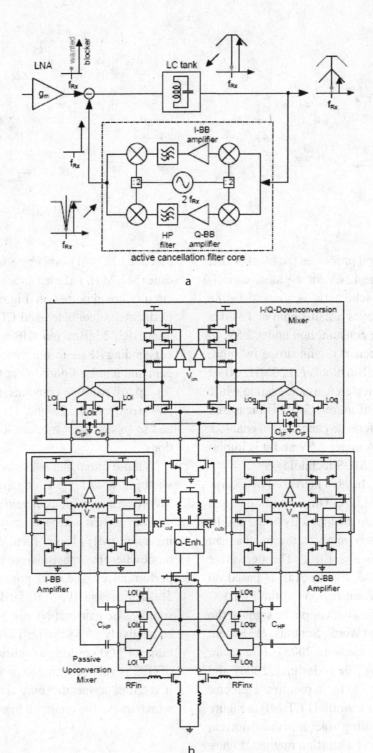

a

b

Figure 3. (a) Derivative superposition LNA; (b) Measurement results (Aparin & Larson, 2005. ©2005, IEEE)

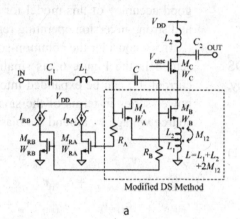

Technology (µm)	0.25
Frequency (GHz)	0.9
S21 (dB)	15.5
NF (dB)	1.65
IIP3 (dBm)	22
Pcons (mW)	25

a

b

Figure 4. (a) Active post-distortion LNA; (b) Measurement results (Kim et al., 2006. ©2005, IEEE)

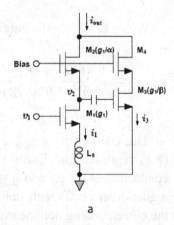

Technology (µm)	0.25
Frequency (GHz)	0.9
S21 (dB)	16.2
NF (dB)	1.2
IIP3 (dBm)	8
Pcons (mW)	31

a

b

Figure 5. (a) Optimum biased LNA; (b) Biasing circuit (Aparin, Brown, & Larson, 2004. ©2004, IEEE)

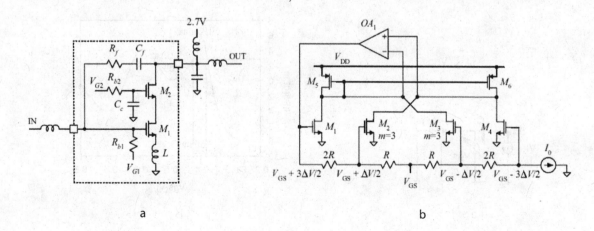

a

b

IIP3 ANALYSIS

IIP3/IM3 Analysis of a Common Source (CS) Amplifier

The expression of drain-source current of a MOS transistor biased in saturation region is given by, (Aparin & Larson, 2005):

$$I_D = \frac{\mu_0 C_{ox}}{2n} \frac{W}{L} \frac{X^2}{1 + \alpha X} \left(1 + \lambda V_{DS}\right)) \qquad (8.1)$$

where

$$X = 2n\varphi_t \ln\left(1 + e^{\frac{(V_{GS} - V_{th})}{(2n\varphi_t)}}\right) \quad \text{and} \quad \alpha = \theta + \frac{\mu_0}{2nv_{sat}L} \qquad (8.2)$$

C_{ox} is the gate oxide capacitance per unit area, $\mu 0$ is the mobility factor, $\phi_t = kT/q$ is the thermal voltage, Vth is the threshold voltage, VGS is the gate-source voltage, and VBS is the drain-source voltage. θ is the mobility-reduction coefficient and vsat is the velocity saturation. The parameter n is the subthreshold slope factor whose value depends on the process, and varies between 1.1

and 1.9.Several simulations and measurements, reported in (Kim, Ko, & Lee, 2000), showed the good accuracy of this model for both moderate and strong inversion operating region.

If we consider the common-source FET presented in the Figure 6, its small signal output current, i_{ds}, can be expanded into the following power series in terms of the small-signal gate-source voltage v_{gs} around the bias point:

$$i_{ds} = c_{(1,0,0)} v_{gs} + c_{(2,0,0)} v_{gs}^2 + c_{(3,0,0)} v_{gs}^3 + c_{(0,1,0)} v_{ds} +$$
$$c_{(0,2,0)} v_{ds}^2 + c_{(0,3,0)} v_{ds}^3 + c_{(0,0,1)} v_{sb} + c_{(0,0,2)} v_{sb}^2 +$$
$$c_{(0,0,3)} v_{sb}^3 + c_{(1,1,0)} v_{gs} v_{ds} + c_{(1,0,1)} v_{gs} v_{sb} + c_{(0,1,1)} v_{ds} v_{sb} +$$
$$c_{(2,1,0)} v_{gs}^2 v_{ds} + c_{(1,2,0)} v_{gs} v_{ds}^2 + c_{(2,0,1)} v_{gs}^2 v_{sb} +$$
$$c_{(1,0,2)} v_{gs} v_{sb}^2 + c_{(0,2,1)} v_{ds}^2 v_{sb} + c_{(0,1,2)} v_{ds} v_{sb}^2 + c_{(1,1,1)} v_{gs} v_{ds} v_{sb}$$
$$(8.3)$$

Where $C_{(m,n,p)}$ coefficients are defined as:

$$c_{(m,n,p)} = \frac{1}{m!} \frac{1}{n!} \frac{1}{p!} \frac{\partial^{(m+n+p)} I_{ds}}{\partial^m V_{gs} \partial^n V_{ds} \partial^p V_{sb}} \qquad (8.4)$$

The coefficients $c_{(1,0,0)}$, $c_{(0,1,0)}$, and $c_{(0,0,1)}$ in (8.1) represent the linear small-signal trans-conductances g_m, g_0, and g_{mb}, respectively. The higher-order coefficients define the strengths of the corresponding nonlinearirties. Among them,

Figure 6. (a) Common-source amplifier with VGS control; (b) Simulated IIP3

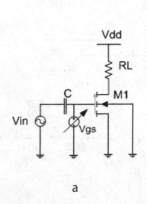

a

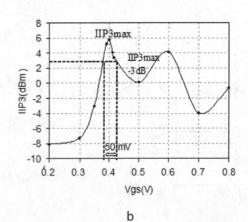

b

C(3,0,0) is particularly important since it controls IMD3 at low signal levels, thus determining IIP3 as it is defined in (8.3).

$$V_{IIP3}^{2} \approx \frac{4}{3}\frac{g_m}{c_{(3,0,0)}} \tag{8.5}$$

According (8.2) the third order coefficient C(3,0,0) is derived in (8.4)

$$c_{(3,0,0)} = -\frac{K\xi\left(1+\lambda V_{DS}\right)}{24\left(n\varphi_t\right)^2\left(1+\xi\right)^3\left(1+\alpha X\right)^4}(24n^2\varphi_t^2\xi^2\alpha - 12n\varphi_t\xi\left(1+\alpha X\right)+X\left(\xi-1\right)\left(2+\alpha X\right)\left(1+\alpha X\right)) \tag{8.6}$$

Where

$$K = \frac{\mu_0 C_{ox}}{2n}\frac{W}{L} \tag{8.7}$$

$$\xi = e^{\frac{\left(V_{GS}-V_{th}\right)}{\left(2n\varphi_t\right)}} \tag{8.8}$$

The simulated IIP3 versus V_{GS} is depicted in Figure 6. Theoretically, the cancellation of $c_{(3,0,0)}$ in (8.3) would lead to an infinite IIP3. However fifth and seventh-order distortions also contribute to IM3 limiting V_{IIP3}^{2}. This first study figures out IIP3 peaks for a specific value of gate-source voltage.

Body Biasing

Studying the expression (8.4) it comes $C_{(3,0,0)}$ is mainly controlled by the gate overdrive voltage V_{od}:

$$V_{od} = (V_{GS}-V_{th}) \tag{8.9}$$

In the previous study the peak of IIP3 is obtained for a specific value of V_{od} tuned by V_{GS} which minimizes $C_{(3,0,0)}$. But V_{od} can be also

adjusted by the bulk-source voltage, V_{BS}, through V_{th} according (8.8).

$$V_{th} = V_{TH0} + \gamma\left(\sqrt{\varphi - V_{bs}} - \sqrt{\varphi}\right) \tag{8.10}$$

Where V_{TH0} is the zero-bias threshold voltage, V_{bs} is the bulk-source voltage, and γ is the body effect coefficient. φ is the surface potential parameter.

However, varying VBS appears to be more intricate since many parameters in (8.4) are no longer constant and should be accounted for a function of it. Among them is the parameter n, defined as follows, (Kim et al., 2006):

$$n = 1 + 0.5\gamma(2\phi_F - V_{BS})^{-0.5} \tag{8.11}$$

Including the contribution of V_{BS} in (8.2), (8.4), and (8.6), a new expression of $C_{(3,0,0)}$ is derived as a function of V_{BS}. Solving (8.12) for V_{BSopt} to minimize $C_{(3,0,0)}$ leads to a maximum of IIP3.

$$c_{(3,0,0)} = -F\left(V_{BS}\right)\begin{bmatrix}24n^2\left(V_{BS}\right)\varphi_t^2\xi^2\left(V_{BS}\right)\alpha\left(V_{BS}\right)-12n\left(V_{BS}\right)\varphi_t\xi\left(V_{BS}\right)\left(1+\alpha\left(V_{BS}\right)X\left(V_{BS}\right)\right)\\+X\left(V_{BS}\right)\left(\xi\left(V_{BS}\right)-1\right)\left(2+\alpha\left(V_{BS}\right)X\left(V_{BS}\right)\right)\left(1+\alpha\left(V_{BS}\right)X\left(V_{BS}\right)\right)\end{bmatrix} \tag{8.12}$$

with

$$F(V_{BS}) = \frac{K(V_{BS})\xi(V_{BS})\left(1+\lambda V_{DS}\right)}{24\left(n(V_{BS})\varphi_t\right)^2\left(1+\xi(V_{BS})\right)^3\left(1+\alpha(V_{BS})X(V_{BS})\right)^4} \tag{8.13}$$

The IIP3 of the circuit presented in the Figure 7(a) has been simulated and is reported in Figure 7(b). As predicted the IIP3 peaks for a specific value of V_{BS}, -110mV. The most interesting result remains the large tuning range, 220mV, of V_{BS} ensuring a significant improvement of IIP3.

Figure 7. Common-source amplifier with VBS control (a) Simulated IIP3 (b)

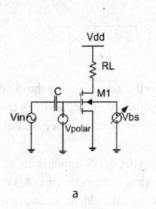

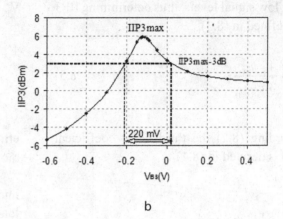

a

b

A 220mV variation around the optimum V_{BS}, Figure 7(b), performs a -3dB attenuation of IIP-3max which is approximately four times larger than the V_{GS} range presented in Figure 6(b). This slower variation of IIP3 comes from the smooth dependence of $C_{(3,0,0)}$ to V_{BS} in (8.6). Optimum body biasing is so less sensitive to process and temperature variations than its optimum gate biasing counterpart. The next section applies this technique to the design of a LNA.

CIRCUIT DESIGN

Cascode LNA

The most popular architecture of LNA is the cascode topology with inductive degeneration (Lee, 1998). It achieves a good reverse isolation, a low NF and a large voltage gain. The simplified schematic of the circuit depicted in the Figure 8(a) has been implemented in a 0.13µm CMOS technology, the chip micrograph is showed in Figure 8(b). It takes place within a 2019 µm × 1000 µm silicon area.

The inductive degeneration allows for a good trade-off between input and noise matching thanks to (L_g, L_s) and M_1 sizing. The input impedance

taking into account the back-gate transconductance g_{mb} is:

$$Z_{in} = R_g + \frac{\omega_T L_s + g_{mb}(\omega L_s)^2}{1 + (g_{mb}\omega L_s)^2} + j\left[-\frac{1}{\omega C_{gs}} + \frac{\omega L_s(1 - g_m \omega L_s)}{1 + (g_{mb}\omega L_s)^2}\right] \quad (8.14)$$

Where $\omega_T = \dfrac{g_{m1}}{C_{gs1}}$, $g_{mb} = \dfrac{\partial I_D}{\partial V_{SB1}}$ and R_g is the gate resistance of M_1

The voltage gain, G_v, is derived as follows:

$$G_v = \frac{v_{out}}{v_{in}} =$$

$$-\frac{[1 + \frac{g_{mb}}{g_m}L_s C_{gs}\omega^2]}{[1 - L_s C_{gs}\omega^2 + j(g_m + g_{mb})L_s\omega]} \times \frac{|jL_d\omega|}{2R_s} \times \frac{\omega_T}{\omega} \quad (8.15)$$

The NF_{min} is simplified to (8.16) under matched conditions:

$$NF_{min} = 1 + \frac{2\sqrt{\frac{\gamma}{\alpha}g_m R_g}}{\frac{\omega_T}{\omega} + g_{mb}\omega L_s} \quad (8.16)$$

Figure 8. (a) Schematic of the cascode LNA with body access; (b) Chip microphotograph of the circuit

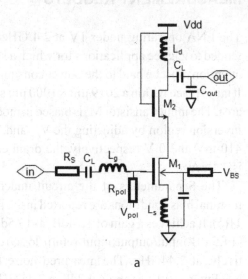

a

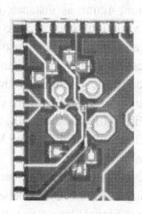

b

It comes from (8.14) to (8.16) that the bulk-source voltage, V_{BS}, through g_{mb}, contributes to the most important characteristics of a cascode LNA. In practice, this contribution remains small since:

$$\frac{\omega_T}{\omega} >> g_{mb}\omega L_s$$

and

$$1 >> (g_{mb}\omega L_s)^2.$$

About the linearity, the IIP3 of a source degenerated cascode LNA differs from a mere common source amplifier because the inductor L_s creates a feedback path for the drain current to v_{gs}. Indeed the 2nd harmonics generated by $C_{(2,0,0)}.v_{gs}^2$ are fed back across the gate and source, adding to the fundamental components of v_{gs}. These spectral components are then mixed in given $C_{(2,0,0)}.v_{gs}^2$ producing harmonics at the same frequency of $C_{(3,0,0)}.v_{gs}^3$ which is the main source of third order nonlinearities in a CS configuration (8.3). Neglecting the contribution of gmb the IIP3 is modeled as proposed in (8.17).

$$IIP_3 = \frac{4C_{(1,0,0)}^2\omega^2 L_s C_{gs}}{3\left|\varepsilon(2\omega)\right|} \qquad (8.17)$$

Where

$$\varepsilon(2\omega) =$$
$$C_{(3,0,0)} - \frac{2}{3}\frac{C_{(2,0,0)}^2}{C_{(1,0,0)} + \frac{1}{j2\omega L_s} + j2\omega C_{gs} + Z_1(2\omega)\frac{C_{gs}}{L_s}} \qquad (8.18)$$

The IIP3 reaches a maximum when $|\varepsilon(2\omega)|$ is minimized. Depending on $C_{(m,0,0)}|_m = 1..3$ coefficients, IIP3 can be still controlled by gate or body biasing.

DIGITAL CONTROL

As demonstrated in section 1.2.1, the peak in IIP3 occurs for a narrow range of V_{GS} making the technique very sensitive to process and temperature variations. In practice it is controlled by a specific biasing circuit, as reported in (Aparin, Brown, & Larson, 2004), which tracks the V_{GSopt}. This extra circuitry, based on device matching, Figure 5(b), is not well suited to modern nanoscale technologies, 65nm, 42nm, as instance, depicting large process variations compared to elder 0.25µm, 0.18µm and 0.13µm. V_{BS} adjusting allows for a four times wider tuning range than V_{GS} as reported in Figure 7(b). It so requires a lower accuracy in the optimum voltage making the control digitally compatible. To demonstrate it the test board of the LNA includes a DAC providing V_{BS} as proposed in Figure 9.

The DAC will be further implemented on-chip. The tuning of the LNA will be so controlled by the Digital Signal Processor (DSP), Figure 10, during the self test procedure of the receiver. In such new approach of radio system the building blocks are digitally controlled allowing for a compensation of technology and temperature variations.

Figure 9. Digital control of body bias through a DAC

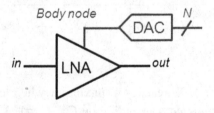

Figure 10. Reconfigurable RF receiver

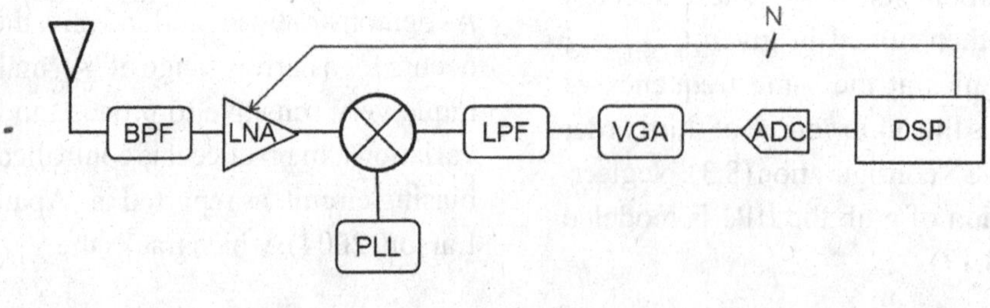

MEASUREMENT RESULTS

The LNA operating under 1V at 2.4 GHz is intended to Zigbee applications for which a special attention must be paid to the power consumption. It takes place within a 2019 µm × 1000 µm silicon area. The input transistor M_1 is biased in moderate inversion region by adjusting the V_{GS} and V_{BS} to 410 mV and 0 V respectively, the drain current is 3.1mA.

The S parameters of the circuit under such nominal bias conditions are reported in the Figure 11(a). It achieves a gain of 12.4dB, a -13.5dB and -14.5 dB input/output input return loss, respectively, at 2.44GHz. The measured noise figure NF, Figure 10(b), is about 4.2dB at 2.35 GHz and 4.35dB at 2.4GHz. This good correlation between the minimum of NF and best input matching is provided by the inductive degeneration.

The IIP3 of a circuit is theoretically the crossing point between the fundamental and third order inter-modulation responses. In practice, this crossing point cannot be directly measured since it occurs beyond the saturation power of the circuit. It is so estimated by interpolating the small signal response to a two tone test. The result depends on the number of collected points making this measurement method inaccurate. Another solution lies on the expression (8.19) which relates the IM3 and IIP3. It is correlated to the power of the input signal, P_{in}, which must be kept low to only characterize the third order inter-modulation and neglect higher order effects. G is the power gain of the circuit.

Figure 11. Measured s-parameters (a) and Noise figure; (b) of the cascode LNA

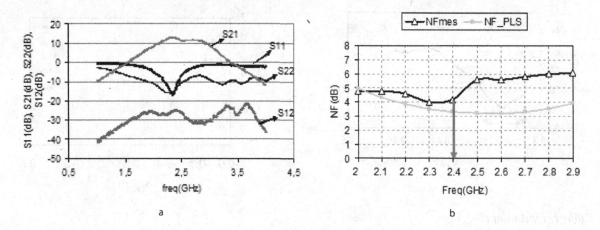

a

b

$$IIP3 = \frac{3}{2}P_{in} + \frac{1}{2}G - \frac{1}{2}IM3 \qquad (8.19)$$

In agreement with (8.19), and assuming G is constant over the sweeping range, the peak of IIP3 matches with a minimum of IM3. The V_{BSopt} performing an IIP3max has been estimated by measuring IM3. A 2.4-2.42GHz two tones test has been applied with V_{GS} kept constant and V_{BS} varying from -0.6 to 0.3 V. In Figure 12, we plotted the measured IM3 as a function of V_{BS}, for an input power of -24.5 dBm. It figures out a minimum of IM3 when the DAC delivers a V_{BS} equals to -0.55V. The corresponding IIP3 is 6

dBm which is a 7 dB improvement of IIP3 under V_{BS}=0V, -1 dBm.

The V_{BS} range around the peak allowing 3dB attenuation is about 80mV in Figure 11. It is 25 mV for a gate biasing as reported in Figure 13. The corresponding IIP3max is 6 dBm in both cases. A first conclusion can be drawn: both optimum gate and body biasing provide the same IIP3 improvement. Furthermore it is demonstrated the body biasing allows for a better adjustment, digitally controlled in this circuit, compared to gate tuning since the adjusting range, providing a significant IIP3 improvement, is almost four times the V_{GS} one.

Figure 12. Measured IM3 vs. VBS

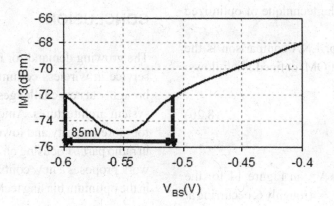

Figure 13. Measured IM3 vs. VGS

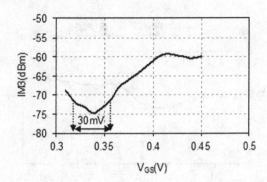

Figure 14. Measured FOM of the LNA vs. VBS

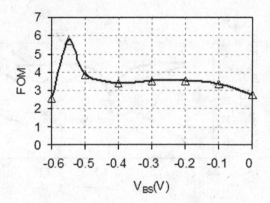

Table 1. Optimum (V_{GS}, V_{BS})

IM3(dBm)	V_{GS} (V)	V_{BS} (V)
-75	0.41	-0.55
-74,33	0.39	-0.45
-74,17	0,37	-0.3
-74,83	0.34	0

In the previous section, dedicated to the cascode LNA, the expressions (8.17) and (8.18) depict the peak of IIP3 is controlled by the coefficients $C_{(m,0,0)}$. So various couples of (V_{GS}, V_{BS}) would achieve the bias condition performing the lowering of $|\varepsilon(2\omega)|$. Table 1 reports on these (V_{GS}, V_{BS}) combinations minimizing the IM3. It comes the optimum biasing conditions are very sensitive to V_{GS} variations, as predicted, but a fine tuning can be applied by adjusting the V_{BS} avoiding the need for a tracking bias circuit. This is the most valuable contribution of optimum body biasing approach compared to the technique of optimized gate biasing.

A useful feature for LNA comparison is the ITRS Figure of Merit (FOM) defined as it follows:

$$FOM = \frac{OIP3}{(F-1)P_{dc}} \qquad (8.20)$$

It is plotted versus V_{BS} in Figure 14 for the tested LNA. The FOM_{max}, a roughly 6, occurring at

IIP3max biasing condition, is two times the FOM under $V_{BS}=0V$ which correspond to the nominal operation of the topology. Hence the technique of optimum biasing also carries out the best tradeoff between the RF performances of a cascode LNA.

The measured characteristics of the LNA: gain, NF, and current consumption, are drawn versus V_{BS} in Figure 15 (a) and (b). The decrease of body bias reduces the drain current thus lessening both the gain and noise figure. However the smooth variation of the RF performances regarding the range of V_{BS}, from 0 to -0.6 V, shows a fair sensitivity of this topology to the body biasing. Indeed the gain decreases from 12.5 to 8.9 dB where as the NF increases from 4.2 to 6.2 dB. The input return loss, Figure 15(b), is frequency shifted. It remains lower than -10 dB over the VBS range ensuring a good input matching.

CONCLUSION

The growing demand for more connectivity and service in wireless communication systems has brought out new challenges for CMOS circuit and system architectures. Among them are the need for more linearity and lower power consumption in radio parts. Focusing on LNA linearization this work proposes a new control of IM3 cancellation in the optimum biasing technique which is known

Figure 15. Measured S_{21}, NF and I_d (a) S_{11} (b) vs. V_{BS}

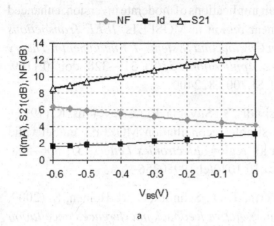

a

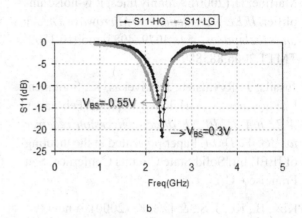

b

for power saving. Based on V_{BS} adjustment it allows for a better tuning of the range performing the IIP3 peak regarding the technique of optimum gate biasing.

After a theoretical review of the IIP3 improvement through optimum biasing, this chapter proposes to analyze its control by either the V_{GS}, already reported in the state of art, either the V_{BS}, demonstrated by the authors for the first time. This new approach is then applied to a 2.4 GHz cascode LNA implemented in a 0.13 μm CMOS technology attended for ZigBee applications.

Operating under 1V, the circuit achieves a 12.4 dB gain, 4.2 dB NF and -1dBm IIP3 for a 3.1mW power consumption without any specific body biasing. By adjusting the V_{BS} through an off-chip DAC, the IIP3 peaks at 6 dBm while consuming a 1.7 mW. The gain and NF are 8.9 dB and 6.2 dB respectively. It so first demonstrates that optimum biasing approach is an efficient and power saving linearization technique. Depicting a four times larger tuning range than V_{GS} control, body effect adjustment does not require additional circuitry to track the optimum. It makes so the technique more reliable and compatible with a digital system control.

ACKNOWLEDGMENT

The authors would like to thank Dr. Olivier Mazoufre for his valuable and helpful advices for the choice and tests of the digital to analog converter suitable for the digital control of the body bias and the whole LNA requirements.

REFERENCES

Aparin, V., Brown, G., & Larson, L. E. (2004). Linearization of CMOS LNA'S via optimum gate biasing. *IEEE Transaction on Circuit and Systems-II, 4*, 748–751.

Aparin, V., & Larson, L. E. (2005). Modified derivative superposition method for linearizing FET low-noise amplifiers. *IEEE Transactions on Microwave Theory and Techniques, 53*(2), 548–551. doi:10.1109/TMTT.2004.840635

Cheng, K.-H., & Jou, C. F. (2005, June). *A novel 2.4 GHz LNA with digital gain control using 0.18μM CMOS*. Paper presented at the meeting of Midwest Symposium, Cincinnati, Ohio

Ganesan, S., Sánchez-Sinencio, E., & Silva-Martinez, J. (2006). A highly linear low-noise amplifier. *IEEE Transactions on Microwave Theory and Techniques*, *54*, 4079–4085. doi:10.1109/TMTT.2006.885889

Jussila, J., Ryynänen, J., Kivekäs, K., Sumanen, L., Pärssinen, A., & Halonen, K. (2001, February). *A 22-mA 3.7dB NF direct-conversion receiver for 3G WCDMA*. Paper presented at the meeting of IEEE Int. Solid State Circuits Confernce, San Francisco, CA.

Kim, B., Ko, J. S., & Lee, K. (2000). A new linearization technique for MOSFET RF amplifier using multiple gated transistors. *IEEE Microwave Guided Wave Letters*, *9*, 371–373.

Kim, N., Aparin, V., Barnett, K., & Persico, C. (2006). A cellular-band CDMA 0.25um CMOS LNA linearized using post-distortion. *IEEE Journal of Solid-state Circuits*, *41*(7), 1530–1534. doi:10.1109/JSSC.2006.873909

Kim, T.-S., & Kim, B.-S. (2008, June). *Linearization of differential CMOS Low Noise Amplifier using cross-coupled post distortion canceller*. Paper presented at the meeting of IEEE Radio Frequency Integrated Circuits Symposium, Atlanta, CA.

Lee, T. H. (1998). The design of narrowband CMOS low-noise amplifiers. In *The design of CMOS radiofrequency integrated circuits* (pp. 272–306). Cambridge University Press.

Lin, M., Wang, H., Li, Y., & Chen, H. (2006). A novel IP3 boosting technique using feedforward distortion cancellation method for 5 GHz CMOS LNA. *Analog Integrated Circuits and Signal Processing*, *46*, 293–296. doi:10.1007/s10470-006-2134-3

Toole, B., Plett, C., & Cloutier, M. (2004). RF circuit implications of moderate inversion, enhanced linear region in MOSFETs. *IEEE Transactions on Circuits and Systems. I, Fundamental Theory and Applications*, *51*(2), 319–328. doi:10.1109/TCSI.2003.822400

Tsividis, Y., Suyama, K., & Vavelidis, K. (1995). A simple reconciliation MOSFET model valid in all region. *Electronics Letters*, *31*, 506–508. doi:10.1049/el:19950256

Werth, T. D., Schmits, C., & Heinen, S. (2009, June). *Active feedback interference cancellation in RF receiver front-ends*. Paper presented at the meeting of IEEE Radio Frequency Integrated Circuits Symposium, Boston, MA.

Zargari, M., Su, D. K., Yue, C. P., Rabii, S., Weber, D., & Kaczynski, B. J. (2002). A 5-GHz CMOS transceiver for IEEE 802.11a wireless LAN systems. *IEEE Journal of Solid-state Circuits*, *37*, 1688–1694. doi:10.1109/JSSC.2002.804353

KEY TERMS AND DEFINITIONS

Body Effect: The modulation of a MOS channel charge applying a C voltage between the body and source node.

ICP1: The maximum input power for which a circuit behaves linearly at its fundamental frequency.

IIP3: Estimates the cross modulations occurring in the circuit because of its non linear response. It is a characteristic of the rejection of the unwanted harmonics fed by the input signal.

Linearity in RF Circuits: Commonly defined throughout the input compression point (ICP1) and the input-referred third-order intercept point (IIP3).

Low Noise Amplifier: The first active circuit that the input signal collected at the Rx antenna enters. According Friis formula it is in charge of the noise figure, and so the sensitivity, of the receiver.

Chapter 2
An All-Inversion-Region g_m/I_D Based Design Methodology for Radiofrequency Blocks in CMOS Nanometer Technologies

Rafaella Fiorelli
University of Seville, Spain & Instituto de Microelectrónica de Sevilla, Spain

Eduardo Peralías
Instituto de Microelectrónica de Sevilla, Spain

Fernando Silveira
Universidad de la República, Uruguay

ABSTRACT

This chapter presents a design optimization methodology for analog radiofrequency (RF) blocks based on the g_m/I_D technique and on the exploration of all-inversion regions (from weak inversion or sub-threshold to strong inversion or above threshold) of the MOS transistor in nanometer technologies. The use of semi-empirical models of MOS transistors and passive components, as inductors or capacitors, assures accurate designs, reducing time and efforts for transferring the initial block specifications to a compliant design. This methodology permits the generation of graphical maps to visualize the evolution of the circuit characteristics when sweeping both the inversion zone and the bias current, allowing reaching very good compromises between performance aspects of the circuit (e.g. noise and power consumption) for a set of initial specifications. In order to demonstrate the effectiveness of this methodology, it is applied in the design of two basic blocks of RF transceivers: low noise amplifiers (LNAs) and voltage controlled oscillators (VCOs), implemented in two different nanometer technologies and specified to be part of a 2.4 GHz transceiver. A possible design flow of each block is provided; resulting designs are implemented and verified both with simulations and measurements.

DOI: 10.4018/978-1-4666-0083-6.ch002

INTRODUCTION

The variety of wireless applications in areas as diverse as medicine, entertainment or environment have originated a wide spectrum of wireless standards and therefore, of circuit specifications. This diversity in the circuit characteristics together with the shrinking time to market results in design challenges. To keep pace with this innovation, RF designers, as never before, need reliable optimization tools helping them from the beginning of the design process.

Some RF standards are very demanding in terms of power consumption but they have relaxed performance requirements e.g. in terms of channel bandwidth or noise and frequency synthesizer spectral purity, as in the case of IEEE 802.15.4 standard (on which ZigBee is based) and low-energy Bluetooth (IEEE 802.15.1-2002). Power consumption constrains the transceiver design and forces to assign carefully the power budget of each block of the chain. It also has a strong influence on the noise, linearity, gain and other characteristics. A well known trade-off is especially noticeable between power and inherent noise of blocks as LNAs, mixers or VCOs. To take advantage of this compromise, the designer needs a deep and accurate knowledge of the block behavior and its devices to reach an optimized design, especially when using nanometer technologies.

The trade-offs between consumption and noise, among other performances, are strongly determined by the characteristics of the active element: the MOS transistor. These characteristics change as a function of the inversion region in which the MOS transistor is biased: strong inversion (above threshold), moderate inversion (approximately "around" threshold) and weak inversion (sub-threshold). In the following section a summary of the characteristics and the implications of working in each of these zones are presented.

When working in radiofrequency, the MOS transistor has been traditionally biased in strong inversion. It is because in this region the transistor has a smaller size and drives a higher current than in moderate or weak inversion. This leads to a reduction of parasitic capacitances and an increment in the transconductance. Therefore, as the MOS transition frequency f_T is proportional to the transconductance and to the inverse of its parasitic capacitance, the maximum frequency of operation increases in strong inversion region. However, as it will be shown later, this increased maximum frequency of operation is obtained at the expense of a very low ratio between transconductance and bias current (below 5 V^{-1} instead of the 38 V^{-1} achievable with a bipolar transistor at ambient temperature). The effect of moving from strong inversion through weak inversion implied a considerable current reduction, but in contrast, parasitic capacitances are higher as transistor dimensions increase. For example, for sub-micrometer technologies the high frequency design in moderate was limited up to one gigahertz (Barboni, Fiorelli & Silveira, 2006).

However, the tremendous channel length reduction to below 100 nm, and the improvement in passive components, i.e. inductors and capacitors, are opening the path to feasible implementations. So, nowadays it is possible to use CMOS technology without increasing the consumption and even reduce it much more by working in the moderate and weak inversion in the range of several gigahertz for minimum length transistor. This can be achieved even considering the MOS transistor working above the quasi-static limit of one tenth of f_T (Tsividis, 2000, p. 492) and therefore greatly simplifying the circuit analysis.

Many implementation examples working in moderate and weak inversion are found in literature. Porret, Melly, Python, Enz and Vittoz (2001) and Melly, Porret, Enz, and Vittoz (2001) presented the design of a receiver and a transmitter, respectively, for 433 MHz in CMOS, working in moderate inversion. Ramos et al. (2004) showed the design of an LNA in 90 nm technology for 900 MHz in moderate/weak inversion. Barboni et al. (2006) utilized the moderate inversion to implement an RF amplifier and a VCO at 900MHz, Shameli and Heydari (2006) designed a CMOS 950 MHz LNA in moderate inversion. Lee and Mohammadi (2007) designed a 2.6 GHz VCO in weak inversion in CMOS. To provide a final example, Jhon, Jung, Koo, Song and Shin (2009) designed a 0.7 V - 2.4 GHz LNA in deep weak inversion. All these works show how, in the last decade, the design in moderate and weak inversion in CMOS at RF became consolidated. Nevertheless, there is a lack of studies that analyze the performance of an RF design in all the inversion regions of the MOS transistor.

In this chapter, we present an RF design systematic approach for all-inversion regions starting from the data provided by the nanometer technology foundries and leading to successfully measured circuits. The basis of this method is the use of the g_m/I_D based tool of the MOS transistor (Silveira, Flandre & Jespers, 1996). As it will be discussed later on, the g_m/I_D ratio is an intrinsic MOS characteristic slightly dependent on the transistor aspect ratio and directly related to the inversion level of the transistor. The inversion level is directly associated with the normalized current or current density, defined as $i=I_D/(W/L)$, and g_m/I_D is one-to-one related with i. Biasing the transistor in strong inversion means low g_m/I_D values and high i currents while working in weak inversion is translated to high g_m/I_D figures and low i values.

Several factors make useful the g_m/I_D parameter. Firstly, the ease to write circuit design expressions as a function of this parameter, since generally the transconductance and the current are part of them. Secondly, its value gives a direct indication of the inversion region and of the efficiency of the transistor in translating current consumption into transconductance. Finally, its variation is constrained to a very small range, efficiently covered with a grid of some tens of values of g_m/I_D (e.g. from 3 V^{-1} to 28 V^{-1} in nanometer bulk CMOS). Utilizing this variable in the circuit expressions and sweeping the g_m/I_D value allows obtaining a

set of design space maps. For example, circuit characteristics as noise, gain, consumption, among others, can be displayed as function of g_m/I_D. This graphical representation helps the designer to study the evolution and trade-offs of some of these characteristics when working in any of the three regions.

Along this chapter, we will state a very general RF design methodology for all-inversion regions of the MOS transistor suitable for RF circuits as diverse as LNAs or VCOs. To develop this design methodology, four general steps should be followed.

Firstly, the DC behavior of MOS transistor has to be captured in curves or expressions of g_m/I_D, g_{ds}, and intrinsic capacitances versus i. This requires a MOS transistor model accurately characterized in all-inversion regions. In addition, good short-channel MOS noise model and their correspondent parameters should be known. All this will be detailed in the section titled MOS Transistor Analysis and g_m/I_D Tool.

Secondly, follows the extraction of passive component models, as will be discussed in the section Passive Component Analysis.

In third place comes the modeling of the RF block with a set of equations modified in order to express them in terms of g_m/I_D or i.

Finally, it is necessary to establish a design flow to arrange the computations, the application of the technological data collected in the two first steps, and the relations between them and the decisions fixed by block specifications and technological constraints. These two last steps are described in the section Proposed Design Methodology through two application examples. Electrical simulations and measurement results of the implementations of these examples, an LNA and a VCO, are also presented in order to show the usefulness and effectiveness of the design methodology.

MOS TRANSISTOR ANALYSIS AND GM/ID TOOL

MOS Operation and Modeling

MOS Transistor Inversion Regions

The simplest, strong inversion model of the MOS transistor considers that when the gate-bulk voltage is lower than the threshold voltage, there is no significant inversion channel in the transistor and therefore the drain current I_D is zero. In practice the inversion charge in the channel is gradually reduced as the gate voltage decreases, as seen in Figure 1(a), where the current I_D versus V_G is plotted in a logarithmic scale. Below the threshold voltage V_{thres} the current is not zero and has an exponential relation with the gate voltage; this current is often referred to as sub-threshold current.

In this sub-threshold region the main current conduction mechanism is through diffusion, where the current is proportional to the charge concentration gradient. The diffusion current component, negligible in the above-threshold operation, is also the main mechanism in a bipolar transistor, which shares with the MOS sub-threshold region the characteristic of having an exponential voltage to current characteristic. Above the threshold, the dominating current conduction mechanism is drift, where the current is proportional to the inversion charge concentration, leading this mechanism to the classic quadratic relationship between gate voltage and drain current.

Summarizing, depending on the value of V_G, three behavioral regions of the saturated MOS transistor, can be distinguished, as Figure 1(a) shows:

- **Strong inversion (S.I.):** when V_G is higher than approximately 100 mV of the threshold voltage V_{thres}, the inversion channel is strongly established, the drift current is the dominant. Here it is the well-known classic quadratic I_D-V_G MOS equations.

- **Weak inversion (W.I.):** for low V_G voltages, far below V_{thres}, the number of free charge is very small, so the inversion in the channel is weak. Here the dominant method of conduction is diffusion and the current I_D has an exponential relationship with V_G ($I_D \propto \exp(V_G/(nU_T))$); that is why $\log(I_D)$ in Figure 1(a) has a constant slope in this zone. Parameter n is called the slope factor and U_T is the thermal voltage.

- **Moderate inversion (M.I.):** when V_G is around V_{thres} both conduction mechanisms are significant and the final effect is a mixture of both. The mathematical expression in this zone is neither quadratic nor exponential.

g_m/I_D Characteristic

As mentioned in the Introduction, the g_m/I_D ratio is a MOS characteristic which is directly related with the inversion region of the transistor. Let us show why this happens.

The coefficient g_m/I_D is the slope of the curve I_D versus V_G in a logarithmic scale because:

$$\frac{g_m}{I_D} = \frac{\partial I_D / \partial V_G}{I_D} = \frac{\partial \log(I_D)}{\partial V_G} \quad (1)$$

As Figure 1(a) shows, the maximum slope of the curve, that is, the maximum g_m/I_D ratio, appears in the weak inversion region, decreasing until reaching strong inversion. Firstly, this means that the weak and moderate inversion regions are more adequate for low power efficient designs. In these regions, the values of gate voltage V_G (around 100 mV below the threshold voltage) and the saturation drain voltage V_{Dsat} (from 100 mV to 150 mV) are very low, which make these zones very adequate for low supply voltage operation.

The g_m/I_D ratio is a measure of the efficiency to translate I_D into the transconductance g_m, because the greater g_m/I_D value the greater transconductance

Figure 1. (a) Drain current I$_D$ versus V$_{GS}$ and g$_m$/I$_D$ vs. I$_D$ (inset) for an nMOS transistor with an aspect ratio of W/L=6μm/100nm. (b) g$_m$/I$_D$ vs. normalized current i and g$_{ds}$/I$_D$ vs. i (inset) for a set of 100nm nMOS transistors with widths in the range of [6μm, 320μm]. (c) Transition frequency f$_T$ and g$_m$/I$_D$ versus I$_D$. (d) Intrinsic capacitance C$_{gs}$'vs. i.

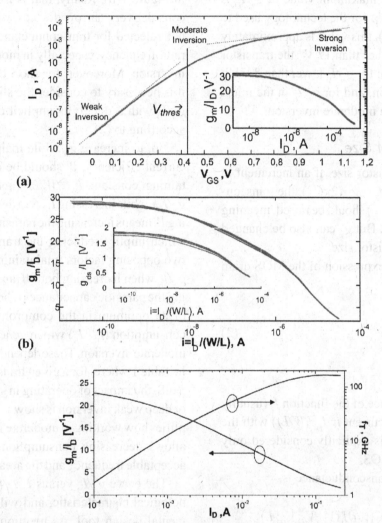

(a)

(b)

(c) © [2011] IEEE. Reprinted, with permission, from (Fiorelli, R., Peralías, E., Silveira, F., 2011).

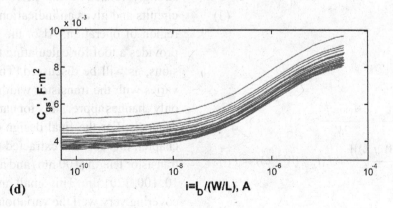

(d)

which can be obtained at a constant current value. The inset of Figure 1(a) shows the g_m/I_D curve as a function of I_D (which is the variable used for MOS biasing). The maximum value of g_m/I_D is approximately $1/nU_T$; for the technology used to generate Figure 1(a), this value is approximately 28 V^{-1}; for g_m/I_D higher than 17 V^{-1} the transistor is in weak inversion; for g_m/I_D lower than 8 V^{-1}, it is in strong inversion, and for g_m/I_D in the midst of this range, it is in moderate inversion.

g_m/I_D vs. Transistor Size

For a specific transistor size, if an increment in the f_T is needed, as $f_T \approx g_m/(2\pi C_{gs})$, the transconductance g_m (and so I_D) should be raised, meaning a reduction in g_m/I_D. But g_m can also be changed modifying the transistor size.

From a general expression of the MOS drain current,

$$I_D = \frac{W}{L} f_1(V_G, V_S, V_D; L), \qquad (2)$$

where the dependence of the function f_1 (usually named normalized current $i=I_D/(W/L)$) with the transistor length L is explicitly considered only for short channel MOS.

The transistor transconductance is,

$$g_m = \partial I_D / \partial V_G = \frac{W}{L} \frac{\partial f_1(V_G, V_S, V_D; L)}{\partial V_G}, \qquad (3)$$

then

$$g_m / I_D = \frac{\partial f_1 / \partial V_G}{f_1} = \frac{\partial(\log f_1)}{\partial V_G} = \frac{\partial(\log(I_D/(W/L)))}{\partial V_G} = f_2(I_D/(W/L)) = f_2(i). \qquad (4)$$

Because $i=f_1$ does not depend on the transistor width W, the g_m/I_D ratio vs. i curve is a constant for MOS transistors with equal length, as shown in Figure 1(b). Really, that is true if you do not consider very narrow devices, which usually are not selected for transconductance generation in radiofrequency, especially in moderate and weak inversion. Moreover, for short channel devices, it is necessary to consider the slight variation of g_m/I_D with L due to its implicit dependence on i according to (2).

So, to increase g_m while maintaining a good current efficiency, W should be increased maintaining constant $I_D/(W/L)$ (and consequently g_m/I_D), while increasing I_D. As a drawback, increasing W means increasing the parasitic capacitances, which implies reducing the transistor f_T. These two opposing factors (maintaining or improving g_m/I_D when increasing both W and I_D but increasing the parasitic capacitances) show the existence of an optimum in the compromise bandwidth-consumption (f_T - I_D) which generally appears in moderate inversion. These dependences are shown in Table 1 where, for a given transconductance of 5 mS, the impact of operating in strong, moderate or deep weak inversion is shown. The table exemplifies how working in moderate inversion region allows decreasing consumption while keeping acceptable frequency and die area characteristics.

The curve g_m/I_D versus $i=I_D/(W/L)$ is a technological characteristic, and will be our fundamental design tool. As mentioned before, it is strongly related to the performance of analog circuits and gives an indication of the transistor region of operation. Also, the g_m/I_D vs. i curve provides a tool for calculating transistor dimensions, as will be discussed. This curve slightly varies with the transistor width and length, and only changes appreciably for narrow or very short channels. For the final design examples of this chapter, this curve is extracted for the minimum transistor length (100 nm) and a set of widths {1, 10, 100, 320} μm. This small range is enough for covering very well the variations of g_m/I_D vs. i in

Table 1. nMOS characteristics for S.I, M.I and W.I.

g_m=5 mS	S.I.	M.I.	W.I.
g_m/I_D, V^{-1}	4	14	25
I_D, A	1.25 m	357 μ	200 μ
i, A	17.8 μ	0.79 μ	12 n
W, m	7 μ	45 μ	1.59 m
$f_T/10$, GHz	16	3	0.2
V_G, V	0.85	0.56	0.36

the whole transistor region. Because of this slight variation in the curve g_m/I_D vs. i with the transistor dimensions, the methodology presented here makes sense. In Figure 1(b), for a 90 nm technology, the behavior of g_m/I_D vs. i when the width of a minimum length transistor changes from W=6 μm to W=320 μm is observed, depicting how little is the change of the g_m/I_D curve for different MOS widths.

g_m/I_D vs. f_T

As well as the g_m/I_D versus i is used to calculate the transistor dimensions, when used together with the transistor gate capacitances versus i, the frequency f_T versus i can be found, as Figure 1(c) shows. This curve gives an idea of the frequency limits of the technology used when different inversion zones are considered. As Figure 1(c) stands, when working with nanometer technologies and in strong inversion, f_T frequencies can reach hundreds of gigahertz whereas in deep weak inversion those frequencies drop down to levels of hundreds of megahertz. For the example of Figure 1(c) and Table 1, and considering again the very restrictive quasi-static limit for the working frequency of one tenth of f_T, for a g_m/I_D around 4 V^{-1} the operating frequency can be up to the tens of gigahertz, whereas with a g_m/I_D around 25 V^{-1} the operating frequency falls to the gigahertz. This simple check lets the designer to know the limitations of the technology in terms of frequency in each level of inversion.

Output Conductance g_{ds} and g_{ds}/I_D

Another small signal parameter required in our methodology to describe the MOS behavior is the output conductance g_{ds}. It dramatically increases in nanometer transistors with respect to micrometer ones, due to the shortening of the channel length L (Tsividis, 2000, page 372). This effect must be taken into account because it begins to influence on certain RF blocks. For example, in an LC tank-VCO, the conductance g_{ds} affects the value of the final g_m chosen, and hence the bias current and the phase noise; in a Common-Source LNA it changes the maximum gain of the circuit. Therefore, a ratio similar to g_m/I_D can be applied (Jespers, 2010) which is the g_{ds}/I_D ratio; it is also very technology dependent. The inset of Figure 1(b) shows the behavior of g_{ds}/I_D versus i, for W in the range of [6, 320] μm. As happens with the g_m/I_D curve, its variation is subtle when changing the width. The variation between strong and weak inversion is small, and similarly to the curve g_m/I_D vs. i, it also decreases when moving towards strong inversion (Tsividis, 2000, page 380).

Intrinsic Capacitances

When working in the radiofrequency range, it is absolutely required the consideration of the transistor intrinsic capacitances. Considering again that the working frequencies are below one tenth of f_T, it is enough to consider the following intrinsic capacitances: C_{gs}, C_{gd}, C_{gb}, C_{bs} and C_{bd}, disregarding the other four capacitances and transcapacitances as well as non-quasistatic effects. These capacitances change with the inversion level, as Tsividis (2000) shows (page 405); and obviously they change with the transistor size. In this work, in order to simplify the modeling, the intrinsic capacitances are considered to be proportional to the gate area (*WL*). This can be done because these capacitances are proportional to the gate oxide capacitance C_{ox} which is, at the same time, proportional to *WL* (Tsividis, 2000, page 391). Hence, each normalized capacitance $C_{ij}' = C_{ij}/(WL)$ is considered to be equal for all transistors in the width range of interest. With this assumption, the intrinsic capacitances are extracted for one representative transistor and normalized to its area. Afterwards, normalized capacitances are applied to estimate the capacitances of other transistors in the considered width range. For example, in Figure 1(d) shows the behavior of the normalized capacitance C_{gs}' versus *i* for a set of widths in a 90 nm technology. As observed, the error is below ±20% of the mean value considering the widths varying between 8 μm and 320 μm, which is acceptable for this methodology. For C_{gd}' and C_{gb}' the error is lower than ±3% of the mean value.

Semi-Empirical Modeling

Analytical compact models —as PSP (Gildenblat et al., 2006), BSIM (BSIM Research Group, 2011), EKV (Enz & Vittoz, 2006) o ACM (Cunha, Schneider & Galup-Montoro, 1998)— have a set of equations more or less complex, consistent in all regions of operation, which describes the MOS transistor. Semi-empirical models use measurement or simulation data to obtain numerically certain characteristics and to build a look-up table.

Despite in the methodology presented here both approaches are valid and can be used indistinctively, in this work we have decided to apply a semi-empirical MOS model, as it jointly considers second and higher order effects which appear in nanometer technologies and it is easily

obtained by extracting MOS characteristics via DC simulation. We discarded the use of analytical compact models, as the fitting of parameters is very time consuming. The semi-empirical model is extracted via an electrical simulator; which, in turn, uses the BSIM (or PSP) model, suitable for RF. The parameters used are provided by the foundry, which means that they are strongly validated. In addition, they are used by designers as the standard verification framework.

MOS Data Acquisition Scheme

As already introduced, for the proposed methodology, three basic characteristics must be considered as a function of the normalized current *i*: (a) the transconductance to current ratio g_m/I_D, (b) the output conductance to current ratio g_{ds}/I_D and (c) the normalized MOS capacitance $C_{ij}' = C_{ij}/(WL)$. To acquire this information, a very simple scheme is utilized: both transistor gate and drain nodes are connected to a DC voltage source, while source and bulk nodes are connected either to ground (nMOS transistor) or to the supply voltage (pMOS transistor). Then, the gate voltage V_G is swept extracting I_D, g_m, g_{ds} and C_{ij}'. For small-signal circuits, the drain voltage is set around its expected DC value. To get a very complete dataset the same simulation must be run for a set of widths (for example, for 1 μm, 10 μm and 100 μm), when a fixed transistor length value is used. Otherwise, following the same idea, a small set of lengths (e.g. 100nm, 1 μm, 10 μm) should be chosen.

Noise in MOS Transistors

In this section, the MOS noise sources used in this chapter to deduce the equations that describe the noise characteristics of the radio-frequency blocks are presented. These sources are the drain current noise (consisting of the white noise and the flicker noise) and the induced gate noise, presented by Galup-Montoro, Schneider and Cunha (1999) and, after by Tsividis, (2000), (Section 8.5); and more recently, for RF models, by Shi, Xiong, Kang, Nan and Lin, (2009).

For the drain-noise current power spectral density two zones are clearly recognized, the white noise zone and the flicker noise zone. The white noise is due to random fluctuations of the charge in the channel; whereas the flicker noise is the result of trapping and detrapping of the channel carriers in the gate oxide. The corner frequency f_c is the frequency of the asymptotic limit between these two zones.

The white noise, for all-inversion regions, is generally expressed as:

$$\overline{i_{d,wn}^2} = 4k_BT\gamma g_{d0}\Delta f = 4k_BT\gamma \frac{g_m}{\alpha}\Delta f, \qquad (5)$$

where k_B is the Boltzmann constant, T is the absolute temperature, γ is the excess noise factor, α is equal to $\alpha = g_m / g_{d0}$, with g_{d0} the output conductance evaluated at $V_{DS}=0$, where the white noise is maximum for all the inversion regions.

The flicker noise is written as:

$$\overline{i_{d,1/f}^2} = \frac{K_F' g_m^2}{WL}\frac{1}{f}\Delta f \qquad (6)$$

with $K_F' = K_F/C_{ox}$, the normalized flicker noise constant, W and L are the transistor width and length, and f is the frequency of study.

The total drain-noise current power spectral density is the sum of (5) and (6), as no correlation is supposed to exist between the white noise and the flicker noise sources.

Finally, for high frequency operation, the induced gate noise must also be considered. This noise appears because random fluctuations of the carriers (generated by the white noise) cause a gate current to flow through the gate, even if no signal current exists. The induced gate noise is written as:

$$\overline{i_g^2} =$$
$$4k_BT\delta\frac{C_{gs}^2}{5g_{d0}}4\pi^2f^2\Delta f = \frac{16}{5}k_BT\delta\,\alpha\pi^2\frac{C_{gs}^2}{g_m}f^2\Delta f, \qquad (7)$$

where δ is the gate noise coefficient.

The gate noise is partially correlated with the drain noise due to the white noise, with a correlation coefficient c given by Van der Ziel (1986):

$$c = \frac{\overline{i_g i_{d,wn}^*}}{\sqrt{\overline{i_g^2}\,\overline{i_{d,wn}^2}}}. \qquad (8)$$

For long channel MOS transistors biased in strong inversion γ is around 2/3, δ is two times γ, α approximately equal to 0.6 and $|c|$ around to 0.4. These variables change its values when working in short-channel devices and when working in moderate and weak inversion. However, in order to simplify the explanation of the methodology, in this work these constants are fixed around the mentioned values. But, to improve the methodology results, the designer should express these constants versus g_m/I_D. Further reading on these topics can be found in the studies presented by Manghisoni, Ratti, Re, Speziali and Traversi (2006) and Scholten et al. (2004). These works quantify the constants of the power spectral densities of MOS noise sources particularly for nanometer technologies.

PASSIVE COMPONENT ANALYSIS

In radiofrequency design, the on-chip passive components need to be correctly characterized, as they are fundamental in the performance of the circuit. For example, in a VCO design, if it is considered an inductor model with a parasitic parallel resistor much lower than the actual one, the VCO could even not oscillate. This section briefly introduces the models and parameters of the passive components we have used in the design examples.

We use semi-empirical models extracted from electrical simulations, the same way we do with the MOS transistor. Depending on the level of accuracy and the available technological information, we use the models provided by the foundry or the ones obtained with electromagnetic simulators as ADS Momentum™ or ASITIC (Niknejad, 2000). The two main drawbacks of electromagnetic simulators are: (1) they need the process technological data and unfortunately this information is not fully available in many cases; and (2) the large computational time. In this work, for the sake of efficiency, the former method is utilized; the library cells supplied by the foundry are simulated using AC analysis at the working frequency obtaining their equivalent complex impedance.

For the design methodology presented in this chapter, simple passive component models, as an ideal inductor in series with a parasitic resistor for on-chip inductors, will be used. Biunivocal relations between the model parameters of the component, as between the inductance and its parasitic serial resistance, are very useful to generate a simple design flow.

The extraction of these models depends on the topological location of the component, for example, if the device has an AC grounded terminal or if it is fully differential. The analysis performed with the electrical simulator logically has to reflect this fact.

Inductor Modeling

In this work, inductors cells provided by the foundry are used. The extracted inductor model consists on an equivalent ideal inductor with a para-

sitic resistor for a particular working frequency f_0. For example, for an inductor with an AC grounded port and using the AC analysis, its serial network is found. It has a complex series impedance $R_{s,ind} + jX_{ind}$, where $R_{s,ind}$ is the series resistance and X_{ind} is its series reactance which divided by $\omega_0 = 2\pi f_0$, is the equivalent series inductance L_{ind}.

Depending on the function of the inductor in the circuit, a serial or a parallel resistance is chosen to describe it. For the previous example, the serial network can be transformed into a parallel network by means of the series quality factor $Q_L = X_{ind}/R_{s,ind}$. The equivalent inductance of the parallel network is $L_{p,ind} = L_{ind}(1 + 1/Q_L^2)$ and the parasitic resistance of the parallel network is $R_{p,ind} = R_{s,ind}(1 + Q_L^2)$. For real on-chip inductors with $Q_L \geq 4$, $L_{p,ind} \approx L_{ind}$. The electrical analysis used have to be run for a large set of inductors to obtain a complete database, including L_{ind}, Q_L, $R_{s,ind}$, and $R_{p,ind}$. It is important to bear in mind that these values will change when the frequency changes or other technology corner is considered, so more than one table should be needed if any of the situations must be taken into account.

To illustrate the modeling procedure in a standard CMOS 90 nm process, extracted L_{ind}, $R_{p,ind}$, and $R_{s,ind}$ are plotted in Figure 2, when both coil conductor width and internal diameter (hence sweeping the number of turns) are swept. The data in these plots show that in this technology the highest parasitic parallel resistances come with the largest inductor values.

Because in this work, we have considered that a good inductor is the one that has a low series resistance or a high parallel resistance, depending on its function in the circuit, we have established some particular biunivocal relations between the data of each simulated inductor in the inductor database, as the highlighted in thick line in Figure 2. In this way, by means of computational routines, it is possible to find, for a given inductance value, the nearest inductor included in the database with

Figure 2. (a) Parasitic parallel resistance $R_{p,ind}$ versus equivalent inductance L_{ind} varying internal inductor radius and inductor coil width; and (b) Parasitic serial resistance $R_{s,ind}$ versus L_{ind} corresponding with inductors in (a). The bold line highlights the inductors with (a) the highest $R_{p,ind}$ and (b) the lowest $R_{s,ind}$

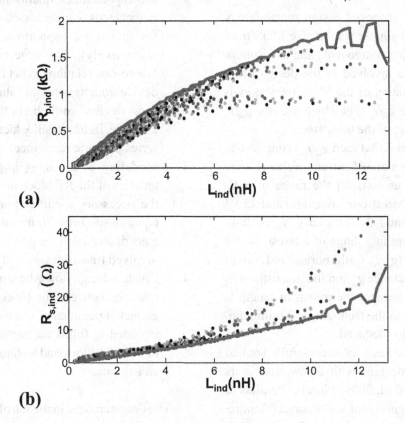

(a)

(b)

the lowest series resistance or the highest parallel resistance.

Capacitor and Varactor Modeling

As well as inductors, capacitors and varactors can be modelled as serial networks which consists of a complex series impedance $R_{s,cap(var)} + jX_{s,cap(var)}$. Again, AC analysis is used to characterize these components.

For practical capacitors used in RF designs, as metal-insulator-metal type, their quality factors are considerably high –above 100 for the technology used here- when we compared them with monolithic inductors, so generally their parasitic resistances will be discarded in the initial design.

On the other hand, varactors, which are generally based on semiconductor devices, have lower quality factor -they can be comparable with high-Q on-chip inductors- and their parasitic resistances suffer from variations when the bias voltage changes the effective capacitance. As a result, an AC behavior study should be done for different biasing conditions. Because the quality factor of the varactor varies with the bias voltage, a conservative yet simple approach is to consider the lowest reachable quality factor value when the bias is swept.

PROPOSED DESIGN METHODOLOGY

The core of the proposed design methodology intends to give a simple way to size MOS transistors and passive components and to visualize the compromises involved in the design of an RF block. The sizing of the MOS transistors is performed by the g_m/I_D tool which uses the g_m/I_D vs. i characteristic of the transistor.

The basic idea is that each g_m/I_D is one-to-one related with a normalized current i value (Figure 1(b)). Then, let us consider the range of g_m/I_D between 3 V^{-1} (deep strong inversion) and 25 V^{-1} (weak inversion) and, that for each g_m/I_D the drain current I_D is swept in a range of interest. So for each defined pair (g_m/I_D, I_D) the normalized current i, the transconductance g_m and the transistor W/L are known and, because the transistor length is set, for example to the technological minimum, the width W is also deduced.

This technique has been successfully applied both in simple designs with a few transistors (Shameli & Heydari, 2006; Fiorelli, Peralías & Silveira, 2011) as in complex structures (Flandre, Viviani, Eggermont, Gentinne & Jespers, 1997; Aguirre & Silveira, 2008; Tanguay & Sawan, 2009).

Despite these examples show the efficient use of the g_m/I_D tool, they lack of a systematic methodology suitable to be employed in RF blocks.

As it was sketched at the end of the chapter Introduction, four steps have to be followed to apply our design methodology for an RF block:

1. DC behavior of MOS transistor has to be captured in curves or expressions. It is necessary to measure or simulate the DC MOS characteristics (g_m, g_{ds}, I_D, C_{ij}) for a small set of transistor sizes and for all-inversion levels to generate the curves g_m/I_D, g_{ds}/I_D and C_{ij}' versus i and W. The parameters corresponding to the noise models should be also extracted.

2. Extraction of parameters of practicable passive components (e.g. parasitic resistances and capacitances, quality factors, effective inductances, capacitances, and resistances for inductors, capacitors, and resistors, respectively). The objective is to have one-to-one relations to get the best feasible device from its nominal value. The qualifier "best device" could be in the sense of, for example, its best quality factor or, its lowest series parasitic resistance.

3. Modeling of the most important characteristics of the RF block and then, perform the necessary modifications to the found equations in order to introduce the parameters described in the previous steps for the involved transistors, as g_m/I_D and g_{ds}/I_D.

4. Create a design flow where it is arranged the relations between the block equations, the extracted parameters and the decisions, all intended to fulfill the particular specifications of the block and technological process constraints.

The final step is the inclusion of characteristics of the modeled circuit in a set of equations. In this way a complete design flow can be developed. In this chapter two examples are provided: a VCO and an LNA. These circuits present a small number of transistors and passive components, so it helps in developing a simple design flow to simplify the reader's comprehension.

Each example begins presenting the relevant equations of the block with no deductions because it is not the scope of this chapter; nevertheless relevant references where these circuits are carefully studied are provided. Where necessary, equations have been modified in order to express them in terms of g_m/I_D and/or g_{ds}/I_D.

The design flows and real implementations in nanometer technologies to work under the 2.4 GHz band of the IEEE 802.15.1 and IEEE 802.15.4 standards are presented. With the design flows, implemented in a computational program, a set

Figure 3. (a) Complementary cross-coupled LC-VCO; (b) LC-VCO small-signal schematic; (c) Inductively degenerated CS-LNA schematic; (d) CS-LNA small-signal schematic

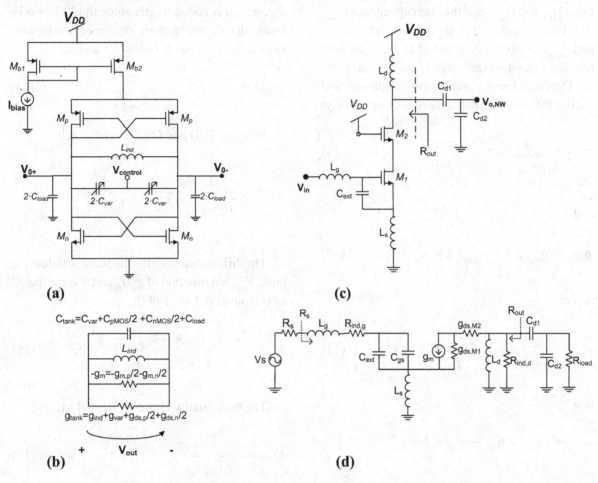

(a)   (b)   (c)   (d)

(a) and (b) © [2011] IEEE. Reprinted, with permission, from (Fiorelli, R., Peralías, E., Silveira, F., 2011).

of design space maps are displayed in order to visualize the trade-offs between consumption and noise and to pick a design point to be fabricated. Implemented circuit simulation data and measurement results are given to show their similarity with the data provided with the methodology.

VCO Example

VCO Modeling[1]

The VCO topology used in this example is depicted in Figure 3(a). It shows a cross-coupled

complementary VCO with an inductor-capacitor tank (LC-VCO), biased with a pMOS current mirror (M_{b1}, M_{b2}). Cross-coupled transistors provide the needed negative feedback whereas a pMOS-nMOS complementary structure increases the VCO transconductance while consuming the same quiescent I_D current (with $I_{bias} = 2 \cdot I_D$). A complete study of this block is developed in the work of Hershenson, Hajimiri, Mohan, Boyd and Lee (1999).

A small-signal simplified model of this LC-VCO is given in Figure 3(b). It comprises: the effective inductance at ω_0 of the differential inductor L_{ind}, the varactor capacitance C_{var}, the parasitic capacitances of the nMOS and pMOS transistors C_{nMOS} and C_{pMOS} and the load capacitance C_{load}. The nMOS and pMOS transconductances, $g_{m,p}$ and $g_{m,n}$ are arbitrarily matched to g_m. Therefore, transistors sizing is adjusted to achieve this.

The well-known oscillation frequency and oscillation condition expressions are respectively:

$$\omega_0 = \frac{1}{\sqrt{L_{ind}C_{tan k}}} \qquad (9)$$

and

$$g_{tank} \leq g_{m,p}/2 + g_{m,n}/2 = g_m \qquad (10)$$

where

$$C_{tan k} = C_{var} + \frac{C_{pMOS} + C_{nMOS}}{2} + C_{load} \qquad (11)$$

and

$$g_{tank} = g_{ind} + g_{var} + g_{ds,p}/2 + g_{ds,n}/2 \qquad (12)$$

where $g_{ds,p}$ and $g_{ds,n}$ are the output parallel conductances of the nMOs and pMOs transistors; g_{ind} and g_{var} are the parasitic parallel conductances of the inductor and varactor respectively. If the MOS transistor intrinsic gain A_i is considered—defined as the ratio between g_m and g_{ds}, i.e. $A_i = g_m/g_{ds} = g_m/I_D/g_{ds}/I_D$ — and as generally g_{var} is negligible compared to g_{ind}, (12) can be rewritten as,

$$g_{tank} \approx g_{ind} + g_{ds,p}/2 + g_{ds,n}/2 =$$
$$g_{ind} + \frac{g_m}{2}\left(\frac{1}{A_{i,p}} + \frac{1}{A_{i,n}}\right). \qquad (13)$$

Inequality (10) can be transformed into an equality using an oscillation safety margin factor k_{osc}, which is added to guarantee the VCO oscillation despite technology or current variations. Generally, k_{osc} goes between 1.5 and 3.

$$g_m = k_{osc}g_{tank}. \qquad (14)$$

Merging (13) and (14), it is obtained,

$$g_m = g_{ind}\left(\frac{1}{k_{osc}} - \frac{1}{2A_{i,p}} - \frac{1}{2A_{i,n}}\right)^{-1} = k'_{osc}g_{ind} \qquad (15)$$

The differential output voltage amplitude at the tank, V_{out}, is a function of g_m/I_D and it is estimated as (Hajimiri & Lee, 1999):

$$V_{out} \approx \frac{8}{\pi}\frac{I_D}{g_{tank}} = \frac{8}{\pi}\frac{k'_{osc}}{g_m/I_D} \qquad (16)$$

The tank quality factor is defined as,

$$Q = \frac{1}{(2\pi f_0 L_{ind}g_{tank})} \qquad (17)$$

Phase noise (PN) is a fundamental characteristic of the VCO that describes the spectral purity around the VCO oscillation frequency f_0 (Leeson, 1966). Considering the frequency offset Δf around f_0, three asymptotic zones are currently defined: very near f_0, in the named $1/f^3$ region, the phase noise decreases proportionally to $1/\Delta f^3$ and it is directly related to the flicker noise of MOS transistors. Then appears the $1/f^2$ region where PN is inversely proportional to Δf^2, caused fundamentally by the white noise of VCO elements. Finally, far from f_0 there is a flat zone, the VCO floor noise, where the external noise sources dominate. Generally it is in the $1/f^2$ zone where the VCO phase noise is specified. The expression of the phase noise in the $1/f^2$ region, derived from the work of Hajimiri and Lee (1999) and modified to express it in terms of the g_m/I_D ratio is presented:

$$PN_{1/f^2} =$$
$$10 \cdot \log \left(k_B T \frac{\pi^2}{64} \left(\frac{\gamma}{\alpha_{eq}} + \frac{1}{k_{osc}} \right) \frac{1}{Q^2} \frac{g_m / I_D}{I_D} \left(\frac{f_0}{\Delta f} \right)^2 \right)$$
$$(18)$$

where k_B is the Boltzmann constant, T is the absolute temperature, Q is the tank quality factor obtained from (17), γ is the excess noise factor, and α_{eq} is defined as $\alpha_{eq} = 2g_m / (g_{d0,n} + g_{d0,p})$, with g_{d0} the output conductance at $V_{DS} = 0$.

Derivation of (18) and a corresponding expression for the $1/f^3$ region can be found in Fiorelli, Peralias and Silveira (2011).

The flicker corner frequency, the asymptotic limit between $1/f^2$ and $1/f^3$ zones, is given by,

$$f_{c,1/f^3} \simeq \frac{k_0}{2\pi} \frac{K'_F \alpha_{eq}}{4 k_B T \gamma} \frac{g_m}{I_D} i \frac{1}{L^2},$$
$$(19)$$

with $k_0 = \Gamma_{av}^2 / (\Gamma_{rms})^2$, where Γ_{av} and Γ_{rms} are the average and the root-mean-square values of the impulse sensitivity function Γ defined in Hajimiri and Lee (1998).

VCO Design Methodology

Now that the basic equations of the VCO model have been listed, the design flow of the VCO is presented through the scheme of Figure 4(a). Each step is itemized below[2]:

Step 1: Lets start fixing a set of initial parameters and limits: the minimum transistor channel length L_{min}, the oscillation safety margin factor k_{osc}, a maximum equivalent inductance $L_{ind,max}$, a minimum varactor capacitance $C_{var,min}$ and C_{load}. Next, set the VCO specifications: the oscillation frequency f_0, a maximum current $I_{D,max}$, a maximum phase noise in the white noise zone PN_{max} at an offset Δf and, a minimum output voltage $V_{out,min}$.

Step 2: Pick a pair of values, an inductance L_{ind} and a g_m/I_D ratio from the technological database of inductors and transistors, which are assumed previously collected.

Step 3: From inductor database, derive the g_{ind} of the selected inductor, assuming that we have the relationship between the maximum parallel resistance versus inductance ($R_{p,ind}^{max}$ vs. L_{ind}). Obtain the normalized currents of nMOS and pMOS i_n and i_p as well as g_{ds}/I_D, from the picked g_m/I_D and the characteristic curves (g_m/I_D vs. i) and (g_{ds}/I_D vs. i). Calculate the intrinsic gains $A_{i,n}$ and $A_{i,p}$. Extract the transistors equivalent capacitance from C'_{nMOS} vs. i and C'_{pMOS} vs i tables.

Step 4: Deduce g_m from (15), k_{osc} and g_{ind}. With g_m and g_m/I_D calculate the bias current I_D, and with (16) compute V_{out}. Then calculate the transistors widths W_n and W_p from i_n and i_p and I_D. Then, compute C_{nMOS} and C_{pMOS}. With (9) and (11), solve for C_{var}. Calculate the flicker frequency corner $f_{c,1/f^3}$ using (19).

Step 5: If $I_D > I_{D,max}$ or $V_{out} < V_{out,min}$ or $C_{var} < C_{var,min}$ or $f_{c,1/f^3} > \Delta f$, return to *Step 2* and change one or both of the values chosen; otherwise continue.

Step 6: Compute Q with (17). Then calculate the phase noise PN using (18) at the frequency offset Δf. If it surpasses PN_{max} return to *Step 2*, otherwise the design is finished.

Following these steps, we have implemented a computational routine both to obtain a VCO design and to study graphically the behavior of the current consumption and PN when we vary the inversion region (i.e. g_m/I_D) and L_{ind}. A 90 nm

Figure 4. (a) LC-VCO design flow; (b) I_D vs g_m/I_D for four inductor values; (c) Design space of PN at 400 kHz offset versus g_m/I_D and L_{ind}; (d) Measured PN at a central frequency of 2.16 GHz; (e) Measured PN at 400 kHz offset varying the current I_D.

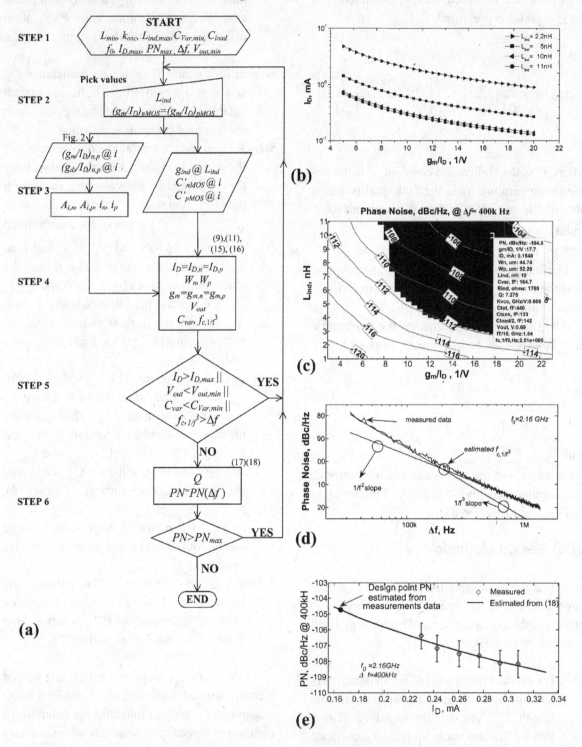

(a), (c) (d) and (e): © [2011] IEEE. Reprinted, with permission, from (Fiorelli, R., Peralías, E., Silveira, F., 2011).

CMOS technology is used, and the noise parameters are set to α=0.65 and γ=0.6. Figure 4(b) presents an example of the plots obtained from the routine. This shows the behavior of the drain current I_D for different inversion zones and for a constrained set inductor values. A reduction in the drain current occurs when g_m/I_D increases, that is, when moving to weak inversion. It happens because g_m is fixed for a fixed inductor and an increment in g_m/I_D means a reduction in I_D. Figure 4(c) displays the phase noise (at an offset of 400 kHz) for different g_m/I_D and inductors values. As expected from (18), *PN* increases when working in moderate and weak inversion as well as when the quality factor of the tank is low.

Figures 4(b) and 4(c) show the power of this methodology, as choosing the g_m/I_D and the inductor it can be obtained jointly the I_D and the phase noise; easily visualizing their trade-offs. Another view of this idea is given in Table 2 where the results of designing in strong, moderate or weak inversion for a hypothetical specification of PN of -114 dBc/Hz affects the consumption, transistors and inductor size. In particular it can be seen that a minimum of consumption exists in the moderate inversion region.

Application Example and Experimental Results

With the VCO methodology presented, a 2.4 GHz LC-VCO has been implemented in a 90 nm CMOS technology. An on-chip differential-pair buffer is included in the design in order to fix C_{load}. To follow the design flow, the technology database (MOS data and inductor data) has been previously collected.

Using the design space of Figure 4(c) the design displayed in the text box has been implemented. The election of this design point was focused on generating a VCO with a PN lower than -100 dBc/Hz at an offset of 400 kHz from the carrier and a total bias current I_{bias} lower than 600 µA, with $I_{bias}=2I_D$. The shadowed area shows the

Table 2. Parameter values of the VCO in S.I., M.I. and W.I.

PN=-114 dBc/Hz @ 400 kHz	S.I.	M.I.	W.I.
g_m/I_D, V^{-1}	7	14	23
L_{ind}, nH	11.2	4.2	1.8
R_p, kΩ	2.0	1.1	0.24
I_D, µA	410	320	840
W_n, µm	4.7	29	3400
W_p, µm	18	35	64000

zone where I_{bias} complies with the latter requirement. The picked point drives an I_{bias} of 310 µA (I_D=155 µA).

With the data provided by the chosen design point, the necessary electrical simulations are performed to do small design adjustments to adapt the design to the desired oscillation frequency and oscillation condition. After the adjustments, the LC-VCO consumes an I_{bias} of 330 µA (I_D=165 µA) with phase noise of -104.3 dBc/Hz at 400 kHz from the 2.4 GHz carrier frequency. The final component sizing is: W_p=54 µm and W_n=46 µm; C_{var}=350 fF and L_{ind}=10 nH.

Measurements

A set of phase noise measurements has been done to the fabricated chip. Due to external interference with the measurement setup, the minimum bias current utilized in the measurements was I_{bias}=440 µA (I_D=220 µA). For this current, the phase noise versus the offset frequency, with the carrier at 2.16 GHz is shown in Figure 4(d). It also shows the measured $1/f^3$ corner frequency, $f_{c,1/f3}$ which is 203 kHz, while the analytical expected one at g_m/I_D = 17.6 V^{-1} is 257 kHz.

The current I_D was also swept up to 310 µA and a set of phase noise measurements at 400 kHz from the carrier were performed, as depicted in Figure 4(e), considering again a carrier frequency around 2.16 GHz (with slight variations due to minor changes in the parasitic capacitances of the MOS). The experimental data were fitted considering γ=0.65, α=0.55 and k_{osc} =3. The fitted model is extended up to the nominal I_D current of 165 μA, obtaining an extrapolated *PN* value of -104.6 dBc/Hz.

LNA Example

LNA Modeling

In order to describe the methodology proposed for RF LNAs implemented in nanometer technologies, the design of an inductively degenerated common-source low noise amplifier (CS-LNA) is utilized, as shown in the schematic of Figure 3(c). The LNA includes an external gate-source capacitor C_{ext} to provide an additional degree of freedom in the design (Andreani & Sjland, 2001). The input stage is composed by the gate inductor L_g, the source inductor L_s, the capacitor C_{ext} and the MOS transistor M_1; whereas the output stage consists of the cascode transistor M_2 and the load inductor L_d. To couple the LNA output resistance R_{out} with the load R_L it is used a matching network, consisting of capacitors C_{d1} and C_{d2}.

This design follows the idea formulated in the work of Belostotski and Haslett (2006). Here, only the parasitic series resistance of the gate inductor $R_{ind,g}$ is considered. The parasitic resistance of the source inductor, as well as the gate-bulk C_{gb} and gate-drain C_{gd} parasitic capacitances are discarded for the sake of facilitating the explanation, as the expressions are considerably simplified and the slight deviation is easily corrected with a minor adjustment in the gate inductance value (Belostotski & Haslett, 2006). To increase as much as possible the circuit gain, the load inductor L_d is chosen to have a very high parallel resistance.

Defining $C_t = C_{gs} + C_{ext}$ and $L_t = L_g + L_s$, the input impedance of the LNA is,

$$Z_{in}(s) = R_{ind,g} + sL_t + \frac{1}{sC_t} + L_s \frac{g_m}{C_t}. \qquad (20)$$

Equation (20) can be divided into real and imaginary parts and evaluated for $s = j\omega_0$, where ω_0 is the working frequency. Assuming matching impedance between the LNA input and the purely resistive input voltage source, i.e. $Z_{in}=R_s$, the following expressions are obtained:

$$R_s = R_{ind,g} + L_s \frac{g_m}{C_t}, \qquad (21)$$

and

$$\omega_0 = 1 / \sqrt{L_t C_t}. \qquad (22)$$

With (21) and (22) a second order equation with C_t as its unique unknown is found:

$$(R_s - R_{ind,g})\omega_0^2 C_t^2 + \omega_0 g_m L_g C_t - g_m = 0. \qquad (23)$$

The effective transconductance of the input stage, evaluated at ω_0, is:

$$G_{eff} = \left| G_{eff}(s) \right|_{s=j\omega_0} = \frac{g_m}{\omega_0 \left(R_{ind,g} C_t + L_s g_m \right)}. \qquad (24)$$

Then the LNA voltage gain is,

$$G = G_{eff} \frac{R_{out}}{2}. \qquad (25)$$

The noise factor expression in ω_0 is (Belostotski & Haslett, 2006):

$$F = \frac{R_{ind,g}}{R_s} \left(1 + \frac{\omega_0 \gamma C_t}{2 G_{eff} \alpha} \chi \right), \qquad (26)$$

with

$$\chi = 1 - 2|c|\sqrt{\frac{\delta\alpha^2}{5\gamma}\frac{C_{gs}^2}{C_t^2} + \frac{\delta\alpha^2}{5\gamma}\left(1 + \frac{1}{\omega_0^2 C_t^2 R_{ind,g}^2}\right)\frac{C_{gs}}{C_t}},$$

(27)

where $|c|$, δ, α and γ are defined in Section 2.1.6.

Finally, the Noise Figure (*NF*) is $NF_{dB} = 10$ log(*F*).

LNA Design Methodology

The proposed design flow optimizes the Noise Figure, considering a power consumption constraint. Its objectives are the correct biasing and sizing of the MOS transistor and the dimensions of L_g, L_s and C_t.

The design flow covers all the possible pairs $(g_m/I_D, I_D)$ with I_D below the maximum acceptable $I_{D,max}$. For each pair, it is necessary to find the gate inductor that minimizes the noise figure among all of a predetermined subset of inductors $\Lambda_L = \{L_{ind,1}, ..., L_{ind,j}, ..., L_{ind,N}\}$. For this inductor, C_{ext}, L_s and G are computed. To build Λ_L the inductors that have the highest parallel resistance are chosen from the whole set of extracted inductors.

Following the above idea, the flow diagram of the methodology is presented in Figure 5(a). It is organized in the following steps:

Step 1: Start by setting the constraints of a minimum transistor length L_{min} and the inductor subset Λ_L, and the specifications: the working frequency ω_0, a maximum transistor bias current I_D^{max}, a maximum noise factor F_{max} and, a minimum gain G_{min}.

Step 2: Pick a pair of I_D and g_m/I_D values, using the transistor technology database, which is assumed previously collected. Pick an inductor L_d included in Λ_L with a high parallel resistance $R_{ind,d}$.

Step 3: With the pair $(g_m/I_D, I_D)$, and the transistor technology database (characteristic curves g_m/I_D vs. i, g_{ds}/I_D vs. i and C_{gs}' vs. i) obtain the normalized current i, the transistor width W, the output conductance g_{ds}, and C_{gs}. Calculate R_{out} with $R_{ind,d}$ and $1/g_{ds}$.

Step 4: Consider each inductor $L_{ind,j}$ of Λ_L as a possible gate inductor L_g. For each $L_{ind,j}$ evaluate its serial resistance $R_{ind,j}$ and apply (21), (24), and (26) to obtain $C_{ext,j}$, $L_{s,j}$ and NF_j. Then, consider as the gate inductor for the selection of *Step 2* the one which provides with the lowest value of *NF*:

$$NF_{min} = \min_j\{NF_j\} \ \& \ j^* = \{j \mid NF_{min} = NF_j\}.$$

That is

$$L_g = L_{ind,j^*}, \ C_{ext} = C_{ext,j^*}$$

If NF_{min} is higher than NF_{max} return to *Step 2*, otherwise continue.

Step 5: Being j^* the index of the selected gate inductor in Λ_L, find in the collection Λ_L the inductor with the nearest inductance to L_{s,j^*} and with the lowest series resistance. If the source inductor is not found in Λ_L, return to *Step 2*.

Step 6: Compute the gain G using (25). If G is lower than G_{min} then return to *Step 2* and choose another pair $(g_m/I_D, I_D)$. Otherwise, end the design.

In order to assess the performance of this design flow, we have implemented it in computational routines. In this way, we can obtain numerically the optimum noise figure for the available range of g_m/I_D versus a wide range of I_D.

We have used the database obtained from a 90 nm CMOS technology. We fix the operating frequency to 2.445 GHz, γ=4/3, δ=0.6, L_{min}=100nm,

Figure 5. (a) CS-LNA design flow. (b) Simulated NF and gain design space versus g$_m$/I$_D$ and I$_D$. Measured S-parameters: (c) LNA gain characteristics, (S$_{21}$), (d) LNA matching characteristics S$_{11}$ and S$_{22}$, and (e) LNA Noise Figure.

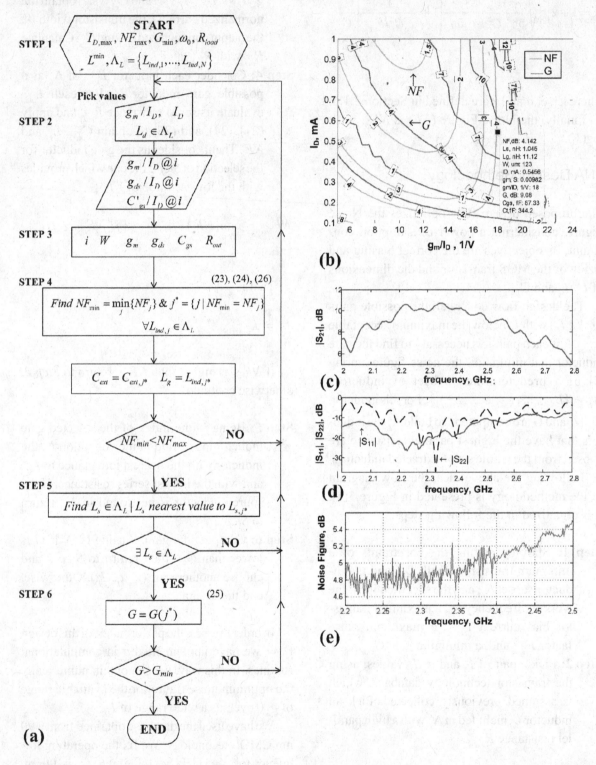

R_s=50Ω, R_{Load}=50Ω, and Λ_L a subset of the inductors of Figure 2.

In Figure 5(b) it is depicted the Noise Figure characteristic and the gain versus g_m/I_D and I_D. As expected, the optimum of Noise Figure respect to the power consumption is in moderate inversion. This trade-off is presented in Table 3, where three design points are compared.

Application Example and Experimental Results

To validate experimentally this LNA design methodology, a differential CS-LNA has been implemented in a 90 nm CMOS technology to be used in a fully differential 2.4 GHz ZigBee receiver. As initial specifications we considered I_D lower than 0.6 mA, G around 10dB, a NF lower than 5 dB, and a 1-dB compression point (P1dB) higher than -15 dBm for 100 Ω input and output impedances. To design a differential circuit based on the method proposed, we obtain the single ended design following the design flow of Figure 5(a), then we mirror the circuit to generate a differential structure. In our differential LNA we employ a differential source inductor; but the L_s calculated by the procedure is single ended; thus we use the double of this value to find a near value differential inductor included in the technology set.

To pick the final design point we use the Noise Figure-Gain space map of Figure 5(b). The displayed text-box lists the computed components sizing, C_t value, current consumption, noise figure, gain, among others. These data were used to implement and simulate the circuit in Cadence SpectreRF.

The final simulation results of the LNA, after minor adjustments in the component sizing, show that it consumes 573 μA, has a voltage gain of 10.7 dB and a NF of 4.5 dB. The nMOS width is 92 μm, C_t/C_{gs} is 4.4, L_g is 11 nH, L_d is 10.5 nH and L_s is 1.5 nH. As expected, under post-layout conditions, only minor adjustments in component sizing were needed to reach the specifications.

Table 3. Parameter values of the LNA in S.I., M.I. and W.I.

I_D=0.6 mA	S.I.	M.I.	W.I.
g_m/I_D, V^{-1}	5	14	19.5
W, μm	4.3	32.4	278
NF, dB	2.6	1.9	9.1
G, dB	0.4	6.6	9.6

Measurements

The measured S-parameters are shown in Figure 5(c) and 5(d). The input and output networks resonant frequencies have a shift around 150MHz, visualized in traces S$_{11}$ and S$_{22}$, where |S$_{11}$|< -10 dB and |S$_{22}$|< -10dB. These shifts reduce the gain in approximately 1 dB and increase the NF value. The LNA isolation is correct as S$_{12}$ is below -35 dB. The gain of the LNA, represented by S$_{21}$ in Figure 5(c), is higher than 9dB in the specified band.

Figure 5(e) depicts the Noise Figure at the band between 2.2 GHz and 2.5 GHz. At 2.445 GHz it shows a value of 5.2 dB, with a minimum of 4.8 dB in the band of interest. This minimum is close to the expected NF value of 4.5 dB obtained in SpectreRF.

Finally, the input third order intermodulation point (IIP3) as well as the 1-dB compression point are measured. The P1dB is found to be -13 dBm. For the IIP3, we measured the amplitude of the fundamental and third order intermodulation tone, where two tones separated 1 MHz with variable amplitude are injected. Extrapolating these curves, the IIP3 is -3.5 dBm.

CONCLUSION

In this chapter we present a design methodology for analog radiofrequency blocks, focused to nanometer technologies and based on the g_m/I_D tool. We review the MOS model in all-inversion regions, studying the curve g_m/I_D versus i and the behavior of f_T when the bias point moves from weak inversion to strong inversion. We show the importance, already highlighted by other works, of working with a MOS transistor model that covers all-inversion regions of operation and therefore exploiting to its maximum the MOS transistor potential and the performance trade-offs. We show that for RF circuits integrated in nanometer technologies, the best trade-off occurs in many cases in the moderate region.

Moreover, this methodology easily presents the trade-offs involved in each particular design and the consequences of modifying the parameters of the RF block. The use of the proposed methodology reduces the design time, as little adjustments are needed after the election of the design point.

We present two examples of RF blocks in which the method is applied. We derive the specific design methodologies for a CS-LNA and an LC-VCO. The key equations of each block were adjusted to express them as a function of the g_m/I_D ratio.

For each circuit, we present how the characteristics change when we utilize a design in weak, moderate or strong inversion.

Considering particularly the VCO, we show graphically the design compromises with respect to the inversion region or the inductor choice. We see that designing in moderate and weak inversion leads to a current reduction and a Phase Noise increment; on the other hand an increment of the inductor value (and hence a raise in its parasitic parallel resistance) contributes to an improvement in the VCO spectral purity.

For the case of the LNA, the design space map is shown displaying the Noise Figure when we vary the inversion level and the drain current. Here we can also appreciate that working in moderate inversion permits to obtain a good compromise between noise figure and gain for a fixed current.

The particular design methodologies of each block are verified in measured prototypes, which show a good agreement between measurements, simulated values and computed results in the design flow.

ACKNOWLEDGMENT

This work was supported in part by FEDER funds through the SR2 project (Catrene2A105SR2 under the Avanza+ Spanish program TSI-020400-2010-55) and the Andalusian Government project P09- TIC-5386; the MOSIS Research Program, the Uruguayan projects PDT 63/361, ANII FCE 2007/501; the bilateral cooperation project CSIC-UR 2009UY0019, and the Spanish Grant MAE-AECID.

REFERENCES

Aguirre, P., & Silveira, F. (2008). CMOS op-amp power optimization in all regions of inversion using geometric programming. *21st Symposium on Integrated Circuits and System Design, SBCCI* (pp. 152–157).

Andreani, P., & Sjland, H. (2001). Noise optimization of an inductively degenerated CMOS low noise amplifier. *IEEE Transactions on Circuits and Systems, 48*(9), 835–841. doi:10.1109/82.964996

Barboni, L., Fiorelli, R., & Silveira, F. (2006). A tool for design exploration and power optimization of CMOS RF circuit blocks. *IEEE International Symposium on Circuits and Systems, ISCAS*, (pp. 2961-2964).

Belostotski, L., & Haslett, J. (2006). Noise figure optimization of inductively degenerated CMOS LNAs with integrated gate inductors. *IEEE Transactions on Circuits and Systems, 53*(7), 1409–1422. doi:10.1109/TCSI.2006.875188

BSIM Research Group. (2009). *BSIM3v3 and BSIM4 MOS model*. Retrieved from http://www-device.eecs.berkeley.edu/~bsim3/bsim4.html

Cunha, A., Schneider, M., & Galup-Montoro, C. (1998). An MOS transistor model for analog circuit design. *IEEE Journal of Solid-state Circuits, 33*(10), 1510–1519. doi:10.1109/4.720397

Enz, C., & Vittoz, E. (2006). *Charge-based MOS transistor modeling.* John Wiley and Sons. doi:10.1002/0470855460

Enz, C. C., Krummenacher, F., & Vittoz, E. A. (1995). An analytical MOS transistor model valid in all regions of operation and dedicated to low voltage and low-current applications. *Analog Integrated Circuits and Signal Processing, 8,* 83–114. doi:10.1007/BF01239381

Fiorelli, R., Peralías, E., & Silveira, F. (2011). LC-VCO design optimization methodology based on the g_m/I_D ratio for nanometer CMOS technologies. *IEEE Transactions on Microwave Theory and Techniques, 59.* doi:10.1109/TMTT.2011.2132735

Flandre, D., Viviani, A., Eggermont, J.-P., Gentinne, B., & Jespers, P. (1997). Improved synthesis of gain-boosted regulated-cascode CMOS stages using symbolic analysis and gm/ID methodology. *IEEE Journal of Solid-state Circuits, 32*(7), 1006–1012. doi:10.1109/4.597291

Galup-Montoro, C., Schneider, M., & Cunha, A. (1999). A current-based MOSFET model for integrated circuit design. In Sánchez-Sinencio, E., & Andreou, A. (Eds.), *Low voltage/low power integrated circuits and systems* (pp. 7–55). IEEE Press.

Gildenblat, G., Li, X., Wu, W., Wang, H., Jha, A., & van Langevelde, R. (2006). PSP: An advanced surface potential- based MOSFET model for circuit simulation. *IEEE Transactions on Electron Devices, 53*(9), 1979–1993. doi:10.1109/TED.2005.881006

Girardi, A., & Bampi, S. (2006). Power constrained design optimization of analog circuits based on physical gm/ID characteristics. *19th Symposium on Integrated Circuits and System Design, SBCCI.*

Hajimiri, A., & Lee, T. (1998). A general theory of phase noise in electrical oscillators. *IEEE Journal of Solid-state Circuits, 33*(2), 179–194. doi:10.1109/4.658619

Hajimiri, A., & Lee, T. (1999). Design issues in CMOS differential LC oscillators. *IEEE Journal of Solid-state Circuits, 34*(5), 717–724. doi:10.1109/4.760384

Hershenson, M., Hajimiri, A., Mohan, S., Boyd, S., & Lee, T. (1999). Design and optimization of LC VCO oscillators. *IEEE/ACM International Conference on Computer-Aided Design,* (pp. 65-69).

Jespers, P. G. (2010). *The gm/ID methodology, a sizing tool for low-voltage analog CMOS circuits.* Springer. doi:10.1007/978-0-387-47101-3

Jhon, H.-S., Jung, H., Koo, M., Song, I., & Shin, H. (2009). 0.7 V supply highly linear subthreshold low-noise amplifier design for 2-4GHz wireless sensor network applications. *Microwave and Optical Technology Letters, 51*(5). doi:10.1002/mop.24333

Lee, H., & Mohammadi, S. (2007). A subthreshold low phase noise CMOS LC VCO for ultra low power applications. *IEEE Microwave and Wireless Component Letters, 17*(11), 796–799. doi:10.1109/LMWC.2007.908057

Leeson, D. (1966). A simple model of feedback oscillator noise spectrum. *Proceedings of the IEEE, 54,* 329–330. doi:10.1109/PROC.1966.4682

Manghisoni, M., Ratti, L., Re, V., Speziali, V., & Traversi, G. (2006). Noise characterization of 130nm and 90nm CMOS technologies for analog front-end electronics. *IEEE Nuclear Science Symposium Conference,* (pp. 214–218).

Melly, T., Porret, A.-S., Enz, C., & Vittoz, E. (2001). An ultralow power UHF transceiver integrated in a standard digital CMOS process: Transmitter. *IEEE Journal of Solid-state Circuits, 36*(3), 467–472. doi:10.1109/4.910485

Niknejad, A. (2000). *Analysis of Si inductors and transformers for IC's (ASITIC)*. Retrieved from http://rfic.eecs.berkeley.edu/niknejad/asitic.html

Porret, A.-S., Melly, T., Python, D., Enz, C., & Vittoz, E. (2001). An ultralow-power UHF transceiver integrated in a standard digital CMOS process: Architecture and receiver. *IEEE Journal of Solid-state Circuits, 36*(3), 452–464. doi:10.1109/4.910484

Ramos, J., Mercha, A., Jeamsaksiri, W., Linten, D., Jenei, S., Rooyackers, R., & Decoutere, S. (2004). 90nm RF CMOS technology for low-power 900MHz applications. *Proceedings of 34th European Solid-State Device Research conference, ESSDERC* (pp. 329-332).

Scholten, A., Tiemeijer, L., van Langevelde, R., Havens, R., Zegers-van Duijnhoven, A., de Kort, R., & Klaassen, D. (2004). Compact modelling of noise for RF CMOS circuit design. *IEE Proceedings. Circuits, Devices and Systems, 151*(2). doi:10.1049/ip-cds:20040373

Shameli, A., & Heydari, P. (2006). A novel power optimization technique for ultra-low power RF ICs. *International Symposium on Low Power Electronics and Design, ISLPED.*

Shi, J., Xiong, Y., Kang, K., Nan, L., & Lin, F. (2009). RF noise of 65-nm MOSFETs in the weak-to-moderate-inversion region. *IEEE Electron Device Letters, 30*(2), 185–188. doi:10.1109/LED.2008.2010464

Silveira, F., Flandre, D., & Jespers, P. G. A. (1996). A gm/ID based methodology for the design of CMOS analog circuits and its applications to the synthesis of a silicon-on-insulator micropower OTA. *IEEE Journal of Solid-State Circuits, 31*(9), 1314–1319. doi:10.1109/4.535416

Tanguay, L.-F., & Sawan, M. (2009). An ultra-low power ISM-band integer-N frequency synthesizer dedicated to implantable medical microsystems. *Analog Integrated Circuits and Signal Processing, 58*, 205–214. doi:10.1007/s10470-007-9123-z

Tsividis, Y. (2000). *Operation and modelling of the MOS transistor* (2nd ed.). Oxford University Press.

Van der Ziel, A. (1986). *Noise in solid state devices and circuits*. New York, NY: Wiley.

KEY TERMS AND DEFINITIONS

All-Inversion Regions: All the MOS transistor channel inversion levels.

Bluetooth: Communication standard defined in the standard IEEE 802.15.1.

CMOS: Complementary Metal Oxide Semiconductor.

Design Methodology: Systematic method used to design a system.

LNA: Low Noise Amplifier.

Low Power Circuits: Circuits consuming power around or below the milliwatt.

Noise Figure: Figure of merit to qualify the intrinsic noisy behaviour of analog RF-blocks.

Phase Noise: Figure of merit to qualify the spectral purity of oscillators.

Radiofrequency: Frequency working-band of the electromagnetic spectrum used in radio-communications.

RF IC Design: Design of radiofrequency integrated circuits.

Sub-Threshold: The bias zone of the MOS transistor channel below the threshold voltage.

Transconductance: Ratio between the output current of a circuit and its input voltage.

Transition Frequency: The frequency where MOS current gain falls to unity.

VCO: Voltage controlled oscillator.

Zigbee: Communication standard defined in the standard IEEE 802.15.4

ENDNOTES

[1] © [2011] IEEE. Reprinted, with permission, from (Fiorelli, R., Peralías, E., Silveira, F., 2011).

[2] © [2011] IEEE. Reprinted, with permission, from (Fiorelli, R., Peralías, E., Silveira, F., 2011).

Chapter 3

Wireless Interface at 5.7 GHz for Intra–Vehicle Communications:
Sensing, Control and Multimedia

J. P. Carmo
University of Minho, Portugal

J. H. Correia
University of Minho, Portugal

ABSTRACT

This chapter presents a wireless interface for intra-vehicle communications (data acquisition from sensors, control, and multimedia) at 5.7 GHz. As part of the wireless interface, a RF transceiver was fabricated in the UMC 0.18 μm RF CMOS process and when activated, it presents a total power consumption of 23 mW with the voltage-supply of 1.5 V. This allows the use of only a coin-sized battery for supplying the interface. The carrier frequency can be digitally selectable and take one of 16 possible frequencies in the range 5.42-5.83 GHz, adjusted in steps of 27.12 MHz. These multiple carriers allow a better spectrum allocation and at the same time will improve the channel capacity due to the possibility to allow multiple accesses with multiple frequencies.

DOI: 10.4018/978-1-4666-0083-6.ch003

INTRODUCTION

Many automobile manufacturers are aiming efforts to reduce vehicle weight in order to improve the fuel economy. Also, the political, business and social need for fuel-efficient and clean vehicles is clear nowadays in many countries, where it is being demanded high environmental performance without trading-off safety, driving performance or cost (Cramer *et al*, 2002). Since the first Velo's prototype presented by Karl Benz in 1894, until the modern Formula 1's Ferrari F-60, an automobile use sensors. Ever since the introduction of the Manifold Air Pressure sensor for engine control in 1979, followed by airbag sensors in the mid-eighties. Integrated microsystems have been increasingly used throughout the vehicle, and the demand of new sensing and management applications leads undoubtedly cars to be more intelligent, and increasing the need of a networking infrastructure to connect the whole range of sensors and actuators. Thus, the system environment of an automobile is becoming more and more complex (Krueger *et al*, 2003). Today, an average car comprises more than 50 sensors and in the luxury segment more than 100 sensors, roughly one third (1/3) might be based on microsystem technologies. Examples of these systems are listed in Table 1 (Krueger *et al*, 2005). Also, while formerly one single supplier delivered all components of an ABS system or all sensors for airbag control, today the networked architecture allows merged sensor systems for different functions. Ambient intelligence, which means an environment of interacting smart devices, is opening up new information sources for the vehicle. With the growing use of bus-systems, building exclusive systems for each function is becoming more and more difficult and too expensive (Krueger *et al*, 2003). A present day wiring harness may have up to 4000 parts, weight as much as 40 kg, and contain more than 1900 wires for up to 4 kilometers of wiring (Ahmed *et al*, 2007). Thus, these networks bring serious drawbacks like reliability,

Table 1. Car functions and the respective sensors (Krueger et al, 2003)

System	Number of sensors
Distronic	3
Electronic controlled transmission	9
Roof control unit	7
Antilock braking system	4
Central locking system	3
Dynamic beam leveling	6
Common-rail diesel injection	11
Automatic air condition	13
Active body control	12
Tire pressure monitoring	11
Electronic stability program	14
Parktronic system	12

maintenance and constraints if the manufacturer plans the addition of new functions. These drawbacks can be avoided with wireless transmission infrastructures. Using multi-chip-module (MCM) techniques, it is possible to assemble in the same microsystem, the sensors, radio-frequency (RF) transceiver, electronics for processing and control, memory, and an associated antenna. In the last years, the potential to use wireless interfaces in the vehicular industry became an important goal (Schoof *et al* 2003, ElBat *et al* 2006, Niu *et al* 2009, Leon *et al* 2001, Tsai *et al* 2007, Flint *et al* 2003, Li *et al* 2006, Niu *et al* 2008, Tsai *et al* 2007, Andreas *et al* 1983).

THE STATE OF THE ART AND SYSTEM OVERVIEW

Advances made in the electronics industry in general, and government legislation towards the increase of comfort and safety in cars, were the main driving forces that leaded to the development of vehicle network technologies. At not so long time ago, the auto-radio was considered the only electronic device in an vehicle, but now almost every existing component in the vehicle has some sort of electronic feature. The engine control module (ECM), the anti-lock braking system (ABS), the transmission control module (TCM) and the body control modules (BCM) are some of the most common electronic systems on the today's vehicles. Electronic modules are placed in the automobile, in order to acquire the measures of the sensors (speed, temperature, pressure, among others) and to be used in computations. The orders received by the various actuators, are given by these same modules, which are responsible for actions, where the switching on the cooling fan, changing gear (in the case of automatic gears) constitutes some examples of actuation. These modules must exchange data between each other, during the normal operation of the vehicle. An example of such a data exchanging, is when a communication between the engine and the transmission of a car, is needed in order to exchange information with other modules when a gear shift occurs. This need of a fast and reliable data exchange lead to the development of vehicle network concept. Moreover, the use of microcomputers, electronic display, and voice output in motor vehicles means greater scope not only for the gathering and processing data, but also for making such data available to the driver (Andreas *et al* 2000). Some years ago, the increased demand for these new applications and needs of electronics in order to increase the passenger's safety and reliability of the vehicles, lead the Toyota company to introduce the model Soarer in the market. For this model was developed a multidisplay system, which employs a 6-inch colour cathode ray tube (CRT) newly developed for automobile application, in which various kinds of useful information such as vehicle conditions and diagnostic data that may be used by service mechanics are compactly and expediently displayed with high legibility (Torri *et al* 1988).

In order to make the different blocks in a car to exchange data between them, some kind of communication network are needed. There are several network types and protocols used in

vehicles by various manufactures. Many companies are encouraging a standard communication protocol, but one has not been settled on. There are several network types and protocols used in vehicles by various manufactures, but the CAN (Controller Area Network), which is an inexpensive low-speed serial bus for interconnecting automotive components, is the most used of all by the vehicular industry. CAN has been running in cars for more than ten years now. But unlike the telecom industry, which has managed to establish a GSM standard where every service provider can use components from the worldwide supplier ecosystem, the car industry has not moved beyond a component standard for CAN. This is going to change with the introduction of LIN (Local Interconnect Network) and FlexRay (adopted in 2007 by BMW), which are defined on a systems level for interoperability of modules (see Figure 1).

Not only are the physical and logical interfaces specified, but in addition the higher protocol software layer APIs, the messaging sequence generation mechanism, diagnostics and conformance test. With these mechanisms in place, it will be possible to generate truly exchangeable electronic components that are independent from the underlying technology. Then the carmaker will be able to source from an ecosystem of suppliers, just like a computer maker is able to source the latest disk-drive technology for its system, thus managing transparent technology transitions (Snook, 2008). The assimilation of multimedia and multimedia communication by industry for applications in design, manufacturing, and training marks a significant turning point. This important and constantly evolving area comprises a number of technologies, including multimedia compression, computer networks, and the transport of multimedia over these networks. The standards and technology for multimedia and multimedia communication are evolving quickly and, therefore, it is challenging to keep pace with the wide spectrum of this rapidly advancing tech-

Figure 1. A backbone-based (on FlexRay) architecture for automotive

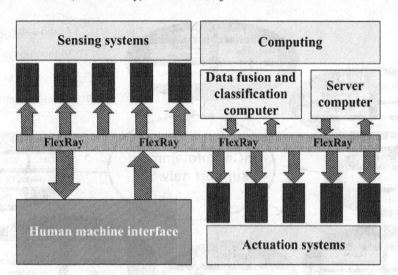

nology. Multimedia and multimedia communication can be globally viewed as a hierarchical system. The multimedia software and applications provide a direct interactive environment for users. When a computer requires information from remote computers or servers, multimedia information must travel through computer networks (Wu *et al*, 1998). The stringent requirements associated to multimedia applications that can't be achieved with traditional automotive networks (the CAN is an example), leaded the automotive industry to respond with the proposition of the MOST (Media Oriented Systems Transport) action. The MOST cooperation is based on a partnership of carmakers, setmakers, system architects and key component suppliers. MOST is a multimedia network optimized for multimedia and infotainment applications. It is a network originally developed by the automotive industry for the automotive industry but with wide-ranging applications in many other industries. Its design allows it to provide a low-overhead and low-cost interface for the simplest of devices, such as microphones and speakers. At the same time, more intelligent devices can automatically determine the features and functions provided by all other devices on the network and establish sophisti-

cated control mechanisms to take away distractions from the driver of the car as different subsystems try to communicate information to him (Allan, 2006). The technology was designed from the ground up to provide an efficient and cost-effective fabric to transmit audio, video, data and control information between any devices attached even to the harsh environment of an automobile. The Figure 2 illustrates an application scenario with a possible MOST-system for a typical in-car infotainment.

In respect of vehicle communication protocol prior art, multiplex vehicle control systems currently use a single channel (wire) for both transmitted and received signals. Such systems are usually microprocessor based and require a slave or satellite module to generate an interrupt function before a particular operation can be undertaken. For example, the operation of braking would entail a signal to be generated upon movement of the brake pedal, the signal serving as an interrupt to the microprocessor, who thereafter would take whatever steps are necessary, such as activation of brakes and/or brake lights. The type of communication used in such systems is usually either all synchronous or all asynchronous. Coupled with the provision of only one transmission/recep-

Figure 2. An exemplary MOST-system view of a typical in-car infotainment application scenario

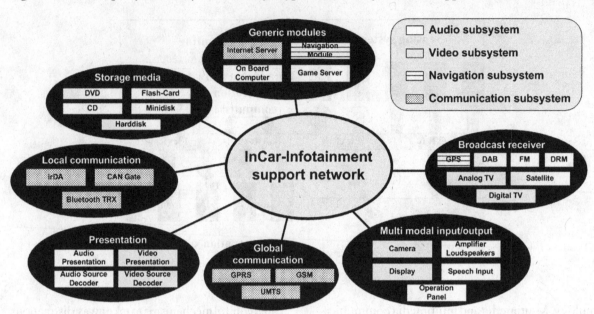

tion channel between the master and each slave module, there has been a need to speed up the rate of data flow. This increased data flow rate has proved necessary as a result of the relatively limited time available for a multiple system to receive, issue and act on commands, for example in the act of braking of the vehicle (Hansen *et al*, 1994). The result of increasing the data flow rate in prior arrangements has been the adoption of higher and more costly technology, and hence relatively more expensive components. Thus, on the whole, vehicle manufacturers have remained with more traditional wiring looms or harnesses as these have proven to date to be more reliable and/or cost effective than multiplex systems previously developed for vehicle application.

The idea to apply wireless links to cable replacement is not new. General Motors Company was the first, if not the only one up to now to got the idea to install wireless links in vehicles, in order to replace cables (Ahmed *et al*, 2007). Mainly, these cables are based in low-current loops that simultaneously feed and acquire data from the sensors. However, the specificity of the

environment in a car addresses aspects that are not present in other type of wireless networks. Thus, a wireless network to connect sensors in a car is not just another type of wireless sensor network. Previous studies conducted in vehicular environment revealed a set of issues, which can't be discarded (Krueger *et al.*, 2003; ElBatt *et al.*, 2006). The most important aspects to be considered when mounting a wireless network in a car include questions like heterogenity, where different sensors and different communications profiles are present (ElBatt *et al.*, 2006). The complete characterization of the wireless channel and the selection of the most suitable modulation are other important and definitive tasks (Niu *et al.*, 2009; Leon *et al.*, 2001; Tsai *et al.*, 2007; Flint *et al.*, 2003; Li *et al.*, 2006; Niu *et al.*, 2008). The work presented conducted by Tsai *et al* (Tsai *et al.*, 2007) showed (at least) for the 915 MHz, using a forward error correction (FEC) code, the network support at least 98% packet reception rate. Moreover, Tsai *et al* also suggest that sacrificing the throughput, by using an automatic repeat request (ARQ) scheme will result in a better packet reception. Also, further works suggest that with ultra-wide-band (UWB) transmission is possible to achieve high data-rates, despite the noisy and fading characteristics of the vehicular environment (Liu *et al.*, 2006; Niu *et al.*, 2008). In spite of an extensive number of studies related to the channel characterisation, it is evident the worry to use the emerging and established technologies, such as the ZigBee and the Bluetooth to put in connection the different sensors, controllers and multimedia systems (Schoof *et al.*, 2003; Flint *et al.*, 2003; Tsai *et al.*, 2007). These two standards have strong points and drawbacks. The ZigBee is a set of protocols (e.g., corresponding to the two lowest layers in the OSI model) that allows to mount a real wireless sensor network in to-pologies ranging from a simple star to complex meshes with the advantage to work for years. This working mode is obtained at the cost to have the wireless nodes to operate in low-duty-cycles. Low-duty-cycles are not tolerable in real-time systems, so the advantage of the ZigBee will fast turns in something to avoid. Alternatively, the Bluetooth allows the use of high-baud-rates, e.g., baud-rates up to 1 Mbps to exchange data between the wireless nodes. However, it is very difficult to have complex mesh topologies and worse, the Bluetooth is a very heavy protocol with a lot of rules, where despite the high-baud-rates available, it will result in high latencies. High latencies are also unacceptable in real-time monitoring and control systems. Thus, the Bluetooth is more suitable in applications such as hand-free sys-tems that allow drivers to keep their hands on the wheel while staying connected to cellular phones. Furthermore, the use of high density of nodes and simple protocols in the vehicular environment was also tried before (Niu *et al.*, 2009; Hill *et al.*, 2000). Several variants for the same solution were proposed and all of the implementations use third-party products such as radios (motes) and sensor interfaces (Hill *et al.*, 2000). The motes are battery-powered devices that run specific software. These motes are ready-to-use wireless modules,

where boards with sensors are attached. Their primary advantage rapidly fades and turns into a severe drawback, beçause the primary goal is to have wireless platforms integrating the vehicular environment. Thus, more compact and low-sized modules are needed. Also, these solutions are much too expensive for high-mass production and thus, for use in cars.

The advantages to have RF transceivers with dimensions comparable to the other elements of the microsystem, such as the sensors and the elec-tronics of processing and control are enormous. Miniaturised microsystems contributes to the mass production with low prices, favoring the spread of applications for these microsystems. Moreover, solutions relying in wireless microsystems, offer a flexibility such as it is possible to chose how many and which are the sensors to be integrated together with the RF transceiver and the remain electronics. Also, it can control the power during the trans-mission and to select what subsystem must be enabled. In terms of project and design, it is easier to provide the supply, when all the system-blocks are integrated together in the same microsystem. Because the feeding points are reduced and the battery coupling is more effective, thus, the key of effective wireless interfaces for vehicles rely on a trade-off between the best possible baud-rates and the best-control features, as it is the case of high-performance embedded systems.

Wireless interfaces can be used to connect the sensors spanned in the car and to transmit the acquired values to a base-station, which stores, process and display the most suitable physical measures, such as the oil level, water tempera-ture in the cooling system, pressures in the tires, beside others. These measures can be monitored and displayed in the front panel of the car, to give information to the driver, while the car is rolling in the road. Another way to use these wireless sensors networks, is when car driver wants to see in a PDA, for example, the oil level of the engine, without the need to move close the car. The Figure 3 shows the system architecture of a wireless interface to mount a wireless sensors network in a car. The wireless interfaces must be deployed closely to the sensors, in order to reduce the interferences caused by the electromagnetic noise generated by the car electrical system and to minimize measuring errors. It is advantageous to have wireless interfaces with plug-and-play features (the modules can be easily placed/removed on/from where and when it is desired without special concerns) for overcoming the gap brought by the previously network standards for cars, thus making possible to have a real network infrastructure coexistent with the sensing sub-system and the Information Communication and Entertainment system (ICE). This allows a common multimedia system platform for integrated information, communication and entertainment applications for use in automotive environments. Typically, the systems offered to the consumer, are made in separate devices for very specific applications (the DVD players is an example). However, the integration of such applications in automotive environments comes with major challenges, such as, system space requirements and overall costs will be too high. Therefore, the use of wireless links to make the integration of different multimedia devices and services into a common system platform for automotive environments don't implies changes in the existent designs of cars, so it is expected to be a valuable option without significant additional costs. Moreover, given the physical way the different interfaces are connected between them, the following hardware requirements for in-car use are easily achieved. These requirements includes modular and extensible hardware concept, in order to be possible to add or remove single hardware components in an easy fashion; suitability for automotive applications, e.g. rigidity, temperature range. To all of this be possible, the wireless interface and the applications must give support for a networked environment. This makes easy the development of a universal system bus, in which can be possible to attach the different products of different suppli-

ers. Another advantage is that modular software architecture for multimedia applications can be designed without strong efforts and cost penalties. This architecture can include features like the possibility to add or remove single software components, upgrade an existing version to a newer or give support to new multimedia services. This constitutes an obvious trend to integrate different new or existing standards in a single device, e.g. Personal Integrated Communicators, Consumer Electronics, in-car Infotainment. Form the part of manufacturers and suppliers, this trend can be seen as a starting point for the convergence of multimedia standards and applications. While the major of the previous specific applications are possibly tolerable in a home environment, for ergonomic, driving safety and limited space reasons, a single infotainment unit is strongly desirable in an automotive environment. Moreover, in the automotive environment additional car-specific applications, like travel information, navigation systems and climate control are expected by the user. The amount of common building blocks between these applications increases the potential for reducing the production costs and the development resources significantly. In addition it is desirable to offer the driver and his passengers a consistent interface to the different applications, using the same display and user interface which will be user adaptable in the future.

RF CMOS TRANSCEIVER DESIGN

Frequency Band Selection

The frequency selection took in account the need to obtain compact and miniaturized solutions. Moreover, the possibility to include chip-size antennas in the RF microsystem was a crucial (and a mandatory) requirement to comply with the former goal. In order to implement efficient power-consumption wireless sensor networks, it was also necessary the development of a low-

Figure 3. The system architecture of a wireless interface for vehicles

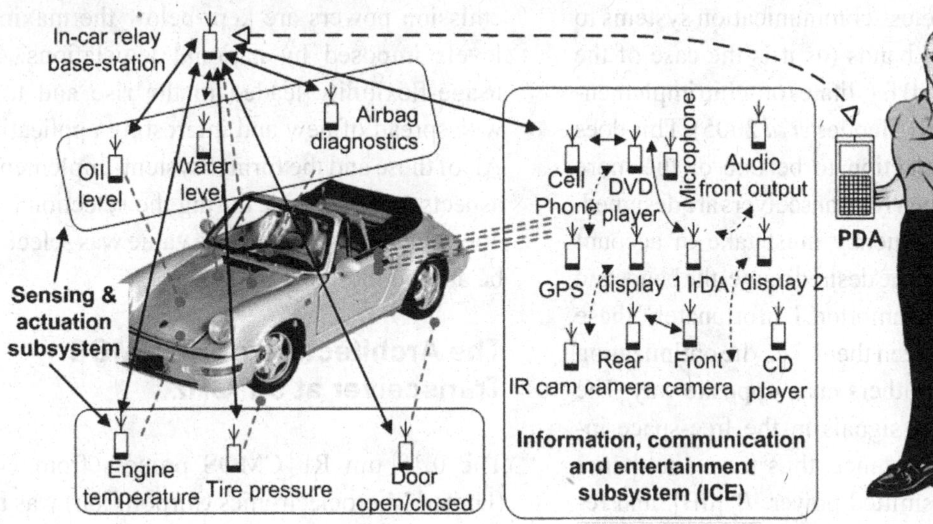

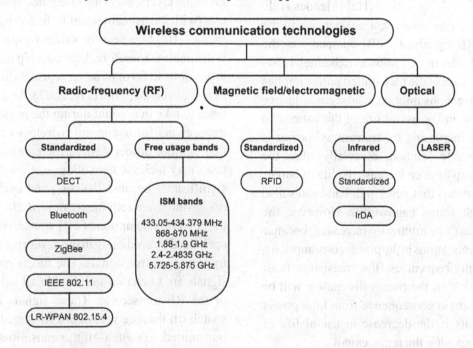

Figure 4. The available frequencies and their respective applications

power/low-voltage RF CMOS transceiver, suitable for mounting in the antenna. In wireless communications, the antenna is one of the most critical subsystem, thus, in order to not compromise the desired miniaturization, the antenna must be small enough to comply with size constraints

of the microsystems. The investigation of new frequency bands (Callaway Jr, 2004) and new geometries (Mackensen *et al.*, 2005) allow to get smaller antennas to integrate in wireless microsystems (Gutierrez *et al* 2001, Enz *et al* 2005). Also, the dimension of an antenna is proportional to the operating wavelength. Thus, the migration of wireless communication systems to higher frequency bands (as it is the case of the 5-6 GHz ISM band) facilitates on-chip implementation of antennas (Mendes *et al* 2005). This does the frequency selection to be one of the more decisive tasks, when RF transceivers are designed. Normally, the frequency must take in account some key-aspects: the desired range, the baud-rate and the power consumption. Unfortunately, these aspects trade between them, i.e., the optimization of one affects the others in an opposite way. The attenuation of RF signals in the free-space increases with the distance, thus for a simultaneously given transmitted power, P_t [dB], and receiver's sensitivity, S_r [dB], the frequency of operation is limited by the range, d_{max} [m], e.g., $f \leq 10^{[(P_t - S_r) - 20\log_{10}(4\pi d_{max})]/20}$ [Hz] (Mendes *et al*, 2002). It must be noted that an increase in the power of RF signals, P_t [dB] compensates the additional losses in the radiowave channel. However, an increase in the transmitted power implies a higher power consumption, whose consequence is a decrease in the useful life of the battery. In conclusion, increasing the transmitted power is an unacceptable solution, especially when the goal is to keep or even increase the life of batteries. Applications that need high baud-rates also require high signal bandwidths. However, the frequency can't be arbitrarily increased, because this have implications in the power consumptions, e.g., at high frequencies, the transistors must switch faster, thus the energy dissipation will be higher. The main consequence from high power consumptions is the decrease in useful life of batteries, imposing the replacement.

The Figure 4 shows the available frequency bands for the different technologies used in wireless communications. The best free-usage frequencies for wireless devices are those belonged to the so called ISM band (Industrial, Scientific and Medical), due to its unregulated usage. This means that these frequencies are not subjected to

standardization and can be freely used, since the emission powers are kept below the maximum levels imposed by national legislations. This usage-flexibility leaded to the rise and to the widespread of new and interesting applications. All of these and the former system-implementing aspects were decisive during the selection of the operating frequency, whose value was selected to be around the 5.7 GHz.

The Architecture of RF CMOS Transceiver at 5.7 GHz

The 0.18 μm RF CMOS process from UMC (United Microelectronics Corporation) was used for the fabrication of a 5.7 GHz RF CMOS transceiver. This process has a polysilicon layer and six metal layers, allowing integrated spiral inductors (with a reasonable quality factor, e.g., in the range 4-10), high resistor values (a special layer is available). Therefore, high on-chip integration is possible, in favor of better repeatability as well as less pin count (Choi *et al*, 2003). An important issue to take in account during the project of RF transceivers for use in any wireless network is that without proper design, the communication tasks may increase network power consumption significantly because listening and emitting are power-intensive activities (Enz *et al*, 2004). Thus, the power consumption of a RF transceiver can be optimized by predicting in the design the possibility to use control signals. The functions of such signals are to enable and disable all subsystems of the RF transceiver. These signals allow to switch-off the receiver when a RF signal is being transmitted, to switch-off the transmitter when a RF signal is being received, and allows the RF transceiver to enter to sleep when RF signals are neither being transmitted, nor being received. The Figure 5 shows the RF CMOS transceiver architecture, which is composed by a receiver, a transmitter, and a frequency synthesizer. The receiver adopts a direct demodulation, by means of envelope detection. The RF CMOS transceiver

Figure 5. The block schematic of the transceiver

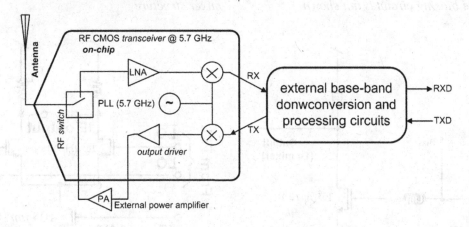

is constituted by a Low-Noise Amplifier (LNA) that provides an input impedance of 50 Ω, the amplified RF signal is directly converted to the baseband with a single balanced active MOS mixer. The internal oscillator at 5.7 GHz is a Phase-Locked Loop (PLL).

The RF CMOS transceiver can operate in the frequency range of 5.42-5.83 GHz. This is done by changing the frequency division ratio in the feedback path of the PLL. The PLL has four digital inputs to select one in sixteen possible division ratios. The output frequency is given by $f_{out} = f_{ref} \times 2 \times (200 + D)$, where D is the equivalent decimal of digital inputs for a reference frequency of $f_{ref} = 13.56$ MHz.

The lowest noise-figure (NF) of LNA is achieved with an inductively degenerated common source amplifier with tuned load. In these conditions, the input impedance at 5.7 GHz for matching with the antenna is easily adjusted to 50 Ω. As it is depicted in the Figure 6, the LNA has a single transistor in the amplifier, thus, the reduction of active devices sacrifices the gain, but achieves lowest NFs. It must be noted that the latter Figure doesn't shows the circuits to provide bias to the LNA.

The upconversion and the downconversion operations are done with two mixers that are ac-coupled to the LNA and are modified versions of

the Gilbert cell (see the Figure 7) (Gramegna *et al*, 2004). Also, both mixers are directly driven by the differential outputs of the on-chip frequency synthesizer.

The Frequency Synthesizer (the PLL)

An on-chip frequency synthesizer provides local versions of the carrier frequencies to both the downconversion and the upconversion mixer. This frequency synthesizer is a Phase-Locked Loop (PLL) with a integer divider in the feedback loop, whose dividing ratio can be digitally programmed to generate local carrier frequencies in the 5.42-5.83 GHz frequency range. The Figure 8 illustrates a block diagram showing the structure of PLL. This the PLL has a reference generator circuit with a crystal based oscillator at 13.56 MHz, followed by a Phase-Frequency Difference Circuit (PFD), a current steering charge pump (CP), a third order passive filter. The passive section output is connected to the VCO, that generates the desired frequency range of 5.42-5.83 GHz. Finally, in order to get the desired frequency in the previous range, this one must be divided by $400 + 2S$, where S is integer and belongs to $\{0, 1, \ldots 15\}$. Then the output of the divider connects to the PFD, closing the loop. The output frequency produced by the PLL depends from the divider ratio, N, and is $f_{out} = f_{ref} N$

Figure 6. The schematic of low-noise-amplifier (LNA) – the biasing circuit is not shown

Figure 7. The electronic schematic showing the mixer structure

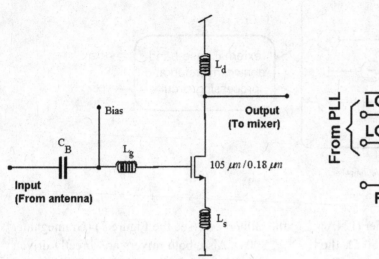

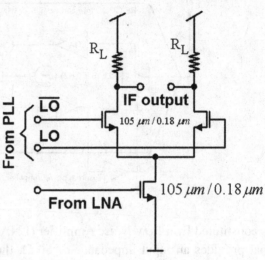

Figure 8. The block diagram of the PLL

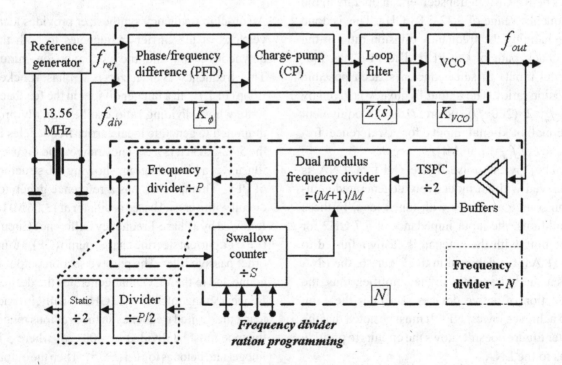

[Hs]. The PLL acts a frequency multiplier of the reference frequency, f_{ref} [Hz].

The Frequency Divider

The PLL is one of the most challenging blocks of RF transceivers because it operates with the highest speed and the stringent trade-off between the speed and the power consumption. To have an ideia, typically, the blocks with higher power consumptions are the Voltage Controlled Oscillator (VCO), the frequency divider and the buffers. Thus, the efforts to reduce the power consumption and increase the speed, must always take place in the design. Also, the most complex and challenging stage of a PLL is the frequency divider, which must be designed with very care in order to keep the power at a low acceptable level, at the same time it meets the speed specifications. In high frequency PLLs, the high power consumption is mainly due to the first stages of the frequency divider that often dissipates half of the total power. The use of conventional static CMOS logic in the first stage is not possible. This is due to the high input frequency (Pellerano *et al.*, 2003). The overall divider has two true-single-phase-clock (TSPC) frequency dividers, that halves the following dividers, which use static logic.

For this PLL, the desired divider ratio, N, in the feedback path is equal to $2(M.P+S)$, where $(M+1)/M$ (with $M=10$) are the variable frequency divider ratios of the prescaler, $S=20$ is the divider ratio of the main counter, and S is the divider ratio of the swallow counter. The main counter has a divider by $P/2=10$ followed by a toggle flip-flop, which makes the feedback signal at the divided input, f_{div}, of the PFD to have a duty-cycle of 50% (as it happens with the reference signal at the main input, f_{ref}, of the PFD). Compared with other situations, where the PFD's inputs have different duty-cycles, this minimises possible delays that can arise, during the locking process of the PLL. This is of special concern in situations when the PLL is turned on or after an order to switch the frequency at its output.

The Figure 9(a) shows the structure of the TSPC frequency divider by two and prescaler. The Figure 9(b) is the schematic of the TSPC divider by two, and the Figure 9(c) is the schematic of the prescaler. The buffers are not shown in the schematics. The frequency at the input of the prescaler is in the range 2712-2915 MHz, and previous measurements for this technology showed that for frequencies above 2 GHz, it is impossible divide higher frequencies with static logic. The TSPC logic must be used to allow the further static logic circuits to work. The TSPC logic was used again to overcome the impossibility to implement the first stage of the prescaler (the frequency divider by 2/3 with modulus control) with static logic in this technology. However, in order to the TSPC dividers work properly, the inputs must be rail-to-rail.

In the global structure of the frequency divider, the swallow counter plays an important role, e.g., the fixed division by 10 or 11 is extremely easy to achieve. The difficulty is to establish the precise intervals in which the division must be made and why. The Figure 10 shows three situations of divisions give by $200=(15\times10)+5\times10$, $203=(3\times11+12\times10)+5\times10$ and $215=(15\times11)+5\times10$ (for the global divisions of 400, 406 and 430), as well as the behaviour of the $(M+1)/M$ control signal to the prescaler. The clock (CLK) signal is the signal at the output of the VCO, VCOout, after to be divided by two in the TSPC frequency divider, thus, this is why half of the counting are refereed and not the exact value. Basically, the idea behind the frequency division is the definition of a general rule to simultaneously make the division of the minimum to the maximum in steps of one (in this case, from 200 to 215), and further in steps of two. In this case, the difference between the two limits is 30 and the swallow counting is from 0 to 15, so the values $11\times S+10\times[\max(S)-S]+50$, with $S\in\{0,1,\ldots,15\}$ and $\max(S)=15$ will be a useful solution to the

Figure 9. The block diagram of (a) the buffers, the TSPC divider by two, followed by the prescaler; (b) the schematic of TSPC divider by two; and (c) the schematic of the prescaler. The buffers are not shown in the schematics.

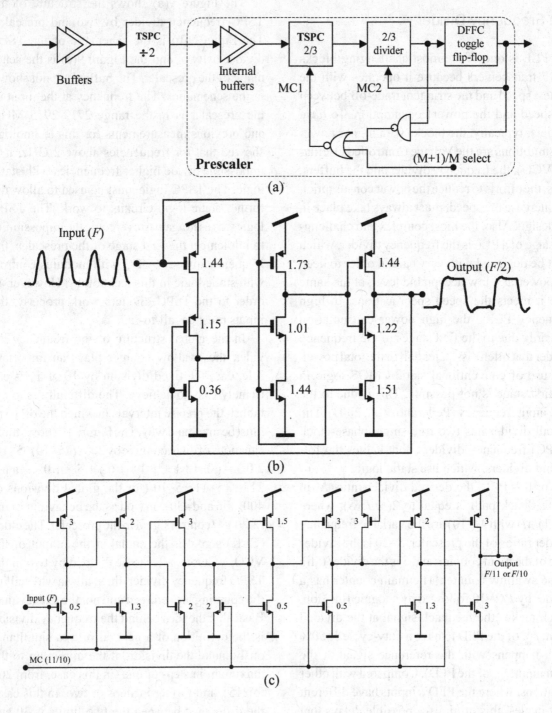

Figure 10. Swallow counting process to generate the appropriate MC signal for the prescaler, for three global division ratios: a) 400, b) 406 and 430

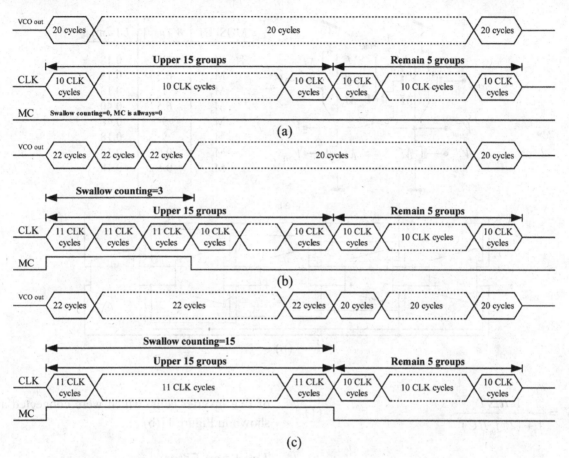

(a)

(b)

(c)

problem. Then the final division ratios in steps of two, are ensured by the first TSPC toggle flip-flop, at the same time the last static toggle flip-flop in the main counter, P, ensures that the divided signal has a duty-cycle of 50%. The swallow counter is essentially a descendent programmable counter and it operates as follows: the counter is initiated to the desired value S, and then it starts to counting in the descending order until zero. Meanwhile, the MC signal is activated then, it falls down, except when S is already initialized at zero.

The Voltage Controlled Oscillator

The VCO is based on a ring-oscillator topology instead of a tuned LC VCO because it is desired to save the on-chip area. Ring oscillators have more phase noise than LC oscillators (Abidi, 2006, Hajimiri, 2000). For overcoming this limitation, the bandwidth of the PLL must be high enough to "clean-up" the output spectrum around the 5.7 GHz interval (Gardener, 1980).

The ring oscillators are classified according theirs switching characteristics, e.g., non-saturated and saturated types (Park *et al.*, 1999). For the non-saturated VCOs, the phase-noise is:

Figure 11. Voltage-control oscillator: a) saturated unity cell, with the MOSFET's dimensions and b) the complete VCO with five inverter cells

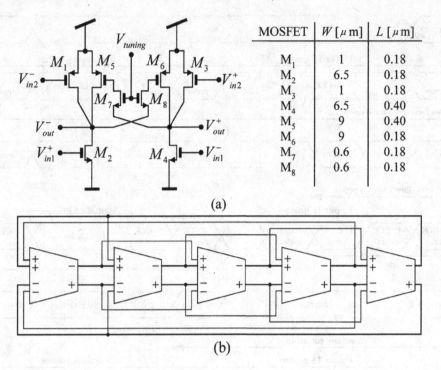

MOSFET	$W\,[\mu m]$	$L\,[\mu m]$
M_1	1	0.18
M_2	6.5	0.18
M_3	1	0.18
M_4	6.5	0.40
M_5	9	0.40
M_6	9	0.18
M_7	0.6	0.18
M_8	0.6	0.18

(a)

(b)

$$N = \frac{4kR\Delta T}{1 + (2\pi f_m RC)^2}, \qquad (1)$$

where ΔT [s] is the on-time of the transistors inside a delay cell, f_m [Hz] is the offset frequency from the carrier, and RC [s] is the equivalent time-constant which is taken from the first-order model of the delay cell. An analysis to the equation (1), reveals that a short on-time is desired to have a low noise power. In order to such a goal be achieved, a simple inverter-based ring oscillator is not suitable, because a full switching never happens, thus a certain kind of anticipation in order to force a full switching must be done. The Figure 11(a) shows an unitary cell of a ring oscillator, which is of differential type and have two cross-connections (M_5/M_7 and M_6/M_8) between its inverter cells (M_1/M_4 and M_2/M_3) in order to make a latch to force the inverters to fully saturate (Park *et al.*, 1999). The complete VCO uses a set

of five inverter cells, which were connected as shown in Figure 11(b).

The Loop-Filter

As previously stated, the ring oscillators have more phase noise than *LC* oscillators (Abidi, 2006, Hajimiri, 2000) thus, a third order passive filter, composed by a second order section (C_1, C_2 and R_2) and a first order section (C_3 and R_3), providing an additional pole it is used. The first order filter reduces spurs caused by the multiples of reference frequency, whose consequence is the increasing of the phase noise at the output. The stability is guaranteed by putting this last pole five times above the PLL bandwidth and below the reference. The stability in the loop is obtained with a phase margin of $\pi/4$ rad or higher. The choice of passive components must obey to the following: given the bandwidth, f_p [Hz], the phase margin ϕ_p [rad], the minimum attenuation, A_{min} [dB], measured at multiples of the spurious reference frequency, f_{ref} [Hz], which is imposed by the low-pass filter R_3C_3, it will result in the five passive components of the loop-filter (Banerje, 2006):

$$C_1 = \frac{\tau_1}{\tau_2} \times \frac{K_\varphi K_{VCO}}{(2\pi f_p)^2 N} \times$$
$$\times \sqrt{\frac{1 + (2\pi f_p)^2 \tau_2^2}{[1 + (2\pi f_p)^2 \tau_1^2] \times [1 + (2\pi f_p)^2 \tau_3^2]}} \quad (2)$$

$$C_2 = C_1 \left(\frac{\tau_2}{\tau_1} - 1 \right) \quad (3)$$

$$R_2 = \frac{\tau_2}{C_2} \quad (4)$$

with τ_1, τ_3 and τ_2 being respectively

$$\tau_2 = \frac{(2\pi f_c)^{-2}}{\tau_1 + \tau_3}, \quad (5)$$

$$\tau_3 = \frac{\sqrt{10^{\frac{A_{min}}{10}} - 1}}{2\pi f_{ref}} = R_3 C_3, \quad (6)$$

and

$$\tau_2 = \frac{(2\pi f_c)^{-2}}{\tau_1 + \tau_3}. \quad (7)$$

Finally, the capacitance C_3 and the resistance R_3 are given by:

$$C_3 \leq \frac{C_1}{10} \text{ and to } R_3 = \frac{\tau_3}{C_3} \quad (8)$$

Table 1 shows some specifications, LF components and the significant results

RESULTS

At frequencies in the range 5.42-5.83 GHz, the LNA has a gain in the range 9.60-9.81 dB (see the Figure 12a), an IP3 of 9.1 dBm (see the Figure 12b), a stabilization factor K of 1.21, making the LNA unconditionally stable ($K>1$). The VCO has a constant $K_{VCO} \approx 2.8$ [GHz/V], obtained from the linear range. The charge-pump has *up* and *down* currents of 269 µA and 201 µA, respectively, and a detector gain constant K_ϕ=75 µA/2π rad. The *up* and *down* currents of 269 µA and 201 µA, respectively, and a detector gain constant K_ϕ=75 µA/2π rad. The LNA showed a power consumption of 9.65 mW. The voltage-to frequency (VF) characteristic is showed in the Figure 13.

The passive components were selected using a custom template spreadsheet. The Table 2 shows some specifications, LF components as well as the significant results, and it can be seen that the PLL has an almost fixed time to lock and independent from the division ratio, e.g., respectively about 10 µs and 7 µs for the first and second filters.

CONCLUSION

The Figure 14 shows the photograph of an encapsulated RF transceiver die, which was fabricated in the 0.18 µm RF CMOS process from UMC and occupies an area of 1.5×1.5 mm². This RF transceiver presents a total power consumption of 23 mW, supplied from a coin-sized battery with 1.5 V. These characteristics fulfill the requirements for short-range communications for using the 5.7 GHz ISM band. This RF transceiver can be integrated as a port of a wireless interface to provide intra-vehicular communications wirelessly of acquired data from sensors, to control actuators and to exchange multimedia data in

Figure 12. The plot of (a) S_{21} [dB] and (b) IP3 parameters

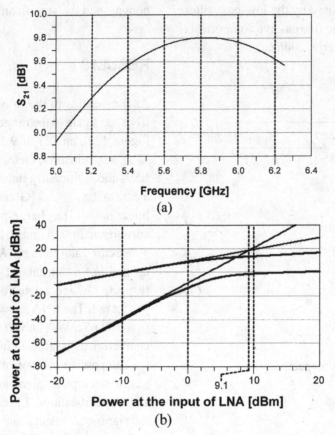

(a)

(b)

Figure 13. The V/F characteristic of the VCO

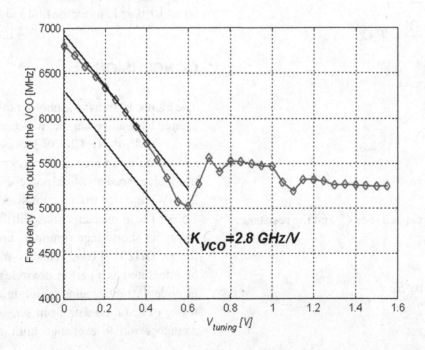

Table 2. Specifications, LF components and most significant results

	Filter	1		Filter	2	
Phase margin - ϕ_p [°]		45			55	
Bandwidth f_p [kHz]		900			900	
Frequency f_c [kHz]		589			540	
Attenuation *attn* [dB]		10			10	
C_1 [pF]		25			21	
C_2 [pF]		200			330	
R_2 [$k\Omega$]		3			3	
C_3 [pF]		2.5			0.7	
R_3 [$k\Omega$]		14			17	
N	400	414	430	400	414	430
Time to converge [μs]	10.6	10.8	11	7.3	7.6	7.7
Actual phase margin [°]	29.34	36.22	35.77	52.28	51.78	51.23
Actual freq. f_c [kHz]	594	286	279	271	264	256
Natural freq. f_n [kHz]	241	237	233	194	191	187
Dumping - ξ	1.823	0.448	0.444	0.605	0.594	0.583

Figure 14. A die photograph of the encapsulated RF CMOS transceiver

information, communication and entertainment systems in (ICEs) cars.

REFERENCES

Ahmed, M., Saraydar, C. U., El Batt, T., Yin, J., Talty, T., & Ames, M. (2007). Intra vehicular wireless networks. In *Proceedings of Globecom, 2007*, 1–9.

Allan, R. (2006, November 6). MOST: A cooperative development effort. *Electronic design - The authority on emerging technologies for design solutions*.

Andreas, P., & Zimdahl, W. (1983). The driver information of the Volkswagen research car auto 2000. *IEEE Transactions on Industrial Electronics, 30*(2), 132–137. doi:10.1109/TIE.1983.356722

Callaway, E. Jr. (2004). The physical layer. In *Wireless sensor networks, architectures and protocols*. CRC Press.

Choi, P., Park, H., Kim, S., Park, S., Nam, I., & Kim, T. W. (2003). An experimental coin-sized radio for extremely low-power WPAN: IEEE 802.15.4. applications at 2.4 GHz. *IEEE Journal of Solid-state Circuits, 8*(12), 2258–2268. doi:10.1109/JSSC.2003.819083

Cramer, D. R., & Taggart, D. F. (2002, February). Design and manufacture of an affordable advanced-composite automobile body structure. In *Proceedings of 19th International Battery, Hybrid and Fuel Cell Electric Vehicle Symposium & Exhibition: 2002 EVS-19*, (p. 12).

ElBatt, T., Saraydar, C., Ames, M., & Talty, T. (2006). *Potential for intra vehicle wireless automotive sensor networks. In Proceedings of Sarnoff Symposium*, (pp. 1-4). March.

Enz, C. C., Hoiydi, A. E., Decotignie, J. D., & Peiris, V. (2004, August). WiseNET: An ultra low-power wireless sensor network solution. *IEEE Computer, 37*(8), 62–67. doi:10.1109/MC.2004.109

Enz, C. C., Scolari, N., & Yodprasit, U. (2005). Ultra low-power radio design for wireless sensor networks. In *Proceedings of IEEE International Workshop on Radio-Frequency Integration Technology: Integrated Circuits for Wideband Communication and Wireless Sensor Networks*, Singapore, December.

Flint, J. A., Ruddle, A. R., & May, A. E. (2003, April). Coupling between Bluetooth modules inside a passenger car. In *Proceedings of IEEE 12th International Conference on Antennas and Propagation, ICAP*, (pp. 397-400).

Gramegna, G., Montagna, G., Bietti, I., Franciotta, M., Baschirotto, A., & Abbotto, G. (2004, July). A 35-mW 3.6-mm^2 fully integrated 0.18-μm CMOS GPS radio. *IEEE Journal of Solid-state Circuits, 39*(7), 1163–1171.

Gutierrez, J. A., Naeve, M., Callaway, E., Bourgeois, M., Mitter, V., & Heile, B. (2001, September). IEEE 802.15.4: Developing standards for low-power low-cost wireless personal area networks. *IEEE Network*, 2–9.

Hansen, S., & Redjepi, J. (1994). *Vehicle communication control system*. Patent WO/1994/026558, World Intellectual Property Organisation.

Hill, J., Szewczyk, R., Woo, A., Hollar, S., Culler, D. E., & Pister, K. S. J. (2000). System architecture directions for networked sensors. In *Proceedings Architectural Support for Programming Languages and Operating Systems*, (pp. 93-104).

Krueger, S., Müller-Fiedler, R., Finkbeiner, S., & Trah, H.-P. (2005, March). Microsystems for automotive industry. *MSTNews - International Newsletter on Microsystems and MEMS*, (pp. 8-10).

Krueger, S., & Solzbacher, F. (2003). Applications in intelligent automobiles. *MSTNews - International Newsletter on Microsystems and MEMS*, (pp. 6-10).

Leon, G., & Heffernan, D. (2001, October). Vehicles without wires. *Computing & Control Engineering Journal*, *12*(5), 205–211. doi:10.1049/cce:20010501

Li, J., & Talty, T. (2006, October). Channel characterization for ultra-wideband intra-vehicle sensor networks. In *Proceedings IEEE Military Communications Conference*, Washington DC, (pp. 1-4).

Mackensen, E., Kuntz, W., & Müller, C. L. (2005). Enhancing the lifetime of autonomous microsystems in wireless sensor actuator networks. In *Proceedings of the XIX Eurosensors*, Barcelona, Spain.

Mendes, P. M., Correia, J. H., Bartek, M., & Burghartz, J. N. (2002). Analysis of chip-size antennas on lossy substrates for short-range wireless Microsystems. In *Proceedings SAFE 2002*, (pp. 51-54). Veldhoven, The Netherlands, November 27-28.

Mendes, P. M., Polyakov, A., Bartek, M., Burghartz, J. N., & Correia, J. H. (2006, January). Integrated chip-size antennas for wireless microsystems: Fabrication and design considerations. *Journal Sensors and Actuators A*, *125*, 217–222. doi:10.1016/j.sna.2005.07.016

Niu, W., Li, J., Liu, S., & Talty, T. (2008, November). Intra vehicle ultra wideband communication testbed. In *Proceedings of IEEE Globecom, 2008*, 1–5.

Niu, W., Li, J., & Talty, T. (2009). Ultra-wideband channel modeling for intravehicle environment. *EURASIP Journal on Wireless Communications and Networking, 2009*. doi:10.1155/2009/806209

Schoof, A., Stadtler, T., & ter Hasborg, J. L. (2003, May). Simulation and measurements of the propagation of Bluetooth signals in automobiles. In *Proceedings IEEE International Symposium on Electromagnetic Compatibility*, (pp. 1297-1300).

Snook, S. (2008, October). A touching display. *Automotive Design*, *12*(9), 20–24.

Torri, T., Azuma, S., & Matsuzaki, Y. (1988, May). Multidisplay system. *IEEE Transactions on Industrial Electronics*, *35*(2), 201–207. doi:10.1109/41.192650

Tsai, H. M. Tonguz, O. K., Saraydar, C., Talty, T., Ames, M., & Macdonald, A. (2007, December). ZigBee based intra car wireless sensor networks: a case study. *IEEE Wireless Communications*, (pp. 67-71).

Tsai, H. M., Viriyasitavat, W., Tonguz, O. K., Saraydar, C., Talty, T., & Macdonald, A. (2007, June). Feasibility of in car wireless sensor networks: a statistical evaluation. In *Proceedings of 4th Annual IEEE Communications Society Conference on Sensor, Mesh and Ad Hoc Communications and Networks* (SECON'07), (pp. 101-111).

UMC. (2001). *0.18μm 1P6M logic process interconnect capacitance model*. UMC Spec. No. G-04-LOGIC18-1P6M-INTERCAP, Ver 1.7, Phase 1, August 2001.

Wu, C. H., & Irwin, J. D. (1998, February). Multimedia and multimedia communication: A tutorial. *IEEE Transactions on Industrial Electronics*, *45*(1), 4–14. doi:10.1109/41.661299

KEY TERMS AND DEFINITIONS

Frequency Divider: An electronic system that picks an input signal with a given frequency and produces an output signal with a smaller (thus, divided) frequency.

Frequency Synthesizer: The same as PLL.

LNA: Low-Noise Amplifier.

Loop Filter: Filter used on a given PLL.

Mixer: A non-linear system that mixes two frequencies.

PLL: Phase-Locked Loop.

Radio-Frequency (RF): Frequencies used to transmit data across the air.

RF Transceiver: Wireless interface sub-system responsible for transmitting/receiving signals.

VCO: Electronic system that generates a periodic signal, whose frequency depends from the input (or the control) voltage.

Wireless Interface: An electronic system for connecting a variety of devices (sensors, multimedia players, computers) to support wireless communications.

Chapter 4
Simulation Techniques for Improving Fabrication Yield of RF–CMOS ICs

Amparo Herrera
University of Cantabria, Spain

ABSTRACT

One of the industry sectors with the largest revenue in the telecommunication field is the wireless communications field. Wireless operators compete for being the first to place their products in the market to obtain the highest revenues. Moreover, they try to offer products that fulfill the user demands in terms of price, battery life, and product quality. All these requirements must be also fulfilled by the designer of the MMIC (Microwave Monolithic Integrated Circuits) circuits that will be used in those wireless terminals, achieving a reliable design, with high performance, low cost, and if possible, in one or two foundry iterations so as to bring the product out to the market as soon as possible. Silicon based technologies are the lowest cost. The demand to use them is simply based on that fact, but their usage in these applications is limited by the ease of use for the designer, in particular, by the lack of adequate simulation models. These technologies don't include some essential components for the design of RF circuits, which leads to measurement results quite different from those simulated. On the other hand, GaAs based technologies, more mature in the RF and microwave field, provide very accurate models, as well as additional tools to verify the design reliability (yield and sensitivity analysis), allowing good results often with only one foundry iteration. The deep study of the problems presented when designing Si-based RF circuits will convince the reader of the need to use special tools as electromagnetic simulation or coo simulation to prevent it. The chapter provides different simulation techniques that help the designer to obtain better designs with a lower cost, as foundry iterations are reduced.

DOI: 10.4018/978-1-4666-0083-6.ch004

INTRODUCTION

Today's communications circuits and systems focus on a mass market in which one of the requirements is the cost, thus pushing towards integration in Silicon technology, most particularly in CMOS technology. In addition, technology tends to associate two techniques SiP (System in Package) and SoC (System on Chip) in these systems to reduce both cost and size. The underlying effects of these requirements are (1) an increase of the circuit complexity; and (2) proximity of the functions, and so the creation of multiple coupling phenomena that are very difficult to diagnose if not known in advance.

At the same time, there is a tendency toward higher working frequencies and for that reason, libraries are very important to help rapid implementation of the functions. The library of a CMOS manufacturer usually consists of active components, MOS transistors or diodes (in which, for example, the effects of interconnecting lines between fingers are not included) and of passive elements, generally the ideal values are used at the start and after layout a parasitic RC extraction is included. Other manufacturers, for these passive components include frequency-dependent models with different levels of complexity depending on the frequency-limit for which they are defined. Moreover, GaAs or SiGe technology fabrication is more expensive but generally provides better performance, and complete active and passive libraries which include frequency-dependent models. In some cases they even provide microstrip line libraries at different levels of metallization as well as possible discontinuities, with real Layout Versus Schematic check and taking into account all of the interconnections. In this case the simulation and measurements can be very close on the first run.

To compensate for this lack of strong library in RF CMOS circuit design, this chapter will propose simulation techniques that allow the designer to take into account all the phenom- ena that appear due to frequency dispersion and coupling, as well as discontinuities. Initially, the typical performance of passive components is shown, including transmission lines, compared with the models provided by the manufacturer or extracted by the layout generation program. Next, typical libraries of these technologies are briefly described, for use with simulation techniques. The techniques to be used are electromagnetic simulation methods combined with circuit simulation techniques, which enable co-simulation to be carried out, taking into account electromagnetic and non linear phenomena.

TRANSMISSION LINE THEORY

In general the books dedicated to electromagnetic signal propagation explain the complete theory of signal transmission in circuits and equipment (Wadell, 1991). All of this theory is applicable to circuits and/or distributed circuits with propagation in mind. On the other hands, circuit theory with localized components (L, C, R) are based on network analysis. For deciding when to use one or the other theory, the operation frequency and the substrate used for transmission must be taken into account.

Next, we will briefly outline one of the theories used to explain electromagnetic signal propagation.

Signal transmission in RF & Microwave circuits or systems takes place through structures that are capable of guiding waves. These structures are basically of two types: transmission lines that guide waves TEM (transverse electromagnetic) between two (or more) conductors, which can be defined and measured in each plane perpendicular to the direction of propagation by the voltage difference between the two conductors. In each transverse plane, the total current flowing through the conductors can also be defined and measured. Otherwise, and more generally, the waveguides are structures that guide electromagnetic signals which are not

Figure 1. Transmission line

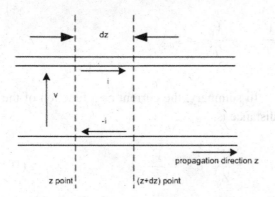

Transmission Line Magnitudes

Assuming a very small section of transmission line (Figure 1), which could be seen as differential, it could be approximated by an L cell as shown in the Figure 2 , where the quantities L, R, G, C are given per unit length

Denominating all Zdz as the impedance per unit length equal to $(R + j\omega L)$ dz and Ydz the admittance per unit length equal to $(G + j\omega C)$ dz, both defined at the frequency ω, the steady state voltage and current can be defined at a particular point on line z applying Kirchoff's laws (Wadell, 1991)

TEM waves. These structures may have one or more dielectric, in the first case, homogeneous structures and the second one inhomogeneous.

For the study of propagation on transmission lines there are two possible approaches: a rigorous one calculating the electromagnetic fields in the structure and thereafter the voltage and current in each transverse plane. The other one is based on the study of the equivalent circuit of a differential segment of transmission line (Figure 1) and then solving the differential equations that appear to apply circuital concepts. Here, the latter method will be used to obtain the main magnitudes of a transmission line.

$$dV = -I \ Z \ dz \Rightarrow \frac{dV}{dz} =$$
$$-I \ Z \Rightarrow \frac{dV(z)}{dz} = -(R + jwL) \ I(z) \tag{1}$$

$$dI = -V \ Y \ dz \Rightarrow \frac{dI}{dz} =$$
$$-V \ Y \Rightarrow \frac{dI(z)}{dz} = -(G + jwC) \ V(z) \tag{2}$$

(1) and (2) could be solved simultaneously and the solution deriving both expressions again with respect to z:

Figure 2. Elementary cell

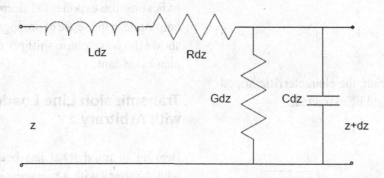

L Conductor Inductance
C Capacitance between conductors
R Resistance of the conductors
G Resistivity of Dielectrics

$$\frac{d^2V}{dz^2} = -Z \frac{dI(z)}{dz} =$$
$$Z \ Y \ V(z) \Rightarrow \frac{d^2V}{dz^2} - Z \ Y \ V(z) = 0 \tag{3}$$

$$\frac{d^2I}{dz^2} = -Y \frac{dV(z)}{dz} =$$
$$Z \ Y \ I(z) \Rightarrow \frac{d^2I}{dz^2} - Z \ Y \ I(z) = 0 \tag{4}$$

This set of equations ((3), (4)) is called the wave equation and is a differential equation whose characteristic equation is $S^2 = ZY$ where:

$$S = \pm\sqrt{ZY} = \pm\gamma = \sqrt{(R + jwL)(G + jwC)} \tag{5}$$

And the solution of this differential equation is:

$$V(z) = V_0^+ \ e^{-\gamma z} + V_0^- \ e^{\gamma z} \tag{6}$$

$$I(z) = I_0^+ \ e^{-\gamma z} + I_0^- \ e^{\gamma z} \tag{7}$$

As
$$d\frac{V(z)}{dz} = \frac{d\left(V_0^+ \ e^{-\gamma z} + V_0^- \ e^{\gamma z}\right)}{dz} = -\gamma\left(V_0^+ \ e^{-\gamma z} - V_0^- \ e^{\gamma z}\right)$$
and substituting into equation (4), we obtain:

$$I(z) = \frac{\gamma}{Z}\left(V_0^+ \ e^{-\gamma z} - V_0^- \ e^{\gamma z}\right) \tag{8}$$

From this equation, the characteristic impedance of the line could be extracted:

$$Z_0 = \frac{Z}{\gamma} =$$
$$\frac{(R + jwL)}{\sqrt{(R + jwL)(G + jwC)}} = \sqrt{\frac{R + jwL}{G + jwC}} \tag{9}$$

since

$$\frac{V_0^+}{I_0^+} = -\frac{V_0^-}{I_0^-} = Z_0$$

In summary, the current as a function of the distance is:

$$I(z) = \frac{V_0^+}{Z_0} \ e^{-\gamma z} - \frac{V_0^-}{Z_0} \ e^{\gamma z} \tag{10}$$

where $e^{-\gamma z}$ represents the propagation on the positive sens of z and $e^{\gamma z}$ represents the negative sens propagation of z, remember that V_0^+ V_0^- and γ are complex numbers and in particular:

$\gamma = \alpha + j\beta$ is the propagation constant

$$Z_{0C} = \sqrt{\frac{Z}{Y}} = R_0 + jX_0 \tag{11}$$

And Z_{0C} is the characteristic impedance which in general is a complex number too. Hence, the solution for the voltage and the current is the superposition of two waves propagating in opposite directions towards and forward the z axis. These waves are affected by the attenuation constant α, indicating the exponential decrease of the wave amplitude in the sense of propagation and β which shows the wave phase shift per unit length called phase constant.

Transmission Line Loaded with Arbitrary z_L

Bearing in mind what has been said, let's see what happens with a transmission line of length l defined by its parameters Z_{0C}, α and β, and connected to an arbitrary load Z_L. In this case it is possible to interpret the reflection coefficient of

Figure 3. Transmission line schema loaded with arbitrary load

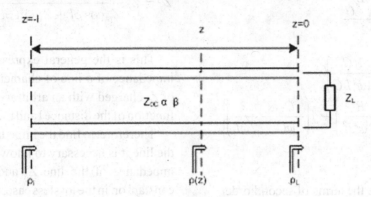

the above-mentioned load at different points of the line as the relationship between the incidental and reflected wave at this point (see Figure 3).

$$\rho_L = \left. \frac{v^-}{v^+} \right|_{z=0} = \frac{V^-}{V^+} \qquad (12)$$

At an arbitrary point z of the line, the reflection coefficient is the coefficient that presents the load ρ_L affected by the phase change produced by the double trip of this line, since the wave goes and returns from z=z to z=0, whose demonstration can be seen next:

$$\rho(z) = \left. \frac{v^-}{v^+} \right|_z = \frac{V^- e^{\gamma z}}{V^+ e^{-\gamma z}} = \frac{V^-}{V^+} e^{2\gamma z} = \rho_L e^{2\gamma z}, \qquad (13)$$

the reflection coefficient at the input will be the particular case when z=-l, expressed as following:

$$\left. \rho_i \right|_{z=-l} = \rho_L e^{-2\gamma l} \qquad (14)$$

Where ρ_L, is the reflection coefficient at the load, defined by:

$$\rho_L = \frac{Z_L - Z_{OC}}{Z_L + Z_{OC}}, \qquad (15)$$

the input impedance of this line with characteristic impedance Z_{OC} loaded with an arbitrary load Z_L is calculated by relating the voltage and the current at the point z =-l, as shown next,

$$Z_i = \left. \frac{V}{I} \right|_{z=-l} = Z_0 \frac{V^+ e^{\gamma l} + V^- e^{-\gamma l}}{V^+ e^{\gamma l} - V^- e^{-\gamma l}} = Z_0 \frac{1 + \rho_L e^{-2\gamma l}}{1 - \rho_L e^{-2\gamma l}}. \qquad (16)$$

Using the impedance instead of the reflection coefficient:

$$Z_i = Z_{0C} \frac{Z_L \cosh \gamma l + Z_{0C} \sinh \gamma l}{Z_{0C} \cosh \gamma l + Z_L \sinh \gamma l}. \qquad (17)$$

In the low losses case and at frequencies where $R \langle\langle wL$ and $G \langle\langle wC$ or $\mu = \frac{R}{wL} \langle\langle 1$ and $v = \frac{G}{wC} \langle\langle 1$

Through power series development of the equations (5) and (9) and ignoring terms third order and above, we obtain:

$$\begin{cases} \alpha = \dfrac{R}{2\sqrt{L/C}} + \dfrac{G\sqrt{L/C}}{2} \\[3mm] \beta = w\sqrt{LC}\left(1 - \dfrac{RG}{4w^2 LC}\right) \\[3mm] Z_{0C} = \sqrt{\dfrac{L}{C}}\left[\left(1 + \dfrac{R^2}{8w^2 L^2}\right) + j\left(\dfrac{G}{2wC} - \dfrac{R}{2wL}\right)\right] \end{cases}$$

If we also ignore the terms of second order

$$\begin{cases} \alpha = \dfrac{R}{2\sqrt{L/C}} + \dfrac{G\sqrt{L/C}}{2} \\[3mm] \beta = w\sqrt{LC} \\[3mm] Z_{0C} = \sqrt{\dfrac{L}{C}}\left[1 + j\left(\dfrac{G}{2wC} - \dfrac{R}{2wL}\right)\right] \end{cases}$$

From the previous equations, we can deduce that the phase constant β is the same in the low-loss case and in the lossless case. In the case of the lossless line, the characteristic impedance of the line is $Z_0 = \sqrt{L/C}$ and $\alpha=0$.

The equations may be rewritten as function of Z_0 as follows:

$$\begin{cases} \alpha = \dfrac{1}{2}\left(\dfrac{R}{Z_0} + GZ_0\right) \\[3mm] \beta = w\sqrt{LC} \\[3mm] Z_{0C} = Z_0\left[1 + j\dfrac{1}{2}\left(\dfrac{G}{wC} - \dfrac{R}{wL}\right)\right] \end{cases}$$

Thus the input impedance of the line in the lossless case is,

$$Z_i = Z_0 \frac{Z_L \cos \beta l + Z_0 \sin \beta l}{Z_0 \cos \beta l + Z_L \sin \beta l}. \qquad (18)$$

This is the general expression for the input impedance of a line of characteristic impedance of Z_0 charged with an arbitrary charge of Z_L as a function of the distance l and the phase constant β.

Therefore, to find the impedance at the input of the line it is necessary to know the characteristic impedance of the line Z_0 and the propagation constant or, in the lossless case, the phase constant β. These characteristics depend on how the line is manufactured. In RF and microwave circuits, nearly all the lines are planar, of which the best known and most frequently used is the microstrip line. There are, however, many others depending on the disposition of the ground plane with respect to the line or what the substrates above and below the metallic strip/s are like. In that case, the distribution of the electromagnetic fields is different and the characteristic impedance and the effective dielectric constant vary, or in other words, the phase constant varies.

Planar Transmission Lines

Figure 4 shows several configurations of lines where there are only two conductors:

There are more different types where other ground planes or other metallic strips are used, but these will not be shown here as they do not provide further information.

The expressions used to calculate the necessary parameters, Z_{0C} and ε_{eff} can be extracted from the extensive pertinent documentation, (Hammerstad & Jensen, 1980; Kirschning & Jansen 1982; Kobayashi 1983). It should be noted that these cyclic equations are interdependent so the solution is not univocal.

Next, we will show the equations solely for the microstrip lines.

Characteristic line impedance Z_{0C}: if $\varepsilon_r \leq 16$ and $0.05 \leq w / h \leq 100 \Rightarrow 0.2\%$ error,

Figure 4. Planar transmission lines

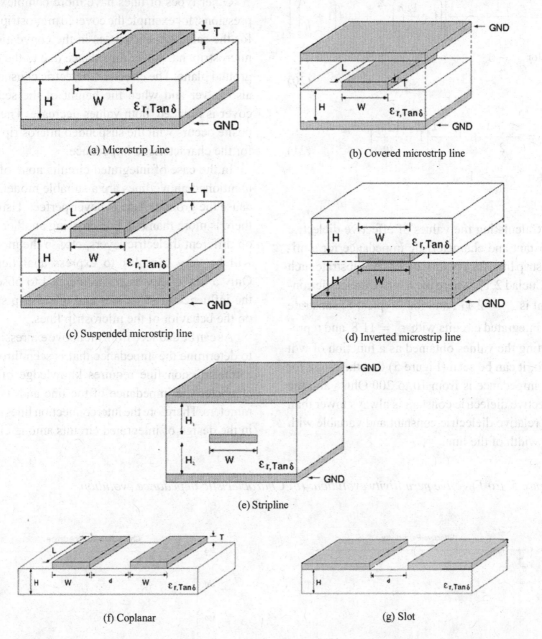

(a) Microstrip Line

(b) Covered microstrip line

(c) Suspended microstrip line

(d) Inverted microstrip line

(e) Stripline

(f) Coplanar

(g) Slot

$$Z_{0C} = \frac{\eta_0}{\sqrt{\varepsilon_{eff}}} K_g =$$

$$\frac{\sqrt{\frac{\mu_0}{\varepsilon_0}}}{2\pi\sqrt{\varepsilon_{eff}}} . \ln\left(\frac{6 + (2\pi - 6).e^{-\left(\frac{30.666h}{w}\right)^{0.7528}}.h}{w} + \sqrt{1 + \frac{4.h^2}{w^2}} \right)$$

(19)

Dielectric constant ε_{eff}: if $\varepsilon_r \leq 16$ and $0.05 \leq w / h \leq 20 \Rightarrow 1\%$ error,

$$\varepsilon_{eff} = \frac{\varepsilon_r + 1}{2} + \frac{\varepsilon_r - 1}{2}\left(\left(1 + \frac{12.h}{w}\right)^{-\frac{1}{2}} + 0.04\left(1 + \frac{w}{h}\right)^2\right)$$

for $\quad \frac{w}{h} \langle 1$

$$(20)$$

$$\varepsilon_{eff} = \frac{\varepsilon_r + 1}{2} + \frac{\varepsilon_r - 1}{2}\left(1 + \frac{12.h}{w}\right)^{-\frac{1}{2}}$$

for $\quad \frac{w}{h} \geq 1$

$$(21)$$

Calculating the values of effective dielectric constant and characteristic impedance for a microstrip line, for a typical dielectric substrate such as Cuclad 2.17, where the relative dielectric constant is $\varepsilon_r = 2.17$, and for a typical Si substrate for integrated circuits with $\varepsilon_r = 11.8$ and representing the values obtained as a function of w/h ratio, it can be seen (Figure 5) that the range for the impedance is from 10 to 200 Ohms and the effective dielectric constant is always lower than the relative dielectric constant and variable with the width of the line.

Other types of lines have more complex expressions: for example the covered microstrip line for the same dimensions as in the conventional microstrip, has lower impedance due to the new ground plane. The effective dielectric constant is also lower and when the height of the second cover is reduced, both values decrease. The opposite occurs with the suspended microstrip line for the characteristic impedance.

In the case of integrated circuits none of the mentioned above lines are a suitable model, because the ground plane is never perfect. Usually there is more than one line crossing another line on different dielectric layers, etc, so the models will be very complex to express analytically. Only a few comparisons are needed to observe the influence of substrates and microstrip stack on the behavior of the microstrip lines.

As can be deduced from the above expressions, to determine the impedance that is seen through a transmission line requires knowledge of the characteristic impedance of the line and its parameters. Therefore the interconnection lines used in the design of integrated circuits among either

Figure 5. (a) Effective permitivity evolution; (b) Characteristic impedance evolution

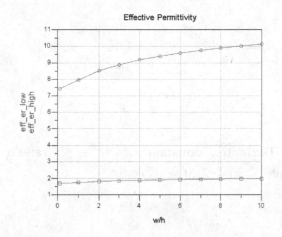

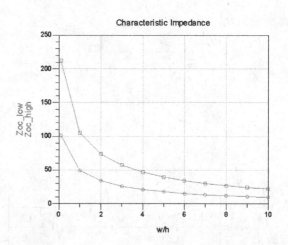

a

υ

active or passive components can vary and can alter the response depending on the frequency and the characteristics of the substrate. Transmission lines in integrated circuits are basically microstrip, or stripline, with non homogeneous substrates.

When the frequencies are sufficiently low so as to assume that the previously mentioned propagation phenomena do not exist, the design of these lines only affects the optimization in the design layout and normally are not taken into account in previous design steps. However as the frequency increases, these phenomena must be considered from the first design stages. In later sections, we will also explain coupling phenomena.

As an example, we will explain how to modify the value of impedance when connecting to one line or another, as well as showing the modification of the possible matching of this impedance when the elements of the matching network are connected at one point or at another.

The study was carried out with a line of 10 μm width and 100 μm length, connected to a load with a resistance of 4 Ohms in series with a capacitance of 250 fF (Figure 6). To observe the influence of the line, two cases were assumed, on the one hand, a line whose ground plane is the global ground of the circuit at 500μm, and a second case, with the ground plane generated from a lower metallization layer at 2μm.

The characteristic impedance and the electrical length of the two lines were calculated changing the substrates in each case. This example enables us to see the influence of this little line depending on the ground plane, as well as the influence on the matching taking into account the effect of this network.

Figure 6. Simulation set-up to compare the variation of the input impedance with a microstrip line

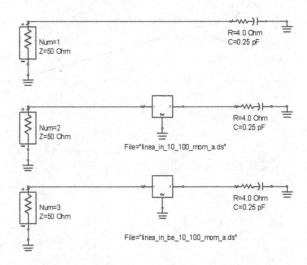

The impedance decreases by 25% in the real part and up to 16% in the imaginary part (Table 1), if an ideal T matching network is used to match to 50 Ohms at 1 GHz (Figure 7), in the no line case a perfect match is obtained as expected, and in the second and third cases a maximum frequency shift of 13 MHz on the optimum match is seen (see Table 2 and Figure 8). If more lines are included more variations could be obtained.

If we study the same problem at 5 GHz with a new matching network (Figure 9) the influences are more significant in the three cases, because the line is electrically larger at 5 GHz than at 1 GHz.

In this case a deviation on the matching frequency is observed of 200 MHz when a frequency sweep is done, or 80% in the real part and

Table 1. Input impedance results, without lines, with line and ground plane at the botton and with line and ground plane at 2 μm under the signal line

freq	zin(S(1,1))	zin(S(2,2))	zin(S(3,3))
1.000 GHz	4.000 – j636.620	3.980 – j610.506	2.941 – j528.522

Figure 7. Simulation set-up to compare the variation of the input impedance with a microstrip line when and input matching network is designed at 1 GHz

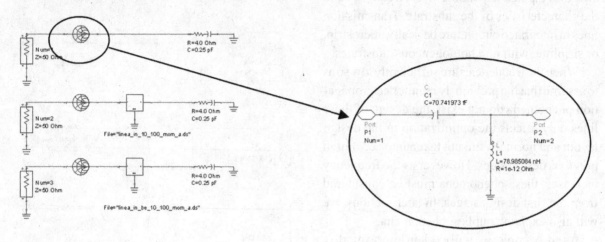

Table 2. Impedance values once matching network is included with and without microstrip lines in the three cases mentioned above at 1 GHz

freq	zin(S(1,1))	zin(S(2,2))	zin(S(3,3))
1.000 GHz	49.978 + j7.842E-5	57.929 + j108.119	75.038 + j318.310

Figure 8. Input return losses in dB when an input matching network in designed for 1 GHz

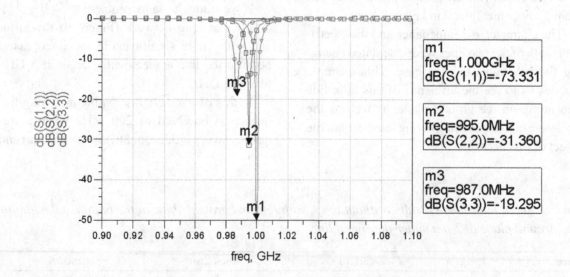

Figure 9. Ideal matching network for 5 GHz operating frequency

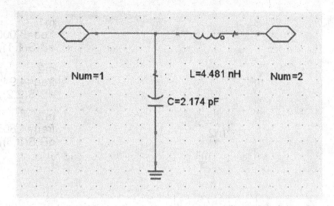

Table 3. Impedance variation with and without lines for 5 GHz operating frequency

freq	zin(S(1,1))	zin(S(2,2))	zin(S(3,3))
5.000 GHz	49.231 + j0.015	44.184 − j33.819	8.039 − j34.915

200000% in the imaginary part of the impedance presented at 5 GHz (see Figure 11).

Another typical example is the unbalance in a differential amplifier. For each differential stage in the ideal or low frequency case the common node voltage is zero, output voltages have the same amplitudes and there is 180° phase difference. In a particular case with two stages operating at 5.8 GHz, we study voltages and currents in each node in the ideal (without interconnection lines) and in the case where 3 small 10X200 μm lines are taken into account to simulate the real non symmetric layout (see Figure 12).

In the first case without lines, it is possible to see a totally symmetric response in voltage and current, and zero voltage is obtained at the common node. (see Table 4)

In that configuration, the output power is 3.9 dBm with a voltage gain of 13.9 dB and current gain of 28.8 dB. When three small lines are introduced into the circuit: the first one in the input (base terminal) of the first stage, the second one

Figure 10. Smith chart representation of the impedance with and without lines for 5 GHz operating frequency

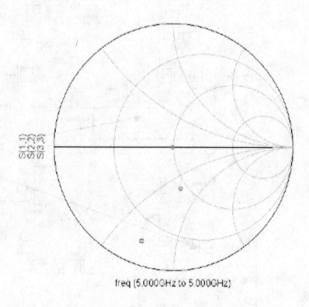

freq (5.000GHz to 5.000GHz)

Figure 11. Input return losses in dB when an input matching network in designed for 5 GHz

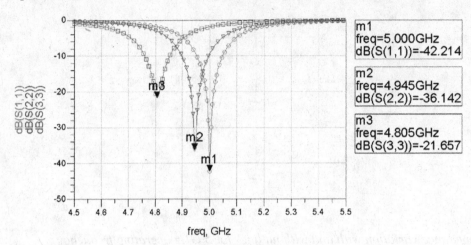

Figure 12. Two stages differential amplifier

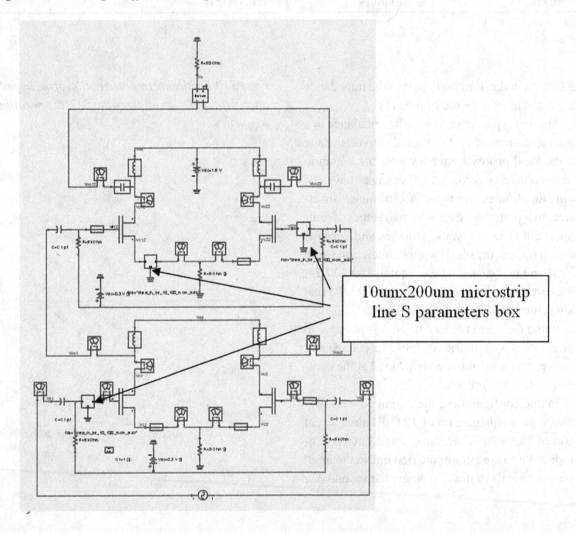

10umx200um microstrip line S parameters box

Table 4. Current and voltages at common node (Vc), output voltages (Voo) and output power and gain voltage for the ideal case (no lines case)

Vc12[1]	I_c12.i[1]	Vc22[1]	I_c22.i[1]
2.742E-13/142.378	0.010/129.743	2.742E-13/142.378	0.010/-50.257
Voo12[1]	**I_oo12.i[1]**	**Voo22[1]**	**I_oo22.i[1]**
0.248/-56.416	0.010/-56.416	0.248/123.584	0.010/123.584
dBm(Vo)[1]	**dB(Voo12/Vii1)[1]**	**dB(I_oo12.i/I_ii1.i)[1]**	**dB(Vo/0.1)[1]**
3.909	13.909	28.816	13.909

in the interconnection of the common node (collector terminal) of the second stage and the third one in the input (base terminal) of the second stage. The most significant difference is the voltage dissymmetry of each branch (Voo12 and Voo22). Moreover, the common node voltage is non-zero Vc12 or Vc22, (see Table 5) all these phenomena cause a voltage gain reduction of 11.8 dB.

These examples validate the possible influence on the response when interconnection lines are not taken into account in the design of RF circuits. It is very important to have the exact information about the lines that interconnect all the passive and active components..

The following sections will deal with describing the models available for transmission lines in the different simulator environments, then the pas-

sive models as well as the electromagnetic simulations with and without co-simulation options.

Typical Transmission Line CAD Models

Cadence-Spectre RF Model

Transmission line modeling is becoming increasingly important as design frequencies increase. So software manufacturers are dedicating more and more effort to it. Spectre, from Cadence, provides an MTLINE component for modeling lossy coupled transmission line structures. It uses sophisticated and robust algorithms that provide accurate and reliable simulation. Among its many capabilities, this model allows dielectric loss to

Table 5. Current and voltages at common node (Vc), output voltages (Voo) and output power and gain voltage for the real case (lines case)

Vc12[1]	I_c12.i[1]	Vc22[1]	I_c22.i[1]
0.007/-161.932	0.010/128.430	0.002/45.192	0.010/-50.540
Voo12[1]	**I_oo12.i[1]**	**Voo22[1]**	**I_oo22.i[1]**
0.184/-60.534	0.010/-57.222	0.307/124.758	0.010/122.778
dBm(Vo)[1]	**dB(Voo12/Vii1)[1]**	**dB(I_oo12.i/I_ii1.i)[1]**	**dB(Vo/0.1)[1]**
3.815	11.831	28.528	13.815

be specified more completely, which improves accuracy and eliminates the causality problem.

In addition, Spectre comes with the Line Model Generator (LMG) utility that allows users to describe a wide variety of transmission line structures graphically; structures such as multi-conductor microstrip, stripline, substrate loss line, and coplanar waveguide, as well as almost any 2-D cross-section of rectangular conductors embedded in layered media. LMG allows users to specify the structure with relatively simple geometric parameters while giving graphical feedback to assure the parameters are correct. It then takes some relatively well-known material properties and generates a complete MTLINE description for the structure that includes frequency dependent loss mechanisms, such as skin effect and dielectric loss, as well as dispersion.

SPICE Model

The uniform RLC/RC/LC/RG transmission line model (referred to as the LTRA model hereafter) models a uniform constant-parameter distributed transmission line. The RC and LC cases may also be modeled using the URC and TRA models; however, the newer LTRA model is usually faster and more accurate than the others. The operation of the LTRA model is based on the convolution of the transmission line's impulse responses with its inputs

ADS Model

The Agilent Technologies ADS simulator has specialized from the early 90s on high-frequency circuits and it has models for various configurations of transmission lines; from ideal transmission lines which allow the designer to work with general characteristics of the lines, to particular transmission lines such as microstrip, striplines, coplanar, etc. In each case the substrate is defined and the physical dimensions of the lines are given, the program uses different models depending

on the line. For example for microstrip Lines the frequency-domain analytical model uses the Hammerstad and Jensen 1980 formula to calculate the static impedance, Z_0, and effective dielectric constant, ε_{eff}. The attenuation factor, α, is calculated using Wheeler's incremental inductance rule (Wheeler 1942). The frequency dependence of the skin effect is included in the conductor loss calculation. Dielectric loss is also included in the loss calculation.

Dispersion effects are included using either the improved version of the Kirschning and Jansen (1982) model, the Kobayashi model (1983-1990), or the Yamashita model (Yamashita, Atshi & Hirachata, 1981), depending on the choice specified in Mod. The default formula is Kirschning and Jansen.

For time-domain analysis, an impulse response obtained from the frequency analytical model is used.

Another characteristic of ADS is that discontinuities are included in the libraries as components, for example the open-end effect in microstrip is modeled in the frequency domain as an extension of the length of the microstrip stub. The microstrip is modeled using the MLIN component, including conductor loss, dielectric loss and dispersion. A correction for finite line thickness is applied to the line width. The length of the microstrip extension, dl, is based on the formula developed by Kirschning, Jansen and Koster (1981). Fringing at the open end of the line is calculated and included in the model.

For the corner discontinuity, the frequency-domain model is an empirically based, analytical model which consists of a static, lumped, equivalent circuit (Figure 13). The equivalent circuit parameters are calculated based on the expressions developed by Kirschning, Jansen and Koster 1983

The microstrip TEE (Figure 14) is modeled in the frequency domain and is an empirically based, analytical model. The model modifies E. Hammerstad model formula to calculate the Tee junction discontinuity at the location defined in the

Figure 13. (a) Microstrip Corner; (b) Equivalent circuit for the discontinuity (extracted from ADS 2009U1 pdf manual)

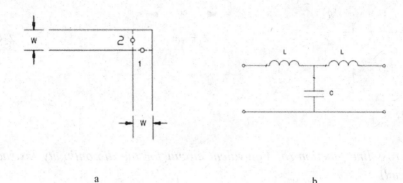

a

b

reference for wide range validity. A reference plan shift is added to each of the ports to make the reference planes consistent with the layout.

The step in width (Figure 15) is a typical discontinuity whose effect is an extra length, so it must be taken into account.

The cross of two microstrip lines (Figure 16) uses the equivalent circuit parameters calculated based on the expressions developed by Gupta et al. The capacitance equations are modified to take into account the relative dielectric constant of the material.

The inductance equations are independent of the relative dielectric constant on the substrate. Dispersion and conductor loss are not included.

ADS offers more than sixty different models on its microstrip library taking into account the majority of discontinuities present on a circuit and the same occurs with the fineline, stripline, suspended substrate and printed circuit board line components that helps the RF designer from the firsts steps of the circuit definition.

Figure 14. (a) Tee junction (b) Equivalent circuit for the discontinuity (extracted from ADS 2009U1 pdf manual)

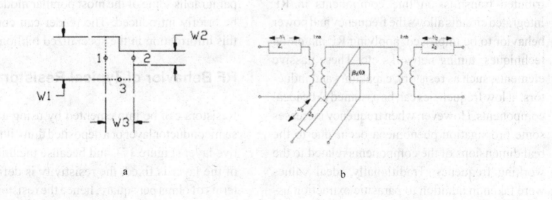

a

b

Figure 15. (a) Step in width (b) Equivalent circuit for the discontinuity (extracted from ADS 2009U1 pdf manual)

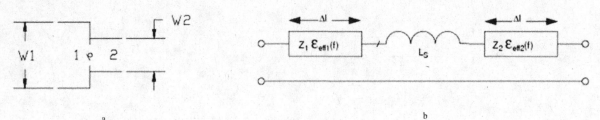

a

b

Figure 16. (a) Cross-line junction (b) Equivalent circuit for the discontinuity (extracted from ADS 2009U1 pdf manual)

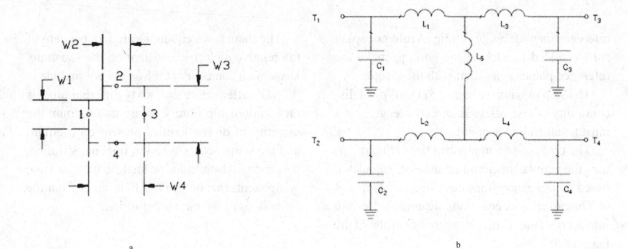

a

b

RF BEHAVIOR OF TYPICAL PASSIVE COMPONENTS

The use of passive components as well as distributed transmission line components in RF integrated circuits allows the frequency and power behavior to be improved, applying RF matching techniques, tuning networks etc. These passive elements, such as resistors, capacitors and inductors, at low frequencies can be assumed to be ideal components. However, when frequency increases some propagation phenomena occur due to the real dimensions of the components related to the working frequency. Traditionally, ideal values were taken in addition to parasitic extraction us-

ing an embedded tool in the simulators, but it is known that this extraction is limited to frequency range validation. Therefore, more complete models must be taken into account. In the next paragraphs some of the most popular models will be briefly introduced. The reader can complete this information in the specialized bibliography.

RF Behavior of Typical Resistor

Resistors can be implemented by using a doped semiconductor layer or a deposited thin-film resistive layer (Figure 17), and because the thickness of the layer is fixed, the resistivity is defined in terms of ohms per square, hence the resistor value

Figure 17. Thick film resistor (a) front view (b) 3D view

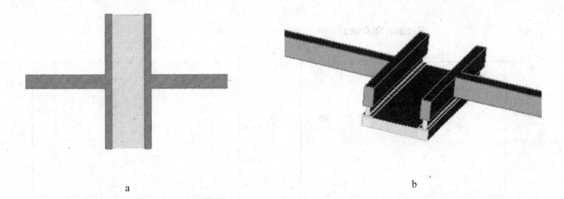

a

b

is defined choosing the dimension W (μm) xL (μm) or the aspect ratio. Depending on the technology, sometimes for large values of resistance, the dimension L is large compared to W, and at the same time it acts like a transmission line, so at high frequencies both phenomena could be taken into account depending on the chosen model.

The most popular model is shown in Figure 18 where L is the equivalent inductance of the line, R is the resistor value and C is the capacitor between each connection and the substrate. This model is limited on frequency because of its lumped characteristic.

Other foundries and authors use distributed models, where the resistor is connected to two transmission lines with the same width and half

length of the resistor dimensions. The substrate definition could be known and in this case frequency dispersion is defined.

Frequency response is shown in the next figure (Figure 19), where we can observe the frequency dispersion on phase and magnitude, which the ideal model (blue line with circles) can't define.

RF Behavior of Typical Capacitor

The capacitor could be made with a dielectric layer between two metallic plates (MIM capacitors) Figure 20, using the coupling effect between two metal sheets on the same plane as an inter-digital capacitor. In the first case, higher values could be obtained depending on the dielectric constant of

Figure 18. Resistor circuit model

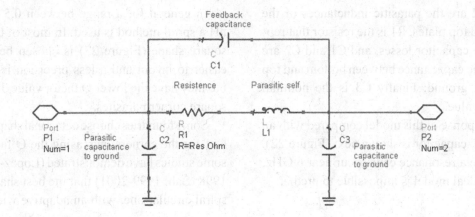

Figure 19. Resistor model S parameters compared with ideal component

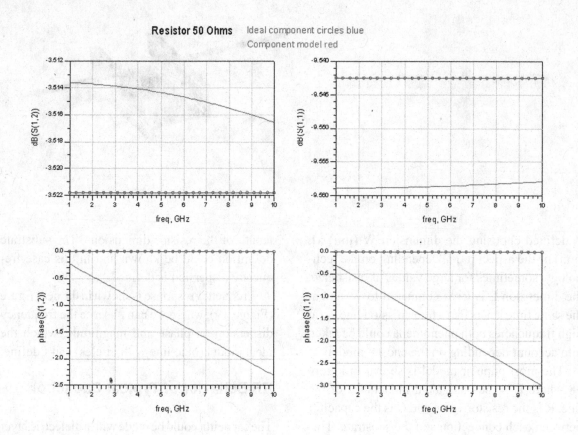

the dielectric layer and in the second one, small and precise values could be obtained depending on the gap precision of the technology. In both cases, as occurs with resistors at high frequency, some other effects could be taken into account that modifies the equivalent value.

A possible model is shown in Figure 21 where L1 and L2 are the parasitic inductances of the bottom and top plates, R1 is the resistor that represents the capacitor losses, and C1 and C2 are the parasitic capacitance between bottom and top plates and ground. Finally C3 is the nominal capacitor value.

The response of this model compared with an ideal 10 pF capacitor is shown next (Figure 22). In this case a resonance cans occur near 6 GHz, since the ideal model is impossible to predict.

Typical Inductor RF Behavior

Finally the inductors used in general for high frequency applications, are made with fine microstrip lines, because more long more inductive is the line obliges to find a solution for obtaining a small shape inductor.

In general for a range between 0.5 nH to 5 nH a spiral method is used. In most of the cases square shape (Figure 23) is chosen because is easier to layout and a less precision is needed, but they have the lower Q factor value due to the square corner parasites.

Some foundries choose octagonal shapes using 45 ° for the corners increasing the Q factor, but some studies have demonstrated (Lopez-Villegas 1998; Bahl 1999-2001) that the best shape is the spiral circular one, with an adaptive width from

Figure 20. MIM capacitor (a) front view, (b) 3D view

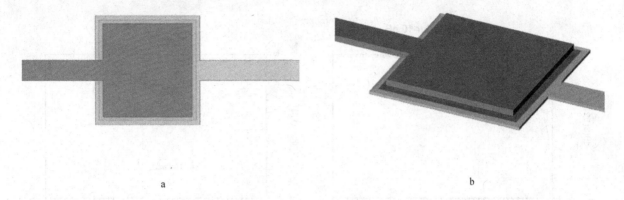

a   b

Figure 21. Capacitor circuit model

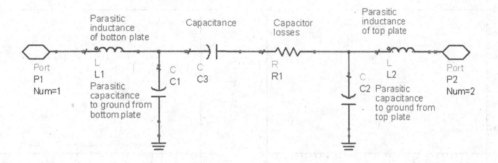

the centre to the external connection that decreases the parasitic capacitor and increases the frequency of operation.

This model (Figure 24) is the simplest one, that in the case of several turns the coupling between a line and the closest is not the same as the coupling with the second line. Most complete models could be found in the literature

If we see in Figure 25 the comparison between ideal and model responses, is possible to appreciate a small difference in the phase of S12 or S11 parameters, but the figure of merit that explain the behavior of and inductor is the quality factor (see Figure 26), and in the ideal case is infinite and in the real one is lower than 4, so in the inductor case the use of a good model could avoid differences between expected and obtained results, because inductors are a key components in matching networks, VCO, etc.

ELECTROMAGNETIC SIMULATIONS

RF integrated circuit designers now require "circuit-level" EM simulation and modeling to provide the accuracy and throughput demands in order to meet aggressive project schedule deadlines. The days of using only flat planar EM simulation solutions for MMIC design are over. Now full 3D geometry modeling of bond wires, via structures, and other 3D structures are a must-have for designers pushing performance. Circuit-level EM simulation captures the true electrical behavior of a design's passive structures including coupling. The active and passive components have interconnections or transmission lines, which are lines that connect different metallization layers, baseband, IF or RF signal lines. The need to decrease the chip size and number of package pins has caused the trend for multi-layers and multichip structures

Figure 22. Capacitor model S param compared with ideal component

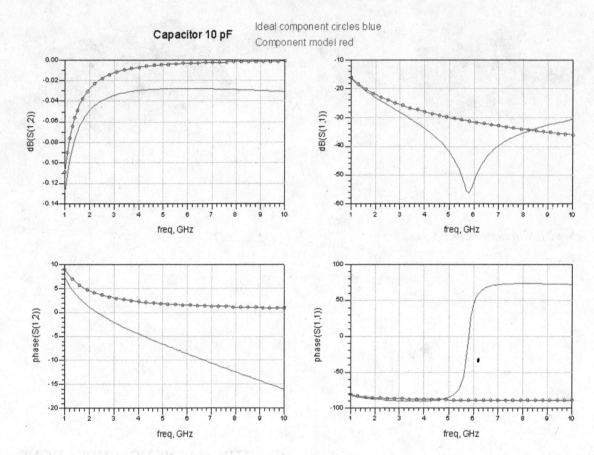

Figure 23. Square spiral inductor a) front view, b) 3D view

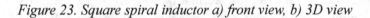

Figure 24. Inductor circuit model

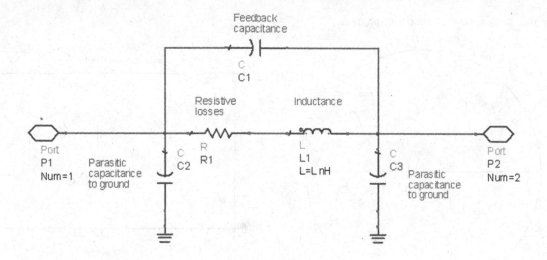

Figure 25. Inductor model S param compared with ideal component

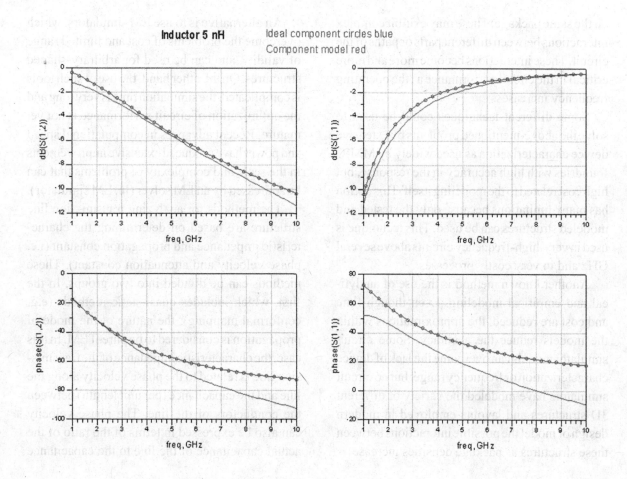

Figure 26. Input impedance comparison and inductor model Q factor

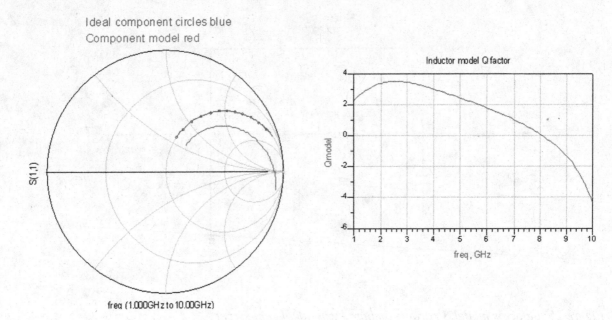

on the same package. These may exhibit complex interactions between different parts or paths of the circuit. These interactions become more and more critical in the circuit performance as the operating frequency increases.

Some different techniques could be used to solve the above-mentioned problems by extensive device characterization as used widely by MMIC foundries with high accuracy in the response, but high cost related to the modeling itself. This option has many limitations because only the tested and modeled structures can be used. This technique is used in very-high-frequency circuits above several GHz and in very costly processes.

Another known method is the use of analytical and empirical modeling. Even though time and cost are reduced, the approximations within the models reduce the accuracy. Some circuit simulator models can overcome the lack of device characterization or frequency range, but no circuit simulators have modeled the variety of different 3D structures and layouts employed in modern design or model the possible interactions between these structures as package densities increase.

An alternative is to use EM simulators, which overcome the problems of cost and limited range of validity, and can be used for arbitrary-shaped structures. On the other hand, the use of such tools is complicated, the simulation time is very long and the optimization of circuit performance is not yet mature. Recent advances in computational speed and power have produced extensive improvements in the scale and complexity of problems that can be addressed by an EM solver (Ie. EM simulator).

The methods for analyzing transmission line structure are based on determining the characteristic impedance and propagation constant (i.e. phase velocity and attenuation constant). These methods can be divided into two groups. In the first, which includes quasi-static methods (e.g. conformal mapping); the nature of the mode of propagation is considered to be pure-TEM. In this case, the characteristic impedance of the transmission line is related to the phase velocity along the line and the capacitance (per unit length) between the conductors of the line. The phase velocity can also be expressed in terms of the ratio of the actual capacitance of the line to the capacitance of the same line in air. Therefore, determining the characteristic impedance and phase velocity of the structure essentially reduces to the problem of finding the capacitance of the line. However, this type of analysis is only suitable for designing lower frequency MMICs, where the strip width and substrate thickness are much smaller than the guided wavelength.

The second group (Ie. full-wave analysis) takes into account the hybrid nature of all the modes of propagation. As a result, an important outcome of this type of analysis is information about the dispersive nature of the line. This gives the frequency variation of the effective permittivity, and therefore the variation in the characteristic impedance and phase velocity.

In general, traditional quasi-TEM approximations, used in the modeling of passive components within many commercially available CAD software packages, cannot accurately account for frequency dispersion. As the design frequency of the MMIC increases, the effects of the associated parasitic effects increase, thus changing the electrical characteristics of the components and associated circuits. For example, this can have the effect of increasing impedance mismatch losses or reducing coupler directivities.

As previously pointed out, the microstrip configuration is not capable of supporting a pure TEM mode. Therefore, this hybrid mode cannot be fully described in terms of static capacitances and inductances only. As a result, one has to consider time-varying electric and magnetic fields, and solve the wave equation subject to appropriate boundary conditions. In general, EM solvers are better when one examines multi-conductor transmission lines, cross-talk effects, ringing effects, skin effect losses and R-C time constant effects of discontinuities. In addition, EM solvers are the only tools that can be used when one considers interconnection and packaging effects.

Nowadays, there are many vendors of EM simulation software. They usually come in two forms: full 3-D EM simulators and 3-D planar simulators.

In spite of the extensive list of possible EM simulators, only two included as they are used on the examples, and offer the possibility of being used integrated in the same environment as circuit design simulators. The Agilent FEM Simulator and Ansoft HFSS are used here, although other programs could equally well be used and may even provide more precise results. However, the author considers that it is also important that the design platforms are uniform so that the designer can easily carry out the opportune simulations without coming out of the working environment, thus making the design process more agile. A more extended description of both programs is presented clarifying the above-mentioned special characteristics they have:

The Agilent FEM Simulator Element (formerly known as EMDS G2) provides full wave 3D EM simulation capabilities based on the Finite Element Method (FEM). This frequency domain simulation technology can be used in both standalone and ADS integrated modes. The FEM Simulator is the second generation of Agilent's FEM 3D EM simulator integrated into the ADS design flow to enable seamless co-simulation of arbitrary 3D structures such as connectors, wire-bonds and packaging with circuit and system components. This allows effects of 3D components previously difficult or tedious to include in a design simulation to be naturally accounted for without leaving your circuit design flow. It is especially convenient for RF module designs where 3D interconnects and packaging must be simulated along with the circuit.

On the other hand, there is Momentum G2, which is the improved second generation of Agilent EEsof EDA's powerful Momentum 3D planar electromagnetic simulator, which is the technology and innovation leader in high-frequency mixed-signal electronic design automation (EDA). Momentum G2 is seamlessly integrated into the Advanced Design System (ADS), the only design simulation platform that enables the co-design of IC, package and board in high-frequency and hi-speed applications. It seamlessly integrates system, circuit and full 3D electromagnetic simulation with Agilent's test instrumentation for you to do single pass successful electronic designs repeatedly.

Momentum G2 is an advanced Method of Moments (MOM) 3D planar electromagnetic simulator, enhanced with the latest NlogN and multi-threading solver algorithms, to deliver the fastest and highest capacity 3D planar EM simulation possible. Integrated within ADS, it allows electromagnetic simulation to be used together with circuit and system co-simulation or co-optimization to take into account proximity or radiation effects of planar structures such as traces or printed antennas. Visualization of the results in terms of surface currents or radiated fields provides insights into where to fix problem areas.

Momentum G2 is paired with an ingenious parameterized passive model generation capability called Advanced Model Composer (AMC). AMC enables you to create EM-based custom libraries of planar 3D models such as transitions, discontinuities or passive components, not available in the standard simulation libraries because of their novel geometries or dimensions, which are beyond the range of validity. AMC libraries retain the accuracy of EM simulation but simulate and optimize at the speed of circuit simulation through smart interpolation across the parameterized EM database.

Ansoft's HFSS TM Engineers rely on the accuracy, capacity, and performance of HFSS to design high-speed components, including on-chip embedded passives, IC packages, PCB interconnects, and high-frequency components such as antennas, RF/microwave components, and biomedical devices. With HFSS, engineers can extract parasitic parameters (S, Y, and Z), visualize 3D electromagnetic fields (near- and far-field) and generate Full-Wave SPICE™ models that link to circuit simulations. Signal Integrity engineers' use HFSS within established EDA design flows to evaluate signal quality, including transmission path losses, reflection loss due to impedance mismatches, parasitic coupling and radiation. HFSS provides unprecedented integration with EDA design flows, allowing engineers to combine complex, highly nonlinear circuits with transistor-level detail and 3D full-wave accurate component models to do challenging high-performance electronic designs. With HFSS Solver on Demand users can operate HFSS from an easy-to-use, stack-up based layout interface, which provides direct import of layered geometry and automated set-up. AnsoftLinks offers another option to transfer 3D ECAD or MCAD component geometry to HFSS.

For in-depth multiphysics analysis, HFSS is integrated with the ANSYS Workbench. HFSS designs exist as data blocks in the ANSYS Workbench interface allowing for easy data exchange with ANSYS Mechanical, ANSYS Icepak and more. This link also provides tighter integration with ANSYS DesignXplorer to facilitate optimization and design of experiment studies

VCO EXAMPLE

Now that the simulators and their capabilities are known, a particular example of a VCO design will be shown (Figure 27). In an oscillator, noise causes quick random fluctuations in the phase of the output signal causing the frequency spectrum to spread around the desired output frequency and making the RF signal detection a very delicate matter. As phase noise is inversely proportional to the quality factor of the resonant circuit, the necessity of high Q inductors to reduce the phase noise level is clear.

Although inductors occupy the largest area and are key components in terms of phase noise, accurate inductor modeling still represents a handicap in the design of VCO at high frequencies (Koutsoyannopoulos & Papananos, 2000).

Figure 27. Differential VCO topology

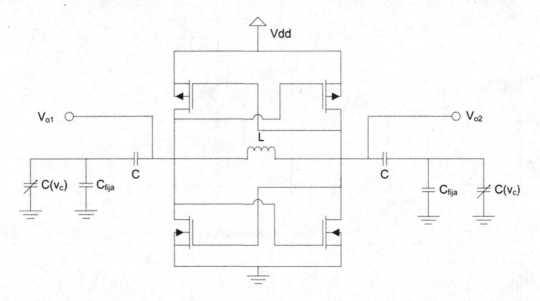

It is difficult to accurately model all the effects in the inductors, especially when the working frequencies are high. One solution is the electromagnetic simulation of the inductor by means of finite element simulators. Planar simulators do not describe the behavior of the inductor accurately enough, but there are 3D simulators which can be more precise 02004).

The shown VCO is a complementary cross-coupled structure suitable for high operation frequencies (Figure 27). It has a good balance between low phase noise and low power consumption. The main disadvantage is the high supply voltage required, in our case 2.5 V. The two NMOS-PMOS pairs provide the negative resistance and the inductor and capacitors at both ends together with the parasitic capacitances make up the resonant circuit (Craninckx, Steyaert, 1997; López-Villegas, et al., 2000). This topology uses only one inductor, in contrast with other crossed MOS pair configurations, significantly reducing the required area. Besides, it does not have a biasing network, simplifying the circuit.

In the first simulations, an electrical inductor model is used and, as the manufacturer does not provide either a substrate model or a library model for the interconnecting microstrip lines, we do not introduce them in the circuit simulations as result of this design procedure no oscillation is observed on the measurements of the prototype of the first run. Then some simulations taking into account the interconnection lines trough EM simulations were done, and it was possible to observe (Figure 28) that the oscillation extinguishes.

In the second run this microstrip lines are taken into account but the simulated tuning range obtained (Figure 29) varies from 10.7 GHz for 5 Volts to 11.7 GHz for 0 Volts of tuning voltage, and in measurement a diminution of 2 GHz is observed on the frequency band.

This time the simulations considered the effect of the microstrip lines. Therefore, the discrepancies between measurements and simulations must be caused by the model of another component. Due to the "low frequency" origins of the CMOS technologies, the inductor is usually poorly modeled at high frequencies. We know the influence of this component in the VCO is important, as it is part of the resonant circuit. Thus, we performed a three dimensional electromagnetic simulation

Figure 28. Simulated differential output first run VCO with lines

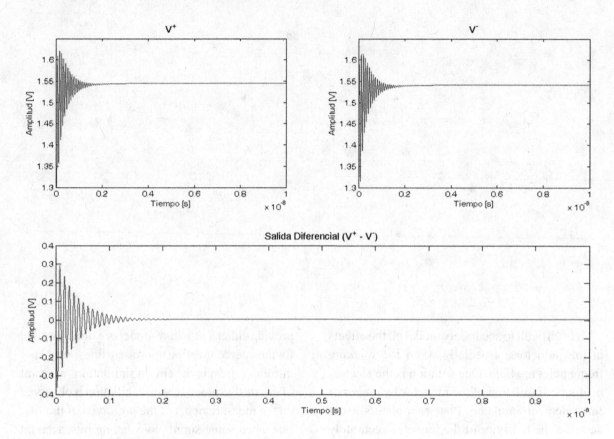

Figure 29. Tuning range comparison simulation-measurement second run VCO

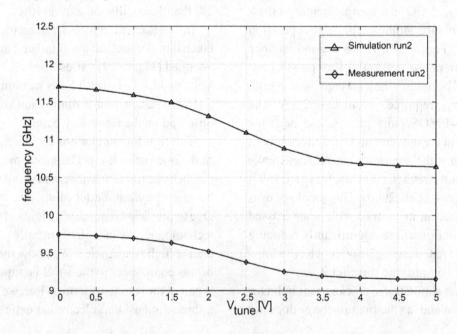

Figure 30. VCO measurement setup

of the inductor alone, in order to obtain a more accurate model to include it in the simulations of the VCO.

Three different simulations of VCO were done and then compared with the measurements. The results are summarized in Figure 31 the diamond line shows the measurement results. The first simulation (squares) corresponds to the VCO simulated with microstrip lines and 3D modeled inductor. It can be seen that this is very close to the measurements' graph. The second simulation (triangles) represents the VCO with the microstrip interconnecting lines, but using the manufacturer's inductor model. The third simulation (circles) corresponds to the VCO with the manufacturer's inductor model and without including the microstrip interconnecting lines. This is the simulation which differs most from the measurements.

We can observe how the simulation using the 3D inductor model is the most similar to the measurements. This demonstrates that the inaccuracy of the inductor model at high frequencies can lead to inexact results and therefore the importance of a reliable model is proven. At the same time, the effect of introducing the intercon-

necting lines is seen as a reduction of the maximum frequency achieved by the VCO.

ELECTROMAGNETIC CO-SIMULATIONS

The electromagnetic simulations of a part of the circuit provide us isolated information about the problem, given that we can find the S parameters of the N-port circuit with the couplings and inter-relations among the different parts of the passive circuit that we saw previously. However, it is insufficient as it is necessary to introduce the file of S parameters from the simulation along with the other active and passive components that are not included in the electromagnetic simulations. Once they are included, the corresponding simulations can be done in order to study the influence of the lines on the final response. If it is considered necessary, some modifications might be made or a new electromagnetic simulation carried out and the process repeated.

Agilent's ADS simulation environment integrates the electromagnetic simulations and the

Figure 31. Effect of the lines and inductor model accuracy on tuning range

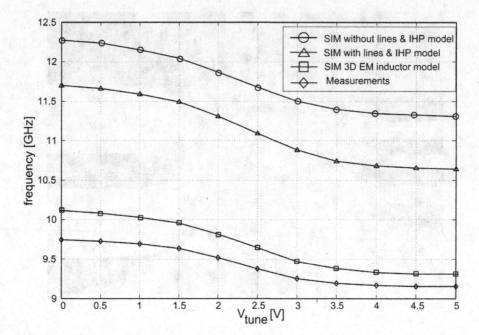

complete circuit simulations enabling the results of the electromagnetic simulations to be used as if they were a library of passive components.

The objective of this section is to define the necessary steps to make a momentum component for use as a circuit component in an ADS circuit simulation environment. A more complete description can be found in the ADS momentum pdf manual 2009

Create a Layout Alike Circuit Design

The first step is to design the circuit, to make a sub circuit on the layout page. It is very interesting if possible to use the microstrip or other strip palette components, in order to make it easier to parameterize the component with variables. Other possibilities exist using the stretching option on the layout page to define the variation on the circuit, see ADS2009 manual

In the following example a GDSII file of a divider is imported and microstrip lines are used

as variable components, then ports are inserted on the same layout layer as the circuit to be connected.

This EM component must be designed (Figure 32) using traditional layout techniques (path or shapes) or using layout library components (microstrip lines, corner, tee, etc) in the corresponding layer, to obtain an exact reproduction of the final circuit for the interconnection lines that is the objective.

Using the corresponding menu, you have access to the definition of the substrate, with their height, permittivity and permeability. Then the definition of the layout layers, to define the circuit layers themselves; that is, where the circuits will be designed, in this case for optimization, only the metal layers are needed. In this case we define the height and the conductivity, if expansion up is chosen (for thick conductors) pay attention to the height of the substrate layer too.

If the sweep or optimize parameters are needed, the first step is to define the variables that we will use. To do this, add each variable with the nominal

Figure 32. Circuit definition

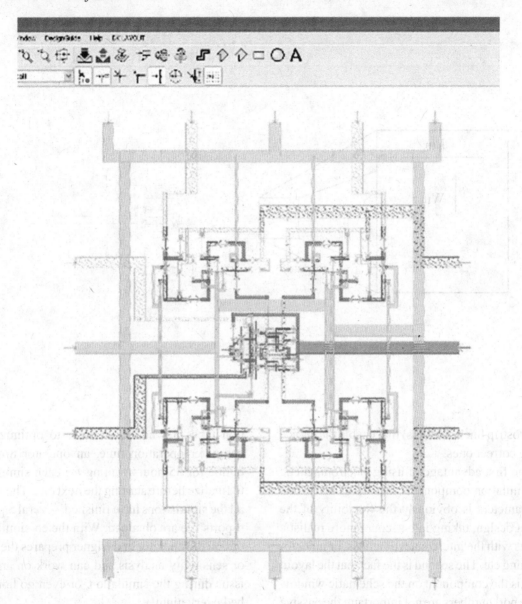

value. If we work with a new design all the lines could be defined as variables.

When all the procedure for the layout component is finished insert it on the schematic page, at this time the component is like a typical circuit component, and the variables are accessible to use as sweep variables, optimization variables, tune variables, statistical variables etc.

In the last case (Figure 33), the influence of the ground line could be studied, varying the Lin variable on the simulation. Other variables could be defined on the momentum component in order to obtain a more flexible circuit simulation environment. The designer has previously carried out some tuning simulations with ideal components

Figure 33. Co-simulation schematic page

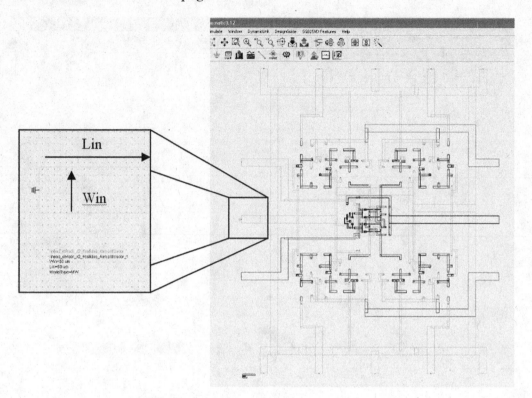

(Microstrip lines or others) that enable the choice of the correct ones.

The first advantage of using electromagnetic co-simulation components instead of black-box S-parameters is obviously the flexibility of the layout design, taking into account more realistic effects with the interconnection lines, or inductor coupling etc. The second is the fact that the layout itself is the component on the schematic window so the port numbers are not important; the passive or active components are connected to the real physical connection and the number of errors in the simulations decreases (Figure 34). The third and most important advantage is that special simulation set-ups including optimizations or Yield, could be defined. These simulations could run in standalone scenarios and no operator is needed. Supposing that the influence of the etching is to be studied, if 10 different electromagnetic simulations must be done and each simula-

tion takes 3.5 hours, in order to optimize the computer operation time, an operator must be online for 35 hours waiting for each simulation to finalize before starting the next one. Then once all the simulations have finished, several S param n-ports file are obtained. With the co-simulation option the operator or designer prepares the yield or sensitivity analysis and can work on another issue during the simulation, or even go home to bed every night!

In Figure 35 and Figure 36 some results of the EM/circuit co-simulations made on the divider, for studying the influence on the auto-oscillation frequency with the length of the ground connection. Related with time domain simulation is possible to see the evolution of the auto-oscillation, from the start-up point trough transitory state and finally the stationary state. In the last case some phase deviations are observed, but is in the fre-

Figure 34. Complete EM/circuit co-simulation set-up where active and layout components are included and linear and non-linear simulations are made

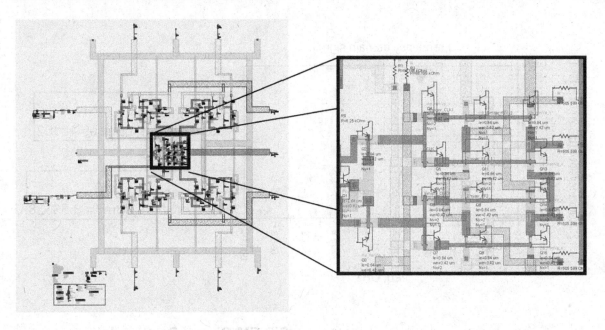

Figure 35. EM/circuit co-simulation time domain results. Somme differences exists on the start-up and the stationary states of the divider auto-oscillation frequency with the ground line length

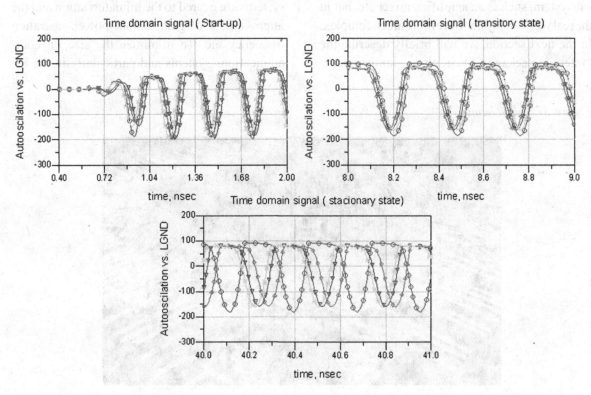

Figure 36. EM/circuit co-simulation frequency domain results. Frequency shift on the divider auto-oscillation frequency is observed with the ground line length

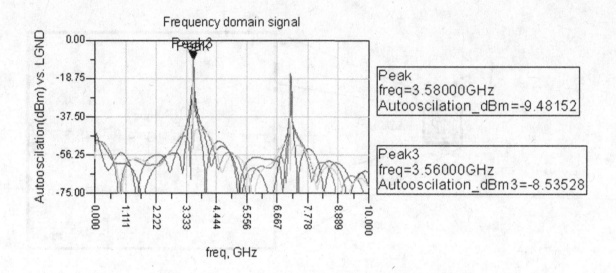

Peak
freq=3.58000GHz
Autooscilation_dBm=-9.48152

Peak3
freq=3.56000GHz
Autooscilation_dBm3=-8.53528

quency domain where we can see frequency shifts only modifying this connection line a few microns.

Up to now, the EM circuit co-simulation environment set-up has been shown as a single subsystem, such as an amplifier, mixer etc. but in the real world the systems are more much complex. In the next section, we will briefly describe the system in package EM circuit co-simulation.

SiP EM/Circuit Co-Simulation

From the beginning of this chapter we have said that the new challenges on current communication systems are geared to the miniaturization and the improvement of gain, output power, operation frequency etc. To minimize the size, in communications systems and particularly in the RF

Figure 37. SiP schema

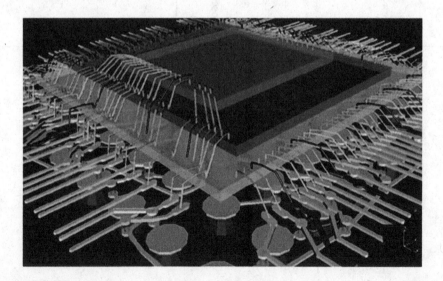

Figure 38. Sip Module Cross Section © 2004 - 2009 ASE Group. All rights reserved.

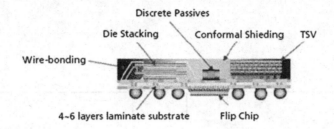

part, in terms of the integration of different parts of the system there are two general possibilities, namely, systems on a chip (SOC) and systems in a single package (SIP). The SOC have been used heavily so far but have a number of disadvantages compared to the SIP. The main advantage is the cost of manufacturing, as a single chip, in general, with thousands of units reduces the cost, that is in general very important, but the electrical performance of the circuits were very dependent on technology, which means for example a low-power technology does not provide enough output power. This also occurs with the noise for the receivers. Moreover, we must take into account the manufacturing and operation yield problems, the bigger the chip, the greater the possibility that it breaks, or some of its specifications are not fulfilled. On the other hand, for verification and test of the functionality of the chip, the bigger it is, the more difficult it is to measure, verify and isolate potential problems.

Finally, there is a lack of flexibility in operation, that is, a system designed and manufactured for a particular application will only be used in this application. For all these reasons, another trend is to minimize the final sizes in the same packaging by integrating different chips, the main advantages are that you can carry out each of the functions in the most appropriate technology, you can measure each of these functions easily and independently, with high flexibility in the use of each function and with the possibility of leveraging each functional block for other applications. The Yield is much higher in the SIP as the individual functions are simpler and smaller, and the development time of each function is less than the total system. As for drawbacks, the main one is due to technological integration itself. In fact, now we can say that there is a new one, namely the successful modeling of such integration. Before explaining how to solve this problem, we present some of the possible types of packaging system (Figure 37)

Figure 39. 3D view of the complete multi-technology EM component

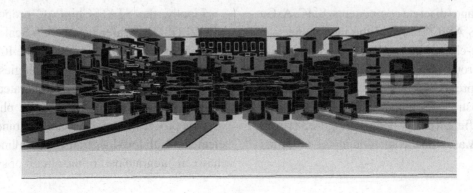

Figure 40. Magnitude in dB of the S parameters of the output power stage amplifier in the undesired mode of operation

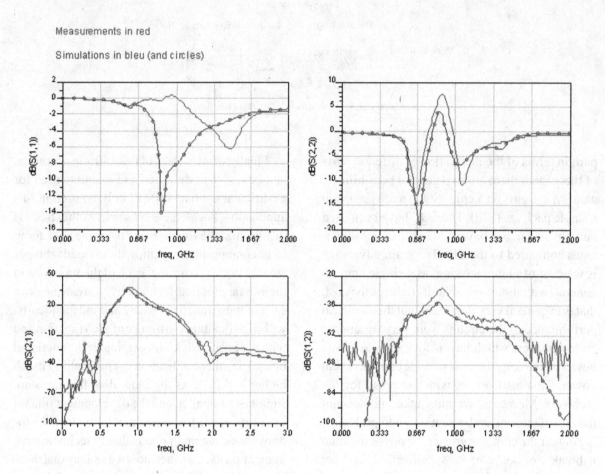

The most popular SiP package is the stacked chip structure, where the interconnection is through bond wires

Another option is the 3D package from ChipSIP The difference with the stacked chip option is that it is possible to integrate different technologies on the same package (discrete components, Si IC, AsGa IC, MEMS ASIC etc.) And the interconnection is with flip-chip, wire bonding, solder mask etc.

ASE Group have another solution that combines both previous solutions through a 4 to 6 layer plastic substrate for making the interconnection between different components see Figure 38 (from http://www.aseglobal.com/content/4-1-6-3.htm)

A similar solution is proposed for SHINKO ELECTRIC INDUSTRIES CO., LTD, they introduce a multilevel multi-technology solution (as well as ASE) but using different substrates and different integration level. (From http://www.shinko.co.jp/english/product/sip/mcep.html)

Finally, the STATSChipPAC proposal with the WLCSMP (Wafer Level Chip Scale Module Package) solution that combines the IC integration using dies on different technologies with the patented Die IPD. IPD means Integrated Passive Device. They make a PCB using a photolithographic process where they can combine passive elements with low-loss transmission lines. Thus, they can integrate part of the circuit or system on

Figure 41. Phase of the S parameters of the output power stage amplifier in the undesired mode of operation

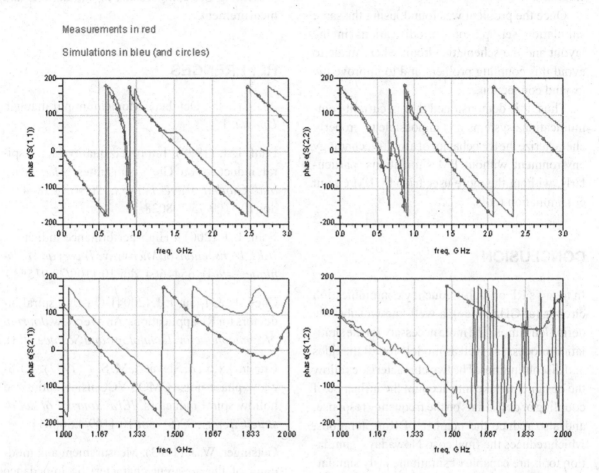

the IPD layer and at the same time interconnect different parts of the circuits or dies with other dies or parts of the circuit. Next, a practical integration example is shown.

In a system of mobile communications utilizing WLCSMP technology, the amplifier output stage frequency response and output power was influenced by the design of the interconnection lines of the output IPD Die and the positioning of the ground bumps. This effect could not be observed until its final integration. Firstly, when each subsystem was previously tested separately, all the functionalities were performed correctly. Therefore, to evaluate where the problem was and to be able to solve it, it was necessary to

use EM/CIRCUIT co-simulation techniques in a complex simulation environment while bearing in mind the effects of the real ground through the Bumps and the PCB in fiberglass as well as the electromagnetic coupling between the different levels, Si-CMOS chip of the RF active part and the passive IPD die. (see Figure 39)

The following graphs (Figure 40, Figure 41) show the simulated/measured coherence, which means that the simulation set-up using the EM/ circuit co-simulation tools enables the prediction of anomalous behavior in a multi-technology environment. In the input port impedance some differences could be appreciated due to the lack of the effect of the whole input circuit in the simulation.

Once the problem was found, using the same simulation set-up, some modifications in the layout and the schematic circuit where made to avoid this coupling problem and to improve the ground connection.

Thus, it is demonstrated that in current communications systems it is impossible to properly characterize the RF behavior of a multi-technology environment without EM simulations, particularly, without the more user-friendly EM/circuit co-simulation tools.

CONCLUSION

In today's RF or high-frequency communication circuits (at GHz range), a well-known substrate definition is more and more necessary for the simulation process, as well as models for all the lines and discontinuities. The two characteristics allow the designer to take into account the influence of coupling or deviations on the frequency response, and also reduce the number of Run iterations, which reduces the final cost. Nowadays, simulation tools are capable of simultaneously simulating active and passive components with layout routing (called electromagnetic co-simulation). In this chapter a short summary of Transmission Line propagation theory is presented, introducing or reminding the reader about the basic equations. Then, some distortion phenomenon's caused by interconnection lines are shown. A short review is provided of library models in order to validate the use of electromagnetic models. Then a guide of electromagnetic simulators with a real example of a CMOS VCO is showed. With this example is justified the need of one more step on the electromagnetic simulation, that is the new possible scenario with circuit/EM co-simulation environment, in this case a short review of how to define the template of a divider including some results is presented, to end with the very useful example of

a system in package of a CMOS power amplifier presenting the comparisons of simulations and measurement.

REFERENCES

ADS. (2009, October). Momentum pdf manual. *Update*, 1.

Bahl, I. J. (1999). Improved quality factor spiral inductors on GaAs substrates. *Microwave and Guided Wave Letters*, *9*(10), 398–400. doi:10.1109/75.798028

Bahl, I. J. (2001). High-performance inductors. *IEEE Transactions on Microwave Theory and Techniques*, *49*(4), 654–664. doi:10.1109/22.915439

Chen, J., & Liou, J. J. (2004). On-chip spiral inductors for RF applications: An overview. *Journal of Semiconductor Technology and Science*, *4*(3).

Craninckx, J., & Steyaert, M. S. J. (1997). A 1.8-z low-phase-noise CMOS VCO using optimized hollow spiral inductors. *IEEE Journal of Solid-state Circuits*, *32*(5). doi:10.1109/4.568844

Getsinger, W. J. (1983). Measurement and modeling of the apparent characteristic impedance of microstrip. *IEEE Transactions on Microwave Theory and Techniques*, *31*, 624–632. doi:10.1109/TMTT.1983.1131560

Gupta, K. C., Garg, R., & Chadha, R. (1981). *Computer-aided design of microwave circuits* (pp. 197–199). Artech House.

Hammerstad, E. (1981). Computer-aided design of microstrip couplers using accurate discontinuity models. *Transactions on Microwave Theory and Techniques Symposium Digest*, (pp. 54-56).

Hammerstad, E., & Jensen, O. (1980). Accurate models for microstrip computer-aided design. *IEEE Microwave Theory and Techniques Symposium Digest*, (pp. 407-409).

Kirschning, M., & Jansen, R. H. (1982). Accurate model for effective dielectric constant of microstrip with validity up to millimetre-wave frequencies. *Electronics Letters, 18*(6), 272–273. doi:10.1049/el:19820186

Kirschning, M., & Jansen, R. H. (1982). Accurate model for effective dielectric constant of microstrip and validity up in millimeter-wave frequencies. *Electronics Letters, 18*, 272–273. doi:10.1049/el:19820186

Kirschning, M., Jansen, R. H., & Koster, N. H. L. (1981). Accurate model for open-end effect of microstrip lines. *Electronics Letters, 17*(3), 123–125. doi:10.1049/el:19810088

Kirschning, M., Jansen, R. H., & Koster, N. H. L. *(1983)*. Measurement and computer-aided modeling of microstrip discontinuities by an improved resonator method. *IEEE Transactions on Microwave Theory and Techniques Symposium Digest,* (pp. 495-497).

Kobayashi, M. (1983, November). Frequency dependent characteristics of microstrips on ansiotropic substrates. *IEEE Transactions on Microwave Theory and Techniques, 30*, 89–92.

Kobayashi, M. (1990, August). A dispersion formula satisfying recent requirements in microstrip CAD. *IEEE Transactions on Microwave Theory and Techniques, 36*, 1246–1370. doi:10.1109/22.3665

Koutsoyannopoulos, Y. K., & Papananos, Y. (2000). Systematic analysis and modeling of integrated inductors and transformers in RF IC design. *IEEE Transactions on Circuits and Systems-II: Analog and Digital Signal Processing, 47*(8).

Ling, F., Song, J., Kamgaing, T., Yang, Y., Blood, W., Petras, M., et al. (2002). *Systematic analysis of inductors on silicon using EM simulations*. Electronic Components and Technology Conference.

Lopez-Villegas, J. M., Samitier, J., Cane, C., & Losantos, P. (1998). Improvement of the quality factor of RF integrated inductors by layout optimization. *Radio Frequency Integrated Circuits (RFIC) Symposium,* (pp. 169-172).

López-Villegas, J. M., Samitier, J., Cané, C., Losantos, P., & Bausells, J. (2000). Improvement of the quality factor of RF integrated inductors by layout optimization. *IEEE Transactions on Microwave Theory and Techniques, 48*(1). doi:10.1109/22.817474

Niknejad, A. M., & Meyer, R. G. (1998). Analysis, design, and optimization of spiral inductors and transformers for Si RF IC's. *IEEE Journal of Solid-state Circuits, 33*(10). doi:10.1109/4.720393

Pérez Serna, E., & Herrera Guardado, A. (2006). *VCO CMOS de Bajo ruido a 10 GHz en Tecnología de SiGe de 0.4 μm. Simposium Nacional de la Unión Científica Internacional de Radio* (pp. 1304–1306). URSI.

Tsang, T. K. K., & El-Gamal, M. N. (2003). *A high figure of merit and area-efficient low-voltage (0.7-1V) 12-GHz CMOS VCO*. IEEE Radio Frequency Integrated Circuits Symposium.

Wadell, B. C. (1991). *Transmission line design handbook*. Boston, MA: Artech House.

Wheeler, A. H. (1942, September). Formulas for the skin effect. *Proceedings of IRE, 30*, 412–424. doi:10.1109/JRPROC.1942.232015

Xue, C., Yaou, F., Cheng, B., & Wang, Q. (2006). Effect of the silicon substrate structure on chip spiral inductor. *Chinese Journal of Semiconductors, 27*(11), 1955–1960.

Yamashita, E., Atshi, K., & Hirachata, T. (1981, June). Microstrip dispersion in a wide frequency range. *IEEE Transactions on Microwave Theory and Techniques, 29*, 610–611. doi:10.1109/TMTT.1981.1130403

KEY TERMS AND DEFINITIONS

Characteristic Impedance: The characteristic impedance (Z0) of a transmission line is a property that is maintained along the length of the line and only depends on the width and height as well as the properties of the substrate used. This means that a line with a specified width on a substrate whose dielectric constant height H and Er has characteristic impedance Z0, if you change any of the above parameters also changes the Z0.

Discontinuities: A transmission line of a given width has a particular characteristic impedance, when the line bends or intersects with another line or change in width, we observe a change on its characteristic impedance and its behavior. All of these effects and some others not mentioned above is what is known as discontinuities.

Effective Dielectric Constant: the dielectric constant also known as epsilon relative (ER) is a material property, because is usually nearly constant with frequency, which is why it is called the dielectric constant. Given that a two-conductor transmission line the propagation wave is transverse electromagnetic (TEM) and is fully encased in a uniform material. But in the case of a non uniform material we must define the effective dielectric constant that takes into account the geometry of a transmission line, which makes it less than ER in many cases. For microstrip, part of the wave is in air, and part is in the substrate material.

Electromagnetic Field: the combination of an electric field produced by stationary charges and a magnetic field produced by moving charges (currents). The way in which charges and currents interact with the electromagnetic field is described by Maxwell's equations and the Lorentz force law.

Fabrication Yield: Once the front-end process has been completed, the devices are subjected to a variety of electrical tests to determine if they function properly. The proportion of devices on the wafer found to perform properly is referred to as the yield. But this yield gives us the information about the fabrication process itself nothing related with the design process. When the complete chip functionality is tested the yield gives us complete information about how precise were the models (active and passive) used in the design, the sensitivity etc. This is the Fabrication Yield we try to improve.

Matching Networks: Provide a transformation of impedance to a desired value to maximize the power dissipated by a load., impedance matching is the practice of designing the input impedance of an electrical load or the output impedance of its corresponding signal source in order to maximize the power transfer and/or minimize reflections from the load. In the case of a complex source impedance ZS and load impedance ZL, matching for maximum power transfer is obtained when ZS=ZL* where * indicates the complex conjugate.

MMIC: In general low frequencies general purposes circuits or multifunction circuits fabricated in CMOS technologies are called integrated circuit IC o ASIC Application-Specific Integrated Circuit, the last ones are (IC) customized for a particular use. When working frequencies are in microwave frequency range and above and other high frequencies technologies are used (i.e. AsGa) the appellation used is MMIC (Microwave Monolithic Integrated Circuits).

Phase Constant: In electromagnetic theory, the phase constant, is the imaginary component of the propagation constant for a plane wave. It represents the change in phase per meter along the path travelled by the wave at any instant and is equal to the angular wave number of the wave. It is represented by the symbol β and is measured in units of radians per meter.

Chapter 5
Σ–Δ Fractional–N Phase–Locked Loop Design Using HDL and Transistor–Level Models for Wireless Communications

Ahmed El Oualkadi
Abdelmalek Essaadi University, Morocco

ABSTRACT

This chapter presents a systematic design of a Σ-Δ fractional-N Phase-Locked Loop based on hardware description language behavioral modeling. The proposed design consists of describing the mixed behavior of this PLL architecture starting from the specifications of each building block. The description language models of critical PLL blocks have been described in VHDL-AMS, which is an IEEE standard, to predict the different specifications of the PLL. The effect of different noise sources has been efficiently introduced to study the overall system performances. The obtained results are compared with transistor-level simulations to validate the effectiveness of the proposed models in the frequency range around 2.45 GHz for wireless applications.

1. INTRODUCTION

The wireless communication market is undergoing a major expansion with the deployment of new technologies and standards opening the prospect of significant impacts in many application areas (security, health, automotive, environment, cold chain management, manufacturing, telecommunications, robotics, etc.). The emerging wireless technologies require architectures with reduced complexity, cost and power consumption; however, they require specific circuits with more accuracy and best performance.

DOI: 10.4018/978-1-4666-0083-6.ch005

The design of state-of-the-art wireless is a challenging task transceivers since many design constraints must be considered, for this reason mixed-signal CAD (Computer- Aided Design) tools are necessary to explore the design space quickly and efficiently. Currently, hardware description languages are widely used in the design of mixed-signal circuits. Indeed, the VHDL-AMS standard allows the implementation of the top-down hierarchical approach for analog and mixed systems (Peterson, 2002). Therefore, it can be used straightforwardly for behavioral modeling and design of a phase locked loop (PLL), which is a key element for any wireless communication system (Hinz, 2000).

With the demand among different applications, standard PLL frequency synthesizers with integer–N dividers must offer a fast-settling time, a good noise performance, and an accurate frequency resolution. Usually, due to the tradeoff between loop bandwidth and channel spacing, fractional-N PLL is a better candidate than integer-N PLL (Riley, 1993). Thus, the fractional-N technique offers wide bandwidth with narrow channel spacing and relaxes PLL design constraints for phase noise (Riley, 2003). The Σ-Δ fractional-N PLL is an attractive solution for agile frequency synthesis or direct modulation schemes (Perrott, 1997).

In this chapter, a Σ-Δ fractional-N PLL is modeled using VHDL-AMS and synthesized for wireless applications. For this study, many HDL models have been studied and tested for different PLL blocks. The VCO and Σ-Δ modulator are the major blocks that affect the PLL phase noise. These blocks are efficiently described and simulated in VHDL-AMS to estimate the PLL phase noise. The proposed PLL models use ELDO scripts (Mentor Graphics, 1998) mixed with VHDL-AMS models which allow the simulation of some PLL blocks at transistor-level and others at behavioral level. Several jitter noise sources are studied based on different noise models (Kundert, 2001) and included into the PLL model to investigate non-ideal effects. These mixed behavioral models enable a fast simulation of the Σ-Δ synthesizer and an accurate phase noise prediction. A comparison with transistor-level simulations validates the proposed models.

The chapter is organized as follows. Section 2 presents the role of the frequency synthesizers in the radio transceivers. Section 3 gives a review about the frequency synthesis techniques. Section 4 describes the fractional-N PLL. Section 5 presents the behavioral models of the PLL building blocks. The PLL system-level design is discussed in section 6. The PLL specifications and the behavioral modeling of noise in PLL are outlined. The system-level simulations results are given in section 7. Finally, section 8 presents the conclusion and some perspectives on future research directions.

2. FREQUENCY SYNTHESIZERS IN RADIO TRANSCEIVERS

The evolution of radio transceiver architectures is derived by the explosive development of standards and applications for wireless communications. Since the first superheterodyne radio receiver presented by Edwin H. Armstrong in the 1920's (Armstrong, 1924), several transceiver architectures have been developed and reported in the literature (Razavi, 1998). The main differences between these topologies concern the implementation techniques of the receiver and the transmitter parts. However, the purpose remains the same. Indeed, the wireless transceivers must be able to generate a wide range of frequencies in order to upconvert the outgoing data for transmission and downconvert the received signal for processing (Lee, 1998). Hence, frequency synthesizers are widely used in modern radio communication systems.

Figure 1 shows an example of superheterodyne receiver which is the most commonly used receiver architecture. The received signal is down mixed to two intermediate frequencies (IF) before it is con-

Figure 1. The superheterodyne receiver architecture

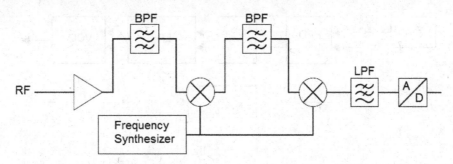

verted to a baseband signal. This architecture uses passives IF SAW (surface acoustic wave) filters as bandpass filters (BPF) which are characterized by a high selectivity. Therefore, the superheterodyne receiver allows a high spectral purity, however, it is very poorly integrable since the SAW filters are off-chip components. Moreover, this architecture need the generation of a wide range of frequencies to ensure the carrier signals for the two IF stages.

The intensive researches for alternative architectures have led to the emergence of the direct conversion transceiver which is the most suitable architecture for full integration (Jussila, 2001). Figure 2 shows the architecture of a direct conversion transceiver. The frequency synthesizer can be used for both to downconvert the received signal directly to around DC and to upconvert the modulated baseband signal to the desired RF frequency. Both the superheterodyne receiver and

Figure 2. The direct conversion transceiver

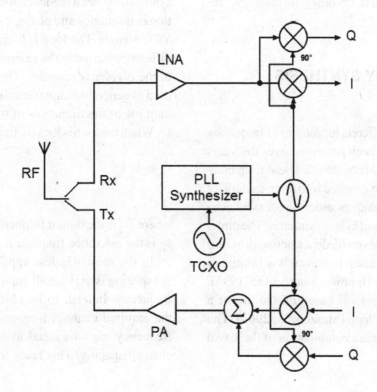

Figure 3. The integer-N PLL frequency synthesizer

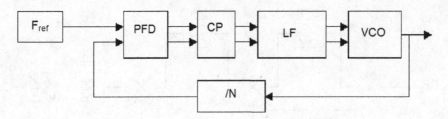

the direct conversion transceiver share the need for frequency synthesis.

However, the frequency synthesizer is the most critical component in a wireless transceiver. This is due to strict noise requirements as well as a high desired frequency of operation with low power consumption. Indeed, the generation of the carrier signal is one of the most challenging aspects in building radio transceivers for the next generation of wireless communications. Recently, the development of multi-standards transceivers has increased the need for the generation of multiple signal frequencies in the same transceiver (Baldwin, 2006). Thus, the demand for frequency synthesis techniques becomes increasingly required.

3. FREQUENCY SYNTHESIS TECHNIQUES

In the literature, different topologies of frequency synthesizers have been presented over the years (Marques, 1998) (Muer, 2008). These frequency synthesizers can be grouped into three categories regarding the techniques used: direct synthesis, indirect synthesis and hybrid synthesis. The direct synthesis which uses no feedback action provides very low settling times; however, it is limited to low frequencies and is power hungry (Tan, 1995). The indirect synthesis is based on the use of a negative feedback loop (Staszewski, 2002). The hybrid synthesis uses a combination of these two

techniques. In this chapter, the focus is on methods of indirect synthesis.

Among the indirect frequency synthesis techniques, PLL represents the most commonly method used in the wireless communication systems. The block diagram in Figure 3 shows the classical PLL frequency synthesizer with integer-N divider. This PLL frequency synthesizer comprises a reference signal generator, a voltage controlled oscillator (VCO), a phase frequency comparator (PFD), a charge pump (CP), a loop filter (LP), and a divider by N. The reference signal is usually derived from a crystal oscillator, which is very stable in frequency. The PLL frequency synthesizer uses a feedback loop for synchronization in frequency and phase, the reference and the VCO signals. The loop is locked when the phase difference between the reference and the output of the divider is constant. The integer-N PLL is used to generate a signal whose frequency f_{vco} is a multiple of the frequency of the reference signal f_{ref}. When the loop is locked, the output is given by:

$$f_{vco} = N f_{ref} \tag{1}$$

where f_{vco} is the output frequency of the VCO and f_{ref} is the reference frequency.

In the most wireless applications, the channel spacing is very small compared to the carrier frequency. Indeed, to be able to synthesize all the required channel frequencies, the reference frequency must be equal to or smaller than the channel spacing. This leads to very high values for the divisor N. Besides; the noise transfer function from the reference to the output multiplies the reference noise by N at offset frequencies smaller than the loop bandwidth. Moreover, the reference frequency of the synthesizer causes normally spurious tones at offsets of $\pm n \cdot f_{ref}$ from the carrier frequency. These spurious tones lie in the middle of the adjacent channels, and thus must be suppressed as much as possible. To guarantee enough of suppression of these spurious, the loop bandwidth must be kept below approximately one tenth of the reference frequency (Ahola, 2005). On the other hand, the switching time of the synthesizer is inversely proportional to the loop bandwidth. The use of a smaller loop bandwidth leads to a longer switching time.

All these problems limit the use of the integer-N PLL for several wireless applications. The fractional-N PLL, with a no constant N division, could be a good solution to these problems caused by the integer division (Riley, 1993).

4. FRACTIONAL-N PLL FREQUENCY SYNTHESIZER

The block diagram of the fractional-N PLL frequency synthesizer is shown in Figure 4. It composed by a set of building blocks. In addition to the blocks of the integer-N PLL (PFD, CP, LP and VCO) the fractional-N PLL uses an N/N+1 frequency divider, and an all-digital Σ-Δ modulator. The modeling concerns of each block are introduced in the next section.

The static input word K is processed by the Σ-Δ modulator to produce an encoded oversampled sequence. This sequence is used to modify the division modulus of a multi-modulus divider in the feedback loop. Essentially, the average value of the encoded Σ-Δ output is equal to the DC input word K, resulting in an output frequency at a fractional multiple of the reference frequency. Consequently, the phase comparison frequency can be much higher than in integer-N synthesizers, and thus the division ratio can be much lower.

The use of fractional-N PLL instead of an integer-N gives more freedom in choosing the

Figure 4. The fractional-N PLL frequency synthesizer

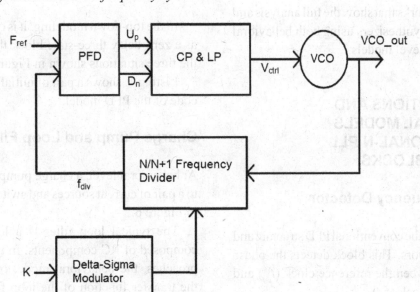

loop bandwidth. Indeed, if a very good reference suppression is required, the loop bandwidth can be made significantly smaller while still meeting the switching time requirements (Pamarti, 2004). Furthermore, the architecture of fractional-N PLL (Figure 4) can still meet requirements such as low-power consumption and simple topology, and is suitable for high-level integration.

The design of fractional-N PLL synthesizers requires an iterative design process due to the large set of system parameters that must be optimized to achieve the desired phase noise, settling time, and fractional spur rejection (Perrott, 1997). In addition, a Σ-Δ modulator, used to instantaneously change the feedback division modulus, introduces excessive phase noise and fractional spurs. A behavioral level simulator is required to reduce the design turnaround time and to understand the contribution of the phase noise of the fractional spur rejection of the Σ-Δ modulator before the physical design phase. The need for a behavioral level simulator is strengthened by the characteristic that both the PLL and the Σ-Δ modulator are nonlinear systems (Milet-Lewis, 2001). In the literature many papers have studied the implementation of the behavioral models of classical PLL systems and Σ-Δ synthesizers (Perrott, 2002). However, there are few works that show the full analysis and design of Σ-Δ synthesizers using both behavioral and transistor-level models.

5. DESCRIPTIONS AND BEHAVIORAL MODELS OF FRACTIONAL-N PLL BUILDING BLOCKS

Phase-Frequency Detector

Figure 5 shows the conventional PFD structure and its ideal behaviors. This block detects the phase difference between the reference clock (f_{ref}) and the feedback clock (f_{div}).

Figure 5. The typical structure of the PFD

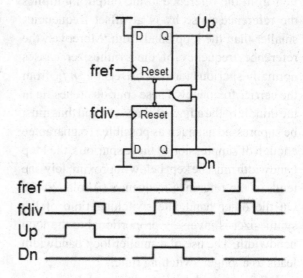

Figure 6. The typical structure of the CP and LF

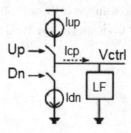

In the top-down modeling, it is only described as a zero-delay three-state block that deals with the three situations shown in Figure 5.

Listing 1. shows a part of initial VHDL-AMS code of the PFD model.

Charge Pump and Loop Filter

At behavioral level, a charge pump is equivalent to a pair of current sources and switches as shown in Figure 6.

The typical loop filter is a low-pass filter composed of RC components. In traditional approaches, the behavioral model only describes the transfer function of the loop filter or keeps the transistor-level descriptions (Mounir, 2003).

Listing 1. A part of initial VHDL-AMS code of the PFD

```
-- **** Entity *****
Entity PFD is
generic (pvdd: real:= 5.0; -- positive supply voltage
pvss: real:= 0.0; -- negative supply voltage
pthreshold: real:= 2.5; -- threshold supply voltage
pdelay: real:= 0.0; -- delay
prisetime: real:= 1.0e-10; -- rise time
pfalltime: real:= 1.0e-10; -- fall time
tresol: real:= 1.0e-12); -- crossing resolution
port (terminal tref, tdiv, tup, tdn: electrical);
end entity PFD;
-- **** ARCHITECTURES *****
Architecture BEHAV of PFD is -- Branch quantities
quantity vup  across iup through tup ;
quantity vdn  across idn through tdn ;
quantity vref across tref ;
quantity vdiv across tdiv ;
-- Signals
    signal sup, sdn: real:= 0.0;
begin – BEHAV
    process (vref'above(pthreshold), vdiv'above(pthreshold)
    variable vxup, vxdn: real:= 0.0;
begin -- process
if (vref'above(pthreshold)) then
    if (vref'above(pthreshold)'event) then
        vxup:= pvdd;
    end if ;
end if;
if (vdiv'above(pthreshold)) then
    if (vdiv'above(pthreshold)'event) then
        vxdn:= pvdd;
    end if ;
end if;
if ((vxup > pvdd/2.0) and (vxdn > pvdd/2.0)) then
    vxup:= pvss;
    vxdn:= pvss;
end if ;
sup <= vxup after pdelay*sec ;
sdn <= vxdn after pdelay*sec ;
end process;
    break on sup, sdn ;
    vup == sup'ramp(prisetime, pfalltime);
    vdn == sdn'ramp(prisetime, pfalltime);
end architecture BEHAV;
```

As mentioned in (Antao, 1998), using transfer function only is not enough for accurate behavioral simulation.

Voltage Controlled Oscillator

The behavioral model of the VCO typically describes the relationship between input control voltage, and output frequency. The range of input operation voltage, the relative output frequency range and the VCO gain are the critical characteristics. In the top-down modeling approach, these parameters are obtained from the design specifications.

A complementary differential CMOS of the LC tuned VCO model has been used for transistor-level simulations (Figure 7). For minimum power consumption and maximum output swing, both the cross-coupled NMOS-transistor and PMOS-transistor generate a negative resistance that compensates the loss of the LC tank (Tiebout, 2011), (El Oualkadi, 2009).

Σ-Δ Modulator and Frequency Divider

The Σ-Δ modulator is a key element in the fractional-N PLL (Kenny, 1999), and it is used to produce the fractional part of the division ratio (Filiol, 1998). Figure 8 shows the architecture of a third order MASH Σ-Δ modulator obtained by cascading three stages of a first order Σ-Δ modulator. The quantization error of every stage is injected to the next one. The corresponding quantized divider can be expressed as,

$$N_3(z) = F(z) + R_3(z) (1-z^{-1})^3 \qquad (2)$$

where $F(z)$ is the fractional input signal, and the last term represents the quantization noise, which is related only to the third stage quantization noise $R_3(z)$ because the noises of the first and second

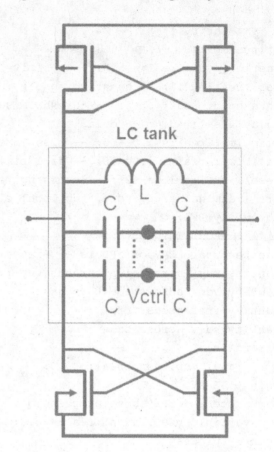

Figure 7. The schematic diagram of the VCO

stages are eliminated in this structure (Filiol, 1998).

The frequency divider is often treated as a pure digital block. The timing information, such as delay time and output transition time, are the critical factors of this block.

The Σ-Δ modulator can be clocked by either the reference clock signal or by the divider output, although using the divider output signal is reported to yield better performance. The scheme presented in this chapter is clocked by the divider output (Fatahi, 2010).

Listing 2 shows a part of VHDL-AMS model that combines together the VCO, the divider and the third order MASH Σ-Δ modulator into a single model.

Figure 8. The third order MASH Σ-Δ modulator structure

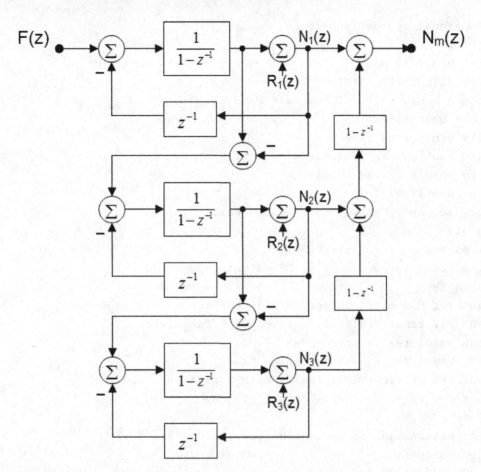

Listing 2. A part of initial VHDL-AMS code that joins together the VCO, the third order MASH Σ-Δ modulator and the divider into a single model.

```
-- **** Entity *****
entity vco_fdiv_MASH is
  generic (fvco_vin0: real:= 1.0e3;    -- free running VCO output frequ
          Kvco: real:= 1.0e3;          -- vco gain
          vcod: real:= 0.5;            -- distortion on voltage-frequency char-
acteristic
          int_div: real:= 1.0;         -- nominal division factor
          pvdd: real:= 3.0;            -- positive supply voltage
          pvss: real:= 0.0;            -- negative supply voltage
          num_bits: integer:= 10;      -- number of bits of the DS accumulators
          phalftref: time:= 0fs;
          fraction: integer:= 0        -- DS input code
          );
  port (terminal tin, tout, tdsclk: electrical;
```

Continued on following page

Listing 2. Continued

```
            signal spy_ds, spy_f: out real:= 0.0
            );
end entity vco_fdiv_MASH;
-- **** ARCHITECTURES *****
architecture behav_ds111 of vco_fdiv_MASH is
  -- branch quantities
  quantity vin across tin;
  quantity vout across iout through tout;
  quantity vdsclk across tdsclk;
  -- free quantities
  quantity xd, nper, arg, phase_total: real:= 0.0;
  -- signals
  signal sdivfactor: real:= int_div;
  signal Sdsout: integer:= 0; -- DS output code
  -- constants
  constant ref_num_bits: integer:= 2**num_bits;
  constant ref_time: real:= 1.0/ (fvco_vin0/int_div);
  constant vmid: real:= (pvdd+pvss)/2.0;
  constant vamp: real:= (pvdd-pvss)/2.0;
  constant two_pi_fvco_vin0: real:= math_2_pi * fvco_vin0;
  constant two_pi_Kvco: real:= math_2_pi * Kvco;
begin
  -- SD output changes instantaneously division factor
  break on Sdsout;
  -- ** VCO & DIVIDER **
     -- distortion on vco transfer characteristic
  if (vcod > 0.0) use
     xd == vcod * tanh(vin/vcod); -- distorts input voltage
  else
     xd == vin;
  end use;
     -- compute divider output phase
  arg == (two_pi_fvco_vin0 + two_pi_Kvco * xd)/(int_div+real(sdsout));
  nper == trunc(arg'integ/math_2_pi);
  phase_total == arg'integ - real(nper)*math_2_pi;
     -- divider output signal
  vout == vmid + vamp * sin(phase_total);
  -- ** DS MASH 111 register-level **
DS_MASH111: process
-- registers
variable ne1, ne2, ne3, ne1_1, ne2_1, ne3_1, d3, d2, d1, d2_1, d3_1, d3_2: in-
teger:= 0;
```

Continued on following page

Listing 2. Continued

```
    begin
    wait until vdsclk'above(vmid);
        -- register like coding for z^-1 blocks
        ne1_1:= ne1;
        ne2_1:= ne2;
        ne3_1:= ne3;
        d3_2:= d3_1;
        d3_1:= d3;
        d2_1:= d2;
    -- 1-bit modulators
    -- First stage
d1:= integer(sign(real(fraction + ne1_1 - ((fraction + ne1_1) mod 2**num_
bits)))); --MSB
ne1:= (fraction + ne1_1) mod 2**num_bits; -- LSB
-- Second stage
d2:= integer(sign(real(ne1 + ne2_1 - ((ne1 + ne2_1) mod 2**num_bits))));
ne2:= (ne1 + ne2_1) mod 2**num_bits;
    -- 3rd stage
d3:= integer(sign(real(ne2 + ne3_1 - ((ne2 + ne3_1) mod 2**num_bits))));
ne3:= (ne2 + ne3_1) mod 2**num_bits;
    -- noise-cancellation logic
Sdsout <= d1 + d2 - d2_1 + d3 - d3_1 - d3_1 + d3_2;
        spy_ds <= real(Sdsout);
        spy_f <= (fvco_vin0+Kvco*xd)/fvco_vin0;
  end process DS_MASH111;
end architecture behav_ds111;
```

Figure 9. The ΣΔ fractional-N PLL modeling approach

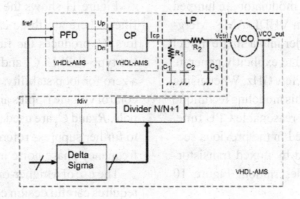

Figure 10. The proposed mixed-signal design flow

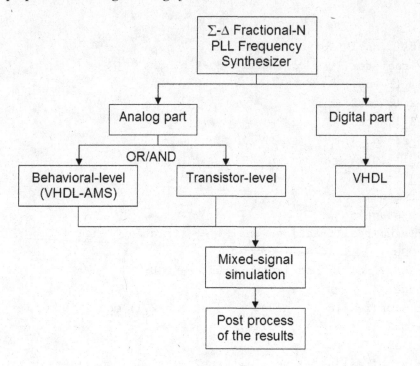

6. PLL SYSTEM-LEVEL DESIGN

In order to validate the ability of VHDL-AMS to successfully describe the ΣΔ fractional-N PLL performance, a common and complex mixed-signal model has been developed. By using VHDL-AMS, the architecture of each block has been defined and simulated. Figure 9 shows the modeling approach used. The CP and PFD are modeled in VHDL-AMS. The loop filter is still modeled in Eldo (only R and C components). The VCO, divider and ΣΔ modulator are lumped into a single model, also in VHDL-AMS. Merging the VCO and the divider into a single model (Listing 1) allows to avoid to explicitly generate the VCO output signal at a few GHz. When using time-domain simulation, this modeling technique is the only way to obtain a reasonable CPU time.

As it has been explained in the previous sections, the PLL is modeled by mixed transistor-level and VHDL-AMS description. Figure 10 shows the mixed-signal design flow proposed for this study.

PLL Specifications

The loop filter deserves a careful study and must undergo a thorough optimization process to match the target specifications for PLL bandwidth, phase margin, and ΣΔ noise suppression. For the sake of simplicity, a third order loop filter has been used in this study.

Figure 11 shows the architecture of this loop filter. There are three capacitors and two resistors. C_1 produces the first pole at the origin for the type-II PLL. C_1 and R_1 are used to generate a zero for loop stability. C_2 is used to smooth the control voltage ripples and to generate the second pole. R_2 and C_3 are used to generate the third pole to further suppress reference spurs and the high-frequency phase noise in the PLL.

The use of a higher-order loop filter, however, requires careful design consideration, as the PLL

Figure 11. The third order passive loop filter for charge-pump PLL

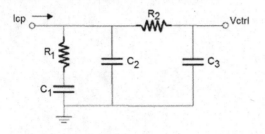

Table 1. The main specifications of ΣΔ fractional-N PLL

Specifications	Values
PLL output frequency (f_{vco})	2.45 GHz
Reference frequency (f_{ref})	26 MHz
Channel spacing	200 KHz
VCO gain (K_{vco})	250 MHz/V
Nominal division ratio (N_{mean} = N + *fraction*)	94.23
Phase margin	60°

is prone to instability. The average current-to-voltage transfer function of the loop filter is

$$F(s) = \frac{V_{out}(s)}{I_{avg}(s)}$$

$$= \frac{D(s + 1/\tau_1)}{\tau_2\tau_3 s^3 + \left[\tau_2 + \left(\frac{D}{R_2}+1\right)\tau_3\right]s^3 + \left(\frac{D\tau_3}{\tau_1 R_2}+1\right)s}$$

(3)

where $D = R_1C_1/(C_1+C_2)$, $\tau_1 = R_1C_1$, $\tau_2 = R_1C_1C_2/(C_1+C_2)$, and $\tau_3 = R_2C_3$.

The open loop transfer function of the PLL can be determined from the following expression,

$$G(s) = \frac{K_d K_{vco} F(s)}{s N_{mean}}$$

(4)

where K_d and K_{vco} are the PFD constant and the VCO gain respectively. N_{mean} is the geometric mean of the maximum and minimum division ratio required to span the desired frequency band (in this case, $N_{mean} = (N + fraction) = 94.23$). Usually, f_{ref} and N_{mean} are defined from the target applications, while K_d and K_{vco} are optimized by the designers.

From equation (4), the PLL bandwidth and phase margin are decided by parameters such as reference frequency f_{ref}, divider ratio N_{mean}, PFD

constant K_d, VCO gain K_{vco} and loop filter transfer function $F(s)$.

The open loop transfer function of the PLL has a zero located at $\omega_z = -1/\tau_1$, two poles at the origin, and two additional high frequency poles, denoted as ω_{p1} and ω_{p2}. Note that as long as $\omega_{p2} >> \omega_{p1}$, the non-zero poles can be approximated by $\omega_{p1} \approx -1/\tau_2$ and $\omega_{p2} \approx -1/\tau_3$.

To achieve a 25 µs settling time acceptable for a wireless application, the unity gain frequency of the open loop transfer function is located at $\omega_u = 2\pi$ 200 Krad/sec. A phase margin of 60° is chosen to provide good settling behavior, dictating that $1/\tau_1 = 2\pi$ 50 Krad/sec and $1/\tau_2 = 2\pi$ 800 Krad/sec. The high frequency pole is located at $1/\tau_3 = 2\pi$ 6.6 Mrad/sec to provide an additional 20 dB attenuation of the reference spurs. With these passive component values, the unity gain frequency is 199.18 kHz and the phase margin is 59.8°.

Model simulation, performed by using ADvance-MS from Mentor Graphics, allows to determine the specifications of the ΣΔ fractional-N PLL. Table 1 summarizes the PLL specifications for a wireless application in the frequency range around 2.45 GHz. These closed-loop simulations take 2 minutes CPU time on a SunBlade 2500 machine.

Behavioral Modeling of Noise in PLL

It is very important to take into account the contribution of noise in the PLL building blocks,

Figure 12. The simulated dynamic of the closed-loop Σ-Δ fractional-N PLL

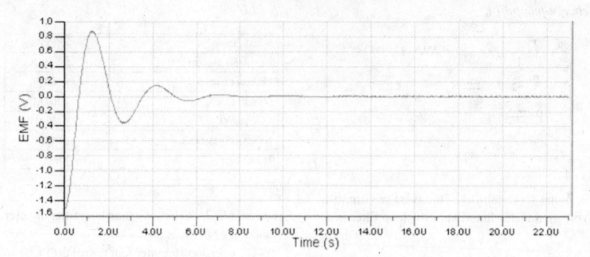

since this noise can directly affect the overall PLL performances and distorts the output spectrum of the PLL system. While it is difficult, for many reasons, to predict the phase noise in traditional circuit simulators (Kundert, 2001), behavioral models can be used straightforwardly to predict the noise contribution in such systems. Kundert (Kundert, 2001) proposed an efficient approach to modeling phase noise in PLL compared to commercial simulators which take a long time to compute the system's dynamic response. Based on Kundert approach (Kundert, 2001), many papers have described the behavioral modeling of noise in the PLL system (Kundert, 2003), (Yang, 2005).

As mentioned in (Kundert, 2001), there are two types of blocks in a PLL system, driven blocks and autonomous blocks. Each type exhibits a different type of jitter. Driven blocks, such as the PFD, CP, and divider are the sources of phase modulation (PM jitter); autonomous blocks, such as the reference oscillator and VCO, are sources of frequency modulation (FM jitter). This approach will be used in this study to simulate the PLL over-all noise.

7. SYSTEM-LEVEL SIMULATIONS RESULTS

To simulate the performances of the Σ-Δ fractional-N frequency synthesizer, all the HDL models must be connected together as described in Figure 9. Using the specifications given in Table I, it is possible to simulate the main characteristics of a Σ-Δ fractional-N PLL for wireless application. These simulations have been performed by using PM (PFD) and FM (VCO) noises sources. A jitter, equal to 2 ps, has been introduced in the HDL models to simulate the physical impact on PLL performances.

To start the closed-loop simulations, a 25 μs transient simulation is performed to achieve the full locking process of the PLL.

Figure 12 shows the transient analysis of the input control voltage (V_{ctrl}) while the PLL is locking. The Σ-Δ fractional-N PLL has no steady-state solution, since the division ratio is changing all the time. Thus the control voltage, even when the PLL is locked, is changing continuously, modulating the VCO output frequency.

Figure 13 shows the PLL output spectrum, with the carrier frequency of 2.45 GHz, obtained by using a FFT algorithm, and Figure 14 shows

Figure 13. The simulated PLL output spectrum

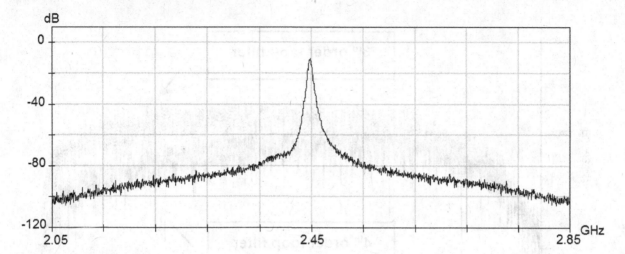

the output code of the Σ-Δ modulator. Since the Σ-Δ modulator is 3rd order, the dithered sequence is {-3, -2, -1, 0, 1, 2, 3}.

The loop filter and the Σ-Δ modulator are important blocks in the Σ-Δ fractional-N frequency synthesizer. To study the order impact of these blocks in the PLL design. Two architectures are simulated and compared using the third and fourth order loop filters. Figures 15 and 16 show the ideal (no noise sources used) simulations results obtained for these two cases.

Figure 15 shows the output filter spectrum obtained with the proposed loop filter compared to that of a fourth order loop filter which uses the same architecture above with an additionally RC branch at the output. As shown in Figure 15, the latter has a better frequency behavior that improves the rejection of the high-frequency spurs.

Figure 16 shows the output spectrums of the third and fourth order ΔΣ modulators. The fourth order modulator presents a low quantization noise in the bandwidth and more noise at high frequencies than the third order modulator.

Figure 14. The simulated output code of the third order Σ-Δ modulator

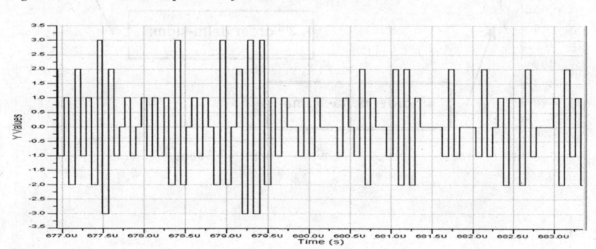

Figure 15. The simulated output spectrums of the third and fourth order filters

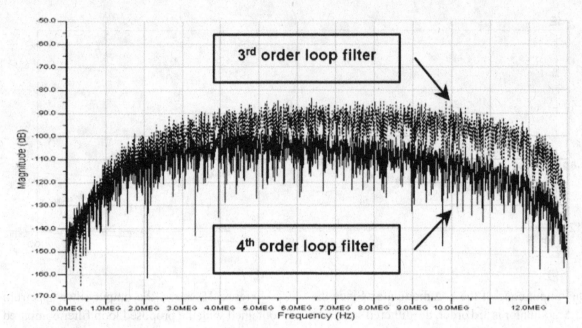

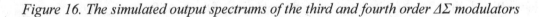

Figure 16. The simulated output spectrums of the third and fourth order ΔΣ modulators

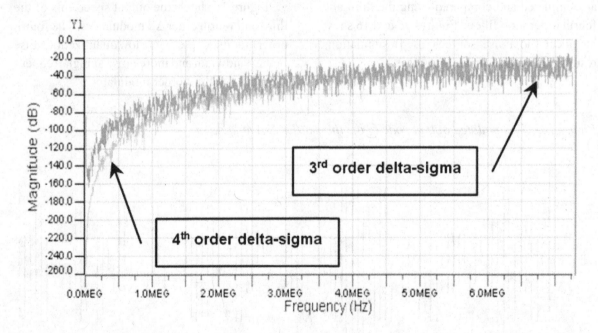

Figure 17. The simulated VCO phase noise at different behavioral levels

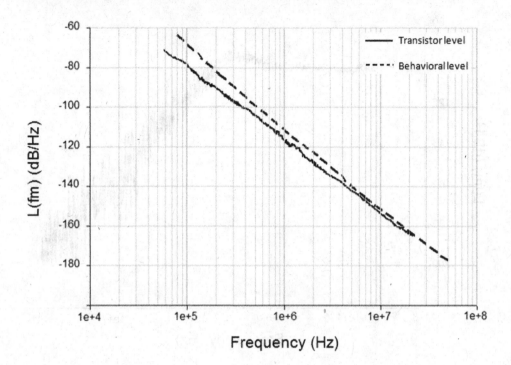

From these simulations results (Figure 15 and Figure 16), it seems that a high order cannot give a significant improvement of the output response. The choice of a third order loop filter and a third order Σ-Δ modulator provides a good trade-off among performance, low power consumption, and ease of implementation.

Noise performance is the most critical specification for a frequency synthesizer. The PLL noise performance depends on all PLL blocks, but mainly on VCO phase noise.

Figure 17 shows the simulated VCO phase noise at both transistor and behavioral levels. The VCO phase noise is obtained by a steady-state 'EldoRF' simulation performed at transistor-level using 130 nm CMOS technology and the topology depicted in Figure 7. The behavioral simulation is carried out by using a FM jitter equal to 2 ps in the VCO HDL model. By comparing the two curves of Figure 17, we note that at low frequencies the behavioral model gives optimistic estimations of

the phase noise since it does not take into account the effects of the 1/f noise.

Figure 18 shows the simulated phase noise of the closed loop PLL. The simulation time is equal to 120 ms for one time step; while the total consumed CPU time is 4 hours. Figure 18 shows the noise contribution of the different building blocks of the PLL. The amount of this contribution depends on the level of jitter exhibited by the divider and PDF/CP.

The phase noise is dominated by the VCO and Σ-Δ modulator in the range that goes from the cutoff frequency up to 10 MHz offset frequency, however the noise from PFD/CP and divider is dominating in the range of cutoff frequency. The reference oscillator noise contribution is clearly visible in the lower frequency range. The fractional spurs out of the loop bandwidth is mainly caused by the Σ-Δ modulator.

Figure 18. The simulated phase noise of the Σ-Δ fractional-N PLL

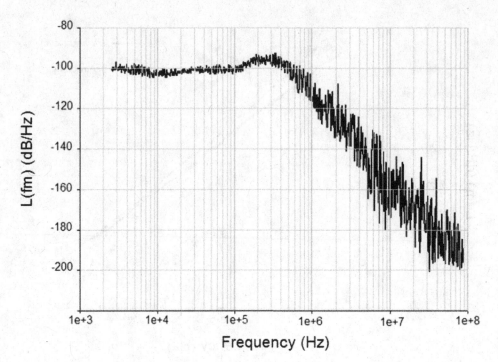

8. CONCLUSION

The evolution of the wireless communications standards and applications has increased the number of constraints concerning the building blocks design of radio transceivers. Over the years, different architectures and methodologies have been proposed. Besides, the constraints of small size and low power consumption, the radio transceivers require additional functionalities to satisfy the demand of the users. The emergence of multi-standards transceivers necessitates the development of reconfigurable architectures of wireless circuits and systems. In this context, the radio frequency synthesizer is a key building block. It should be able to generate multiple signal frequencies in the same transceiver.

Among the various frequency synthesizers, the Σ-Δ fractional-N PLL offers a wide bandwidth with narrow channel spacing and relaxes the PLL design constraints for phase noise. Moreover, the architecture of this kind of PLL can still meet

requirements such as low-power consumption and simple topology, and is suitable for high-level integration. Therefore, the Σ-Δ fractional-N PLL could be an attractive solution for agile frequency synthesis.

This chapter has demonstrated the behavioral modeling and systematic mixed-design of ΔΣ fractional-N PLL using hardware description language (VHDL-AMS). The behavioral modeling can provide a fast estimation of PLL performances when compared to transistor-level simulation. These HDL behavioral models can be successfully mixed with some circuit blocks (transistor-level) to rapidly evaluate the contribution of each noise source and non-ideal element. This can help designers to test ΔΣ fractional-N PLLs, for a given wireless application, accurately with a minimum CPU time.

REFERENCES

Ahola, R. (2005). *Integrated radio frequency synthesizers for wireless applications*. Ph.D. thesis. Helsinki University of Technology, Electronic Circuit Design Laboratory, Helsinki, Finland.

Antao, B. A. A., El-Turky, F. M., & Leonowich, R. H. (1996). Behavioral modeling phase-locked loops for mixed-mode simulation. *Analog Integrated Circuits and Signal Processing*, 10.

Armstrong, E. H. (1924). The super-heterodyne - Its origin, development, and some recent improvements. *Proceedings of the IRE, 50*, 539–552. doi:10.1109/JRPROC.1924.219990

Baldwin, G., & Ruiz, L. (2006, May). *Reconfigurable transceiver architecture: Front end hardware requirements*. Colloquium on Physical Layers Wireless Communications.

El Oualkadi, A. (2009). *5-GHz low phase noise CMOS LC-VCO with pgs inductor suitable for ultra-low power applications*. IEEE Mediterranean Microwave Symposium (MMS'09), Tangiers, Morocco.

Fatahi, N., & Nabovati, H. (2010). *Sigma-delta modulation technique for low noise fractional-n frequency synthesizer*. 4th International Symposium on Communications, Control and Signal Processing, ISCCSP 2010, Limassol, Cyprus.

Filiol, N. M., Riley, T. A. D., Plett, C., & Copeland, M. A. (1998). An agile ISM band frequency synthesizer with built-in GMSK data modulation. *IEEE Journal of Solid-state Circuits, 7*(33), 998–1008. doi:10.1109/4.701242

Jussila, J., Ryynänen, J., Kivekäs, K., Sumanen, L., Pärssinen, A., & Halonen, K. (2001). A 22mA 3.7dB NF direct conversion receiver for 3G WCDMA. *ISSCC 2001 Digest of Technical Papers*, San Francisco, USA, (pp. 284-285).

Kenny, T. P., Riley, T. A. D., Filiol, N. M., & Copeland, M. A. (1999). Design and realization of a digital ΔΣ modulator for fractional-n frequency synthesis. *IEEE Transactions on Vehicular Technology, 2*(48), 510–521. doi:10.1109/25.752575

Kundert, K. S. (2001). *Modeling and simulation of jitter in phase-locked loops*. San Jose, CA: Cadence Design Systems. Hinz, M., Konenkamp, I., & Horneber, E. H. (2000). *Behavioral modeling and simulation of phase-locked loops for RF front ends*. IEEE Midwest Symposium on Circuits and Systems.

Lee, T. H. (1998). *The design of CMOS radio-frequency integrated circuits*. Cambridge University Press.

Marques, A., Steyaert, M., and Sansen, W. (1998). Theory of PLL fractional-N frequency synthesizers. *Journal Wireless Networks - Special Issue VLSI in Wireless Networks, 1*(4), 79–85.

Mentor Graphics. (1998). *Eldo user's manual.*

Milet-Lewis, N., Monnerie, G., Fakhfakh, A., et al. (2001). *A VHDL-AMS library of RF blocks models*. IEEE International Workshop on Behavioral Modeling and Simulation.

Mounir, A., Mostafa, A., & Fikry, M. (2003). *Automatic behavioural model calibration for efficient PLL system verification*. Design, Automation and Test in Europe Conference and Exhibition.

Muer, B. D., & Steyaert, M. (2008). *CMOS fractional-N frequency synthesizers*. Dordrecht, The Netherlands: Kluwer Academic Publishers.

Pamarti, S., Jansson, L., & Galton, I. (2004). A wideband 2.4-GHz delta-sigma fractional-N PLL with 1-Mb/s in-loop modulation. *IEEE Journal of Solid-state Circuits, 1*(39), 49–62. doi:10.1109/JSSC.2003.820858

Perrott, M. H. (2002). Fast and accurate behavioral simulation of fractional-N frequency synthesizers and other PLL/DLL circuits. *Proceedings of the 39th Design Automation Conference.*

Perrott, M. H., Tewksbury, T. L., & Sodini, C. G. (1997). A 27-mW CMOS fractional-N synthesizer using digital compensation for 2.5-Mb/s GFSK modulation. *IEEE Journal of Solid-state Circuits*, *12*(32), 2048–2060. doi:10.1109/4.643663

Perrott, M. H., Trott, M. D., & Sodini, C. G. (2002). A modeling approach for Σ-Δ fractional-n frequency synthesizers allowing straightforward noise analysis. *IEEE Journal of Solid-state Circuits*, *8*(37), 1028–1038. doi:10.1109/JSSC.2002.800925

Peterson, G., Ashenden, P. G., & Teegarden, D. A. (2002). *The system designer's guide to VHDL-AMS: Analog, mixed-signal, and mixed-technology modeling*. Morgan Kaufmann Publishers.

Razavi, B. (1998). *RF microelectronics*. USA: Prentice Hall.

Riley, T. A. D., Copeland, M. A., & Kwasniewski, T. A. (1993). Delta–sigma modulation in fractional-N frequency synthesis. *IEEE Journal of Solid-state Circuits*, *5*(28), 553–559. doi:10.1109/4.229400

Riley, T. A. D., Filiol, N. M., Du, Q., & Kostamovvra, J. (2003). Techniques for in-band phase noise reduction in ΣΔ synthesizers. *IEEE Transactions on Circuits and Systems II-Analog and Digital Signal Processing*, *50*(11), 794–803. doi:10.1109/TCSII.2003.819132

Staszewski, R. B. (2002). *Digital deep-submicron CMOS frequency synthesis for RF wireless applications*. Ph.D. thesis, The University of Texas at Dallas, USA.

Tan, L. K., & Samueli, H. (1995). A 200 MHz quadrature digital synthezier/mixer in 0.8μm CMOS. *IEEE Journal of Solid-state Circuits*, *3*(30), 193–200.

Tiebout, M. (2001). Low-power low-phase-noise differentially tuned quadrature VCO design in standard CMOS. *IEEE Journal of Solid-state Circuits*, *7*(36), 1018–1024. doi:10.1109/4.933456

Yang, L., Wakayama, C., & Shi, R. C. (2005). Noise aware behavioral modeling of the ΣΔ fractional-n frequency synthesizer. *Proceedings of the Great Lakes Symposium on VLSI*.

KEY TERMS AND DEFINITIONS

Σ-Δ Modulation: A method for encoding high resolution signals into lower resolution signals using pulse-density modulation.

Behavioral Modeling: The operation that reproduces the required behavior of the original analyzed system.

CAD: is Computer-Aided Design.

Fractional-N PLL: A PLL with a fractional division.

Frequency Synthesizer: An electronic system for generating any of a range of frequencies from a single fixed timebase or oscillator.

Mixed-Signal Design: Any integrated system that has both analog circuits and digital circuits on a single semiconductor die.

Phase-Locked Loop: A control system that tries to generate an output signal whose phase is related to the phase of the input "reference" signal. It is an electronic circuit consisting of a variable frequency oscillator and a phase detector. This circuit compares the phase of the input signal with the phase of the signal derived from its output oscillator and adjusts the frequency of its oscillator to keep the phases matched. The signal from the phase detector is used to control the oscillator in a feedback loop.

VHDL-AMS: A derivative of the hardware description language VHDL. It includes analog and mixed-signal extensions (AMS) in order to define the behavior of analog and mixed-signal systems.

Voltage-Controlled Oscillator: An electronic oscillator designed to be controlled in oscillation frequency by a voltage input.

Section 2
RF–MEMS and Passive Devices

Chapter 6
RF–MEMS Based Oscillators

Anis Nurashikin Nordin
International Islamic University Malaysia, Malaysia

ABSTRACT

Today's high-tech consumer market demand complex, portable personal wireless consumer devices that are low-cost and have small sizes. Creative methods of combining mature integrated circuit (IC) fabrication techniques with innovative radio-frequency micro-electro-mechanical systems (RF-MEMS) devices has given birth to wireless transceiver components, which operate at higher frequencies but are manufactured at the low-cost of standard ICs. Oscillators, RF bandpass filters, and low noise amplifiers are the most critical and important modules of any wireless transceiver. Their individual characteristics determine the overall performance of a transceiver. This chapter illustrates RF-oscillators that utilize MEMS devices such as resonators, varactors, and inductors for frequency generation. Emphasis will be given on state of the art RF-MEMS components such as film bulk acoustic wave, surface acoustic wave, flexural mode resonators, lateral and vertical varactors, and solenoid and planar inductors. The advantages and disadvantages of each device structure are described, with reference to the most recent work published in the field.

OSCILLATOR FUNDAMENTALS

The increasing demand for portable, small-sized, personal wireless consumer devices, wireless sensor nodes coupled with emerging field of radio-frequency micro-electro-mechanical systems (RF-MEMS) has fueled exciting research on the complete integration of wireless transceivers (Deparis, 2008; Santos, 2004). Recent advancement of silicon based radio-frequency (RF) electronics have driven the innovation of CMOS-based, low-cost, high technology and portable consumer devices. The escalating need for more and more wireless circuits to be portable has highlighted the importance of low power consumption to enable long operating lifetime for such circuits (Tsung-

DOI: 10.4018/978-1-4666-0083-6.ch006

Figure 1. RF-front end receiver using a heterodyne architecture

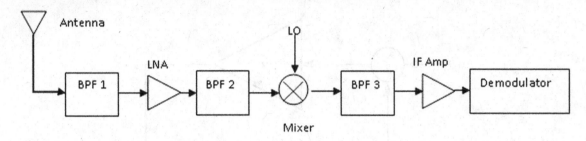

Hsien et al., 2004). This chapter deals with the RF-MEMS oscillators, where RF-MEMS devices such as inductors, varactors and resonators are explained in detail. The focus of this chapter is how the usage of RF-MEMS components can benefit and greatly improve the performance of RF-circuits.

Wireless communication systems have evolved dramatically in the last few decades generating multi-standard wireless systems which have high speed data rates and a multitude of applications. Current trends require multi-standard wireless systems (WLAN, GSM, GPS, WCDMA, DCS and Bluetooth) to operate using multiple frequency bands. Such demands place stringent requirements on handheld mobile terminals to be able to switch from one standard to another and also simultaneously be capable of accessing different networks. Specifications for multi-band RF front-end transceiver devices are more complex since such capabilities also imply increase or reduction of current consumption to meet concurrent operational requirements (Tasic et al., 2007). Novel adaptive RF circuits are a popular solution to meet the stringent RF requirements such as high gain, low noise figure with the added variable power consumption (Tasic et al., 2007).

Modern wireless transceiver circuits can be categorized into either analog front-end circuits or digital baseband circuits. Figure 1 illustrates a typical RF front end receiver circuit. Analog front-ends basically perform three important functions namely: frequency selection, amplification and frequency translation. Mixers with appropriate local oscillators typically perform frequency translation as required by the transceiver during signal transmission and reception. The challenge here is to design oscillators that meet the strict requirements imposed by different wireless standards. For example, the new IEEE 802.11a standard WLAN operates at 5.15 to 5.35 GHz and 5.725 to 5.875 GHz bands, with maximum data rates of 54 Mbps. Bluetooth on the other hand, operates at frequencies ranging from 2.4 to 2.4835GHz with data rates of 720 Kbps. On top of this are the general requirements for oscillators to be low cost, have low power consumption, small in size, multi-band (tunability) capabilities and silicon-compatible. This results in large chip area and high power requirement to allow multi-band/mode function. Area optimization and maximum block reusability for multiple mode of operation are the main challenges for System-on-Chip wireless transceiver designs (van Der Tang et al., 2003). One of the proposed solutions to this problem is to design an adaptive or reconfigurable RF circuit (Okada et al., 2005; Tasic et al., 2007; Yoshihara et al., 2004).

As shown in Figure 1, the local oscillator (LO) is a key component in a transceiver which generates a carrier signal (sinusoidal signal) as described in (1), from no input signal other than the dc bias. The LO input to the mixer allows the incoming RF signals to be downconverted to a lower frequency (kHz), which relaxes the complexity of

Figure 2. Block Diagram of feedback system

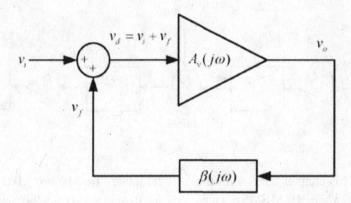

the subsequent circuits. An ideal oscillator has an ideal output,

$$V_{out} = A\cos(\omega_{osc}t) \tag{1}$$

Ideally, all signal power is located at the oscillating frequency, ω_{osc}. Unfortunately, in practice it is not possible to generate a noise free signal at a specific frequency. Real oscillator outputs are accompanied by unwanted harmonics. Carrier power is now distributed over the carrier frequency's bandwidth and its harmonics, leading to power reduction at the wanted frequency.

Oscillators are typically used to select a particular frequency in a transceiver. Transceivers catering to different standards require tunable oscillators to synthesize or generate different frequencies. In such cases, the tuning voltage, (V_{ctrl}) determines the oscillation frequency. In this case the oscillator output voltage is expressed as,

$$V_{out} = A\cos[2\pi(k_{vco}V_{ctrl} + f_{osc})t] \tag{2}$$

where k_{vco} is the tuning constant.

Besides the harmonics, practical oscillators also suffer from phase noise sidebands or jitter in time domain. To incorporate phase noise and jitter, the output signal of practical oscillator can be written as

$$V_{out} = A\cos\left(\omega_{osc}t + \theta\right), \tag{3}$$

where θ is stochastic variable presenting the phase uncertainty due to the presence of jitter.

To generate a pure sinusoidal signal from noise, oscillators employ feedback systems. Figure 2 illustrates a conventional oscillator block diagram which consists of a positive feedback amplifier $A_v(j\omega)$, a frequency-determining network $\beta(j\omega)$ and the noise input v_i.

The input voltage, v_i and the output voltage, v_o can be related as follows:

$$v_o = \frac{A_v(j\omega)}{1 - \beta(j\omega)A_v(j\omega)}v_i. \tag{4}$$

Where, $A_v(j\omega)$, $\beta(j\omega)$ are the amplifier gain and feedback transfer function respectively. $\beta(j\omega)A_v(j\omega)$ is known as the loop gain. From this relation it is possible to derive the close loop gain $[A_{vf}(j\omega)]$ of the feedback system as follows

$$A_{vf}(j\omega) = \frac{v_o}{v_i} = \frac{A_v(j\omega)}{1 - \beta(j\omega)A_v(j\omega)} \qquad (5)$$

To achieve oscillation from the feedback system (finite v_o) the denominator of (5) has to be zero. The loop gain, $\beta(j\omega)A_v(j\omega)$ must be unity. This relation is known as the Barkhausen criterion.

$$1 - \beta(j\omega)A_v(j\omega) = 0 \qquad (6)$$

$$\beta(j\omega)A_v(j\omega`) = 1 \qquad (7)$$

This relation can be expressed in polar form as follows:

$$\left|\beta(j\omega)A_v(j\omega`)\right|\langle(\beta(j\omega)A_v(j\omega`)) = 1 \qquad (8)$$

Hence,

$$\left|\beta(j\omega)A_v(j\omega`)\right| = 1$$

and

$$\langle\beta(j\omega)A_v(j\omega`) = \pm n360$$

where n=0,1,2,3,...

The above mentioned condition implies that any feedback system with unity loop gain and phase shift of $\pm n360$ can oscillate. To achieve oscillation, the Barkhausen criterion is necessary but not sufficient (Meyer, 1992.). To ensure oscillation in the presence of temperature and process variation the loop gain has to be chosen at least twice or three times the required value (Razavi et al., 1998).

In any transceiver system it is vital that the oscillators autonomously start oscillating, usu-ally triggered by noise, when the system is switched on. To guarantee oscillator start-up, the open loop gain must initially be larger than unity. This requirement is called the "start-up condition": $\left|\beta(j\omega)A_v(j\omega`)\right| > 1$, and the open loop gain ranges typically from 2 to 5 for self-limiting oscillators to ensure start-up.

RF-MEMS DEVICES

Microelectromechanical Systems (MEMS) is an enabling technology which allows the integration of mechanical elements, sensors, actuators and electronics on a common substrate using micro fabrication techniques (G M Rebeiz, 2003). Conventional integrated circuit (IC) fabrication techniques such as CMOS, Bipolar, SiGe are technologically mature, capable of mass producing complex circuits on a small area at a low cost. Due to its focus on manufacturing two-dimensional devices, conventional IC fabrication techniques have difficulty fabricating three-dimensional mechanical devices. To bridge this gap, RF-MEMS processing techniques such as surface and bulk micromachining can be utilized. Surface micromachining or 'additive' processing typically starts with a silicon substrate and the electro-mechanical structures are added on top of the substrate through a series of thin film deposition and patterning. Bulk micromachining on the other hand, creates electro-mechanical devices in the substrate itself through removing selected areas of the substrate. These processing techniques can be utilized to create crucial RF-system components such as filters, inductors, varactors and resonators.

Traditionally, frequency selective components for oscillators are realized using highly lossy integrated passive LCs or high Q discrete crystals (N S Khan, 2009). Discrete quartz crystals have technical maturity, high frequency-temperature stability and are widely available, but are several orders of magnitude bigger than MEMS resonators

(Euisik et al., 2005; Nabki et al., 2009). Integrated LC resonators can be easily fabricated on-chip as series or parallel tank circuits for frequencies lower than 100 MHz. Above this frequency, the physical dimensions of the LC resonators are the order of the signal wavelength, $\lambda = c/f$. When this occurs, current and voltages in the LC circuit are no longer constant and do not obey the distributed-circuit regime (Santos, 2004). At such physical dimensions radiation and skin effects are also dominant, causing the circuits to become lossy and they no longer behave as efficient storage elements. Resonant frequencies generated by integrated LCs are highly dependent on IC manufacturing tolerances and temperature-induced drifts, making it difficult to generate precise and highly stable frequencies (Santos, 2004).

Integrated MEMS resonators formed using vibrating beams and acoustic wave devices have become a promising solution in such conditions. It has been reported that MEMS resonators can be scaled to vibrate over a very wide frequency range from 1 KHz to over 1 GHz, making them ideal for highly stable oscillators (C. Nguyen, 2002). RF-MEMS devices have the potential of replacing many RF components such as switches, inductors, capacitors, phase shifters, surface acoustic wave (SAW) devices and ceramic filters used in today's mobile communication (N S Khan, 2009). Usage of integrated MEMS devices over their discrete counterparts benefit from batch processing, higher reliability, smaller footprint of the overall system which eventually result in an overall cost reduction (Nickel et al., 2005).

Issues in CMOS Integration

Traditionally, bipolar RF-front ends have shown low current consumption compared to their CMOS counterparts, especially for cellular applications which has complex network environments (Qiuting et al., 1999). CMOS technology has been a mainstream process in the digital design community, but it has not been considered as an adequate process for RF circuit modules due to its high noise, low operating frequency, and small transconductance. Recent technological developments in fabrication of complementary metal-oxide semiconductor (CMOS) have led to a marked improvement in the performance of CMOS devices in the RF range (Burghartz, 2001; Hassan et al., 2004; Hiroshi, 2004; Shi, 2001). The performance enhancement of RF-CMOS devices is largely attributed to the aggressive downsizing of the CMOS transistors' gate widths to 0.25 μm and 0.18 μm (Burghartz, 2001; Hassan et al., 2004; Hiroshi, 2004; Iwai, 2000; Manku, 1999; Shi, 2001) leading to improvement in the transistors cutoff frequency (f_r), and maximum frequency (f_{max}). The increased capabilities of these CMOS devices have led to the successful design and implementation of major RF transceiver building blocks such as low-noise amplifiers (LNAs), power amplifiers, mixers and local oscillators (LOs) (Huang et al., 1998; T. H. Lin et al., 1998; M. S. J. Steyaert et al., 2002). Recently, the demand for system integration in wireless communications has attracted RF designers to build extensive RF circuit blocks using CMOS processes with performance improvement due to the deep sub micrometer CMOS technologies. Silicon-based RF front ends have been successfully implemented in (Abidi et al., 1997) and (M. Steyaert et al., 1998). Competitive low-power CMOS RF-front end transceivers, which have comparable performance to their BJT counterparts have been described in (Qiuting et al., 1999).

To date, the major hurdle in achieving a completely silicon transceiver is the off-chip resonators, which usually cannot be fabricated using standard integrated circuit (IC) compatible fabrication methods (Sanduleanu et al., 2008). A key component in the heterodyne transceiver system, these resonators are often used for frequency selection in the radio-frequency (RF) and intermediate-frequency (IF) stages. MEMS devices show promising prospects to meet all these demands. Although typically optimized for integrated circuits, a wide variety of novel MEMS devices have been successfully implemented using CMOS fabrication techniques (Baltes et al., 2005; Baltes et al., 1998; Milanovic et al., 1997; Tea et al., 1997). Recent advances in the IC-compatible micromachining technologies, yield microscale silicon based resonators that have brought us closer to achieving the ultimate objective of a single-chip transceiver (A. N. Nordin et al., 2007). Complete integration of the resonators with the RF circuits using the same CMOS fabrication process eliminates the need for lossy wire-bonds to connect the passive device to the circuits, reduces the parasitics, attenuation and thus improving the performance of the system.

RF-MEMS Resonators

In general, there are two major categories of MEMS resonators used in oscillator circuits. A purely mechanical resonator or flexural mode resonator can be formed using a beam or disk which will vibrate at a specific frequency. Electro-mechanical resonators on the other hand, are usually formed using a piezoelectric membrane which is electrically excited to produce a traveling mechanical acoustic wave at a specific resonant frequency. The performance of the resonators is highly dependent both on the structure and design parameters of the resonator (Rebeiz, 2003). The essential requirements of a resonator with wireless applications include having precise series and parallel resonant frequencies (*fs, fp*), low insertion losses, and high quality factors (*Q*) (Zhou, 2009).

Efficiency of acoustic wave propagation in a piezoelectric material is measured by its electromechanical coupling coefficient κ^2, or the efficiency of the transformation of the electrical input into mechanical acoustic waves. κ^2 can be defined in terms of the piezoelectric coefficient *e*, elastic constant *c* and dielectric permittivity ε as shown in (Hara et al., 2003):

$$\kappa^2 = \frac{e^2}{c\varepsilon} \tag{9}$$

Quality factor (*Q*) is the ratio of the stored energy over the lost energy or $Q = E/\Delta E$ where *E* is the stored vibration energy and ΔE is the energy lost per cycle of vibration (Zhou, 2009). Two most widely used acoustic-wave resonators are the film bulk acoustic wave resonator (FBAR) and the surface acoustic wave resonator (SAWR).

The acoustic wave resonators are typically named according their acoustic wave propagation modes; bulk and surface. Bulk wave devices have the acoustic waves propagating through the substrate. Surface wave resonators have the acoustic waves propagating along the top surface of the device. In the next sections we first illustrate current activities in the acoustic wave resonators (film and surface) followed by the flexural mode resonators.

Film Bulk Acoustic Wave Resonator (FBAR)

BAW resonators are typically formed by two metal layers sandwiching a piezoelectric layer. The metal electrodes can be formed using highly conductive metals such as Au, Mo or Pt. The typical cross-section of a FBAR is shown in Figure 3.

Acoustic waves are excited by the metal electrodes and propagate unguided through the volume of the piezoelectric substrate. Bulk acoustic wave resonant frequencies are characterized by the thickness of the piezoelectric material as shown in (10):

$$f_r = \frac{v}{2d}, \tag{10}$$

where f_r is the resonant frequency, *v* is the acoustic wave velocity and *d* is the thickness of the piezoelectric material. Based on (10) a resonator with

Figure 3. Cross-section of film bulk acoustic wave resonator (FBAR)

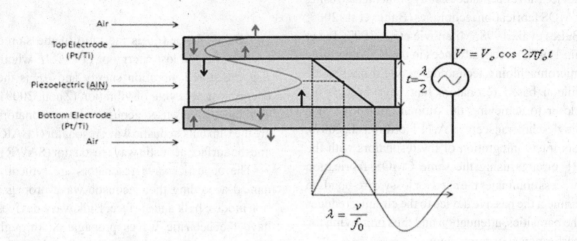

a thick piezoelectric layer or large mass will be characterized by a low resonant frequency and vice-versa.

There has been a lot of interest to integrate silicon-based FBARs with CMOS circuits. Numerous silicon FBARs have been successfully fabricated, typically using AlN as its piezoelectric material (Campanella et al., 2008; Hara et al., 2003; B. P. Otis et al., 2003; Zuo, Van der Spiegel et al., 2010). Research done by (Hara et al., 2003) describes the development of AlN FBARs on silicon substrates using CMOS-compatible MEMS techniques. To reduce spurious responses, losses and to obtain high Q factor the FBAR has to be isolated acoustically from the lossy substrate. Three different structures are possible for acoustic isolation namely; the acoustic diaphragm type resonator, air gap type resonator (AGR) and solidity mounted type resonator (SMR). The AGR is the more preferred structure since acoustic isolation is achieved using an air-gap which theoretically allows a higher Q factor than the SMR structure. The fabricated resonator shown in Figure 4 achieved a resonant frequency of 2 GHz, a Q factor of 780 and an effective electromechanical coupling constant (k_{eff}) of 5.36%. Although this work indicated good quality factor and high

coupling constant at resonance frequencies of 2 GHz, the FBAR is difficult to fabricate. CMOS-compatibility requires a temperature limit of less than 200°C for fabrication, the usage of AlN as a piezoelectric layer has temperature stability and reliability issues.

An improved FBAR with Q factors in the order of 100 has been demonstrated in (Chee et al., 2005; B. P. Otis et al., 2003). As shown in Figure 5, this 1.9 GHz FBAR is formed using a sandwich of metal electrodes and AlN thin film on top of a back-etched Si substrate. The Butterworth-Van Dyke circuit is used to model FBAR as shown in Figure 6. The motional LCR circuit describes the resonant frequency and was placed in parallel with parasitic capacitance, inductance and resistances of the device structure. This equivalent circuit model was useful for the design of the low-power oscillator circuit. The Q factor of this resonator was measured to be 1200, and its motional resistance, R_m to be 300 Ohms (B. P. Otis et al., 2003). Low R_m places less stringent requirements on the feedback amplifier which is necessary that the loop gain =1.

In this instance, the simple Pierce topology was used where an inverting amplifier consisting of two transistors formed the feedback loop to the

Figure 4. Structure for FBAR

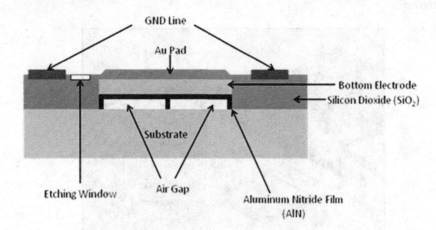

Figure 5. Cross-section of FBAR (Chee et al., 2005), (© [2005] IEEE). Used with permission.

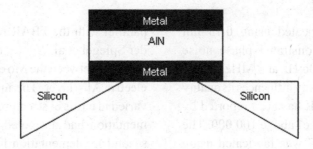

Figure 6. Left: FBAR Equivalent circuit model. Right: Oscillator Circuit (Chee et al., 2005), (© [2005] IEEE). Used with permission.

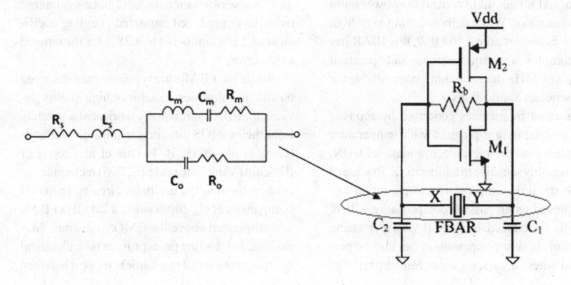

Figure 7. SEM micrograph of an I-shaped bulk acoustic wave resonator (Ho et al.), (© [2010] IEEE). Used with permission.

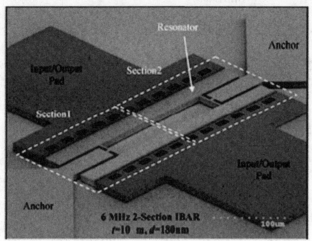

FBAR. The circuit fabricated using 0.13 μm CMOS technology demonstrated phase noise characteristics of -138 dBc/Hz at 1 MHz.

The FBAR's shape greatly influences its quality factor. An I-shaped FBAR has been reported by (Ho et al.) with Q factors of above 100 000. The IBAR shown in Figure 7 was fabricated using single crystal silicon on a silicon-on-insulator (SOI) substrate. The IBAR demonstrated Q factors of 112 000 at 5.75 MHz. To form an oscillator, the IBAR was connected to a transimpedance amplifier to sustain oscillation and an automatic level control (ALC) circuit to control the power input to the resonator. While demonstrating very high quality factors of above 100 000, this IBAR has very complex fabrication methods and operate at a very low MHz range, making it unsuitable for most wireless applications.

Resonant frequencies generated by acoustic wave resonators are plagued with temperature dependency as the piezoelectric material (AlN, ZnO) is highly sensitive to temperature. To achieve device stability, temperature compensation can be achieved using passive compensation where oxide is introduced in the FBAR layer stack. Electronic tuning compensation can also be performed where a varactor array can be placed in

parallel with the FBAR resonator. In (Zuo, Van der Spiegel et al., 2010), the oxide layer was inserted in between the Mo electrode and the piezoelectric AlN layer. The inserted oxide layer was varied in terms of structure, where the first implementation had a tapered layer oxide while the second implementation had a symmetric oxide layer in the FBAR stack. From the experimental results, it was observed that the tapered oxide layer produced better temperature coefficient of frequency (TCF) of 0 ppm/°C compared to -6 ppm/°C for the symmetric oxide layer. The low TCF is a performance tradeoff since symmetric oxide layer produced improved coupling coefficient of 5.6% compared to 4.28% for the tapered oxide layer.

While the FBARs are typically manufactured on silicon substrates, to achieve high quality devices, the FBARs are usually fabricated separately from their CMOS circuitry, requiring wirebonds (Chee et al., 2005; B. P. Otis et al., 2003) or flip-chip (Vanhelmont et al., 2006) techniques to connect them to the oscillator circuits. In his (H Campanella et al., 2008) work, a 2.5 GHz FBAR was suspended above the CMOS substrate. Mechanical conducting posts provide both electrical interconnection and mechanical support between

Figure 8. Cross-sectional view of the heterogeneous integration process of FBAR to CMOS substrate

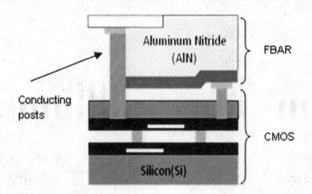

the FBAR and CMOS substrate. The cross-section of the device is shown in Figure 8. Such vertical integration has several advantages. The first is that larger FBAR electrodes can be fabricated which in turn results in better Q factor of the device. Flipping the FBAR structures on top of the CMOS substrate allows removal of the lossy Si attached to the FBAR, which also improves the Q-factor of the device. Finally, the placement of the FBAR on top of the CMOS circuits forms a protective package that encapsulates the circuits.

Surface Acoustic Wave Resonators (SAWR)

SAW acoustic resonators are formed using interdigitated (IDT) arrays of electrodes on top of a piezoelectric layer as shown in Figure 9. Sinusoidal electrical excitation is placed at the input IDTs which produce spatially non-uniform time varying electric fields in the piezoelectric layer underneath. These electric fields generate local stresses in the form of elastic waves on the surface of the piezoelectric material. The propagating elastic waves are detected and translated back into electrical signals at the output port. Using this concept, SAW devices are capable of performing powerful signal processing and have been successfully functioning as filters, resonators and duplexers for the past 60 years.

The series resonant frequency (f_s) of a SAW resonator is related to the frequency of the propagating acoustic wave. The frequency of the surface acoustic wave is dependent both on the

Figure 9. Schematic of a surface acoustic wave device

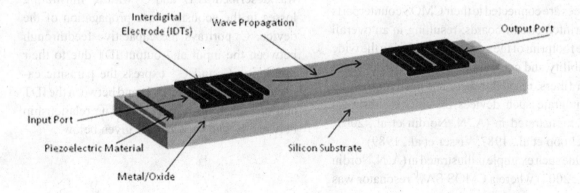

Figure 10. (a) Cross section of CMOS SAW resonator; (b) Cross section of CMOS SAW resonator with increased height reflectors

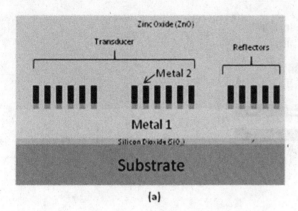

(a)

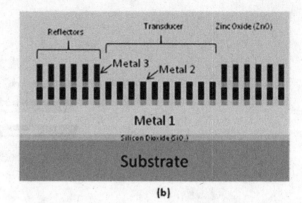

(b)

velocity of the acoustic wave (*v*) and the periodicity of the IDTs (11) as follows,

$$\lambda = \frac{v}{f_s}. \qquad (11)$$

To improve resonance and to contain the waves within a cavity, shorted metal electrodes or reflectors can be placed at both ends of the device. Such device is known as a SAW resonator and has demonstrated higher quality factors compared to SAW devices without reflectors.

Although SAW devices are technological mature and have served the telecommunication industry for more than 50 years, these devices are typically fabricated on piezoelectric substrates and are packaged as discrete components. Very little silicon integration is achieved since these devices are connected to their CMOS counterparts on printed circuit boards, resulting in an overall large footprint of the system. Considering the wide flexibility and capabilities of the SAW device to form filters, resonator there has been motivation to integrate such devices on silicon substrates as demonstrated in (A. N. Nordin et al., 2007; Vellekoop et al., 1987; Visser et al., 1989).

One such example is illustrated in (A. N. Nordin et al., 2007) where a CMOS SAW resonator was

fabricated using 0.6 μm AMIs CMOS technology process with additional MEMS post-processing. The traditional SAW structure of having the piezoelectric at the bottom was inverted. Instead, the IDTs were cleverly manufactured using standard CMOS process and the piezoelectric layer was placed on the top. Active circuitry can be placed adjacent to the CMOS resonator and can be connected using the integrated metal layers. The height of the reflectors was varied to investigate the effect of the reflector height on the containment of the acoustic waves. The cross-section of the device is shown in Figure 10.

Similar to the FBAR structure, an equivalent circuit model was developed for the CMOS SAW resonator as shown in Figure 11. The two main components in the circuit model are the acoustic and parasitic components. Acoustic resonance was described as L_x and C_x with R_x illustrating losses in the acoustic wave propagation of the device. C_f portrays the capacitive feedthrough between the input and output IDT due to their proximity. C_t and C_{ox} express the parasitic capacitance between two IDTs and between the IDT and the substrate respectively. The relationship between L_x and C_x with Q is given below.

Figure 11. Left: Cross section of CMOS fabrication layers and equivalent circuit model of the two-port acoustic wave resonator (A. N. Nordin et al., 2007). Right: Scanning Electron Microscope image of fabricated 3 GHz CMOS SAW Resonator (A.N. Nordin, 2008), (© [2008] IEEE). Used with permission.

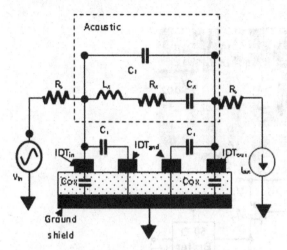

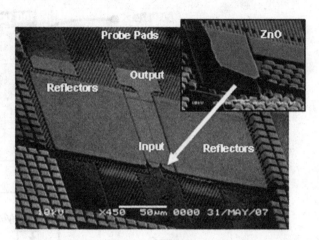

C_I: Static capacitance between IDT_{in} and IDT_{gnd}
C_{oxi}: Oxide capacitance between IDT_{in} and ground shield

$$L_x = \frac{R_x\, Q}{2\pi f_s} \tag{12}$$

$$C_x = \frac{1}{L_x \left(2\pi f_s\right)^2} \tag{13}$$

The fabricated resonators had operating frequencies in the range of 600 MHz to 1 GHz. Although the measured Q factors were relatively low (order of 100s) compared FBARs, these CMOS SAW resonators indicated that fully monolithic implementations of SAW devices are possible.

A much improved SAW resonator, with Q factors in the order of 1000 has been successfully fabricated recently (Zuo, Van der Spiegel et al., 2010). This lateral-field-excited resonator was formed using similar layers as an FBAR, with Pt electrodes on top of AlN thin films situated directly on Si substrates. The usual bottom electrode of the FBAR is not required in the SAW device,

Figure 12. Cross-section of a lateral-field-excited resonator (Zuo, Van der Spiegel et al., 2010), (© [2010] IEEE). Used with permission.

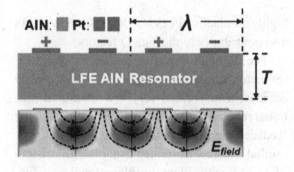

greatly relaxing alignment requirements. The cross-section of this device is shown in Figure 12. As expected of a SAW resonator, the resonant frequency of the LFE resonator is dependent on the periodic spacing of the IDT or λ. High electromechanical coupling coefficient of 1.20% was achieved by depositing the AlN directly on the Si wafers and later dry-etching the lossy Si substrate to release the membrane. The usage of

Figure 13. Micrograph of LFE resonator wirebonded to CMOS chip. Bottom: Equivalent circuit of LFE resonator and Pierce oscillator schematic (Zuo, Van der Spiegel et al., 2010), (© [2010] IEEE). Used with permission.

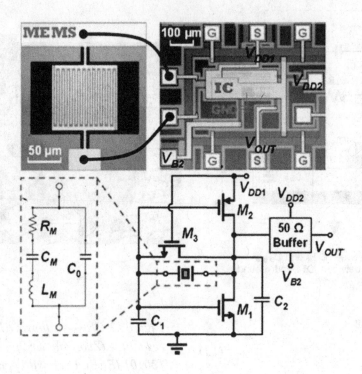

highly conductive Pt electrodes to form the IDTs also contributes to the high Q factors.

The equivalent circuit model for the LFE resonators are shown in Figure 13. These high Q devices demonstrated very low measured motional resistance, R_m, making it easy to design the feedback amplifier of the oscillator circuit. The oscillator core was formed using two transistors M_1 and M_2 in the Pierce oscillator topology (Zuo, Van der Spiegel et al., 2010). M_3 acts as MOSFET resistor to bias M_1 and M_2 at half of V_{DD1}. The gain of the amplifier is proportional to the transconductance of M_1 and M_2, which can be tuned by varying V_{DD1}. Having variable gain allows the same oscillator circuit to be reused for different resonators of assorted frequencies. V_{DD1} affects the DC bias current and can be tuned such that M_1 and M_2 achieve critical transconductance necessary for the oscillations to start. The measured

LFE oscillators indicated phase noise of -140dBc/Hz at 100kHz.

A hybrid of a SAW resonator and an FBAR, also fabricated on silicon has been reported in (Harrington et al.; Lavasani et al.) with even better performance characteristics. The extensional thin-film piezoelectric-on-substrate (TPoS) resonator has an unloaded quality factor (Q) of 6700 in air and operates at 1 GHz. Its resonance frequency is inversely proportional to the pitch of the IDTs or

$$2\pi f_s = (\pi/\lambda) \sqrt{(E_{eff}/\rho_{eff})} \qquad (14)$$

Where E_{eff} and ρ_{eff} are the effective Young's Modulus and density of the composite structure, respectively. The TPoS resonator shown in Figure 14 has Molybdenum electrodes on top AlN, which is suspended above the Si substrate. Isolation from the lossy Si substrate allows the device to

Figure 14. Schematic for 7th order TPoS devices with one pair (top) and two pairs (bottom) of support tethers

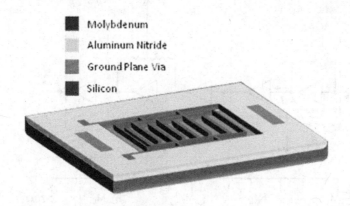

Molybdenum
Aluminum Nitride
Ground Plane Via
Silicon

have very low motional resistance of 160 Ohms. The suspended AlN and Mo is tethered to the substrate using Mo anchors on both sides. This work also evaluated the effect of having single versus multiple pairs of tethers. It was reported that having multiple supports causes the resonator plate to become more rigid and suppresses the spurious modes (Harrington et al.). As a result, the near resonance response is cleaner and the Q factor is increased up to 57%.

To counteract the motional resistance of the TPoS resonators, a high-gain transimpedance amplifier (TIA) was designed in the feedback loop of the oscillator (Lavasani et al.). The TIA shown in Figure 15 is complex with three stages namely the current-to-voltage converter, bandwidth enhancement and 50 Ohm buffer. The TPoS resonator provides the input current to the first stage which amplifies the current before converting it to voltage. The voltage amplifier of the second stage uses the common-source topology with shunt-shunt feedback to achieve high output swing with increased bandwidth. Finally the 50 Ohm buffer is designed as a common-source stage to obtain 50 Ohm matching with the measurement equipment.

Flexural Mode Resonators

Flexural mode resonators operate on a different concept compared to acoustic wave resonators. Instead of generating acoustic waves in piezoelectric material, the entire mechanical structure (beam or disks) vibrate when driven using AC electrical signals. The flexural mode resonators can be fabricated using single-crystal silicon (Ayazi et al., 2000) or polysilicon (Bannon et al., 2000). A schematic of a typical clamped-clamped beam is shown in Figure 16 (Ruther et al., 2005).

A dc bias voltage is applied between the beam and the substrate. AC electrical signals are placed between the drive electrode and the substrate. This creates an electrostatic force which causes the beam to vibrate and the capacitance between the output electrode and the beam (C_b) to vary. The resonant frequency can be monitored by measuring the current at the output or sensing electrode, which is dependent on the capacitance change as given by,

$$I_{ac} = V_{bias} \frac{dC_b}{dt}. \tag{15}$$

The resonant frequency of the clamped-clamped beam resonator is related to the Young's

Figure 15. Trans-impedance amplifier (Lavasani et al.), (© [2011] IEEE). Used with permission.

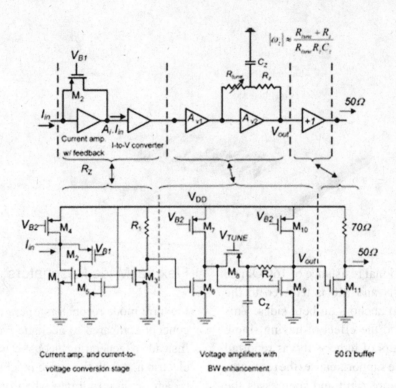

Figure 16. Schematic of Clamped-clamped beam resonator (Ruther et al., 2005), (© [2005] IEEE). Used with permission.

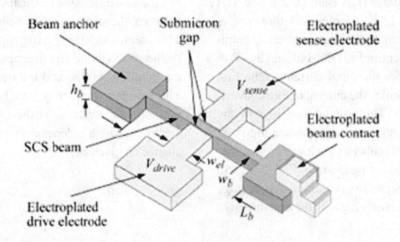

Figure 17. SEM micrograph of the clamped-clamped beam resonator (Ruther et al., 2005), (© [2005] IEEE). Used with permission.

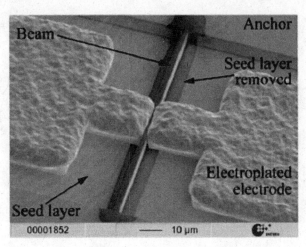

modulus (E), material density (ρ) and dimensions of the device w_b and L_b which are shown in Figure 16.

$$f_{res} = \frac{1}{2}\sqrt{\frac{E}{\rho}\frac{w_b}{L_b^2}} \qquad (16)$$

As can be seen in (35), the resonance frequency of the vibrating device is inversely proportional to the length of the structure. Operation at high frequencies (MHz or GHz) requires the beam length to be of µm length. Such miniature structures are sensitive to air or gas molecules surrounding it which exert Brownian force and manifests as noise during movement of the structure (Santos, 2004). This results in fluctuations in the resonant frequency. The sensitivity of the beam structure to ambient air or gas molecules also affect the Q factor of the device, where it can be seen that beams operating at atmospheric structure have Qs of 100 while those operating under vacuum have Qs up to 80 000 (Santos, 2004).

The resonator structure shown in Figure 17 was fabricated using single-crystal silicon (SCS) on silicon on insulator (SOI) substrates. To ensure CMOS compatibility, all post-CMOS MEMS pro-

cessing techniques were done at low processing temperatures. These include patterning the SOI wafer using deep reactive ion etching (DRIE) and chemical vapor deposition (CVD) of the sacrificial oxide layer. The fabricated resonator operates at low frequencies of 420 kHz but have high Q factors of 50 000 (Ruther et al., 2005).

An interesting method to push the operating frequency of the clamped-clamped beam to the MHz without significant reduction in size was shown in (Bannon et al., 2000). Two clamped-clamped beams were coupled together using a flexural mode beam and suspended on top of a silicon substrate. The resonant frequency of the coupled clamped-clamped beams is determined by the resonant frequencies of each beam which obey (35) (Bannon et al., 2000). The bandwidth (B) of the frequency response is related to the stiffness of the coupling spring as shown below,

$$k_{e12} = k_{re}\left(\frac{B}{f_{res}}\right)k_{12}. \qquad (17)$$

Where k_{re} is the resonator's stiffness at the coupling location, k_{12} is the normalized coupling coefficient and k_{e12} is the coupling spring constant.

Figure 18. SEM Micrograph of the Dual Clamped-clamped beam resonator (Bannon et al., 2000), (©[2000] IEEE). Used with permission.

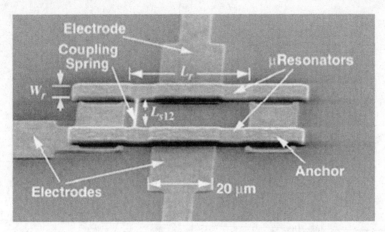

The coupling beam also adds mass to each of the clamped resonators and affect the resonant frequencies calculated using (35). Solution of the resonant frequency can be calculated using a mechanical transmission line in the form of an impedance matrix (Bannon et al., 2000).

The coupled clamped-clamped beams were fabricated using thick polysilicon suspended on top of Silicon substrate. The 2 μm thick polysilicon layer was deposited on top of sacrificial oxide via LPCVD at high temperatures and patterned using reactive-ion-etching. The sacrificial layer was later removed using HF wet-etching to yield the suspended beams as shown in Figure 18. This structure operates at 7.81 MHz with a high Q factor of 8000. Unlike the implementation shown in (Ruther et al., 2005), the dual clamped-clamped beam is not CMOS-compatible due to the required high processing temperatures to fabricate the structures.

Much higher (GHz) resonance frequencies can be achieved using disk-shaped micromechanical resonators (Y. W. Lin et al., 2004). Bulk-mode or disk resonators have very high stiffness, resulting in high Qs and resonators that are less susceptible to the pressure of the surrounding environment (Ho et al.). Disk resonators can be vibrated in a variety of modes namely (i) flexural; (ii) breath-

ing; and (iii) wine-glass. All three modes can generate GHz resonance frequencies, but the wine-glass mode has been reported to produce highest Qs (> 150 000). Both breathing and flexural mode resonators can achieve Q's in the order of 10 000 at GHz frequencies even when operating in air (Y. W. Lin et al., 2004). Breathing mode resonators have the highest stiffness amongst the three modes which translates into highest resonance frequencies (~ 1.5 GHz) but are more difficult to fabricate (Nguyen, 2007).

An example of a radial disk resonator is shown in Figure 19. This type of resonator vibrates in the flexural mode has its resonance frequency governed by,

$$f_{res} = 0.253 \frac{h}{R^2} \sqrt{\frac{E}{\rho}} \qquad (18)$$

Where E, ρ and σ are Young's modulus, density and Poisson's ratio respectively, h and R are the thickness and radius respectively (Tzuen-Hsi et al., 2008). Flexural mode resonators have the advantage of very higher Qs compared to the wine glass disk resonators (Tzuen-Hsi et al., 2008). However, flexural mode resonators have very high motional resistance, which are in the order of 10 000. The drive for low motional impedance

Figure 19. Left: SEM Micrograph of a radial disk resonator. Right: Simulated orthogonal flexural mode shapes of the resonator (Demirci et al., 2005)., (© [2005] IEEE). Used with permission.

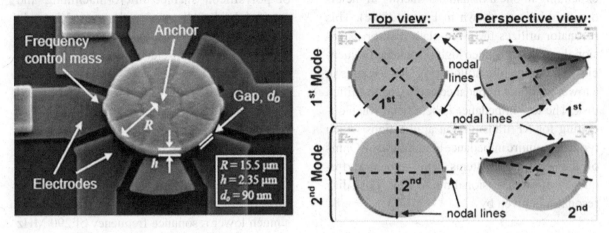

or resistance is especially important when the resonators are connected to amplifier circuits to function as oscillators. Having large motional resistance, R_m will heavily load the amplifier and degrade the Q of the oscillator. When connected RF front-end system components, RF-MEMS resonators are also required to match the front-end system impedance of 50 Ω (Xie et al., 2008). Motional resistance in the kΩ will create mismatch and deter maximum power transfer. As such researchers have explored several methods to reduce

R_m in disk resonators such as resonator array (Tzuen-Hsi et al., 2008) or using hollow ring resonators (Xie et al., 2008) to reduce motional resistance of the resonators. The nickel disk resonators can be arranged in an array to function as a single mode resonator or a multi-pole filter as shown in Figure 20. The advantage of having an array of *n* resonators allows larger current handling and reduces the overall motional resistance by a factor of *n* (Tzuen-Hsi et al., 2008).

Figure 20. Left: SEM Micrograph of an array of flexural mode radial disk resonators. Right: Measured frequency response of a single and an array of flexural mode disk resonator (Tzuen-Hsi et al., 2008), (© [2008] IEEE). Used with permission.

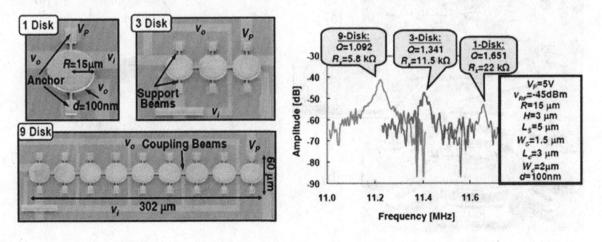

The wine glass disk mode shape has the disk expanding in one axis and contracting in the orthogonal axis as shown in Figure 28 (c). This resonator utilizes the wine-glass disk or extensional mode to produce high resonance frequencies. The usage of a hollow ring shape results in a lower motional impedance compared to a filled disk. The low impedance is beneficial when operating for RF transmission applications which typically require impedance matching to 50 Ohms of the front-end systems. The resonance frequency of an extensional mode wine glass disk resonator is given by

$$f_{res} = \frac{h}{2\pi} \sqrt{(E / \rho(1 - \sigma^2))} \qquad (19)$$

Where E, ρ and σ are Young's modulus, density and Poisson's ratio respectively. h is the determinant of the 4x4 H matrix which is a function of the ring's device parameters and Bessel functions. Using these equations, a 220 MHz ring resonator with dimensions of 2 μm thickness, 30.5 μm inner radius and 50 μm outer radius was successfully designed. The RF ring resonators (200 MHz to 1.5 GHz) were fabricated using a combination of polysilicon surface micro-machining and sacrificial sidewall spacer techniques (Xie et al., 2008). The Qs of these devices range from 2800 to 3500. The scanning electron micrographs of the fabricated ring resonators are shown in Figure 21 (a) and (b). The ring resonators were fabricated using a series of complex surface micro-machining process to fabricate the self-aligned phosphorus-doped polysilicon microstructures (Wang, Ren et al., 2004; Xie et al., 2008).

Commercial CMOS technology can also be used to fabricate the ring resonators, although at a much lower resonance frequency of 290 MHz (Teva et al., 2008). Fabrication of RF-MEMS in standard CMOS technology offer possibility of full integration with RF-CMOS circuitry and batch fabrication. In this work, the standard CMOS AMS 0.35 μm technology were used to fabricate both a clamped-clamped beam and a ring resonator. In this design, existing CMOS layers such as poly1 was used as the structural material for the ring, poly2 was chosen for the electrode and the anchors were realized using a set of vias between the metals as shown in Figure 22 (Teva et al.,

Figure 21. (a) and (b) SEM Micrograph of extensional mode wine glass resonators (Xie et al., 2008); (c) Simulation of wine-glass mode shape (Pakdast, 2008), (© [2008] IEEE). Used with permission.

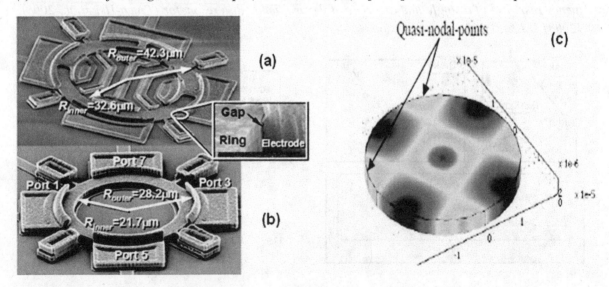

Figure 22. (a) Top view of ring resonator. (b) Cross-section of CMOS process for RF-MEMS ring resonator. (c) S_{21} transmission characteristics of ring resonator. (d) Micrograph of the ring resonator (Teva et al., 2008), (© [2008] IEEE). Used with permission.

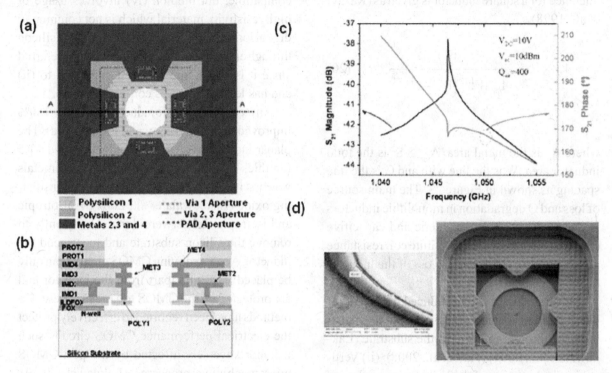

2008). Anchoring the structure using a different material (metal) than the structural material (poly1) minimizes the losses (Wang, Butler et al., 2004). An annular ring resonator with inner radius of 5 μm and outer radius of 8.56 μm was successfully fabricated as shown in Figure 22(d). The Q-factor of this CMOS resonator in air is 400 which is very low compared to its non-CMOS counterparts.

RF-MEMS Inductors

Inductors are a crucial component of RF systems, be it as an on-chip matching network, passive filter or a frequency selecting component for voltage controlled oscillators (VCOs) (Liu et al., 2008). Taking into account that the inductors are often coupled with RF circuits, monolithic implementations are preferred compared to bondwires which are area intensive and have inductance values

which are difficult to control. On-chip CMOS inductors often suffer from parasitic, metallic, substrate proximity losses and limited fabrication geometries (Okoniewski et al., 2006). Recent advances in reduction of interconnect resistance combined with improved RF-MEMS techniques have allowed fabrication of high Q inductors with low series resistance. High-Q inductors improve the phase noise and power in VCOs, figure of merit for low noise amplifiers and reduce the losses of bandpass filters (Lakdawala et al., 2004).

The rectangular spiral inductor is the preferred structure for monolithic inductors operations below 20 GHz. This structure shown in Figure 30 occupies smaller area compared to transmission line inductors and can be fabricated as planar (Euisik et al., 2005), solenoid (Lee et al., 2008) or bimorph (Chang et al., 2006) structures. Circular inductors approximated using hexagons or octagons, have less metal resistance for the same amount of inductance and metal width (Razavi et al., 1998). A simplified formula to calculate inductance for a square inductor is given as (Razavi et al., 1998),

$$L \approx 1.3 \times 10^{-7} \frac{A_m^{5/3}}{A_{tot}^{1/6} W^{1.75} \left(W + G\right)^{0.25}} \quad (20)$$

where A_m is the metal area, $A_{tot} \cong S^2$ is the total inductor area, W is the line with and G is the line spacing as shown in Figure 23. The main source of loss and Q degradation in monolithic inductors is due to the substrate magnetic and capacitive coupling. To a lesser degree, finite coil resistance also contribute to I^2R energy loss of the inductor (Lakdawala et al., 2004).

Substrate losses can be reduced using a number of methods namely (i) Suspending the planar inductor through removal of the substrate (Lakdawala et al., 2004) (Park et al., 2008), (ii) Vertical implementation of the inductor as a solenoid (Lee et al., 2008), (iii) Placing patterned ground shields underneath the inductor (Yue et al., 1998)

Figure 23. Key dimensions of a rectangular spiral inductor

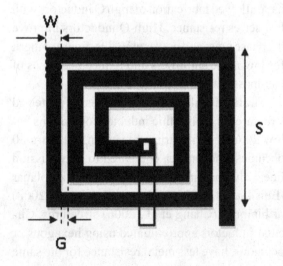

and (iv) Increasing the substrate resistance (Ashby et al., 1996). Methods (i) to (iii) are CMOS compatible, but method (iv) involves usage of high resistivity material which is not common to digital logic CMOS processes. Removal of silicon through either dry or wet-etching is often preferred since it is easily implemented compared to (ii) and has lesser parasitics compared to (iii).

An etched monolithic inductor with $100 - 180\%$ improved Q factor is shown in Figure 24 (a). The planar inductor with 20 μm wide turns and ~1.5 μm thick metal formed using CMOS top metals was first reactive ion etched to remove the insulating oxide (Lakdawala et al., 2004). Anisotropic and isotropic etches were done subsequently to remove the silicon substrate and to suspend the inductor. Accompanying CMOS circuits can only be placed > 30 μm apart from the inductor and are protected by the CMOS top metal. These two methods have been reported to effectively protect the electrical performance CMOS circuits such it is not adversely affected by the post-CMOS micromachining processes (Lakdawala et al., 2004). The fabricated inductors have indicated inductance values of $3 - 5$ nH with Q factors of less than 20 (Lakdawala et al., 2004).

Suspended inductors can also be surface micromachined on silicon substrates. This process is complex and requires thick photoresist mold to form the 3-D inductor structures of < 10 nH. A combination of electro-plating, vacuum deposition and mechanical polishing is required to shape the inductors in the mold. 10 μm thick inductors as shown in Figure 24(b) can be fabricated using this method. The thick (10 μm) inductors and large gap (50 μm) between the inductor and the substrate allows this type of inductor to achieve a much higher Q of 70 compared to the CMOS counterpart (Euisik et al., 2005).

While suspended inductors offer relatively high Q factors, they are area intensive and often consume a large chunk of the die area. To reduce substrate losses, while minimizing the area, solenoids or vertical inductors have been fabricated

Figure 24. (a)Bulk-etched, suspended CMOS spiral inductor (Lakdawala et al., 2004), (© [2002] IEEE) (b)Microphotograph of surface-micromachined inductor (Euisik et al., 2005), (© [2002] IEEE). Used with permission.

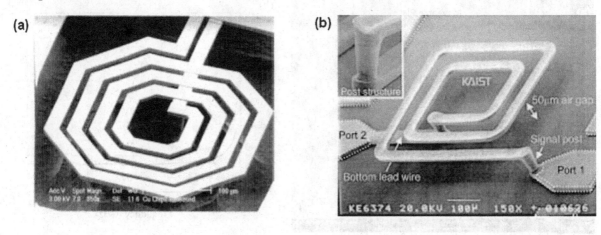

Figure 25. (a)-(d) SEM images of solenoid with integrated magnetic core. (e) Calculated and measured values of resistance and Q factors of the solenoid at varying frequencies (Lee et al., 2008), (© [2008] IEEE). Used with permission.

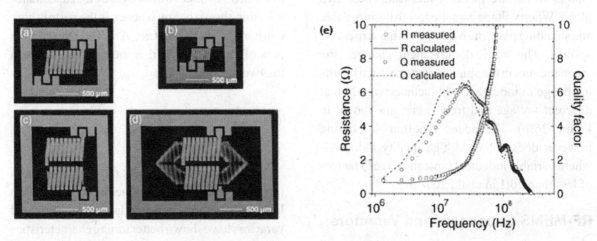

(Lee et al., 2008). In Figure 25, vertical copper inductors were fabricated on high resistivity silicon wafers using a series of electroplating, polyimide coating and planarization process. The solenoid wraps around a magnetic core, which helps to increase inductance since the magnetic material adds a factor of μ_r compared to an air core. The inductors were 5 μm thick, 350 μm long and yielded much higher inductances of 150 nH. The Q factors are relatively low (< 10) but the inductance density is very high (219 nH/mm²) which is much higher than the typical values of 20 – 40 nH/mm² for planar structures.

Variable inductors can also be fabricated using RF-MEMS processes. Tunable inductors provide added functionality to RF-circuit components such as VCOs, power amplifiers, matching networks and filters. Figure 26 (a) illustrates an electrostatically actuated tunable inductor. The moveable and shielding plate moves vertically

Figure 26. (a) Micrograph of the tunable inductor. (b) Inductance versus frequency at different voltage values (Liu et al., 2008), (© [2010] IEEE). Used with permission.

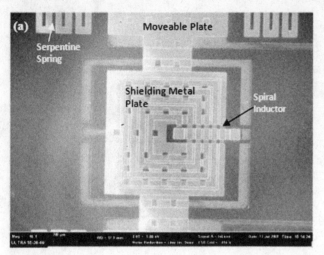

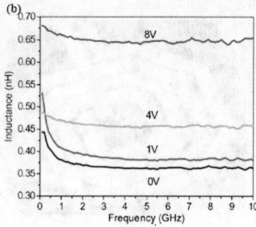

and is controlled by parallel plate capacitive actuators which are placed underneath these two plates. When voltage is applied, both the moveable and shielding plates move down via the serpentine springs. The vertical movement changes the magnetic flux in the spiral inductor, which results in change in inductance. Inductance variation at different voltage and frequencies are shown in Figure 26(b). The added flexibility of tuning however does not yield high quality inductors, where variable inductors typically have Q factors of less than 20(Liu et al., 2008).

RF-MEMS Capacitors and Varactors

Like inductors, capacitors play an important role in RF circuits and are often employed in filters, matching networks and VCOs. Capacitors can be easily implemented as parallel metal plates or interdigitated metal finger capacitors (MFC) in standard CMOS technology, but its MEMS counterparts offer tunable and higher capacitance density. In general, MEMS capacitors can be classified into three categories namely (i) Parallel plates, (ii) Lateral or interdigitated capacitors and (iii) Vertical capacitors. In this section, recent

work in RF-MEMS capacitors are reviewed and discussed. All three structures obey the capacitance equation shown below where ε is the permittivity constant of the dielectric, A is the overlapping area of the plates and d is the distance between the two parallel plates.

$$C = \frac{\varepsilon A}{d}. \tag{21}$$

Parallel capacitive plates have higher Q factors and lower parasitic inductance compared to lateral capacitors. However, lateral interdigitated varactors have shown better tuning characteristics than their parallel counterparts. To ensure compatibility with CMOS, RF-MEMS parallel capacitors are usually formed using standard CMOS metal and poly layers, but are released from the silicon substrates using MEMS processing techniques. A novel curled-plate varactor shown in Figure 27 was fabricated in standard TSMC 0.35 μm CMOS technology followed by a series of reactive ion etching and isotropic etching of the silicon substrate to release the structure (Bakri-Kassem et al., 2008). The curled-varactor operates in three states: zero-bias and two other DC bias collapse

Figure 27. (a)-(c) Three main states of the tri-state varactor zero dc bias, 1st collapse point and 2nd collapse point (b) SEM image of the fabricated tri-state varactor (Bakri-Kassem et al., 2008), (© [2008] IEEE). Used with permission.

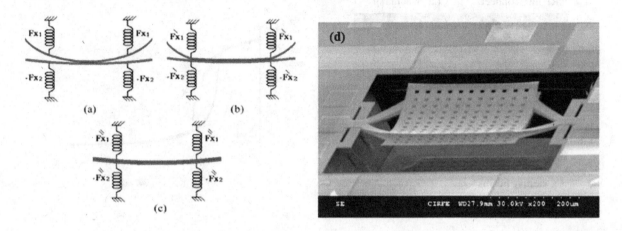

Figure 28. Simulated and measured capacitance at different bias voltage (Bakri-Kassem et al., 2008), (© [2008] IEEE). Used with permission.

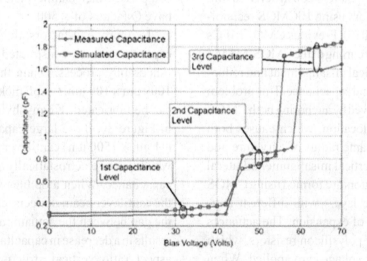

points, 50V and 60V. By applying different DC voltages to the curled-varactor, both plates adopt different curvatures and therefore different capacitance values as shown in Figure 28. Through this method, the capacitance can be varied from 0.4 to 1.8 pF with Q factors of < 500.

Lateral MEMS CMOS capacitors are usually in the form of interdigitated metal finger capacitors (MFCs). Each metal finger is formed by a composite of CMOS metal and oxide layers, and creates a vertical plate. Vertical capacitors are created when the metal fingers are placed close to each other, where the capacitance is a function of the lateral gap between the fingers. Due to their vertical structures, MFCs offer higher capacitance density compared to parallel plates. To realize varactors, two sets of MFCs are placed opposite of each other and electrothermal actuators are

Figure 29. Left micrograph of CMOS-MEMS lateral varactor. Right: Capacitance versus actuator power (Reinke et al., 2010), (© [2010] IEEE). Used with permission.

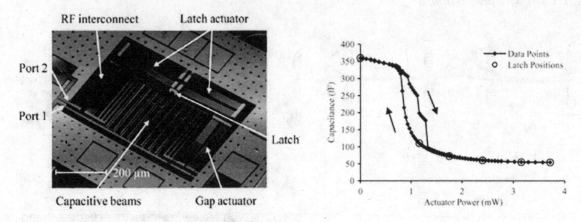

used to control the gap between them. Figure 29 illustrates an electrothermally actuated CMOS-MEMS variable capacitor constructed using metal finger capacitors using BiCMOS technology (Reinke et al., 2010). Previous CMOS MFCs have been plagued by curling of the CMOS-MEMS beams, causing vertical misalignment and reduction of overlap area and capacitance. This problem has been recently solved by anchoring both CMOS MFCs at the same location, which causes both beams to have the same radius of curvature and therefore reduced vertical misalignment. Lateral electrothermal actuators are formed using CMOS metal and dielectric layers with different temperature coefficient of expansion. The actuators are placed on top of polysilicon resistors, which act as heaters when voltages are applied. When the actuators are heated, they force the MFCs to move, causing the overlap area and the capacitance to change. The usage of electrothermal actuators allow a wide range of capacitive tuning (50 – 350 fF) at a low voltage of 0 - 3 V. This is in contrast with electrostatically actuated lateral varactors which require 30 – 70V for tuning. Figure 29 illustrates the different capacitance values at vari-

ous voltages. As expected, these lateral CMOS MEMS capacitors have lower Q factors of (< 100) compared to their parallel plate counterparts which have Q factors of < 500.

To improve Q-factors, thick vertical variable capacitors can be constructed using deep X-ray lithography process. Using this technique large 1000 μm x 100 μm, 0.9 pF nickel-gold capacitors can be fabricated (Klymyshyn et al.). As shown in Figure 30, these large capacitors have a thin (11 μm × 1500 μm) cantilever beam in the center which can be electrostatically actuated to vary the capacitance. When a dc bias voltage is applied, the cantilever beam deflects, causing a change in the gap between the actuator and the beam. This results in a decrease in capacitance. The tall, high-aspect ratio vertical structure of the moving cantilever beam allows it to be electrostatically actuated at low voltages (< 20V). Typical tuning voltages for electrostatically actuated capacitors require ~80V. A wide capacitive tuning range between 0.68 pF to 0.86 pF is reported using this structure using 0 – 20 V tuning voltage. At frequencies < 5GHz, these thick vertical varactors show impressive high Qs of < 500.

Figure 30. SEM of vertical variable capacitors (Reinke et al., 2010), (© [2010] IEEE). Used with permission.

La = Actuator
Electrode
Length
= 1.5mm

Lc = Capacitor
Electrode
Length
= 1.5mm

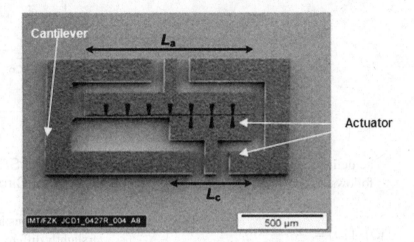

RF-MEMS-BASED OSCILLATORS

In this section, we wish to detail the implementations of MEMS devices in oscillator circuits. To function as a reference oscillator in wireless communication transceiver, the requirements of the resonator is very stringent. Quality factors have to be in the order of 10 000 and temperature stability has to be better than 35 ppm over 0°C to 70°C (Y. W. Lin et al., 2004) to compete with the existing off-chip quartz crystals. On-chip tank circuits such as spiral LC tanks and active biquads typically have Qs in the order of 100 in the frequency of interest. MEMS devices such as wine glass (Xie et al., 2008), FBAR (Campanella et al., 2008), clamped-clamped beam (Ruther et al., 2005) and SAW resonators (A. N. Nordin et al., 2007) all have Qs higher than 100s, making them a promising solution for on-chip integration.

The mechanical resonance in MEMS devices can be modeled using a series RLC circuit as shown in Figure 31 where the series resonant frequency,

$$f_s = \frac{1}{2\sqrt{LC}} \qquad (22)$$

Figure 31. General block diagram for a series-resonant oscillator (Y. W. Lin et al., 2004), (© [2004] IEEE). Used with permission.

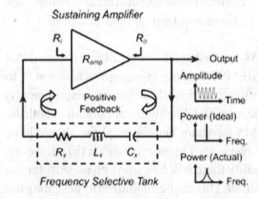

The motional resistance, R_x is related to the losses and the Q factor of the device. The sustaining amplifier acts to counteract the losses due to R_x. In general, to achieve sustained oscillation, the following conditions have to be met:

a. In accordance to (7), the loop gain of the system $\beta(j\omega)A(j\omega)$ shown in Figure 27 should be greater than 1. The loop gain can

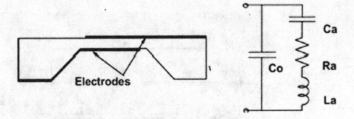

be defined with reference to Figure 27 as follows:

$$A(j\omega)^2 (j\omega) = \frac{R_{amp}}{R_i + R_o + R_x} \quad (23)$$

where R_{amp} is the gain and R_I, R_O is the input and output impedance of the amplifier respectively.

b.   The total phase shift of in the closed-feedback loop should be 0° or multiples of it.

As can be deduced from (23), it is desired that the MEMS frequency selecting tank have low R_x to relax the conditions (have low gain requirements) of the amplifier. Ideally, the phase shift of both the MEMS resonator and the amplifier should have zero phase shift to meet condition (b). However, in reality there will be a finite phase shift for the amplifier. This can be minimized by designing the amplifier bandwidth to be 10 times greater than the oscillation frequency (Y. W. Lin et al., 2004).

In this section we will first detail the oscillator circuits used for the acoustic wave resonators namely the FBARs and SAW resonators. Next, we will describe the oscillator circuits used for purely mechanical resonators such as the clamped-clamped beams and the wine glass resonators. Finally we will describe the typical techniques to design voltage controlled oscillators using MEMS devices.

FBAR and SAW Resonator Oscillator Circuits

Film bulk acoustic wave resonators (FBARs) have a slightly different equivalent circuit compared to the basic RLC circuit shown in Figure 31. Due to the structure of the FBAR (Figure 32) which consists of two electrodes sandwiching the dielectric piezoelectric material, capacitance C_0 exists between the top and bottom electrode as shown in Figure 28 (Lakin, 2005).

Similarly, SAW and lateral field-excited resonators have the input and output IDTs close to each other, which also can be modeled as a parallel feedthrough capacitor C_f or C_o which is across the series RLC as shown in Figure 18. The parallel capacitor produces the parallel resonance (f_p) which is the point of maximum loss, as opposed to the series resonance (f_s) which is the point of minimum loss of the device's frequency response as shown in Figure 33.

Having two distinct minimum and maximum values allows the designer to choose the oscillator to work at either f_s or f_p depending on the resistance values at each resonance point. The equivalent resistance at either f_s or f_p depends on their Quality factors. The Q factors of FBARs normally are in the order of 1000 (Chee et al., 2005; Zou et al.) translating to low values of resistance of less than 1 kΩ. Due to the high Q, it is not too difficult to obey (40), requiring simple feedback oscillator circuits such as Pierce oscillator as shown in Figure 13 for FBAR and 19 for

Figure 33. Frequency response of a SAW resonator with f_s and f_p (A. N. Nordin et al., 2007), (© [2007] IEEE). Used with permission.

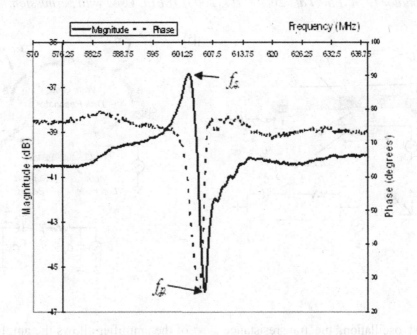

LFE resonator. This method is similar to the small-signal analysis of three-point oscillators described by Vittoz (Vittoz et al., 1988). The core of the Pierce oscillator is an inverting amplifier formed by M_1 and M_2. The combined transconductance (g_m) of both transistors M_1 and M_2 is used to counteract the losses caused by the motional resistance R_x and the parasitic capacitances C_1 and C_2 (Zuo, Sinha et al., 2010). Pierce oscillators have excellent phase noise characteristics due to the low number of transistors used (B.P. Otis, 2005). Only three transistors were used for the feedback amplifier to minimize phase noise in the circuits in the topologies shown in (Chee et al., 2005; Zuo, Van der Spiegel et al., 2010). Typical phase noise characteristics for Pierce oscillators are between -68 dBc/Hz (Zuo, Sinha et al., 2010) to −140dBc/Hz (B.P. Otis, 2005) at 1MHz offset.

Wine-Glass and Clamped-Clamped Beam Oscillator Circuits

Clamped-clamped-beam (CC-beam) micromechanical resonator has an output current due to the time-varying capacitance described in (34). Depending on the structure of the CC-beam, it also may have a parallel capacitor C_0 across the series RLC network due to the overlap of the input electrode and the CC-beam as shown in Figure 30 (Y. W. Lin et al., 2004). The wine glass disk resonator also has an output current but does not have the parallel capacitor C_0 since there are no overlapping metal structures as shown in Figure 34 (Y. W. Lin et al., 2004). Unlike FBARs, flexural mode resonators have high motional resistances, R_x, in the range of 1 kΩ to 10 kΩ. The design of feedback amplifier is not so trivial. With reference to Figure 35, transresistance amplifiers are popularly used as the feedback amplifier since it has low input R_i and output R_o impedances and does not degrade the Q of the resonator. To

Figure 34. (a) Perspective view and equivalent circuit of a clamped-clamped beam (Y. W. Lin et al., 2004)., (© [2004] IEEE). Used with permission. (b) Perspective view and equivalent circuit of a wine glass disk resonator (Y. W. Lin et al., 2004)., (© [2004] IEEE). Used with permission.

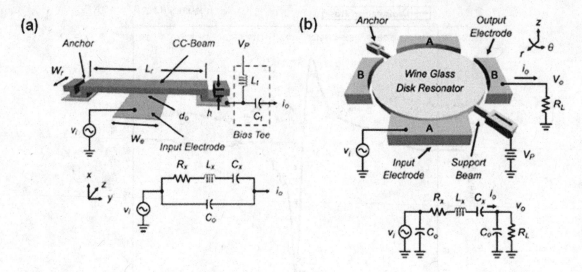

have sustained oscillation, the transresistance amplifier must have 0° phase shift and also have sufficient gain to obey (40). On top of all these conditions, it is also desirable that the complex oscillator have minimum phase noise and low power consumption.

Figure 35 illustrates a single stage transresistance amplifier that can be hooked up to either a wine glass disk or a CC-beam resonator. The amplifier is fully differential and has 180° phase shift. Connecting one of the outputs to the input

of the amplifier allows the amplifier to have an added 180° phase shift, resulting in a total of 0° phase shift from the input to the output. To obtain 0° phase shift, as a rule of thumb, the bandwidth of the amplifier should be 10x the oscillation frequency. The amplifier gain, R_{amp} is largely dependent on the feedback resistance R_f. Unfortunately, increasing R_{amp} increases the amplifier gain but decreases the bandwidth. Another method of increasing bandwidth is to decrease C_{in}. The input and output impedances (R_i and R_o)

Figure 35. Left: Schematic of single-stage transresistance amplifier. Right: ALC circuit (Y. W. Lin et al., 2004), (© [2004] IEEE). Used with permission.

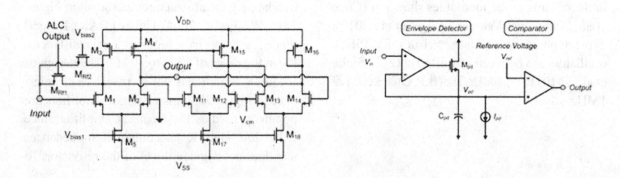

of the amplifier is proportional to the transconductance, g_m of M_1, indicating that a larger bias current through M_1 would reduce loading on the Q of the resonator. This is a performance tradeoff since larger bias current would also increase power consumption. To ensure that oscillator limiting is done using electronic methods instead of via the resonator's nonlinearity, an automatic level control (ALC) circuit was implemented. Limiting through the resonator's nonlinearity adds a $1/f^3$ phase noise component that dominates near the frequency of interest. The ALC circuit consists of an envelope detector and a comparator. The envelope detector measures the oscillation amplitude. The comparator feeds back a voltage close to V_{ref} to the mechanical resonator. This scheme effectively ensures that the oscillator has low phase noise. Measured phase noise for both the CC-beam and the wine-glass disk resonator range from -116 dBc/Hz to -147 dBc/Hz @ 100 kHz (Y. W. Lin et al., 2004).

MEMS-based Voltage Control Oscillators

In general MEMS-based oscillators produce fixed oscillation frequencies as the resonant frequencies are controlled by the device dimensions such as film thickness for FBARs and IDT spacing for SAW resonators. Tuning of MEMS-based oscillators is not as simple as tuning LC-based oscillators, where varying the voltage in a varactor can easily change the resonant frequency of the tank circuit. Most of the MEMS-based voltage controlled oscillators (VCO) are actually LC-based VCOs, where either the variable inductor or the varactor is fabricated using MEMS techniques (Chen et al., 2005; Dec et al., 2000; Sheng-Lyang et al.; Tzuen-Hsi et al., 2008). As mentioned earlier, at high radio frequencies, the skin effect of inductors are highly dominant, causing integrated inductors to have low Qs (less than 100) and are very lossy. In (Chen et al., 2005), 7μm thick MEMS Cu inductors were used instead of standard CMOS

Al inductors to improve the Q of the inductors and to achieve low phase noise. Frequency tuning of 390 MHz at 2.38 GHz is achieved using varactors and a low phase noise of -122 dBc/Hz @ 600kHz was obtained. A similar quadrature VCO using MEMS inductors was implemented in (Sheng-Lyang et al.), but instead of standard CMOS Al inductors were used, but the inductors were suspended and back-etched to remove the lossy silicon substrate. Frequency tuning of 280 MHz at 5 GHz was also achieved using varactors. This suspended L, CMOS VCO produced phase noise of -125 dBc/Hz @ 1MHz.

A different method of frequency tuning through the usage of MEMS switchable inductors was explored in (Tzuen-Hsi et al., 2008). The MEMS inductors were fabricated using the thick top metal layer in the standard CMOS process. Anisotropic and isotropic etching were performed to release the inductor from the isolating oxide layer and the silicon substrate. Adding both an NMOS switch across the inductors and also varactors in the cross-coupled VCO circuit allow a large tuning range of 470 MHz (from 5.13 GHz to 5.60 GHz). A multi-band VCO was introduced in (Zhang et al., 2008) where a differential Colpitts circuit uses MEMS switches and varactors to perform frequency tuning. The inductors and varactors are the standard integrated LCs but the MEMS switch is a CMOS-based thermally actuated bimorph beam. When voltage is applied to the switch, a polysilicon strip heats the beam and causes the beam to curl (OFF switch). The cantilever beam is a composite of Al-SiO_2-polysilicon CMOS layers which is released from the substrate through a sequence of anisotropic and isotropic reactive-ion-etching. The tuning range of this VCO was simulated to be from 1.8 GHz to 1.31 GHz.

A bulk acoustic wave (BAW) based quadrature VCO was introduced by (Rai et al., 2007). The usage of BAW instead of LC as the frequency selector is to capitalize on the high Qs of BAW devices (~1000) as opposed to Q ~ 10 of integrated LCs. To tune the resonant frequency of the BAW, a digitally controlled capacitor bank was connected at the output node of the quadrature VCO. Although the BAW has extremely high Q factors which should translate to low phase noise of the VCO, when compared to an LC implementation of the same circuit, the BAW VCO produced phase noise of -143 dBc/Hz while the LC VCO produced a phase noise of -110.7 dBc/Hz. The tuning range of the BAW VCO is also very limited to 60 kHz while the LC VCO had a tuning range of 300 MHz.

In another MEMS-based VCO, MEMS varactors fabricated using multi-user MEMS process (MUMPs) surface polysilicon micromachining technology was used to tune the VCO's frequency (Dec et al., 2000). The MEMS varactor consists of two parallel plates, where the top plate is supported by a spring while the bottom plate is fixed to the substrate. When a dc bias voltage is applied across the two plates, the top plate is attracted to the bottom plate, changing the capacitance between the two plates. For this device the maximum tuning voltage was 5 V which causes the capacitance to vary from 1.4 to 1.9 pF and translates into tuning range of 80 MHz for the 2.4 GHz VCO. The usage of MEMS varactors reduced the phase noise to -122 dBc/Hz @ 1 MHz.

CONCLUSION

This chapter has dealt with important RF-MEMS devices used in VCOs, namely resonators, inductors and varactors. Each component was described in depth, where their operation, specifications and fabrication methods are detailed. A large part of this chapter has focused on RF-MEMS resonators, which had been classified into three major categories according to their actuation methods, bulk acoustic, surface acoustic and flexural mode resonators. The advantages and disadvantages of each structure are described, with reference to the most recent work published in the field. It can be summarized that the RF-MEMS techniques will play a key role in fabrication methods of silicon compatible components. RF-CMOS components are popular amongst RF-circuit designers, but are plagued with poor performance due to the lossy silicon substrates. The usage of RF-MEMS post-processing techniques such as surface and bulk micromachining allow designers to improve the performance characteristics of purely CMOS devices. These results in RF-MEMS components which are highly silicon compatible, but have low insertion losses and high Q factors.

REFERENCES

Abidi, A., Rofougaran, A., Chang, G., Rael, J., Chang, J., Rofougaran, M., et al. (1997, 6-8 February). *The future of CMOS wireless transceivers.* Paper presented at the 1997 43rd ISSCC IEEE International Solid-State Circuits Conference, Digest of Technical Papers.

Ashby, K. B., Koullias, I. A., Finley, W. C., Bastek, J. J., & Moinian, S. (1996). High Q inductors for wireless applications in a complementary silicon bipolar process. *IEEE Journal of Solid-state Circuits, 31*(1), 4–9. doi:10.1109/4.485838

Ayazi, F., & Najafi, K. (2000). High aspect-ratio combined poly and single-crystal silicon (HARPSS) MEMS technology. *Journal of Microelectromechanical Systems, 9*(3), 288–294. doi:10.1109/84.870053

Bakri-Kassem, M., Fouladi, S., & Mansour, R. R. (2008). Novel high-Q MEMS curled-plate variable capacitors fabricated in 0.35- m CMOS technology. *IEEE Transactions on Microwave Theory and Techniques, 56*(2), 530–541. doi:10.1109/TMTT.2007.914657

Baltes, H., Brand, O., Fedder, G., Hierold, C., Korvink, J., & Tabata, O. (2005). *CMOS MEMS* (*Vol. 2*). Weinhem, Germany: Wiley-VCH.

Baltes, H., Paul, O., & Brand, O. (1998). Micromachined thermally based CMOS microsensors. *Proceedings of the IEEE, 86*(8), 1660–1678. doi:10.1109/5.704271

Bannon, F. D., Clark, J. R., & Nguyen, C. T. C. (2000). High-Q HF microelectromechanical filters. *IEEE Journal of Solid-state Circuits, 35*(4), 512–526. doi:10.1109/4.839911

Burghartz, J. N. (2001). *Tailoring logic CMOS for RF applications.* Paper presented at the VLSI Technology Systems and Applications.

Campanella, H., Cabruja, E., Montserrat, J., Uranga, A., Barniol, N., & Esteve, J. (2008). Thin-film bulk acoustic wave resonator floating above CMOS substrate. *Electron Device Letters, 29*(1), 28–30. doi:10.1109/LED.2007.910751

Chang, S., & Sivoththaman, S. (2006). A tunable RF MEMS inductor on silicon incorporating an amorphous silicon bimorph in a low-temperature process. *Electron Device Letters, 27*(11), 905–907. doi:10.1109/LED.2006.884712

Chee, Y. H., Niknejad, A. M., & Rabaey, J. (2005, 12-14 June 2005). *A sub-100 μW 1.9-GHz CMOS oscillator using FBAR resonator.* Paper presented at the Radio Frequency integrated Circuits (RFIC) Symposium, 2005, Digest of Papers.

Chen, H. C., Chien, C. H., Chiu, H. W., Lu, S. S., Chang, K. N., & Chen, K. Y. (2005). A low-power low-phase-noise LC VCO with MEMS Cu inductors. *Microwave and Wireless Components Letters, 15*(6), 434–436. doi:10.1109/LMWC.2005.850565

Dec, A., & Suyama, K. (2000). Microwave MEMS-based voltage-controlled oscillators. *IEEE Transactions on Microwave Theory and Techniques, 48*(11), 1943–1949. doi:10.1109/22.883875

Demirci, M. U., & Nguyen, C. T. C. (2005). *Single-resonator fourth-order micromechanical disk filters.* Paper presented at the IEEE Micro Electro Mechanical Systems Conference.

Deparis, N. (2008). UWB in millimeter wave band with pulsed ILO. *IEEE Transactions on Circuits and Systems II, 55*(4), 339–343. doi:10.1109/TCSII.2008.918977

Euisik, Y., & Kwang-Seok, Y. (2005, 5-9 June 2005). *Development of a wireless environmental sensor system and MEMS-based RF circuit components.* Paper presented at The 13th International Conference on Solid-State Sensors, Actuators and Microsystems, 2005, Digest of Technical Papers.

Hara, M., Kuypers, J., Abe, T., & Esashi, M. (2003). *MEMS based thin film 2 GHz resonator for CMOS integration.* Paper presented at the 2003 IEEE MTT-S International Microwave Symposium Digest.

Harrington, B. P., Shahmohammadi, M., & Abdolvand, R. (24-28 January, 2010). *Toward ultimate performance in GHZ MEMS resonators: Low impedance and high Q.* Paper presented at the 2010 IEEE 23rd International Conference on Micro Electro Mechanical Systems (MEMS).

Hassan, H., Anis, M., & Elmasry, M. (2004). *Impact of technology scaling on RF CMOS.* Paper presented at the IEEE SOC Conference

Hiroshi, I. (2004). *RF CMOS technology.* Paper presented at the IEEE Asia-Pacific Radio Science Conference.

Ho, G. K., Sundaresan, K., Pourkamali, S., & Ayazi, F. (2010). Micromechanical IBARs: Tunable High-Q resonators for temperature-compensated reference oscillators. *Journal of Microelectromechanical Systems, 19*(3), 503–515. doi:10.1109/JMEMS.2010.2044866

Huang, Q., Piazza, F., Orsatti, P., & Ohguro, T. (1998). The impact of scaling down to deep submicron on CMOS RF circuits. *IEEE Journal of Solid-state Circuits, 33*(7), 1023–1036. doi:10.1109/4.701249

Iwai, H. (2000). *CMOS technology for RF application.* Paper presented at the 22nd International Conference on Microelectronics (MIEL 2000). Klymyshyn, D. M., Borner, M., Haluzan, D. T., Santosa, E. G., Schaffer, M., Achenbach, S., et al. Vertical High-Q RF-MEMS devices for reactive lumped-element circuits. *IEEE Transactions on Microwave Theory and Techniques, 58*(11), 2976-2986.

Lakdawala, H., & Fedder, G. K. (2004). Temperature stabilization of CMOS capacitive accelerometers. *Journal of Micromechanics and Microengineering, 14.*

Lakin, K. M. (2005). Thin film resonator technology. *IEEE Transactions on Ultrasonics, Ferroelectrics, and Frequency Control, 52*(5), 707–716. doi:10.1109/TUFFC.2005.1503959

Lavasani, H. M., Wanling, P., Harrington, B., Abdolvand, R., & Ayazi, F. (2011). A 76 dB Ohm 1.7 GHz 0.18 um CMOS tunable TIA using broadband current pre-amplifier for high frequency lateral MEMS oscillators. *IEEE Journal of Solid-state Circuits, 46*(1), 224–235. doi:10.1109/JSSC.2010.2085890

Lee, D. W., Hwang, K. P., & Wang, S. X. (2008). Fabrication and analysis of high-performance integrated solenoid inductor with magnetic core. *IEEE Transactions on Magnetics, 44*(11), 4089–4095. doi:10.1109/TMAG.2008.2003398

Lin, T. H., Sanchez, H., Rofougaran, R., & Kaiser, W. J. (1998). *Micropower CMOS RF components for distributed wireless sensors.* Paper presented at the IEEE Radio Frequency Integrated Circuits (RFIC) Symposium.

Lin, Y. W., Lee, S., Li, S. S., Xie, Y., Ren, Z., & Nguyen, C. T. C. (2004). Series-resonant VHF micromechanical resonator reference oscillators. *IEEE Journal of Solid-state Circuits, 39*(12), 2477–2491. doi:10.1109/JSSC.2004.837086

Liu, J.-Q., Fang, H.-B., Xu, Z.-Y., Mao, X.-H., Shen, X.-C., & Chen, D. (2008). A MEMS-based piezoelectric power generator array for vibration energy harvesting. *Microelectronics Journal, 39*(5), 802–806. doi:10.1016/j.mejo.2007.12.017

Manku, T. (1999). Microwave CMOS-device physics and design. *IEEE Journal of Solid-state Circuits, 34*(3), 277–285. doi:10.1109/4.748178

Meyer, N. M. N. R. G. (1992). Start-up and frequency stability in high frequency oscillation. *IEEE Journal of Solid-State Circuit, 27*, 810–820. doi:10.1109/4.133172

Milanovic, V., Gaitan, M., Bowen, E. D., Tea, N. H., & Zaghloul, M. E. (1997). *Design and fabrication of micromachined passive microwave filtering elements in CMOS technology.* Paper presented at the IEEE Solid State Sensors and Actuators.

Nabki, F., Allidina, K., Ahmad, F., Cicek, P. V., & El-Gamal, M. N. (2009). A highly integrated 1.8 GHz frequency synthesizer based on a MEMS resonator. *IEEE Journal of Solid-state Circuits, 44*(8), 2154–2168. doi:10.1109/JSSC.2009.2022914

Nguyen, C. T. C. (2007). MEMS technology for timing and frequency control. *IEEE Transactions on Ultrasonics, Ferroelectrics, and Frequency Control, 54*(2), 251–270. doi:10.1109/TUFFC.2007.240

Nickel, N. H., & Terukov, E. (2005). *Zinc oxide - A material for micro and optoelectronic applications.* New York, NY: Springer. doi:10.1007/1-4020-3475-X

Nordin, A. N. (2008). *Design, implementation and characterization of temperature compensated SAW resonators in CMOS technology for RF oscillators*. Washington, DC: George Washington University.

Nordin, A. N., & Zaghloul, M. E. (2007). Modeling and fabrication of CMOS surface acoustic wave resonators. *IEEE Transactions on Microwave Theory and Techniques, 55*(5), 992–1001. doi:10.1109/TMTT.2007.895408

Okada, K., Yoshihara, Y., Sugawara, H., & Masu, K. (2005). *A dynamic reconfigurable RF circuit architecture*.

Okoniewski, M., & McFeetors, G. (2006). *Radio frequency microelectromechanical systems components*. Paper presented at the International Conference on Microwaves, Radar & Wireless Communications.

Otis, B. P. (2005). *Ultra low power wireless technologies for sensor networks*. Berkeley: University of California.

Otis, B. P., & Rabaey, J. M. (2003). A 300-/spl mu/W 1.9-GHz CMOS oscillator utilizing micromachined resonators. *IEEE Journal of Solid-state Circuits, 38*(7), 1271–1274. doi:10.1109/JSSC.2003.813219

Pakdast, H. (2008). Development and characterization of high frequency bulk mode resonators. *DTU Nanotech, June*.

Park, D., Jeong, Y., Lee, J.-B., & Jung, S. (2008). Chip-level integration of RF MEMS on-chip inductors using UV-LIGA technique. *Microsystem Technologies, 14*(9), 1429–1438. doi:10.1007/s00542-007-0532-9

Qiuting, H., Orsatti, P., & Piazza, F. (1999). GSM transceiver front-end circuits in 0.25-μm CMOS. *IEEE Journal of Solid-State Circuits, 34*(3), 292–303.

Rai, S., & Otis, B. (2007, 11-15 Feb. 2007). *A 1V 600&mu W 2.1GHz quadrature VCO using BAW resonators*. Paper presented at the Solid-State Circuits Conference, 2007. ISSCC 2007. Digest of Technical Papers. IEEE International.

Razavi, B., & Behzad, R. (1998). *RF microelectronics*. Upper Saddle River, NJ: Prentice Hall.

Rebeiz, G. M. (2003). *RF MEMS: Theory, design, and technology*. John Wiley and Sons. doi:10.1002/0471225282

Reinke, J., Fedder, G. K., & Mukherjee, T. (2010). CMOS-MEMS variable capacitors using electro-thermal actuation. *Journal of Microelectromechanical Systems, 19*(5), 1105–1115. doi:10.1109/JMEMS.2010.2067197

Ruther, P., Bartholomeyczik, J., Buhmann, A., Trautmann, A., Steffen, K., & Paul, O. (2005). Microelectromechanical HF resonators fabricated using a novel SOI-based low-temperature process. *IEEE Sensors Journal, 5*(5), 1112–1119. doi:10.1109/JSEN.2005.851009

Sanduleanu, M. A. T., Vidojkovic, M., Vidojkovic, V., Roermund, A. H. M. v., & Tasic, A. (2008). Receiver front-end circuits for future generations of wireless communications. *IEEE Transactions on Circuits and Systems II, 55*(4), 299–303. doi:10.1109/TCSII.2008.919566

Santos, H. J. d. l. (2004). *Introduction to microelectromechanical microwave systems*.

Sheng-Lyang, J., Chih-Chieh, S., Cheng-Chen, L., & Miin-Horng, J. (2010). A 0.18um CMOS quadrature VCO using the quadruple push-push technique. *IEEE Microwave and Wireless Components Letters, 20*(6), 343–345. doi:10.1109/LMWC.2010.2047525

Shi, B. (2001). *Challenges in RF analog integrated circuits*. Paper presented at the IEEE 4th International Conference on ASIC.

Steyaert, M., Borremans, M., Janssens, J., de Muer, B., Itoh, I., Craninckx, J., et al. (1998, 5-7 February). *A single-chip CMOS transceiver for DCS-1800 wireless communications.* Paper presented at the Solid-State Circuits Conference, 1998, Digest of Technical Papers. 1998 IEEE International.

Steyaert, M. S. J., De Muer, B., Leroux, P., Borremans, M., & Mertens, K. (2002). Low-voltage low-power CMOS-RF transceiver design. *IEEE Transactions on Microwave Theory and Techniques, 50*(1), 281–287. doi:10.1109/22.981281

Tasic, A., Lim, S. T., Serdijn, W. A., & Long, J. R. (2007). Design of adaptive multimode RF front-end circuits. *IEEE Journal of Solid-state Circuits, 42*(2), 313–322. doi:10.1109/JSSC.2006.889387

Tea, N. H., Milanovic, V., Zincke, C. A., Suehle, J. S., Gaitan, M., & Zaghloul, M. E. (1997). Hybrid postprocessing etching for CMOS-compatible MEMS. *Journal of Microelectromechanical Systems, 6*(4), 363–372. doi:10.1109/84.650134

Teva, J., Abadal, G., Uranga, A., Verd, J., Torres, F., Lopez, J. L., et al. (2008). *From VHF to UHF CMOS-MEMS monolithically integrated resonators.*

Tsung-Hsien, L., Kaiser, W. J., & Pottie, G. J. (2004). Integrated low-power communication system design for wireless sensor networks. *IEEE Communications Magazine, 42*(12), 142–150. doi:10.1109/MCOM.2004.1367566

Tzuen-Hsi, H., & Jay-Jen, H. (2008). 5-GHz Low phase-noise CMOS VCO integrated with a micromachined switchable differential inductor. *IEEE Microwave and Wireless Components Letters, 18*(5), 338–340. doi:10.1109/LMWC.2008.922125

van Der Tang, J., Kasperkovitz, D., & van Roermund, A. H. M. (2003). *High-frequency oscillator design for integrated transceivers*. Kluwer Academic Publishers.

Vanhelmont, F., Philippe, P., Jansman, A. B. M., Milsom, R. F., Ruigrok, J. J. M., & Oruk, A. (2006, 2-6 October). *4D-3 A 2 GHz reference oscillator incorporating a temperature compensated BAW resonator.* Paper presented at the Ultrasonics Symposium, 2006. IEEE.

Vellekoop, M. J., Nieuwkoop, E., Haartsan, J. C., & Venema, A. (1987). *A monolithic SAW physical-electronic system for sensors.* Paper presented at the IEEE Ultrasonics Symposium.

Visser, J. H., Vellekoop, M. J., Venema, A., Drift, E. d., Rek, P. J. M., & Nederhof, A. J. (1989). *Surface acoustic wave filter in ZnO-SiO2-Si layered structures.* Paper presented at the IEEE Ultrasonics Symposium.

Vittoz, E. A., Degrauwe, M. G. R., & Bitz, S. (1988). High-performance crystal oscillator circuits: Theory and application. *IEEE Journal of Solid-state Circuits, 23*(3), 774–783. doi:10.1109/4.318

Wang, J., Butler, J. E., Feygelson, T., & Nguyen, C. T. C. (2004). *1.51-GHz nanocrystalline diamond micromechanical disk resonator with material-mismatched isolating support.* Paper presented at the Micro-Electro-Mechanical Systems.

Wang, J., Ren, Z., & Nguyen, C. T. C. (2004). 1.156-GHz self-aligned vibrating micromechanical disk resonator. *IEEE Transactions on Ultrasonics, Ferroelectrics, and Frequency Control, 51*(12), 1607–1628. doi:10.1109/TUFFC.2004.1386679

Xie, Y., Li, S. S., Lin, Y. W., Ren, Z., & Nguyen, C. T. C. (2008). 1.52-GHz micromechanical extensional wine-glass mode ring resonators. *IEEE Transactions on Ultrasonics, Ferroelectrics, and Frequency Control, 55*(4), 890–907. doi:10.1109/TUFFC.2008.725

Yoshihara, Y., Sugawara, H., Ito, H., Okada, K., & Masu, K. (2004). *Reconfigurable RF circuit design for multi-band wireless chip.*

Yue, C. P., & Wong, S. S. (1998). On-chip spiral inductors with patterned ground shields for Si-based RF ICs. *IEEE Journal of Solid-state Circuits*, *33*(5), 743–752. doi:10.1109/4.668989

Zhang, S., Su, W., & Zaghloul, M. E. (2008). *Low noise multi-band voltage controlled oscillator using MEMS technology.*

Zhou, W. (2009). *Integration of MEMS resonators within CMOS technology.* Cornell.

Zou, Q., Lee, D., Bi, F., Ruby, R., Small, M., Ortiz, S., et al. *High coupling coefficient temperature compensated FBAR resonator for oscillator application with wide pulling range.*

Zuo, C., Sinha, N., Van der Spiegel, J., & Piazza, G. (2010). Multifrequency Pierce oscillators based on piezoelectric AlN contour-mode MEMS technology. *Journal of Microelectromechanical Systems*, *19*(3), 570–580. doi:10.1109/JMEMS.2010.2045879

Zuo, C., Van der Spiegel, J., & Piazza, G. (2010). 1.05-GHz CMOS oscillator based on lateral-field-excited piezoelectric AlN contour-mode MEMS resonators. *Chengjie Zuo*, 15.

KEY TERMS AND DEFINITIONS

Acoustic Wave Resonator: Acoustic wave resonator requires both a transducer (metal) and a piezoelectric membrane. Electrical excitation applied at the transducer generates traveling acoustic waves within the piezoelectric material.

Clamped-Clamped Beam Resonator: Beam resonators which are fixed at both ends and vibrates when driven using AC electrical signals.

Disk Resonator: Circular (disk shape) resonator which vibrates when driven using AC electrical signals.

Oscillator: A device that can generates a pure sinusoidal signal from no input signal other than the dc bias.

Varactor: Variable capacitors formed using parallel plates, lateral or interdigitated capacitors and vertical capacitors.

Voltage Controlled Oscillator: A variable frequency oscillator which can be tuned by applying different voltage.

Wine-Glass Resonator: Hemispherical resonator which vibrates when driven using AC electrical signals.

Chapter 7
RF–MEMS Components for Wireless Transceivers

Masoud Baghelani
Sahand University of Technology, Iran

Habib Badri Ghavifekr
Sahand University of Technology, Iran

Afshin Ebrahimi
Sahand University of Technology, Iran

ABSTRACT

The application of Micro-Electro-Mechanical-Systems (MEMS) in the fields of radio frequency and microwave is offensively spreading. Nowadays a large amount of scientists and research centers worldwide are involved with development, design, and fabrication of MEMS components for RF applications. RF-MEMS show numerous capabilities for improving the performance of RF transceivers. Their excellent features such as extremely low power consumption, low loss, simple and cheap fabrication process, the ability to work at UHF and SHF frequencies, and compatibility with standard CMOS process make them ideal devices replacing the bulky off-chip components and enhancing the performance of on-chip circuits of transceivers. Therefore they can realize the idea of a transceiver on a chip. The aim of this chapter is to provide a reader with deep information in the field of RF-MEMS, covering their current and possible applications, design, modeling, and simulation. Also their problems such as power handling, packaging, frequency extension, et cetera, are discussed. In addition, this chapter will introduce case studies in RF-MEMS area for researchers.

DOI: 10.4018/978-1-4666-0083-6.ch007

INTRODUCTION

Nowadays MEMS technology finds numerous applications in technology and science. These applications spread from everyday supplies such as toys, civil engineering monitoring, automotive industries, biotechnology, medical, energy conservation, and etc. to military and aerospace applications as both sensors and actuators. MEMS is an enabling technology for smaller device sizes, batch processing for low cost and uniform productions, distributed device placement and more precise sensing and actuating.

One of the most important research areas in the field of wireless RF transceivers is miniaturization. Miniaturization (integration) has significant benefits such as lightness, reducing the costs and improving the shape factors. For example, in the last decades, communication systems were bulky, heavy and without suitable shape and also required large batteries. But nowadays, they become small and light systems with wide variety of abilities with tiny and rechargeable batteries. These tremendous progresses are as the result of integration. But, nevertheless, there are some barriers against fully miniaturization of RF transceivers on a single chip. There are many off-chip components on the transceiver board which cannot be integrated alongside the state of the art CMOS technology, such as high Q off-chip crystals and quartz filters, high Q inductors and capacitors.

RF-MEMS is an advanced branch of MEMS technology which can provide necessary components for RF transceiver's integration. This technology introduces very high performance components such as filters, switches, inductors and varactors which all are capable of integration alongside CMOS transistors and hence can realize monolithic RF transceivers.

This chapter is organized as follows; the next section introduces RF-MEMS components where the most important components such as resonators, switches, inductors and varactors are discussed. The third section is concerning RF-MEMS ap-

plications in wireless transceivers and describes some RF building blocks realizable by MEMS technology such as filters, mixer-filters, oscillators and VCOs, switchable filters and duplexers followed by a conclusion in the last section.

RF-MEMS COMPONENTS

RF-MEMS Resonators

Because micro-electro-mechanical resonators exhibit some degrees of order of Q more than their electrical counterparts, could be excellent alternatives in today and next generation wireless systems. Due to recent progresses in MEMS technology, their working frequencies extended from 1KHz to several GHz. RF MEM resonators are categorized to several classes according to their resonating frequencies.

Types of Resonators

Comb-Drive Resonators

One of the earliest surface micromachined resonator designs is comb-drive resonator (Nguyen, 1995, 1999). This resonator comprises of two electrostatic comb structures, one working as sensor and another as actuator, Figure 1. The structure is biased by a DC voltage source applied on its anchors and therefore constructs a DC – biased variable capacitor. An AC voltage applied on its input port causes a relatively linear movement along its fingers. This movement causes variation in the biased capacitor which in turn produces an output current which itself can be translated to voltage by a trans – impedance amplifier. The output current formulation is as follows:

$$i_{out} = \frac{dQ}{dt} = \frac{d(CV)}{dt} = V_{DC}\frac{dC}{dt} = V_{DC}\frac{\partial C}{\partial x}\cdot\frac{\partial x}{\partial t}.$$

$$(1)$$

Figure 1. A typical comb driven resonator

Figure 1. A typical comb driven resonator

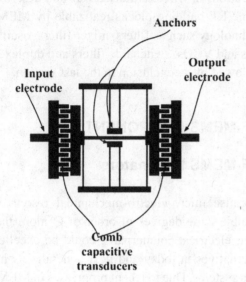

Figure 2. A typical frequency response of the resonator shown in Figure 1

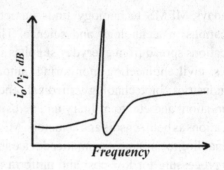

This equation is applicable to all electrostatic actuated RF-MEMS resonators. If the exciting frequency be far from the resonator's natural frequency (or on the other word "resonance frequency") of the resonator, the term $\frac{\partial x}{\partial t}$ and hence the output current is very small and negligible for lots of applications. But, when the exciting frequency is equal to the resonance frequency of the resonator, the structure will resonate with relatively large amplitude and hence produce a strong output current. Figure 2 sketches a typical output spectrum of such a resonator.

Resonance frequency of these resonators is calculates by (Nguyen 1999):

$$f_r = \frac{1}{2\pi} \sqrt{\frac{K_{tot}}{m_p + 0.25 m_c + 0.34 m_b}}. \qquad (2)$$

Where K_{tot} is the system's spring constant, m_p is the mass of shuttle, m_c is the mass of connector, and m_b is the mass of spring beams where their formulations can be found in some technical papers (Jing et al., 2002), (Ong et al., 2007). Resonance frequency of such devices starts from

1KHz and is limited to less than 20MHz (Tang et al., 1990; Wang et al., 1999), with quality factors more than 50000 in vacuum, but due to their low resonance energy, when working in air, the air damping decrease their Q to less than 100! Thus vacuum packaging is essential to commercialize these resonators.

Beam Resonators

Clamped-clamped resonators are actually guitar strings which are scaled down to μm dimensions to achieve several MHz frequencies. Their working frequencies range from 10KHz (MF range) (Pourkamali et al., 2003) up to 100MHz (VHF range) (Nguyen, 2002) sustaining Q in the order of several thousands. Their resonating energy is more than comb-drive resonators so their Q in air is still considerable (Bannon et al., 1996). According to their clamping status, beam resonators branch to two major categories: Clamped- clamped (C-C) and free-free (F-F) beam resonators. C-C beam resonators can provide Q's in the range of 10000 in HF frequencies. But they suffer from anchor losses in higher frequencies e.g. in VHF range (Nguyen, 2000). Figure 3 illustrates a typical C-C beam resonator. The structure is a suspended beam with both ends anchored (clamped) to the substrate. A DC biasing voltage is applied to its anchors by an inductive coupling to bias the variable capacitor and isolates DC from HF circuits. The exciting AC electrode is placed underneath the beam and

Figure 3. A simple clamped – clamped beam resonator

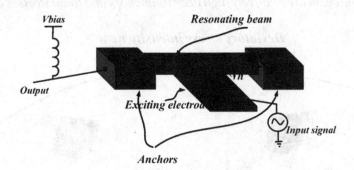

constructs a pre – DC – biased capacitor alongside with beam structure.

Like comb-drive resonators, when input frequency is far from the natural frequency of the beam, the structure moves slightly in perpendicular direction and according to equation (1) produces a negligible output current which passes through the anchor which connected to the output. When the exciting frequency is equal to the resonance frequency of the beam, the structure's movement is amplified by the Q of the beam and produces a strong current. The resonance frequency of such a structure is calculated as below (Nguyen, 2000):

$$f_0 = \frac{1}{2\pi}\sqrt{\frac{K_m}{m_r}} = 1.03\kappa\sqrt{\frac{E}{\rho}}\cdot\frac{h}{L^2}. \qquad (3)$$

Where K_m and m_r denote stiffness and effective mass of the resonator at the beam's center location respectively. E and ρ are respectively the Young modulus and density of structural material, and h and L_r are specified in Figure 3. Finite element analysis (FEA) shows considerable stresses near the anchor of these resonators which cause increasing the insertion loss and therefore decreasing the Q. This problem becomes more critical when we want to scale the beam down to achieving higher frequencies. Hence C-C beam resonators are not suitable for up VHF and UHF ranges, see Figure 4.

For overcoming this problem, another branch of beam resonators was introduced. Called F-F beam resonators, are beam resonators which their anchors are located at their nodal vibration points. Nodal points are points at which the movement of the structure is zero. Hence they are virtually suspended without anchor, Figure 5. Instead of this characteristic, F-F beams have similar operation to C-C beams. Figure 6 shows FEA for a typical F-F beam resonator. The whole structure has four nodal points. Four supporting strings are connected to these nodal points and effectively isolate the resonator from anchors. The resonator works in flexural mode. Due to attaching supporting beams to completely nodal points, F-F resonator exhibit several times of Q more than C-C beams with comparable stiffness (Wang et al., 2000; Demirci et al., 2003; Ferguson et al., 2005). Also, due to decreasing of the anchor losses, the resonance frequency of such resonators can extend toward VHF range.

Disk and Ring-Shaped Resonators

A preliminary work which can be done to increase the resonance frequency of RF-MEMS resonators is scaling down which lowers the effective mass, and hence increase the frequency due to the principal equation of mechanical resonators:

$$f_r = \frac{1}{2\pi}\sqrt{\frac{K}{m}} \qquad (4)$$

Figure 4. FEA analysis of a beam clamped at its ends. As shown the deviatory stresses, which cause decreasing the Q of the beam are relatively high near its anchors and these stresses arise with frequency

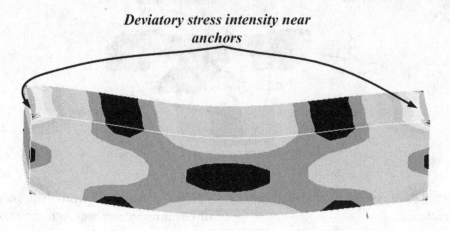

Deviatory stress intensity near anchors

Figure 5. Free-free beam resonator

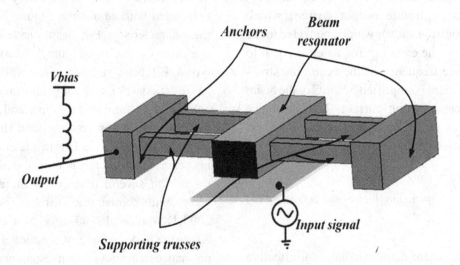

Vbias

Output

Anchors

Beam resonator

Input signal

Supporting trusses

But unfortunately, this approach in addition to technological difficulties has other drawbacks such as environmental sensitivity (due to ultra low weight structure), power handling abilities, insertion loss increasing and etc. Another method is changing the structural material from polysilicon to materials with more acoustic velocities such as silicon carbide (Huang et al., 2003; Azevedo et al., 2007) and poly-crystalline diamond (Butler et al., 2004; Gurbuz et al., 2005). This approach

encountered with high price, expensive technology and less compatibility with standard CMOS techniques. The other method for frequency extension of resonators is use of resonators in their high stiffness mode shapes. Hence, according to their ultra high stiff structures, contour mode disk and wine-glass resonators are excellent candidates for this purpose. Contour mode disk and wine glass mode resonators have been extensively studied in recent years (Clark et al., 2000; Piazza et al.,

Figure 6. FEA analysis of a typical F-F beam resonator. As shown, there are very small stresses on the attaching points because of the connections provided at the nodal points of the beam

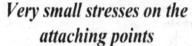

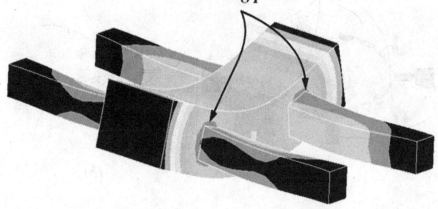

2006; Piazza et al., 2007; Stephanou et al., 2007; Baghelani et al., 2010). These resonators have been designed from VHF toward up UHF frequencies. They exhibit Q's more than 10000 even in GHz ranges. Contour mode disk resonators (CMDR) with polycrystalline diamond and piezoelectric structural materials are also fabricated and tested (Butler et al 2004).

Figure 7 illustrates a typical wine – glass resonator (WGR) and the modal analysis results by FEA. It can be seen that, there are four nodal points on the perimeter of the WGR structure which can be considered as anchor locations. WGRs have relatively small output impedance in comparison with other resonators (Wang et al., 2004). The resonance frequency of these resonators can be calculates from (Johnson, 1983);

$$\left[\Psi_n\left(\frac{\zeta}{\xi}\right) - n - q\right]\left[\Psi_n(\xi) - n - q\right] = (nq - n)^2 \tag{5}$$

$$q = \frac{\zeta}{n^2 - 2} \tag{6}$$

$$\zeta = 2\pi f_0 R \sqrt{\frac{\rho(2 + 2\nu)}{E}} \tag{7}$$

$$\xi = \sqrt{\frac{2}{1 - \nu}}, \qquad n = 2 \tag{8}$$

Where Ψ is a modified Bessel function quotient. Disk and WGR resonators have been fabricated to work at frequencies up to 1.5GHz.

Another structure which can work in UHF frequencies with high Q is CMDR. Figure 8(a) shows a CMDR anchored at its nodal point (center of the disk). The DC voltage is applied to its anchor and biases the surrounding capacitors. When an AC signal is applied to the input electrode with equal frequency to natural frequency of the disk, the structure will resonate in its contour mode and expand and contract periodically and produce an output current in the output electrode according to equation (1). The resonance frequency of such resonators is calculated from (Johnson 1983);

$$J_0\left(\frac{\zeta}{\xi}\right) = 1 - \nu \tag{9}$$

Figure 7. A typical wine glass mode resonator, the excitation schematic (a) and the FEA analysis of the mode shape (b)

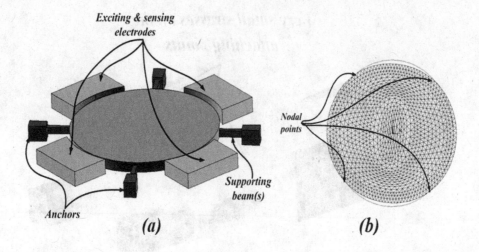

(a) *(b)*

Figure 8. (a) The perspective view of a typical disk micro resonator; (b) and Contour plots of a disk vibrating in second radial contour mode (Baghelani & Ghavifekr, 2010)

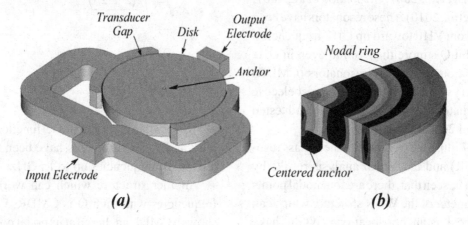

(a) *(b)*

$$\zeta = 2\pi f_0 R \sqrt{\frac{\rho(2 + 2\nu)}{E}} \qquad (10)$$

$$\xi = \sqrt{\frac{2}{1 - \nu}} \qquad (11)$$

Where R, E, v and ρ are disk radius, Young modulus, Poisson coefficient, and material density, respectively. $J_0(.)$ is Bessel function of zero order and f_0 is the resonance frequency. For at-

taining even more frequencies we can use higher modes, e.g. second mode (Clark et al., 2005), which is shown in Figure 8(b). In this mode there is a nodal ring instead of a nodal point, which can be considered as the anchor location. Also, the central area of the disk can be removed to some extent; we will calculate the exact value of removable central area. By these changes, new structure is achieved which is shown in Figure 9 (Baghelani & Ghavifekr, 2010). The resonance frequency of this device can be calculated as below:

Figure 9. (a) The ring shape anchored CMDR; (b) and the contour plot of its resonance mode (Baghelani & Ghavifekr, 2010)

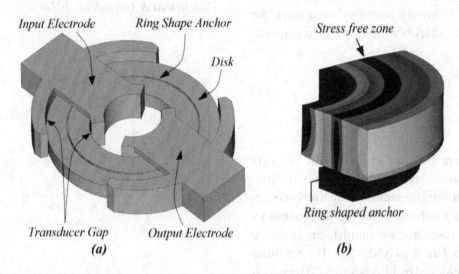

(a)

(b)

$$r^2 \frac{d^2 R(r)}{dr^2} + rv \frac{dR(r)}{dr} + \left(k_r^2 r^2 - v \right) R(r) = 0$$

(12)

$$k_r = 2\pi f_r \sqrt{\frac{\rho_0 \left(1 - v^2 \right)}{E}}$$

(13)

Although their very high Q's in frequencies spreading from MF to UHF, RF-MEMS resonators suffer from some non-idealities such as their relatively high output impedance which is still too high to be used in standard wireless systems, spurious modes which can be very close to desired mode and can affect the operation of resonator (Baghelani & Ghavifekr, 2009), and reliability problems of a micrometer dimension structures which expands and contracts several million to more than one billion times per second and is anchored only by very thin stems. Researchers are going on to overcome these non-idealities. Table 1 summarizes the operation frequencies of RF-MEMS resonators.

Table 1. Operating frequencies range of different RF-MEMS resonators

Resonator type	Frequency range
Comb-drive	LF – MF
Clamped-clamped beam	MF – HF
Free-free beam	MF – VHF
Square shaped	HF – high VHF
Wine glass mode disk	HF – UHF
Contour mode disk	HF – UHF

Design Example

Here we prepare a design example of a resonator for a specific application and describe design procedure step-by-step. We want to design a resonator to be used in GSM receiving band (935-960 MHz (Razavi, 1998)) for example 940MHz. Because of its excellent reliability and ability to work in GHz frequencies with relatively large dimension, we choose ring shape anchored resonator (Baghelani & Ghavifekr, 2010). We should work with equations (8 and 9 by choosing a proper value for inner radius. The higher the value of the inner radius, the lower the output resistance but closer spurious modes. So, we should choose it as moderate value e.g. 12μm. Now, by solving equations (8) and (9), by following boundary conditions, the outer radius and anchor location are determined:

$$\begin{cases} R\left(r_{in}\right) = R_0 \\ \left.\dfrac{dR(r)}{dr}\right|_{r=r_{in}} = 0 \end{cases} \tag{14}$$

Results are sketched in Figure 10. The first minimum value is outer radius which is 16.8μm. Anchor location is the radius where $R(r)$ becomes zero (14.4μm). After determining the dimensions of designed resonator, we simulate the structure by a FEA tool such as ANSYS®. The resulting frequency achieved by FEA is 938.87MHz which deviates just 0.12% from analytical approach. This difference comes from neglecting the anchor width in analytical solution.

RF-MEMS Switches

Electrical signal paths are controlled by different types of switches in many applications. But RF and microwave applications require special switches which must be able to control both phase and frequency in addition to signal path. Traditional solid state switches such as FET transistors and PIN diodes are less applicable in such ultra high frequencies due to their insertion losses (Rebeiz, 2003).

Methods of Switching

Progressively miniaturizing the communication systems and military radars need smaller switches with less power consumption. According to their excellent characteristics, RF-MEMS switches are inimitable candidates for these applications. In accordance with the method of their placement in the circuit, RF-MEMS switches are categorized to two classes: shunt and series.

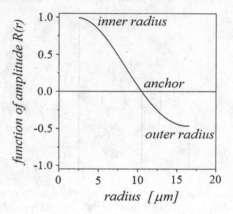

Figure 10. Determining the dimensions of the desired resonator from equations (8), (9) and (14) (Baghelani & Ghavifekr, 2010)

MEMS Shunt Switches

Shunt switches are placed in shunt with the signal path as shown in Figure 11a. The structure is a sustained bridge which connects to the circuit's ground over the transmission line. An electrode is located beneath the structure. When a DC voltage is applied to the beneath electrode, an electrostatic force is generated and tries to pull the bridge down to the waveguide. If the applied force is strong enough, the upper bridge is pulled down and connects the transmission line to the ground. Figure 11b illustrates the equivalent circuit of a shunt switch.

MEMS Series Switches

The operation of MEM series switches is similar to shunt counterparts instead of the placement the switch as a part of transmission line. Hence the structure is often a sustained cantilever anchored at one (both) end(s), Figure 12a. The equivalent circuit of a series switch is shown in Figure 12b.

Regardless of their connection being series or shunt, MEM switches are clustered to two categories according to the type of their contacts: direct or capacitive.

Figure 11. (a) Schematic of a typical shunt switch; (b) Equivalent circuit of a shunt switch

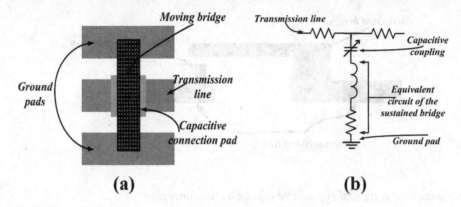

(a)　　　　**(b)**

Figure 12. (a) Schematic of a typical series switch; (b) Equivalent circuit of a series switch

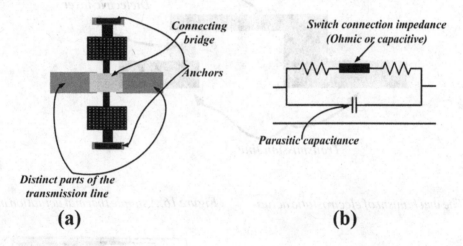

(a)　　　　**(b)**

Direct Contact MEMS Switches

In the direct contact or so called Ohmic contact RF MEM switches, as obvious from their name, the contact between movable sustained part and transmission line is provided by direct metallic connection, Figure 13. Therefore they can work from DC to microwave frequencies (Wang et al., 2006; Lee et al., 2007).

Capacitive Contact MEMS Switches

In this kind of MEM switches, a dielectric layer is deposited between metallic connectors form a capacitor, Figure 14. In microwave and RF fre-

quencies, signal's energy is coupled between them through the resulting capacitor. Hence their low operation frequencies limited by capacitance and hence this kind of switches cannot work below RF frequencies (Gue et al., 2003).

Different Activation Mechanisms of RF-MEMS Switches

RF-MEMS switches use various excitation methods such as electrostatic, thermal, magnetic, piezoelectric and etc. these mechanisms are described in following.

Figure 13. Schematic of a typical direct (metallic or Ohmic) connection

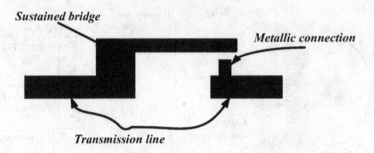

Figure 14. Schematic of a typical capacitive (dielectric) connection

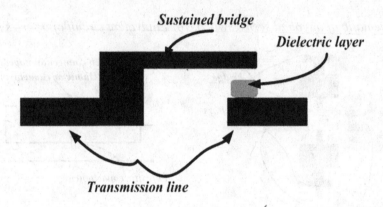

Figure 15. The mechanism of electrostatic actuation

Figure 16. A simple thermal actuation mechanism

Electrostatic Excitation

The most popular method for exciting RF-MEMS switches is electrostatic. This method is based on the generated energy in the result of an applied electrical voltage between fixed and movable electrodes. When this energy is strong enough, the movable electrode pulled down to fixed one and establishes either capacitive or Ohmic contact, depending on the contact mechanism. When the actuating energy is removed restoring energy, which stored in the holding springs, returns the movable electrode back to its *resting* position. Figure 15 illustrates the mechanism of electrostatic actuation (Chen et al., 2007).

Thermal Actuation

Despite thermal – mechanical mechanisms are mostly used for sensing applications; they also can be used for actuation. Figure 16 shows a simple thermal actuation mechanism. As shown, there are

Figure 17. Electromagnetic excitation mechanism

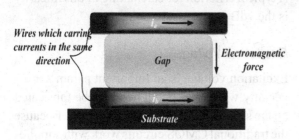

Figure 18. Piezoelectric excitation mechanism, before applying voltage (top) and after applying voltage (bottom)

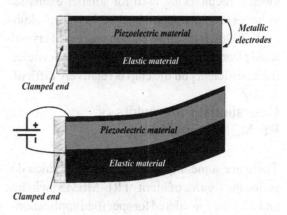

thin and thick arms placed in series with control voltage. The thin arm has more resistance than the thick one, therefore passing the same current through them causes more heat in the thin arm. Then, the thin arm (hot arm) tries to expand more than the thick arm (cold arm). Because they join together at their end, the structure bends toward the thick arm. This bending could be used for various applications such as switching.

Another approach is use of bi – material with different expansion coefficients. When these layers become hot, the layer with larger expansion coefficient tries to expand more while the other one resists, hence the structure bends toward the layer with smaller expansion coefficient.

Various designs for thermal actuators are available with the ability to be displaced in several directions (Zelinski, 2001).

Magnetic Excitation

According to the Ampere low, when two conductors carry currents in the same directions in the presence of magnetic field, an absorbent force is produced which depends directly to the current of conductors and inversely proportional to their distances. This mechanism can perform as a switch as illustrated in Figure 17. The external magnetic field can be realized on-chip by on-wafer integrated magnets (Hartley et al., 2008).

Piezoelectric Excitation

Piezoelectric materials produce electrical charges in the result of applying mechanical stress and

inversely mechanical strain in the result of applying electrical field. Piezoelectric material is sandwiched between two thin film layers construct an actuator. When an electrical field applied (Figure 18), a voltage related deformation is yelled which can be used in various applications e.g. switching (Lee et al., 2007).

Characteristics of Excitation Methods

There are two important subjects associated with electrostatic actuated RF-MEMS switches: excitation voltage and lifetime. High excitation voltages result in more charge trapping which shorten the lifetime. On the other hand, low excitation voltages need springs with low stiffness (loose springs) which may cause the switch breakdown in the operation time. Hence, if one can design an electrostatic excitation method with low excitation voltage and more reliability, electrostatic actuation will be the best method.

In thermal actuators, the excitation power is more than the other methods. The speed of such actuators is specified by thermal time constant and therefore these actuators have slower dynamics. But, this method doesn't suffer from static electrical charge problems and doesn't require high actuating voltages. The excitation power for electromagnetic actuated switches is considerably more than the electrostatic method which limited the application of this kind of excitations. Piezoelectric methods are used for smaller excitation voltages in comparison with the others (Kawakubo et al., 2006), but the fabrication process of crystallized piezoelectric materials with large piezoelectric coefficients on the chip is relatively difficult.

Operational Parameters of RF-MEMS Switches

There are some important parameters which describe the figures of merit of RF-MEMS switches and must be considered for specified applications.

Isolation

Isolation is a criterion which determines the power leakage from one port to another. This leakage could be caused by capacitive coupling, conductive losses of the surface or mismatch resulting losses.

Insertion Loss

Insertion loss is the dissipated power by the switch in its "on" state. This power is calculated by the ratio of the input power to the output power and is expressed by dB.

Transition Time

Transition time is a touch store of the speed and determines the consumed time by the switch to change its state.

Switching Rate

Switching time is the needed time for a complete switching cycle including the time taken by the switch to response to the control signal. Switching time is always longer than the transition time (Varadan et al., 2002).

Power Control

Determines the maximum tolerable RF input power, while the output power follows it linearly.

A typical criterion for calculating of this linearity is the 1dB compression point.

Excitation Voltage

Excitation voltage is an important parameter especially when the switch needs to be fabricated on the same chip with transistor circuits. Because the traditional CMOS circuits work with supplies less than 2V, large voltages required for actuation of RF-MEMS switches are provided by charge pump circuits.

Impedance Matching

Impedance matching is a prominent subject for all RF circuits. The switch must be matched in its both ports with the impedance of its preceding and succeeding stages.

Bandwidth

The traditional bandwidth description is the frequency range between the upper and lower 3dB frequencies, which is not a useful statement for switches. Cut–off frequency is a more admissible concept for describing the frequency operation of switches and demonstrates the frequency where the ratio of off – state to on – state impedances falls to unity. The cut – off frequency for RF-MEMS switches is more than 9000GHz which is more than 10 times of its FET and PIN diode counterparts.

Reliability

Reliability or lifetime is another important parameter of switches which is more considered in recent years (Chan et al., 2003; Matmat et al., 2009). Lifetime is denoted by billions switching cycles and is in the order of hundred billions for RF-MEMS switches.

Self Resonance Frequency

Like any mechanical structures, RF-MEMS switches have natural frequencies and if the frequency of high power RF signal is equal to that

Figure 19. The schematic of the designed switch (Mahmoudi et al., 2010)

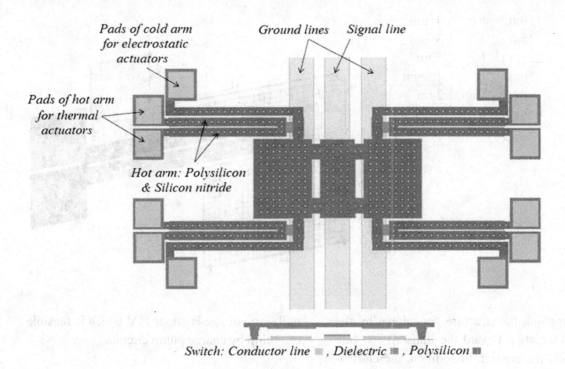

Switch: Conductor line ■ *, Dielectric* ■ *, Polysilicon* ■

resonance frequency, the structure may resonates and even unwanted pull – downs may occurred. Therefore this effect must be considered during designing a switch for a certain frequency and application.

Switch Sticking as the Result of High Power RF Frequencies

If the power of RF signal is strong enough, this phenomenon can taken place. When a switch pulls down as the consequence of DC control signal, if the power of RF signal is high enough, while removing the DC control, the RF signal may absorb the bridge and not let it go up by supporting springs. This phenomenon is called RF sticking and must be considered in high power RF applications. The supporting springs must be stiff enough to be able to evoke the bridge when DC control is removed, but not so stiff to need very high DC voltage for pulling down.

Design Example

As mentioned before, RF-MEMS switches have very wide frequency ranges and could work in all their frequency bands without any problems (which is in opposition with narrow band resonators).

Due to its long life, less charge accumulation and relatively low actuation voltages, electro – thermal mechanism is selected. The sample switch designed in (Mahmoudi et al., 2010) is considered here. Figure 19 illustrates its schematic of the mentioned switch. The switch is completely symmetric and hence its ¼ structure can be used for simplifying the simulations.

As one can see, its springs are like the one shown in Figure 17 with little modifications. The switch's arms are anchored at their ends and constructed from polysilicon and silicon – nitride layers to form bi-material structure with different thermal expansion coefficients. When a DC volt-

Figure 20. The schema of ¼ of the designed structure and related dimensions (Mahmoudi et al., 2010)

L_4	15µm	h_4	45µm
L_5	215µm	h_5	35µm
L_6	225µm	h_6	5µm
L_7	25µm	h_7	100µm
W_{switch}	2µm	Gap	2µm
W_{cond}	0.5µm	K	4.6N/µm

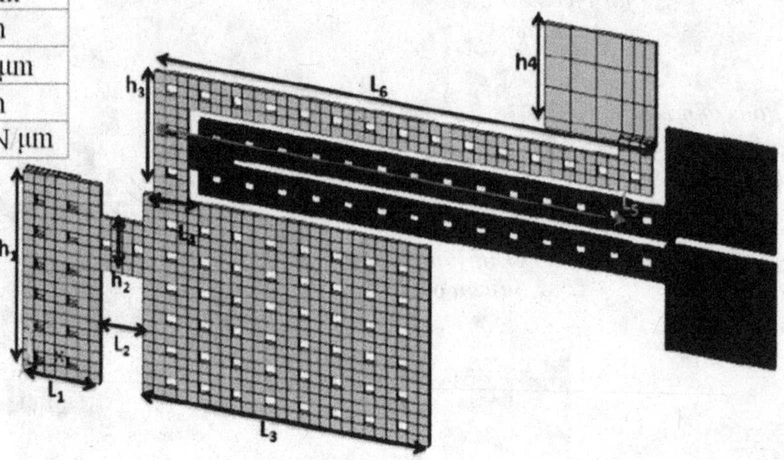

age is applied, the structure goes down by the thermal actuation toward the transmission line and closes the contact. In addition, the electrostatic actuation is applied to making the closing process much faster. After closing the switch, applied voltage is removed from thermal arms which reduce the power consumption, and electrostatic force holds the switch closed. For releasing the switch and opening the contact, it is enough to remove the electrostatic force.

Figure 20 shows the ¼ schema of the designed switch. The holes of the structure are created to reduce the coupling between the transmission line and the switch and increasing the isolation. Also, these holes ease the releasing of the beneath sacrificial layer in the fabrication process. To prevent the sticking, the width of the contacting plane is selected greater than that of the transmission line. FEA analysis is shown in Figure 21.

Another important parameter which must be considered is the natural frequency of the switch which must be very far from the operating frequency (e.g. near 1GHz for GSM). From the modal analysis the natural frequency of the designed switch is calculated as about 35KHz which satisfies the above condition, as well. Required

pull – in voltage is about 11V which is feasible on – chip by charge pump circuits.

RF-MEMS Inductors

Paying attention to a typical wireless transceiver, one can easily find out that lots of inductors are used in that circuit. Inductors are basic electronics components with the least compatibility for integration alongside CMOS transistors (Gijs et al., 2006). In addition to compatibility with CMOS transistors, the state – of – the art RF transceivers need inductors with high inductance values, high quality factors and very high self resonance frequencies. Traditional on – chip inductors have relatively very high self – resonance frequencies, but they have large losses and therefore low Q (less than 10!) and also have low inductance values (less than 20nH) (Wu et al., 2003). Due to its ability for building astonishing structures, MEMS technology can give a hand to help the CMOS technology for improving its performance by introducing RF-MEMS inductors. MEMS inductors have been designed and fabricated in various frequency ranges with excellent specifications (Weon et al., 2007; Tseng et al., 2007). We

Figure 21. Displacement contour plot of the switch after achievement of the contact (Mahmoudi et al., 2010)

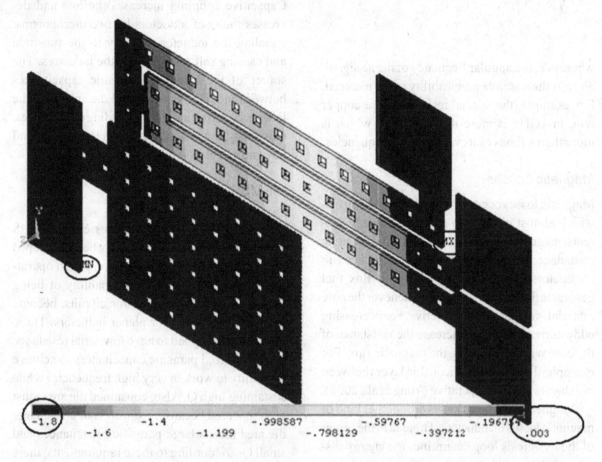

start this concept by studying the loss mechanisms in solid state on – chip inductors.

Loss Mechanisms in On – Chip Inductors

Ideal inductor is a basic electrical component which can store the energy by a magnetic field built in its coil with infinity quality factor. But real inductors suffer from some dissipation such as resistive and capacitive losses which decrease the Q of the inductors.

Ohmic Losses

Inductors are typically constructed by windings which their structural material is copper and hence

their Ohmic (resistive) losses are negligible in DC frequencies (the special resistance of copper in these frequencies is about $2\mu\Omega$cm). By increasing the frequency, due to skin effect, the resistance of inductors is increased which causes more losses decreasing the Q. The special resistance of a conductor for alternative currents is:

$$\rho_{ac} = \frac{\rho_{dc}}{\delta}, \tag{15}$$

where ρ_{dc} is the special resistance at zero frequency, and δ is a quantity called skin depth and calculated from:

171

$$\delta = \sqrt{\frac{2\rho}{\omega\mu}}, \qquad (16)$$

where ω is the angular frequency of the ac signal, and μ is the absolute permeability of the material. For example, the special resistance of a copper wire in 1GHz is more than $8.8\mu\Omega$cm which is more than 4 times of its value in low frequencies.

Magnetic Losses

Magnetic losses occur through three mechanisms which almost all refer to core losses; eddy currents, magnetic hysteresis losses ad ferromagnetic resonance losses. Eddy currents are induced in conductors to oppose the changes in flux that generates them. The loss occurs whenever the core material is electrically conductive. For decreasing eddy currents, one can increase the resistance of the core without affecting the magnetic flux. For example, deposition of silicon thin layers between iron layers could be operative (Yong et al., 2008).

Magnetic hysteresis losses are another kind of magnetic losses in inductors. The area in the center of the hysteresis loop determines the energy dissipated as heat. The last class of magnetic losses is referred to ferromagnetic resonant losses, and is as the result of permeability dropping in high frequencies. The resonance frequency is:

$$\omega_{res} = 2\pi f_{res} = \frac{2\gamma K_1}{\mu_0 M_s}, \qquad (17)$$

where K_1 is anisotropy constant, γ is the gyromagnetic constant and M_s is the saturation magnetization.

As said, all magnetic loss mechanisms occur in the core which is essential for attaining high value inductors, therefore inductors with magnetic core may not be suitable for UHF frequencies and higher.

Capacitive Coupling Losses

Capacitive coupling increases the loss and decreases the Q of inductors by two mechanisms: coupling the inductor's energy to the substrate and causing self resonance of the inductors. The source of the former is parasitic capacitances between inductor's metals and the substrate, the latter occurred by inductor's winding capacitances. Obviously, both occurred in high frequencies and have no effect in low frequency operations.

MEMS Inductors

According to enormous progresses in MEMS technology, MEMS inductors have been developed with high Qs, high values and very high operating frequencies, and due to capability of being integrated alongside transistor circuits, become suitable alternatives for planar inductors. These devices are designed to have low serial resistance and minimized parasitic capacitances to achieve the ability to work in very high frequencies while sustaining high Q. Also, consumed die area must be considered because, regardless of costs, large die area means large parasitic capacitances and small Qs. According to these requirements, there are several methods for design and fabrication of MEMS inductors for specific applications.

A useful method for increasing the Q of inductors is employing thick metals to decrease the resistive losses and isolation of the inductor by a thick polyamide layer from the substrate to reduce parasitic capacitances and hence increase the self resonance frequency (Figure 22). For inductors which wanted to work in microwave frequencies, substrate etching technique is appropriate. KOH anisotropic etching is almost a favorite etching technique due to its simplicity and efficiency. Substrate etching reduces parasitic capacitances by a significant factor and therefore pushes the resonance frequency to high microwave frequencies, see Figure 23.

Figure 22. The schematic of a MEMS inductor utilizing thick metal method

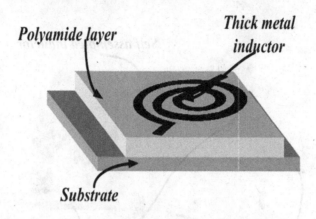

Figure 23. The schematic of a substrate etched MEMS inductor

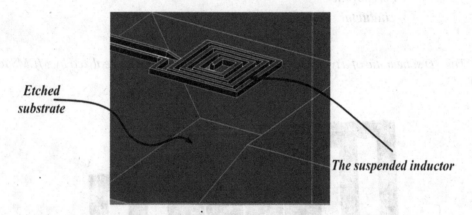

Self assembly technique is another method for construction of MEMS inductors. This method is based on creating a residual stresses during fabrication. When preventing sacrificial oxide layers are released, these residual stresses make the structure to be self–assembled above the substrate (Figure 24).

By restriction of a magnetic field inside a solenoid type welding, one can achieve higher inductance values (Figure 25). Even larger inductances could be attained by using a metallic core inside that solenoid. The fabrication process of these types of MEMS inductors is relatively expensive because of the need for direct laser lithography processes.

Overall, our requirements such as inductance value, maximum quality factor, operating frequency and etc. determine the inductor's type. For example, thick copper electroplating method is suitable for 0.2 – 5GHz, elevated inductors are good for small inductances but high frequencies and substrate etching is preferred when the operating frequency is increased. Table 1 summarizes different methods and their specifications.

RF-MEMS Varactors

One of the most important building blocks in RF transceivers is Voltage Controlled Oscillator (VCO) which determines the overall performance of the transceiver. In VCOs, the oscillation fre-

Figure 24. The schematic of a self – assembled inductor

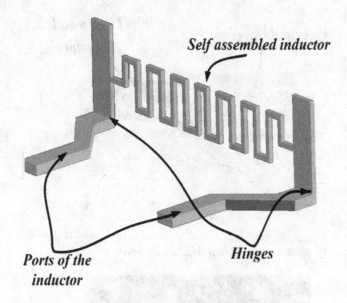

Figure 25. The 3D schematic of a typical solenoid type on – chip inductor realized by MEMS technology

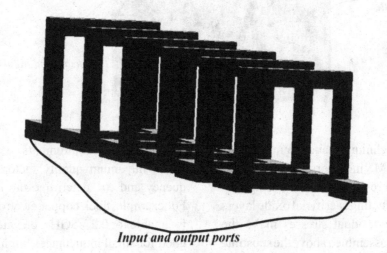

Table 1. Summarizing the specification of different MEMS inductors

Method	Operating frequency	Typical inductor size	Q
Thick metal (Pinel et al., 2003)	0.2 – 6GHz	<50j	20 – 50
Substrate etching (Tseng et al., 2007)	1 – 40GHz	<900j	10 – 50
Self assembling (Dahlmann et al., 2001)	2 – 20GHz	<60j	3 – 20
Solenoid (Gao et al., 2006)	1 – 10GHz	<120j	20 – 40
Elevated (Yoon et al., 1999)	1 – 7GHz	<100j	20 – 50

quency is controlled by the resonance frequency of their LC tank. Changing in resonance frequency is mostly performed by change in tank's variable capacitor called varactor.

Traditional varactors are inverse biased PN junctions, MOS transistors in their inversion mode and MOS transistors in accumulation mode where, inversion mode MOS varactors are most common because of their compatibility with CMOS fabrication technology (Musah, 2005).

The most important characteristic of varactors is tuning in the effect of applied control voltage which determines the ability to change the tank's resonance frequency and finally the dynamic range of VCO. Tuning is stated by capacitance ratio which is calculated as follows:

$$CR = \frac{C_{max}}{C_{min}}, \tag{18}$$

where C_{max} and C_{min} are the maximum and minimum capacitances of the varactor respectively. Another important parameter of varactors is their quality factor which plays a significant role in the oscillator's phase noise characteristic (Hajimiri et al 1998). Although the Q of varactors is considerably more than that of inductors and indeed the Q of inductor determines the overall Q of the tank, but in high frequencies roles are changed, and the Q of inductors becomes comparable with that of varactors (Razavi, 2006).

In spite of low operation frequencies (up to 10 GHz) and little tuning range (1.2 – 2.5) in comparison with solid state varactors (4 – 6) and affecting from Brownian, acceleration, acoustic and bias noises, MEMS varactors have very high Qs (100 – 400) in mm wave frequencies and large IIP3 in addition to low cost production (Rebeiz, 2003).

Types of MEMS Varactors

MEMS varactors are categorized to three major branches: electrostatic parallel plates, thermal and piezo parallel plates and inter digital capacitors.

Electrostatic Parallel Plates

Like RF-MEMS capacitive switches, electrostatic parallel plate varactors are mostly constructed by two parallel plates which one is fixed and another is movable, actuated by electrostatic force which is produced by applying a DC voltage between plates (Figure 26). Several designed RF-MEMS varactors by this method have been published by scientists (Young et al., 1996; Dec et al., 1997; Borwick et al., 2002) with Qs from 30 to 600, tuning ratios from 1.2 to 4.2 and operation frequencies from 1 GHz to 90 GHz.

Thermal and Piezoelectric Parallel Plate Varactors

Thermal actuation technique needs lower control voltage and has more linear C – V curve and (like RF-MEMS switches) avoids the static charges to be collected on the capacitor plates. Thermal actuated varactors use *bi-metal* technique which cause deflections in varactor arms and change the movable plate's position and hence the capacitance, see Figure 27. Piezoelectric actuation is similar to thermal actuation, instead of using piezoelectric arms in place of bimetal.

Tunable Inter Digital Capacitors

Large tuning ranges and large capacitance values are characteristics of tunable inter digital capacitors. The capacitor plates are placed in parallel horizontally. Figure 28 illustrates this kind of varactors conceptually with their excitation scheme.

Table 2 summarizes some results of RF-MEMS varactors with different excitation and design methods.

Figure 26. 3D schematic of a parallel plate MEMS varactor

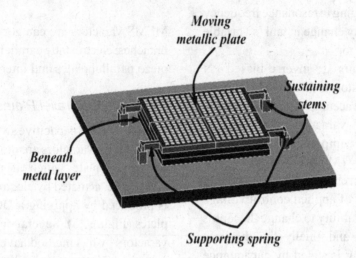

Figure 27. The schema and FEA analysis of a thermal actuated MEMS varactor. The side view (a) shows the bending of the top plate as the result of thermal actuation and the top view (b) illustrates the temperature distribution of the varactor

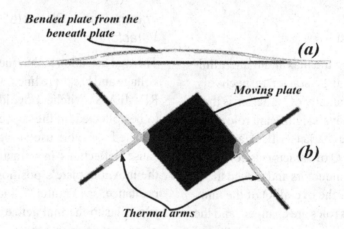

Design Example

As mentioned before, Electrostatic actuated RF-MEMS varactors consume very low power and achieve high qualities. The most important obstacle of this kind of varactors is their low tuning ratios. Here we design an electrostatic actuated RF-MEMS varactor with very wide tuning range.

The pull – down phenomenon is preventing high tuning ratios for varactors. But there may be some techniques to overcome this problem such as changing the stiffness coefficient of supporting springs during the varactor's work. A pioneering work is done by (Thielicke et al., 2003) which employed dimpling techniques for MEMS switches. Such a technique can be utilized by varactors, too with some modifications.

Figure 29 illustrates this technique conceptually. As shown, at the initial location of the movable plate (top), the only first spring with the anchored end is engaged. This spring could be chosen loose to decrease the requiring actuation

Figure 28. An inter digital MEMS varactor

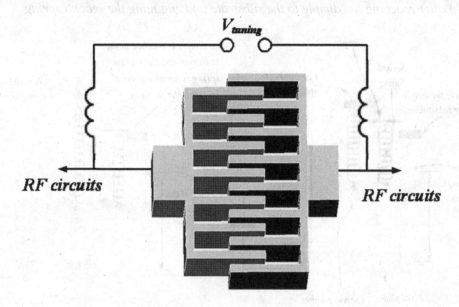

voltage. Before achieving the mentioned critical point (the 1/3 of the gap) the second spring is paralleled to the first one and constructs a strong spring. This means at this point the dimple reaches to the substrate, and constructs an anchor for the second spring. The resulting spring must be much stiffer than the first one to prevent the structure to go to the unstable region. One can assume the resulting combination as the new initial state of a new system, which has its own unstable boundary. By employing 3 steps, large tuning ratios as 3.375:1 are achievable. Figure 30 shows the resulting varactor in different views. Both inside and outside dimples and their related springs are magnified. At the initial state, both the dimples are suspended and just long and weak springs are engaged. By pulling down the movable plate to 1/3 of the total gap, the inside dimple reaches to the substrate and makes a new initial condition. After moving down of the plate to the 1/3 of the

Table 2. Some fabricated varactors with different excitation methods

Method	Bias (V)	Q	Frequency	C	Tuning ratio	Area(μm^2)
Electrostatic (Young et al 1996)	3	60	1 GHz	2.35 pF	1.175	200X200
Electrostatic (Dec et al 1998)	5.5	23	2 GHz	1.9 pF	1.35	400X400
Electrostatic (Barker et al 1999)	8.5	660	100 GHz	40 fF	1.35	140X140
Electrostatic (Hung et al 1998)	40	N.A.	1 GHz	1 pF	1.81	400X90
Electrostatic (Ketterl et al 2001)	40	30	4 GHz	460 fF	3.53	700X150
Electrostatic (Zou et al 2001)	40	N.A.	N.A.	32 fF	1.65	90X90
Thermal (Feng et al 1999)	2.7	100	20 GHz	0.1 pF	2.7	200X300
Piezo (Park et al 2001)	6	210	10 GHz	0.1 pF	3.1	150X150
Inter digital (Yao et al 1998)	5	160	6 GHz	12 pF	8.4	N.A.

Figure 29. Conceptual representation of the described technique (a) before reaching the dimple to the substrate, (b) after reaching the dimple to the substrate and engaging the second spring

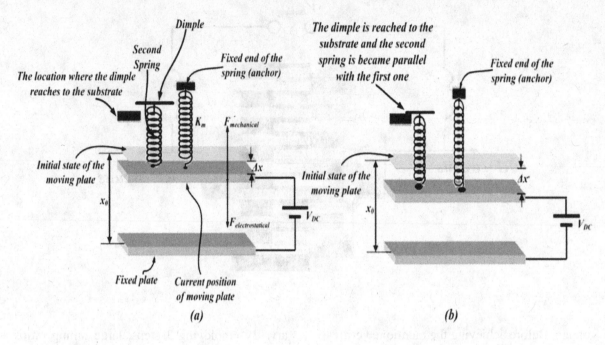

(a) *(b)*

Figure 30. The described varactor and its different parts

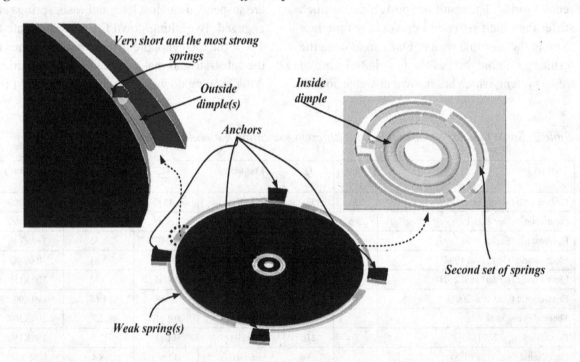

new gap, the outer dimples reach to the substrate, and long springs are removed, and short and very strong springs are paralleled with internal springs which make new initial conditions. The resulting system can move down about 1/3 of the remaining gap before instability. Hence, it can be seen that with such a technique one can achieve tuning ratios as large as 3.375:1. For achieving much larger tuning ratios with electrostatic actuation, employing more steps could work.

RF-MEMS APPLICATIONS IN WIRELESS TRANSCEIVERS

Due to their nominated and excellent features, RF-MEMS components have many applications in RF transceivers such as filters, mixers, oscillators and VCOs, switchable filter banks and etc. We describe some below.

RF-MEMS Filters

Although it's very high quality factor, a single RF-MEMS resonator can't be a good filter by its own because a suitable filter for RF transceivers require a relatively flat and precise pass-band, high stop-band rejection and sharp transition band. For making high Q RF-MEMS resonators to become suitable and high performance monolithic filters, one can couple a number of resonators properly.

By modeling of MEMS resonators as LC tanks, we can observe the effect of coupling (Figure 31). If strong coupling is employed, two far resonance frequencies are achieved for two identical resonators where the resulting system is not suitable for being a good filter. By weakening the coupling, these two resonance frequencies move toward each other, and for sufficiently weak coupling, coupled resonators construct an excellent filter with precise and flat pass-band. Also, the stop-band rejection is enhanced by increasing the number of well – coupled resonators.

The insertion loss characteristic of the resulting filter depends on the quality factor of individual resonators (Pourkamali et al., 2005a, b). Furthermore, paralleling of several resonators causes decreasing the output impedance of the filter which is an important parameter of RF transceiver's building blocks, and is essential for impedance matching (Li et al., 2007).

In the mechanical point of view, weak coupling translates to low velocity coupling (Wang et al., 1999) i.e. the coupling performed by connecting of two resonators at the position with low resonance speed and amplitudes in comparison with other parts of resonators. For example, low velocity coupling can be accomplished for beam resonators by connecting a spring between the resonant mass of the resonators near their anchors (the region with low resonant speed and amplitude) (Lee et al., 2004).

The length of the coupling beam for accommodating the use of the resonators with the same resonance frequencies must correspond to the effective quarter wavelength of the operation frequency.

There are specific regions for combdrive (Wang et al., 1999), beam (Lee et al., 2004), square (Demirci et al., 2006) and wine glass resonators (Shalaby et al., 2009) to accomplishing mentioned low velocity coupling, but it is critical for contour mode disk resonators because there is no low velocity regions at the perimeter of this kind of resonators. Figure 32 illustrates the low velocity coupling strategy for beam resonators.

RF-MEMS Mixers

Frequency translation is an essential process in RF transceivers accomplished by building blocks called mixers. In these blocks, both up – conversion (in transmitter) and down – conversion (in receivers) are carried out. After mixing, almost a filtering process must be performed to select the desired translated frequency component. Due to their excellent properties, RF-MEMS devices can

Figure 31. Equivalent circuit of two mechanically coupled resonators (a) and the SPICE simulation results of the circuit for different coupling strengths; (b) As shown for weak coupling (which is translated to low velocity coupling in the mechanical point of view) two strikes become very close to one another

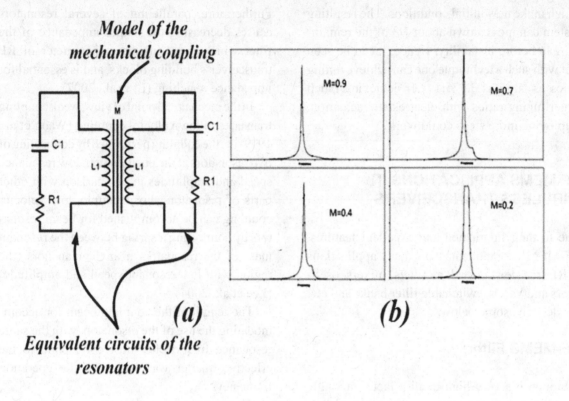

Model of the mechanical coupling

Equivalent circuits of the resonators

(a)

(b)

Figure 32. Low velocity coupling of two beam resonators

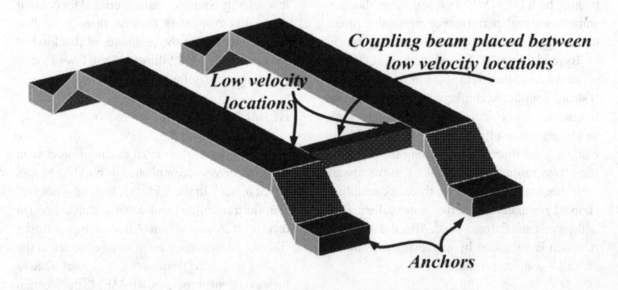

Coupling beam placed between low velocity locations

Low velocity locations

Anchors

Figure 33. Schematic of a mixer - filter constructed by MEMS C-C beam resonators

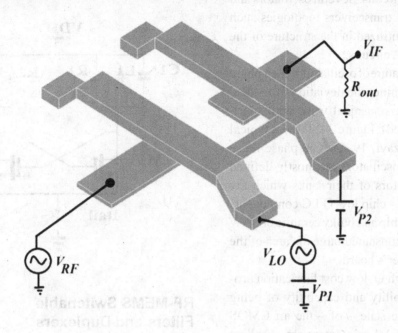

construct a fully electromechanical mixer – filter structure and therefore decrease the consumed power, insertion loss and required die area and increase the functionality.

Super heterodyne transceiver architecture requires two steps of down conversion for its receiver, one for RF to IF (Intermediate frequency) and another for IF to base band conversions. Hence, MEMS mixer – filter structure could much decrease the chip area of the transceiver with less insertion loss and power consumption.

Figure 33 illustrates a typical structure of a MEMS mixer – filter device. If the RF signal is applied to the input and local oscillator output is applied to the anchor in addition to the DC bias voltage, the capacitive transducer acts as the voltage to force convertor, according to the square form of the voltage to force transfer function; the following result is achieved (Wong et al 2004):

$$F_2 = \frac{1}{2}\left(V_P + v_{LO} - v_{RF}\right)^2 \left(\frac{\partial C}{\partial z}\right) =$$

$$\cdots - \frac{1}{2} V_{LO} V_{RF} \frac{\partial C}{\partial z} \cos\left(\omega_{RF} - \omega_{LO}\right)t + \cdots$$

$$(19)$$

where

$$v_{RF} = V_{RF} \cos\left(\omega_{RF}t\right)$$

and

$$v_{LO} = V_{LO} \cos\left(\omega_{LO}t\right).$$

This force signal passes through MEMS filter comprises of several connected RF-MEMS resonators which are adjusted on the desired frequency as described in the previous section. UHF mixer – filter are attainable by more stiff resonators such as hollow disks (Li et al., 2005) which make RF to IF down conversion by MEMS technology to be feasible.

RF-MEMS Oscillators and VCOs

Reference oscillators and Voltage Controlled Oscillators (VCO) are hearts of electronic circuits. Any deviation of the oscillation frequency of the oscillators causes significant errors in the operation of electronic circuits. Several oscillators and VCOs are used in transceivers topologies such as LO and VCOs utilized in the structure of the channel select PLL circuits.

An important feature of oscillators is their phase noise which determines the deviation from ideal oscillation (a pure sinusoidal wave with spurious modes excluded). Figure 34 shows a typical CMOS VCO (Razavi, 1998). The phase noise characteristics of oscillators are mostly defined by the quality factors of their tanks which are constructed by on – chip low Q LC components or by high Q off – chip and bulky ceramic or SAW resonators which consumed large die area of the precious transceiver's board.

Due to their high Q, low cost fabrication process and compatibility and capability of being integrated with the state – of – the art CMOS transistors, RF-MEMS resonators are excellent alternatives for low power, monolithic and low phase noise reference oscillators (Lin et al., 2004; Lee et al., 2001; Nguyen et al., 1999; Huang et al., 2008). For example, they can provide about 50dB improvement in the phase noise in comparison with their LC counterparts in the same frequency and the same offset (Nguyen, 2007).

But unfortunately, RF-MEMS resonators are not tunable in UHF frequencies because of the ultra high stiffness disk resonators required for these applications are not easily tunable. Therefore, RF-MEMS resonators are not suitable for VCOs which need high tuning ranges.

Luckily, MEMS technology has a solution for this problem; high Q inductors and varactors. As mentioned before, MEMS varactors have the great and linear dynamic range placed in parallel with high Q MEMS inductors and can construct high Q tanks which result highly tunable and low phase noise VCOs.

Figure 34. The circuit of a CMOS basic LC VCO

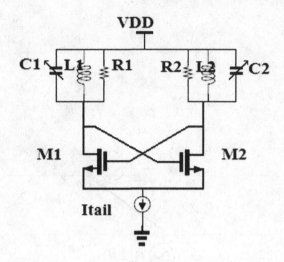

RF-MEMS Switchable Filters and Duplexers

A duplexer is a device that allows bidirectional (transmission and receiving) communication over a single channel. Duplexer must be designed to support frequency bands of the transmitter and the receiver distinctly, and also provide sufficient isolation to prevent receiver desensitization (Razavi, 1998). Duplexers can be realized by MEMS technology by a switchable filter system with low insertion loss and small area.

Channel selection (instead of band selection) is the ambition of RF designers, because the unwanted in – band signals are not important any more here, and direct down conversion becomes easily possible. Hence, the dynamic range of the succeeding critical electronic blocks such as LNA and mixer becomes relaxed. Therefore, the robustness of the receiver is enhanced and power consumption is decreased. Also, because of the rejection of in – band interferences as the result of channel selection, the phase noise of the LO is not very critical (Huang et al., 2008).

But, channel selection require tunable resonators with Qs>10000 (Nguyen, 2005). As said, RF-MEMS resonators can achieve Qs in the range

Figure 35. MEMS based multi standard monolithic transceiver. (Green blocks can be fully implemented and yellow blocks can be partially implemented by described MEMS technology)

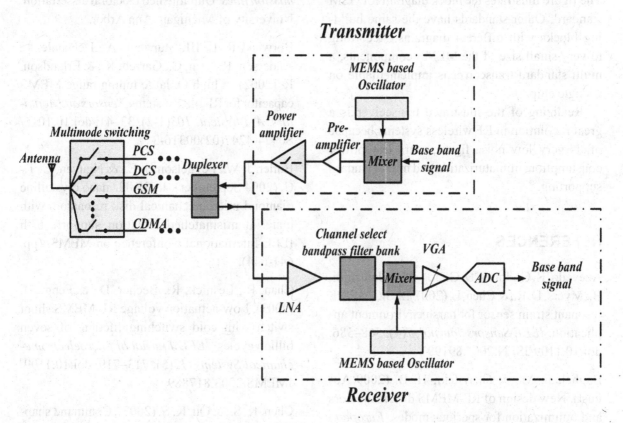

of ten thousands at GHz frequencies, but unfortunately, are not tunable. By combining RF-MEMS high performance switches with RF-MEMS high Q resonators, the channel select architecture is feasible. There are many standards for RF transceiver systems which all together (for realizing multi mode transceiver on a chip) require hundreds of these switchable filters each used for a specific channel. If we consider currently off chip and bulky filters utilized by ceramic and SAW technologies, the transceiver board area increases drastically and the resulting transceiver may not be portable anymore! But MEMS switchable filter banks are feasible in a single chip due to tiny on chip high performance switches and resonators.

CONCLUSION

Due to their various types and applications and their excellent performances, RF-MEMS devices are superior alternatives for off – chip devices or low performance on – chip elements and circuits in transceiver boards. Introduced components and circuits such as resonators, switches, inductors, varactors, filters, mixer-filters, oscillators, VCOs, switchable filter banks and duplexers could be utilized in RF transceivers with excellent performance. By considering the mentioned applications, monolithic multi standard channel select RF transceivers can be realized by RF-MEMS technology. Figure 35 shows a block diagram of a monolithic transceiver realized by RF-MEMS components and circuits (Nguyen et al 1998), where the green blocks are fully and yellow ones are partially realizable by RF-MEMS technology. The figure illustrates the block diagram for GSM standard. Other standards have the same building blocks with different diagrams. According to very small size of the MEMS components, a multi standard transceiver is implementable on a single chip.

Realizing of the illustrated transceiver is a great revolution in RF wireless systems because of its very low noise figure, extra low power consumption, miniaturization and multi standard supporting.

REFERENCES

Azevedo, R. G., Jones, D. G., Jog, A. V., Jamshidi, B., Myers, D. R., & Chen, L. (2007). A SiC MEMS resonant strain sensor for harsh environment application. *IEEE Sensors Journal, 7*(4), 568–586. doi:10.1109/JSEN.2007.891997

Baghelani, M., & Ghavifekr, H. B. (2009 August). New design of RF-MEMS disk resonators and optimization for spurious modes. *European Conference on Circuit Theory and Design*, (pp. 894-897). Antalya, Turkey.

Baghelani, M., & Ghavifekr, H. B. (2010 May). A new high reliable structure of micro-electro-mechanical radial contour mode disk resonators for UHF application. *18th Iranian Conference on Electrical Engineering* (ICEE), (pp. 386-390). Isfahan, Iran.

Baghelani, M., & Ghavifekr, H. B. (2010). Ring shape anchored RF-MEMS contour mode disk resonator for UHF communication applications. *Microsystem Technologies, 16*(12), 2123–2130. doi:10.1007/s00542-010-1143-4

Bannon, F. D., III, Clark, J. R., & Nguyen, C. T.-C. (1996 December). High frequency micromechanical IF filters. *International Electronic Devices Meeting*, (pp. 773 – 776). San Francisco, CA.

Barker, N. S. (1999). *Distributed MEMS transmission lines*. Unpublished Doctoral dissertation, University of Michigan, Ann Arbor.

Borwick, R. L. III, Stupar, P. A., DeNatale, J., Anderson, R., Tsai, C., Garrett, K., & Erlandson, R. (2002). A high Q, large tuning range MEMS capacitor for RF filter systems. *Sensors and Actuators. A, Physical, 103*(1-2), 33–41. doi:10.1016/S0924-4247(02)00316-3

Butler, J. W., Feygelson, J. E., & Nguyen, C. T.-C. (2004 September). 1.51 GHz nano crystalline diamond micromechanical disk resonators with material mismatched isolation support. 17th IEEE International Conference on MEMS, (pp. 641-644).

Chan, R., Lesnick, R., Becher, D., & Feng, M. (2003). Low-actuation voltage RF-MEMS shunt switch with cold switching lifetime of seven billion cycles. *IEEE Journal of Microelectromechanical Systems, 12*(5), 713–719. doi:10.1109/JMEMS.2003.817889

Chen, K. S., & Ou, K. S. (2007). Command shaping techniques for electrostatic MEMS actuator analysis and simulation. *IEEE Journal of Microelectromechanical Systems, 16*(3), 537–549. doi:10.1109/JMEMS.2007.893512

Clark, J. R., Hsu, W.-T., Abdelmoneum, M. A., & Nguyen, C. T.-C. (2005). High q UHF micromechanical radial contour mode disk resonators. *IEEE Journal of Microelectromechanical Systems, 14*(6), 1298–1310. doi:10.1109/JMEMS.2005.856675

Clark, J. R., Hsu, W.-T., & Nguyen, C. T.-C. (2000 December). High-Q VHF micromechanical contour-mode disk resonator. *Technical Digest, IEEE International Electronic Devices Meeting*, (pp. 493-496). San Francisco, CA.

Dahlmann, G. W., Yeatman, E. M., Young, P. R., Robertson, I. D., & Lucyszyn, S. (2001, August). MEMS high Q microwave inductors using solder surface tension self-assembly. *IEEE International Microwave Symposium*, (vol. 1, pp. 329-332). Phoenix, AZ.

Dec, A., & Suyama, K. (1997). Micromachined varactor with wide tuning range. *Electronics Letters*, *33*(11), 922–924. doi:10.1049/el:19970628

Dec, A., & Suyama, K. (1998). Micromachined electro-mechanically tunable capacitors and their applications to RF IC's. *IEEE Transactions on Microwave Theory and Techniques*, *46*(12), 2587–2596. doi:10.1109/22.739251

Demirci, M. U., & Nguyen, C. T.-C. (2003 Mars). Higher-mode free-free beam micromechanical resonators. Proceeding of the IEEE International Symposium on Frequency Control, (pp. 810–818).

Demirci, M. U., & Nguyen, C. T.-C. (2006). Mechanically corner-coupled square micro resonator array for reduced series motional resistance. *IEEE Journal of Microelectromechanical Systems*, *15*(6), 1419–1436. doi:10.1109/JMEMS.2006.883588

Feng, Z., Zhang, W., Su, B. H., & Gupta, K. F. K.C., Bright, V., & Lee, Y.C. (1999, August). Design and modeling of RF-MEMS tunable capacitors using electro-thermal actuators. *IEEE International Microwave Symposium*, (vol 4, pp. 1507-1510). Anaheim, CA.

Ferguson, A. T., Li, L., Nagaraj, V. T. B., Piekarski, B., & DeVoe, D. L. (2005). modeling and design of composite free-free beam piezoelectric resonators. *Sensors and Actuators. A, Physical*, *118*(1), 63–69. doi:10.1016/S0924-4247(04)00540-0

Gao, X. Y., Cao, Y., Zhou, Y., Ding, W., Lei, C., & Chen, J. A. (2006). Fabrication of solenoid-type inductor with electroplated NiFe magnetic core. *Journal of Magnetism and Magnetic Materials*, *305*(1), 207–211. doi:10.1016/j.jmmm.2005.12.014

Gijs, M. A. M. (2006). MEMS inductors: Technology and applications. *Conference of the NATO Advanced Study Institute on Magnetic Nanostructures for Micro-Electromechanical Systems and Spintronic Applications*, (pp. 127-152).

Guo, F. M., Zhu, Z. Q., Long, Y. F., Wang, W. M., Zhu, S. Z., & Lai, Z. S. (2003). Study on low voltage actuated MEMS RF capacitive switches. *Sensors and Actuators. A, Physical*, *108*(1-3), 128–133. doi:10.1016/S0924-4247(03)00372-8

Gurbuz, Y., Esame, O., Tekin, I., Kang, W. P., & Davidson, J. L. (2005). Diamond semiconductor technology for RF device applications. *Solid-State Electronics*, *49*(7), 1055–1070. doi:10.1016/j.sse.2005.04.005

Hajimiri, A., & Lee, T. H. (1998). A general theory of phase noise in electrical oscillators. *IEEE Journal of Solid-state Circuits*, *33*(2), 179–194. doi:10.1109/4.658619

Hartley, A. C., Miles, R. E., Corda, J., & Dimitrakopoulos, N. (2008). Large throw magnetic microactuator. *Mechatronics*, *18*(9), 459–465. doi:10.1016/j.mechatronics.2008.05.012

Huang, W. L., Ren, Z., Lin, Y. W., Chen, H. Y., Lahann, J., & Nguyen, C. T.-C. (2008 January). Fully monolithic CMOS nickel micromechanical resonator oscillator. 21th IEEE International Conference on MEMS, (pp. 10-13). Tucson, AZ

Huang, X. M. H., Zorman, C. A., Mehregany, M., & Roukes, M. L. (2003 July). Quality factor issues in silicon carbide nano mechanical resonators. 12th International Conference on Transducers, Solid State Sensors, Actuators and Microsystems, (vol. 1, pp. 722–725).

Hung, E. S., & Senturia, S. D. (1998). Tunable capacitors with programmable capacitance-voltage characteristic. *Solid-State Sensors and Actuators Workshop*, (pp. 292–295).

Johnson, R. A. (1983). *Mechanical filters in electronics*. New York, NY: Wiley.

Kawakubo, T., Nagano, T., Nishigaki, M., Abe, K., & Itaya, K. (2006). RF-MEMS tunable capacitor with 3V operation using folded beam piezoelectric bimorph actuator. *IEEE Journal of Microelectromechanical Systems, 15*(6), 1759–1765. doi:10.1109/JMEMS.2006.885985

Ketterl, T., Weller, T., & Fries, D. (2001 August). A micromachined tunable CPW resonator. *IEEE International Microwave Symposium*, (vol. 1, pp. 345-348). Phoenix, AZ.

Lee, H. C., Park, J. H., & Park, Y. H. (2007). Development of shunt type Ohmic RF-MEMS switches actuated by piezoelectric cantilever. *Sensors and Actuators. A, Physical, 136*(1), 282–290. doi:10.1016/j.sna.2006.10.050

Lee, S., Demirci, M. U., & Nguyen, C. T.-C. (2001). A 10-MHz micromechanical resonator Pierce reference oscillator for communications. *Digest of Technical Papers, the 11th International Conference on Solid-State Sensors & Actuators* (Transducers'01), (pp. 1094-1097).

Lee, S., & Nguyen, C. T.-C. (2004 April). Mechanically-coupled micromechanical resonator arrays for improved phase noise. *Proceedings of IEEE International Symposium on Frequency Control*, (pp. 144-150).

Li, S. S., Lin, Y. W., Ren, Z., & Nguyen, C. T.-C. (2007 June). An MSI micromechanical differential disk-array filter. *International Conference on Transducers, Solid State Sensors, Actuators and Microsystems*, (pp. 307 –311). Lyon.

Li, S. S., Lin, Y. W., Xie, Y., Ren, Z., & Nguyen, C. T.-C. (2005 March). Small percent bandwidth design of a 431-MHz notch-coupled micromechanical hollow-disk ring mixer-filter. *Proceedings of the IEEE International Ultrasonics Symposium*, (pp. 1295-1298).

Mahmoudi, P., Ghavifekr, H. B., & Najafiaghdam, E. (2010). A combined thermo-electrostatic MEMS-based switch with low actuation voltage. *Sensors & Transducers, 115*(4), 61–70.

Matmat, M., Coccetti, F., Marty, A., Plana, R., Escriba, C., Fourniols, J. Y., & Esteve, D. (2009). Capacitive RF-MEMS analytical predictive reliability and lifetime characterization. *Microelectronics and Reliability, 49*(9-11), 1304–1308. doi:10.1016/j.microrel.2009.06.049

Musah, T. (2005). Mos varactors in weak inversion for 0.5 v analog filters. *National Conference on Undergraduate Research*, (pp. 1-8).

Nguyen, C. T.-C. (1995). Micromechanical resonators for oscillators and filters. *Proceeding of IEEE Ultrasonics Symposium*, (vol. 1, pp. 489-499).

Nguyen, C. T.-C. (1999). Frequency selective MEMS for miniaturized low power communication devices. *IEEE Transactions on Microwave Theory and Techniques, 47*(8), 1486–1503. doi:10.1109/22.780400

Nguyen, C. T.-C. (2000). Micromechanical circuits for communication transceivers (invited). *Proceedings Bipolar/BiCMOS Circuits and Technology Meeting* (BCTM), (pp. 142-149).

Nguyen, C. T.-C. (2002). *MEMS for wireless communications. Technical Report*. University of Michigan.

Nguyen, C. T.-C. (2005). Vibrating RF-MEMS overview: Applications to wireless communications. *Proceedings of the Society for Photo-Instrumentation Engineers, 5715*, 11–25.

Nguyen, C. T.-C. (2007). MEMS technology for timing and frequency control. *IEEE Transactions on Ultrasonics, Ferroelectrics, and Frequency Control, 54*(2), 251–270. doi:10.1109/TUFFC.2007.240

Nguyen, C. T.-C., & Howe, R. T. (1999). An integrated CMOS micromechanical resonator high-Q oscillator. *IEEE Journal of Solid-state Circuits, 34*(4), 440–455. doi:10.1109/4.753677

Nguyen, C. T.-C., Katehi, L. P. B., & Rebeiz, G. M. (1998). Micromachined devices for wireless communications. *Proceedings of the IEEE*, *86*(8), 1756–1768. doi:10.1109/5.704281

Ong, A. O., & Tay, F. E. H. (2007). Motion characterizations of lateral micromachined sensor based on stroboscopic measurements. *IEEE Sensors Journal*, *7*(2), 163–171. doi:10.1109/JSEN.2006.886871

Park, J. Y., Yee, Y. J., Nam, H. J., & Bu, J. U. (2001 August). Micromachined RF-MEMS tunable capacitors using piezoelectric actuator. IEEE International Microwave Symposium, (vol. 3, pp. 2111-2114). Phoenix, AZ.

Piazza, G., Stephanou, P. J., & Pisano, A. P. (2006). Piezoelectric aluminum nitride vibrating contour-mode MEMS resonators. *IEEE Journal of Microelectromechanical Systems*, *15*(6), 1406–1418. doi:10.1109/JMEMS.2006.886012

Piazza, G., Stephanou, P. J., & Pisano, A. P. (2007). Single chip multiple frequency AlN MEMS filters based on contour mode piezoelectric resonators. *IEEE Journal of Microelectromechanical Systems*, *16*(2), 319–328. doi:10.1109/JMEMS.2006.889503

Pinel, S., Cros, F., Nuttinck, S., Yoon, S.-W., Allen, M. G., & Laskar, J. (2003 June). Very high-Q inductors using RF-MEMS technology for system-on-package wireless communication integrated module. *IEEE International Microwave Symposium*, (vol. 3, pp. 1497-1500).

Pourkamali, S., & Ayazi, F. (2005). Electrically coupled MEMS bandpass filters: Part I: With coupling element. *Sensors and Actuators. A, Physical*, *122*(2), 307–316. doi:10.1016/j.sna.2005.03.038

Pourkamali, S., & Ayazi, F. (2005). Electrically coupled MEMS bandpass filters: Part II. Without coupling element. *Sensors and Actuators. A, Physical*, *122*(2), 317–325. doi:10.1016/j.sna.2005.03.039

Pourkamali, S., Hashimura, A., Abdolvand, R., Ho, G. K., Erbil, A., & Ayazi, F. (2003). High-Q single crystal silicon HARPSS capacitive beam resonators with self-aligned sub-100-nm transduction gaps. *IEEE Journal Microelectromechanical System*, *12*(4), 487–496. doi:10.1109/JMEMS.2003.811726

Razavi, B. (1998). *RF microelectronics*. NJ: Prentice Hall PTR.

Razavi, B. (2006). A 60-GHz CMOS receiver front-end. *IEEE Journal of Solid-state Circuits*, *41*(1), 17–22. doi:10.1109/JSSC.2005.858626

Rebeiz, G. M. (2003). *RF-MEMS, theory, design and technology*. NJ: John Wiley & Sons. doi:10.1002/0471225282

Shalaby, M., Abdelmoneum, M., & Saitou, M. A. K. (2009). Design of spring coupling for high- Q high-frequency MEMS filters for wireless applications. *IEEE Transactions on Industrial Electronics*, *56*(4), 1022–1030. doi:10.1109/TIE.2009.2014671

Stephanou, P. J., Piazza, G., White, C. D., Wijesundara, M. B. J., & Pisano, A. P. (2007). Piezoelectric aluminum nitride MEMS annular dual contour mode filter. *Sensors and Actuators. A, Physical*, *134*(1), 152–160. doi:10.1016/j.sna.2006.04.032

Tang, W. C., Nguyen, T. C. H., Judy, M. W., & Howe, R. T. (1990). Electrostatic comb drive of lateral polysilicon resonators. *Sensors and Actuators. A, Physical*, *21*(1-3), 328–331. doi:10.1016/0924-4247(90)85065-C

Thielicke, E., & Obermeier, E. (2003). A Fast switching surface micromachined electrostatic relay. *The 12th International Conference on Solid State Sensors, Actuators and Microsystems*, (pp. 899-902).

Tseng, S. H., Hung, Y. J., Juang, Y. Z., & Lu, M. S.-C. (2007). A 5.8-GHz VCO with CMOS-compatible MEMS inductors. *Sensors and Actuators. A, Physical*, *139*(1-2), 187–193. doi:10.1016/j.sna.2006.12.014

Varadan, V. K., Vinoy, K. J., & Jose, K. A. (2002). *RF-MEMS and their applications*. England: John Wiley & Sons. doi:10.1002/0470856602

Wang, J. Butler, J. E., Hsu, D. S. Y., &Nguyen, T.-C. (2002 August). CVD polycrystalline diamond high-Q micromechanical resonators. *The 5th IEEE International Conference on Micro Electro Mechanical Systems*, (pp. 657 – 660). Las Vegas, NV.

Wang, J., Ren, Z., & Nguyen, C. T.-C. (2004). 1.156-GHz self-aligned vibrating micromechanical disk resonator. *IEEE Transactions on Ultrasonics, Ferroelectrics, and Frequency Control, 51*(12), 1607–1628. doi:10.1109/TUFFC.2004.1386679

Wang, K., Bannon, F. D., III, Clark, J. R., & Nguyen, C. T.-C. (1997). Q-enhancement of microelectromechanical filters via low-velocity spring coupling. *Proceedings of IEEE Ultrasonics Symposium,* (vol. 1, pp. 323-327).

Wang, K., & Nguyen, C. T.-C. (1999). High order medium frequency micromechanical electronic filters. *IEEE Journal Microelectromechanical System, 8*(4), 534–556. doi:10.1109/84.809070

Wang, K., Wong, A. C., & Nguyen, C. T.-C. (2000). VHF free-free beam high q micromechanical resonators. *IEEE Journal Microelectromechanical System, 9*(3), 347–360. doi:10.1109/84.870061

Wang, L., Cui, Z., Hong, J. S., McErlean E. P., Greed, R. B., & Voyce, D. C. (2006). Fabrication of high power RF-MEMS switches. *Microelectronics Engineering, 83*(4-9), 1418-1420.

Weon, D. H., Jeon, J. H., & Mohammadi, S. (2007). High-Q micromachined three-dimensional integrated inductors for high-frequency applications. *Journal of Vacuum Science & Technology B Microelectronics and Nanometer Structures, 25*(1), 264–270. doi:10.1116/1.2433984

Wong, A. C., & Nguyen, C. T.-C. (2004). Micromechanical mixer-filters ("mixlers"). *IEEE Journal of Microelectromechanical Systems, 13*(1), 100–112. doi:10.1109/JMEMS.2003.823218

Wu, C. H., Tang, C. C., & Liu, S. I. (2003). Analysis of on-chip spiral inductors using the distributed capacitance model. *IEEE Journal of Solid-state Circuits, 38*(6), 1040–1044. doi:10.1109/JSSC.2003.811965

Yao, J. J., Park, S., & Natale, D. (1998). High tuning ratio MEMS-based tunable capacitors for RF communications applications. *Solid State Sensors and Actuators Workshop*, (pp. 124-127).

Yong, Z., Zhou, Z. M., Cao, Y., Gao, X. Y., & Ding, W. (2008). Fabrication and performance of Fe-based magnetic thin film inductor for high-frequency application. *Journal of Magnetism and Magnetic Materials, 320*(20), 963–966. doi:10.1016/j.jmmm.2008.04.136

Yoon, J. B., Han, C. H., Yoon, E., & Kim, C. K. (1999 January). Monolithic integration of 3-D electroplated microstructures with unlimited number of levels using planarization with a sacrificial metallic mold (PSMM). *IEEE International Conference on MEMS*, (pp. 624-629). Orlando, FL.

Young, D. J., & Boser, B. E. (1996). A micromachined variable capacitor for monolithic low-noise VCOs. *Technical Digest, IEEE Solid-state Sensor and Actuator Workshop*, (pp. 86-89).

Zelinski, S. (2001). Design of vertical-lateral thermal actuators for MEMS. *Sensors and Actuators. A, Physical, 90*, 38–48.

Zou, J., Liu, C., & Ainé, J. E. S. (2001). Development of a wide-tuning-range two-parallel-plate tunable capacitor for integrated wireless communication systems. *International Journal of RF and Microwave Computer-Aided Engineering, 11*(5), 322–329. doi:10.1002/mmce.1040

Chapter 8
Passive Components for RF–ICs

Gianluca Cornetta
Universidad San Pablo-CEU, Spain & Vrije Universiteit Brussel, Belgium

David J. Santos
Universidad San Pablo-CEU, Spain

José Manuel Vázquez
Universidad San Pablo-CEU, Spain

ABSTRACT

The modern wireless communication industry is demanding transceivers with a high integration level operating in the gigahertz frequency range. This, in turn, has prompted intense research in the area of monolithic passive devices. Modern fabrication processes now provide the capability to integrate onto a silicon substrate inductors and capacitors, enabling a broad range of new applications. Inductors and capacitors are the core elements of many circuits, including low-noise amplifiers, power amplifiers, baluns, mixers, and oscillators, as well as fully-integrated matching networks. While the behavior and the modeling of integrated capacitors are well understood, the design of an integrated inductor is still a challenging task since its magnetic behavior is hard to predict accurately. As the operating frequency approaches the gigahertz range, device nonlinearities, coupling effects, and skin effect dominate, making difficult the design of critical parameters such as the self-resonant frequency, the quality factor, and self and mutual inductances. However, despite the parasitic effects and the low quality-factor, integrated inductors still allow for the implementation of integrated circuits with improved performances under low supply voltage. In this chapter, the authors review the technology behind monolithic capacitors and inductors on silicon substrate for high-frequency applications, with major emphasis on physical implementation and modeling.

DOI: 10.4018/978-1-4666-0083-6.ch008

INTRODUCTION

During the last decade, the unprecedented growth of the wireless market and the demand for high-performance and low-cost RF transceivers to support the broad range of new wireless communication applications have prompted an intense research in the development of new technologies and fabrication processes aimed at providing the designers with a rich set of analog features integrated on a single silicon substrate. State-of-the-art RF-CMOS processes comes with libraries of monolithic passive devices such as resistors, inductors, and capacitors, and CAD tools allow the possibility to synthesize automatically more complex devices such as tapped inductors and multi-port transformers. The capability to implement lumped elements such as inductors, capacitors, and resistors has been crucial for the development of such low-cost transceivers.

Monolithic fabrication technologies for RF and microwave circuits provide the end user with the possibility to integrate on chip either lumped elements (i.e., components with electrical dimensions less than approximately 0.1 times the wavelength of the RF signal) or distributed elements (i.e., components that consist of transmission line sections). The choice between lumped or distributed elements depends on the frequency of operation. Lumped elements are suitable for designs up to approximately 20 GHz; however, in the practice, it is difficult to realize a "pure" monolithic lumped element because of the parasitic effects introduced by ground or substrate coupling which affect the performances of any on-chip component. For implementations that operate at frequencies beyond 20 GHz and into the millimeter-wave band, distributed elements are probably the best option to guarantee a manufacturable design.

Although lumped elements typically exhibit a lower quality factor Q than distributed circuits, due to smaller element dimensions and to the parasitic introduced by the multilevel fabrication process, they have the advantage of smaller size, lower cost, smaller phase delays, and good frequency behavior. In addition, lumped elements simplify circuit analysis and design since allow the possibility to use conventional low-frequency techniques also at RF. Finally, since lumped elements are much smaller than the signals wavelength, coupling effects between them when they are placed in proximity are smaller than those of distributed elements.

The availability of monolithic lumped elements allows the possibility to implement on-chip matching networks as well as a wide range of transceivers of fully-monolithic building blocks such as Gilbert-cell mixers, oscillators, filters, phase splitters, and tuned amplifiers. At RF and the low end of the microwave band, the use of lumped elements contributes to significantly reduce the chip size without appreciably affecting system performance and RF behavior; the higher integration level, in turn helps to reduce the production costs drastically.

The purpose of this chapter is to present a comprehensive review of technology and design of monolithic lumped elements for RF application with special emphasis on capacitor and inductor design. The Monolithic Capacitors section deals with capacitor design. The basic definition of capacitor parameters, the analysis of parallel plate capacitors, voltage and current ratings, as well as the electrical representation are issued. MIM and MOM capacitors are discussed as well, and new device topologies such as interdigitated and woven capacitors are also addressed. Monolithic Inductors and Transformers are analyzed in their eponymous section. Self-inductance estimation methods for different monolithic inductor topologies is thoroughly analyzed, as well as the effect of parasitic and Q enhancement techniques. The basic theory of transformers is also discussed, with special emphasis on the applications. Finally, conclusions are given in the last section.

Figure 1. Cross-connected metal layers

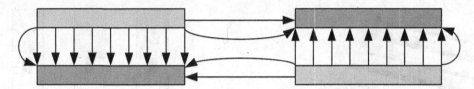

MONOLITHIC CAPACITORS

Capacitors are one of the fundamental elements in integrated circuits, and are used extensively in many applications. In radio frequency transceivers it is the basic component of many elementary building blocks such as oscillators, low-noise amplifiers, and mixers. RF-CMOS processes dispose either of specific (i.e., MIM capacitors) or native devices (i.e., MOM capacitors). Metal-insulator-metal (MIM) capacitors are implemented using extra masks, whereas metal-oxide-metal (MOM) capacitors exploit inter-metal parasitic capacitances and hence do not require any additional processing step.

Capacitors can occupy considerable area and this problem is even more important in deep submicron technology nodes, since the inter-metal dielectric thickness does not scale much if at all. Native capacitors are formed by stacking two or more metal layers; they exhibit excellent linearity, high quality factor Q, and very small temperature variations. Unfortunately, the capacitance density is not excessively high (about 1.5 fF/μm^2) due to the relatively thick inter-metal oxide layers. The problem becomes more severe with scaled technologies since the vertical spacing of the metal layers is relatively constant; nonetheless, this problem is partially mitigated by the high number of metal layers available in modern processes, and by the metal thickness that allows exploiting fringe fields to increase the overall capacitance. As a result, standard parallel plate capacitors consume a larger percentage of silicon area.

In a standard parallel plate capacitor, two different metal layers are used to create a vertical flux; however, as process technologies continue to scale down, lateral fringing fields are becoming dominant and can be used to implement capacitors using a single metal layer. Lateral flux capacitor have excellent matching properties (i.e., very small tolerances) because metal spacing in a same layer can be controlled better than inter-metal oxide thickness during the lithography. The lateral spacing of the metal layers gets smaller with scaling, whereas the thickness of the metal layers and the vertical spacing of the metal layers are relatively constant. This means that structures exploiting lateral flux will achieve vey high capacitance densities in deep submicron technology nodes.

Very high capacitances can be implemented by combining vertical and lateral fluxes using cross connected structures as depicted in Figure 1.

The plates are broken into separate sections that are cross-connected (Akcasu, 1993). In the scheme of Figure 1 the plates are implemented with metal stripes located in different layers and forming a cross-coupled structure that allows exploiting both vertical and lateral fluxes. To emphasize the cross-coupled connection, the capacitor plates are represented with two different shades. Very high capacitance values can be achieved by stacking more than two metal layers as shown in Figure 2. To maximize the lateral flux, each layer is formed by an interdigitized structure

The capacity of a lateral flux capacitor depends on its perimeter; hence, to maximize the capacity, fractal geometries that increase the perimeter length have been proposed (Samavati et al., 1998). Another structure that allows the implementation

Figure 2. Lateral flux capacitor: (a) Stacked implementation; and (b) Cross-section

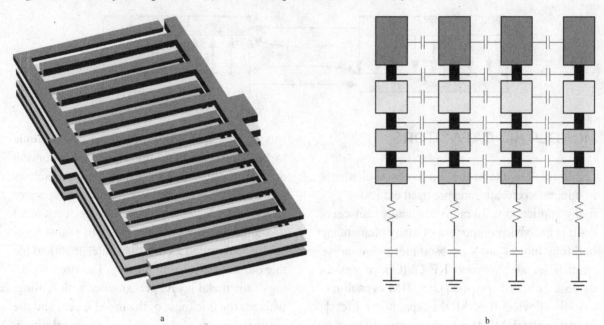

a

b

of very high capacitances is the woven capacitor depicted in Figure 3.

A woven capacitor exhibits a parasitic inductance and resistance much lower than that of a capacitor with an interdigitized layout; this, in turn results in a higher self-resonance frequency and a better quality factor. This characteristic is of paramount importance in radio frequency circuits. Nonetheless, the major shortcoming of this topology is the lower capacity density compared with the interdigitized structure with the same metal spacing, because of the reduced contribution of the vertical fields.

MIM Capacitors

Some fabrication processes, either CMOS, BiC-MOS, or bipolar, provide the end user with high quality metal-insulator-metal (MIM) capacitors. Typical applications of MIM capacitors are RF coupling, and RF bypass in oscillators, resonator circuits, and matching networks. The key attributes of MIM capacitors are high linearity over broad voltage ranges, low series resistance, good

matching properties and dielectric reliability, small temperature coefficients, low leakage currents, high breakdown voltage. The price to pay for these excellent performances is a higher fabrication cost since, typically, three extra masks are necessary to fabricate this kind of device.

Figure 4 depicts the structure of a typical MIM capacitor. The capacitor is implemented between two native metal layers. To reduce parasitic substrate coupling and achieve high quality factors, it is preferable to implement the MIM capacitor plates into upper metallization levels.

One of the major drawbacks of MIM capacitors is their small capacitance density, typically around 2 fF/μm^2. The strive for cost reduction has led to an increasing demand for high-density MIM capacitors to reduce silicon area; however, further thinning of the traditionally used Si-oxide or Si-nitride dielectrics is no longer feasible because of increased leakage currents and reduced dielectric reliability. Therefore, new high-κ dielectric materials, such as Al_2O_3, Ta_2O_5, Nb_2O_5, etc. or laminated layer stacks of different materials are being evaluated as MIM dielectrics and many

Figure 3. Woven capacitor

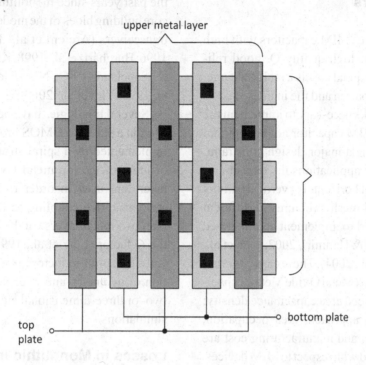

promising integrations schemes of high-κ materials have been demonstrated in the literature (Mahnkopf et al., 1999; Schiml et al., 2001; Miyashita et al., 2001; Lin et al., 2001; Kar-Roy et al., 1999; Liu et al., 2000; Armacost et al., 2000; Zurcher et al., 2000; van Huylenbroeck et al., 2009; Ng et al., 2002). Large decoupling capacitors with capacitance density of about 8 fF/µm²

have been demonstrated for a 90 nm SOI process (Roberts et al., 2005; Sanchez et al., 2005), and an innovative 3D damascene MIM capacitor concept that requires only one added mask compared to the standard CMOS process flow where investigated in (Thomas et al., 2007; Jeannot et al., 2007), achieving capacitance densities up to 30 fF/µm².

Figure 4. Cross section of a MIM capacitor

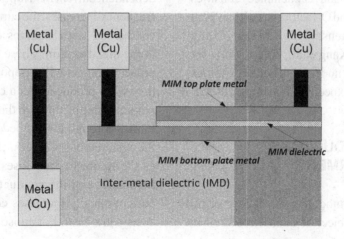

MOM Capacitors

The manufacturing of MIM capacitors with high capacitance density, high quality Q, good reliability and low additional cost is a real challenge. The high area occupation and the increased costs due to the extra masks necessary to implement the device, make the MIM capacitor not the optimal choice if low cost is a major design constraint. Therefore, in many applications the parasitic or native capacitance of horizontal or vertical parallel plates or comb and mesh structures in different metal levels are used to implement an integrated capacitor (Aparicio & Hajimiri, 2002; Kim et al., 2003; Zamdmer et al., 2004). These capacitors are also known as MOM (Metal Oxide Metal) capacitors and have a reduced area capacitance density; however, with this approach, area occupation, process complexity, and manufacturing cost are dramatically reduced with respect to MIM devices. Since MOM capacitors can be fabricated using conventional processes, they can be optimized by design and layout techniques only, without adding extra steps to the standard wafer manufacturing process. In addition, the continued scaling of the on-chip interconnects and the increasing number of interconnect layers in current and future CMOS technology nodes makes MOM capacitors more and more competitive, even from a capacitance density per chip area point of view. For the 65 nm and 45 nm technology nodes, native capacitors with good linearity, and capacitance densities larger than 2 fF/μm^2 and Q-factors larger than 20 at 1 GHz have been demonstrated (Kim et al., 2007; Fischer et al., 2008; Kang et al., 2009), while for the 32 nm technology node, capacitance densities above 4 fF/μm^2 are expected (Wu et al., 2007).

MONOLITHIC INDUCTORS AND TRANSFORMERS

Implementation and modeling of on-chip spiral inductors has been object of intense research in the past years since monolithic inductors are the core building block of the modern radio-frequency transceivers (Arcioni et al., 1998; Ashby et al., 1996; Burghartz et al., 1998; Kim & O, 1997; Long & Copeland, 1997; Niknejad, & Meyer, 1998; O, 1998; Yim et al., 2002; Yue, & Simon, 1998).

Several topologies have been proposed; however, in a standard CMOS process, an inductor is implemented by a spiral structure that uses two or more of the top metal layers. The top metal layers are used in order to minimize resistive and capacitive coupling to the substrate. More than two metal layers can be utilized to increase the Q factor (Lutz et al., 1999). The inductance value of spiral inductors is a complicated function of geometry and is usually estimated from two- or three-dimensional electromagnetic (EM) simulations.

Losses in Monolithic Inductors

A passive device such as an inductor, is constructed using one or more metal layers (typically aluminum, or copper for more expensive processes) provided by the target technology. Hence the device exhibits a non-ideal behavior due to the metal parasitic resistance that makes the quality factor Q to decrease. Metal is thus the primary source of resistive losses, and part of the magnetic energy is dissipated as heat by the device itself. However, the inductor also exhibits a frequency-dependent current distribution. As the operational frequency increases, the current distribution in the conducting layer changes due to eddy currents in the metallization. These currents, generate an induced magnetic flux opposing the one by which they were produced. As a consequence, the currents circulating through the conductor are forced to flow through low-impedance paths situated in the outer regions (Cao et al., 2003). Consequently, as the frequency increases, the effective cross-section area of the conductor decreases and the current density increases converting even more energy into heat. For an isolated conductor (Fig-

Figure 5. Current distribution in the case of (a) skin effect; (b) proximity effect (identical current flows), and (c) proximity effect (opposite current flows)

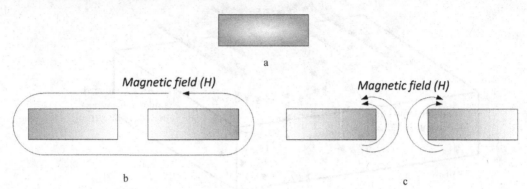

ure 5 (a)), this increase of the AC resistance is also known as *skin effect*, since the current tends to flow mainly at the surface of the conductor, and the skin depth δ is a measure of the distance at which the current density decays to $1/e$ of its original value:

$$\delta = \sqrt{\frac{2\rho}{2\pi f \mu}}$$

where ρ is the resistivity of the conductor, μ the absolute magnetic permeability of the conductor, and f the frequency.

In a multi-conductor system (Figures 5 (b) and (c)), the magnetic field in the proximity of a given conductor is the sum of two contributions: the self-induced magnetic field, and the magnetic field induced by the neighboring conductor. In this case, the increase of the AC resistance is due not only to skin effect, but also to the *proximity effect*, i.e. the effect of the conductor nearby. This means that the AC resistance will increase even further with respect to the case of an isolated conductor. Unfortunately this is the case of a spiral inductor.

The silicon substrate is a major source of resistive losses and frequency limitation in RF integrated circuits. The main drawback of the Si substrate when compared to other technologies such as GaAs or SOI is its conductive nature (Yue & Simon, 1998). The coupling between the electromagnetic field and the substrate induces in it two kinds of parasitic currents: the displacement currents and the eddy currents (see Figure 6). Eddy currents are induced by the magnetic field while displacement currents are induced by the time-varying displacement electric field associated to the magnetic field. The displacement currents flow perpendicularly to the spiral segments, either in the substrate surface or bulk to nearby grounds. Eddy currents, depicted in Figure 6 in the case of a spiral inductor, always flow parallel to the spiral segments creating a parasitic return path to signal.

In CMOS technologies, the largest losses result from eddy currents flow in the low-resistivity substrate, often dominating and masking the effects of the displacement current and of the inductor primary current. (Kuhn & Ibrahim, 2001). In modern CMOS processes two kinds of substrate are available: lightly doped and heavily doped. Lightly doped substrate (i.e., high resistivity) faces eddy current problem, whereas heavily doped substrate (i.e., low resistivity) faces displacement current problem. The substrate losses can be mitigated by shielding (Yue & Wong, 2000) the price of reduced self-resonant frequency.

To summarize, inductor Q is limited by resistive physical phenomena that convert electromagnetic energy into heat. At lower frequencies, the

Figure 6. Substrate induced displacement and eddy currents

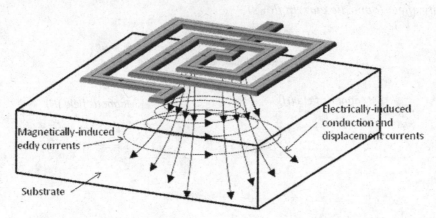

series resistance of the coil is a dominant factor in determining the quality factor Q; whereas, at higher frequencies, eddy currents in metal layers (skin and proximity effects) reduce current flow to smaller areas increasing heat conversion and limiting Q. In addition, the silicon substrate is source of additional resistive losses. Electrically-induced currents flow into the lossy substrate through displacement current injection, and additional losses occur for significantly conductive substrates due to magnetically-induced currents (eddy currents) severely limiting Q.

In a complex mixed-signal system, noise current is injected into the substrate through various mechanisms by the different digital and analog blocks that form the system (Su et al., 1993). This current flows vertically and horizontally towards points of low potential in the substrate, such as substrate taps and ground. Analog blocks are very sensitive to this coupling current that can result in a gain reduction or even instability. Particularly problematic in a mixed-signal IC are the possible interaction between digital logic and sensitive analog blocks. Digital gates switch in a pseudo-random manner and each gate transition results in some energy transfer to the substrate. This energy can couple with the analog circuits (such as LNAs and VCOs) decreasing the signal-to-noise ratio (Colvin et al., 1999). The effects of substrate noise injection can be mitigated or eliminated by using appropriate layout techniques. Guard rings around sensitive analog circuits provide a low resistance path to AC ground to substrate noise. Shielding decouples passive RF components or bus lines from the noisy substrate. Deep trench guards (Kim et al., 2001) can suppress inductor-substrate coupling, and can isolate noisy blocks in mixed-signal ICs. Finally, on-chip decoupling capacitors can reduce ground-bouncing effect as well as supply-voltage noise.

Modeling of Square Spiral Inductors

The extensive research and development in the modeling area recently carried out (Scuderi et al., 2004; Koutsoyannopoulos & Papananos, 2000; Yue & Wong, 2000; Cao et al., 2003; Talwalkar et al., 2005; Chao et al., 2002) has led to development of the π model, an inductor compact model that works well with the recently developed EM simulators. High-frequency behavioral modeling of an inductor is very difficult due to the effects of eddy currents and substrate losses. The first step toward the construction of a compact but accurate circuit model of a monolithic inductor consists in detecting the relevant parasitic elements and how do they affect the actual inductor. An ideal inductor is a lossless energy-storing device; however, the actual inductor exhibits parasitic resistances and capacitances. Resistances produce energy losses by means of power dissipation, whereas the capacitances store electrical energy.

Koutsoyannopoulos and Papananos (2000) provide detailed guidelines for modeling integrated inductors and transformers. Design parameters such as the quality factor Q, or the self-resonance frequency f_{SR} depend on device geometry, dimensions, type of material used for coils, and substrate.

Inductor compact models allow fast device characterization in detriment of results accuracy, since, in general, a compact model provides a good device characterization up to the self-resonance frequency. For this reason, when using a compact model, care should be taken in using the inductor at an operating frequency sufficiently far from its self-resonance frequency. Despite its limitation, the key advantage of a compact model is its scalability, which allows a fast estimation of the self inductance of devices of various sizes. Compact models use a reduced number of lumped elements to model the parasitic effects of CMOS fabrication process (see Figure 7). A simple and widely-used model (Yue & Wong, 2000) for square inductors relies on six elements: the device total series inductance L_s, resistance R_s, and capacitance C_s, the oxide parasitic capacitance C_{ox}, and the silicon substrate parasitic capacitance and resistance (indicated with C_{Si} and R_{Si} respectively).

Figure 8 depicts the equivalent electrical circuit of the model by Yue and Wong (2000).

Series Inductance

The series inductance of the model is computed as proposed by Greenhouse (1974). Greenhouse, using the inductance calculation formulas proposed by Grover (1946), developed an algorithm to estimate the inductance value of a planar integrated inductor. The Greenhouse method states that the overall series inductance of a square-shaped spiral inductor is the sum of two contributions: the wire self inductance L_{self}, and the positive or

negative mutual inductances among all possible wire segments.

The DC self inductance of a wire with a rectangular cross section can be computed as:

$$L_{self} = 2 \cdot l \cdot \left(\ln \frac{2 \cdot l}{w + t} + 0.5 + \frac{w + t}{3 \cdot l} \right),$$

where L_{self} is the self inductance in nH, l is the wire length in cm, w the wire width in cm, and t the wire thickness in cm.

The mutual inductance between two wires depends on their angle of intersection, length, and separation. Two wires orthogonal to each other have no mutual coupling. The current flow directions in the wires determine the sign of coupling. The coupling is positive if the currents in the two wires flow in the same direction, and negative otherwise. To evaluate the overall inductance of a N–turn square spiral, it involves the computation of $4N$ self-inductance terms, $2N(N\text{-}1)$ positive mutual-inductance terms, $2N^2$ and negative mutual-inductance terms. The mutual inductance M (in nH) between two parallel wires can be computed as:

$$M = 2 \cdot l \cdot m,$$

where l is the wire length in cm, and m the mutual inductance parameter that can be calculated as:

$$m = \\ \ln \left[\frac{l}{GMD} + \sqrt{1 + \left(\frac{l}{GMD} \right)^2} \right] - \sqrt{1 + \left(\frac{GMD}{l} \right)^2} + \frac{GMD}{l}$$

GMD denotes the geometric mean distance among the wire segments, which is approximately equal to the pitch of the wires. A more precise

Figure 7. Inductor (a) electrically-induced losses; and (b) physical parasitic

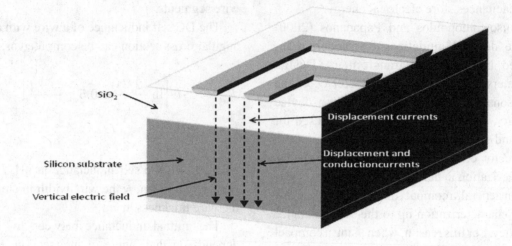

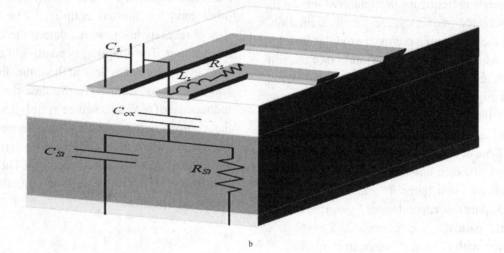

estimation of GMD is given by the following expression:

$$\ln GMD =$$
$$\ln d - \frac{w^2}{12d^2} - \frac{w^4}{60d^4} - \frac{w^6}{168d^6} - \frac{w^8}{360d^8} - \frac{w^{10}}{660d^{10}} - \cdots$$

where w is the width of a wire in cm, and d is the pitch between two wires in cm.

The self and mutual inductances of two wires are related by:

$$M = k\sqrt{L_1 \cdot L_2}$$

where k is the mutual coupling coefficient, and L_1 and L_2 the self inductances of the wires.

Series Capacitance

The series capacitance C_s models the parasitic capacitive coupling between input and output ports of the inductor. This capacitance forwards the signal directly to the output port without passing through the spiral inductor. The forward-

Figure 8. Inductor simple electrical model

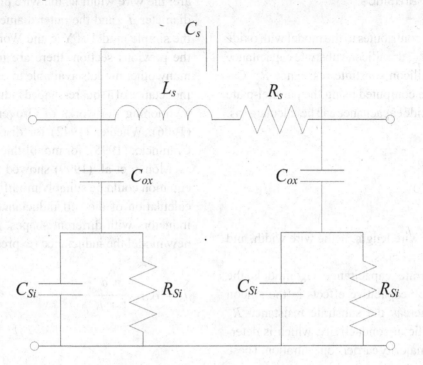

ing mechanism is due to both crosstalk through the coupling capacitance between two adjacent turns, and the overlap between the spiral and the underpass. However, the crosstalk impact can be cancelled by increasing wire pitch and is, in most cases, negligible. The effect of overlap capacitance is more significant because of the larger potential difference between the spiral and the underpass. The series capacitance can be computed as:

$$C_S = n \cdot w^2 \frac{\varepsilon_{ox}}{t_{ox,M}}$$

where n is the number of overlaps, w the wire width, and $t_{ox,M}$ the oxide thickness between the spiral and the underpass.

Series Resistance

The series resistance R_s models the frequency-dependent behavior of current density in a wire. As frequency increases, current distribution becomes non uniform due the magnetic fields generated by the self-induced eddy currents. As stated before, eddy currents manifest themselves as skin and proximity effects that can be modeled by a resistance increase. The series resistance can be computed as:

$$R_S = \frac{\rho \cdot l}{w \cdot t_{eff}} = \frac{\rho \cdot l}{w \cdot \delta \cdot \left(1 - e^{-t/\delta}\right)}$$

where ρ is the wire resistivity, l the wire length, w the wire width, δ the skin depth, and t_{eff} the effective thickness.

Substrate Parasitics

The substrate contributes to the model with oxide capacitance C_{ox}, the silicon substrate capacitance C_{Si}, and the silicon substrate resistance R_{Si}. Capacitances are computed using the parallel-plate model. The oxide capacitance can be calculated as:

$$C_{ox} = \frac{1}{2} \cdot l \cdot w \cdot \frac{\varepsilon_{ox}}{t_{ox}}$$

where l is the wire length, w the wire width, and t_{ox} the oxide thickness.

The substrate capacitance C_{Si} models the high-frequency capacitive effects in the silicon substrate, whereas the substrate resistance R_{Si} models the silicon conductivity, which is determined by the majority carrier concentration. These parameters can be computed as:

$$C_{Si} = \frac{1}{2} \cdot l \cdot w \cdot C_{sub}$$

and

$$R_{Si} = \frac{2}{w \cdot l \cdot G_{sub}}$$

where C_{sub} is substrate capacitance per unit area, G_{sub} is substrate conductance per unit area.

Other Inductors Topologies

In the previous section we dealt with modeling issues for square-shaped inductors. However, automatic synthesis tools offer the possibility of implementing inductors with various shapes: hexagonal, octagonal, and even circular (see Figure 9). The geometrical parameters of an inductor are: the wire width w, the wire pitch s, the inner diameter d_{in}, and the outer diameter d_{out}. Beside the simple model of Yue and Wong discussed in the previous section, there are in the literature many other models available to estimate the self inductance of a square-shaped inductor. It is worth mentioning the works of Grover (1946), Rosa (1906), Wheeler (1942) for discrete inductors, Craninckx (1995), for monolithic inductors.

Mohan et al. (1999) showed that Wheeler's equation could be suitably modified to allow the calculation of the self inductance of integrated inductors with different shapes. According this new model the inductance (expressed in H) is:

$$L = K_1 \mu_0 \frac{n^2 d_{avg}}{1 + K_2 \rho}$$

where $d_{avg} = 0.5 \cdot (d_{out} + d_{in})$ is the average diameter, μ_0 the vacuum permeability, n is the number of turns, and ρ is *fill ratio* defined as:

$$\rho = \frac{d_{out} - d_{in}}{d_{out} + d_{in}}$$

The fill ratio represents how hollow the inductor is. If ρ is small (i.e., $d_{out} \approx d_{in}$), the inductor is hollow, otherwise, if ρ is large (i.e., $d_{out} \gg d_{in}$), the inductor is full. The full inductor has a smaller inductance because its inner turns are closer to the center of the spiral and so they contribute less positive mutual inductance and more negative mutual inductance. Coefficients K_1 and K_2 depend on the inductor shapes and are shown in Table 1 for several layouts.

In the same work, Mohan et al. also proposed another simple model based on current sheet approximation (Rosa, 1906). The resulting inductance expression is:

Figure 9. Inductor topologies: (a) Square, (b) Hexagonal, (c) Octagonal, and (d) Circular

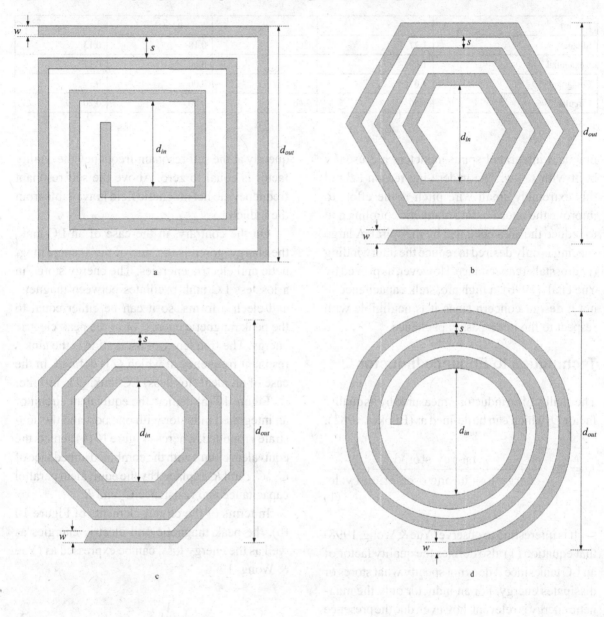

$$L = \frac{\mu \cdot n^2 \cdot d_{avg} \cdot c_1}{2}\left(\ln\left(\frac{c_2}{\rho}\right) + c_3\rho + c_4\rho^2\right),$$

where coefficients c_i are layout-dependent and are reported in Table 2. Although, as reported in (Mohan et al., 1999), the accuracy of this expression worsens as the ratio s/w becomes large; for $s \leq 3w$ the maximum measured error is of 8%, and

Table 1. Coefficients for the modified Wheeler's expression

Layout	K_1	K_2
Square	2.34	2.75
Hexagonal	2.33	3.82
Octagonal	2.25	3.55

Table 2. Coefficients for the current sheet expression

Layout	c_1	c_2	c_3	c_4
Square	1.27	2.07	0.18	0.13
Hexagonal	1.09	2.23	0.00	0.17
Octagonal	1.07	2.29	0.00	0.19
Circular	1.00	2.46	0.00	0.20

practical integrated spiral inductors are usually built with $s \leq w$. The underlying reason behind this extremely small wire pitch is the effort to improve the interwinding magnetic coupling and to reduce the area occupied by the spiral. A large spacing is only desired to reduce the interwinding (or crosstalk) capacitance. However, as proved by Yue et al. (1996), a high crosstalk capacitance in not a design concern since it is negligible with respect to the underpass capacitance.

Techniques to Enhance Inductor Q

The quality of an inductor is measured by its quality factor Q, which can be defined as (Booker, 1982):

$$Q = 2\pi \cdot \frac{\text{energy stored}}{\text{energy loss in one oscillation cycle}} \tag{1}$$

It is interesting to observe (Yue & Wong, 1998) that equation (1) also defines the quality factor of an LC tank since it does not specify what stores or dissipates energy. For an inductor only the magnetic energy is relevant; however, due the presence of resistive parasitic elements, there is also some energy stored in the inductor's electric field that reduces the theoretical maximum Q achievable:

$$Q = 2\pi \cdot \frac{\text{peak magnetic energy - peak electric energy}}{\text{energy loss in one oscillation cycle}} \tag{2}$$

An inductor is at self-resonance when the peak magnetic and electric energies are equal, conse-

quently at the self resonant frequency the quality factor is equal to zero. Above the self resonant frequency, no net magnetic field is available from the inductor.

On the contrary, in the case of an LC tank, the energy stored is the sum of the average magnetic and electric energies. The energy stored in a lossless LC tank oscillates between magnetic and electric forms, so it can be either equal to the peak magnetic energy, or to the peak electric energy. The frequency of oscillation is the tank's resonant frequency at which Q is defined. In the case of an ideal (lossless) LC tank, Q is infinite.

Figure 10 (a) depicts the equivalent circuit of an integrated inductor with one port and the substrate grounded, whereas Figure 10 (b) depicts the equivalent circuit with the combined impedance of C_{ox}, C_{Si}, and R_{Si} replaced by the equivalent parallel capacitance and resistance C_p and R_p.

In terms of the circuit elements of Figure 10 (b), the peak magnetic and electric energies as well as the energy loss, can be expressed as (Yue & Wong, 1998):

$$E_{peak,magnetic} = \frac{V_0^2 L_s}{2 \cdot \left[(\omega L_s)^2 + R_s^2\right]} \tag{3}$$

$$E_{peak,electric} = \frac{V_0^2 \left(C_s + C_p\right)}{2} \tag{4}$$

and

Figure 10. (a) Lumped equivalent circuit of a monolithic inductor; (b) Lumped model with equivalent parallel resistance and capacitance

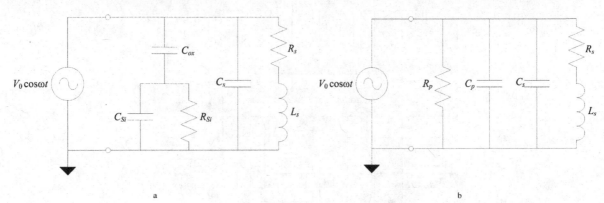

$$E_{loss} = \frac{2\pi}{\omega} \cdot \frac{V_0^2}{2} \cdot \left[\frac{1}{R_p} + \frac{R_s}{\left(\omega L_s\right)^2 + R_s^2} \right], \qquad (5)$$

where

$$R_p = \frac{1}{\omega^2 C_{ox}^2 R_{Si}} + \frac{R_{Si}\left(C_{ox} + C_{Si}\right)^2}{C_{ox}^2}$$

$$C_p = C_{ox} \cdot \frac{1 + \omega^2\left(C_{ox} + C_{Si}\right)C_{Si}R_{Si}^2}{1 + \omega^2\left(C_{ox} + C_{Si}\right)^2 R_{Si}^2}$$

and V_0 denotes the peak voltage across the inductor terminals. The inductor Q can be derived by substituting equations (3) to (5) into equation (2), thus obtaining:

$$Q = \frac{\omega L_s}{R_s} \cdot \frac{R_p}{R_p + \left[\left(\frac{\omega L_s}{R_s}\right)^2 + 1\right]R_s} \cdot \left[1 - \frac{R_s^2\left(C_s + C_p\right)}{L_s} - \omega^2 L_s\left(C_s + C_p\right)\right] =$$

$$= \frac{\omega L_s}{R_s} \cdot \text{substrate loss factor} \cdot \text{self-resonance factor}$$

The substrate loss factor represents the energy dissipated in the conductive silicon substrate,

whereas the self-resonance factor models the Q reduction due to the increase of the peak electric energy as the frequency increase, leading to Q vanishing at the self-resonant frequency. Finally, the term $\omega L_s/R_s$ accounts for the magnetic energy stored in the inductor and the ohmic losses in the parasitic series resistance.

In order to maximize the inductor Q, the two degradation factors (substrate loss factor and self-resonance factors) must be equal to one at the inductor working frequency. This means, according to the above discussion, that R_p must approach infinity and $(C_s + C_p)$ must approach zero. This is accomplished when the substrate resistance R_{Si} approaches either zero or infinity. Using high-resistivity silicon (for example SOI processes) or etching away the silicon (like in MEMS processes) is equivalent to make the substrate an open circuit. Another approach consists in shorting the substrate to eliminate resistive losses. This can be accomplished by inserting a ground plane that prevents the inductor electric field from entering the silicon substrate.

Solids ground shields for reducing silicon parasitic (Rofougaran et al., 1996; Tsukahara & Ishikawa, 1997) either in metal or in polysilicon can be detrimental for the shielded device since the induced eddy currents limit the magnetic field of the inductor they are supposed to protect.

Figure 11. Patterned ground shield layout

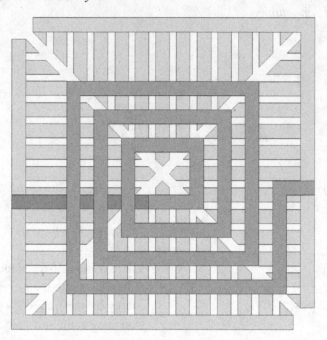

To avoid the formation of eddy currents, the shield can be patterned with slots orthogonal to the inductor turns as depicted in Figure 11 (Kim & O, 1997; Yue & Wong, 1998; O, 1998; Chen et al., 2001; Yim et al., 2002). The shield can be implemented with metal, polysilicon or *n+* diffusion strips, being the last the implementation considered most effective (Bahl, 2003). The slots in the shield act as an open circuit to break the flow of the induced eddy current; however, the slots must be narrow enough to prevent the vertical electric field from leaking through the shield down in the silicon substrate. On the other side, the ground strips act as the termination for the electric field. The ground strips are merged together around the four outer edges of the spiral inductor. The separation between the merged path and the spiral is not critical; however, care must be taken to avoid closed loop in the merged path so that to avoid the formation of eddy currents. In addition, the shield should be strapped with metal to provide a low-impedance path to ground (Yue & Wong, 1998).

According to Yue and Wong (1998), the shield resistance and the shield thickness are other critical design parameters. As stated before, the purpose of the patterned ground shield is to provide a good short to ground for the electric field. However, the resistance of the shield itself contributes to the energy loss of the inductor and must be kept minimal. To minimize the shield resistive losses its resistance should be negligible when compared to the reactance of the oxide parasitic capacitance. A typical monolithic inductor may have a parasitic capacitance in the range of 0.25 to 1 pF depending on the size and the oxide thickness (Yue & Wong, 1998), consequently the corresponding reactance in the frequency range of 1 to 2 GHz is on the order of 100 Ω, and a shield parasitic resistance of few ohms is sufficient to minimize the voltage drop across the shield minimizing the losses.

As the magnetic field crosses the patterned ground shield, the skin effect due to the induced magnetic currents in the shield originates an opposite magnetic flux that causes a decrease in the inductance (Wheeler, 1942). To avoid this attenu-

Figure 12. (a) Mesh-like deep trenches; (b) Side view of the deep trenches

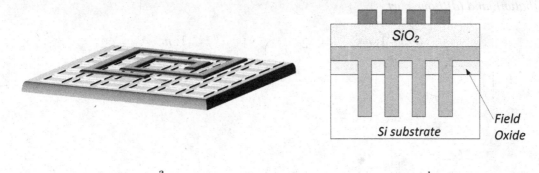

a

b

ation, the shield must be significantly thinner than the skin depth at the frequency of interest.

Another way to enhance Q is to increase the substrate resistance. In order to make substrate resistance to approach infinity, one idea is to use an insulator as substrate. Quartz or glass show better Q and higher self-resonant frequency than silicon-based substrates (Burghartz, 1998). On the other hand, in a standard CMOS process it is not possible to use a high resistive silicon substrate as an effective RF ground. Nonetheless, instead of building the whole circuit on a low resistive substrate, we can make a region with high resistivity for placing the inductor (Chan et al., 2003). A method to reduce substrate parasitic capacitance and improve the Q and increase the self-resonant frequency of an integrated inductor is the use of deep trenches (Yoshida et al., 1998). This option is not available in standard CMOS, but only BiCMOS and HBT fabrication processes. As depicted in Figure 12 (a), mesh-like narrow deep trenches are used to reduce substrate parasitic capacitance under a monolithic inductor, as well as the substrate-injected noise from other blocks of a complex mixed-signal system-on-chip. Figure 12 (b) depicts the side view of the deep trenches. Silicon substrate is etched to create the trenches that are filled with a combination of insulating materials. The advantage of a deep-trench mesh structure is twofold: first the capacitive coupling with the substrate decreases and the self-resonant

frequency increases by 10%, and second the resistive losses decreases and the peak quality factor increased by 15% (Tu & al., 2006).

Transformers and Baluns

Transformers are widely used in RF and microwave circuits for various applications including impedance matching, power dividers/combiners, double balanced mixers, power amplifiers, signal coupling, and phase shifting. Multiport transformers are also known as baluns (balanced-unbalanced) and are used to convert a single-ended signal into a differential signal and vice versa. A typical application could be, for example, the conversion of the single-end LNA output into a differential signal to be fed into the double-balanced down-conversion mixer. A major challenge in monolithic transformers is maintaining low parasitic capacitances and series resistances in order to operate these components at higher frequencies with low insertion loss. In general, the use of integrated transformers is limited to the frequency range between 1 and 3 GHz (Long, 2000).

The terminal currents and voltages of an ideal two-port transformer are related as follows:

$$\begin{bmatrix} V_1 \\ V_2 \end{bmatrix} = \begin{bmatrix} j\omega L_1 & j\omega M \\ j\omega M & j\omega L_2 \end{bmatrix} \begin{bmatrix} I_1 \\ I_2 \end{bmatrix}$$

Figure 13. Transformer configurations: (a) Two-port inverting, (b) Two-port non-inverting, (c) Three-port (balun), and (d) Four-port

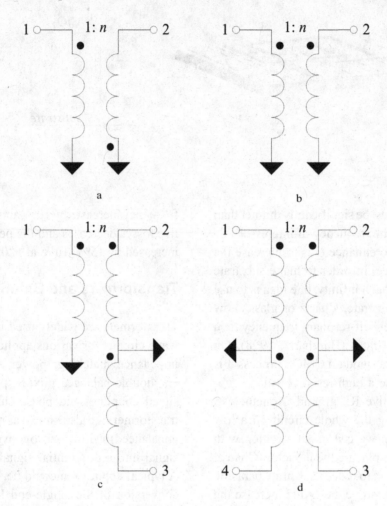

where L_1 and L_2 are the self-inductances of the primary and of the secondary port, respectively, M is the mutual inductance between the primary and the secondary, I_1 is the current flowing in the primary windings, I_2 is the current flowing in the secondary windings, V_1 is the voltage at the primary, and V_2 is the voltage at the secondary.

The magnetic coupling coefficient k is given by:

$$k = \frac{M}{\sqrt{L_1 L_2}}$$

For an ideal transformer, $k = 1$, whereas for most monolithic transformers k falls in the range within 0.3 and 0.9, due to the leakage of the magnetic flux. A monolithic transformer suffers from the same non-idealities of the integrated inductors, namely: parasitic capacitances, losses due to parasitic resistances, eddy currents, skin effect, and proximity effect.

Another parameter of interest is the turn ratio n, defined as:

$$n = \sqrt{\frac{L_2}{L_1}} = \frac{V_2}{V_1} = \frac{I_1}{I_2}$$

Figure 13 shows the possible transformer configurations. A transformer can be configured as a two-port, three-port or four-port device. The two-port inverting transformer is in general implemented as a symmetric inductor with the center tap grounded. It is used in as the load inductors or the source degenerated inductors in many differential LNA schemes. The two-port non-inverting transformer usually has smaller effective inductance, thus the self-resonant frequency is usually high. The three-port transformer is used as a single-ended to differential converter (balun) in LNAs and PAs. Finally, the four-port transformer has two pairs of differential ports and is used in differential mixers.

The coupling coefficient k, the turn ratio n, and other transformer parameters may vary considerably depending on the transformer topology. In addition, transformers may be divided in two categories: *planar* if lateral magnetic coupling is used, and *stacked* if vertical magnetic coupling is used. Figure 14 depicts several planar transformer implementations (Long, 2000). The tapped two-port transformer represented in is Figure 14 (a), in practice, an inductor with a middle tap. This topology is not a symmetric design but allows a wide range of turn ratios, although the coupling coefficient k is usually small (between 0.3 and 0.5).

Figure 14 (b) shows another asymmetric implementation, the parallel transformer. Although in this topology the number of turns of the primary and of the secondary are exactly the same, this is not the case for the self inductances; as a consequence, for this topology $n \neq 1$.

Figure 14 (c) shows the interwinded transformer; the layout is symmetrical with respect to the center of the device; however, it is not suitable for multi-port implementation due to the difficulty for connecting either primary or secondary center taps. The implementations represented in Figures 14 (d) to (f) are, on the contrary designed for multi-port applications with the center taps located at about half of the physical length. The

implementations shown in Figures 14 (b) to (f) are all interleaved transformer variations. They have moderate coupling (k approximately equal to 0.7) with reduced self-inductances and larger terminal-to-terminal capacitances.

A stacked transformer using three metal layers is shown in Figure 15. Both vertical and lateral magnetic coupling is utilized; as a consequence, self-inductance and coupling coefficients are high (k about 0.9). The lowest metal layer acts like a shield to mitigate the substrate effect to the upper layers.

Due to the reduced inter-layer distance, the device exhibits high coupling capacitances. To mitigate this problem several solutions have been proposed such as shifting the middle traces to reduce the overlap area or using alternate metal layers to increase the thickness of the inter-metal dielectric. The overlap capacitance can be computed as reported by Zolfaghari et al. (2001), and it is inversely proportional to the square of the number of metal layers used. Compared to planar transformers, the stacked implementation is more compact; however, a major shortcoming of a multi-level implementation is that in state-of-the-art processes the different metal layers have different thicknesses, with the top layer (also known as analog metal) usually thicker than the others. This, in turn, complicates the estimation of the transformer figures of merit and of the parasitic parameters.

CONCLUSION

The capability to fabricate passive components compatible with standard low-cost CMOS processes is a major breakthrough achieved by the semiconductor industry in this decade. This has enabled a wide number of new applications and allowed the implementation of fully-monolithic, low-cost wireless transceivers. On chip inductors and capacitors are the key elements to implement radio-frequency circuits, especially in the

Figure 14. Planar transformer topologies: (a) Tapped, (b) Parallel, (c) Interwinded, (d) Symmetric, (e) Step-up, and (f) Step-up variation

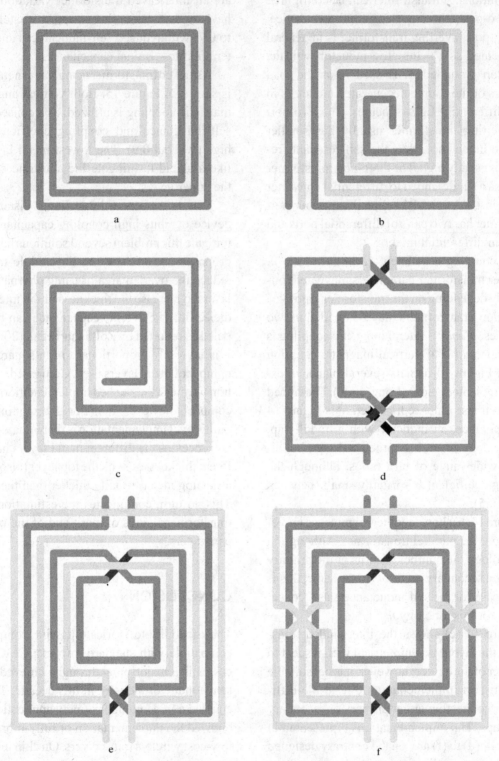

Figure 15. (a) Stacked transformer, and (b) circuit model

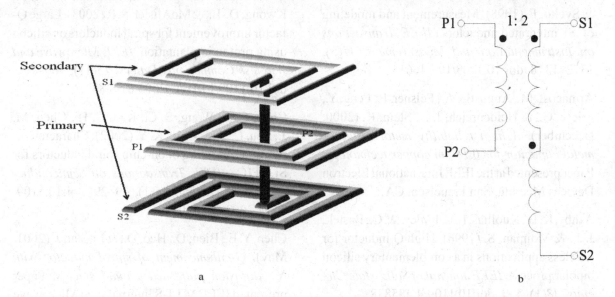

gigahertz range where off-chip inductors are not effective since their inductance values are comparable with bondwire parasitic inductances. When incorporating passive components into a standard CMOS process, it is likely that additional photolithography and processing steps are necessary. x Moreover, new materials like high-κ dielectrics may be required to improve passive elements performance. This is the case, for example, of MIM capacitors. Therefore, processing cost must be traded-off for device performance. As a matter of fact, in low-cost designs using MOM capacitors is the best option. Nonetheless, this is quite a complex and application-dependent design choice. In fact, on one hand capacitors and inductors usually occupy much more silicon area than active devices, but on the other, optimization schemes that require extra processing steps are basically aimed at reducing the area overhead of the passive devices. Consequently, implementing extra process steps or adding process complexity to increase the unit capacitance could lead to a smaller die size, reducing the overall implementation costs, and must be carefully evaluated during the design planning. The major issue in inductor

design in with CMOS technologies is the resistive nature of the substrate which introduces losses that are detrimental for the quality factor of the device. Several solutions have been proposed to tackle the Q problem in inductor design relying either on patterned shields or on the introduction of specific process steps aimed at increasing substrate resistivity. Long-term challenges for passive elements implementation will include the need to integrate new materials in a cost-effective manner to realize compact high quality-factor (Q) inductors and high-density metal-insulator-metal (MIM) capacitors.

REFERENCES

Akcasu, O. E. (1993). *High capacitance structures in a semiconductor device.* (U.S. Patent 5 208 725).

Aparicio, R., & Hajimiri, A. (2002). Capacity limits and matching properties of integrated capacitors. *IEEE Journal of Solid-state Circuits, 37*(3), 384–393. doi:10.1109/4.987091

Arcioni, P., Castello, R., De Astis, G., Sacchi, E., & Svelto, F. (1998). Measurement and modeling of Si integrated inductors. *IEEE Transactions on Instrumentation and Measurement*, *47*(5), 1372–1378. doi:10.1109/19.746613

Armacost, M., Augustin, A., Felsner, P., Feng, Y., Friese, G., & Heidenreich, J. ... Stein, K. (2000, December). *A high reliability metal insulator metal capacitor for 0.18 μm copper technology.* Paper presented at the IEEE International Electron Devices Meeting, San Francisco, CA.

Ashby, K. B., Kuollias, I. A., Finley, W. C., Bastek, J. J., & Moinian, S. (1996). High Q inductor for wireless applications in a complementary silicon bipolar process. *IEEE Journal of Solid-state Circuits*, *33*(1), 4–9. doi:10.1109/4.485838

Bahl, I. J. (2003). *Lumped elements for RF and microwave circuits*. Norwood, MA: Artech House.

Booker, H. G. (1982). *Energy in electromagnetism*. London, UK: Peter Peregrinus (on behalf of the IEE).

Burghartz, J. N. (1998, December). *Progress in RF Inductors on silicon-understanding substrate losses.* Paper presented at the IEEE International Electron Devices Meeting, San Francisco, CA.

Burghartz, J. N., Edelstein, D. C., Souyer, M., Ainspan, H. A., & Jenkins, K. A. (1998). RF circuit aspects of spiral inductors on silicon. *IEEE Journal of Solid-state Circuits*, *33*(12), 2028–2034. doi:10.1109/4.735544

Cao, Y., Groves, R. A., Zamdmer, N. D., Plouchart, J. O., Wachnik, R. A., & Huang, X. (2003). Frequency-independent equivalent circuit model for on-chip spiral inductors. *IEEE Journal of Solid-state Circuits*, *38*(3), 419–426. doi:10.1109/JSSC.2002.808285

Chan, K. T., Huang, C. H., Chin, A., Li, M. F., Kwong, D.-L., & McAlister, S. P. (2003). Large Q-factor improvement for spiral inductors on silicon using proton implantation. *IEEE Microwave and Wireless Components Letters*, *13*(11), 460–462. doi:10.1109/LMWC.2003.819383

Chao, C. J., Wong, S. C., Kao, C. H., Chen, M. J., Leu, L. Y., & Chiu, K. Y. (2002). Characterization and Modeling of on-chip spiral inductors for Si RFICs. *IEEE Transactions on Semiconductor Manufacturing*, *15*(1), 19–29. doi:10.1109/TSM.2002.983440

Chen, Y. E., Bien, D., Heo, D., & Laskar, J. (2001, May). *Q-enhancement of spiral inductor with N+ diffusion patterned ground shields.* Paper presented IEEE MTT-S International Microwave Symposium, Phoenix, AZ.

Colvin, J. T., & Bhatia, S. S., & O, K. (1999). Effect of substrate resistances on LNA performance and a bondpad structure for reducing the effects in a silicon bipolar technology. *IEEE Journal of Solid-state Circuits*, *34*(9), 1339–1344. doi:10.1109/4.782095

Craninckx, J., & Steyart, M. S. J. (1995). A 1.8 GHz CMOS low noise voltage-controlled oscillator with prescalar. *IEEE Journal of Solid-state Circuits*, *30*(12), 1474–1482. doi:10.1109/4.482195

Fischer, A. H., Lim, Y. K., Riess, P., Pompl, T., Zhang, B. C., & Chua, E. C. ... von Glasow, A. (2008, April). *TDDB robustness of highly dense 65NM BEOL vertical natural capacitor with competitive area capacitance for RF and mixed-signal applications.* Paper presented at the IEEE International Reliability Physics Symposium, Phoenix, AZ.

Greenhouse, H. M. (1974). Design of planar rectangular microelectronic inductors. *IEEE Transactions on Parts, Hybrids, and Packaging*, *10*(2), 101–109. doi:10.1109/TPHP.1974.1134841

Grover, F. W. (1946). *Inductance calculation: Working formulas and tables*. NJ: Van Nostrand.

Jeannot, S., Bajolet, A., Manceau, J.-P., Cremer, S., Deloffre, E., & Oddou, J.-P. ... Bruyere, S. (2007, December). *Toward next high performances MIM generation: up to 30fF/μm² with 3D architecture and high-κ materials.* Paper presented at the IEEE International Electron Devices Meeting, San Francisco, CA.

Kang, I. M., Jung, S.-J., Choi, T.-H., Jung, J.-H., Chung, C., & Kim, H.-S. (2009). RF model of BEOL vertical natural capacitor (VNCAP) fabricated by 45-nm RF CMOS technology and its verification. *IEEE Electron Device Letters, 30*(5), 538–540. doi:10.1109/LED.2009.2015781

Kar-Roy, A., Chun, H., Racanelli, M., Compton, C. A., Kempf, P., & Jolly, G. ... Yin, A. (1999, May). *High density metal insulator metal capacitors using PECVD nitride for mixed signal and RF circuits.* Paper presented at the IEEE International Interconnect Technology Conference, San Francisco, CA.

Kim, C. S., Park, P., Park, J.-W., Hwang, N., & Yu, H. K. (2001, May). *Deep trench guard technology to suppress coupling between inductors in silicon RF ICs.* Paper presented at the IEEE MTT-S International Microwave Symposium, Phoenix, AZ.

Kim, D., Kim, J., Plouchart, J.-O., Cho, C., Trzcinski, R., Kumar, M., & Norris, C. (2007). Symmetric vertical parallel plate capacitors for on-chip RF circuits in 65-nm SOI technology. *IEEE Electron Device Letters, 28*(7), 616–618. doi:10.1109/LED.2007.899464

Kim, J., Plouchart, J.-O., Zamdmer, N., Sherony, M., Lu, L.-H., & Tan, Y. ... Wagner, L. (2003, June). *3-dimensional vertical parallel plate capacitors in an SOI CMOS technology for integrated RF circuits.* Paper presented at the IEEE Symposium on VLSI Circuits, Honolulu, HI.

Kim, K., & O. K. (1997). Characteristics of an integrated spiral inductor with an underlying n-well. *IEEE Transactions on Electron Devices, 44*(9), 1565–1567. doi:10.1109/16.622620

Koutsoyannopoulos, Y. K., & Papananos, Y. (2000). Systematic analysis and modeling of integrated inductors and transformers in RF IC design. *IEEE Transactions on Circuits and Systems-II: Analog and Digital Signal Processing, 47*(8), 699–713. doi:10.1109/82.861403

Kuhn, W. B., & Ibrahim, N. M. (2001). Analysis of current crowding effects in multiturn spiral inductors. *IEEE Transactions on Microwave Theory and Techniques, 49*(1), 31–38. doi:10.1109/22.899959

Lin, C. C., Hsu, H. M., Chen, Y. H., Shih, T., Jang, S. M., Yu, C. H., & Liang, M. S. (2001, June). *A full Cu damascene metallization process for sub-0.18 /spl mu/m RF CMOS SoC high Q inductor and MIM capacitor application at 2.4 GHz and 5.3 GHz.* Paper presented at the IEEE International Interconnect Technology Conference, San Francisco, CA.

Liu, R., Lin, C.-Y., Harris, E., Merchant, S., Downey, S. W., & Weber, G. ... Gregor, R. (2000, June). *Single mask metal-insulator-metal (MIM) capacitor with copper damascene metallization for sub-0.18 μm mixed mode signal and system-on-a-chip (SoC) applications.* Paper presented at the IEEE International Interconnect Technology Conference, San Francisco, CA.

Long, J. R. (2000). Monolithic transformers for silicon RF IC design. *IEEE Journal of Solid-state Circuits, 35*(9), 1368–1382. doi:10.1109/4.868049

Long, J. R., & Copeland, M. A. (1997). The modeling, characterization, and design of monolithic inductors for silicon RF ICs. *IEEE Journal of Solid-state Circuits, 32*(3), 257–369. doi:10.1109/4.557634

Lutz, R. D., Hahm, Y., Weisshaar, A., Tripathi, V. K., Wu, H., & Kanaglekar, N. (1999, June). *Modeling and analysis of multilevel spiral inductors for RF ICs.* Paper presented at the IEEE MTT-S International Microwave Symposium, Anaheim, CA.

Mahnkopf, R., Allers, K.-H., Armacost, M., Augustin, A., Barth, J., & Brase, G. ... Chen, B. (1999, December). *System on a chip technology for 0.18-μm digital, mixed signal and eDRAM applications.* Paper presented at the IEEE International Electron Devices Meeting, San Francisco, CA.

Miyashita, K., Nakayama, T., Oishi, A., Hasumi, R., Owada, M., & Aota, S. ... Kakumu, M. (2001, June). *A high performance 100 nm generation SOC technology (CMOS IV) for high density embedded memory and mixed signal LSIs.* Paper presented at the IEEE Symposium on VLSI Technology, Kyoto, Japan.

Mohan, S. S., Hershenson, M., Boyd, S. P., & Lee, T. H. (1999). Simple accurate expressions for planar spiral inductances. *IEEE Journal of Solid-state Circuits, 34*(10), 1419–1424. doi:10.1109/4.792620

Ng, C. H., Chew, K. W., Li, J. X., Tjoa, T. T., Goh, L. N., & Chu, S. F. (2002, December). *Characterization and comparison of two metal-insulator-metal capacitor schemes in 0.13 μm copper dual damascene metallization process for mixed-mode and RF applications.* Paper presented at the IEEE International Electron Devices Meeting, San Francisco, CA.

Niknejad, A., & Meyer, R. (1998). Analysis, design, and optimization of spiral inductors and transformers for Si RF ICs. *IEEE Journal of Solid-state Circuits, 33*(10), 1470–1481. doi:10.1109/4.720393

O, K. (1998). Estimation methods for quality factors of inductors fabricated in silicon integrate circuit process technologies. *IEEE Journal of Solid-State Circuits, 33*(8), 1249–1252.

Roberts, D., Johnstone, W., Sanchez, H., Mandhana, O., Spilo, D., & Hayden, J. ... White, B.E. (2005, December). *Application of on-chip MIM decoupling capacitor for 90 nm SOI microprocessor.* Paper presented at the IEEE International Electron Devices Meeting, San Francisco, CA.

Rofougaran, A., Chang, J. Y.-C., Rofougaran, M., & Abidi, A. A. (1996). A 1 GHz CMOS RF front-end IC for a direct-conversion wireless receiver. *IEEE Journal of Solid-state Circuits, 31*(7), 880–889. doi:10.1109/4.508199

Rosa, E. B. (1906). Calculation of the self-inductance of single-layer coils. *Bulletin of the Bureau of Standards, 2*(2), 161–187.

Samavati, H., Hajimiri, A., Shahani, A. R., Nasserbakht, G. N., & Lee, T. H. (1998). Fractal capacitors. *IEEE Journal of Solid-state Circuits, 33*(12), 2035–2041. doi:10.1109/4.735545

Sanchez, H., Mandhana, O. P., Johnstone, B., Roberts, D., Siegel, J., & Melnick, B. ... White, B. (2007, June). *Technology and design cooperation: High-K MIM capacitors for microprocessor, IO, and clocking.* Paper presented at the IEEE International Interconnect Technology Conference, San Francisco, CA.

Schiml, T., Biesemans, S., Brase, G., Burrell, L., Cowley, A., & Chen, K. C. ... Leung, P. (2001, June). *A 0.13 μm CMOS platform with Cu/low-k interconnects for system on chip applications.* Paper presented at the IEEE Symposium on VLSI Technology, Kyoto, Japan.

Scuderi, A., Biondi, T., Ragonese, E., & Palmisano, G. (2004). A lumped scalable model for silicon integrated spiral inductors. *IEEE Transactions on Circuits and Systems-I, 51*(6), 1203–1209. doi:10.1109/TCSI.2004.829301

Su, D. K., Loinaz, M. J., Masui, S., & Wooley, B. A. (1993). Experimental results and modeling techniques for substrate noise in mixed-signal integrated circuits. *IEEE Journal of Solid-state Circuits, 28*(4), 420–430. doi:10.1109/4.210024

Talwalkar, N. A., Yue, C. P., & Wong, S. S. (2005). Analysis and synthesis of on-chip spiral inductors. *IEEE Transactions on Electron Devices, 52*(2), 176–182. doi:10.1109/TED.2004.842535

Thomas, M., Farcy, A., Deloffre, E., Gros-Jean, M., Perrot, C., & Benoit, D. … Torres, J. (2007, June). *Impact of TaN/Ta copper barrier on full PEALD TiN/Ta2O5/TiN 3D damascene MIM capacitor performance.* Paper presented at the IEEE International Interconnect Technology Conference, San Francisco, CA.

Thomas, M., Farcy, A., Perrot, C., Deloffre, E., Gros-Jean, M., & Benoit, D. … Torres, J. (2007, June). *Reliable 3D damascene MIM architecture embedded into Cu interconnect for a Ta$_2$O$_5$ capacitor record density of 17 fF/μm^2.* Paper presented at the IEEE Symposium on VLSI Technology, Kyoto, Japan.

Tsukahara, T., & Ishikawa, M. (1997, February). *A 2 GHz 60 dB dynamic-range Si logarithmic/limiting amplifier with low-phase deviations.* Paper presented at the IEEE International Solid-State Circuits Conference, San Francisco, CA.

Tu, H.-L., Chen, I.-S., Yeh, P.-C., & Ciuou, H.-K. (2006). High performance spiral inductor on deep-trench-mesh silicon substrate. *IEEE Microwave and Wireless Components Letters, 16*(12), 654–656. doi:10.1109/LMWC.2006.885608

van Huylenbroeck, S., Decoutere, S., Venegas, R., Jenei, S., & Winderickx, G. (2009). Investigation of PECVD dielectrics for nondispersive metal-insulator-metal capacitors. *IEEE Electron Device Letters, 23*(4), 191–193. doi:10.1109/55.992835

Wheeler, H. A. (1942). Formulas for skin effect. [IRE]. *Proceedings of the Institute of Radio Engineers, 30*(9), 412–424.

Wu, S.-Y., Chou, C. W., Lin, C. Y., Chiang, M. C., Yang, C. K., & Liu, M. Y. … Liang, M. S. (2007, December). *A 32nm CMOS Low power SoC platform technology for foundry applications with functional high density SRAM.* Paper presented at the IEEE International Electron Devices Meeting, San Francisco, CA.

Yim, S.-M., & Chen, T., & O, K. (2002). The effects of a ground shield on the characteristics and performance of spiral inductors. *IEEE Journal of Solid-state Circuits, 37*(2), 237–244. doi:10.1109/4.982430

Yoshida, H., Suzuki, H., Kinoshita, Y., Fujii, H., & Yamazaki, T. (1998, December). *An RF BiCMOS process using high f_{SR} spiral inductor with premetal deep trenches and a dual recessed bipolar collector sink.* Paper presented at the IEEE International Electron Devices Meeting, San Francisco, CA.

Yue, C. P., Ryu, C., Lau, J., Lee, T. H., & Wong, S. S. (1996, December). *A physical model for planar spiral inductors on silicon.* Paper presented at the IEEE International Electron Devices Meeting, San Francisco, CA.

Yue, C. P., & Wong, S. S. (1998). On-chip spiral inductors with patterned ground shields for Si-based RF ICs. *IEEE Journal of Solid-state Circuits, 33*(5), 743–752. doi:10.1109/4.668989

Yue, C. P., & Wong, S. S. (2000). Physical modeling of spiral inductors on silicon. *IEEE Transactions on Electron Devices, 47*(3), 560–568. doi:10.1109/16.824729

Zamdmer, N., Kim, J., Trzcinski, R., Plouchart, J.-O., Narasimha, S., Khare, M., et al. (2004, June). *A 243-GHz F$_t$ and 208-GHz F$_{max}$, 90-nm SOI CMOS SoC technology with low-power millimeter-wave digital and RF circuit capability.* Paper presented at the IEEE Symposium on VLSI Technology, Kyoto, Japan.

Zolfaghari, A., Chan, A., & Razavi, B. (2001). Stacked inductors and transformers in CMOS technology. *IEEE Journal of Solid-state Circuits, 36*(4), 620–628. doi:10.1109/4.913740

Zurcher, P., Alluri, P., Chu, P., Duvallet, A., Happ, C., Henderson, R., et al. (2000, December). *Integration of thin film MIM capacitors and resistors into copper metallization based RF-CMOS and Bi-CMOS technologies.* Paper presented at the IEEE International Electron Devices Meeting, San Francisco, CA.

KEY TERMS AND DEFINITIONS

Balanced-Unbalanced (Balun): It is a type of electrical transformer than can convert an input differential signal (i.e., a signal that is balanced with respect ground) into an output single-ended (i.e., unbalanced) signal and vice versa.

Bipolar-CMOS (BiCMOS): It is an integrated circuit technology that allows the integration on a single silicon substrate of both bipolar and MOS devices.

Heterojunction Bipolar Transitor (HBT): An improved bipolar devices that can handle signals at very high frequencies (up to several hundred GHz) and it is commonly used in many radio-frequency applications.

Low Noise Amplifier (LNA): It is an electronic amplifier designed to amplify very weak signal like those captured by an antenna in a radio-frequency receiver. It is located very close to the antenna to reduce the losses. In order to reduce the overall noise figure of the down-conversion chain it must have very high gain and very low noise figure.

Quality Factor: In engineering and physics, the quality factor (Q) is a dimensionless parameter that describes the amount of energy loss in a LC resonator.

Voltage Controlled Oscillator (VCO): It is an electronic oscillator whose oscillation frequency is controlled by an external DC voltage.

Section 3
Baseband Processing and Wireless Standards

Chapter 9
Frequency Synchronization for OFDM/OFDMA Systems

Javier González Bayón
Universidad Politécnica de Madrid, Spain

Carlos Carreras Vaquer
Universidad Politécnica de Madrid, Spain

Angel Fernández Herrero
Universidad Politécnica de Madrid, Spain

ABSTRACT

Orthogonal frequency division multiplexing (OFDM) has been the focus of many studies in wireless communications because of its high transmission capability and its robustness to the effects of frequency-selective multipath channels. However, it is well known that OFDM systems are much more sensitive to a carrier frequency offset (CFO) than single carrier schemes with the same bit rate. Therefore, a frequency synchronization process is necessary to overcome this sensitivity to frequency offset. Synchronization is performed in two stages: acquisition and tracking. After a first estimation and correction of the CFO performed in the acquisition stage, there still remains a residual frequency offset (RFO) due to real system conditions. Therefore, the RFO tracking has to be performed for all the receiving data. Frequency synchronization is even more complicated for uplink communications in OFDMA (orthogonal frequency division multiple access) systems because the base station (BS) has to deal with signals from different users in the same bandwidth. Each user's data is affected by a different CFO. Because of this, estimation and correction of the CFOs cannot be accomplished by the same methods as in OFDM systems.

DOI: 10.4018/978-1-4666-0083-6.ch009

INTRODUCTION

OFDM has, with substantial progress in digital signal processing, become an important part of the telecommunications arena. This is because its ability to transform a wideband frequency-selective channel to a set of parallel flat-fading narrowband channels, which substantially simplifies the channel equalization problem. Several existing standards, among them WiFi 802.11g/n (802.11n, 2009), WiMAX 802.16d/e (802.16d, 2004; 802.16e, 2005) or DVB-T (DVB-T, 2004), are based on the OFDM concept. This chapter will focus on these standards when explaining the frequency synchronization process.

CFO synchronization turns out to be a critical issue for *multicarrier* systems. This CFO can appear because of two reasons: due to an offset between the frequencies of the local oscillator of the transmitter and the receiver or due to the Doppler effect. The CFO causes loss of orthogonality of the multiplexed signals that produces an *inter-carrier interference (ICI)* noise, an amplitude reduction and, also, a constant increment in the phase of the samples. Therefore a frequency synchronization process is necessary to overcome this sensitivity to frequency offset.

Frequency synchronization is often performed in two phases: *acquisition* and *tracking*. At the start of the sequence the acquisition stage is used to perform a first estimation of the CFO of the signal (Beek, 1997; Schmidl, 1997; Speth, 2001; Moose, 1994). In a circuit-switched system the acquisition phase can be fairly long since it only represents a small percentage of the total transmitted sequence. Some systems like DVB-T and cellular systems are circuit-switched. In packet-switched systems, as 802.16d and 802.11g/n, the acquisition phase is more important since the transmission sequences are short. The most common approach in such systems is to use a preamble for acquisition. As it will be shown, the acquisition stage is a well defined task that can be easily adapted to all standards being considered. Most of the CFO is

usually corrected at the acquisition stage, but there still remains the problem with the residual ICI and the increasing phase of the samples.

After acquisition, the tracking problem has to be solved. Since acquisition is never performed perfectly and real world conditions are not static, there still remains a RFO. If the RFO is not tracked and corrected, oscillator instabilities and/or Doppler effect can make the CFO estimation from the acquisition stage to become obsolete, thus increasing the residual ICI and decreasing the receiver performance. The constellation points will also suffer a rotation due to this RFO and will eventually cross the decisor boundaries, thus causing the system performance to become unacceptable. This rotation affects mostly to OFDM packet based systems as 802.11g/n or 802.16d/e. This is because, for these standards, the channel estimation is only performed at the beginning of the frame since the packet length is short enough to assume a constant channel during the length of the packet. Therefore, channel estimation can not correct the constant rotation produced by the CFO. In addition, the residual ICI will also affect the performance of the systems. It is mandatory to correct this impairment for all the technologies that use OFDM.

The tracking stage can be non data-aided (Kuang, 2005), when no extra information is included in the transmitted data (as in decision-directed methods) or data-aided (Speth, 2001; González-Bayón, 2007), when periodically transmitted training symbols and/or known pilot subcarriers are used.

The increasing demand for multimedia communications with variable data rates and different quality of service (QoS) requirements has recently led to a strong interest in OFDMA. This transmission technique has been chosen for mobile wireless metropolitan area network as in 802.16e-2005 (mobile WiMAX). In OFDMA, subcarriers are grouped into sets, each of which is assigned to a different user. Block, interleaved, random or clustered tiled assignment schemes can be used for this purpose. Unfortunately, OFDMA is particularly sensitive to the different CFOs caused by oscillator mismatches between the users with respect to the base station and/or by doppler shifts. All the users transmitting in the uplink signal have to be synchronized with the BS in order to prevent ICI, multiple access interference (MAI), signal attenuation and a constant increment in the phase of the subcarriers. ICI is caused by the leakage or interference between a users own subcarriers, whereas MAI is caused by the power leakage from other users subcarriers.

Frequency synchronization in OFDMA systems is based on a three-step procedure. In the first step, each user performs CFO estimation in the downlink. This operation reduces the CFO and can be easily accomplished using techniques applied in OFDM systems. The obtained CFO estimates are used as synchronization references in the subsequent uplink transmission. Due to estimation errors in the first step and/or oscillator instabilities and/or Doppler effects, uplink signals arriving at the base station may be affected by some residual CFOs, which not only introduce ICI and MAI, but also cause a phase rotation in the subcarriers, thus producing incorrect data decisions after a few OFDM symbols. Hence, the second necessary step corresponds to CFO estimation in the uplink. The third step is the compensation of the CFO at the receiver, which also requires different techniques than those used in OFDM systems. This chapter will focus in the second and third steps when referring to frequency synchronization in OFDMA systems.

Pun (2007) proposed a complete OFDMA detection scheme, but the complexity of the calculations makes impossible its practical implementation. In (Zeng, 2009; Morelli, 2007; Pun, 2006; Nguyen, 2008) a preamble amended at the beginning of the uplink frame is used to perform CFO estimation in the time domain. However, there is no preamble at the beginning of the uplink frame in the 802.16e standard. This standard supports optional repeating short pre-ambles, called midambles, one out of 4, 8 or 16 OFDM symbols. Though these midambles could support the implementation of these estimation methods, they also decrease the throughput of the system. In addition, the number of computations required by these schemes is still quite high. In (Sun, 2009), pilot subcarriers are used to estimate and correct the CFOs by performing an iterative process. This process is composed of an exhaustive search step and a frequency correction step by using the ICI matrix defined by Cao (2004). Again, an exhaustive search is a very expensive approach in terms of the required computations. Although a limited sweep is proposed to alleviate this problem, the tradeoff between accuracy and complexity remains uncharacterized. In (Cao, 2004; Yücek, 2007), compensation methods for the different CFOs are proposed. However, the estimation part is not included in these works. The method proposed by Yücek (2007) reduces the number of computations required in (Cao, 2004) by taking advantage of the physical frame of the 802.16e standard, where subcarriers are grouped into tiles.

FREQUENCY SYNCRONIZATION IN OFDM SYSTEMS

In this section, we review briefly the basics of OFDM and focus in the study of the frequency synchronization methods. Clearly, issues such as timing recovery and channel estimation are important, but will not be treated here. We assume perfect frame and time synchronizations in the equations of this section.

The OFDM Signal

Figure 1 shows the block diagram of an OFDM system. The data source emits symbols (d'_i) which belong to a QPSK, 16-QAM or 64-QAM constellation and are assumed to be equiprobable and statistically independent. The sequence d_i is

Figure 1. Block diagram of an OFDM system

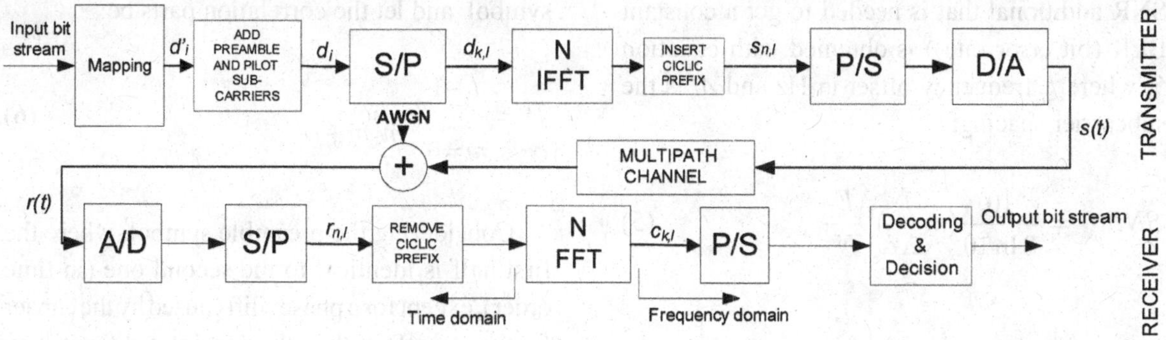

converted into parallel blocks of N symbols ($d_{k,l}$ denotes the k_{th} symbol of the l_{th} block, $k=0,...,N-1$ and $l=-\infty,...,+\infty$) which are generated with period $T_s=T+T_g$ (T: useful period, T_g: guard interval). After an inverse FFT (IFFT) of length N is applied, a cyclic prefix (CP) is inserted by prefixing the resulting N samples with a replica of the last N_g samples. Thus, each block consists of $N_s=N+N_g$ samples and is called "OFDM symbol".

The received OFDM signal can be represented as:

$$r(t)=e^{j2\pi\Delta ft}s(t)*h(t,\tau)+w(t) \qquad (1)$$

where $w(t)$ is the additive white Gaussian noise (AWGN), $s(t)$ is the transmitted baseband OFDM signal, $h(t,\tau)$ is the channel complex impulse response with τ being the delay spread, Δf is the carrier frequency difference between the transmitter and the receiver, and "*" denotes linear convolution.

Assuming that $r(t)$ is sampled at the transmit interval $T'=T/N$ with perfect timing, the samples corresponding to the l_{th} FFT are:

$$r_{n,l} = r((n + N_g + lN_s)T')0 \leq n < N \quad -\infty < l < +\infty \qquad (2)$$

Once the FFT is performed, the resulting samples are (Beek, 1997):

$c_{k,l} =$

$$e^{j\pi\left(\frac{N-1}{N}\right)\varepsilon} e^{j2\pi\left(\frac{lN_s+N_g}{N}\right)\varepsilon} \frac{\sin(\pi\varepsilon)}{N\sin\frac{\pi\varepsilon}{N}}H_{k,l}d_{k,l} + ICI_{k,l} + W_{k,l}$$

$$0 \leq k < N \qquad -\infty < l < +\infty$$

$$(3)$$

where $\varepsilon=\Delta fT$ is the CFO normalized with respect to the subcarrier spacing. Likewise, $H_{k,l}$ is the channel coefficient on the k_{th} subcarrier under the assumption that the channel is stationary during at least one symbol, $ICI_{k,l}$ is the intercarrier interference noise due to loss of orthogonality, and $W_{k,l}$ is a zero-mean stationary complex process. The first term is the data value $d_{k,l}$ modified by the channel transfer function, experiencing an amplitude reduction and phase shift due to the frequency offset.

This phase shift is given by:

$$2\pi\varepsilon(\frac{lN_s + N_g}{N} + \frac{N-1}{2N}) \qquad (4)$$

A small CFO of $\varepsilon=0.003$ accumulates a phase shift of 55° at the end of the 50th OFDM symbol in a WiMAX receiver if a synchronization process is not enabled.

There are two studies performed by Moeneclaey (1995) and Van Nee (1995) about the noise introduced by the CFO and how it degrades the

OFDM system. The loss of SNR (SNRloss - la SNR additional that is needed to get a constant BER (bit error rate)) is obtained with equation 5, where f_o frequency offset in Hz and Δf is the subcarrier spacing:

$$SNR_{loss} = \frac{10}{3 \ln 10} (\pi \frac{f_o}{\Delta f})^2 \frac{E_s}{N_o} \qquad (5)$$

Acquisition of the CFO

Most of the solutions for acquisition use the aid of pilot symbols (as a preamble), which are assumed to be known at the receiver. An alternative technique is to use the redundant information included in the CP (Beek, 1997). Furthermore, CFO acquisition can be divided in two steps as explained in (Schmidl, 1997: Speth, 2001). In the first step, the fractional part of the CFO is estimated and corrected, allowing, if it is necessary, for the integer part of the CFO to be estimated and corrected in the second step.

Acquisition of the Fractional CFO

The Moose (1994) algorithm performs the fractional acquisition stage by using a repeated OFDM symbol. This algorithm can be also performed using an OFDM symbol with symmetry in the time domain or by using the cyclic prefix and its repeated pattern. It is important to remark that the fractional CFO acquisition is performed in the time domain, since it is necessary to correct the ICI noise before the channel estimation.

The 802.11g and 802.16d standards include a preamble at the beginning of the frame. This preamble has an OFDM symbol with a repeated pattern in the time domain (before the FFT of the receptor) that can be used by the Moose algorithm. Next equations will show this algorithm using this preamble or training OFDM symbol. Let there be

L complex samples in each half of the training symbol, and let the correlation parts be:

$$P = \sum_{m=0}^{L-1} (r_m^* r_{\dot{m}+L}) \qquad (6)$$

Considering the preamble symbol, where the first half is identical to the second one (in time order), except for a phase shift caused by the carrier frequency offset, then the normalized frequency offset estimate is:

$$\varepsilon = \frac{angle(P)}{\pi} \qquad (7)$$

It is important to notice that the angle function in (7) has a range of:

$$angle(P) \le |\pi| \qquad (8)$$

Therefore, the range of estimation of the normalized CFO using this method and this preamble is $|\varepsilon| \le 1$. Depending of the symmetry of the preamble it is possible to obtain a greater range. The performance of the estimation using (7) is expressed by Schmidl (1997):

$$Var[\hat{\varphi} / \pi] = \frac{1}{\pi^2 LSNR} \qquad (9)$$

where L is the distance in samples of the two parts that we want to correlate (as in equation (6)). The block diagram of the fractional acquisition is shown in Figure 2.

DVB-T does not include a preamble in its frame so the Moose method should be performed using the cyclic prefix and its repeated pattern. Similar equations are needed in this case. But, instead of performing the correlation of equation

Figure 2. Block diagram of the fractional CFO acquisition scheme

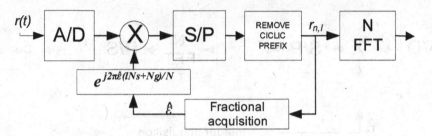

Acquisition of the Integer CFO

After the fractional CFO acquisition, there still remains the integer CFO acquisition, as previously mentioned. However, integer CFO acquisition is not always necessary. Subcarrier spacing for 802.11g is 312.5 KHz. Assuming a 25 ppm (parts per million) local oscillator and a carrier frequency of 2.4 GHz, the signal can experience a CFO of less than ±0.6 times the subcarrier spacing. Thus, the integer estimation of the CFO can be avoided for this technology. Similar calculations and conclusions can be obtained for 802.16d. Therefore, for these two standards, the Moose algorithm, that has a range of normalized CFO estimation of 1 using the preamble, is enough for the acquisition stage.

Subcarrier spacing in DVB-T systems is 4.5 KHz for the 2K mode. This is a low value, thus normalized CFO can be higher than one. Therefore, for this standard, a complete acquisition, with fractional and integer steps is required.

According to (Speth, 2001), for DVB-T systems, first the fractional part of the CFO can be estimated by using the cyclic prefix allocated in the OFDM symbol as shown in equations (6) and (7), where r_m and r_{m+L} are now the cyclic prefix and its copy, and $L=N$. After that, the fractional CFO is corrected and integer estimation can be performed in the frequency domain by using the algorithm described by Speth (2001). This algorithm uses the pilot subcarriers of two consecutive OFDM symbols. It is important that the pilot subcarriers are always placed in the same position. Otherwise, this method will not work. This algorithm is shown in the next two equations:

$$x_k = p_{l,k} \cdot p_{l-1,k} \tag{10}$$

$$\hat{n}_I = \arg\max \left| \sum_{\substack{k \in cp+m \\ m \in I}} x_k \right| \tag{11}$$

where $p_{l,k}$ are the boosted pilot subcarriers inserted in the l_{th} OFDM symbol, and I is determined from $[-n_{max}, n_{max}]$. The n_{max} value is chosen by the designer considering that, this value can not be higher than the minimum separation between the subcarriers in the frequency domain. For DVB-T, the minimum distance between the subcarriers is high, therefore, no problems are expected. Also, it is important to notice that it is necessary a buffer to store the OFDM symbols until the integer estimation can be performed and the CFO corrected. This buffer has a length of two OFDM symbols for DVB-T. The block diagram of the integer CFO acquisition scheme is shown in Figure 3.

The main differences between integer estimation in DVB-T and other physical frames are the length of the cyclic prefix and the number of pilot subcarriers. These parameters can vary depending of the transmission mode or the technology, thus increasing or decreasing the CFO esti-

Figure 3. Block diagram of the integer CFO acquisition scheme

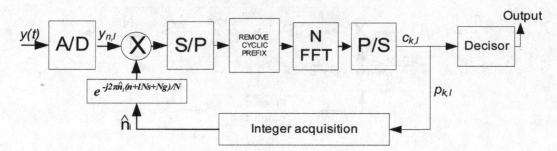

mation performance and its computational complexity.

It can be concluded that the same algorithm (6, 7) can be applied in the different OFDM standards for fractional CFO acquisition by using the cyclic prefix or the available preamble, whereas the scheme described in equations (10) and (11) can be used for integer acquisition in DVB-T or where it is needed.

Tracking of the RFO

After acquisition, there still remains a residual CFO. Furthermore, this RFO can increase due to oscillator instabilities or to the Doppler effect. If this RFO is not tracked and corrected, the ICI and the rotation caused by the RFO can decrease the performance of the OFDM system.

Depending of the OFDM standard, the RFO rotation or the ICI can become more or less important. That can vary the method to perform the RFO tracking.

Tracking for Packet Based OFDM Systems

In packet-based OFDM systems, as 802.11g or 802.16d, the rotation introduced by the RFO leads to a performance degradation of the OFDM system, because the channel estimation is performed only at the beginning of the frame by using the preamble. Therefore, the rotation, that increases with each OFDM symbol, is not corrected un-less a RFO tracking or phase error tracking is performed. Otherwise, the constellation points will fall in a different quadrant after a number of OFDM symbols thus significantly degrading the system performance.

For example, a small CFO of $\varepsilon=0.003$ accumulates a phase shift of 55° at the end of the 50th OFDM symbol in a WiMAX receiver if a tracking process is not enabled. Thus, accuracy and speed of convergence are important when implementing the RFO tracking closed-loop. Furthermore, this residual CFO also introduces ICI that can not be considered negligible.

In this subsection, we will show a complete example of a tracking scheme for a packet-switched system. This method is called the Decision-Directed Time-Frequency Loop (DD-TFL) and it was proposed by Kuang (2005) for RFO tracking in the 802.11g standard. The so-called decision-directed methods (non-data-aided methods) compare the received data subcarriers with sliced versions (as fed from the demapper) to give a larger number of estimates. This scheme is based on two feedback loops in the time and the frequency domain and it uses all the data subcarriers to perform the estimations.

The DD-TFL scheme is composed of two tracking loops as it can be observed in Figure 4. The frequency loop uses the information provided by the output of the demapper to build the tracking system. This demapper is allocated in the decision-directed phase error detector (DD-PED).

Figure 4. Block diagram of the DD-TFL tracking method

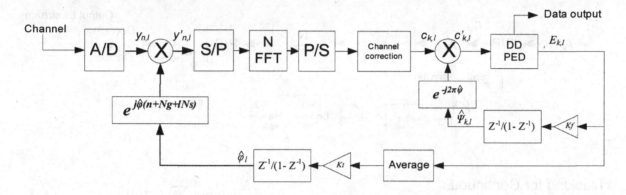

The sequence $c_{k,l}$ after the FFT at the receiver is modified at every subcarrier as:

$$c'_{k,l} = c_{k,l} e^{-j\Psi_{k,l}} \qquad 0 \leq k \leq N \qquad (12)$$

The corrected data symbols $c'_{k,l}$ may then be demapped to a bit stream. In the phase error detector (PED), the data subcarrier, $c_{k,l}$, are used for extracting the error increment $E_{k,l}$ according to one of the algorithms proposed in (Moridi, 1985). In particular, the algorithm selected here to extract the error increment computes:

$$e^I_{k,l} = imag(c_{k,l}) - imag(c'_{k,l}) \qquad (13)$$

$$e^{QI}_{k,l} = real(c_{k,l}) - real(c'_{k,l}) \qquad (14)$$

$$E_{k,l} = e^Q_{k,l}\,sgn(real(c_{k,l})) - e^I_{k,l}\,sgn(imag(c_{k,l})) \qquad (15)$$

where $c'_{k,l}$ are the data subcarriers and *sgn()* is the sign function. After error extraction, the error increment $E_{k,l}$ is attenuated and enters the filter directly. Then, the estimated phase error $\Psi_{k,l}$ is applied to the post-FFT data symbol $c_{k,l}$. Therefore, phase error correction is updated as many times as data subcarriers are inserted in the OFDM

symbol. It is important to observe that frequency loop is only able to correct the phase error caused by the RFO.

In the time loop, the error $E_{k,l}$ estimated by the DD-PED is fed to the time loop and is averaged before entering the filter. As a result, the pre-FFT sample $r_{n,l}$ is rotated as:

$$r'_{k,l} = r_{k,l} e^{-j(n+Ng+lNs)\Psi_l} \qquad 0 \leq n \leq N \qquad (16)$$

This time loop is able to correct the ICI introduced by the residual CFO. An important point to remark is that by using algorithm described in equations (13) to (15) no complex multiplications are needed. This is an important improvement over classical tracking schemes as in (Speth, 2001). One of the main drawbacks of DD-TFL is that is sensitive to mistakes in the demapping of the subcarriers. Therefore, its performance degrades for low SNR (signal to noise ratio) values. Adaptations of this scheme for the 802.16d standard are found in (González-Bayón, 2007), where the Data-Aided Time Frequency Loop (DA-TFL) scheme is presented. By using DA-TFL, the pilot subcarriers inserted in the data stream are used instead of the data subcarriers to perform the CFO estimations. DA-TFL aims at reducing the CFO tracking computational complexity with no performance penalty.

Figure 5. Block diagram of DA-TL-2

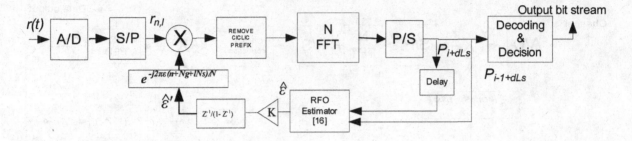

Tracking for Continuous Based OFDM Systems

The previous subsection was focused in packet-switched systems. But for continuous based systems different tracking methods should be used. The main aim of the frequency tracking for these systems is to correct the ICI produced by the RFO. This is because in continuous transmission systems, as in DVB-T, channel equalization is continuously performed and it will correct the phase rotation produced by the RFO. However, if channel equalization is not performed continuously, this phase rotation must be taken into account and the speed of convergence of the RFO tracking closed-loop becomes a critical parameter.

The tracking scheme in (Fechtel, 2006) and (Speth, 2001) estimates the RFO by using L_s OFDM symbols. The post-FFT correlation at the k_{th} pilot subcarrier is:

$$C_d(k) = \sum_{i=1}^{L_s-1} P_{i+dL_s}(k) P^*_{i+dL_s}(k) \qquad (17)$$

where $d=0,1,2,\ldots$ indicates the d_{th} RFO estimation in a tracking feedback loop, and L_s is the number of OFDM symbols in the data stream. Notice that, for all L_s values, each term in equation (17) is obtained by multiplying two consecutive OFDM symbols. This scheme is proposed by Speth (2001) for $L_s = 2$. The estimated RFO results:

$$\varepsilon_d = \frac{N}{4\pi N_T} \left[\arg\left\{ \sum_{k \in CPS} C_d(k) \right\} \right] \qquad (18)$$

where CPS are the continual pilot subcarriers defined in DVB-T for synchronization purposes. Unlike Speth (2001), in equation (18) there is only one summation since the sampling clock error tracking is being performed along with the RFO tracking. This method is called DA-TL-2 in this chapter. Figure 5 shows the system block diagram when using this scheme.

When the RFO is relatively small, the difference of the rotated phases between two adjacent symbols is very small. This results in poor estimation accuracy. Consequently, You (2008) proposes a method which extends the difference of the rotated samples by first adding $L_a < L_s$ consecutive pilot subcarriers as:

$$A_n(k) = \sum_{i=0}^{L_s-1} P_{n+i}(k) \qquad (19)$$

and then multiplying by the CPS of the next successive OFDM symbol. Therefore, the post-FFT correlation becomes:

$$C_d(k) = \sum_{n=0}^{L_s-L_a-1} P_{n+dL_s+L_a}(k) A^*_{n+dL_s}(k) \qquad (20)$$

Similarly to equation (18), the estimated RFO becomes:

Figure 6. Block diagram of DA-TL-L_s.

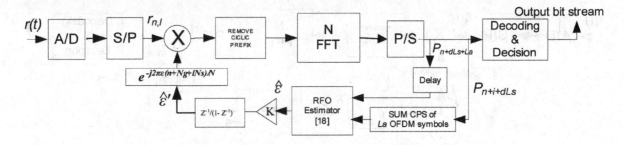

$$\varepsilon_d = \frac{N}{2\pi(L_a+1)N_s}\left[\arg\left\{\sum_{k\in CPS}C_d(k)\right\}\right] \qquad (21)$$

$$\Phi_3 = 2\pi\frac{2N_T}{N}\varepsilon = 4\pi(1+\frac{N_g}{N})\varepsilon \qquad (23)$$

Figure 6 shows the system block diagram when using this scheme. It is important to notice that, in order to obtain a RFO estimation using (5) or (8), a latency of L_s OFDM symbols is required and the channel has to remain quasi-static for these symbols. For DA-TL-2, the minimum latency obtaining a RFO estimation is two OFDM symbols, while the method in (You, 2008) has a minimum latency of three OFDM symbols. This last method is called DA-TL-L_s in this chapter.

The method proposed by González-Bayón (2010) starts from the same observation than DA-TL-L_s: the phase rotation of two consecutive OFDM symbols can be relatively small, so estimations can be inaccurate in noisy environments. However, the idea of using the phase rotations of several consecutive OFDM symbols is taken one step further. In essence, rather than adding the consecutive pilot subcarriers, the accumulated rotation is directly considered.

The phase rotation between two consecutive OFDM symbols due to the RFO is:

$$\Phi_2 = 2\pi\frac{N_T}{N}\varepsilon = 2\pi(1+\frac{N_g}{N})\varepsilon \qquad (22)$$

The phase rotation between the first and third OFDM symbols in a sequence of consecutive OFDM symbols becomes:

Since the phase in (23) is twice the phase in (22), more accurate RFO estimations can be performed with (23) than with (22). Thus the RFO can be estimated comparing phases of the pilot subcarriers of two OFDM symbols separated L_s OFDM symbols by (González-Bayón, 2010):

$$C_d(k) = P_{dL_s}(k)P^*_{dL_s+L_s-1}(k) \qquad (24)$$

$$\varepsilon_d = \frac{N}{2\pi(L_s-1)N_s}\left[\arg\left\{\sum_{k\in CPS}C_d(k)\right\}\right] \qquad (25)$$

This method is called Data-Aided Phase Incremental Technique (DA-PIT) and Figure 7 shows its block diagram. It is important to notice that the number of computations using equations (24) and (25) does not increase if L_s increases as it is the case with equations (17) to (21).

An important concern using DA-PIT, and also using methods DA-TL-2 and DA-TL-L_s, is that the channel must be quasi-static during L_s OFDM symbols. It is also interesting to note that DA-TL-L_s and DA-PIT become DA-TL-2 when L_s=2.

One of the main disadvantages of the schemes presented so far is that the d_{th} RFO estimation can only be updated every L_s OFDM symbols ($L_s>1$). If a rapid convergence of the RFO is needed in a

Figure 7. Block diagram of DA-PIT

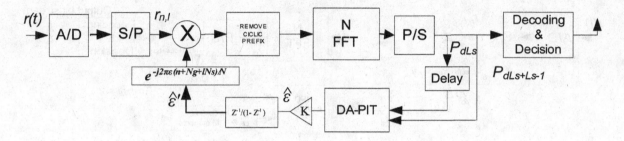

closed-loop tracking, a method that updates the RFO every OFDM symbol would be desirable.

The next method proposed in (González-Bayon, 2010) applies to this scenario, where a rapid convergence is required. This proposed scheme is based on the same algorithm described in (17) and (18) but, instead of correlating the CPS of two OFDM symbols, the correlation is performed with the known value of the CPS. Taking this into account, the correlation in equation (17) for the d_{th} RFO estimation in a feedback loop becomes:

$$C_d(k) = P_d(k)H^*(k)P_k^*$$ (26)

where P_k is the known value of the pilot subcarrier at the k_{th} position and $H(k)$ is the value of the channel at the pilot subcarrier position. If a quasi-static channel is assumed over M OFDM symbols and there is one channel estimation in that period, equation (18) becomes:

$$C_d(k) = P_d(k)H_j^*(k)P_k^*$$ (27)

where j increases after M RFO estimations. For DVB-T, the value of P_k is ±4/3 [1]. Taking equation (3) into account and assuming $N-1/N \approx N$, the estimated RFO becomes:

$$\varepsilon_d \approx \frac{N}{\pi(2mN_s + N_g)}\left[\arg\left\{\sum_{k \in CPS} C_d(k)\right\}\right]$$ (28)

$$m = d \bmod M = 0, 1, 2 ..., M - 1$$ (29)

This scheme is called Data-Aided Phase Pilot Technique (DA-PPT) and Figure 8 shows its system diagram. The accuracy of RFO estimation using the proposed method increases with m. Moreover, less noise is introduced in equation (27) when compared to (18), (20) and (24), since P_k is noise free. Furthermore, with this scheme, RFO estimation can be performed on each OFDM

Figure 8. Block diagram of DA-PPT

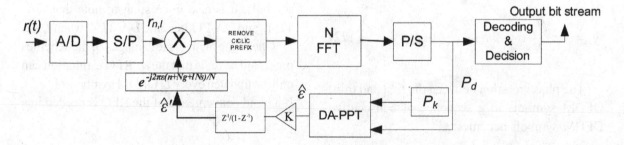

Figure 9. Diagram of an OFDMA system

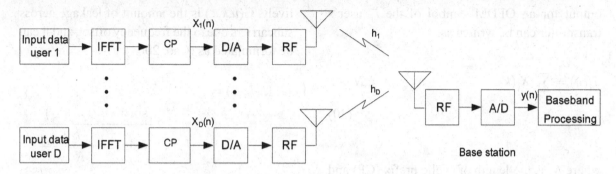

symbol for any value of M. It is important to remind that RFO estimation can not be performed every OFDM symbol when using the other tracking schemes mentioned in this subsection.

Notice that in this scheme it is necessary to know the $H(k)$ values. If channel estimations can not be performed before the RFO tracking in the same OFDM symbol, channel estimates from the previous OFDM symbol can be used.

After evaluating the different RFO tracking methods and comparing their responses in terms of MSE accuracy, convergence and complexity, a new optimized technique for RFO tracking in DVB-T was proposed by Gonzalez-Bayón (2010). This technique divides RFO tracking in two stages: "fast" and "slow".

In the "fast" stage, DA-PPT is used to obtain a rapid convergence and avoid performance losses in the system due to high residual ICI noise or phase rotation. This stage is performed just after CFO acquisition and until convergence is obtained. Simulations performed in (Gonzalez-Bayón, 2010) with RFO<0.1 and $K=1/4$ show that the steady state is reached between the 5th and the 12th OFDM symbols. At this point, RFO tracking switches to the "slow" stage. In this stage, the goal is to use an estimator that reduces the number of calculations needed to a minimum. Taking all this into account, DA-PIT appears as the best option for this stage since it improves both accuracy and complexity, compared to DA-TL-2 and DA-TL-L_s, as it was shown by Gonzalez-Bayón

(2010). This new procedure is called Two-Stage Tracking (TST).

By using TST, a rapid convergence and a high accuracy for the steady-state are obtained with minimum resources. Since DA-PIT and DA-PPT perform a similar number of operations, there is no problem in sharing resources when switching between both methods.

FREQUENCY SYNCRONIZATION IN OFDMA SYSTEMS

This section of the chapter focuses in the estimation and correction of the CFOs in the uplink of an 802.16e OFDMA system. Several approaches have been presented for interleaved or block subcarrier assignments, but just a few methods are available for the random and clustered cases. The 802.16e physical frame groups its subcarriers in clusters. Furthermore, these methods can be divided in CFO estimation or correction. However, it is also possible to find iterative methods that perform both, estimation and correction.

The OFDMA Signal

An OFDMA system with D simultaneously active users and N subcarriers is considered. The Figure 9 shows a diagram of an OFDMA system.

The inverse discrete Fourier transform (IDFT) output for an OFDM symbol of the i_{th} user's transmitter can be written as:

$$x_i(n) = \sum_{k \in \Gamma_i} X_i(k) e^{-j\frac{2\pi kn}{N}} \qquad -N_g < n < N-1$$

(30)

where N_g is the length of cyclic prefix (CP) and $X_i(k)$, $k \in \Gamma_i$, is the value of the transmitted data on the k_{th} subcarrier. The set of subcarriers assigned to user i is denoted as Γ_i. These sets satisfy $\cup_{i=1}^{D} \Gamma_i = \{0,1,\ldots,N-1\}$ and $\Gamma_i \cap \Gamma_j = \emptyset$ if $i \neq j$. Vectors and matrices are denoted by bold-face letters in the following equations. Assuming perfect time synchronization, the discrete-time model of the received signal at the BS after removal of the CP can be written in matrix form as:

$$y = \sum_{i=1}^{D} D(\varepsilon_i) P(x_i) h_i + w$$

(31)

where $y = \{y_0, \ldots, y_{N-1}\}$, $D(\varepsilon_i) = \text{diagonal}\{1, e^{j2\pi\varepsilon_i/N}, \ldots, e^{j2\pi(N-1)\varepsilon_i/N}\}$, h_i is a vector of dimension L that encapsulates the channel response for the i_{th} user, $P(x_i)$ is a $N \times L$ matrix with entries $[P(x_i)]_{k,l} = x_i(k-l)$ for $0 < k < N-1$ and $0 < l < L-1$, w is the complex additive Gaussian noise (AWGN) sample with variance σ^2, and $\varepsilon_i = \Delta f / f_{sub}$ is the carrier frequency offset normalized for the i_{th} user with respect to the subcarrier spacing. The receiver applies a DFT to the signal y to obtain the frequency domain symbols. The DFT output at the k_{th} subcarrier can be obtained as:

$$Y(k) = \sum_{i=1}^{D} \left(\sum_{u \in \Gamma_i} X_i(u) H_i(u) G(u,k,\varepsilon_i) \right) + W(k)$$

(32)

where H_i and W are the DFTs of h_i and w, respectively. $G(u,k,\varepsilon_i)$ is the amount of leakage across subcarriers due to the frequency offset, and it can be formulated as (Cao, 2004):

$$G^m(u,k,\varepsilon_i) = e^{j\pi(u-k+\varepsilon_i)\frac{N-1}{N}} e^{j2\pi\frac{mNs+Ng}{N}\varepsilon_i} \frac{\sin \pi (u-k+\varepsilon_i)}{N \sin \frac{\pi(u-k+\varepsilon_i)}{N}}$$

(33)

where $N_s = N_g + N$, and m is the OFDM symbol index. Assuming $k \in \Gamma_i$, the received signal in the k_{th} subcarrier can be written as:

$$Y(k) = \underbrace{X_i(k)}_{Desired\ Value} H_i(k) e^{j2\pi\frac{mNs+Ng}{N}\varepsilon_i} G(k,k,\varepsilon_i) +$$
$$\underbrace{\sum_{\substack{u \in \Gamma_i \\ u \neq k}} X_i(u) H_i(u) G(u,k,\varepsilon_i)}_{ICI} +$$
$$\underbrace{\sum_{\substack{j=1 \\ j \neq i}}^{D} \sum_{u \in \Gamma_i} H_j(u) X_j(u) G(u,k,\varepsilon_j) + W(k)}_{MAI}$$

(34)

where the first term is the desired signal ($u=k$) with amplitude reduction and phase distortion, while the second and third terms represent the ICI and the total MAI, respectively. The system model considered so far is independent of the subcarrier allocation method.

The 802.16e Physical Frame

The IEEE 802.16e standard defines a physical layer that can use 128, 512, 1024 or 2048 subcarriers, which are modulated with BPSK, QPSK or 16-QAM constellations. A number of boosted subcarriers are allocated for pilot signals and a number of the highest and lowest frequency subcarriers

Figure 10. Tile structure for the UL PUSC 802.16e

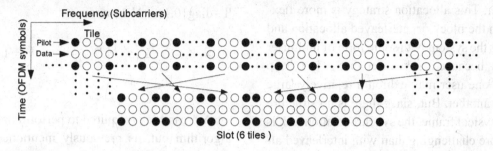

are null. A subchannel is a logical collection of subcarriers that is assigned to a specific user.

The number and exact distribution of the subcarriers that constitute a subchannel depends on the subcarrier permutation mode. There are two types of subcarrier permutations for subchannelization: diversity and contiguous. The diversity permutation includes UL PUSC (uplink partially used subcarrier), ULO-PUSC (optional uplink partially used subcarrier) and also several downlink modes. UL PUSC splits the time-frequency grid into tiles. This permutation mode can be observed in Figure 10. Six tiles are grouped to form a slot. The slot comprises 48 data subcarriers and 24 pilot subcarriers in three OFDM symbols. The minimum frequency-time resource unit of subchannelization is one slot. In a similar way, UL OPUSC is composed of tiles of eight data subcarriers and one pilot subcarrier in three OFDM symbols. The contiguous permutation (also called UL AMC) groups a block of nine contiguous subcarriers in a symbol, with eight subcarriers assigned to data and one subcarrier assigned to a pilot.

CFO Estimation Schemes

As previously mentioned, CFO estimation and correction in OFDMA are closely connected to the subcarrier allocation. The simplest way to allocate the subcarriers is grouping them in blocks or subbands. Therefore, all the subcarriers of a user are grouped together. The subcarriers that are at the edges of this block are the only ones affected

for the MAI. In this case, it is usual to introduce a guard band between the blocks of the different users to alleviate this MAI noise. Because of this allocation, it is possible to reconstruct the signal of each user by using band-pass filters. This can not be done perfectly, but due to this filtering it is possible to estimate and correct the CFOs for the different users by using frequency synchronization techniques similar to OFDM systems as by Barbarossa (2002).

Other way to allocate the subcarriers in an OFDMA system is to use interleaved subcarrier allocation. In this case, each user modulates an exclusive set of subcarriers which are uniformly spaced in the frequency domain at a certain distance. By using this technique, the frequency synchronization is more complicated than with block allocation. That is because the MAI noise is affecting to all the subcarriers and it is not possible to separate them using band-pass filters. However, it is possible to use this special pattern to implement an estimation scheme. This is done in (Cao, 2004a) where a frequency estimation scheme based on the principle of multiple signal classification (MUSIC) is proposed. This algorithm does not need a preamble or subcarriers to perform the CFO estimation but the CFOs have to be, at least, half of the subcarrier spacing. However, this method only works for this allocation pattern.

The third possible way to allocate the subcarriers is to use a generalized allocation. To perform this, it is necessary that the base station uses its knowledge of the channel responses to assign the best subcarriers that are currently available for the next user. This allocation strategy is more flexible than the block or interleaved allocation and provides the system with some form of multiuser diversity because a subcarrier that is in a deep fade for one user may exhibit a relatively large gain for another. But, since there is no structure in the physical frame, the synchronization task is even more challenging than with interleaved allocation. The physical frame of the 802.16e uses a tile structure to allocate the subcarriers. This tile organization is a mixture, combination of the block and the generalized allocations.

A CFO synchronization scheme for generalized subcarrier allocation in OFDMA systems has been proposed by Pun (2007). In (Morelli, 2007), same authors have published a tutorial about CFO synchronization techniques in OFDMA systems. This method tries to solve the log-likelihood function for unknown parameters ε_i using this preamble. Unfortunately, to solve this equation would require an exhaustive search over the parameter space which is prohibitely complex for practical implementation. To circumvent this obstacle, (Morelli, 2007) proposes an iterative scheme, in which a space-alternating generalized expectation-maximization (SAGE) algorithm proposed by Fessler (1994) is first used to extract the contribution of each user, say r_i. Each r_i is then used to estimate ε_i by following an expectation-conditional maximization (ECM) approach (Feder, 1998). This leads to a procedure consisting of iterations, where a update ε of a given user is obtained after C cycles. This scheme is called expectation maximization acquisition (EMA). After some calculations and supposing that the channel is perfectly estimated and corrected by the receiver, it is obtained that the CFO estimation during the c_{th} iteration (where C is a design parameter) in an OFDM symbol is:

$$\hat{\varepsilon}_i^{(c+1)} = \hat{\varepsilon}_i^{(c)} + \frac{real(\hat{r}_i^{(c)H}\Gamma'(\hat{\varepsilon}_i^{(c)})D(x_i))}{imag(\hat{r}_i^{(c)H}\Gamma''(\hat{\varepsilon}_i^{(c)})D(x_i))} \quad (35)$$

where $\Gamma'(\hat{\varepsilon}_i^{(c)}) = \Psi\Gamma(\hat{\varepsilon}_i^{(c)})$, $\Gamma''(\hat{\varepsilon}_i^{(c)}) = \Psi^2\Gamma(\hat{\varepsilon}_i^{(c)})$, Ψ=diag$\{0,1,...,N-1\}$ and:

$$\hat{r}_i^c = Y - \sum_{k\neq i}\Gamma\left(\varepsilon_k^{c-1}\right)D(x_k) \qquad k = 1,2...,D \quad (36)$$

A preamble is required to perform the SAGE algorithm but, as previously mentioned, there are standards like 802.16e where no preamble is included at the beginning of the uplink frame. However, it is possible to use optional midambles defined in mobile WiMAX at the cost of decreasing the throughput of the system. These midambles can be inserted every 4, 8 or 12 OFDM symbols.

CFO Correction Schemes

After the CFOs estimation still remains an important task: the CFOs correction. To perform CFO cancellation, the total ICI (and MAI) matrix can be computed and a maximum likelihood (ML) correction can be performed as in (Cao, 2004b). This method works for any subcarrier distribution. The ICI matrix can be calculated as follows:

$$\prod = \sum_{i=1}^{D}\Pi_i \quad (37)$$

where $\Pi_i(u,k)=G(u,k,\varepsilon_i)$ and G is given in equation (33) and has a size of $N{\times}N$. To construct the orthogonal spectral signals is to construct s from the received y. In (Cao, 2004b), two different criteria are applied: least squares (LS) and minimum mean squared error (MMSE). The linear model minimizes the sum of noise energy in one OFDMA symbol. The solution to the cost function formulated based on the LS criterion is:

$$s_{LS} = \prod^{-1} y \quad (38)$$

In MMSE, the second-order statistics of the signals and noise are assumed to be known to the base station. Let the noise on each subcarrier be additive white Gaussian with zero mean and variance σ_n^2 such that $\mathrm{E}\left[zz^H\right] = \sigma_n^2 I$, where I is a $N \times N$ identity matrix, and E[] denotes the expectation operator. Based on the orthogonality principle, the MMSE solution is:

$$s_{MMSE} = R\Pi^H (\Pi R \Pi^H + \sigma_n^2 I)^{-1} y \qquad (39)$$

where $\mathbf{R}=\mathrm{E}[ss^H]$ is the autocorrelation matrix of the orthogonal spectral signal s.

However, these two correction methods require obtaining the inverse of the ICI matrix and that implies a large number of computations due to its size of $N \times N$. A banded matrix to approximate the interference matrix is proposed by Cao (2004b). Still, the number of computations required to perform this correction is too high for implementation purposes.

There is another option to correct the effect of the CFO, taking into account the tile structure of the OFDMA 802.16e frame (Yücek, 2007). By using this method, an iterative compensation scheme that uses a small ICI matrix is performed. In this scheme an interference matrix is built for each group of K subcarriers that forms a tile or cluster. For example, for UL PUSC the interference matrix has a size of 4×4, e.g., $K=4$, as shown in Figure 10. ICI interference is removed in each tile by multiplying the subcarriers of the tile by the inverse of this small ICI matrix. This stage is called decorrelation. Then, using the channel knowledge, the receiver can detect the transmitted information. After detection is performed, the transmitted signal is reconstructed with a QAM modulator and the channel knowledge. This reconstructed signal is used to remove the MAI of the current tile on the other tiles in a procedure called successive cancellation. The whole method is called Decorrelation Sucessive Cancellation (DC-SC) scheme.

The $K \times K$ matrix Π is the interference matrix whose entries are $\Pi_i(u,k)=G(u,k,\varepsilon_i)$ where G is given in equation (33). This method reduces the number of computations compared to the method described in equations (37) to (39), but channel knowledge is needed.

In the DC-SC scheme, the clusters are first sorted in descending order according to their average power. Then, starting from the cluster c with the largest power, decorrelation is applied to every subcarrier in the cluster and decisions are made. This is represented by the following equation:

$$\hat{Y}(c) = \Pi_i^{-1} Y(c) \qquad c \in \Gamma_i^c \qquad (40)$$

After obtaining partially corrected subcarriers in the current cluster, the MAI for the neighboring clusters is reconstructed using the knowledge of the frequency offset value, and subtracted to cancel its MAI. The u_{th} subcarrier value after removal of the MAI from the c_{th} cluster becomes (Yücek, 2007):

$$\hat{Y}(u) = Y(u) - (\hat{X}\hat{H})_c^T g_{c,u} \qquad (41)$$

where $g_{c,u}=[G(k,u,\varepsilon_i), G(k+1,u,\varepsilon_i)\dots G(k+K,u,\varepsilon_i)]$ and X is the signal originally transmitted that is calculated assuming that the decisions are correct. After this, the second cluster is decorrelated, and the MAI is calculated and substracted from the other subcarriers. This process is performed for all the clusters and its diagram is shown in Figure 11. This method reduces the number of computations compared to the method proposed by Cao (2004b). This is because the interference matrix used in equation (40) is much smaller than the matrix used in equations (38) or (39).

Figure 11. Block diagram of the DC-SC OFDMA correction method

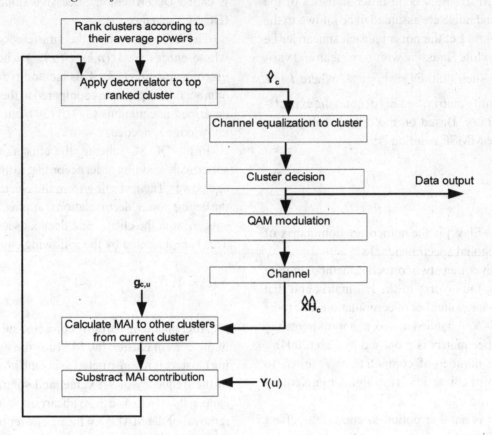

Figure 12. Block diagram of the APFE method

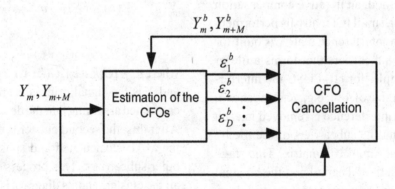

Iterative CFO Estimation and Correction

Sun (2009) proposed a synchronization method that estimates and compensates for the CFO. It is called Alternating-Projection Frequency Estima-

tor (APFE). The diagram of this iterative process is shown in Figure 12.

This work proposes a physical frame composed of frequency domain tiles of five subcarriers with one pilot subcarrier in the middle. The synchronization is performed by an iterative joint CFO estimation and compensation scheme. The CFO of an individual user is determined from a one dimensional search where the MAI from other users is treated as noise. CFO estimation in APFE is performed by applying a non-linear least squares algorithm where an exhaustive search needs to be performed. CFO estimates are then exploited to compensate for the ICI and MAI in the next iteration, and the corrected signal is used to estimate the residual CFOs. CFO compensation is performed by using the method in (Cao, 2004), where the effect of CFO is represented as an interference matrix. This compensation scheme requires the inversion of the large interference matrix, which is computationally demanding as the size of the matrix is determined by the number of subcarriers (N) in one OFDM symbol.

APFE is performed in the frequency domain and uses the pilot subcarriers of the tiles avoiding the use of midambles. However, its computational complexity is extremely high, possibly preventing any practical implementation.

In (Nguyen, 2008) a method that also estimates and corrects the CFOs iteratively is proposed. The first step in the first iteration is composed of a CFO estimation using the method described by (Moose, 1994) for OFDM systems. Therefore, this estimation is applied in the time domain and a preamble with time symmetry is needed. In the second step of the iterative process, the CFOs are corrected in the time domain. In the next iteration the same two steps are performed but the estimation has better performance because the CFO is reduced from the previous iteration.

However, this method needs to separate the time samples of the different users. Therefore, it is mandatory to perform a different FFT for each user. Otherwise, the CFO correction for a user would interfere in the signal of other user that is affected from a different carrier frequency offset. Unfortunately, this requires a high amount of resources for implementing the different FFTs, especially for a high number of users. Besides, results from this work show poor performance

results for subcarrier allocation different than contiguous subcarriers.

CONCLUSION

In this chapter, a review of the frequency synchronization in OFDM/OFDMA systems has been performed. In OFDM systems, the literature has provided suitable schemes for CFO acquisition and RFO tracking. Acquisition can be divided into fractional (Moose, 1994) or integer (Speth, 2001) CFO estimation.

For packet-based systems, as 802.11g and 802.16d, some tracking schemes can be found that focus in the phase impairment caused by the RFO (Kuang, 2005; González-Bayón, 2007), while for continuous-based systems, as DVB-T, the tracking schemes focus in correcting the ICI noise (Speth, 2001; You, 2008; González-Bayon, 2010).

In OFDMA systems, frequency estimation is a more complicated task than in OFDM. This is because the base station receives signals from different users in the same bandwidth. Each user can be affected by a different CFO. Estimation and correction techniques depend on the subcarrier allocation policy. For the 802.16e standard, the technique in (Morelli, 2007) can be used, although the data rate decreases because it is necessary to include midambles in the data frame. The correction can be performed with (Cao, 2004b), but Yücek (2007) reduces the number of computations compared with the former scheme. However, it can be concluded that frequency synchronization in OFDMA systems is a difficult task in terms of computational complexity and additional research is needed in this area.

Future work of frequency synchronization in OFDM systems is focusing, mainly, in multiuser OFDMA systems since the high number of the computations needed makes difficult its implementation in hardware. Therefore, new proposals focus in the reduction of the algorithm complexity with no performance penalty if possible.

ACKNOWLEDGMENT

The work presented in this paper has been supported in part by the Spanish Ministry of Science and Innovation under project TEC2009-14219-C03-02.

REFERENCES

Barbarossa, S., Pompili, M., & Giannakis, G. B. (2002, February). Channel-independent synchronization of orthogonal frequency division multiple access systems. *IEEE Journal on Selected Areas in Communications, 20*(2), 474–486. doi:10.1109/49.983375

Beek, J., Sandell, M., & Borjesson, P. O. (1997, July). ML estimation of time and frequency offset in OFDM systems. *IEEE Transactions on Signal Processing, 45*, 1800–1805. doi:10.1109/78.599949

Cao, Z. T., & Yao, Y. D. (2004a, September). Deterministic multiuser carrier frequency offset estimation for interleaved OFDMA uplink. *IEEE Transactions on Communications, 52*(9), 1585–1594. doi:10.1109/TCOMM.2004.833183

Cao, Z. T., Yao, Y. D., & Honan, P. (2004b, November). Frequency synchronization for generalized OFDMA uplink. *Proceedings of IEEE Global Telecomunications Conference*, (vol. 2, pp. 1071-1075).

ETSI. (2004). *Digital video broadcasting (DVB): Frame structure, channel coding and modulation for digital terrestrial television (DVB-T)*. ETSI EN 300 744, November 2004.

Fechtel, S. A. (2000, August). OFDM carrier and sampling frequency synchronization and its performance on stationary and mobile channels. *IEEE Transactions on Consumer Electronics, 54*(3).

Feder, M., & Weinstein, E. (1988, April). Parameter estimation of superimposed signals using the EM algorithm. *IEEE Transactions on Acoustics, Speech, and Signal Processing, 36*(12), 477–489. doi:10.1109/29.1552

Fessler, J., & Hero, A. (1994, October). Space-alternating generalized expectation maximitation algorithm. *IEEE Transactions on Signal Processing, 42*(10), 2664–2677. doi:10.1109/78.324732

González-Bayón, J., Carreras, C., & Fernández-Herrero, A. (2007, December). Comparative evaluation of carrier frequency offset tracking schemes for WiMAX OFDM systems. *IEEE Symposium on Signal Processing and Information Technology ISSPIT 2007.*

González-Bayón, J., Fernández-Herrero, A., & Carreras, C. (2010 May). Improved schemes for tracking residual frequency offset in DVB-T systems. *IEEE Transactions on Consumer Electronics.*

IEEE. (2004). *IEEE standard for local and metropolitan area networks part 16: Air interface for fixed broadband wireless access systems.* IEEE 802.16, 2004.

IEEE. (2005). *Amended to 802.16e: IEEE standard for local and metropolitan area networks part 16: Air interface for fixed broadband wireless access systems. Amendment for physical and medium access control layers for combined fixed and mobile operation in licensed bands and corrigendum 1.* IEEE 802.16-2005, December 2005.

IEEE. (2009). *IEEE draft standard for Information Technology-Telecommunications and information exchange between systems-Local and metropolitan area networks-Specific requirements-Part 11: Wireless LAN medium access control (MAC) and physical layer (PHY) specifications amendment: Enhancements for higher throughput.* June 2009.

Kuang, L., Ni, Z., Lu, J., & Zheng, J. (2005, March). A time- frequency decision-feedback loop for carrier frequency offset tracking in OFDM systems. *IEEE Transactions on Wireless Communications, 4*(2).

Moeneclae, M., Pollet, M., & Van Bladel, T. (1995, February-April). Ber sensitivity of OFDM systems to carrier frequency offset and Wiener phase noise. *IEEE Transactions on Communications, 45*(2-5), 191–193.

Moose, P. (1994, October). A technique for orthogonal frequency division multiplexing frequency offset correction. *IEEE Transactions on Communications, 42*, 2908–2914. doi:10.1109/26.328961

Morelli, P., Jay Kuo, C.-C., & Pun, M.-O. (2007, July). Synchronization techniques for orthogonal frequency division multiple access (OFDMA): A tutorial review. *Proceedings of the IEEE, 95*(7). doi:10.1109/JPROC.2007.897979

Moridi, S., & Sri, H. (1985, June). Analysis of four decision feedback carrier recovery loops in the presence of inter-symbol interference. *IEEE Transactions on Communications, 33*, 543–550. doi:10.1109/TCOM.1985.1096331

Nguyen, H. C., de Carvalho, E., & Prasad, R. (2008, September). A generalized carrier frequency offset estimator for uplink OFDMA. *IEEE 19th International Symposium on Personal, Indoor and Mobile Radio Communications,* (pp. 1-5).

Pun, M., Morelli, M., & Kuo, C. (2006, April). Maximum-likelihood synchronization and channel estimation for OFDMA uplink transmissions. *IEEE Transactions on Communications, 54*(4), 726–736. doi:10.1109/TCOMM.2006.873093

Pun, M.-O., Morelli, M., & Jay Kuo, C.-C. (2007, February). Iterative detection and frequency synchronization for FDMA uplink transmissions. *IEEE Transactions on Wireless Communications, 6*(2). doi:10.1109/TWC.2007.05368

Schmidl, T., & Cox, D. (1997, December). Robust frequency and timing synchronization for OFDM. *IEEE Transactions on Communications, 45*, 1613–1621. doi:10.1109/26.650240

Speth, M., Fechtel, S., Fock, G., & Meyr, H. (2001, April). Optimum receiver design for OFDM-based broadband transmission part II: A case study. *IEEE Transactions on Communications, 49*(4). doi:10.1109/26.917759

Sun, P., & Zhang, L. (2009, July). Low complexity pilot aided frequency synchronization for OFDMA uplink transmission. *IEEE Transactions on Wireless Communications, 8*(7), 3758–3769. doi:10.1109/TWC.2009.081005

Van Nee, R., & Prasad, R. (1995, February-April). OFDM for wireless multimedia communications. *IEEE Transactions on Communications, 45*(2-5), 191–193.

You, Y. H., Lee, K.-T., & Kang, S.-J. (2008, August). Pilot-aided frequency offset tracking scheme for OFDM-based DVB-T. *IEEE Transactions on Consumer Electronics, 46*, 438–441.

Yücek, T., & Arslan, H. (2007, October). Carrier frequency offset compensation with successive cancellation in uplink OFDMA systems. *IEEE Transactions on Wireless Communications, 6*, 3546–3551. doi:10.1109/TWC.2007.060273

Zeng, X. N., & Ghrayeb, A. (2009, May). Joint CFO and channel estimation for OFDMA uplink: An application of the variable projection method. *IEEE Transactions on Wireless Communications, 8*(5). doi:10.1109/TWC.2009.081100

KEY TERMS AND DEFINITIONS

Carrier Frequency Offset (CFO): An offset between the frequencies of the local oscillator of the transmitter and the receiver because oscillator instabilities or because of the Doppler effect.

Frequency Acquisition: First estimation of the CFO that is affecting an OFDM system. It is performed at the beginning of the frame.

Frequency Tracking: Estimation of the residual carrier frequency offset that remains after the acquisition. It is performed during all the frame length.

Intercarrier Interference (ICI): Noise caused by the loss of orthogonality between the subcarriers in an OFDM system. It can be caused by a CFO impairment.

Multiple Access Interference (MAI): Noise caused by the power leakage from other users subcarriers in an OFDMA system.

Orthogonal Frequency Division Multiple Acces (OFDMA): Similar to OFDM but in this modulation several users share the same bandwidth.

Orthogonal Frequency Division Multiplexing (OFDM): Parallel modulation scheme with high transmission capability and its robustness to the effects of frequency-selective multipath channels.

Chapter 10
Design Issues for Multi-Mode Multi-Standard Transceivers

Gianluca Cornetta
Universidad San Pablo-CEU, Spain & Vrije Universiteit Brussel, Belgium

David J. Santos
Universidad San Pablo-CEU, Spain

José Manuel Vázquez
Universidad San Pablo-CEU, Spain

ABSTRACT

Multi-mode and multi-band transceivers, i.e., transceivers with the capability to operate in different frequency bands and to support different waveforms and signaling schemes, are objects of intense study. In fact, hardware reuse among different standards would help to reduce production costs, power consumption, and to increase the integration level of a given implementation. The design of such transceivers is indeed very complex, because it not only implies the choice of the architecture more suitable for the target application, but also the choice and the design of reconfigurable building blocks to perform tuning among the different standards and signaling schemes. In addition, different standards may have considerably different requirements in terms of receiver sensitivity, linearity, input dynamic range, error vector magnitude (EVM), signal bandwidth, and data rate, which in turn make the design of a multi-mode reconfigurable transceiver a very challenging task. In this chapter, the authors present the most common techniques and architecture schemes used in modern wireless communication systems supporting standards for cellular, wireless local area networks (WLAN), and wireless personal area networks (WPAN), i.e., GSM, WCDMA, IEEE 802.11 (Wi-Fi), IEEE 802.15.1 (Bluetooth), IEEE 802.15.4 (Zigbee), and IEEE 802.15.3 (UWB). State-of-the-art techniques for multi-standard cellular, WLAN, and WPAN transceivers are thoroughly analyzed and reviewed with special emphasis on those relying on bandpass sampling and multi-rate signal processing schemes.

DOI: 10.4018/978-1-4666-0083-6.ch010

1. INTRODUCTION

The widespread use of wireless communications has prompted an ever increasing demand for radio frequency transceivers. Until now, a rich variety of wireless technologies have been standardized and commercialized; however, no single solution is considered the best to satisfy all the communication needs and target applications due to different coverage, power consumption, and bandwidth limitations. Therefore, internetworking between heterogeneous wireless networks is extremely important for achieving ubiquitous and high performance wireless communications. Many studies dedicated to the internetworking of 3G cellular networks and WLAN are available in the literature (Ala-Laurila, et al., 2001; Pahlavan et al., 2000; Salkintzis et al., 2002; Buddhikot et al., 2003), and the support for heterogeneous network interconnection has been finally standardized by the Third Generation Partnership Project (2004). Nonetheless, a wireless device operating under multiple network protocols must mandatorily rely on a multi-standard transceiver (Agnelli et al., 2006).

In modern communication systems, the co-existence of numerous cellular systems requires multi-mode, multiband, and multi-standard mobile terminals that have the capability to process heterogeneous information, i.e., text, voice, audio, and video using different standards, and support seamless handover among different networks with different data rates. This requires a careful design in which the number of the handset components shared by the different standards must be maximized, and the power consumption must be minimized in order to slow down battery depletion and prolong talk time without degrading the performance compared to that of a conventional single-standard transceiver. The simplest way to implement a multi-standard design is by duplicating more than one transceiver; however, this solution is economically unfeasible as well as

highly inefficient under the power consumption point of view (Ryynänen et al., 2000).

When different standards do not operate simultaneously, circuit blocks of a multi-standard handset can be shared. This consideration is marking the trend in the design of state-of-the-art reconfigurable and adaptive modules for RF IC. Several multi-mode, multi-band integrated implementations of low-noise amplifiers (Hashemi & Hajimiri, 2001), oscillators (Tasić, Serdijn, & Long, 2005), power amplifiers (Imanishi et al., 2010) and transceivers (Hueber & Staszewski, 2011) are reported in the literature.

Adaptivity and reconfigurability should be implemented at baseband frequencies as well. After a signal is down-converted to the baseband, it must be filtered, amplified and digitized before further processing. To accommodate on a single monolithic transceiver multiple radio standards with different bandwidths and modulation schemes, such receivers should require channel and image reject filters with tunable bandwidths, as well as analogue-to-digital converters with programmable resolutions and dynamic ranges.

The mainstream techniques for implementing multi-mode multi-standard reconfigurable transceivers rely on the Software-defined Radio approach (Burns, 2002; Reed, 2002; Dillinger, Madani, & Alonistioti, 2003). A Software-Defined Radio system (SDR), is a radio communication system where modulation and demodulation operations typically performed by analog components (e.g. mixers, filters, amplifiers, etc.) are instead implemented by means of digital reconfigurable and programmable hardware. Although, a fully digital implementation is actually not possible due to the accuracy and conversion rate limitations of the Analog-to-Digital (ADC) and Digital-to-Analog (DAC) Converters, SDR techniques can be used to replace most of the expensive analog blocks with low-cost reconfigurable digital blocks. However this task is not easy and requires a deep understanding of the basic transceiver architectures and of the standard requirements; in addition, switching from the analog to the digital domain requires a careful trade-off between cost and design efficiency. The goal of a SDR system is to convert a signal to a digital format as close to the antenna as possible, to eliminate from the transceiver the largest number of analog components maximizing the transceiver reconfigurability. Due to the aforementioned ADC and DAC limitations, the conversion must be carried out at an intermediate frequency (IF). If the designer is not concerned with recovering the carrier frequency, the incoming signal can be undersampled provided the sampling frequency is at least twice the signal bandwidth. This class of receivers is known as bandpass or subsampling transceivers. This chapter aims at reviewing the fundamental aspects in the design of such kind of transceivers.

The rest of the chapter is organized as follows. In Section 2 we review the main characteristics of the different receiver and transmitter architectures; in Section 3 bandpass sampling is analyzed in depth, whereas in Section 4 multi-rate signal processing techniques are analyzed. Multi-rate signal processing is an effective and low-cost technique in multi-mode receivers to change system sampling rate so that multiple receivers at the back-end could share the same ADC. Finally, in Section 5 concluding remarks and future research trends are given.

2. CONVENTIONAL AND MULTI-STANDARD TRANSCEIVER ARCHITECTURE

In order to properly decide which is the transceiver architecture more suitable for a given target application, a thorough knowledge about the most widely used architectures is required. In addition, the analysis of these architectures also provides useful information about the major challenges that exist in wireless communication systems design.

The wireless medium is extremely noisy and crowded by many RF signals, and imposes severe constraints on the transceiver design. Limited bandwidth allocation, multipath fading in indoor environments, low power consumption, and reciprocal mixing with strong interferers are only some of the problems that have to be tackled during the design.

The heterodyne architecture is still widely used in wireless systems, mainly because of its high performance. It has been the dominant choice in RF systems until recently (Razavi, 1998). However, this architecture is bulky and expensive. The designers strive for low-cost and low power consumption and the widespread of CMOS processes as the dominant technologies also for analog RF designs, has enabled the use of other architectures more suitable for fully monolithic implementation such as homodyne and Low-IF (Razavi, 1998).

Receiver Architectures

The architecture of a superheterodyne receiver is depicted in Figure 1 (a). Out of band interferers probably generated by other standards are rejected by a wide bandpass filter covering the entire spectrum of interest. The available bandwidth is usually divided into narrow-band channels that can be selected using a channel-select bandpass filter.

Unfortunately, the implementation of such filters is a major bottleneck. In fact, the selection of a channel with high center frequency surrounded by adjacent channels requires filters with a high quality factor (Q) which is difficult to achieve even with external Surface Acoustic Wave (SAW) devices (Razavi, 1998) and impossible to realize in fully monolithic implementations. The major improvement introduced by the superheterodyne architecture is a partial down-conversion of the incoming signal to an intermediate lower frequency in order to relax the channel selection filter specifications. The choice of the intermediate frequency IF is a critical trade-off in superheterodyne receiver design: choosing IF high

Figure 1. Receiver architectures: (a) Superheterodyne, (b) Weaver, and (c) Homodyne or Zero-IF

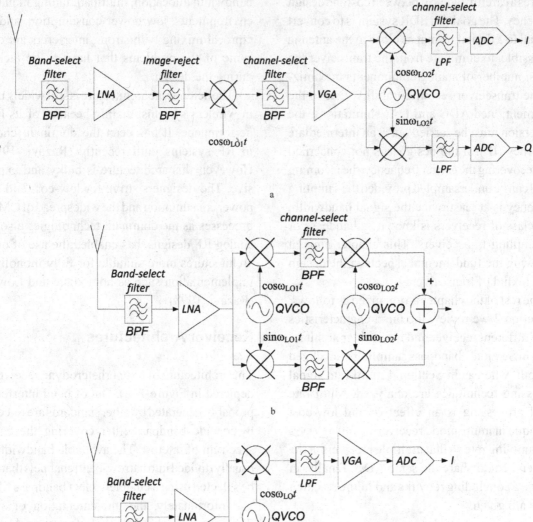

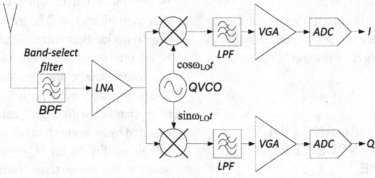

eases image rejection, whereas a low IF eases adjacent channels suppression.

To avoid the image problem, Hartley (1928) proposed a receiver architecture in which the desired channel and its image were processed so that the image could eventually be eliminated by

signal cancellation. However due device mismatch practical image rejections are low and in the range between 30 and 40 dB.

Weaver architecture (1956) depicted in Figure 1 (b), is an improvement of the Hartley demodulation scheme. The only difference is that in the

Weaver scheme the 90° phase shifter is replaced by a quadrature down-converter. The key advantage of the Weaver scheme with respect the Hartley implementation is the wideband behavior of the down-converter that can perform image rejection over a larger bandwidth. However, the Weaver implementation doubles the silicon area and the power consumption with respect to Hartley scheme.

Both Hartley and Weaver schemes are more suitable for fully monolithic implementation that the superheterodyne receiver that, instead, requires external components. Nonetheless, the difficulty in matching the I and Q paths in this class of receivers results in phase and gain mismatches that lead to incomplete image rejection and may put severe or even unpractical design constraints on other components (Razavi, 1997).

The homodyne architecture depicted in Figure 1 (c) is another cheap alternative to superheterodyne architecture since it avoids the use of any type of off-chip components and it is suitable for fully monolithic implementation. As shown in Figure 1 (c), the desired channel is shifted from RF to baseband using only one down-conversion stage (Razavi, 1998). This architecture has several advantages: there is no image frequency since the signal is directly down-converted to baseband, channel selection is performed by a low-pass filter rather than a bandpass one, and digitization and post-processing are at baseband, relaxing the ADC specifications. However, the homodyne architecture has some limitations as well. The down-conversion process overlaps negative and positive parts of the input spectrum; this is not a problem for DSB (Double Side-Band) signals (for example, AM signals) since both sides of the spectrum carry the same information. Unfortunately, other modulation schemes such as phase or frequency modulation make use of all the bandwidth, i.e., the two side-bands carry different information (this type of signals are usually referred as Single Side-Band –SSB). For these types of modulations, the down-conversion

must provide quadrature outputs to avoid loss of information. This quadrature modulation is also referred to as I/Q modulation.

Finally, homodyne architecture is very sensitive to low-frequency interferences (i.e., DC offsets and $1/f$ noise) that may cause a substantial degradation of the signal-to-noise ratio (SNR) or a complete desensitization of the receiver if the baseband gain is too high. The direct conversion architecture poses severe linearity constraints on LNAs (Low Noise Amplifiers) and Mixers, and requires high-frequency oscillators with precise quadrature, and very low offsets and $1/f$ noise. Unfortunately, all these requirements are difficult to fulfill simultaneously (Oliveira et al., 2008).

The Low-IF architecture (Crols & Steyaert, 2002) depicted in Figure 2 has the same key advantages of the direct conversion scheme, but is less sensitive to low-frequency interference at the expense of a harder constraints for image rejection.

The desired channel is down-converted to a very low frequency very close to DC (typically from half to few channels spacing). After that, the base-band conversion is performed digitally by the ADCs. Image cancellation is performed in the digital domain by special mixing circuits, thus avoiding the use of a high-Q image-reject filter. Finally, Table 1 summarizes the main characteristics of the receiver architectures analyzed so far.

Transmitter Architecture

Figure 3 (a) depicts the architecture of a superheterodyne transmitter. Conceptually, the scheme resembles its receiving counterpart with the basic operations performed in reverse order. In a transmitter only one channel is up-converted, thus the power level is well determined and there is no need for Variable Gain Amplifiers (VGA) in the up-conversion chain, provided the power control could be implemented by the Power Amplifier (PA).

Figure 3 (b) shows the architecture of a two-step up transmitter. The up-conversion is per-

Figure 2. Low-IF receiver

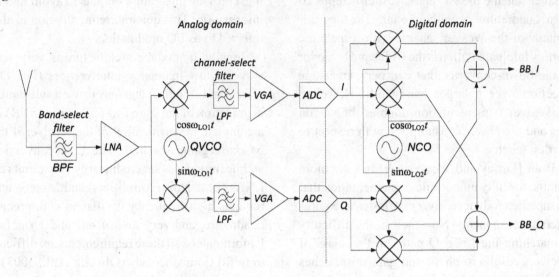

formed in two steps: the first in the digital domain, the second in the analog domain. The advantage of this configuration is an improved I/Q matching and no LO (Local Oscillator) pulling when compared with a direct-up transmission since the out-band noise of the PA is far from the natural oscillation frequency of the QVCO (Quadrature Voltage Controlled Oscillator).

Finally, Figure 4 shows the architecture of a direct-up transmitter. In this scheme the up-conversion is performed in only one step. The advantage of this configuration is its high integra-

bility due to the reduced number of components. Nonetheless, a direct-up transmitter has important shortcomings such as LO pulling that may corrupt the QVCO making it to lock on a different oscillation frequency, and LO leakage that may corrupt RF output. To avoid these problems, techniques such as VCO (Voltage Controlled Oscillator) and LO-leakage calibration are necessary in this transmission scheme. Finally, Table 2 summarizes the main characteristics of the transmitter architectures analyzed so far.

Table 1. Summary of the characteristics of the receiver architectures

Architecture	Advantages	Drawbacks
Superheterodyne	☺ Reliable performances ☺ No DC-offsets and $1/f$ noise	☹ Expensive and bulky ☹ High power consumption ☹ Not suitable for multi-standard
Image-reject (Hartley and Weaver)	☺ Low cost ☺ No DC-offsets and $1/f$ noise ☺ Suitable for monolithic implementation	☹ Requires quadrature down-conversion ☹ Suffer from first and secondary images ☹ Narrowband (Hartley) ☹ Requires high I/Q matching
Zero-IF	☺ Low cost ☺ No image problem ☺ Suitable for monolithic implementation ☺ Easily adaptable to multi-standard	☹ Requires quadrature down-conversion ☹ DC-offsets and $1/f$ noise
Low-IF	☺ Low cost ☺ Small DC-offsets and $1/f$ noise ☺ Suitable for monolithic implementation	☹ Requires quadrature down-conversion ☹ Double quadrature for image rejection ☹ Suffer from image frequency

Figure 3. Transmitter topologies: (a) Superheterodyne, and (b) Two-step up

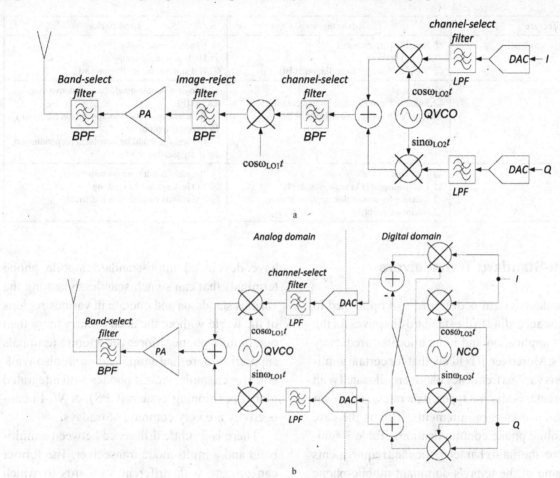

Figure 4. Direct-up transmitter

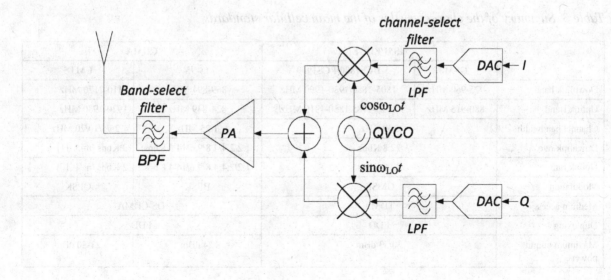

Table 2. Summary of the characteristics of the receiver architectures

Architecture	Advantages	Drawbacks
Superheterodyne	☺ Reliable performances ☺ No LO leakage ☺ Simple DC offset cancellation at BB	☹ Expensive and bulky ☹ High power consumption ☹ Not suitable for multi-standard
Two-step up	☺ Low cost ☺ Suitable for monolithic implementation ☺ Simple DC offset cancellation at BB	☹ Requires double-quadrature up-conversion (DC to IF) ☹ Requires quadrature up-conversion (IF to RF) ☹ Image is a problem ☹ LO leakage could be a problem (depending on the IF frequency)
Direct-up	☺ Low cost ☺ Easily adaptable to multi-standard ☺ Suitable for monolithic implementation ☺ No image problem	☹ Requires quadrature up-conversion ☹ LO leakage and LO pulling ☹ DC offsets cancellation is difficult

Multi-Standard Transceivers

A wireless system is designed and optimized to operate according to the standard directives for the target application and in its allocated frequency bands. Moreover, it is likely that for certain applications various frequency bands are allocated with different modulation types, data rates, and power emission ratings requirements. This is the case of mobile phone communications. Table 3 summarizes the main characteristics and requirements of some of the today's dominant mobile-phone standards to demonstrate this concept. To support these different sets of standards, manufactures have developed multi-standard mobile phone terminals that can switch seamlessly among the various standards and operate in various regions of the world without the need to carry more than one mobile phone. Moreover, mobile terminals supporting more than an application are also available; for example, mobile phones with integrated global positioning system (GPS), or Wi-Fi connectivity are very common nowadays.

There is a subtle difference between a multi-band and a multi-mode transceiver. The former can operate with different standards to which different bands are allocated; on the other hand,

Table 3. Summary of the characteristics of the main cellular standards

	GSM/EDGE		CDMA	
	GSM	DCS1800/PCS1900	IS-95	UMTS
Downlink band	925-960 MHz	1805-1880/1930-1990 MHz	869-894 MHz	2110-2170 MHz
Uplink Band	880-915 MHz	1710-1785/1850-1910 MHz	824-849 MHz	1920-1980 MHz
Channel bandwidth	200 KHz		1.25 MHz	1.25/5/10/20 MHz
Downlink rate	22.8 Kbps		1.2/2.4/4.8/9.6/14.4 Kbps	2^n Kbps (n=5..11)
Uplink rate	22.8 Kbps		1.2/2.4/4.8/9.6/14.4 Kbps	2^n Kbps (n=4..10)
Modulation	GMSK		BPSK	QPSK
Medium access	TDMA		DS-CDMA	
Duplexing	FDD		FDD	
Maximum output power	30/33 dBm		24 dBm	23-30 dBm

Table 4. Summary of the characteristics of the main wireless network standards

	ISM			UNII
Frequency	2400-2483.5 MHz			5150-5250/5250-5350 MHz
Standard	ZigBee	Bluetooth	802.11b (Wi-Fi)	802.11a (Wi-Fi)
Medium access	DSSS/TDD	FHSS/TDD	DSSS	OFDM
Modulation	OQPSK	GFSK	CCK	64 QAM
Channel bandwidth	2 MHz	1 MHz	5 MHz	16.6 MHz
Maximum data rate	250 Kbps	1 Mbps	11 Mbps	54 Mbps
Output power	-3 – 0 dBm	0 – 20 dBm	30 dBm	16 dBm (5150-5250 MHz) 23 dBm (5250-5350 MHz)
Range	10 – 100m	1 – 100 m	100 m	50 m
Application	Industrial/remote sensing	Short range/cable replacement	High-speed WLAN	High-speed WLAN

the latter can operate with different standards to which the same band is allocated.

Beside cellular communications, wireless networking is another market segment which is demanding transceivers with multi-standard capability; however, since the great majority of the wireless network standards are designed to operate in the unlicensed 2400 MHz ISM band, the multi-mode capability is preferable in this case. Table 4 summarizes some of the specifications of these standards. Obviously, since all these standards are intended for short-range applications, their radio interface specifications are more relaxed when compared to those of the cellular standards.

Several multi-standard transceivers for cellular, WPAN/WLAN and WLAN applications are reported in the literature. However, in spite of the multi-mode or multi-band features, all the implementation reported rely on the classical transceiver topologies described in Sections 2.1 and 2.2.

Ryynänen et al. (2003) described a monolithic direct conversion receiver for cellular applications supporting GSM, DCS, PCS, and WCDMA. Cho et al. (2003) proposed a multi-mode transceiver supporting Bluetooth and 802.11b. The transceiver relies on a two-step topology on both the transmit and the receive side. Since Bluetooth and 802.11b share the same frequency band, most of the components of the transceiver are shared by the two standards. Filtering and signal amplification is instead performed by reconfigurable devices to match the different standard requirements. Brandolini et al. (2005) proposed an implementation of a low-IF transceiver supporting several cellular, WLAN, and WPAN standards, namely Bluetooth, 802.11a/b/g, DCS, and PCS. The Bluetooth interface provides a wireless link between the radio terminal and other peripherals (i.e., the headset) and is active all the time, whereas the other standards are activated by an RF switch. The implementation of a multi-mode transceiver for Bluetooth and 802.11b proposed by Jung et al. (2003) utilizes instead direct up and down-conversion at the transmit and the receive side respectively. Darabi et al. (2003) presented multi-mode transceiver for Bluetooth and 802.11b. The implementation relies on a direct-up transmitter, on a low-IF receiver for Bluetooth, and on a direct-conversion receiver for 802.11b.

This work does not pretend to give an exhaustive review of all the implementations available in the literature. The interested reader may refer to (Hashemi, 2003) or to (Mak, U, & Martins, 2007) for a more comprehensive review of multi-mode and multi-band transceivers.

All the architectures reviewed in this section require a careful frequency planning and implement the multi-standard function by optimally sharing the available hardware resources, and by using tunable devices. This, in turn, considerably reduces area occupation and power consumption, which is a key aspect in the design of portable and battery-operated devices. Among all the topologies analyzed so far, the homodyne (Zero-IF) and the Low-IF architectures are those more suitable for multi-band, multi-mode radio communications. In fact, the key advantage of these topologies is that the A/D conversion is performed very close to the antenna, reducing the number of the analog components, and allowing to perform signal processing, modulation and demodulation by low-cost, compact, and low-power digital programmable hardware functions. In the case of the homodyne transceiver the sampling operation is performed in the baseband, whereas, in the case of the Low-IF transceiver the sampling is performed in the pass-band, i.e. at the intermediate down-conversion frequency IF. However, there is another front-end architecture we have not yet considered and that is also appealing for the implementation of multi-mode, multi-band radios: we refer to the bandpass sampling (or subsampling) radio.

The Low-IF architecture may result in imperfect image rejection if the intermediate frequency IF is too close to the baseband, and could be impractical if the intermediate frequency IF is too close to the RF frequency, due to the limitations of the analog-to-digital converter (linearity, dynamic range, etc.). However, if the target application does not require reconstructing the carrier, the IF signal can be sampled below the Nyquist frequency. In fact, Shannon's theorem states that the minimum sampling frequency necessary to reconstruct a signal is not only a function of the maximum frequency, but also of the signal bandwidth. Consequently, undersampling the carrier and oversampling the signal will still allow signal reconstruction.

Subsampling (or bandpass sampling) the IF signal relaxes the requirements of the ADC, and allows the implementation of a front-end architecture very close to the design paradigm of the ideal Software Defined Radio (Mitola, 1995). For this reason, in spite of the limitations and drawbacks that will be discussed in the sequel, subsampling radios are a valid alternative to homodyne and Low-IF architectures.

Software Defined Radio (SDR) can be considered as the second great radio evolution after the transition from analog to digital communication systems. It is a new design paradigm, originally developed for military applications, in which radio functionalities are extensively defined by software. It consists of a single radio transceiver that allows the communications among different types of military radios using different frequency bands and modulation schemes (Lackey & Upmal, 1995). This concept has been gradually introduced in modern commercial designs that are now a mix of analog hardware, digital hardware, and software functions.

In the following section we will briefly review the main characteristics of the subsampling architecture, whereas in Section 3 we will discuss both practical and theoretical aspects behind the design of subsampling front-ends with particular emphasis on the ADC requirements. Finally, since the operation in a multi-mode, multi-band fashion requires a change of the system sampling rate, in Section 4 we will review the main techniques to implement low-cost multi-rate processing schemes.

Bandpass-Sampling Radio Architecture

Until now we have dealt basically with standard transceiver topologies. Most of them rely almost exclusively on analog blocks to perform basic signal processing, modulation, and demodulation. Although all the implementations we have reviewed are fully monolithic, the passive com-

Figure 5. Architecture of a bandpass sampling (subsampling) receiver

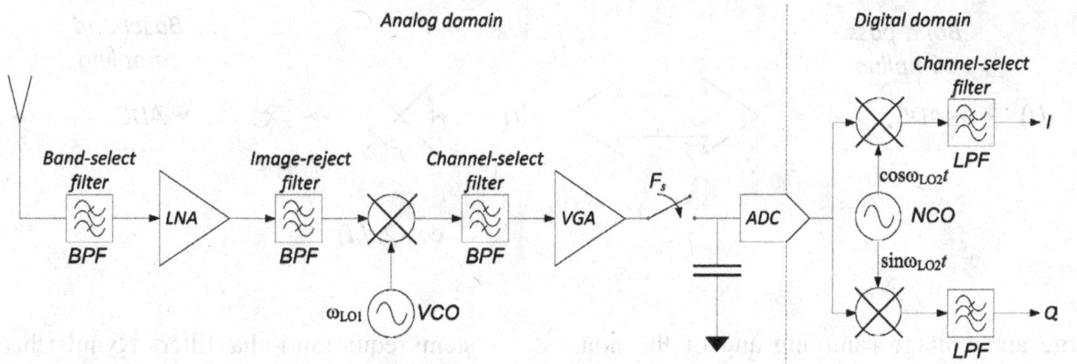

ponents (inductors and capacitors) that implement on-chip matching networks, and LC tanks for the oscillators, introduce a high area penalty that limits the integration level. As mentioned in the previous section, bandpass sampling is one of the possible design alternatives to mitigate the noise and the area overhead of the analog blocks.

The design of a multi-standard subsampling fully monolithic transceiver is a challenging task due to the limitations imposed by noise aliasing (Vaughan et al., 1991; Sun & Signell, 2005). However, several designs of subsampling receivers have been reported, tackling GSM (Muhammad et al., 2005), Bluetooth (Muhammad et al., 2004; Muhammad et al., 2005), and 802.11b (Jakonis, 2004; Jakonis et al., 2005).

More recently, also multi-standard implementations like (Barrak et al., 2006; Barrak et al., 2009) and (Bechir & Rida, 2010) have been reported. Barrak et al. (2006, 2009) present an architecture for GSM, UMTS, and 802.11b, based on two cascaded subsampling stages, the former with a fixed RF subsampling frequency, and the latter with a variable IF subsampling frequency that depends on the considered standard. The RF frequency is designed to down-convert multiple-standard waveforms into the same IF band. Two tunable bandpass filters at RF and IF reject wideband noise and perform anti-aliasing function as well. Bechir and Ridha (2010) present a dual-mode receiver

for GSM and WCDMA based on a fourth-order subsampling continous-time $\Sigma\Delta$ modulator.

Figure 5 depicts the architecture of a subsampling receiver. Baseband conversion is performed in two steps, the first in the analog domain, and the second in the digital domain by a quadrature digital low-frequency mixer, improving the I/Q matching of the receiver. Moreover, performing final down-conversion and demodulation in the digital domain limits the number of analog components with high area overhead, drastically reduces the system costs, making this topology very attractive for CMOS monolithic implementation. Since the down-conversion is performed in two steps, the receiver does not suffer from problems due to DC offsets and $1/f$ noise; however, the sampling operation produces aliasing and noise folding that negatively affect the SNR of the receiver. To avoid noise folding, the sample & hold and the ADC must run at a high clock frequency; this, on one hand puts severe constraints on the ADC design, and, on the other hand increases power consumption.

There are two possible sampling techniques: charge sampling and voltage sampling (Xu & Yuan, 2000). For example, the scheme proposed by Muhammad et al. (2005) and that by Karvonel et al. (2006) rely on charge sampling, whereas the implementation of Jakonis et al. (2005) relies on voltage sampling. A comprehensive study of

Figure 6. Advantages of bandpass sampling

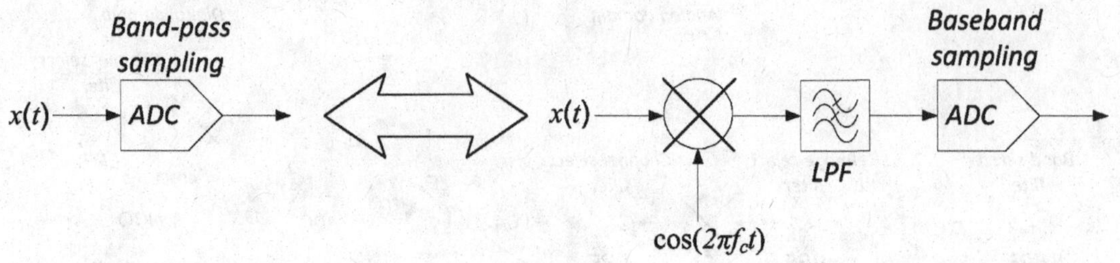

charge and voltage sampling and of the non-idealities of bandpass sampling systems (spectral overlapping, noise aliasing, and sampling timing jitter) can be found in (Karvonen, 2006; Sun, 2006).

3. DESIGN CONSIDERATIONS IN BANDPASS SAMPLING RADIOS

The bandpass sampling, also known as *harmonic sampling* or *subsampling*, is a technique that consists in sampling the incoming signal at rates lower than the highest frequency of interest to perform signal down-conversion from RF to low IF or baseband through intentional aliasing. In this scheme, sampling rate requirements do not depend on the carrier, but rather on the signal bandwidth, thus relaxing the processing requirements of the system.

Sampling an analog signal with maximum frequency f_0, at a sampling rate F_s, produces two aliased components: the former at F_s+f_0 and the latter at F_s-f_0. However, it is only the lower-frequency alias component which may cause problems because it can fall within the Nyquist bandwidth and corrupt wanted signals. Due to the aliasing phenomenon of sampling systems, the Nyquist criteria requires sampling signals at a rate of $F_s > f_0$ to avoid the folding of the aliased components into the first Nyquist zone. To prevent unwanted interference, any signals which fall outside the bandwidth of interest should be filtered before sampling. This is the reason why many sampling systems require anti-alias filters. Nyquist theorem assumes that the desired information bandwidth is equal to the Nyquist bandwidth or half the sampling frequency. However, according to Shannon's theorem, the required minimum sampling frequency is a function of the input signal bandwidth and not only of the maximum frequency. An analog signal with a bandwidth B, must be sampled at a rate of $F_s > 2B$ in order to avoid the loss of information. Nonetheless, the signal bandwidth may extend from DC to B (in the case of baseband sampling) or from f_L to f_H where $B = f_H - f_L$ (in the case of bandpass sampling or undersampling). In general the sampling rate must be at least twice the signal bandwidth and the sampled signal must not cross an integer multiple of $F_s/2$ to prevent overlapping of the aliased components.

A bandpass sampling analog-to-digital converter (ADC) is equivalent to a down-conversion mixer followed by a baseband-sampling ADC, as depicted in Figure 6. However, in the case of bandpass sampling, the down-conversion is carried-out by intentional spectral folding. Bandpass sampling has a clear advantage over conventional techniques, namely a drastic reduction of component counts that leads to architecture simplification and costs drop.

However, sampling-rate requirements of a bandpass ADC are much more exigent when compared with its baseband counterpart.

Due to harmonic sampling or subsampling, every ADC input frequency component outside the Nyquist bandwidth is always folded back into the first Nyquist zone. The process of subsampling or folding can be thought of as mixing the ADC input signal with the sampling frequency and its harmonics. This means that many frequencies can be down-converted to DC and their original frequency can no longer be determined. For this reason subsampling cannot be used if the original input frequency must be determined at the ADC output, because the Nyquist criterion is violated. However, subsampling is a very effective technique when there is no need to determine the carrier frequency at the ADC output. This is the case of many communication systems such as cellular base-station receivers, since the receiver only needs to recover the information on the carrier and not the carrier itself.

Fundamentals

According to the Nyquist theorem, to avoid aliasing and to reconstruct the signal, the sampling frequency must be at least twice the signal bandwidth. However, the RF signals used in many wireless communication schemes are typically narrowband in nature since the signal bandwidths rarely exceeds the 0.2% of their carrier frequencies. Under these conditions, the minimum sampling rate to avoid aliasing depends on the signal bandwidth B and not on the highest frequency. The theoretical minimum sampling rate $F_{s,min}$ can be as low as twice the signal bandwidth, i.e. $F_{s,min} = 2 \times B$. Nonetheless, practical sampling rates are larger than $F_{s,min}$ to take into account imperfections of the implementation that could cause aliasing.

The sampling operation of signal $x_b(t)$ by a uniform train of impulses produces shifted replicas of the signal' spectrum $X_b(f)$ at multiples of the sampling frequency F_s, namely:

$$x(t) = x_b(t) \sum_{n=-\infty}^{\infty} \delta(t - nT_s) =$$
$$\sum_{n=-\infty}^{\infty} x_b(t) \delta(t - nT_s) =$$
$$\sum_{n=-\infty}^{\infty} x_b(nT_s) \delta(t - nT_s)$$

The spectrum of the sampled signal can be obtained taking the Fourier transform,

$$X(f) = X_b(f) * \left[\frac{1}{T_s} \sum_{n=-\infty}^{\infty} \delta(f - nF_s) \right] =$$
$$\frac{1}{T_s} \sum_{n=-\infty}^{\infty} X_b(f - nF_s)$$

This scenario is depicted graphically in Figure 7.

The sampling operation converts the signal spectrum to baseband. Observe that Nyquist zones divide the spectrum into regions with width $F_s/2$, and that contain either a copy or a mirrored copy of the signal spectrum.

If f_H is an integer multiple n of the signal band B, and n is odd, the Nyquist zone 1 contains the exact replica of the signal spectrum. Otherwise, if n is even, Nyquist zone 1 contains a flipped version of the signal spectrum.

Let now consider the general case in which $f_H \neq nB$, and $B = f_H - f_L$. The bandpass analog signal can be exactly reconstructed after sampling and digitization if the sampling frequency F_s meets the following conditions:

$$\frac{(n-1)F_s}{2} < f_L. \tag{1}$$

and

$$f_H < \frac{nF_s}{2}, \tag{2}$$

Where n is an integer such that

$$n = \left\lfloor \frac{f_H}{B} \right\rfloor = \left\lfloor \frac{f_H}{f_H - f_L} \right\rfloor.$$

Figure 7. Bandpass sampling of RF signals

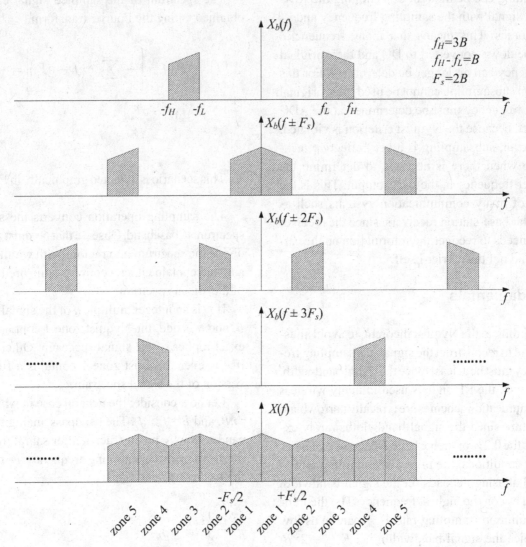

From inequalities (1) and (2) it is possible to determine the upper and lower bounds for aliasing-free sampling rate:

$$\frac{2f_H}{n} \le F_s \le \frac{2f_L}{n-1} \tag{3}$$

The allowable range of sampling frequencies can be estimated in terms of the difference of the maximum and minimum allowed sampling rates:

$$\Delta F_s = \frac{2\left(f_H - B\right)}{n-1} - \frac{2f_H}{n}$$

Equation (3) is depicted graphically in Figure 8 for several values of *n*. The graphic represents the normalized sampling frequency versus the normalized highest frequency. The shaded areas represent the forbidden sampling rates, i.e. the rates at which aliasing is produced.

The white areas are the permissible zones. Observe that, the smaller the integer number *n*,

Figure 8. Allowed zones for aliasing-free sampling

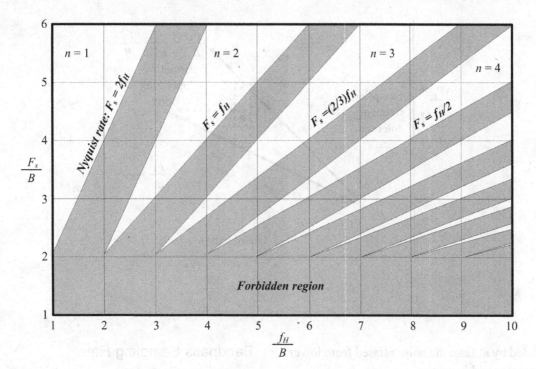

the broader is the aliasing-free region. The value of n is usually low and less than 10.

For a given f_H/B ratio (i.e., for a given value of the number n), the sampling rate F_s must be chosen so that the operating point falls within the aliasing-free region. In order to assure a correct behavior, fluctuations of the sampling rate due to clock jitter and other circuit non-idealities must be taken into account as depicted in Figure 9.

Vaughan et al. (1991) observed that sampling at non-minimum rates is equivalent to increase the signal bandwidth with a total guard band $B_G = \Delta B_L + \Delta B_H = F_s - 2B$. The lower and upper bounds of the overall bandwidth (signal plus total guard-band) are:

$$f_L' = f_L - \Delta B_L$$

and

$$f_H' = f_H + \Delta B_H$$

Consequently the lower order wedge is given by:

$$n' = \left\lfloor \frac{f_H'}{B + B_G} \right\rfloor$$

and the allowable range of sampling frequencies becomes:

$$\Delta F_s' = \frac{2f_L'}{n' - 1} - \frac{2f_H'}{n'}$$

Design Considerations

The bandpass sampling shifts the RF bandpass signal to IF or baseband. The resulting signal-to-noise ratio is poorer than that of a standard quadrature analog receiver because the SNR is

Figure 9. Parameters for the nth wedge

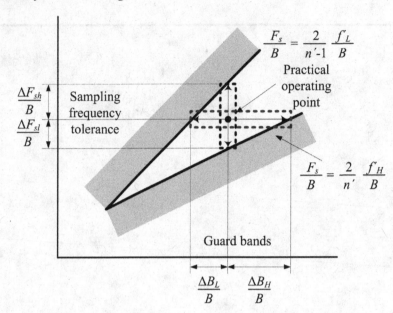

degraded by at least the noise aliased from lower frequencies and becomes:

$$SNR = \frac{P_S}{P_{N,inband} + (n-1)P_{N,outband}}$$

where P_S is the power spectral density of the pass-band signal, $P_{N,inband}$ is the power spectral density of the in-band noise, and $P_{N,outband}$ is the power spectral density of the out-band noise. In general the main source of degradation is the in-band noise (i.e., $P_{N,inband} \gg P_{N,outband}$).

The performance of a bandpass sampling architecture transceiver depends mainly on the performance of the ADC and DAC of the reception and transmission chains respectively. This means that a bandpass architecture is feasible for a particular standard only if we are able to design and implement high-performance ADC and DAC running at IF frequency with reasonably low power consumption.

Bandpass Sampling Rate

It can be shown (Kester, 2003) that the ratio of the root-mean-square (rms) value of a full scale sine wave to the value of the quantization noise (expressed in dB) is:

$$SNR_{ADC} = 6.02b + 1.76 \text{ dB},$$

where b is the number of bits of the ideal ADC. This equation is valid only for base-band sampling and when the noise is measured over the entire Nyquist bandwidth from DC to $F_s/2$. In the case of bandpass sampling, the previous equation must be suitably modified to take into account the maximum frequency f_H of the bandpass signal:

$$SNR_{ADC} = 6.02b + 1.76 + 10\log\left(\frac{F_s}{2f_H}\right) \text{ dB}$$

The third term represents the SNR improvement or degradation due to over or under sampling.

It is clear that the signal-to-noise ratio of the ADC output decreases as the ratio f_H/F_s increases. Selecting large n results in low sampling rate; nonetheless there are some limitations: first, the allowable range for F_s established by (3) becomes very small requiring a highly accurate sampling clock and selective channel filters; second, the signal-to-noise ratio worsens since $(n-1)$ noise bands between DC and f_L are aliased into the signal band. In this aspect, bandpass sampling differs from signal down-conversion with an analog mixer, because this process preserves the signal-to-noise ratio. To keep the ADC dynamic range high and the noise figure low it is desirable to sample the pass-band signal with a low harmonic of the Nyquist sampling rate.

ADC Requirements

As stated before, noise behavior is a major shortcoming of bandpass sampling because of the aliasing, especially in the case of high-order harmonic sampling. In a transceiver, the noise behavior is expressed by means of the noise figure NF. In the case of an ADC, the equivalent noise figure can be estimated as (Gu, 2005):

$$NF_{ADC} =$$
$$10\log\left[1+\left(\frac{2f_H}{F_s}-1\right)+\frac{1}{4kTR_s}\left(P_{Nq}+P_{Nj}\right)\left(1+\frac{R_s}{R_L}\right)^2\right]$$

where $k = 1.38\times10^{-23}$ J/K, $T = 300$ K, R_s is the source resistance, R_L is the load impedance (i.e., the ADC input impedance), P_{Nq} is the quantization noise density, and P_{Nj} is the jitter noise density.

The quantization noise density can be expressed as:

$$P_{Nq} = \frac{V_{pp}^2}{L_q^2 6F_s}\left(\frac{2f_H}{F_s}\right)$$

where V_{pp} is the maximum peak-to-peak voltage swing of the ADC, and L_q the number of quantization levels. The jitter noise density P_{Nj} is typically assumed to be half of a LSB.

The noise figure of a state-of-the-art high-resolution ADC bandpass sampling at a rate of hundreds of MSamples/s is usually in the range of 20 to 30 dB depending on the value of the ratio $2f_H/F_s$. The high equivalent noise introduced by the ADC puts severe constraints on the analog front-end of the receiver that must have a very low noise figure and a high gain (around 30 dB) to achieve good receiver sensitivity.

Another important design parameter is the ADC dynamic range. The dynamic range of the ADC depends on the strength of the interferer and the sensitivity of the receiver. The lower bound for the dynamic range is:

$$DR_{ADC,\min} =$$
$$S_I - S_d + CNR + \Delta G_{LNA} + PAR_{Rx} + \Delta S_F,$$

where S_I is the strength of the interfering signal (expressed in dBm), S_d is the strength of the desired signal (expressed in dBm), CNR is the carrier-to-noise ratio, ΔG_{LNA} is a possible variation of the LNA gain, PAR_{Rx} is the peak-to-average ratio of the received signal, and ΔS_F is a possible magnitude variation due to constructive fading.

For example, for a CDMA receiver, the desirable ADC dynamic range should be around 90 dB, which in turn requires an ADC resolution of 15 bits. On the other hand, for a short-range WPAN the desirable ADC dynamic range should be around 60 dB, which requires 10-bit resolution.

The linearity of a bandpass receiver can be characterized by its third-order input-referred intercept point IIP_3; however, in the case of a bandpass sampling architecture, the ADC is directly connected to the analog front-end without any channel filter. This, in turn, requires extremely-linear

ADCs when compared to heterodyne or homodyne receivers. The overall third-order input intercept point of the receiver $IIP_{3,Rx}$ is determined by:

$$IIP_{3,Rx} = \left(\frac{1}{IIP_{3,FE}} + \frac{G_{FE}}{IIP_{3,ADC}} \right)^{-1},$$

where $IIP_{3,FE}$ and $IIP_{3,ADC}$ are the third-order intercept point of the front end and of the ADC respectively. The $IIP_{3,ADC}$ can be as high as 14 to 15 dBm.

Automatic Gain Control (AGC)

The overall dynamic range DR_{Rx} of the receiver (in dB) is the sum of the ADC effective dynamic range and of the AGC range of the LNA, that is:

$$DR_{Rx} = DR_{ADC} + \Delta G_{LNA}$$

The AGC system of a bandpass sampling receiver is simpler that its counterparts in heterodyne or homodyne receivers. In fact, in bandpass sampling no variable gain amplifiers are required since the receiver dynamic range can be covered by controlling and combining the LNA automatic gain and the ADC dynamic.

4. MULTIRATE SIGNAL PROCESSING

Digital signal processing in high-complexity applications cannot be performed using a single sampling rate. In order to reduce the computational complexity and to use simple digital signal processing hardware, it is beneficial to use variable sampling rates at the different stages of the system. A digital signal processing scheme that relies on variable sampling rates is called *multirate digital signal processing*.

Multirate signal processing can be effectively used in multi-mode receivers to share the same ADC among multiple receiver implementations. At the receiver, a signal is typically digitized at a sampling rate much higher than its bandwidth in order to relax the specifications of the ADC anti-aliasing filter. After digitization, the signal is immediately down-converted to the minimum sampling rate in order to reduce computational complexity. On the other hand, on the transmitter side, signals are created at the minimum sampling rate; however, the sampling rate is increased before the DAC to relax the specifications of the interpolation filter.

Multirate signal processing relies on two basic operations: decimation and interpolation. Decimation (or down-sampling) is the process by which high-frequency spectral components are eliminated from the signal to reduce the sampling rate. On the other hand, interpolation (or up-sampling) is the process to increase the number of points per unit time of a given signal to increase the sampling rate.

In the sequel we will review the basic hardware structures used to implement decimation and interpolation in digital transceivers.

Multi-Stage Sampling Rate Conversion

When large changes in sampling are required, cascading multiple sample-rate converters is the best solution. In fact, many practical implementations employ multi-stage structures to relax the specifications of anti-aliasing (decimation) or anti-imaging (interpolation) filters when compared to a single stage implementation (see Figure 10).

The condition that must be accomplished to implement a multi-stage decimator is that the decimation factor M can be expressed as:

$$M = \prod_{j=1}^{K} M_j = M_1 \times M_2 \times \ldots \times M_K$$

Figure 10. Multi-stage down-sampling chain

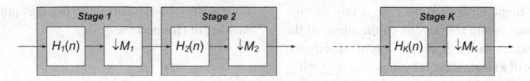

Where $M_1, M_2,...,M_k$ are the decimation factors of the individual stages. Moreover, the original sampling frequency F_s and the sampling frequency of the k-th decimator stage are related by the following expression:

$$F_{s,K} = \frac{F_s}{M} = \frac{F_s}{\prod_{j=1}^{K} M_j}$$

The sampling frequencies of two adjacent decimation stages are related by:

$$F_{s,j} = \frac{F_{s,j-1}}{M_j}$$

Consider a three-stage decimator: input data are sampled at $F_{s,1}$, whereas output data are sampled at $F_{s,3}$. The pass-band frequency is f_{pass}, whereas the stop-band frequency is f_{stop}. The goal of the last stage of the decimator is limiting the signal bans so that $f_{stop} \leq F_{s,3}/2$. In general, to prevent signal degradation due to aliasing, the cut frequency of the last stage must comply with the Nyquist theorem, i.e.:

$$f_{stop} \leq \frac{F_{s,K}}{2}$$

This scenario is depicted in Figure 11. Moreover, to assure that the aliased signal do not fall into the pass-band, the j-th stage, the following relation must hold:

$$f_{stop,j} \leq F_{s,j} - f_{stop}$$

From this relation, the stop-band of the last stage can be computed as:

$$f_{stop,K} = F_{s,K} - f_{stop} = 2f_{stop} - f_{stop} = f_{stop}$$

Figure 11. Bandwidth requirement of the cascaded decimating filters

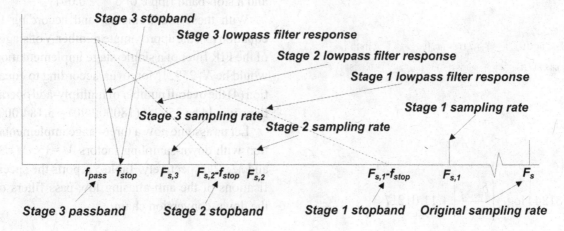

Other design goal is assuring that the overall filter ripple be limited by $1+\delta_{pass}$; this, in turn, imposes severe restrictions on the ripple of the individual stages. A simple way to specify the ripple of a single stage is by imposing $\delta_{pass,j} = \delta_{pass}/K$. However, this specification does not guarantee that the ripples of the different stages are phase-aligned. Analogously, it must be guaranteed that the cumulative ripple in the stop-band does not exceed δ_{stop}. Each stage of the decimator must be designed so that the stop-band ripple is $\delta_{stop,j} = \delta_{stop}$.

To estimate the order of the decimation filter, a transition band Δf_j from pass to stop-band must be defined. The width of the transition band is normalized with respect to the sampling frequency of the stage considered:

$$\Delta f_j = \frac{\left(F_{s,j} - f_{stop}\right) - f_{pass}}{F_{s,j-1}} \tag{1}$$

Rabiner (1973) demonstrated that the optimum number of taps of a low-pass FIR (Finite Impulse Response) filter is:

$$N_{j,optimum} = \frac{D_\infty\left(\delta_{pass,j}, \delta_{stop,j}\right)}{\Delta f_j} - f\left(\delta_{pass,j}, \delta_{stop,j}\right)\Delta f_j + 1 \tag{2}$$

where:

$$D_\infty\left(\delta_{pass,j}, \delta_{stop,j}\right) = \left[5.309\times10^{-3}\left(\log_{10}\delta_{pass,j}\right)^2 + 7.114\times10^{-2}\left(\log_{10}\delta_{pass,j}\right) - 0.4761\right]\times\left(\log_{10}\delta_{stop,j}\right) - \left[2.66\times10^{-3}\left(\log_{10}\delta_{pass,j}\right)^2 + 0.5941\times10^{-2}\left(\log_{10}\delta_{pass,j}\right) - 0.4278\right]$$

and

$$f\left(\delta_{pass,j}, \delta_{stop,j}\right) = 0.51244\log_{10}\left(\frac{\delta_{pass,j}}{\delta_{stop,j}}\right) + 11.01217$$

Observe that when the decimation rate is high, the transition band is narrow, so that the optimum number of taps becomes:

$$N_{j,optimum} \approx \frac{D_\infty\left(\delta_{pass,j}, \delta_{stop,j}\right)}{\Delta f_j} \tag{3}$$

The goal of a multi-stage decimator is reducing the overall number R_{total} of multiply-add operations:

$$R_{total} = \sum_{j=1}^{K} R_j$$

Where R_j is the number of multiply-add operation performed by the j-th stage of the decimator. Assuming a direct-form FIR filter with $N_{j,optimum}$ coefficients, the overall number R_j of multiply-add operation of the j-th stage is:

$$R_j = \frac{N_{j,optimum}F_{s,j}}{M_j} \tag{4}$$

As an example, assume having a discrete time signal with a sampling rate of 180 KHz. The signal has a pass-band of 900 Hz and a transition band from 900 Hz to 1 KHz. The signal has to be decimated by a factor of 90 and the required tolerances are a pass-band ripple of $\delta_{pass} = 0.003$ and a stop-band ripple of $\delta_{stop} = 0.001$.

With these requirements, and according to equation (3), the approximate number N of stages of the FIR filter of a single-stage implementation would be $N\approx2592$. Moreover, according to equation (4) the overall number of multiply-add operations would be $2592 \times (180000/90) = 5.184.000$.

Let us assume now a three-stage implementation with down-sampling factors $M_1=15$, $M_2=3$, and $M_3=2$ respectively. Table 5 reports the specifications of the anti-aliasing low-pass filters of the down-conversion chain.

Table 5. Specifications of the decimator stages

Stage	Specifications
1	$\delta_{pass1} = 0.003/3 = 0.001$ (0.0087 dB)
	$\delta_{stop1} = 0.001$
	$f_{pass1} = 900$ Hz
	$f_{stop1} = 1000$ Hz
	$F_s = 180$ KHz
	$F_{s1} = 180000/15 = 12$ KHz
2	$\delta_{pass2} = 0.003/3 = 0.001$ (0.0087 dB)
	$\delta_{stop2} = 0.001$
	$f_{pass2} = 900$ Hz
	$f_{stop2} = 1000$ Hz
	$F_{s2} = 12$ KHz
	$F_{s2} = 12000/3 = 4$ KHz
3	$\delta_{pass1} = 0.003/3 = 0.001$ (0.0087 dB)
	$\delta_{stop1} = 0.001$
	$f_{pass1} = 900$ Hz
	$f_{stop1} = 1000$ Hz
	$F_s = 4$ KHz
	$F_{s1} = 4000/2 = 2$ KHz

The number of taps of the anti-aliasing filters of the decimator are $N_1 = 57$, $N_2 = 20$, and $N_3 = 133$ respectively. Consequently, the number of multiply-add operations of each individual stage of the decimator are $R_1 = N_1 \times (F_s/M_1) = 720.000$, $R_2 = N_2 \times (F_{s1}/M_2) = 80.000$, and $R_3 = N_3 \times (F_{s2}/M_3) = 266.000$. The total number of multiply-add operation is $R_{total} = R_1 + R_2 + R_3 = 720.000 + 80.000 + 266.000 = 1.066.000$, thus, using three decimating stages leads to an overall reduction of the multiply-add operations by a factor of almost 5.

Cascaded Comb Integrator Filters

In multi-standard systems, sample rate changes can be very large, whit changes ranging from few tenths of KHz to some MHz. This, in turn, requires large order and high sampling-rate digital filters that can degrade system performance. To reduce the computational demand a Cascaded Comb

Integrator (CIC) can be used, since in this case up- and down-sampling can be implemented only with sum operations.

The integrator section of the decimating or interpolating CIC of Figure 12 (c) and (d) is implemented by cascading several simple integrating stages like that depicted in Figure 12 (a). On the other hand, the comb section is implemented by cascading the simple comb stage of Figure 12 (b). A typical comb stage has a differential delay of R samples per stage with R between 1 and 3.

The integrator section of a decimating CIC filter is the cascade of N simple integrator stages operating at the sampling frequency F_s. The transfer function is:

$$H_I\left(z\right) = \left(\frac{1}{1 - z^{-1}}\right)^N$$

The comb section is obtained by cascading N simple comb sections operating at the sampling frequency F_s/M.

$$H_C\left(z\right) = \left(1 - z^{-R}\right)^N$$

Applying the Noble identity to the comb section, the CIC filter transfer function can be expressed as:

$$H\left(z\right) = H_I\left(z\right)H_C\left(z\right) = \left(\frac{1 - z^{-RM}}{1 - z^{-1}}\right)^N$$

The filter response in the frequency domain is:

$$H\left(e^{j\omega T_s}\right) = \left(\frac{\sin\left(\frac{\omega T_s RM}{2}\right)}{\sin\left(\frac{\omega T_s}{2}\right)}\right)^N$$

Figure 12. (a) Integrator stage, (b) Comb stage, (c) Down-sampling CIC, and (d) Up-sampling CIC

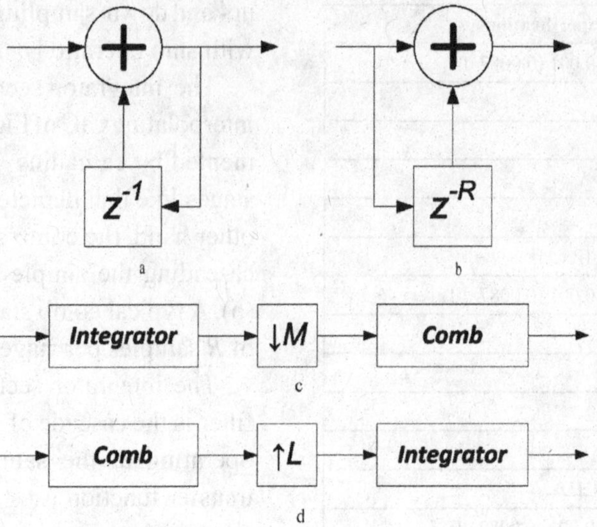

This is the typical response of low-pass filter with lineal phase. The response can be also expressed as a function of the decimated sampling frequency F_s/M:

$$H\left(e^{j\frac{\omega}{M}T_s}\right) =$$

$$\left(\frac{\sin\left(\dfrac{\dfrac{\omega}{M}T_s R}{2}\right)}{\sin\left(\dfrac{\omega}{M}\dfrac{T_s}{2M}\right)}\right)^N \approx R^N M^N \left(\frac{\sin\left(\dfrac{\omega T_s R}{2M}\right)}{\dfrac{\omega T_s R}{2M}}\right)^N$$

Increasing the number N of stages of the filter improves the anti-aliasing characteristics in detriment of the low-pass response. Moreover, as R, M, and N increase, the filter DC gain also increases requiring large registers to hold the output result. If b_i is the size of the filter input word, the number of bits b_o of the output word is:

$$b_o = b_i + \left\lceil N \log_2\left(RM\right)\right\rceil$$

Polyphase Filtering

Decimation and interpolation processes can be simplified by using the polyphase filter structures. Decimating a discrete signal $x(n)$ by a factor of M consists in processing only those samples that are integer multiples of M, consequently the relevant filter outputs after decimation are:

$$y\left(m\right) = \sum_{k=0}^{N-1} h\left(k\right) x\left(mM - k\right)$$

Let $k=qM+p$, then:

$$y\left(m\right) = \sum_{p=0}^{M-1} \sum_{q=0}^{\left\lceil\frac{N}{M}-1\right\rceil} h\left(qM + p\right) x\left(\left(m - q\right)M - p\right)$$

Defining

$$h_p\left(q\right) = h\left(qM + p\right)$$
$$x_p\left(q\right) = x\left(qM - p\right)$$

Figure 13. (a) Polyphase decimator, and (b) polyphase interpolator

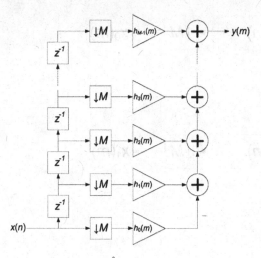

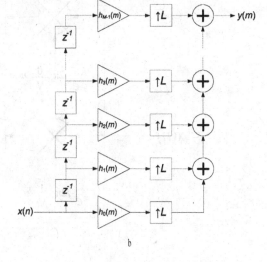

a

b

We obtain:

$$y\left(m\right) =$$

$$\sum_{p=0}^{M-1} \sum_{q=0}^{\left\lfloor \frac{N}{M}-1 \right\rfloor} h_p\left(q\right) x_p\left(m-q\right) = \sum_{p=0}^{M-1} h_p\left(m\right) * x_p\left(m\right)$$

Hence, the decimation operation can be decomposed into a sum of M parallel filtering operations, where each filter $h_p(m)$ is obtained by decimating by a factor of M the time-shifted version of $h(m)$. Implementing the decimation operation within the filter structure like depicted in Figure 13 (a) will reduce the number of multiply-add operation by a factor of M without affecting filter complexity since a decimation operation only implies the reduction by M of the sampling clock frequency.

A polyphase interpolator can be built using analogous considerations. In the case of a zero-insertion interpolator with an interpolation factor of L, the circuit must insert L-1 zeros between two consecutive samples. Inserting the interpolator within the filter structure as depicted in Figure 13 (b), will reduce the number of multiplications since all those by zero samples do not need to be performed. In addition, the filter will work at a lower frequency compared to the case with an external interpolator, thus reducing overall power consumption.

Digital Filter Banks

Digital filter banks can be used to split a wideband signal into multiple bands or channels. Each channel can be processed individually with lightweight signal processing techniques to reduce the hardware complexity of the implementation. In addition, digital filter banks can be used also to implement transmultiplexers to perform data channelization and implement TDM (Time Division Multiplexing) to FDM (Frequency Division Multiplexing) conversion and vice versa.

A digital filter bank comes into two different forms: (1) the analyzer for decomposing the wideband input into several narrowband output channels, and (2) the synthesizer for reconstructing the wideband output by combining several narrowband input channels.

In the analyzer, the input signal is divided into N channel, demodulated and shifted to baseband (i.e. frequency shifted by $\omega_k = 2\pi k/N$, with $k = 0$, $1,..., N$-1), filtered using an array of complex low-pass filters $H_0(\omega)$, and then down-sampled

Figure 14. Digital filter bank analyzer

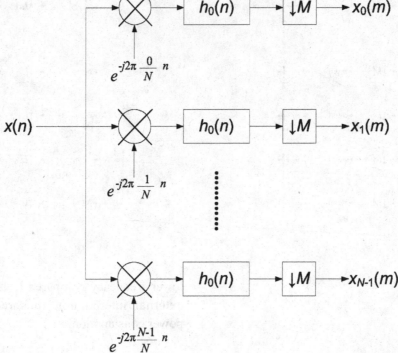

by a factor M as depicted in Figure 14 (when $M = N$ the system is critically sampled).

In the synthesizer, the input signal is up-sampled and interpolated using a complex low-pass filter $H_0(\omega)$. After that, the narrowband signal is modulated and converted into a pass-band signal (i.e., frequency shifted by $\omega_k = 2\pi k/N$, with $k = 0, 1,..., N-1$), and finally combined with the other up-converted signals to form the wideband output as represented in Figure 15.

4.5 Timing Recovery in Digital Receivers

Multirate signal processing can be used to design flexible and fully-digital timing-recovery circuits for radios supporting multiple standards and hence multiple waveforms. In a standard quadrature receiver, a PLL (Phase Locked Loop) is used to control the phase of a VCO that controls the sampling rate at the output of the analog matched filter.

On the other hand, in modern digital receivers like that depicted in Figure 16, the signal is sampled in the analog domain but matched filtering is performed in the digital domain. However, in this scheme the timing recovery requires a feedback between the analog and the digital domain that complicates the implementation.

In order to avoid the need to implement a feedback loop between the digital and the analog domains, the digitized signal can be interpolated using a polyphase filter (Reed, 2002). The optimum sampling time is that of the sample with maximum energy. The incoming signal can be sampled either at the Nyquist rate or at a higher rate. In the first case the samples are interpolated using a polyphase filter with a sampling frequency higher than the Nyquist rate, and then down-sampled to the symbol rate by selecting the optimum sampling time for a symbol. In the second case, the polyphase filter is used to decimate the input signal to the desired symbol rate.

Figure 15. Digital filter bank synthesizer

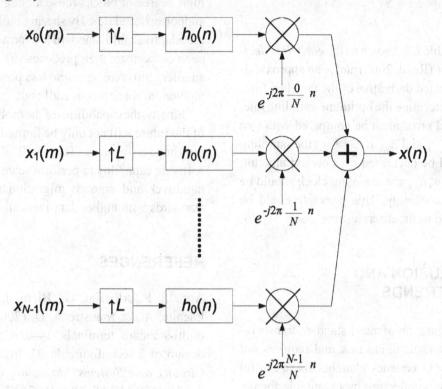

Figure 16. Timing recovery in digital receivers

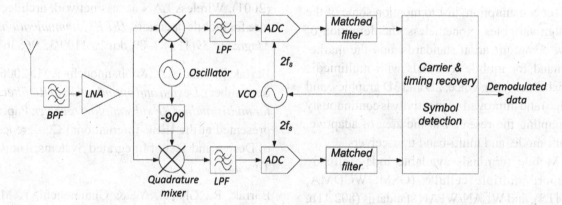

Timing information is recovered by controlling the starting index of the samples at the polyphase filter input by means of a programmable tapped-delay chain.

Timing information can be recovered by exploiting the symmetry of the match-filtered signal $S(t)$. The optimal timing is achieved when $S(t)$ is sampled at $t=T_{opt}$. If we take two samples $S(T-\Delta)$ and $S(T+\Delta)$ at the instants $T-\Delta$ and $T+\Delta$ respectively, and if $T=T_{opt}$, the two samples are equal and the optimum sampling time is halfway between the samples. Using this property it is possible to define an error signal E that controls the timing-recovery loop:

$$E = S\left(T_{opt} + \Delta\right) - S\left(T_{opt} - \Delta\right)$$

The variable E is known as the *early/late decision statistics* (Reed, 2002) and is an approximation of the scaled derivative of the matched filter output. To determine the optimum sampling rate, the measured error must be compared with two thresholds E_{early} and E_{late}. If $E > E_{early}$ the sampling clock should be decreased by a certain amount, whereas if $E < E_{late}$ the sampling clock should be increased accordingly. This principle could be extended also to the discrete-time case.

5. CONCLUSION AND FUTURE TRENDS

The implementation of multi-standard transceivers is a very challenging task and requires not only a detailed frequency plan, but also a careful choice of the architecture more suitable for the target application as well as a constant trade-off among noise, performance, area occupation and power consumption, just to mention some of the design variables. Nonetheless, the definition of new communication standards, and the market demand for mobile terminals with multimedia capabilities (text, voice, 2D and 3D graphics, and video) and improved connectivity is continuously prompting the research in the area of adaptive, multi-mode, and multi-band transceivers.

Mobile terminals available today, already support multiple cellular (GSM, WCDMA, UMTS), and WLAN/WPAN standards (802.11b, Bluetooth) for broadband internet access or communication with other devices, and this trend is likely to increase in the future to support new applications and telecommunication services.

The potentiality of the future devices will be limited only by the integration factor and by the power consumption, for this reason it is crucial to put even more effort to investigate the feasibility of new adaptive front-ends dominated by tunable digital hardware and software blocks, and with a high degree of blocks reuse among the different supported standards. By sharing building blocks, the adaptive multi-standard low-power radios will soon outperform their predecessors as they use a smaller chip area, consume less power, and have a potential for lower overall cost.

Finally, the capabilities of the mobile terminals of the future will not only be limited to enhanced multimedia features. They will also have the software capability to perform seamless network handover and smooth migration toward new standards with higher data-rates and capacities.

REFERENCES

Agnelli, F., Albasini, G., Bietti, I., Gnudi, A., Lacaita, A., & Manstretta, D. (2006). Wireless multi-standard terminals: system analysis and design of a reconfigurable RF front-end. *IEEE Circuits and Systems Magazine, 6*(1), 38–59. doi:10.1109/MCAS.2006.1607637

Ala-Laurila, J., Mikkonen, J., & Rinnemaa, J. (2001). Wireless LAN access network architecture for mobile operators. *IEEE Communications Magazine, 39*(11), 82–89. doi:10.1109/35.965363

Barrak, R., Ghazel, A., & Ghannouchi, F. M. (2006, September). *Design and optimization of RF filters for multistandard RF subsampling receiver.* Paper presented at the IEEE International Conference of Design and Test of Integrated Systems, Tunis, Tunisia.

Barrak, R., Ghazel, A., & Ghannouchi, F. M. (2009). Optimized multistandard RF subsampling receiver architecture. *IEEE Transactions on Wireless Communications, 8*(6), 82–89. doi:10.1109/TWC.2009.070584

Bechir, D. M., & Ridha, B. (2010, April). *On the RF subsampling continuous-time ΣΔ downconversion stage for multistandard receivers.* Paper presented at the IEEE Conference on Computer Engineering and Technology, Tunis, Tunisia.

Brandolini, M., Rossi, P., Manstretta, D., & Svelto, F. (2005). Toward multistandard mobile terminals—Fully integrated receivers requirements and architectures. *IEEE Transactions on Microwave Theory and Techniques, 53*(3), 1026–1038. doi:10.1109/TMTT.2005.843505

Buddhikot, M., Chandranmenon, G., Han, S., Lee, Y.-W., Miller, S., & Salgarelli, L. (2003). Design and implementation of a WLAN/CDMA2000 interworking architecture. *IEEE Communications Magazine, 41*(11), 90–100. doi:10.1109/MCOM.2003.1244928

Burns, P. (2002). *Software defined radio for 3G.* Boston, MA: Artech House.

Cho, T., Kang, D., Dow, S., Heng, C. H., & Song, B. S. (2003, February). *A 2.4 GHz dual-mode 0.18 µm CMOS transceiver for Bluetooth and 802.11b.* Paper presented at the IEEE International Solid-State Circuits Conference, San Francisco, CA.

Crols, J., & Steyaert, M. (1997). *CMOS wireless transceiver design.* Dordrecht, The Netherlands: Kluwer Academic Publishers.

Darabi, H., Chiu, J., Khorram, S., Kim, H.-J., Zhou, Z., & Chien, H.-M. (2005). A dual-mode 802.11b/Bluetooth radio in 0.35 µm CMOS. *IEEE Journal of Solid-state Circuits, 40*(3), 698–706. doi:10.1109/JSSC.2005.843597

Dillinger, M., Madani, K., & Alonistioti, N. (2003). *Software defined radio: Architectures, systems, and functions.* New York, NY: Wiley.

Gu, Q. (2005). *RF system design of transceivers for wireless communication.* New York, NY: Springer.

Hartley, R. (1928). *Modulation system.* U.S. Patent 1.666.206.

Hashemi, H. (2003). *Integrated concurrent multi-band radios and multiple-antenna systems.* Unpublished doctoral dissertation, California Institute of Technology, Pasadena.

Hashemi, H., & Hajimiri, A. (2001, June). *Concurrent dual-band LNAs and receiver architectures.* Paper presented at IEEE Symposium on VLSI, Kyoto, Japan.

Hueber, G., & Staszewski, R. B. (2011). *Multimode / multi-band RF transceivers for wireless communications: Advanced techniques, architectures, and trends.* New York, NY: Wiley.

Imanishi, D., Hong, J. Y., Okada, K., & Matsuzawa, A. (2010, January). *A 2-6 GHz fully integrated tunable CMOS power amplifier for multi-standard transmitters.* Paper presented at the Asia and South Pacific Design Automation Conference, Taipei, Taiwan.

Jakonis, D. (2004). *Direct RF sampling receivers for wireless systems in CMOS technology.* Unpublished doctoral dissertation, Linköping University, Sweden.

Jakonis, D., Folkesson, K., Dabrowski, J., Eriksson, P., & Svensson, C. (2005). A 2.4-GHz RF sampling receiver front-end in 0.18µm CMOS. *IEEE Journal of Solide-State Circuits, 40*(6), 1265–1277. doi:10.1109/JSSC.2005.848027

Jung, Y.-J., Jeong, H., Song, E., Lee, J., Lee, S.-W., & Seo, D. ... Kim, W. (2003, September). *A dual-mode direct-conversion CMOS transceiver for Bluetooth and 802.11b.* Paper presented at the IEEE European Solid-State Circuits Conference, Lisbon, Portugal.

Karvonen, S. (2006). *Charge-domain sampling of high-frequency signals with embedded filtering.* Unpublished doctoral dissertation, University of Oulu, Finland.

Karvonen, S., Riley, T. A. D., Kurtti, S., & Kostamovaara, J. (2006). A quadrature charge-domain sampler with embedded FIR and IIR filtering functions. *IEEE Journal of Solid-state Circuits, 41*(2), 507–515. doi:10.1109/JSSC.2005.857357

Kester, W. (2003). *Mixed-signal and DSP design techniques*. Burlington, MA: Newnes.

Lackey, R. J., & Upmal, D. W. (1995). Speakeasy: The military software radio. *IEEE Communications Magazine, 33*(5), 56–61. doi:10.1109/35.392998

Mak, S.-P. U., & Martins, R. P. (2007). Transceiver architecture selection: Review, state-of-the-art survey and case study. *IEEE Circuits and Systems Magazine, 7*(2), 6–24. doi:10.1109/MCAS.2007.4299439

Mitola, J. (1995). The software radio architecture. *IEEE Communications Magazine, 33*(5), 26–38. doi:10.1109/35.393001

Muhammad, K., Leipold, D., Staszewski, B., Ho, Y.-C., Hung, C.-M., & Maggio, K. … Friedman, O. (2004, February). *A discrete-time Bluetooth receiver in a 0.13μm digital CMOS process*. Paper presented at the IEEE International Solid-State Circuits Conference, San Francisco, CA.

Muhammad, K., Staszewski, R. B., & Leipold, D. (2005). Digital RF processing: Toward low-cost reconfigurable radios. *IEEE Communications Magazine, 43*(8), 105–113. doi:10.1109/MCOM.2005.1497564

Oliveira, L. B., Fernandes, J. R., Filanovsky, I. M., Verhoeven, C. J., & Silva, M. M. (2008). *Analysis and design of quadrature oscillators*. Berlin, Germany: Springer. doi:10.1007/978-1-4020-8516-1

Pahlavan, K., Krishnamurthy, P., Hatami, A., Yli-anttila, M., Makela, J., Pichna, R., & Vallström, J. (2000). Handoff in hybrid mobile data networks. *IEEE Personal Communications, 7*(2), 34–47. doi:10.1109/98.839330

Rabiner, L. R. (1973). Approximate design relationships for low-pass FIR digital filters. *IEEE Transactions on Audio and Electroacoustics, 21*(5), 456–460. doi:10.1109/TAU.1973.1162510

Razavi, B. (1997). Design considerations for direct-conversion receivers. *IEEE Transaction on Circuits and Systems II: Analog and Digital Signal Processing, 44*(6), 428–435. doi:10.1109/82.592569

Razavi, B. (1998). *RF microelectronics*. Upper Saddle River, NJ: Prentice Hall.

Reed, J. H. (2002). *Software radio: A modern approach to radio engineering*. Upper Saddle River, NJ: Prentice Hall.

Ryynänen, J., Kivekäs, K., Jussila, J., Pärssinen, A., & Halonen, K. (2000, May). *A dual band RF front-end for WCDMA and GSM applications*. Paper presented at the IEEE Custom Integrated Circuits Conference, Orlando, FL.

Ryynänen, J., Kivekäs, K., Jussila, J., Sumanen, L., Pärssinen, A., & Halonen, K. (2003). A single-chip multimode receiver for GSM900, DCS1800, PC1900, and WCDMA. *IEEE Journal of Solid-state Circuits, 38*(4), 594–602. doi:10.1109/JSSC.2003.809511

Salkintzis, A. K., Fors, C., & Pazhyannur, R. (2002). WLAN-GPRS integration for next-generation mobile data networks. *IEEE Wireless Communications, 9*(5), 112–124. doi:10.1109/MWC.2002.1043861

Sun, Y.-R. (2006). *Generalized bandpass sampling receivers for software defined radio*. Unpublished doctoral dissertation, Royal Institute of Technology (KTH), Sweden.

Sun, Y.-R., & Signell, S. (2005). Effects of noise and jitter in bandpass sampling. *Journal of Analog Integrated Circuits and Signal Processing, 42*(1), 85–97. doi:10.1023/B:ALOG.0000042331.21974.85

Tasić, A., Serdijn, W. A., & Long, J. R. (2005). Design of multi-standard adaptive voltage controlled oscillators. *IEEE Transactions on Microwave Theory and Techniques, 53*(2), 556–563. doi:10.1109/TMTT.2004.840648

Third Generation Partnership Project. (2004). *3GPP system to wireless local area network (WLAN) interworking.* System description TS 23.234, v6.0.0, 3GPP2 Technical Specifications.

Vaughan, R. G., Scott, N. L., & White, D. R. (1991). The theory of bandpass sampling. *IEEE Transactions on Signal Processing, 39*(9), 1973–1984. doi:10.1109/78.134430

Weaver, D. (1956). A third method of generation and detection of single sideband signals. *Proceedings of the IRE, 44*(12), 1703–1705. doi:10.1109/JRPROC.1956.275061

Xu, G., & Yuan, J. (2000, August). *Comparison of charge sampling and voltage sampling.* Paper presented at the IEEE Midwest Symposium on Circuits and Systems, Lansing, MI.

KEY TERMS AND DEFINITIONS

Binary Phase Shift Keying (BPSK): The simplest form of phase shift keying (PSK). It uses two phases which are separated by 180° to encode the 0 bit and the 1 bit.

Complementary Code Keying (CCK): A modulation scheme used in wireless LANs that employ the IEEE 802.11b specification. CCK was adopted in 1999 to replace the Barker code and to achieve data rates higher than 2 Mbps at the expense of shorter transmission range. It

has a shorter chipping sequence compared with Barker code (8 bits versus 11 bits), this makes this modulation scheme faster, but also more sensitive to narrowband interference, resulting in a shorter transmission range.

Frequency-Division Multiplexing (FDM): A type of signal multiplexing which assigns non-overlapping frequency bands to different signals in order to allow simultaneous access to the shared medium.

Gaussian Minimum Shift Keying (GMSK): A type of digital continuous-phase frequency modulation used in the Global System for Mobile Communications (GSM).

Quadrature Phase Shift Keying (QPSK): A digital modulation that uses four possible phase values (equispaced around a circle) to encode an alphabet of four two-bit symbols.

Surface Acoustic Wave (SAW): Filters are high-Q electromechanical resonators. The incoming electrical signal is converted into an acoustic wave and delayed as it propagates through de device. The delayed outputs are recombined at the filter output to produce the same effect of a Finite Impulse Response (FIR) filter. SAW filters are limited to frequencies up to 3 GHz.

Time-Division Multiplexing (TDM): A type of digital multiplexing in which the communication channel is shared among multiple bit-streams. Each bit-stream is allocated a given time slot of fixed length during which it can access the medium.

Chapter 11
Design and Implementation of Hardware Modules for Baseband Processing in Radio Transceivers:
A Case Study

Angel Fernández Herrero
Universidad Politécnica de Madrid, Spain

Gabriel Caffarena Fernández
Universidad San Pablo-CEU, Spain

Alberto Jiménez Pacheco
École Polytechnique Fédérale de Lausanne, Switzerland

Juan Antonio López Martín
Universidad Politécnica de Madrid, Spain

Carlos Carreras Vaquer
Universidad Politécnica de Madrid, Spain

Francisco Javier Casajús Quirós
Universidad Politécnica de Madrid, Spain

ABSTRACT

In this chapter, the main aspects of the design of baseband hardware modules are addressed. Special attention is given to word-length optimization, implementation, and validation tasks. As a case study, the design of an equalizer for a 4G MIMO receiver is addressed. The equalizer is part of a communication system able to handle up to 32 users and provide transmission bit-rates up to 125 Mbps. The word-length optimization process will be explained first, as well as techniques to reduce computation times. Then, the case study will be presented and analyzed, and the different tasks and tools required for its implementation will be explained. FPGAs are selected as the target implementation technology due to their interest from the DSP community.

DOI: 10.4018/978-1-4666-0083-6.ch011

1. INTRODUCTION

The design of communication systems is a challenging task that includes many complex stages. It requires performing accurate simulations of the hardware involved along with the physical environment (modeling of radio channels, analog circuitry with corresponding non idealities, etc.), designing hardware for both analog and digital blocks and testing the final implementation in a realistic framework.

In radio communications, baseband processing refers to the algorithms applied to the useful signal, previously to carrier modulation. Nowadays, it is usually carried out digitally by applying sometimes very complex or computation-intensive Digital Signal Processing (DSP) techniques. Depending on the considered transmission scheme, it can include algorithms for Fast Fourier Transforms (FFT), time and frequency synchronization, channel estimation and equalization, channel coding and decoding, correction of front-end impairments, etc.

This chapter is focused on the development tasks performed for the design, implementation and validation of a Fourth Generation (4G) MIMO communication system in the framework of the European Project 4MORE (Stefan Kaiser et al., 2004). Baseband processing was able to provide the high data rates and spectral efficiency expected from 4G wireless multi-user communication systems, merging state-of-the-art techniques, as multiple antennas (MIMO), with MC-CDMA and other advanced signal processing methods. Additional details and references on these topics will be provided in Section 4.

The complexity of the digital signal processing involved in baseband processing imposes the use of dedicated hardware that can handle the computation power by means of highly parallelized architectures. The preferred target technologies are ASICs and FPGAs. The first ones provide the best performance at a cost of very long and expensive design cycles. The latter ones, originally intended for prototyping, still provide good performances with reduced design cycles and, for that reason, they have been massively used during the last decade. Basically, FPGAs are composed of thousands of configurable logic blocks (LUTs: look-up tables) that can be *programmed* and interconnected at pleasure, as opposed to ASICs, where the architecture cannot be modified after manufacturing. Once a suitable digital architecture is envisioned by the designer, available commercial tools handle most of the optimization tasks required to obtain high-performance architectures. Thus, the design cycle is highly reduced.

In order to keep the cost of the hardware system (i.e. area and power consumption) to practical bounds, it is necessary to translate the original floating-point description of the algorithms to fixed-point arithmetic, which is more suitable for high-speed and low-power systems. This translation is known as quantization and it aims at finding the minimum precision that the mathematical operation requires to reduce cost, while matching the application quality standards. Reducing the precision implies decreasing the number of bits of each signal (word-length) and, thus, reducing the silicon area and power consumption of the arithmetic operators. Once the word-lengths are determined, the hardware designer must deal with the architectural issues. Several optimizations can be applied in order to produce an efficient implementation of DSP algorithms (pipelining, parallelization, etc.) with the help of electronic design tools.

In this chapter, we present the main tasks involved in the digital design of baseband modules and illustrate them with a case study. Special attention is given to the process of Word-Length Optimization (WLO), as this task is very time-consuming due to a lack of a clear methodology and to the use of simulation-based approaches. A methodology for fast WLO is presented. Then, the complete design of a channel equalizer is addressed. The tools used, as well as the engineering decisions taken, are explained, to provide

Figure 1. Schematic diagram of the design methodology

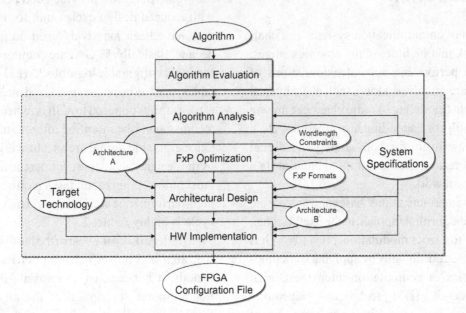

the DSP engineer with interesting insights on hardware design that can be directly applied to similar design tasks.

The chapter is organized as follows. Section two is an introduction to baseband hardware design, where the main design tasks are explained. Section three deals with Fixed-Point Optimization (FPO) and presents a technique to enable the fast estimation of mathematical precision loss due to the use of finite precision or Fixed-Point (FxP) arithmetic. In Section four, an equalizer for a 4G MIMO receiver is introduced as a case study, and several architectural considerations are made. The ideas on FPO from previous sections are then applied to the equalizer in Section five. There, all the design tasks are covered. In Section six, the block is implemented using FPGA technology and performance results in terms of silicon area and Bit Error Rate (BER) are presented. Finally, Section seven concludes the chapter.

2. BASEBAND HARDWARE DESIGN

Hardware design of communication systems is known to be a tough task, since it is necessary to translate the usually complex mathematical specification of a DSP algorithm into a practical hardware implementation. Modeling of the system is essential to assess the quality of the resulting implementation compared to the initial specifications of the system (Cranickx & Donnay, 2003). It is also important to perform a thorough analysis of the selected architecture in order to achieve the high throughput required. Prior to hardware design, an algorithm evaluation is carried out (Figure 1), where several alternatives are assessed under different scenarios to find the most suitable one that complies with system requirements. Once the algorithm and its parameters are defined, and the system specifications are selected, hardware design starts.

Basically, the design process is divided into two major tasks: *quantization* (or *fixed-point optimization*) and *architectural design*. The first one deals with the translation of a floating-point arithmetic description of the algorithm into a finite precision one, given an upper bound on the permitted error. The second deals with the mapping of the algorithm operations and variables into hardware resources. Figure 1 shows our approach to the hardware design of wireless communication systems.

The methodology is divided into four stages:

1. Algorithm analysis
2. Fixed-point optimization
3. Architectural design
4. Hardware implementation

First, the algorithm is analyzed in order to make high-level decisions regarding its final implementation using microelectronic devices (e.g. FPGAs). These decisions take into account technology mapping issues. As a result, a new version of the algorithm (architecture A), which is assured to comply with timing constraints, word-length (WL) constraints on signals, and binding between operations and hardware resources, is produced. Next, fixed-point optimization based on simulations and analytical techniques is applied. Given the quantized algorithm, where all the variables are assigned a finite-precision format (i.e., fixed-point format), and the resource binding, which relates the original mathematical description with the actual hardware resources that are to execute them, architectural optimization techniques are applied to produce the final architecture of the system (architecture B). Finally, the system is implemented using Electronic Design Automation (EDA) tools that enable to go from hardware-oriented languages, such as VHDL, to a physical hardware implementation of the system. Depending on the target technology, the latter can be a circuit layout or an FPGA configuration file.

3. FIXED-POINT OPTIMIZATION

The original infinite precision version of an algorithm based on the use of real arithmetic must be reduced to the practical precision bounds imposed by digital computing systems. Word-length optimization aims at the selection of variables' word-lengths of an algorithm to comply with a certain output noise constraint while optimizing the characteristics of the implementation (e.g., area, speed or power consumption). Normally, the precision loss is computed by using a double precision floating-point arithmetic description of the algorithm as a reference and, although there are some works on quantization for custom floating-point arithmetic (Fang & Rutenbar, 2003; Gaffar, Mencer, Luk, Cheung & Shirazi, 2002; Gaffar, Mencer, Luk & Cheung, 2004), the common approach is to implement the system using fixed-point arithmetic, since this leads to lower cost implementations in terms of area, speed, and power consumption (Caffarena, Constantinides, Cheung, Carreras & O. Nieto-Taladriz, 2006; Catthoor, De Man & Vandewalle, 1988; Constantinides, Cheung & Luk, 2003; Sung & Kum, 1995). Thus, WLO is commonly referred to as Fixed-Point Optimization (FPO).

The starting point of FPO is a representation of the algorithm by means of a set of equations. Formally, a signal flow graph $G(V, S)$ is generated from the original description. This graph contains information about signal Fixed-Point (FxP) formats and data dependencies. FxP formats of signals enable the computation of statistical parameters of quantization noises introduced by them, and data dependencies are essential to obtain a noise model that relates signals' noise parameters to the overall noise at the output of the algorithm. Set V holds the operations of the algorithm: additions/subtractions, constant multiplications, multiplications, divisions, and unit delays. Set S contains the signals that carry data values among these.

The FxP format of a number is defined by means of a pair (p, n), where p represents the num-

Figure 2. Fixed-point format: p represents the MSBs, n the word-length, and S is the sign bit

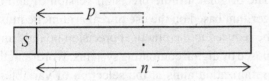

ber of bits from the Most Significant Bit (MSB) to the binary point, and *n* is the total number of bits without the sign bit (see Figure 2). The FxP formatting of a signal requires two FxP formats: one before quantization (p_{pre}, n_{pre}) and another after quantization (p, n) (Constantinides et al., 2003). The quantization of the signal is performed only if these two formats are not equal. Initially, the FxP format of signals is unknown and it is the task of FPO to find a suitable set that minimizes the total cost. The FxP format not only determines the quantization error generated by a quantized signal, but also the number of bits of each signal, and, therefore, the size of required hardware resources. The size of a resource ultimately determines its area, delay and power.

During FPO, the optimization is guided by means of the cost function and the output error obtained from different FxP formats tried through successive iterations.

Figure 3 depicts the typical FPO diagram. FPO is composed of the stages of *scaling*, which determines the set of p's, and *word-length selection*, which determines the set of n's. This subdivision allows simplifying FPO, while still providing significant cost reductions. A wrap-around scaling strategy is usually adopted, since it requires less hardware than other approaches (e.g., saturation techniques). After scaling, the values of p's are the minimum possible values that avoid overflow of signals or, at least, those that reduce the likelihood of overflow to a negligible value. Simulations in conjunction with analytical techniques are used to carry out scaling (Sung & Kum, 1995).

Once scaling has been performed, the values of p's can be fixed during word-length selection. The right side of Figure 3 shows the basic blocks for word-length selection. The main idea is to iterate trying different word-length (i.e., n) combinations until the cost is minimized. Each time the word-length of a signal or a group of signals

Figure 3. Fixed-point optimization diagram

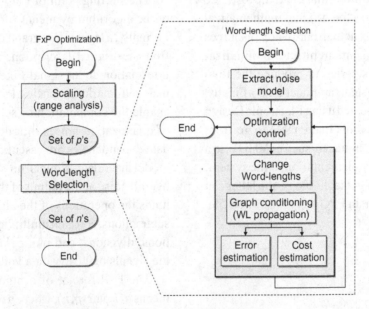

is changed, the word-lengths must be propagated throughout the graph, task referred to as graph conditioning (Constantinides et al., 2003), in order to update the rest of word-lengths. The optimization control block selects the size of the word-lengths using the values of the previous error and cost estimations and decides when the optimization procedure has finished. The role of the first block in the diagram is the generation of a model for the quantization noise (parameterization) at the output due to the FxP format of each signal. This enables to perform quick error estimation within the optimization loop. The implications of using a fast error estimator are twofold. On the one hand, it is possible to reduce FPO time. On the other hand, more complex optimization techniques can be applied in standard computation times.

3.1. Fast Estimation

FPO is a slow process due to the fact that the optimization is very complex, actually NP-hard (Constantinides & Woeginger, 2002), and also because of the necessity of a continuous assessment of the algorithm accuracy, which may involve a high computational load. This estimation is normally performed by adopting a simulation-based approach (Sung & Kum, 1995; Caffarena, Fernández, Carreras & Nieto-Taladriz, 2004; Cantin, Savaria & Lavoie, 2002), which leads to exceedingly long design times. However, in the last few years, there have been attempts to provide fast estimation methods based on analytical techniques. These approaches can be applied to Linear Time-Invariant (LTI) systems (Constantinides et al., 2003; López, Caffarena, Carreras & Nieto-Taladriz, 2008) and to differentiable nonlinear systems (Constantinides, 2003; Menard, Rocher, Scalart & Sentieys, 2004; Shi & Brodersen, 2004; Caffarena, Carreras, López, Fernández, 2010). As for the noise metric used, they are based on the peak value (Shi & Brodersen, 2004) and on the computation of SQNR (Constantinides et al., 2003; López, Caffarena, Carreras & Nieto-Taladriz, 2008; Constantinides, 2003; Menard et al., 2004; Shi & Brodersen, 2004). Since SQNR is a very popular error metric within DSP systems, we support fast SQNR estimation techniques for LTI and differentiable nonlinear systems.

LTI Methods

Let us start with LTI-oriented methods. Given an algorithm with $|S|$ signals, where each signal s_i is quantized to n_i bits, it is possible to relate the number of bits to the power of the noise at the output of the algorithm in steady state by means of the following expression:

$$P_o =$$
$$\sum_{i=0}^{|S|-1} \sigma_i^2 \frac{1}{2\pi} \int_{-\pi}^{\pi} \left| G_i\left(e^{j\Omega}\right)\right|^2 d\Omega + \left(\sum_{i=0}^{|S|-1} \mu_i G_i\left(e^{j0}\right)\right)^2,$$

(1)

where G_i is the transfer function from signal s_i to output o, and σ_i^2 and μ_i are the variance and mean of the quantization noise associated to signal s_i, which are related to n_i. Expression (1) can be rewritten more compactly using vectors σ^2, v, μ, and m as:

$$P_o = \sigma^2 \cdot \mathbf{v}^T + \left(\mu \cdot \mathbf{m}^T\right)^2,$$

(2)

where:

$$\mu \equiv \left\langle \mu_0, \dots, \mu_{|S|-1}\right\rangle,$$

(3)

$$\sigma^2 \equiv \left\langle \sigma_0^2, \dots, \sigma_{|S|-1}^2\right\rangle,$$

(4)

$$\mathbf{v} \equiv$$

$$\left\langle \frac{1}{2\pi} \int_{-\pi}^{\pi} \left| G_0 \left(e^{j\Omega} \right) \right|^2 d\Omega, \cdots, \frac{1}{2\pi} \int_{-\pi}^{\pi} \left| G_{|S|-1} \left(e^{j\Omega} \right) \right|^2 d\Omega \right\rangle,$$

$$(5)$$

$$\mathbf{m} \equiv \left\langle G_0 \left(e^{j0} \right), \ldots, G_{|S|-1} \left(e^{j0} \right) \right\rangle. \qquad (6)$$

Note that v and m can be computed by means of a graph analysis and, once they are determined, the output noise power can be estimated from σ^2 and μ.

In (Constantinides et al., 2003) a two-step method is applied where, first, vectors v and m are computed, and then, expression (2) is used to estimate the output noise power during FPO. Parseval's Theorem (Oppenheim & Schafer, 1987) is applied in order to compute expression (5), since it is possible to obtain an equivalent expression that makes use of the impulse response $g_i[n]$ from signal s_i to the output of the system, instead of using G_i. This highly simplifies the computational cost. If the length of input vectors is long enough, expression (1) can be estimated with high precision, leading to highly accurate quantization noise estimations.

An Affine Arithmetic (AA) based approach is presented in (López et al, 2008). The approach is based again on the computation of $g_i[n]$ for each signal. Due to the characteristics of AA, it is possible to compute all $g_i[n]$ simultaneously. In this case, the process has not been divided into parameterization (extraction of vectors v and m) and noise estimation. Instead, everything is computed at once. The computational cost is similar to that obtained in (Constantinides et al., 2003) (i.e., parameterization plus estimation times). Also, the quality of the estimates is high, since they are based on (1).

The approach in (Menard & Sentieys, 2002) also relies on (1) to present a two-step estimation method. The parameterization is based on the ap-

plication of graph transforms that allow obtaining the vectors v and m (5) and (6). Its performance in terms of computation time and accuracy is equivalent to the other two approaches.

Non-Linear Systems

The approaches aimed at nonlinear systems are mainly based on perturbation theory, where the effect of the quantization of each algorithm's signal on the quality of the output signal is supposed to be small. This allows applying a first-order Taylor expansion to each nonlinear operation in order to characterize the effect of the quantization of the inputs of the operations. This constrains the application to algorithms composed of differentiable operations. The existent methods enable us to obtain an expression similar to (2), which relates the word-lengths of signals to the power (also mean and variance) of the quantization noise at the output. This will be further explained in Section 3.3.

In (Constantinides, 2003) a hybrid method which combines simulations and analytical techniques to estimate the variance of the noise is proposed. The estimator is suitable for non-recursive and recursive algorithms. The parameterization phase is relatively fast, since it requires $|S|$ simulations for an algorithm with $|S|$ variables. The noise model is based on (Constantinides, Cheung & Luk, 1999) and second-order effects are neglected by applying first-order Taylor expansions. However, the paper seems to suggest that the contributions of the signal quantization noises at the output can be added, assuming that the noises are independent. In nonlinear systems, this is a strong assumption that leads to variance underestimation. The accuracy of the method is not supported with any empirical data.

In (Shi & Brodersen, 2004) another method suitable for non-recursive and recursive algorithms is presented. Here, $|S|^2/2$ simulations as well as a curve fitting technique (with $|S|^2/2$ variables) are required to parameterize quantization noise. On the one hand, the noise produced by each signal is modeled following the traditional quantization noise model from (Jackson, 1970; Oppenheim & Weinstein, 1972), which is less accurate than (Constantinides et al., 1999), and, again, second order statistics are neglected. On the other hand, the expression of the estimated noise power accounts for noise interdependencies, which is a better approach than (Constantinides, 2003). The method is tested with an LMS adaptive filter and the accuracy is evaluated graphically. There is no information about computation times.

Finally, in (Menard et al., 2004) the parameterization is performed by means of $|S|$ simulations and the estimator is suitable only for non-recursive systems. The accuracy of this approach seems to be the highest, since it uses the model from (Constantinides et al., 1999) and it accounts for noise interdependencies. Although the information provided about accuracy is more complete, it is not sufficient yet, since the estimator is tested in only a few SQNR scenarios.

In this chapter we focus on the work from (Caffarena et al., 2010). The approach, presented in 3.3, tries to overcome most of the drawbacks of the works presented above. It deals with non-recursive and recursive systems using the accurate noise model from (Constantinides et al., 1999) and also accounting for noise interdependencies.

3.2. Affine Arithmetic

Affine Arithmetic (AA) (Stolfi & Figuereido, 1997) is an extension of Interval Arithmetic (IA) (Hayes, 1999) aimed at the fast and accurate computation of the ranges of signals in a particular mathematical description of an algorithm. Its main feature is that it automatically cancels the linear dependencies of the included uncertainties along the computation path, thus avoiding the oversizing produced by IA approaches (López, 2004). It has been applied to both scaling computation (Lee et al., 2006; López, 2004; López, Carreras & Nieto-Taladriz, 2007) and word-length allocation

(Fang & Rutenbar, 2003; Lee et al., 2006; López, 2004). Also, a modification called Quantized Affine Arithmetic (QAA) has been applied to the computation of limit cycles (López, Caffarena, Carreras & Nieto-Taladriz, 2004) and dynamic range analysis of quantized LTI algorithms (López et al., 2007).

The mathematical expression of an affine form is:

$$\hat{x} = x_0 + \sum_{i=0}^{N-1} x_i \varepsilon_i, \tag{7}$$

where x_0 is the central value of $\hat{x}$, and ε_i and x_i are its ith noise term identifier and amplitude, respectively. In fact, $x_i \varepsilon_i$ represents the interval $[-x_i, +x_i]$, so an affine form describes a numerical domain in terms of a central value and a sum of intervals with different identifiers. Affine operations are those which operate affine forms and produce an affine form as a result. Given affine forms $\hat{x}$, $\hat{y}$, and $\hat{c} = c_0$, the affine operations are:

$$\hat{x} \pm \hat{c} = x_0 \pm c_0 + \sum_{i=0}^{N-1} x_i \varepsilon_i,$$

$$\hat{x} \pm \hat{y} = x_0 \pm y_0 + \sum_{i=0}^{N-1} \left(x_i \pm y_i \right) \varepsilon_i, \tag{8}$$

$$\hat{x} \cdot \hat{c} = x_0 c_0 + \sum_{i=0}^{N-1} c_0 x_i \varepsilon_i$$

These operations are sufficient to model any LTI algorithm. Differentiable operations can be approximated using a first-order Taylor expansion:

$$f(\hat{x}, \hat{y}) =$$

$$f(x_0, y_0) + \sum_{i=0}^{N-1} \left(\frac{\partial f(x_0, y_0)}{\partial \hat{x}} x_i + \frac{\partial f(x_0, y_0)}{\partial \hat{y}} y_i \right) \varepsilon_i \tag{9}$$

3.3. Fast Estimation Based on Affine Arithmetic

In this section, we present a method able to estimate the quantization noise power from a single AA simulation. The noise estimation is not based on (1), since this equation only applies to LTI systems in steady state and our proposal is more general, covering both LTI and nonlinear algorithms. Also, the parameterization method does not lead to (2)–(6), since these are also aimed at LTI algorithms in steady state. The fast estimator is suitable to perform FxP design of hardware modules for baseband processing in communication systems.

Noise estimation is based on the assumption that the quantization of a signal s_i from n_{pre} bits to n bits can be modeled by the addition of a uniformly distributed white noise with the following statistical parameters (Constantinides et al., 1999):

$$\sigma_i^2 = \frac{2^{2p_i}}{12}\left(2^{-2n_i} - 2^{-2n_i^{pre}}\right), \quad \mu_i = -2^{p_i-1}\left(2^{-n_i} - 2^{-n_i^{pre}}\right). \tag{10}$$

This noise model, which is referred to as the *discrete noise model*, is an extension of the traditional modeling of quantization error as an additive white noise (Jackson, 1970; Oppenheim & Weinstein, 1972) (*continuous noise model*). In (Constantinides et al., 1999), it is shown that the continuous model can produce an error of up to 200% in comparison to the discrete model.

In (López et al, 2008) it was proved that the effect of the deviation from the original behavior of an algorithm with feedback loops can be modeled by adding an affine form $\hat{e}_i[k]$ to each signal s_i at each simulation time instant k. If every error term ε is assigned a uniform distribution, the affine form $\hat{e}_i$ models a quantization noise with mean μ_i and variance σ_i^2, and can be expressed:

$$\hat{e}_i[k] = \mu_i + \sqrt{12\sigma_i^2}\,\varepsilon_{i,k}' \tag{11}$$

Thus, it is possible to know at each moment the origin of a particular error term (i) and the moment when it was generated (k). The AA-based simulation can be made independent on the particular statistical parameters of each quantization thanks to error term ε'. This is desirable in order to obtain a parameterizable noise model. This error term encapsulates the mean value and the variance of the error term ε, and now it can be seen as a random variable with variance σ_i^2 and mean μ_i. This is a reinterpretation of AA, since the error terms are not only intervals, but they also have a probability distribution associated. Once the simulation is finished, it is possible to compute the impact of the quantization noise produced by signal i on the output of the algorithms by checking the values of $x_{i,k}$ (see (7)). This enables the parameterization of the noise.

Once the parameterization is performed, the estimation error produced by any combination of (p, n) can be easily assessed replacing all $\varepsilon'_{i,k}$ by the original expression that accounts for the mean and variance $(\mu_i + \sqrt{12\sigma_i^2}\,\varepsilon_{i,k}')$, thus enabling a fast estimation of the quantization error. We will see all the process in the next paragraphs.

The expression of a given output $\hat{Y}$ of an algorithm with $|S|$ noise sources is:

$$\hat{Y}[k] = Y_0[k] + \sum_{i=0}^{|S|-1}\sum_{j=0}^{k} Y_{i,j}[k]\varepsilon_{i,j}', \tag{12}$$

where $Y_0[k]$ is the value of the output of the algorithm using floating-point arithmetic and the summation is the contribution of the quantization noise sources. Note that $Y_{i,j}[k]$ is a function that depends on the inputs of the algorithm.

The error $\hat{Err}_Y$ at the output is:

$$\hat{Err}_Y[k] = Y_0[k] - \hat{Y}_0[k] = -\sum_{i=0}^{|S|-1}\sum_{j=0}^{k} Y_{i,j}[k]\varepsilon'_{i,j}.$$

(13)

The value of the error is formed by a collection of affine forms at each time step. The power of the quantization noise of the output can be approximated by the Mean Square Error (MSE), which is estimated as the mean value of the expectancy of the power of the summations of the uniform distributions at each time step m as in (14). The estimation is performed using an AA simulation during K time steps:

$$P\left(\hat{Err}_Y[k]\right) = \frac{1}{K}\sum_{m=0}^{K-1} E\left[\left(\hat{Err}_Y[m]\right)^2\right]$$
$$= \frac{1}{K}\sum_{m=0}^{K-1}\left(Var\left(\hat{Err}_Y[m]\right) + E\left(\hat{Err}_Y[m]\right)^2\right)$$

(14)

This equation relies on the fact that error terms $\varepsilon_{i,n}$ are uncorrelated to each other, which is a sensible assumption in quantized DSP systems (Jackson, 1970; Oppenheim & Weinstein, 1972). Also, the uncorrelation between quantization noises enables to express the variance of a summation of random variables as the summation of the variance of each random variable. The two main terms in (14) are developed as follows:

$$Var\left[\hat{Err}_Y[m]\right] = Var\left(-\sum_{i=0}^{|S|-1}\sum_{j=0}^{m} Y_{i,j}[m]\varepsilon'_{i,j}\right)$$
$$= \sum_{i=0}^{|S|-1}\sum_{j=0}^{m} Var\left(-Y_{i,j}[m]\varepsilon'_{i,j}\right)$$
$$= \sum_{i=0}^{|S|-1}\sigma_i^2\sum_{j=0}^{m} Y_{i,j}^2[m]$$

(15)

$$E\left[\hat{Err}_Y[m]\right] = E\left(-\sum_{i=0}^{|S|-1}\sum_{j=0}^{m} Y_{i,j}[m]\varepsilon'_{i,j}\right)$$
$$= -\sum_{i=0}^{|S|-1}\mu_i^2\sum_{j=0}^{m} Y_{i,j}[m]$$

(16)

Combining (14), (15) and (16):

$$P\left(\hat{Err}_Y[k]\right) =$$
$$\frac{1}{K}\sum_{m=0}^{K-1}\left(\sum_{i=0}^{|S|-1}\sigma_i^2\sum_{j=0}^{m} Y_{i,j}^2[m] + \left(\sum_{i=0}^{|S|-1}\mu_i^2\sum_{j=0}^{m} Y_{i,j}[m]\right)^2\right)$$

(17)

The output noise power (17) can be expressed more compactly by using vectors v, m, and matrix M as shown in (18)–(21). Once vectors v matrix M are computed, the estimation of the quantization noise does not require a simulation, but the computation of expressions (18)–(21), which is a much faster process:

$$P_0 = \frac{1}{K}\left(\sigma^2 \cdot \mathbf{v}^T + \mu \cdot M\mu^T\right)$$

(18)

$$\mathbf{v} \equiv \left\langle \sum_{k=0}^{K-1}\sum_{j=0}^{k} Y_{0,j}^2[k], \ldots, \sum_{k=0}^{K-1}\sum_{j=0}^{k} Y_{|S|-1,j}^2[k]\right\rangle$$

(19)

$$\mathbf{M} \equiv \begin{bmatrix} m_{0,0} & \cdots & m_{|S|-1,0} \\ & \ddots & \\ m_{0,|S|-1} & \cdots & m_{|S|-1,|S|-1} \end{bmatrix}$$

(20)

$$\mathbf{m}_{i_1,i_2} \equiv \sum_{k=0}^{K-1}\left(\sum_{j_1=0}^{k} Y_{i_1,j_1}[k]\sum_{j_2=0}^{k} Y_{i_2,j_2}[k]\right)$$

(21)

The parameterization process is then composed of the following steps:

1. Perform a K-step AA simulation adding an affine form $\hat{n}_i$ to each signal i,

2. Compute (19)–(21) using previously collected $Y_{i,j}[k]$.

The error estimation phase can now be executed very quickly by applying (18).

Please note that expressions (18)–(21) can be applied to DSP algorithms including differentiable operations (e.g., multiplications, divisions, etc.) by means of (9) due to 1st order approximation.

The estimator was implemented using C/C++ and tested with several DSP algorithms (adaptive filters, vector multiplication, etc.) showing an average computation time acceleration of ×1500 with respect to simulations, while keeping the accuracy of the estimates down to an average of 4% of error (Caffarena et al., 2010).

4. CASE STUDY: EQUALIZER FOR 4G MIMO COMMUNICATIONS

In this section, we deal with the design and implementation of an equalizer for a 4G MIMO receiver in a Mobile Terminal (MT) (Fernández-Herrero, Jiménez-Pacheco, Caffarena, Casajús, 2006). The MT is able to provide the high data rates and spectral efficiency expected from 4G wireless multi-user communication systems. It combines multiple antenna communications with MC-CDMA and other advanced signal processing techniques. The design of this system was carried out in the framework of the European Project 4MORE (Stefan Kaiser et al., 2004).

The MT performance and its feasibility of implementation is tested by means of modeling a complete 4G system composed of an MT with two antennas and a Base Station (BS) with four antennas. Some key parameters of the system include a channelization bandwidth of 50 MHz, a spreading factor in frequency $S_f = 32$, and raw bit-rates up to 125 Mbps for the downlink, depending on the modulation format (QPSK, 16-QAM or 64-QAM), and number of active users (up to 32).

MC-CDMA, based on the serial combination of direct sequence CDMA and OFDM, has been considered for the physical layer because it derives benefits from both technologies. On one side, OFDM provides robustness against multipath, avoiding intersymbol interference, whereas, on the other, CDMA provides frequency diversity and multiple user flexibility. Moreover, the use of multiple antenna systems (MIMO) helps to exploit spatial diversity, to increase capacity, and to mitigate the effects of fading.

It is not the purpose of this chapter to go deeper into the intricacies of the signal processing technologies that push the nowadays wireless communication systems, but there are many interesting references on these subjects, both papers and books: OFDM and MC-CDMA (Hara, S., and Prasad, R., 1997; Van Nee, R., and Prasad, R., 2000; Hanzo, L.L., and Keller, T., 2006), MIMO (Stuber, G.L., Barry, J.R., McLaughlin, S.W., Ye Li, Ingram, M.A., Pratt, T.G., 2004; Paulraj, A.J., Gore, D.A., Nabar, R.U., Bolcskei, H., 2004; Ming Jiang, Hanzo, L., 2007; Tse, D., and Viswanath, P., 2005) and combinations (Juntti, M., Vehkapera, M., Leinonen, J., Zexian, V., Tujkovic, D., Tsumura, S., Hara, S., 2005).

In the next subsections, details are given on the receiver and equalizer, as well as the design steps followed to implement the last one.

4.1. Overview of the Receiver

A simplified diagram of the receiver holding the equalizer is depicted in Figure 4. Analog signals received by both antennas are downconverted to baseband by twin RF front-ends and sampled at 61.44 MHz. To ensure that the whole dynamic range of the analog-to-digital converters is used, an Automatic Gain Control (AGC) is implemented in baseband. Next, there comes a module that corrects RF impairments caused by the zero-IF architecture of the front-ends. At this stage, time and frequency synchronization must also be performed in order to minimize misalignments with the transmitting BS.

An FFT operation is required per each antenna branch to perform OFDM demodulation and to recover the symbols in the frequency domain. Next, pilot symbols are separated from information symbols by the de-framing module.

Figure 4. Structure of the mobile receiver (MAC stands for Medium Access Control)

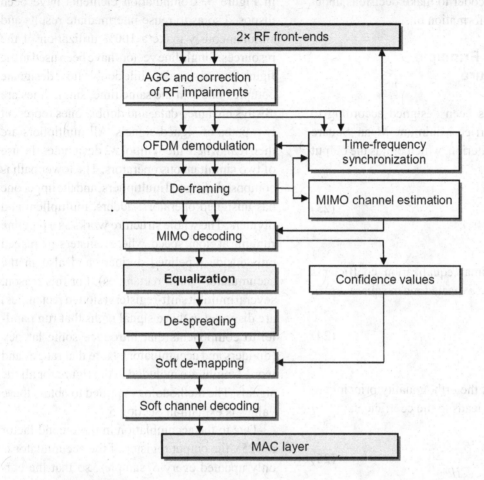

The MIMO decoding module (Jiménez-Pacheco, Fernández-Herrero, & Casajús, 2008) performs linear processing of the signals received on both antennas as specified by the Alamouti space-time block coding scheme (Alamouti, 1998), and aided by channel coefficients obtained by the MIMO channel estimator using the pilot symbols.

Hence, at the output of the MIMO decoder we recover a single stream Z_l of complex symbols (Le Nir, Hélard, & Le Gouable, 2003):

$$Z_l = H_l Y_l + N_l \qquad (22)$$

where Y_l is the complex information transmitted on the l-th subcarrier of a given MC-CDMA symbol ($1 \leq l \leq S_f$), N_l is a Gaussian distributed equivalent noise term, and H_l is the channel as seen after space-time combining, which turns out to be real and is also evaluated by the MIMO decoder.

According to (22), since H_l is real, phase distortion has already been dealt with by the MIMO decoder. However, equalization is still required, so that outputs Z_l and H_l of the MIMO decoder are passed on to the equalizer module, to be described in detail in the following sections.

After equalization, a de-spreading process is required to split the signals of the different users before sending the information to the soft de-mapper. Finally, the output of this module is sent to the channel decoder to make decisions about the transmitted information bits.

4.2. Equalizer Principle and Architecture

The equalizer has been designed according to the linear per-carrier Minimum Mean Square Error (MMSE) criterion, which builds the output signal as:

$$\hat{Y}_l = G_l \cdot Z_l \tag{23}$$

and chooses optimal equalization coefficients G_l to minimize the expected mean square error:

$$E\left\{\left|\hat{Y}_l - Y_l\right|^2\right\} \tag{24}$$

Application of the orthogonality principle to linear model (22) leads to the coefficients:

$$G_l = \frac{1}{H_l + \lambda} \cdot \frac{S_f}{\displaystyle\sum_{i=1}^{S_f} \frac{H_i}{H_i + \lambda}} \tag{25}$$

where $\lambda = 1/SNR_c$ is the inverse of the signal-to-noise ratio per subcarrier. Although the MIMO combined samples Z_l are complex, the equalization coefficients turn out to be real, because the channel H_l is real.

The second factor in (25) is a normalization term that remains constant for S_f contiguous carriers (same MC-CDMA symbol). It is necessary to appropriately scale the de-spread signal at the input of the soft de-mapper, but the equalizer seems the right place to evaluate it, since reuse of the dividers is then possible.

The architecture considered for the implementation of equations (23) and (25) is depicted

in Figure 5. Computation elements have been disposed so as to reuse intermediate results and simultaneously make a 100% utilization of the resources. Single line vectors have been used in the figure for real signals, while double lines designate complex ones. At the same time, single lines are always unsigned data, and double ones represent two paths of signed signals. All multipliers are then real, where the symbol ×2 designates the use of two simultaneous operators. The lower path is composed of signed multipliers, and the upper one has unsigned operators: adders, multipliers and dividers. The whole structure works as a pipeline running at clock speed, where registers are placed only inside pipelined dividers and also in the accumulator (small rectangles). For this reason, several multibit shift-registers (slotted rectangles) are disposed in those signal paths that run parallel to components that introduce some latency (dividers and accumulator). Note that ranges and word-lengths are included in the figure for all the signals. The methodology applied to obtain these values is explain in Section 5.

Due to the accumulation in the second factor of (25), the output register of the accumulator is only updated every S_f samples, so that the corresponding divider has not a 100% utilization. For this reason, a specific type of divider can be selected, which computes one result out of several clock cycles, saving an important amount of area.

As can be seen in the diagram, the architecture begins computing the first factor in (25) and directly applying it to the input complex signal. This factor is then reused to perform the accumulation specified in the second one, which, after a new division, is finally applied to the intermediate complex signal to get equalized results.

Figure 5. Architecture, dynamic ranges and word-lengths

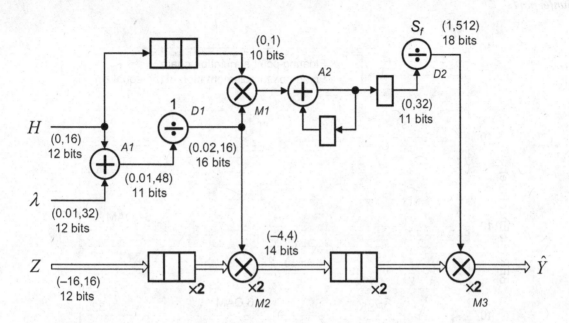

5. FIXED-POINT OPTIMIZATION OF THE EQUALIZER

The fixed-point design was accomplished following three steps:

1. Determining the dynamic range of each signal involved in the equalizer (*scaling*).
2. Obtaining the number of bits required for them (*word-length selection*).
3. Testing the design for robustness by performing BER simulations.

Following this process we seek to obtain a low cost, performance effective implementation of the hardware module. In this section we detail the design considering analytical as well as simulation based techniques (Sung & Kum, 1995; Caffarena et al., 2004). Final results regarding FPO can be found in Figure 5, where dynamic ranges and word-lengths are shown for all the signals.

Table 1. Parameters for the considered modes

Number of users (N_u)	Modulation	Coding Rate (R_{cc})
1 to 32	QPSK (*b*=2)	1/2
1 to 32	16-QAM (*b*=4)	2/3
1 to 32	64-QAM (*b*=6)	3/4

5.1. Analysis of Dynamic Ranges

In the first place, dynamic ranges for the inputs *H*, *Z* and *λ* must be determined. This was accomplished by means of a SystemC-based floating-point software simulator, developed within the project, which accurately models the behavior of all the modules in the communication system, also including a realistic MIMO channel model.

Ranges of Input Signals H and Z

Ranges for *H* and *Z* were determined by examination of the histograms of large data records obtained using the SystemC simulator. In Table 1 we show the most important parameters for the

Figure 6. BER degradation comparing the floating-point version of the equalizer and its fixed-point counterpart

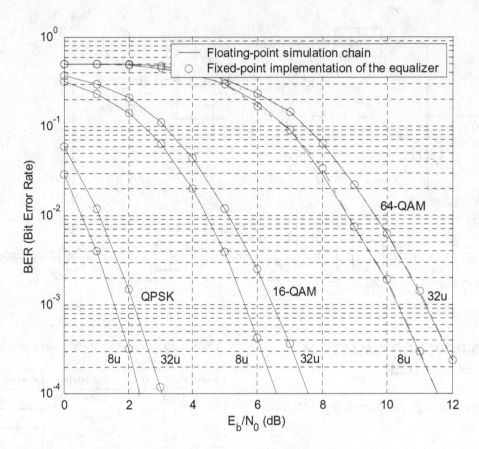

working modes implemented in the system. While dynamic margin for input H is independent of the mode, the maximum margin for Z is attained when the maximum number of users is present in the system. Therefore, we obtained data records running simulations with 32 users and 64-QAM modulation.

According to the collected histograms, the dynamic range for the channel H was $(0, 8)$, but we added an extra margin of 6 dB and considered it to be $(0, 16)$, trying to take into account some variability of the channel that might have not been captured in our data records. Similarly, ranges for real and imaginary parts of Z turned out to be ± 16.

Range of Input λ

As it will be shown later (Figure 6), according to the results obtained from the floating-point simulator, the value of the signal-to-noise ratio per information bit, E_b/N_0, should be in the range from 0 to 14 dB for a target BER of 10^{-4}. The expected range for input λ can then be obtained:

$$SNR_c = 10^{\frac{E_b/N_0 \, (dB)}{10}} \cdot b \cdot R_{cc} \cdot \frac{N_u}{S_f} \qquad (26)$$

which relates SNR_c to E_b/N_0 and parameters in Table 1. The input range for λ turns out to be about $(0.01, 32.0)$.

Ranges for Intermediate and Output Signals

Depending on the case, ranges for intermediate and output signals were obtained by considering histograms or by taking into account theoretical margins that result when operating with inputs whose range is already known. For example, considering equation (25), it is evident that the output of multiplier $M1$ lies in the range $(0, 1)$.

As a different example, due to the existence of hidden correlations between H and Z (there are common inputs employed by the MIMO decoding module to obtain these signals), histograms show that, with very high probability, the output of multiplier $M2$ lies within the range ± 4, instead of the theoretical one ± 256.

Inverters are the most critical operands. The maximum output of $D1$ will be reached when $H = 0$ and $\lambda = 0.01$, implying a theoretical value of 100. However, the true minimum of H will be different from 0, since this would correspond to a complete simultaneous fade of all paths between transmitter and receiver. This minimum is difficult to determine, so that we set $\lambda = 0.01$ and observed the histogram of the inverter output. The maximum value was around 6. Again, we added an extra margin and considered the maximum output to be 16. Similar reasoning was performed for inverter $D2$.

5.2. Selection of Word-Lengths

For this task, we developed a tool able to simulate both floating and fixed-point descriptions of algorithms as well as to extract the values of v and M, thus providing a fast FxP effect estimator. The steps followed were:

1. Extract the FxP estimation model.
2. Perform word-length selection using a gradient-descent algorithm considering a target minimum SQNR.
3. Check the accuracy of estimator using a single FxP simulation.

The first step follows the technique explained in Section 3.3. The input vectors were extracted from the SystemC simulation chain that contains the complete communication system, and the fast estimator only needs to use the portion of code that describes the equalizer.

The second step makes use of expression (18) within an optimization loop of hundreds of iterations. The optimization starts with the minimum word-length that applied to all signals complies with the target SQNR. Then it starts reducing the word-lengths following a gradient-descent scheme until the SQNR is minimized. The SQNRs obtained by each independent decrease of word-length are stored and the signal that obtained the better SQNR is reduced permanently. The process goes on until it is not possible to meet the noise constraints. A target SQNR of 40 dB was chosen, since the maximum SNR_c, from equation (26), is 20 dB (Fernández-Herrero et al., 2006), and we can consider the quantization effect negligible as the quantization noise is much smaller than the receiver noise.

Finally, since the fast estimator commits some error, the actual quality is checked by performing a single FxP simulation.

The aforementioned three steps where repeated several times, setting λ to its maximum or minimum, and the most restrictive FxP formats where selected for each signal (the FxP with a greater number of bits). Once the word-lengths of all signals were determined, we simultaneously applied the whole set of fixed-point formats, getting $SNR_c = 38$ dB, safely larger than the 20 dB constraint and close enough to the previously set temptative target of 40 dB.

The use of the fast estimator during FPO led to a speedup in computation time of $\times 904$ over the simulation-based approach. The final set of word-lengths and ranges can be seen in Figure 5.

5.3 Validation in Terms of BER Performance

As a final step, the SystemC simulation chain was used to validate the decisions concerning signal ranges and word-length selection in terms of BER performance (see Figure 5 for the final dynamic ranges and word-lengths). For this purpose, a complete fixed-point software model of the equalizer was developed, which is bit-accurate with the VHDL source code to be implemented in the FPGA. By substituting the original floating-point equalizer module with its fixed-point counterpart in the SystemC simulator, and including appropriate floating/fixed-point interfaces between modules, we checked that the BER performance degradation was negligible. This is shown in Figure 6, where the bit error rate performance of different modes implemented on the system has been evaluated for 8 and 32 users.

6. IMPLEMENTATION AND RESULTS

Tools used during the design were Xilinx ISE 7.1 with XST engine for VHDL synthesis and place-and-route, and ModelSim SE 6.0d to run simulations. The architecture of the equalizer was described using VHDL and synthesized by means of the XST tool. Before continuing with the implementation process, a behavioral simulation was performed using ModelSim. Then, after checking that the architecture was correct, the system was implemented by means of the synthesis and place-and-route processes. These select the particular resources of the FPGA that are used to map the different architecture elementary blocks and interconnect them efficiently, so that the speed requirements are met. Finally, a post-place-and-route simulation was performed using ModelSim to get the final check of the hardware module.

Target FPGAs considered for the implementation were Xilinx Virtex-4, specifically, XC4V-LX100 devices. These devices are suitable for high-performance DSP since they are composed of 49,152 logic blocks (slices), 96 DSP blocks and 240 18Kb memory blocks. DSP blocks are capable of performing 18×18 multiplications. Most of the arithmetic operators from Figure 5 were directly described using standard VHDL commands (e.g., a<=b+c implies an addition, a<=b*c implies a multiplication) and the ISE tool is able to map them onto logic or DSP blocks. However, inverters were implemented as cores (Xilinx Pipelined Divider v3.0) using the Xilinx Core Generator tool. This provides with predesigned arithmetic cores that can be customized in terms of word-length and processing speed, leading to highly optimized results. Inverter *D1* gives one result per clock cycle, while *D2*, which follows the accumulator, produces one result every 8 cycles, thus making possible to select different architectures for each inverter. *D2* can then be implemented with a core that requires less area. It is important to reduce the area of dividers, since they require a high number of LUTs.

Table 2 shows FPGA resources used by the equalizer. Usage of datapath LUTs is distributed as 361 for logic, 184 for shift registers and 3 for route-thru tasks. It can be seen that the percentage of resource usage is very small: 1% of logic resources and 5% of DSP blocks. In order to build the bitstream for the FPGA, we used a constraint of 100 MHz for the clock frequency, resulting in

Table 2. Use of resources in the Virtex-4 FPGA

	Slices	Flips-Flops	LUTs	DSPs
Control	30	22	54	0
Datapath	532	847	548	5

a minimum clock cycle of 9.720 ns. Thus, speed requirements were also met.

Quantized outputs from the MIMO decoding module of the SystemC simulator were used to perform the functional validation of the hardware implementation. The outputs of VHDL simulations were compared for equality with those obtained by the bit-accurate software model of the equalizer, the aforementioned SystemC-based framework (see Section 5), when driven by the same patterns, thus validating the design.

In summary, the implementation widely met system requirements. The processing speed was met by means of performing a thorough quantization and by using a highly parallel architecture (pipeline). The resource usage of the equalizer was quite reduced, again, due to the fixed-point optimization and the wise use of DSP blocks and optimized dividers.

7. CONCLUSION

In this chapter, we have addressed the main aspects of the design of baseband hardware modules. We have focused on word-length optimization, implementation and validation. These concepts have been applied to the design of an equalizer for 4G MIMO communications.

A robust simulation framework, able to simulate both floating-point and fixed-point descriptions, has proven to be essential in the design of the system. The architecture of the system has been optimized to comply with the throughput requirements, as well as to reduce implementation area. The design of wireless systems usually involves a simulation-based fixed-point translation approach which, given the nature of the input data, leads to exceedingly high word-length optimization times. In order to ease this issue, the fixed-point translation presented here has combined both analytical and simulation-based techniques. This has enabled the reduction of the total number of bit-true simulations needed for the computation of

the signal ranges, and the computation reduction of the word-length selection task by means of a fast SQNR estimator. Implementation results using Xilinx Virtex-4 devices show that the equalizer requires a limited number of FPGA resources while achieving a high performance.

ACKNOWLEDGMENT

This work was supported in part by Research Projects USP-BS PPC05/2010 (Banco Santander and University CEU San Pablo) and TEC2009-14219-C03 (Spanish Ministry of Science and Innovation).

REFERENCES

Alamouti, S. M. (1998). A simple transmit diversity technique for wireless communications. *IEEE Journal on Selected Areas in Communications*, *16*(8). doi:10.1109/49.730453

Caffarena, G., Carreras, C., López, J. A., & Fernández, A. (2010). SQNR estimation of fixed-point DSP algorithms. *EURASIP Journal on Advances in Signal Processing*, 2010.

Caffarena, G., Constantinides, G. A., Cheung, P. Y. K., Carreras, C., & Nieto-Taladriz, O. (2006). Optimal combined word length allocation and architectural synthesis of digital signal processing circuits. *IEEE Transactions on Circuits and Systems II*, *53*(5), 339–343. doi:10.1109/TC-SII.2005.862175

Caffarena, G., Fernández, A., Carreras, C., & Nieto-Taladriz, O. (2004). Fixed-point refinement of OFDM-based adaptive equalizers: a heuristic approach. In *European Signal Processing Conference* (pp. 1353–1356).

Cantin, M.-A., Savaria, Y., & Lavoie, P. (2002). A comparison of automatic word length optimization procedures. In *IEEE International Symposium on Circuits and Systems* (pp. 612–615).

Catthoor, F., De Man, H., & Vandewalle, J. (1988). Simulated annealing based optimization of coefficient and data wordlengths in digital filters. *International Journal of Circuit Theory and Applications, 16*(4), 371–390. doi:10.1002/cta.4490160404

Constantinides, G. (2003). Perturbation analysis for word-length optimization. In *IEEE Symposium on Field-Programmable Custom Computing Machines* (pp. 81–90).

Constantinides, G. A., Cheung, P. Y. K., & Luk, W. (1999). Truncation noise in fixed-point SFGs. *Electronics Letters, 35*(23), 2013–2014. doi:10.1049/el:19991375

Constantinides, G. A., Cheung, P. Y. K., & Luk, W. (2003). Wordlength optimization for linear digital signal processing. *IEEE Transactions on Computer-Aided Design of Integrated Circuits and Systems, 22*(10), 1432–1442. doi:10.1109/TCAD.2003.818119

Constantinides, G. A., & Woeginger, G. J. (2002). The complexity of multiple wordlength assignment. *Applied Mathematics Letters, 15*(2), 137–140. doi:10.1016/S0893-9659(01)00107-0

Cranickx, J., & Donnay, D. (2003). 4G terminals: How are we going to design them? In *Design and Automation Conference* (pp. 79-84).

Fang, C. F., Chen, T., & Rutenbar, R. A. (2003). Floating-point error analysis based on affine arithmetic. In *IEEE International Conference on Acoustics, Speech, and Signal Processing* (pp. 561–564).

Fernández-Herrero, A., Jiménez-Pacheco, A., Caffarena, G., & Casajus Quiros, J. (2006). Design and implementation of a hardware module for equalisation in a 4G MIMO receiver. In *International Conference on Field Programmable Logic and Applications* (pp. 765–768).

Gaffar, A., Mencer, O., Luk, W., & Cheung, P. Y. K. (2004). Unifying bit-width optimisation for fixed-point and floating-point designs. In *IEEE Symposium on Field-Programmable Custom Computing Machines* (pp. 79–88).

Gaffar, A., Mencer, O., Luk, W., Cheung, P. Y. K., & Shirazi, N. (2002). Floating-point bitwidth analysis via automatic differentiation. In *International Conference on Field Programmable Technology* (pp. 158–165).

Hanzo, L. L., & Keller, T. (2006). *OFDM and MC-CDMA: A primer*. Wiley-IEEE Press. doi:10.1002/9780470031384

Hara, S., & Prasad, R. (1997, December). Overview of multicarrier CDMA. *IEEE Communications Magazine*.

Hayes, B. (1999). A lucid interval. *American Scientist, 91*(6), 484–488.

Jackson, L. B. (1970). Roundoff-noise analysis for fixed-point digital filters realized in cascade or parallel form. *IEEE Transactions on Audio and Electroacoustics, 18*(2), 107–122. doi:10.1109/TAU.1970.1162084

Jiang, M. Hanzo, L. (2007). Multiuser MIMO-OFDM for next-generation wireless systems. *Proceedings of the IEEE,* July 2007.

Jiménez-Pacheco, A., Fernández-Herrero, A., & Casajús-Quirós, J. (2008). Design and implementation of a hardware module for MIMO decoding in a 4G wireless receiver. *VLSI Design, 2008*, 312614. doi:10.1155/2008/312614

Juntti, M., Vehkapera, M., Leinonen, J., Zexian, V., Tujkovic, D., Tsumura, S., & Hara, S. (2005, February). MIMO MC-CDMA communications for future cellular systems. *IEEE Communications Magazine*.

Kaiser, S., et al. (2004). 4G MC-CDMA multi antenna system on chip for radio enhancements (4MORE). *Proceedings of the 13th IST Mobile and Wireless Communications Summit*, June 2004.

Le Nir, V., Hélard, M., & Le Gouable, R. (2003). *Space-time block coding applied to turbo coded MC-CDMA*. In Vehicular Technology Conference.

Lee, D.-U., Gaffar, A. A., Cheung, R. C. C., Mencer, O., Luk, W., & Constantinides, G. A. (2006). Accuracy-guaranteed bit-width optimization. *IEEE Transactions on Computer-Aided Design of Integrated Circuits and Systems, 25*(10), 1990–1999. doi:10.1109/TCAD.2006.873887

López, J. (2004). *Evaluación de los efectos de cuantificación en las estructuras de filtros digitales mediante técnicas de simulación basadas en extensiones de intervalos*. Ph.D. thesis, Universidad Politécnica de Madrid, Spain.

López, J. A., Caffarena, G., Carreras, C., & Nieto-Taladriz, O. (2004). Analysis of limit cycles by means of affine arithmetic computer-aided tests. In *European Signal Processing Conference* (pp. 991–994).

López, J. A., Caffarena, G., Carreras, C., & Nieto-Taladriz, O. (2008). Fast and accurate computation of the round-off noise of linear time-invariant systems. *IET Circuits. Devices and Systems, 2*(4), 393–408. doi:10.1049/iet-cds:20070198

López, J. A., Carreras, C., & Nieto-Taladriz, O. (2007). Improved interval-based characterization of fixed-point LTI systems with feedback loops. *IEEE Transactions on Computer-Aided Design of Integrated Circuits and Systems, 26*(11), 1923–1933. doi:10.1109/TCAD.2007.896306

Menard, D., Rocher, R., Scalart, P., & Sentieys, O. (2004). SQNR determination in non-linear and non-recursive fixed-point systems. In *European Signal Processing Conference* (pp. 1349–1352).

Menard, D., & Sentieys, O. (2002). A methodology for evaluating the precision of fixed-point systems. In *IEEE International Conference on Acoustic, Speech, and Signal Processing* (pp. 3152–3155).

Oppenheim, A. V., & Schafer, R. W. (1987). *Discrete-time signal processing*. Prentice-Hall.

Oppenheim, A. V., & Weinstein, C. J. (1972). Effects of finite register length in digital filtering and the fast Fourier transform. *Proceedings of the IEEE, 60*(8), 957–976. doi:10.1109/PROC.1972.8820

Paulraj, A. J., Gore, D. A., Nabar, R. U., & Bolcskei, H. (2004). An overview of MIMO communications – A key to gigabit wireless. *Proceedings of the IEEE*, (February): 2004.

Shi, C., & Brodersen, R. W. (2004). A perturbation theory on statistical quantization effects in fixed-point DSP with nonstationary inputs. In *IEEE International Symposium on Circuits and Systems*, vol. 3, (pp. 373–376).

Stolfi, J., & Figueiredo, L. H. (1997). Self-validated numerical methods and applications. In *Brazilian Mathematics Colloquium Monograph*. IMPA.

Stuber, G. L., Barry, J. R., McLaughlin, S. W., Li, Y., Ingram, M. A., & Pratt, T. G. (2004). Broadband MIMO-OFDM wireless communications. *Proceedings of the IEEE*, (February): 2004.

Sung, W., & Kum, K. (1995). Simulation-based word-length optimization method for fixed-point digital signal processing systems. *IEEE Transactions on Signal Processing, 43*(12), 3087–3090. doi:10.1109/78.476465

Tse, D., & Viswanath, P. (2005). *Fundamentals of wireless communication*. Cambridge University Press.

Van Nee, R., & Prasad, R. (2000). *OFDM for wireless multimedia communications*. Artech House.

KEY TERMS AND DEFINITIONS

Code-Division Multiple-Access (CDMA): A signaling technique used in digital communications to allow several users to share the same channel. It is based on spreading the spectrum of each transmission by using specific orthogonal codes and merging them together.

Fixed-Point Arithmetic: It is a way of computing with real numbers in digital systems, where the internal representation for numbers is based on finite word-lengths with fixed positions for radix points.

Field-Programmable Gate Array (FPGA): Electronic devices that are composed of a miriad of fine-grain programmable logic blocks and some coarse-grain specialized blocks (e.g. DSP blocks, RAM blocks, etc.). Their capabilities are in the middle of those of Aplication-Specific Integrated Circuits (ASICs) and microprocessors (µPs), since they support massive parallelism while enabling the reconfiguration of its functionality.

MC-CDMA: Multi-Carrier CDMA is a signaling scheme that completes OFDM with multiple user capabilities by combination with direct sequence CDMA techniques.

Multiple-Input Multiple-Output (MIMO): A recently developed communication technique based on the simultaneous use of several antennas in the transmitter and/or receiver sides of the radio link. It allows taking advantage of spatial diversity in multipath environments, both to increase capacity and mitigate the effects of fading.

Orthogonal Frequency-Division Multiplexing (OFDM): A signaling scheme for wideband digital communications. It provides robustness against severe multipath channels, avoiding intersymbol interference and simplifying equalization tasks.

Signal to Quantization-Noise Ratio (SQNR): Given a signal that is truncated by means of quantization, SQNR is the ratio between the mean power of the original signal and the mean power of the quantization error introduced after the quantization process. It is used as a metric ton guide word-length optimization.

VHDL: Very high speed Hardware Description Language is a language commonly used in the design of integrated circuits and FPGA-based circuits.

Word-Length Optimization (WLO): The process that finds optimal FxP formats for signals of an algorithm that is originally described using real arithmetic. It is an essential step in order to obtain a digital implementation of any numeric algorithm.

Chapter 12
System Design Perspective:
WiMAX Standards and IEEE 802.16j
Based Multihop WiMAX

Hrishikesh Venkataraman
Dublin City University (DCU), Ireland

Bogdan Ciubotaru
Dublin City University (DCU), Ireland

Gabriel-Miro Muntean
Dublin City University (DCU), Ireland

ABSTRACT

The next generation of cellular networks has evolved from voice-based to data-centric communication. The recent focus has been mainly on high data-rate services like mobile gaming, high quality music, Internet browsing, video streaming, etcetera, which consumes lots of bandwidth. This puts a severe constraint on the available radio resource. In this chapter, the IEEE 802.16 based multihop WiMAX networks (802.16j) is introduced, and the system design is explained in detail. The chapter outlines the background and the importance of multihop wireless networks, especially in the cellular domain. Different types of multihop design for WiMAX are explained, along with a detailed analysis of the effect of the number of hops in the WiMAX networks. Further, in order to support next generation rich media services, the system design requirements, and challenges for real-time video transmission are explained.

INTRODUCTION TO WiMAX

The Worldwide Interoperability for Microwave Access, abbreviated commonly as WiMAX is a wireless technology aimed to provide a standard based solution for broadband data access to fixed, portable and mobile devices. WiMAX has gained significant prominence from 2005, since the origin of WiMAX certified products. The mobile WiMAX air interface is designed based on orthogonal frequency division multiplexing (OFDM) technique. Importantly, it relies on the IP network architecture and is mainly developed to realize the convergence of fixed and mobile

DOI: 10.4018/978-1-4666-0083-6.ch012

Figure 1. Different sub-groups within 802.16 WiMAX networks

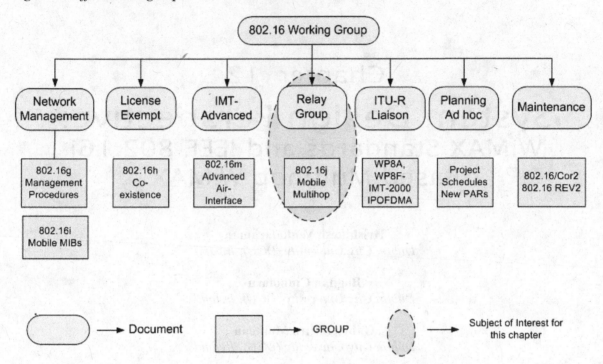

broadband in the wireless cellular network. The WiMAX air interface is developed by the IEEE 802.16 working group established by the IEEE Standards Board in 1999. The IEEE 802.16 standards define the structure of the PHY layer (layer 1) and MAC layer (layer 2) operations that occur between the mobile subscriber stations and BSs over the air while the upper layer signaling over the air is considered to be out of scope of the IEEE 802.16 definition.

Sub-Groups in WiMAX

The initial versions of the standard focus 802.16/a/d focused on the fixed access and the later versions include many new features and functionalities needed to support enhanced QoS, increased coverage, better mobility and high security (Etemad, 2002). The work group organization of IEEE 802.16 and the different sub groups are shown in Figure 1. The 802.16 working group has different sub-groups, the 802.16g, 802.16h,

80.216m, etc. each designed for different purpose that includes advanced air interface, co-existence, etc. Given the importance of high rate communications in the next generation wireless network, the *"relay group"* proposed the IEEE 802.16j mobile multihop sub-division, as a method to integrate multihop *ad hoc* networking into cellular networks.

Why Multihop WiMAX?

The network operators and the service providers constantly look for higher system capacity and network coverage, while at the same time aim to reduce the cost of cell-site developments and maintenance. Due to the varying topography and constant irregularities in the coverage area, novel mechanisms have to be proposed in order to increase the system capacity. In this context, a relay based cellular network is a key architectural advancement towards the next generation wireless networks. The next generation broadband wireless network would comprise of both multihop capabilities and infrastructure-based communication. Services like video-on-demand and real-time multimedia streaming over broadband and/or IP based networks would drive the demand for high data rate and high bandwidth applications. The architecture would target a communication environment wherein a wireless terminal can communicate with another terminal through an *ad hoc* network via multihop routing and at the same time establish contact with a gateway to download a file from an Internet server or make contact with another far-off device through cellular networks. In case of the multihop design, the relaying hops put a lot of burden on the overhead requirements. Also, a channel distortion in a single unreliable link in the end-to-end multihop scenario might create severe QoS issues. Hence, it is necessary to take into account the channel characteristics in designing multihop wireless networks (Tonguz, 2006). At the same time, the relaying hops put a lot of burden on the overhead requirements and designing an optimum radio resource scheme in the multihop network design. Also, since the same resources are reused for some other communication pair, the performance of the multihop wireless network is sensitive to the quality of all the relaying routes and simultaneously communicating pairs. It can be seen that the subgroup on '*relay task*' have come up with the standards for 802.16j mobile multihop infrastructure

COMPONENT DESIGN FOR MULTIHOP WiMAX (IEEE 802.16j BASED NETWORKS)

Multihop Wireless Networks

A multihop wireless network, by definition is one wherein the source and destination terminals communicate with each other in multiple hops. There are an infinitely large number of dimensions to the design space of multihop wireless networks (Murthy, 2004). Consider for example, whether the range of wireless transmission should be large or small compared to the geographical distribution of the mobile wireless terminals. If all the wireless terminals are within transmission range of each other, no multihop relaying is needed and the wireless network is, by definition, fully connected. The wireless nodes can directly send packets to their destination via single-hop routing as long as the link signal-to-interference-noise ratio (SINR) is above some minimal threshold. The standard technique for long distance wireless communication (in the range of 2-20 kms) that has been prevalent in the last decade has been the single-hop cellular communication with direct transmission between mobile station (MS) and base station (BS). In this mode, the BSs are connected by a backbone wired network or a broadband wireless microwave link access. However, apart from the limitation of not being able to provide high data rates over long distances, such a network frequently encounters problems like *dead zones* (areas without coverage) and *hot spots* (congestion of traffic in a particular cell) around the BSs, thus causing inefficient spatial reuse of resources and leading to sub-optimal system capacity (Li, 2003).

In a multihop wireless network, the packets are forwarded from source to destination through intermediate relay nodes. Since path loss causes an exponential decrease in the received power as a function of distance, using intermediate nodes can greatly reduce the transmit power for the entire source and relay nodes. This approach reduces the interference experienced by other nodes in the system which in-turn results in an increase in the system capacity. A fundamental issue in multihop wireless networks is that the performance degrades sharply as the number of hops traversed increases. For example, in a network of nodes with identical and omni-directional radio ranges, going from a single hop to two hops halves the throughput of a flow because wireless interference dictates that only one of the two hops can be active at a time (Jain, 2003). Similarly, there is another fundamental question that has been the focus of researchers in recent years, "*What is the optimal capacity of a multihop wireless network?*". In case of a single-hop cellular network, this question is analyzed on a cell-by-cell basis, by considering the multiple access channel from the mobile users to the BS (uplink), and the broadcast channel from the BS(s) to the users (downlink). This area of research has been very active over the last couple of decades and is relatively well understood. The case of multihop wireless networks is more recent, and thus less well understood. The difficulty stems from the fact that in a multihop wireless network, any kind of cooperation between the users is permissible. Hence, a node in the multihop network has substantially more degrees of freedom than a single hop cellular network. For example, in a multihop cellular network, all the nodes that communicate to the BS (uplink) in multiple hops would first communicate to the relay node. For this transmission between the mobile and the relay node, the relay would act as a receiver. At the next time instant, the relay node would then act as a transmitter and transmit this signal to the BS. This relay could be a fixed terminal mounted over a roof top or a mobile node that has its own data to transmit to some destination. At the same time, this problem is extremely severe in multihop *ad hoc* networks where there is no central coordinator and hence any node in the network can act both as a terminal (sender/receiver of data) and as a relay for other transmission. Similarly, lack of any centralized control and possible node mobility gives rise to many issues at the network, medium access and physical layers, which have no counterpart in the wired or cellular networks. In order to understand in detail the different research problems in the field of multihop wireless networks, the description of the multihop network is divided into two sections: multihop *ad hoc* network and multihop hybrid wireless network.

Spatial Reuse and QoS in Multihop Wireless Networks

One of the most challenging problems in multihop wireless networks is to guarantee a certain quality of service (QoS). This problem is usually considered in the MAC layer. Traditionally, MAC protocols for wireless networks are based on dynamic access methods such as carrier sense multiple access (CSMA), e.g., the IEEE 802.11 standard (IEEE, 2011). Although efforts have been made to guarantee QoS in CSMA based MAC protocols, dynamic methods are inherently inappropriate for providing QoS guarantees (Sobrinho, 1999). One of the most important QoS in many applications is delay guarantee, i.e., the upper bound on the time it takes to transmit a message from the source to destination. This is useful when transmitting delay sensitive traffic such as voice or video. One approach where delay bounds can be guaranteed is a TDMA-based network. Unfortunately, this is usually inefficient in sparsely connected networks. However, due to multihop properties, the TS(s) can often be shared by more than one user without conflicts. Therefore, the spatial resources can be reused in any TS of a TDMA system, in order to increase the network capacity.

Spatial reuse in a TDMA based multihop packet radio networks was first studied more than two decades back in (Chlamtac & Kutten, 1985) and (Chlamtac &Lerner, 1985) wherein it was introduced as a collision free access scheme for multihop *ad hoc* networks. The concept of spatial reuse channel access schedule for multihop radio networks was formalized by Nelson and Kleinrock (1985). The idea was to let spatially separated radio terminals reuse the same TS(s) when the resulting interferences are not severe. Such a protocol is called spatial reuse TDMA, or STDMA. The gain from spatial reuse must however outweigh the additional number of transmissions required between the source and destination node, in order to achieve an improvement in the throughput performance. A STDMA schedule describes the transmission rights for each TS. In the literature, various algorithms for generating reuse schedules have been proposed. Centralized algorithms for multihop networks have been proposed in (Funabiki, 1993) and (Hajek, 1998) and distributed algorithms in (Chlamtac and Pinter, 1987).

Most of the early work in the literature have in common that the reuse schedule is designed from the graph-model of the network, wherein the radio terminals that are located beyond a certain distance could communicate simultaneously. The graph-scheduling technique is therefore based exactly on the same principle as the interference-avoidance *Protocol Model* that has been introduced in the landmark paper of Gupta and Kumar (2000). Zander (1991) proposed an alternative interference model where the signal-to-interference ratio (SIR) is used to describe the interferences in the network. The schedule was defined to be conflict-free if the SIR does not fall below a certain threshold. It has been shown in (Samaribba, 1995) that under the full interference environment, the STDMA schedules result in conflict-free approach in terms of SIR. Further, (Groenkvist & Hansson, 2001) shows that under complete knowledge of the interference environment, interference-based scheduling can improve the network performance by up to one third, as compared to the graph-based scheduling. However, the main disadvantage of the interference based STDMA scheduling is the increased network complexity and the control overhead, as the interference has to be calculated at the receiver of every potential communication pair. Also, the relaying of traffic causes a considerable variation in the traffic of the communicating pairs in the network. This results in "*bottle neck*" effects at busy nodes which in turn results in long packet delays. In fact, it is shown in (Arikon, 1984) that for a wireless network with large number of wireless terminals, it is an NP-hard problem to determine the optimum STDMA scheduling.

Interference Models for Multihop Wireless Networks

Consider a multihop wireless network with n nodes in the system. Let Xi and Xj denote two wireless nodes and also the location of the nodes. Suppose node Xi transmits over a particular sub-channel to node Xj. The distance between the two nodes would be given by, $|Xi - Xj|$. Let there be nt concurrent transmitters over the same sub-channel, all of them transmitting with the same power level, P_T.

Protocol Model

The transmission from node, Xi, is successfully received by node, Xj if

$$\left| X_s - X_j \right| \geq (1 + \Delta)\left| X_i - X_j \right|$$

For every other node Xk, (where $k \neq j$ and $k \in nt$), simultaneously transmitting over the same sub-channel. The quantity Δ models situations where an exclusion region (or a guard zone) is specified by the protocol to prevent a neighboring node from transmitting on the same sub-channel at the same time. It is to be noted that under this condition, a node may not send and receive at the same time nor transmit to more than one other node at the same time. Also, it is to be noted that this model differs from the popular 802.11 MAC in an important way—it requires only the receiver to be free of interference, instead of requiring that both the sender and the receiver be free of interference.

Physical Model

The transmission from a node Xi, is successfully received by node Xj if

$$\frac{\dfrac{P_T}{\left|X_i - X_j\right|^\alpha}}{P_N + \sum_{s=1,s\neq i}^{n_t} \dfrac{P_T}{\left|X_s - X_j\right|^\alpha}} \geq \beta$$

Here, β is the minimum signal-to-interference-noise ratio required at the receiver for successful reception of the signal, P_N is the ambient noise power level and α is the propagation loss coefficient. It can be observed that the constraints defined by the *Protocol Model* are local. They only require certain localities of transmitters to be free of receivers. On the other hand, the *Physical Model* considers the cumulative interference due to all the nodes in the network. Thus, intuitively it appears that the *Physical Model* is a much more restrictive model, and would entail lower capacity. However, it has been shown in Theorem 4.1 in (Arikon, 1984) that the exclusion range concept of the *Protocol Model* (also known as interference avoidance model) results in a more restrictive bound on the system throughput in comparison to the *Physical Model*. Also, in a multihop design, especially in multihop *ad hoc* networks, it is very difficult in practice to calculate the total interference across each of the communicating pairs, and then select a new simultaneously communicating pair, based on the interference across the receiver of each pair. On account of this, an interference avoidance *Protocol Model* is considered in most practical scenarios.

Relays in Multihop Wireless Networks

Gastpar and Vetterli (2002) extended the work of Gupta and Kumar (2000) in a different direction. Instead of the simple point-to-point coding assumption which treats each transmitter-receiver pairs to be independent of other pairs, they consider a network coding model where nodes could cooperate in arbitrary ways. In this scheme, there is only one source-destination pair while all others act as relays that assist the transmission between the source and destination. The optimum throughput capacity under these conditions is $\theta(\log(n))$. In the landmark paper of Gupta and Kumar (2000), they also point out that, if m additional homogeneous nodes are deployed as pure relays in random positions, with no independent traffic of their own, then the throughput that can be furnished to each of the n sources is

$$\Theta\left(\frac{(n + m)}{n\sqrt{(n + m)\log(n + m)}}\right)$$

There is however a severe cost of providing this increase in throughput. The number of additional relay nodes that need to be deployed to gain an appreciable increase in the capacity for the source nodes may be very large. The addition of m relay nodes provide less than $\sqrt{[(m/n) + 1]}$ fold increase in throughput. Also, the lack of any centralized control and possible node mobility gives rise to many issues at the network, medium access and physical layers, which have no counterpart in wired networks like internet, or in the cellular networks. This gives rise to one of its most serious drawbacks, the limitation in providing global connectivity. This is the reason why few real world applications of mobile *ad hoc* networks have been developed or deployed outside the military environment. In all practical and realistic applications that have been designed so far, an infrastructure based network is considered in the backbone of the multihop *ad hoc* networks. An "anytime – anywhere" connectivity between two mobile devices is obtained by having the multihop *ad hoc* network combined with infrastructure based cellular networks (or any other centralized control) and is known as "multihop hybrid wireless networks"; and this is precisely the concept of IEEE802.16j networks.

Figure 2. A multihop hybrid transmission: A link communicates in either ad hoc mode or in cellular mode

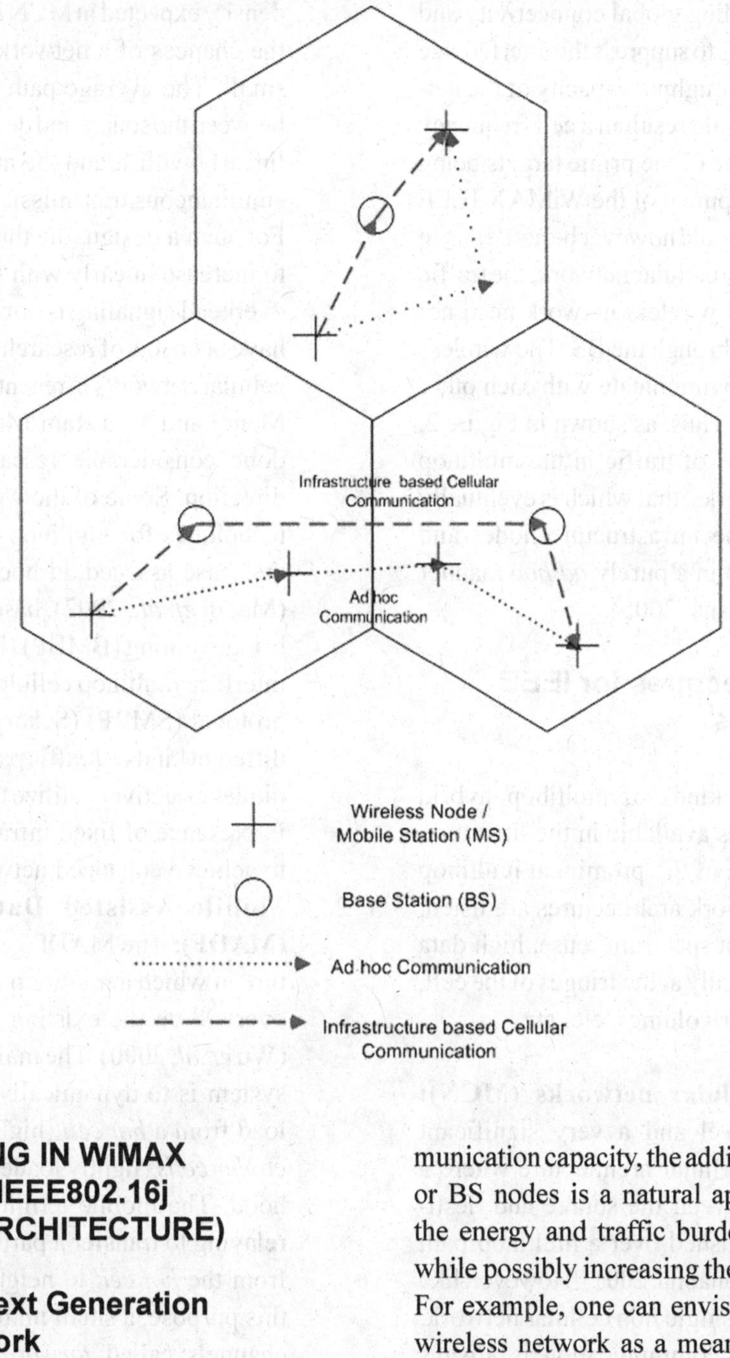

Infrastructure based Cellular
Communication

Ad hoc
Communication

─┼─ Wireless Node /
     Mobile Station (MS)

◯   Base Station (BS)

·········▶ Ad hoc Communication

─ ─ ─ ─▶ Infrastructure based Cellular
          Communication

MULTIHOPPING IN WiMAX NETWORKS (IEEE802.16j CELLULAR ARCHITECTURE)

Multihop in Next Generation Cellular Network

A multihop hybrid wireless network model overcomes the limitation posed by the *ad hoc* networks and the single hop cellular networks. Since wireless units are typically energy constrained and *ad hoc* networks have limited communication capacity, the addition of infrastructure or BS nodes is a natural approach of reducing the energy and traffic burden on *ad hoc* nodes while possibly increasing the system throughput. For example, one can envisage a hybrid *ad hoc* wireless network as a means to enable sharing of information between possibly mobile sensor nodes or gathering of sensed information toward query points on a wire-line network (Zemlinanov & Veciana, 2005). Alternatively, one can view multihop cellular network model as a means to extend the communication coverage of wireless cellular infrastructure. Such a hybrid network model aims at providing global connectivity and at the same time, seeks to suppress the interference and maximize the throughput capacity of the network. This in turn would result in a cell frequency reuse ratio of *one,* one of the prime targets being aimed for the development of the WiMAX/IEEE 802.16j standard. It should however be noted that in contrast to single-hop cellular network, the traffic in a multihop hybrid wireless network need not be always mediated through the BS. The wireless nodes that wish to communicate with each other might do so directly. Thus, as shown in Figure 2, there are two "types" of traffic in the multihop hybrid cellular networks: that which is eventually mediated through the infrastructure nodes and that which is relayed in a purely *ad hoc* manner (Zemlinanov & Veciana, 2005).

Different Architectures for IEEE 802.16j Networks

There are different kinds of multihop hybrid wireless architectures available in the literature. In this section, some of the prominent multihop hybrid wireless network architectures are listed, based on the efficient spectrum reuse, high data rate capability especially at the fringes of the cell, support for large user volumes, etc. etc.

1. **Multihop cellular networks (MCN):** MCN is a novel and a very significant design in the cellular architecture where a connection between the source and destination is established over a multihop path (Ananthapadmanabha, 2001). However, like in a traditional single hop cellular network, the end-to-end communication is always between the MS and BS. MCN suggests that the transmission power of the mobile node and the BS over the data channel be reduced to a fraction $1/k$ where k is referred to as the reuse factor of the cell radius, r. This means that more than one node can transmit simul-

taneously on the same channel. The node density expected in MCN is quite high, hence the chances of a network partition is quite small. The average path length, for a path between the source and destination, increases linearly with k, and the number of possible simultaneous transmissions increases as k^2. For such a design, the throughput is shown to increase linearly with k, if the additional overhead signaling is not considered. There have been lots of research work on multihop cellular networks in recent years (Liu, 2006). Manoj and Siva Ram Murthy (2002) have done considerable research work in this direction. Some of the well-known routing techniques for multihop cellular networks are: base assisted ad hoc routing (BAAR) (Manoj *et. al.*, 2002), base-driven multihop bridge routing (BMBP) (Lin, 2000), single-interface multihop cellular network routing protocol (SMRP) (Sekar *et. al.*, 2006), for different kinds of traffic patterns. These techniques effectively utilize the *ad hoc* relaying in presence of fixed infrastructure in order to achieve enhanced network capacity.

2. **Mobile Assisted Data Forwarding (MADF):** The MADF is a hybrid architecture in which a multihop relaying system is overlaid on the existing cellular networks (Wu *et. al*, 2000). The main objective of this system is to dynamically divert the traffic load from a *hot cell* (highly loaded cell) to *cooler cells* (lightly loaded) in its neighborhood. The mobile terminals use multihop relaying to transfer a part of the traffic load from the *hot cell* to neighboring cells. For this purpose, a small number of designated channels called *forwarding channels* are used to establish multihop paths.

3. **Integrated Cellular *ad hoc* Relay system, (iCAR):** iCAR, (Wu *et. al.*, 2001), is a next generation wireless architecture that can easily evolve from the existing cellular infrastructure. In particular, it enables a cel-

lular network to achieve a throughput closer to its theoretical capacity by dynamically balancing the load among different cells. In a normal single-hop cellular network, even if the network load does not reach the network capacity, several calls may be blocked or dropped because of isolated instances of congestion in the system. To counter this, iCAR uses fixed relays over and above the infrastructure based cellular system that dynamically routes the traffic. This architecture eliminates the problem of hot spots by employing different kinds of routing (primary routing, secondary routing and tertiary routing) and by allowing high data rates to be transmitted over long distances with the help of multiple hops between the source and destination.

4. **Multihop Hybrid Cellular Network:** A multihop hybrid cellular network with both BS(s) and dedicated relays have been considered by Vishwanathan and Mukherjee (2005). The dedicated relay stations are used to store and forward data from the BS to the wireless terminals and vice-versa. Like in the case of multihop *ad hoc* network, the relays in the multihop hybrid wireless network rely on the wireless transmission to communicate to either the MS or the BS. Deploying relays and employing multihop transmission in the cellular architecture results in simultaneous transmission by both the BS and the relays. This would therefore clearly improve the performance of the system as compared to a multihop ad hoc network or the standard single hop cellular network. Routing in the traditional single-hop cellular networks is fairly simple and does not extend to multihop hybrid wireless networks due to multihop transmission and high routing overhead. There has been lots of research done with regard to routing in ad hoc networks and extending the same to multihop hybrid wireless architectures. It is observed that routing

efficiency is higher in iCAR as compared to other hybrid wireless architectures [28]. The hybrid wireless network design has shown significant capacity improvement over the single-hop cellular network and the ad hoc network model, and is explained in detail in the next subsection.

System Model

A mobile coverage area comprising a hexagonal cellular structure is considered here, as shown in Figure 3. The circular coverage area has a radius, R, while each of the hexagonal cells has a side length, r. 1000 MSs are assumed to be uniformly distributed in the coverage area. An interference avoidance *Protocol Model* is considered for a hybrid cellular design, such that no MS except the desired transmitter can transmit within that circular region. The area of one exclusion range circle is given by $B = \pi ((1+ \Delta) dc)^2$, where dc is the transmission distance between the transmitter and receiver and Δ is the exclusion range ratio/ spatial protection margin added to the transmission distance. In the single-hop model, there are no relays, and all MSs communicate with the BS in single-hops. In case of a multihop model, the mobile terminal located between the source and destination is selected as the relay node, such that, the total end-to-end transmission distance between the source and destination node is minimized. This relay selection mechanism is known as shortest total distance (STD) selection scheme. If there are $n \in N$ possible routes for a M-hop communication between the source and destination node, and $dc_{n1}, dc_{n2}, dc_{n3}, \dots dc_{nM}$ are the distances of the M hops of the nth route, then the selected route, rs, as per the STD selection scheme is given by,

$$r_s = \min_{\forall n \in N} \sum_{i=1}^{M} ((d_{c_{ni}}))$$

Figure 3. A multi-cell scenario for an IEEE802.16 based cellular network

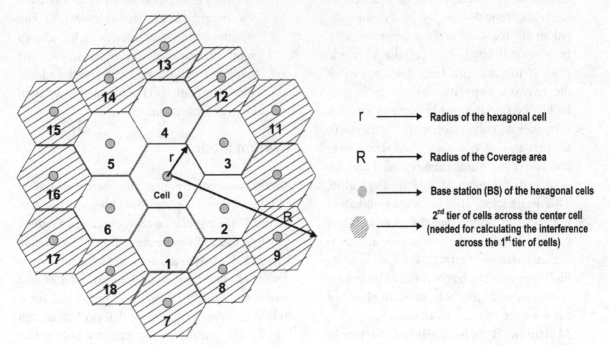

A typical example for a multihop cellular communication model under the STD selection scheme is shown in Figure 4 and Figure 5. In Figure 4, the MS communicates with the BS in 2 hops, with a single relay between the source and destination, whereas, in Figure 5, there are two relays between the MS and BS. It can be observed that the relays are not on the same line as the source and destination node. But, out of the all possible routes, the selected route has the shortest total distance between the source and destination. At this stage, the STD algorithm is considered throughout the analysis, for all *M*-hop cellular model. In the next subsection, the performance of multihop cellular networks is studied for a different number of multiple hops per link, and for a different number of BSs in the system.

System Capacity Variation

In order to determine the system performance of multihop cellular networks, the variation of system capacity with the number of hops per link is studied

for different number of BSs in the coverage area. A constant coverage area is considered and the performance of the multihop cellular network is analyzed for varying number of BSs. In the initial stages, two different scenarios are considered in detail in the system design, depending on the relation between the radius of the hexagonal cell, *r*, and the radius of the coverage area, *R*.

1. The radius of the hexagonal cell, *r*, is ¼ of the radius of the coverage area, *R*, i.e., *r* = *R*/4. This results in 19 hexagonal cells in the system with a center cell surrounded by 2 tiers of 6 and 12 cells respectively.
2. *r* = *R*/5. This would result in 30 hexagonal cells in the system.

Figure 6 and Figure 7 show the plot of variation in the system capacity with different number of multiple hops per link when the number of BSs in the system are 19 and 30 respectively. Both the figures indicate that, irrespective of the path loss exponent, *α*, the system capacity increases

Figure 4. Relay selection mechanism for a 2-hop cellular network using the shortest total distance method

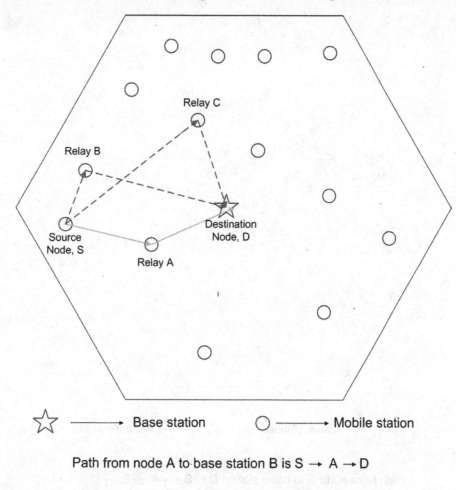

Path from node A to base station B is S → A → D

Path from S to D, following the shortest total distance method

Paths from S to D. These paths are not selected as per the shortest total distance selection scheme

with an increase in the number of multiple hops per link. This is because, with an increase in the number of multiple hops per link, the transmission distance of each communicating pair reduces which in turn reduces the exclusion region around every communicating pair. This in-effect increases the spatial reuse of resources which results in an increase in the system capacity. However, it should be noted that the increase in capacity is not linear. With an increase in the number of multiple hops, the system capacity saturates. This is because, as the number of multiple hops per link is linearly increased, the improvement in spatial reuse efficiency reaches a constant which in-turn saturates the system capacity. In fact, it is observed in Figure 6 that for 19 cells in the coverage area, the average system throughput for a single-hop system is 1.1bps/Hz, whereas for a system with 4-hop per link, the system throughput is 2.2 bps/Hz, which is *twice* the increase over a single-hop system. If the number of hops per link is increased to 10 hops, the system capacity saturates to 2.8 bps/Hz,

Figure 5. Relay selection mechanism for a 3-hop cellular network using the shortest total distance method

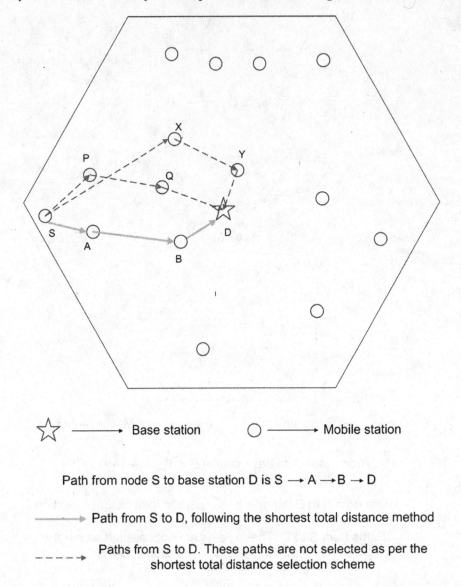

Path from node S to base station D is S → A → B → D

Path from S to D, following the shortest total distance method

Paths from S to D. These paths are not selected as per the shortest total distance selection scheme

an increase of only 27% over the 4-hop per link system, and that is without considering any loss of capacity due to additional overhead signals. Figure 8 shows the capacity gain obtained from a multihop cellular network when a 10% overhead is considered for each of the multiple hops of the communication link. It can be observed from Figure 7 that the capacity gain is highest when the maximum number of multiple hops between the MS and the BS is either two or three hops. For

higher number of multiple hops, the total amount of overhead signal required also increases which reduces the increase in the system capacity. Hence, in a practical system, it is not practical to have more than 3 to 4 hops per link. In addition, as the number of multiple hops per link is increased, the end-to-end delay between the source and destination also increases. The effect of delay is however not considered in this research work. Also, in practice, it is very difficult to maintain

Figure 6. System capacity variation for different number of multiple hops per link and for different values of path-loss exponent, α, for a system with 19 BSs in the coverage area

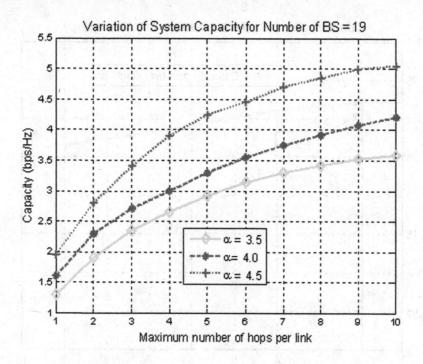

Figure 7. System capacity variation for different number of multiple hops per link and for different values of path-loss exponent, α, for a system with 30 BSs in the coverage area

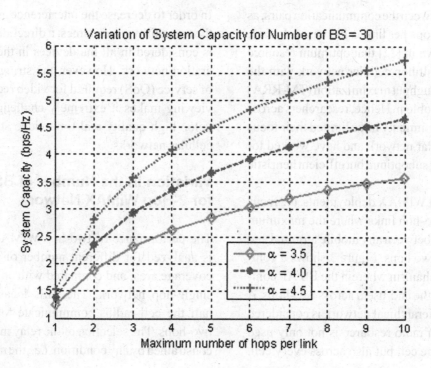

Figure 8. Capacity gain for a multihop multi-cellular system (19 BSs in the coverage area) with 10% overhead for each of the multiple hops

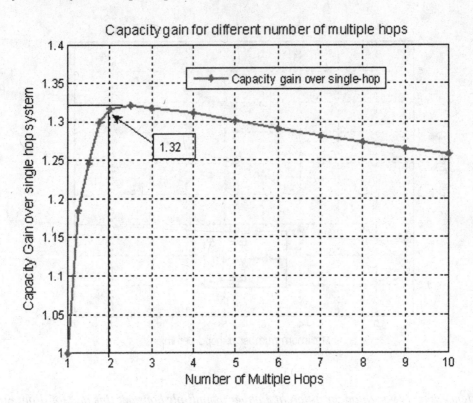

co-operation between the communication pairs, as the number of hops per link is increased. In fact, it has been shown in [22] that optimum resource allocation in multihop cellular network with the objective of throughput maximization (TM-RRA) is an NP-hard problem. Hence, researchers across the scientific community have limited their focus to a 2-hop cellular network and have worked towards designing suboptimal but efficient heuristic algorithms.

In the current WiMAX deployments, the focus mainly is on two-hop links where the maximum number of hops between any mobile terminal and the BS is only two hops. Figure 3 shows a communication mechanism wherein the BS/AP communicates with the end-users across two-hops. A multi-cellular hierarchical network is considered wherein a given radio resource is not only used twice in the same cell but also across every cell.

In order to decrease the interference and increase the reusability of resources, a directional antenna is considered in all the devices in the next generation network. However, the stringent quality of service (QoS) required for video reception and viewing makes it extremely challenging to develop high quality real-time video streaming in cellular networks.

Variation in the Number of BSs for 2-Hop WiMAX Network

The performance of two-hop WiMAX network is analyzed for different number of BSs in the coverage area, and compared with an equivalent single-hop network. The MSs located beyond half the cell radius communicate to the BS in two-hops. The selection of the relay mobile is not constrained by any condition, i.e., the mobile node

Figure 9. System capacity variation with number of BSs in the coverage area for single-hop and 2-hop cellular network

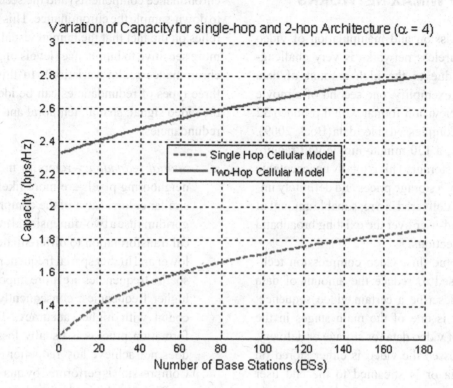

that is selected as a relay for a particular end-to-end link could be equidistant from the source and destination, or it could be very close to the source or destination. This flexibility in the selection of relay provides a wide range of choice as to which a mobile terminal could be selected as a relay. A deeper study in the selection of relays will be described later in the chapter, while developing the cluster-based architecture. The main aim of this subsection is to evaluate the performance of a two-hop cellular network with different numbers of BSs in the system.

It can be observed from Figure 9 that as the number of BSs in the given coverage area is increased, the system capacity increases for both single-hop and two-hop cellular network. However, the rate of capacity increase is much higher for single-hop network than for two-hop design. With an increase in the number of BSs from 18 to 180, the capacity of single-hop cellular network

increases from 1.38 bps/Hz to 1.87 bps/Hz, an increase of 35.5%. However, for the two-hop cellular design, this increase is only 14.6%, (2.4 bps/Hz to 2.81 bps/Hz). This is because, for a two-hop design, the relays help in balancing the traffic. In case a relay node is over-loaded, the wireless terminals communicate through another relay node that has less traffic. This is implemented by checking the buffer of each possible relay node, before selecting the particular wireless terminal as the relay node. The node that has the least number of packets in its buffer to be transmitted, and the node which is in the direction of the destination node is selected as the relay node, for a given communication link. Hence, the rate of increase of the system capacity is much lower for the two-hop design.

VIDEO TRANSMISSION OVER MULTIHOP WiMAX NETWORKS

Video transmission and manipulation of video content in wireless networks is very challenging, mainly due to the high amount of data involved. To exemplify, one second of a movie in standard television format would produce 32 Mbytes of uncompressed video data (Bock, 2009). Consequently, a 120 minute movie will require 230 Gbytes of storage. This is totally unacceptable even for today's storage prices and definitely impossible to be delivered in a reasonable amount of time to the end-user over the existing broadband Internet connections.

To overcome this, video compression techniques are used to reduce the amount of data required to describe a certain video sequence. Compression is one of the main stages in the preparation of video data for storage or delivery. Once compressed the video is either stored on various media or is streamed to the end user over wired or wireless networks. Unlike storage media, transport networks may introduce certain level of unreliability leading to possible delays in delivering chunks of video data or even total loss of data. As a consequence the compressed video has to be further prepared for transmission in the form of data streams composed of data packets with specific formats and bearing specific information regarding synchronization, loss and error detections as well as error concealment. In the following sections, video compression and content delivery over various types of networks is discussed.

Principles of Video Compression

Video compression algorithms rely on a good understanding of the human psycho-visual perception system which permits the exploitation of redundancies in the video signals. Based on this knowledge, one of the first steps in video compression is to use the YUV format (where Y denotes and the luminance and U and V are the chrominance components) and the second step is to down-sample the chrominance. This technique relies on the fact that the human visual system is more sensitive to luminance (levels of gray) than chrominance (color variation). In this context, three types of redundancies can be identified in the video signal: spatial, temporal and statistical redundancies.

a. *Spatial redundancy* refers to the fact that neighboring pixels are more likely to have similar colors. Most of the compression algorithms use a two-dimensional mathematical transformation to differentiate between lower and higher spatial frequencies. Lower spatial frequencies are more important than higher frequencies; consequently they are coded with higher accuracy. The transformation process is usually loss-less and does not achieve any reduction in bitrate. Compression is performed by quantizing the coefficients obtained after the transformation process. Quantization involves loss of information; consequently the decompressed image will be different to a certain extent from the original image. The most popular transformation is the discrete cosine transform (DCT) used by the MPEG compression algorithms and is usually applied on blocks of 8×8 pixels. However the size of the blocks can be varied to trade efficiency for complexity and spatial variation.

b. *Statistical redundancy* is exploited by assigning shorter codewords to symbols appearing more often longer codewords to less often ones. After the quantization process is performed each block in the transform domain will contain a large number of zero coefficients, mostly corresponding to the higher frequencies. Special coding techniques have been developed to combine a number of zero coefficients with the level of the next non-zero coefficients in a single codeword.

Various combinations of zero and non-zero coefficients are assigned variable-length codes (VLC) according to their frequency of apparition. The block in transform domain is scanned from low to high frequencies in such a way that the last non-zero coefficient is reached as soon as possible.

c. *Temporal redundancy* relies on the fact that usually there is little difference between consecutive frames in a video sequence. Based on this, by calculating the difference between the frame to be encoded and the previous frame the bitrate is reduced by encoding only this prediction error, as the frame difference requires fewer coefficients to encode. If the motion level is too high and the inter-frame difference is significantly greater, the compression efficiency of this technique is rapidly lost. To overcome this, motion compensation is used. Motion compensation is a technique which compares the currently processed block of pixels with a reference block taken from a different location in the previous frame. The reference block is searched in a larger area in the previous frame in order to estimate the motion within the video sequence. The position of the chosen reference block is then sent to the decoder as a motion vector. The motion prediction can also be performed by comparing the current frame with future frames. Consequently there is a forward, backward and bi-directional motion prediction.

Although most of the existing video encoders exploit the same redundancies in the video signal there are various approaches and algorithms which led to the development of different video encoding standards both public and proprietary. Among the best known standards are the MPEG family developed by the Moving Picture Experts Group (MPEG) which includes MPEG1, MPEG2, MPEG3 and MPEG4. The H.26x family of video encoding standards is also well known and was developed by International Telecommunication Union (ITU) through the Telecommunication Standardization Sector (ITU-T). This family includes ITU-T R. H.261, ITU-T R. H.262, ITU-T R. H.263 and the latest standard which is ITU-T R. H.264. These standards have been developed in parallel with the MPEG working group and sometimes the two organizations have jointly coordinated their activities leading to H.26x standards to be similar and sometimes identical with the MPEG standards.

Video Content Delivery

Multimedia content delivery is well known from the days of TV broadcasting services. However, currently, with the development of other multimedia based services like video-on-demand or video conferencing, unicast and multicast content delivery becomes increasingly popular approach to multimedia content delivery. *Broadcasting* has the main advantage of cost effectiveness in terms of bandwidth. Delivering the same content to multiple users in the same time significantly reduces network resource utilization. The users are more likely to prefer video-on-demand services (Hartung *et. al.*, 2007); consequently this may decrease the popularity of broadcasting services. *Unicast* has the main advantage of supporting video-on-demand services as well as broadcast services. Another benefit of unicast is that network resources are used only when there is a user requiring a certain service (Hartung *et. al.*, 2007). In the context of multimedia delivery to mobile devices unicast presents the benefit of supporting content adaptation for each user separately in order to meet their device capabilities and networking resources. *Multicast* is beneficial especially for group content delivery in applications like video conferencing. However the management of multicast groups is difficult and complex. Various wireless solutions have been proposed to address multimedia content delivery to mobile users. Three typical categories can be identified: DVB-based solutions which enhance the Digital Video Broadcasting standard for mobile devices (handheld), solution enhancing the third generation cellular networks including UMTS with Multimedia Broadcast Multicast Service (MBMS) support and content delivery solutions exploiting the widespread popularity of WLAN (802.11 - WiFi).

Multimedia Streaming in Cellular Networks

In cellular networks, multimedia delivery has been introduced starting from the 2.5G technologies and continuing with current 3G technologies and towards the emerging 4G networks. The packet-switched streaming (PSS) standard developed by the Third Generation Partnership Project (3GPP) provides the means of content transportation for streaming and downloading applications. PSS uses various protocols for content delivery and information exchange. Content is delivered using Real Time Transport Protocol (RTP) over User Datagram Protocol (UDP) as underlying transport protocol. Other types of media including text and graphics are delivered over the HTTP protocol. The Real Time Streaming Protocol (RTSP) is used for control information exchange. PSS supports user quality of experience monitoring which permits content adaptation for improved user satisfaction. Apart from the transport mechanisms, PSS also specifies a set of media codecs including Adaptive Multi-rate (AMR), H.263, H.264, MPEG-4 Advanced Video Codec (AVC) and MPEG-4. For further improvement of user perceived quality PSS also includes an Adaptive Streaming feature (Frojdh *et al.*, 2006) which is useful for adapting the content to network condition variations as well as variations in network characteristics due to handovers between systems (Hartung *et al.*, 2007) like GPRS to WCDMA and vice-versa. The IP Multimedia Subsystem (IMS) (Cuevas *et al.*, 2006) was developed within 3GPP as a service platform to provide multimedia services over 3G networks.

IMS uses the Session Initiation Protocol (SIP) for signaling and session control, RTP for media transport and IPv6 at the network layer. The IMS platform is not directly involved in media transport (only in session control) (Cuevas *et. al.*, 2006), but QoS is maintained by collaboration between the IMS platform and the transport network. The Policy Decision Function (PDF) is the IMS sub-module which is responsible for QoS negotiation according to the application requirements. 3GPP also proposed the Multimedia Broadcast/Multicast Service (MBMS) for UMTS (3GPP, 2006). MBMS delivers multimedia content to a group of users in a point-to-multipoint manner using UMTS MBMS transmission bearer. MBMS is composed of two modules, the MBMS bearer service which deals with transmission procedures below the IP layer and the MBMS user service which manages streaming and downloading methods and procedures. The streaming methods used by MBMS are similar to PSS in terms of transfer protocols (e.g. RTP) and codecs. Broadcast and Multicast Services (BCMCS) (3GPP2, 2006) protocol is similar with MBMS but was developed by 3GPP2 for the CDMA2000 protocol family for 3G networks. Similar to MBMS, BCMCS provides point-to-multipoint content delivery and guarantees QoS for two way multimedia applications. Content adaptation may be performed using SVC which was also introduced in MPEG-4 standard as FGS (MPEG-4 FGS) (Kang & Kim, 2009).

DVB-Based Multimedia Delivery

The Digital Video Broadcasting (DVB) standards offer point-to-multipoint data services with high data rates for multimedia (especially TV) content delivery to end users. Apart from the satellite versions (DVB-S), DVB also standardized a terrestrial wireless data service through DVB-T. Although DVB-T broadcasts multimedia content to static and mobile users, including vehicular receivers, it is not optimized for highly mobile handheld devices. Consequently, Digital Video Broadcasting (DVB)

Project has developed DVB-H (handheld) (DVB, 2004) for multimedia content delivery to mobile devices. DVB-H specifies only the protocol layers below the network layer; consequently an Internet Protocol (IP) interface for higher transport layers which are defined by the IP-based Data Broadcast (IP Datacast) specification was introduced. IP Datacast specified the protocols for higher layers in concordance with the Internet protocol stack. For transport layer UDP was chosen with RTP for real-time media broadcasting and File Delivery over Unidirectional Transport (FLUTE) for non real-time data transfer like download-based media delivery. For media encoding DVB-H aims for high compatibility between network components and terminals. Therefore MPEG-4/H.264 has been chosen for video encoding as well as the Microsoft Windows Media 9 based VC-1 codec. For audio, MPEG 4 AAC+ is recommended. IP Datacast has been developed towards a hybrid interoperability of several types of networks in order to benefit of their advantages and balance their disadvantages. DVB-H has the advantage of being highly scalable with the number of users unlike cellular networks or WLANs which are basically point-to-point and suffer from severe QoS drops when congested. On the other hand DVB-H interactivity is quite limited. Considering these aspects using a hybrid solution where the content management layer decides which network to use for delivery of a certain service depending on its popularity (the number of users requesting the same service at the same time) or its interactivity requirements may improve the overall quality of the service as perceived by the user.

Multimedia Delivery over Multihop Wireless Networks

In a multi-hop network the source and destination communicate with each other over multiple hops, each hop being represented by a client node or a dedicated router in charge of relaying the traffic as part of one or several paths or routes. As men-

tioned before, multi-hop wireless networks have the advantage of flexibility as well as cheap and easy deployment. However this type of network suffers from a lack of QoS guarantee, especially in terms of delay. Under these circumstances a packet transporting video data has to travel over multiple wireless links from its source (e.g., media server) to the destination (i.e., end-user). Each link being shared by other neighboring nodes the issue of link congestion and quality appears separately for each hop. This may affect significantly the packet delay and packet delay jitter. Each separate hop being a wireless link is prone to transmission errors leading to packet loss.

Depending on the specific of the application and the video content, especially the encoding scheme used, these aspects concerning QoS levels offered by the multi-hop network may negatively affect the video quality of the delivered content. For example, a video conferencing application where interaction between users is important the delay in delivering data packets may have a strong negative impact. The same would happen in the case of on-line gaming applications. On the other hand, a video-on-demand application may not be affected so severely by the packet delay as user interaction with the application is minimal. However delay jitter may have more significant impact as it may determine some packets to arrive too late to be decoded and displayed adding in this way to the packet loss levels. Packet loss on the other hand has a significant impact on video quality and consequently on user satisfaction.

All these effects can be minimized by using intelligent routing mechanism and minimizing the number of hops between the source and destination. By maintaining the number of hops to a minimum, the QoS levels received by the two pairs can be improved while still benefiting from the advantages of using multi-hop wireless networks. However, on the other hand, disseminating video content over large multihop may benefit from the existence of various chunks of the same video in transit. In this way several users demanding the same content at different time may aggregate the packets in transit at their nearest neighbors avoiding the delays and maybe packet loss involved by transiting the data over multiple hops separately.

CONCLUSION

This chapter introduces the IEEE 802.16 standards and its different sub-groups. Further, the chapter explains the importance of 802.16j multihop WiMAX standard and its different components, that includes relaying concept, spatial reuse and interference modeling. Importantly, the wireless cellular network is analyzed in detail for different number of multiple hops. It is found that the system capacity of a multihop network initially increases exponentially (till 3 to 4 hops) and then linearly (till around 6 hops), after which it remains almost constant. This is an interesting result, which indicates that multihop WiMAX holds great significance, as long as the number of multiple hops is not increased beyond a certain value. Also, the complexity of dynamic and adaptive resource allocation over a generalized multihop networks is a major issue that hinders its implementation. Hence, the focus in practical design of multihop WiMAX has been geared towards two-hop networks. Notably, a two-hop WiMAX network shows a significantly superior performance, up to 2.5 times as compared to a single-hop network, and the exact improvement depends on the number of BSs in the network. At the same time, video transmission, though well developed on its own, is a huge challenge to implement in multihop networks, especially in case of real-time transmission. This is still an open problem that would have to be investigated further over the coming years.

REFERENCES

Ananthapadmanabha, R., Manoj, B. S., & Murthy, C. S. R. (2001, October). Multihop cellular networks: The architecture and routing protocol. In *Proceedings of IEEE International Symposium on Personal Indoor Mobile Radio Communications* (PIMRC'01), San Diego, USA, (vol. 2, pp. 78–82).

Arikon, E. (1984, July). Some complexity results about packet radio networks. *IEEE Transactions on Information Theory*, *30*(4), 910–918.

Bock, A. M. (2009). *Video compression systems. Institution of Engineering & Technology*. IET.

Chlamtac, I., & Kutten, S. (1985, January). A spatial reuse TDMA/FDMA for mobile multi-hop radio networks. In *Proceedings of IEEE International Conference on Computer Communications* INFOCOM), Washington DC, USA, (vol. 1, pp. 389–394).

Chlamtac, I., & Lerner, A. (1985, December). *A link allocation protocol for mobile multihop radio networks*. In *Proceedings of IEEE Global Communications Conference* (GLOBECOM), New Orleans, Los Angeles, USA, (vol. 1, pp. 238-242).

Chlamtac, I., & Pinter, S. (1987, June). Distributed nodes organization algorithm for channel access in a multihop dynamic radio network. *IEEE Transactions on Computers*, *36*(6), 728–737. doi:10.1109/TC.1987.1676965

Cuevas, A., Moreno, J., Vidales, P., & Einsiedler, H. (2006, August). The IMS service platform: A solution for next-generation network operators to be more than bit pipes. *IEEE Communications Magazine*, *44*(8), 75–81. doi:10.1109/MCOM.2006.1678113

DVB. (2004, November). *Transmission system for handheld terminals (DVB-H)*. ETSI EN 302304 v1.1.1. Digital Video Broadcasting (DVB) Std.

Etemad, K., & Lai, M. Y. (2010). *WiMAX technology and network evolution*. IEEE Communication Society Press. doi:10.1002/9780470633021

Frojdh, P., Horn, U., Kampmann, M., Nohlgren, A., & Westerlund, M. (2006, March). Adaptive streaming within the 3GPP packet-switched streaming service. *IEEE Network*, 20(2), 34–40. doi:10.1109/MNET.2006.1607894

Funabiki, N., & Takefuji, Y. (1993). A parallel algorithm for broadcast scheduling problems in packet radio networks. *IEEE Transactions on Communications*, 41(6), 828–831. doi:10.1109/26.231903

Gastpar, M., & Vetterli, M. (2002, June). On the capacity of wireless networks: The relay case. In *Proceedings of IEEE International Conference on Computer Communications* (INFOCOM), 23-27 June 2002, (vol. 3, pp. 1577–1586).

3GPP2. (2006, April). *Broadcast multicast service for CDMA2000 1x systems C.S0077 rev. 1.0.* 3GPP2 Std.

3GPP. (2006, March). *Multimedia broadcast/multicast service (MBMS): Stage 1 (release 7).* (Tech. Rep. 3G TS 22.146 V7.1.0). 3GPP Std.

Groenkvist, J., & Hansson, A. (2001, October). Comparison between graph based and interference based STDMA scheduling. In *Proceedings of ACM International Symposium on Mobile Ad hoc Networking and Computing* (MOBIHOC), Long Beach, California, USA, (pp. 255–258).

Gupta, P., & Kumar, P. R. (2000, February). The capacity of wireless networks. *IEEE Transactions on Information Theory*, 46(2), 388–404. doi:10.1109/18.825799

Hajek, B., & Sasaki, G. (1998, September). Link scheduling in polynomial time. *IEEE Transactions on Information Theory*, 34(5), 910–917. doi:10.1109/18.21215

Hartung, F., Horn, U., Huschke, J., Kampmann, M., Lohmar, T., & Lundevall, M. (2007, March). Delivery of broadcast services in 3G networks. *IEEE Transactions on Broadcasting*, 53(1), 188–199. doi:10.1109/TBC.2007.891711

IEEE. (2011, February). *IEEE Get Program*. Retrieved from http://standards.ieee.org/about/get/802/802.11.html

Jain, K., Padhye, J., Padmanabhan, V., & Qiu, L. (2003, September). Impact of interference on multi-hop wireless network performance. In *Proceedings of ACM Mobile Computing and Networking* (MOBICOM), San Diego, USA, (vol. 2, pp. 66–80).

Kang, K., & Kim, T. (2009, January). Improved error control for real-time video broadcasting over CDMA2000 networks. *IEEE Transactions on Vehicular Technology*, 58(1), 188–197. doi:10.1109/TVT.2008.926077

Li, H., Yu, D., & Chen, H. (2003, September). New approach to multihop - Cellular based multihop network. In *Proceedings of IEEE International Symposium on Personal Indoor and Mobile Radio Communications* (PIMRC'03), Beijing, China, (vol. 2, pp. 1629–1633).

Lin, Y. D., Hsu, Y. C., Oyang, K. W., Tsai, T. C., & Yang, D. S. (2000, December). Multihop wireless IEEE 802.11 LANs: A prototype implementation. *Journal of Communications and Networks*, 2(4).

Liu, Y., Hoshyar, R., Yang, X., & Tafazolli, R. (2006, November). Integrated radio resource allocation for multihop cellular networks with fixed relay stations. *IEEE Journal on Selected Areas in Communications*, 24(11), 2137–2146. doi:10.1109/JSAC.2006.881603

Manoj, B. S., Ananthapadmanabha, R., & Murthy, C. S. R. (2002, March). Multi-hop cellular networks: The architecture and routing protocol for best-effort and real-time communication. In *Proceedings of Inter Research Institute Student Seminar in Computer Science*. Bangalore, India: IRISS.

Manoj, B. S., & Murthy, C. S. R. (2002, June). *A high-performance wireless local loop architecture utilizing directional multi-hop relaying*. Department of Computer Science and Engineering, Indian Institute of Technology, Madras, India, Technical Report.

Murthy, C. S. R., & Manoj, B. S. (2004). *Ad hoc wireless networks: Architectures and protocols*. Prentice Hall.

Nelson, R., & Kleinrock, L. (1985, September). Spatial TDMA: A collision free multihop channel access protocol. *IEEE Transactions on Communications*, *33*(9), 934–944. doi:10.1109/TCOM.1985.1096405

Samaribba, O. (1995, October). *Multihop packet radio systems in rough terrain*. Department of S3, Radio Communication Systems, Stockholm, Sweden, Tech. Lic, Thesis SE 10044.

Sekar, V., Manoj, B. S., & Murthy, C. S. R. (2003, May). *Routing for a single interface MCN architecture and pricing schemes for data traffic in multihop cellular networks*. In *Proceedings of IEEE International Conference on Communications* (ICC'03), Alaska, USA, (vol. 2, pp. 969–973).

Sobhrinho, J., & Krishnakumar, A. (1999, August). Quality-of-service in ad hoc carrier sense multiple access wireless networks. *IEEE Journal on Selected Areas in Communications*, *17*(8), 1353–1368. doi:10.1109/49.779919

Tonguz, O. K., & Ferrari, G. (2006). *Ad hoc wireless networks: A communication-theoretic perspective*. John Wiley and Sons, Ltd. doi:10.1002/0470091126

Vishwanathan, H., & Mukherjee, S. (2005, September). Performance of cellular networks with relays and centralized scheduling. *IEEE Transactions on Wireless Communications*, *4*, 2318–2328. doi:10.1109/TWC.2005.853820

Wu, H., Qao, C., De, S., & Tonguz, O. (2001, October). Integrated cellular and ad hoc relaying systems. *IEEE Journal on Selected Areas in Communications*, *19*(10), 2105–2115. doi:10.1109/49.957326

Wu, X., Chan, S. H. G., & Mukherjee, B. (2000, September). MADF: A novel approach to add an ad hoc overlay on a fixed cellular infrastructure. In *Proceedings of IEEE Wireless Communications and Networking Conference* (WCNC'00), Chicago, USA, (pp. 549–554).

Zander, J. (1991, October). Jamming in slotted ALOHA multihop packet radio networks. *IEEE Transactions on Communications*, 39.

Zemlinanov, A., & Veciana, G. (2005, March). Capacity of ad hoc wireless networks with infrastructure support. *IEEE Journal on Selected Areas in Communications*, *23*(3), 657–667. doi:10.1109/JSAC.2004.842536

KEY TERMS AND DEFINITIONS

Air-Interface: Radio-based communication link between the mobile station and the active base station.

Cellular Networks: Radio network distributed over land areas called cells, each served by at least one fixed-location transceiver known as a cell site.

Interference: Interference is the unwanted signal/information that interferes and disturbs the desired signal.

Multihop Networks: A communication mechanism wherein the information is transmitted from transmitter to receiver in multiple hops, through intermediate nodes.

Multimedia Delivery: Information delivered over different medium like voice, images, video, audio, etc.

Radio Resource: A time/frequency or any other resource over which the information is transmitted.

Spatial Reuse: Reusability of resources across space.

System Capacity: Ability of the medium to carry information per unit resource.

Video Compression: Reduce the size of the video file without significantly reducing the video quality.

WiMAX: New global wireless standard by the name "Worldwide Interoperability for Microwave Access".

Compilation of References

3GPP. (2006, March). *Multimedia broadcast/multicast service (MBMS): Stage 1 (release 7).* (Tech. Rep. 3G TS 22.146 V7.1.0). 3GPP Std.

3GPP2. (2006, April). *Broadcast multicast service for CDMA2000 1x systems C.S0077 rev. 1.0.* 3GPP2 Std.

Abidi, A., Rofougaran, A., Chang, G., Rael, J., Chang, J., Rofougaran, M., et al. (1997, 6-8 February). *The future of CMOS wireless transceivers.* Paper presented at the 1997 43rd ISSCC IEEE International Solid-State Circuits Conference, Digest of Technical Papers.

ADS. (2009, October). Momentum pdf manual. *Update*, 1.

Agnelli, F., Albasini, G., Bietti, I., Gnudi, A., Lacaita, A., & Manstretta, D. (2006). Wireless multi-standard terminals: system analysis and design of a reconfigurable RF front-end. *IEEE Circuits and Systems Magazine*, 6(1), 38–59. doi:10.1109/MCAS.2006.1607637

Aguirre, P., & Silveira, F. (2008). CMOS op-amp power optimization in all regions of inversion using geometric programming. *21st Symposium on Integrated Circuits and System Design, SBCCI* (pp. 152–157).

Ahmed, M., Saraydar, C. U., El Batt, T., Yin, J., Talty, T., & Ames, M. (2007). Intra vehicular wireless networks. In [November.]. *Proceedings of Globecom, 2007*, 1–9.

Ahola, R. (2005). *Integrated radio frequency synthesizers for wireless applications.* Ph.D. thesis. Helsinki University of Technology, Electronic Circuit Design Laboratory, Helsinki, Finland.

Akcasu, O. E. (1993). *High capacitance structures in a semiconductor device.* (U.S. Patent 5 208 725).

Ala-Laurila, J., Mikkonen, J., & Rinnemaa, J. (2001). Wireless LAN access network architecture for mobile operators. *IEEE Communications Magazine*, 39(11), 82–89. doi:10.1109/35.965363

Alamouti, S. M. (1998). A simple transmit diversity technique for wireless communications. *IEEE Journal on Selected Areas in Communications*, 16(8). doi:10.1109/49.730453

Allan, R. (2006, November 6). MOST: A cooperative development effort. *Electronic design - The authority on emerging technologies for design solutions.*

Ananthapadmanabha, R., Manoj, B. S., & Murthy, C. S. R. (2001, October). Multihop cellular networks: The architecture and routing protocol. In *Proceedings of IEEE International Symposium on Personal Indoor Mobile Radio Communications* (PIMRC'01), San Diego, USA, (vol. 2, pp. 78–82).

Andreani, P., & Sjland, H. (2001). Noise optimization of an inductively degenerated CMOS low noise amplifier. *IEEE Transactions on Circuits and Systems*, 48(9), 835–841. doi:10.1109/82.964996

Andreas, P., & Zimdahl, W. (1983). The driver information of the Volkswagen research car auto 2000. [May.]. *IEEE Transactions on Industrial Electronics*, 30(2), 132–137. doi:10.1109/TIE.1983.356722

Antao, B. A. A., El-Turky, F. M., & Leonowich, R. H. (1996). Behavioral modeling phase-locked loops for mixed-mode simulation. *Analog Integrated Circuits and Signal Processing*, 10.

Aparicio, R., & Hajimiri, A. (2002). Capacity limits and matching properties of integrated capacitors. *IEEE Journal of Solid-state Circuits*, *37*(3), 384–393. doi:10.1109/4.987091

Aparin, V., Brown, G., & Larson, L. E. (2004). Linearization of CMOS LNA'S via optimum gate biasing. *IEEE Transaction on Circuit and Systems-II*, *4*, 748–751.

Aparin, V., & Larson, L. E. (2005). Modified derivative superposition method for linearizing FET low-noise amplifiers. *IEEE Transactions on Microwave Theory and Techniques*, *53*(2), 548–551. doi:10.1109/TMTT.2004.840635

Arcioni, P., Castello, R., De Astis, G., Sacchi, E., & Svelto, F. (1998). Measurement and modeling of Si integrated inductors. *IEEE Transactions on Instrumentation and Measurement*, *47*(5), 1372–1378. doi:10.1109/19.746613

Arikon, E. (1984, July). Some complexity results about packet radio networks. *IEEE Transactions on Information Theory*, *30*(4), 910–918.

Armacost, M., Augustin, A., Felsner, P., Feng, Y., Friese, G., & Heidenreich, J. ... Stein, K. (2000, December). *A high reliability metal insulator metal capacitor for 0.18 µm copper technology.* Paper presented at the IEEE International Electron Devices Meeting, San Francisco, CA.

Armstrong, E. H. (1924). The super-heterodyne □ Its origin, development, and some recent improvements. *Proceedings of the IRE*, *50*, 539–552. doi:10.1109/JRPROC.1924.219990

Ashby, K. B., Kuollias, I. A., Finley, W. C., Bastek, J. J., & Moinian, S. (1996). High Q inductor for wireless applications in a complementary silicon bipolar process. *IEEE Journal of Solid-state Circuits*, *33*(1), 4–9. doi:10.1109/4.485838

Ayazi, F., & Najafi, K. (2000). High aspect-ratio combined poly and single-crystal silicon (HARPSS) MEMS technology. *Journal of Microelectromechanical Systems*, *9*(3), 288–294. doi:10.1109/84.870053

Azevedo, R. G., Jones, D. G., Jog, A. V., Jamshidi, B., Myers, D. R., & Chen, L. (2007). A SiC MEMS resonant strain sensor for harsh environment application. *IEEE Sensors Journal*, *7*(4), 568–586. doi:10.1109/JSEN.2007.891997

Baghelani, M., & Ghavifekr, H. B. (2009 August). New design of RF MEMS disk resonators and optimization for spurious modes. *European Conference on Circuit Theory and Design*, (pp. 894-897). Antalya, Turkey.

Baghelani, M., & Ghavifekr, H. B. (2010 May). A new high reliable structure of micro-electro-mechanical radial contour mode disk resonators for UHF application. *18th Iranian Conference on Electrical Engineering* (ICEE), (pp. 386-390). Isfahan, Iran.

Baghelani, M., & Ghavifekr, H. B. (2010). Ring shape anchored RF MEMS contour mode disk resonator for UHF communication applications. *Microsystem Technologies*, *16*(12), 2123–2130. doi:10.1007/s00542-010-1143-4

Bahl, I. J. (1999). Improved quality factor spiral inductors on GaAs substrates. *Microwave and Guided Wave Letters*, *9*(10), 398–400. doi:10.1109/75.798028

Bahl, I. J. (2001). High-performance inductors. *IEEE Transactions on Microwave Theory and Techniques*, *49*(4), 654–664. doi:10.1109/22.915439

Bahl, I. J. (2003). *Lumped elements for RF and microwave circuits*. Norwood, MA: Artech House.

Bakri-Kassem, M., Fouladi, S., & Mansour, R. R. (2008). Novel high-Q MEMS curled-plate variable capacitors fabricated in 0.35- m CMOS technology. *IEEE Transactions on Microwave Theory and Techniques*, *56*(2), 530–541. doi:10.1109/TMTT.2007.914657

Baldwin, G., & Ruiz, L. (2006, May). *Reconfigurable transceiver architecture: Front end hardware requirements.* Colloquium on Physical Layers Wireless Communications.

Baltes, H., Brand, O., Fedder, G., Hierold, C., Korvink, J., & Tabata, O. (2005). *CMOS MEMS (Vol. 2)*. Weinhem, Germany: Wiley-VCH.

Baltes, H., Paul, O., & Brand, O. (1998). Micromachined thermally based CMOS microsensors. *Proceedings of the IEEE*, *86*(8), 1660–1678. doi:10.1109/5.704271

Bannon, F. D., III, Clark, J. R., & Nguyen, C. T.-C. (1996 December). High frequency micromechanical IF filters. *International Electronic Devices Meeting*, (pp. 773–776). San Francisco, CA.

Bannon, F. D., Clark, J. R., & Nguyen, C. T. C. (2000). High-Q HF microelectromechanical filters. *IEEE Journal of Solid-state Circuits, 35*(4), 512–526. doi:10.1109/4.839911

Barbarossa, S., Pompili, M., & Giannakis, G. B. (2002, February). Channel-independent synchronization of orthogonal frequency division multiple access systems. *IEEE Journal on Selected Areas in Communications, 20*(2), 474–486. doi:10.1109/49.983375

Barboni, L., Fiorelli, R., & Silveira, F. (2006). A tool for design exploration and power optimization of CMOS RF circuit blocks. *IEEE International Symposium on Circuits and Systems, ISCAS*, (pp. 2961-2964).

Barker, N. S. (1999). *Distributed MEMS transmission lines*. Unpublished Doctoral dissertation, University of Michigan, Ann Arbor.

Barrak, R., Ghazel, A., & Ghannouchi, F. M. (2006, September). *Design and optimization of RF filters for multistandard RF subsampling receiver.* Paper presented at the IEEE International Conference of Design and Test of Integrated Systems, Tunis, Tunisia.

Barrak, R., Ghazel, A., & Ghannouchi, F. M. (2009). Optimized multistandard RF subsampling receiver architecture. *IEEE Transactions on Wireless Communications, 8*(6), 82–89. doi:10.1109/TWC.2009.070584

Bechir, D. M., & Ridha, B. (2010, April). *On the RF subsampling continuous-time ΣΔ downconversion stage for multistandard receivers.* Paper presented at the IEEE Conference on Computer Engineering and Technology, Tunis, Tunisia.

Beek, J., Sandell, M., & Borjesson, P. O. (1997, July). ML estimation of time and frequency offset in OFDM systems. *IEEE Transactions on Signal Processing, 45,* 1800–1805. doi:10.1109/78.599949

Belostotski, L., & Haslett, J. (2006). Noise figure optimization of inductively degenerated CMOS LNAs with integrated gate inductors. *IEEE Transactions on Circuits and Systems, 53*(7), 1409–1422. doi:10.1109/TCSI.2006.875188

Bock, A. M. (2009). *Video compression systems. Institution of Engineering & Technology.* IET.

Booker, H. G. (1982). *Energy in electromagnetism.* London, UK: Peter Peregrinus (on behalf of the IEE).

Borwick, R. L. III, Stupar, P. A., DeNatale, J., Anderson, R., Tsai, C., Garrett, K., & Erlandson, R. (2002). A high Q, large tuning range MEMS capacitor for RF filter systems. *Sensors and Actuators. A, Physical, 103*(1-2), 33–41. doi:10.1016/S0924-4247(02)00316-3

Brandolini, M., Rossi, P., Manstretta, D., & Svelto, F. (2005). Toward multistandard mobile terminals – Fully integrated receivers requirements and architectures. *IEEE Transactions on Microwave Theory and Techniques, 53*(3), 1026–1038. doi:10.1109/TMTT.2005.843505

BSIM Research Group. (2009). *BSIM3v3 and BSIM4 MOS model.* Retrieved from http://www-device.eecs.berkeley.edu/~bsim3/bsim4.html

Buddhikot, M., Chandranmenon, G., Han, S., Lee, Y.-W., Miller, S., & Salgarelli, L. (2003). Design and implementation of a WLAN/CDMA2000 interworking architecture. *IEEE Communications Magazine, 41*(11), 90–100. doi:10.1109/MCOM.2003.1244928

Burghartz, J. N. (1998, December). *Progress in RF Inductors on silicon-understanding substrate losses.* Paper presented at the IEEE International Electron Devices Meeting, San Francisco, CA.

Burghartz, J. N. (2001). *Tailoring logic CMOS for RF applications.* Paper presented at the VLSI Technology Systems and Applications.

Burghartz, J. N., Edelstein, D. C., Souyer, M., Ainspan, H. A., & Jenkins, K. A. (1998). RF circuit aspects of spiral inductors on silicon. *IEEE Journal of Solid-state Circuits, 33*(12), 2028–2034. doi:10.1109/4.735544

Burns, P. (2002). *Software defined radio for 3G.* Boston, MA: Artech House.

Butler, J. W., Feygelson, J. E., & Nguyen, C. T.-C. (2004 September). 1.51 GHz nano crystalline diamond micromechanical disk resonators with material mismatched isolation support. 17th IEEE International Conference on MEMS, (pp. 641-644).

Caffarena, G., Fernández, A., Carreras, C., & Nieto-Taladriz, O. (2004). Fixed-point refinement of OFDM-based adaptive equalizers: a heuristic approach. In *European Signal Processing Conference* (pp. 1353–1356).

Caffarena, G., Carreras, C., López, J. A., & Fernández, A. (2010). SQNR estimation of fixed-point DSP algorithms. *EURASIP Journal on Advances in Signal Processing*, 2010.

Caffarena, G., Constantinides, G. A., Cheung, P. Y. K., Carreras, C., & Nieto-Taladriz, O. (2006). Optimal combined word length allocation and architectural synthesis of digital signal processing circuits. *IEEE Transactions on Circuits and Systems II*, 53(5), 339–343. doi:10.1109/TCSII.2005.862175

Callaway, E. Jr. (2004). The physical layer. In *Wireless sensor networks, architectures and protocols*. CRC Press.

Campanella, H., Cabruja, E., Montserrat, J., Uranga, A., Barniol, N., & Esteve, J. (2008). Thin-film bulk acoustic wave resonator floating above CMOS substrate. *Electron Device Letters*, 29(1), 28–30. doi:10.1109/LED.2007.910751

Cantin, M.-A., Savaria, Y., & Lavoie, P. (2002). A comparison of automatic word length optimization procedures. In *IEEE International Symposium on Circuits and Systems* (pp. 612–615).

Cao, Z. T., Yao, Y. D., & Honan, P. (2004b, November). Frequency synchronization for generalized OFDMA uplink. *Proceedings of IEEE Global Telecomunications Conference*, (vol. 2, pp. 1071-1075).

Cao, Y., Groves, R. A., Zamdmer, N. D., Plouchart, J. O., Wachnik, R. A., & Huang, X. (2003). Frequency-independent equivalent circuit model for on-chip spiral inductors. *IEEE Journal of Solid-state Circuits*, 38(3), 419–426. doi:10.1109/JSSC.2002.808285

Cao, Z. T., & Yao, Y. D. (2004a, September). Deterministic multiuser carrier frequency offset estimation for interleaved OFDMA uplink. *IEEE Transactions on Communications*, 52(9), 1585–1594. doi:10.1109/TCOMM.2004.833183

Catthoor, F., De Man, H., & Vandewalle, J. (1988). Simulated annealing based optimization of coefficient and data wordlengths in digital filters. *International Journal of Circuit Theory and Applications*, 16(4), 371–390. doi:10.1002/cta.4490160404

Chang, S., & Sivoththaman, S. (2006). A tunable RF MEMS inductor on silicon incorporating an amorphous silicon bimorph in a low-temperature process. *Electron Device Letters*, 27(11), 905–907. doi:10.1109/LED.2006.884712

Chan, K. T., Huang, C. H., Chin, A., Li, M. F., Kwong, D.-L., & McAlister, S. P. (2003). Large Q-factor improvement for spiral inductors on silicon using proton implantation. *IEEE Microwave and Wireless Components Letters*, 13(11), 460–462. doi:10.1109/LMWC.2003.819383

Chan, R., Lesnick, R., Becher, D., & Feng, M. (2003). Low-actuation voltage RF MEMS shunt switch with cold switching lifetime of seven billion cycles. *IEEE Journal of Microelectromechanical Systems*, 12(5), 713–719. doi:10.1109/JMEMS.2003.817889

Chao, C. J., Wong, S. C., Kao, C. H., Chen, M. J., Leu, L. Y., & Chiu, K. Y. (2002). Characterization and Modeling of on-chip spiral inductors for Si RFICs. *IEEE Transactions on Semiconductor Manufacturing*, 15(1), 19–29. doi:10.1109/TSM.2002.983440

Chee, Y. H., Niknejad, A. M., & Rabaey, J. (2005, 12-14 June 2005). *A sub-100 μW 1.9-GHz CMOS oscillator using FBAR resonator.* Paper presented at the Radio Frequency integrated Circuits (RFIC) Symposium, 2005, Digest of Papers.

Chen, Y. E., Bien, D., Heo, D., & Laskar, J. (2001, May). *Q-enhancement of spiral inductor with N+ diffusion patterned ground shields.* Paper presented IEEE MTT-S International Microwave Symposium, Phoenix, AZ.

Cheng, K.-H., & Jou, C. F. (2005, June). *A novel 2.4 GHz LNA with digital gain control using 0.18μM CMOS.* Paper presented at the meeting of Midwest Symposium, Cincinnati, Ohio

Chen, H. C., Chien, C. H., Chiu, H. W., Lu, S. S., Chang, K. N., & Chen, K. Y. (2005). A low-power low-phase-noise LC VCO with MEMS Cu inductors. *Microwave and Wireless Components Letters*, 15(6), 434–436. doi:10.1109/LMWC.2005.850565

Chen, J., & Liou, J. J. (2004). On-chip spiral inductors for RF applications: An overview. *Journal of Semiconductor Technology and Science*, 4(3).

Chen, K. S., & Ou, K. S. (2007). Command shaping techniques for electrostatic MEMS actuator analysis and simulation. *IEEE Journal of Microelectromechanical Systems*, *16*(3), 537–549. doi:10.1109/JMEMS.2007.893512

Chlamtac, I., & Kutten, S. (1985, January). A spatial reuse TDMA/FDMA for mobile multi-hop radio networks. In *Proceedings of IEEE International Conference on Computer Communications* INFOCOM), Washington DC, USA, (vol. 1, pp. 389–394).

Chlamtac, I., & Lerner, A. (1985, December). *A link allocation protocol for mobile multihop radio networks*. In *Proceedings of IEEE Global Communications Conference* (GLOBECOM), New Orleans, Los Angeles, USA, (vol. 1, pp. 238-242).

Chlamtac, I., & Pinter, S. (1987, June). Distributed nodes organization algorithm for channel access in a multihop dynamic radio network. *IEEE Transactions on Computers*, *36*(6), 728–737. doi:10.1109/TC.1987.1676965

Cho, T., Kang, D., Dow, S., Heng, C. H., & Song, B. S. (2003, February). *A 2.4 GHz dual-mode 0.18 µm CMOS transceiver for Bluetooth and 802.11b*. Paper presented at the IEEE International Solid-State Circuits Conference, San Francisco, CA.

Choi, P., Park, H., Kim, S., Park, S., Nam, I., & Kim, T. W. (2003). An experimental coin-sized radio for extremely low-power WPAN: IEEE 802.15.4. applications at 2.4 GHz. *IEEE Journal of Solid-state Circuits*, *8*(12), 2258–2268. doi:10.1109/JSSC.2003.819083

Clark, J. R., Hsu, W.-T., & Nguyen, C. T.-C. (2000 December). High-Q VHF micromechanical contour-mode disk resonator. *Technical Digest, IEEE International Electronic Devices Meeting*, (pp. 493-496). San Francisco, CA.

Clark, J. R., Hsu, W.-T., Abdelmoneum, M. A., & Nguyen, C. T.-C. (2005). High q UHF micromechanical radial contour mode disk resonators. *IEEE Journal of Microelectromechanical Systems*, *14*(6), 1298–1310. doi:10.1109/JMEMS.2005.856675

Colvin, J. T., & Bhatia, S. S., & O, K. (1999). Effect of substrate resistances on LNA performance and a bondpad structure for reducing the effects in a silicon bipolar technology. *IEEE Journal of Solid-state Circuits*, *34*(9), 1339–1344. doi:10.1109/4.782095

Constantinides, G. (2003). Perturbation analysis for word-length optimization. In *IEEE Symposium on Field-Programmable Custom Computing Machines* (pp. 81–90).

Constantinides, G. A., Cheung, P. Y. K., & Luk, W. (1999). Truncation noise in fixed-point SFGs. *Electronics Letters*, *35*(23), 2013–2014. doi:10.1049/el:19991375

Constantinides, G. A., Cheung, P. Y. K., & Luk, W. (2003). Wordlength optimization for linear digital signal processing. *IEEE Transactions on Computer-Aided Design of Integrated Circuits and Systems*, *22*(10), 1432–1442. doi:10.1109/TCAD.2003.818119

Constantinides, G. A., & Woeginger, G. J. (2002). The complexity of multiple wordlength assignment. *Applied Mathematics Letters*, *15*(2), 137–140. doi:10.1016/S0893-9659(01)00107-0

Cramer, D. R., & Taggart, D. F. (2002, February). Design and manufacture of an affordable advanced-composite automobile body structure. In *Proceedings of 19th International Battery, Hybrid and Fuel Cell Electric Vehicle Symposium & Exhibition: 2002 EVS-19*, (p. 12).

Cranickx, J., & Donnay, D. (2003). 4G terminals: How are we going to design them? In *Design and Automation Conference* (pp. 79-84).

Craninckx, J., & Steyaert, M. S. J. (1997). A 1.8-z low-phase-noise CMOS VCO using optimized hollow spiral inductors. *IEEE Journal of Solid-state Circuits*, *32*(5). doi:10.1109/4.568844

Craninckx, J., & Steyart, M. S. J. (1995). A 1.8 GHz CMOS low noise voltage-controlled oscillator with prescalar. *IEEE Journal of Solid-state Circuits*, *30*(12), 1474–1482. doi:10.1109/4.482195

Crols, J., & Steyaert, M. (1997). *CMOS wireless transceiver design*. Dordrecht, The Netherlands: Kluwer Academic Publishers.

Cuevas, A., Moreno, J., Vidales, P., & Einsiedler, H. (2006, August). The IMS service platform: A solution for next-generation network operators to be more than bit pipes. *IEEE Communications Magazine*, *44*(8), 75–81. doi:10.1109/MCOM.2006.1678113

Cunha, A., Schneider, M., & Galup-Montoro, C. (1998). An MOS transistor model for analog circuit design. *IEEE Journal of Solid-state Circuits, 33*(10), 1510–1519. doi:10.1109/4.720397

Dahlmann, G. W., Yeatman, E. M., Young, P. R., Robertson, I. D., & Lucyszyn, S. (2001, August). MEMS high Q microwave inductors using solder surface tension self-assembly. *IEEE International Microwave Symposium*, (vol. 1, pp. 329-332). Phoenix, AZ.

Darabi, H., Chiu, J., Khorram, S., Kim, H.-J., Zhou, Z., & Chien, H.-M. (2005). A dual-mode 802.11b/Bluetooth radio in 0.35 μm CMOS. *IEEE Journal of Solid-state Circuits, 40*(3), 698–706. doi:10.1109/JSSC.2005.843597

Dec, A., & Suyama, K. (1997). Micromachined varactor with wide tuning range. *Electronics Letters, 33*(11), 922–924. doi:10.1049/el:19970628

Dec, A., & Suyama, K. (1998). Micromachined electro-mechanically tunable capacitors and their applications to RF IC's. *IEEE Transactions on Microwave Theory and Techniques, 46*(12), 2587–2596. doi:10.1109/22.739251

Dec, A., & Suyama, K. (2000). Microwave MEMS-based voltage-controlled oscillators. *IEEE Transactions on Microwave Theory and Techniques, 48*(11), 1943–1949. doi:10.1109/22.883875

Demirci, M. U., & Nguyen, C. T. C. (2005). *Single-resonator fourth-order micromechanical disk filters.* Paper presented at the IEEE Micro Electro Mechanical Systems Conference.

Demirci, M. U., & Nguyen, C. T.-C. (2003 Mars). Higher-mode free-free beam micromechanical resonators. Proceeding of the IEEE International Symposium on Frequency Control, (pp. 810–818).

Demirci, M. U., & Nguyen, C. T.-C. (2006). Mechanically corner-coupled square micro resonator array for reduced series motional resistance. *IEEE Journal of Microelectromechanical Systems, 15*(6), 1419–1436. doi:10.1109/JMEMS.2006.883588

Deparis, N. (2008). UWB in millimeter wave band with pulsed ILO. *IEEE Transactions on Circuits and Systems II, 55*(4), 339–343. doi:10.1109/TCSII.2008.918977

Dillinger, M., Madani, K., & Alonistioti, N. (2003). *Software defined radio: Architectures, systems, and functions.* New York, NY: Wiley.

DVB. (2004, November). *Transmission system for hand-held terminals (DVB-H).* ETSI EN 302304 v1.1.1. Digital Video Broadcasting (DVB) Std.

El Oualkadi, A. (2009). *5-GHz low phase noise CMOS LC-VCO with pgs inductor suitable for ultra-low power applications.* IEEE Mediterranean Microwave Symposium (MMS'09), Tangiers, Morocco.

ElBatt, T., Saraydar, C., Ames, M., & Talty, T. (2006). *Potential for intra vehicle wireless automotive sensor networks.* In *Proceedings of Sarnoff Symposium,* (pp. 1-4). March.

Enz, C. C., Scolari, N., & Yodprasit, U. (2005). Ultra low-power radio design for wireless sensor networks. In *Proceedings of IEEE International Workshop on Radio-Frequency Integration Technology: Integrated Circuits for Wideband Communication and Wireless Sensor Networks,* Singapore, December.

Enz, C. C., Hoiydi, A. E., Decotignie, J. D., & Peiris, V. (2004, August). WiseNET: An ultra low-power wireless sensor network solution. *IEEE Computer, 37*(8), 62–67. doi:10.1109/MC.2004.109

Enz, C. C., Krummenacher, F., & Vittoz, E. A. (1995). An analytical MOS transistor model valid in all regions of operation and dedicated to low voltage and low-current applications. *Analog Integrated Circuits and Signal Processing, 8,* 83–114. doi:10.1007/BF01239381

Enz, C., & Vittoz, E. (2006). *Charge-based MOS transistor modeling.* John Wiley and Sons. doi:10.1002/0470855460

Etemad, K., & Lai, M. Y. (2010). *WiMAX technology and network evolution.* IEEE Communication Society Press. doi:10.1002/9780470633021

ETSI. (2004). *Digital video broadcasting (DVB): Frame structure, channel coding and modulation for digital terrestrial television (DVB-T).* ETSI EN 300 744, November 2004.

Euisik, Y., & Kwang-Seok, Y. (2005, 5-9 June 2005). *Development of a wireless environmental sensor system and MEMS-based RF circuit components*. Paper presented at The 13th International Conference on Solid-State Sensors, Actuators and Microsystems, 2005, Digest of Technical Papers.

Fang, C. F., Chen, T., & Rutenbar, R. A. (2003). Floating-point error analysis based on affine arithmetic. In *IEEE International Conference on Acoustics, Speech, and Signal Processing* (pp. 561–564).

Fatahi, N., & Nabovati, H. (2010). *Sigma-delta modulation technique for low noise fractional-n frequency synthesizer*. 4th International Symposium on Communications, Control and Signal Processing, ISCCSP 2010, Limassol, Cyprus.

Fechtel, S. A. (2000, August). OFDM carrier and sampling frequency synchronization and its performance on stationary and mobile channels. *IEEE Transactions on Consumer Electronics, 54*(3).

Feder, M., & Weinstein, E. (1988, April). Parameter estimation of superimposed signals using the EM algorithm. *IEEE Transactions on Acoustics, Speech, and Signal Processing, 36*(12), 477–489. doi:10.1109/29.1552

Feng, Z., Zhang, W., Su, B. H., & Gupta, K. F. K. C., Bright, V., & Lee, Y.C. (1999, August). Design and modeling of RF MEMS tunable capacitors using electro-thermal actuators. *IEEE International Microwave Symposium,* (vol 4, pp. 1507-1510). Anaheim, CA.

Ferguson, A. T., Li, L., Nagaraj, V. T. B., Piekarski, B., & DeVoe, D. L. (2005). modeling and design of composite free-free beam piezoelectric resonators. *Sensors and Actuators. A, Physical, 118*(1), 63–69. doi:10.1016/S0924-4247(04)00540-0

Fernández-Herrero, A., Jiménez-Pacheco, A., Caffarena, G., & Casajus Quiros, J. (2006). Design and implementation of a hardware module for equalisation in a 4G MIMO receiver. In *International Conference on Field Programmable Logic and Applications* (pp. 765–768).

Fessler, J., & Hero, A. (1994, October). Space-alternating generalized expectation maximitation algorithm. *IEEE Transactions on Signal Processing, 42*(10), 2664–2677. doi:10.1109/78.324732

Filiol, N. M., Riley, T. A. D., Plett, C., & Copeland, M. A. (1998). An agile ISM band frequency synthesizer with built-in GMSK data modulation. *IEEE Journal of Solid-state Circuits, 7*(33), 998–1008. doi:10.1109/4.701242

Fiorelli, R., Peralías, E., & Silveira, F. (2011). LC-VCO design optimization methodology based on the g_m/I_D ratio for nanometer CMOS technologies. *IEEE Transactions on Microwave Theory and Techniques, 59*. doi:10.1109/TMTT.2011.2132735

Fischer, A. H., Lim, Y. K., Riess, P., Pompl, T., Zhang, B. C., & Chua, E. C. … von Glasow, A. (2008, April). *TDDB robustness of highly dense 65NM BEOL vertical natural capacitor with competitive area capacitance for RF and mixed-signal applications*. Paper presented at the IEEE International Reliability Physics Symposium, Phoenix, AZ.

Flandre, D., Viviani, A., Eggermont, J.-P., Gentinne, B., & Jespers, P. (1997). Improved synthesis of gain-boosted regulated-cascode CMOS stages using symbolic analysis and gm/ID methodology. *IEEE Journal of Solid-state Circuits, 32*(7), 1006–1012. doi:10.1109/4.597291

Flint, J. A., Ruddle, A. R., & May, A. E. (2003, April). Coupling between Bluetooth modules inside a passenger car. In *Proceedings of IEEE 12th International Conference on Antennas and Propagation, ICAP,* (pp. 397-400).

Frojdh, P., Horn, U., Kampmann, M., Nohlgren, A., & Westerlund, M. (2006, March). Adaptive streaming within the 3GPP packet-switched streaming service. *IEEE Network, 20*(2), 34–40. doi:10.1109/MNET.2006.1607894

Funabiki, N., & Takefuji, Y. (1993). A parallel algorithm for broadcast scheduling problems in packet radio networks. *IEEE Transactions on Communications, 41*(6), 828–831. doi:10.1109/26.231903

Gaffar, A., Mencer, O., Luk, W., & Cheung, P. Y. K. (2004). Unifying bit-width optimisation for fixed-point and floating-point designs. In *IEEE Symposium on Field-Programmable Custom Computing Machines* (pp. 79–88).

Gaffar, A., Mencer, O., Luk, W., Cheung, P. Y. K., & Shirazi, N. (2002). Floating-point bitwidth analysis via automatic differentiation. In *International Conference on Field Programmable Technology* (pp. 158–165).

Galup-Montoro, C., Schneider, M., & Cunha, A. (1999). A current-based MOSFET model for integrated circuit design. In Sánchez-Sinencio, E., & Andreou, A. (Eds.), *Low voltage/low power integrated circuits and systems* (pp. 7–55). IEEE Press.

Ganesan, S., Sánchez-Sinencio, E., & Silva-Martinez, J. (2006). A highly linear low-noise amplifier. *IEEE Transactions on Microwave Theory and Techniques, 54*, 4079–4085. doi:10.1109/TMTT.2006.885889

Gao, X. Y., Cao, Y., Zhou, Y., Ding, W., Lei, C., & Chen, J. A. (2006). Fabrication of solenoid-type inductor with electroplated NiFe magnetic core. *Journal of Magnetism and Magnetic Materials, 305*(1), 207–211. doi:10.1016/j.jmmm.2005.12.014

Gastpar, M., & Vetterli, M. (2002, June). On the capacity of wireless networks: The relay case. In *Proceedings of IEEE International Conference on Computer Communications* (INFOCOM), 23-27 June 2002, (vol. 3, pp. 1577–1586).

Getsinger, W. J. (1983). Measurement and modeling of the apparent characteristic impedance of microstrip. *IEEE Transactions on Microwave Theory and Techniques, 31*, 624–632. doi:10.1109/TMTT.1983.1131560

Gijs, M. A. M. (2006). MEMS inductors: Technology and applications. *Conference of the NATO Advanced Study Institute on Magnetic Nanostructures for Micro-Electromechanical Systems and Spintronic Applications*, (pp. 127-152).

Gildenblat, G., Li, X., Wu, W., Wang, H., Jha, A., & van Langevelde, R. (2006). PSP: An advanced surface potential- based MOSFET model for circuit simulation. *IEEE Transactions on Electron Devices, 53*(9), 1979–1993. doi:10.1109/TED.2005.881006

Girardi, A., & Bampi, S. (2006). *Power constrained design optimization of analog circuits based on physical gm/ID characteristics*. 19th Symposium on Integrated Circuits and System Design, SBCCI.

González-Bayón, J., Carreras, C., & Fernández-Herrero, A. (2007, December). Comparative evaluation of carrier frequency offset tracking schemes for WiMAX OFDM systems. *IEEE Symposium on Signal Processing and Information Technology ISSPIT 2007*.

González-Bayón, J., Fernández-Herrero, A., & Carreras, C. (2010 May). Improved schemes for tracking residual frequency offset in DVB-T systems. *IEEE Transactions on Consumer Electronics*.

Gramegna, G., Montagna, G., Bietti, I., Franciotta, M., Baschirotto, A., & Abbotto, G. (2004, July). A 35-mW 3.6-mm² fully integrated 0.18-µm CMOS GPS radio. *IEEE Journal of Solid-state Circuits, 39*(7), 1163–1171.

Greenhouse, H. M. (1974). Design of planar rectangular microelectronic inductors. *IEEE Transactions on Parts, Hybrids, and Packaging, 10*(2), 101–109. doi:10.1109/TPHP.1974.1134841

Groenkvist, J., & Hansson, A. (2001, October). Comparison between graph based and interference based STDMA scheduling. In *Proceedings of ACM International Symposium on Mobile Ad hoc Networking and Computing* (MOBIHOC), Long Beach, California, USA, (pp. 255–258).

Grover, F. W. (1946). *Inductance calculation: Working formulas and tables*. NJ: Van Nostrand.

Guo, F. M., Zhu, Z. Q., Long, Y. F., Wang, W. M., Zhu, S. Z., & Lai, Z. S. (2003). Study on low voltage actuated MEMS RF capacitive switches. *Sensors and Actuators. A, Physical, 108*(1-3), 128–133. doi:10.1016/S0924-4247(03)00372-8

Gupta, K. C., Garg, R., & Chadha, R. (1981). *Computer-aided design of microwave circuits* (pp. 197–199). Artech House.

Gupta, P., & Kumar, P. R. (2000, February). The capacity of wireless networks. *IEEE Transactions on Information Theory, 46*(2), 388–404. doi:10.1109/18.825799

Gu, Q. (2005). *RF system design of transceivers for wireless communication*. New York, NY: Springer.

Gurbuz, Y., Esame, O., Tekin, I., Kang, W. P., & Davidson, J. L. (2005). Diamond semiconductor technology for RF device applications. *Solid-State Electronics, 49*(7), 1055–1070. doi:10.1016/j.sse.2005.04.005

Gutierrez, J. A., Naeve, M., Callaway, E., Bourgeois, M., Mitter, V., & Heile, B. (2001, September). IEEE 802.15.4: Developing standards for low-power low-cost wireless personal area networks. *IEEE Network*, 2–9.

Hajek, B., & Sasaki, G. (1998, September). Link scheduling in polynomial time. *IEEE Transactions on Information Theory*, *34*(5), 910–917. doi:10.1109/18.21215

Hajimiri, A., & Lee, T. (1998). A general theory of phase noise in electrical oscillators. *IEEE Journal of Solid-state Circuits*, *33*(2), 179–194. doi:10.1109/4.658619

Hajimiri, A., & Lee, T. (1999). Design issues in CMOS differential LC oscillators. *IEEE Journal of Solid-state Circuits*, *34*(5), 717–724. doi:10.1109/4.760384

Hajimiri, A., & Lee, T. H. (1998). A general theory of phase noise in electrical oscillators. *IEEE Journal of Solid-state Circuits*, *33*(2), 179–194. doi:10.1109/4.658619

Hammerstad, E. (1981). Computer-aided design of microstrip couplers using accurate discontinuity models. *Transactions on Microwave Theory and Techniques Symposium Digest,* (pp. 54-56).

Hammerstad, E., & Jensen, O. (1980). Accurate models for microstrip computer-aided design. *IEEE Microwave Theory and Techniques Symposium Digest,* (pp. 407-409).

Hansen, S., & Redjepi, J. (1994). *Vehicle communication control system*. Patent WO/1994/026558, World Intellectual Property Organisation.

Hanzo, L. L., & Keller, T. (2006). *OFDM and MC-CDMA: A primer*. Wiley-IEEE Press. doi:10.1002/9780470031384

Hara, M., Kuypers, J., Abe, T., & Esashi, M. (2003). *MEMS based thin film 2 GHz resonator for CMOS integration*. Paper presented at the 2003 IEEE MTT-S International Microwave Symposium Digest.

Hara, S., & Prasad, R. (1997, December). Overview of multicarrier CDMA. *IEEE Communications Magazine*.

Harrington, B. P., Shahmohammadi, M., & Abdolvand, R. (24-28 January, 2010). *Toward ultimate performance in GHZ MEMS resonators: Low impedance and high Q*. Paper presented at the 2010 IEEE 23rd International Conference on Micro Electro Mechanical Systems (MEMS).

Hartley, R. (1928). *Modulation system*. U.S. Patent 1.666.206.

Hartley, A. C., Miles, R. E., Corda, J., & Dimitrakopoulos, N. (2008). Large throw magnetic microactuator. *Mechatronics*, *18*(9), 459–465. doi:10.1016/j.mechatronics.2008.05.012

Hartung, F., Horn, U., Huschke, J., Kampmann, M., Lohmar, T., & Lundevall, M. (2007, March). Delivery of broadcast services in 3G networks. *IEEE Transactions on Broadcasting*, *53*(1), 188–199. doi:10.1109/TBC.2007.891711

Hashemi, H. (2003). *Integrated concurrent multi-band radios and multiple-antenna systems*. Unpublished doctoral dissertation, California Institute of Technology, Pasadena.

Hashemi, H., & Hajimiri, A. (2001, June). *Concurrent dual-band LNAs and receiver architectures*. Paper presented at IEEE Symposium on VLSI, Kyoto, Japan.

Hassan, H., Anis, M., & Elmasry, M. (2004). *Impact of technology scaling on RF CMOS*. Paper presented at the IEEE SOC Conference

Hayes, B. (1999). A lucid interval. *American Scientist*, *91*(6), 484–488.

Hershenson, M., Hajimiri, A., Mohan, S., Boyd, S., & Lee, T. (1999). Design and optimization of LC VCO oscillators. *IEEE/ACM International Conference on Computer-Aided Design,* (pp. 65-69).

Hill, J., Szewczyk, R., Woo, A., Hollar, S., Culler, D. E., & Pister, K. S. J. (2000). System architecture directions for networked sensors. In *Proceedings Architectural Support for Programming Languages and Operating Systems,* (pp. 93-104).

Hiroshi, I. (2004). *RF CMOS technology*. Paper presented at the IEEE Asia-Pacific Radio Science Conference.

Ho, G. K., Sundaresan, K., Pourkamali, S., & Ayazi, F. (2010). Micromechanical IBARs: Tunable High-Q resonators for temperature-compensated reference oscillators. *Journal of Microelectromechanical Systems*, *19*(3), 503–515. doi:10.1109/JMEMS.2010.2044866

Huang, W. L., Ren, Z., Lin, Y. W., Chen, H. Y., Lahann, J., & Nguyen, C. T.-C. (2008 January). Fully monolithic CMOS nickel micromechanical resonator oscillator. 21th IEEE International Conference on MEMS, (pp. 10-13). Tucson, AZ

Huang, X. M. H., Zorman, C. A., Mehregany, M., & Roukes, M. L. (2003 July). Quality factor issues in silicon carbide nano mechanical resonators. 12th International Conference on Transducers, Solid State Sensors, Actuators and Microsystems, (vol. 1, pp. 722–725).

Huang, Q., Piazza, F., Orsatti, P., & Ohguro, T. (1998). The impact of scaling down to deep submicron on CMOS RF circuits. *IEEE Journal of Solid-state Circuits, 33*(7), 1023–1036. doi:10.1109/4.701249

Hueber, G., & Staszewski, R. B. (2011). *Multi-mode / multi-band RF transceivers for wireless communications: Advanced techniques, architectures, and trends.* New York, NY: Wiley.

Hung, E. S., & Senturia, S. D. (1998). Tunable capacitors with programmable capacitance-voltage characteristic. *Solid-State Sensors and Actuators Workshop,* (pp. 292–295).

IEEE. (2004). *IEEE standard for local and metropolitan area networks part 16: Air interface for fixed broadband wireless access systems.* IEEE 802.16, 2004.

IEEE. (2005). *Amended to 802.16e: IEEE standard for local and metropolitan area networks part 16: Air interface for fixed broadband wireless access systems. Amendment for physical and medium access control layers for combined fixed and mobile operation in licensed bands and corrigendum 1.* IEEE 802.16-2005, December 2005.

IEEE. (2009). *IEEE draft standard for Information Technology-Telecommunications and information exchange between systems-Local and metropolitan area networks-Specific requirements-Part 11: Wireless LAN medium access control (MAC) and physical layer (PHY) specifications amendment: Enhancements for higher throughput.* June 2009.

IEEE. (2011, February). *IEEE Get Program.* Retrieved from http://standards.ieee.org/about/get/802/802.11.html

Imanishi, D., Hong, J. Y., Okada, K., & Matsuzawa, A. (2010, January). *A 2-6 GHz fully integrated tunable CMOS power amplifier for multi-standard transmitters.* Paper presented at the Asia and South Pacific Design Automation Conference, Taipei, Taiwan.

Iwai, H. (2000). *CMOS technology for RF application.* Paper presented at the 22nd International Conference on Microelectronics (MIEL 2000). Klymyshyn, D. M., Borner, M., Haluzan, D. T., Santosa, E. G., Schaffer, M., Achenbach, S., et al. Vertical High-Q RF-MEMS devices for reactive lumped-element circuits. *IEEE Transactions on Microwave Theory and Techniques, 58*(11), 2976-2986.

Jackson, L. B. (1970). Roundoff-noise analysis for fixed-point digital filters realized in cascade or parallel form. *IEEE Transactions on Audio and Electroacoustics, 18*(2), 107–122. doi:10.1109/TAU.1970.1162084

Jain, K., Padhye, J., Padmanabhan, V., & Qiu, L. (2003, September). Impact of interference on multi-hop wireless network performance. In *Proceedings of ACM Mobile Computing and Networking* (MOBICOM), San Diego, USA, (vol. 2, pp. 66–80).

Jakonis, D. (2004). *Direct RF sampling receivers for wireless systems in CMOS technology.* Unpublished doctoral dissertation, Linköping University, Sweden.

Jakonis, D., Folkesson, K., Dabrowski, J., Eriksson, P., & Svensson, C. (2005). A 2.4-GHz RF sampling receiver front-end in 0.18μm CMOS. *IEEE Journal of Solide-State Circuits, 40*(6), 1265–1277. doi:10.1109/JSSC.2005.848027

Jeannot, S., Bajolet, A., Manceau, J.-P., Cremer, S., Deloffre, E., & Oddou, J.-P. … Bruyere, S. (2007, December). *Toward next high performances MIM generation: up to 30fF/μm^2 with 3D architecture and high-κ materials.* Paper presented at the IEEE International Electron Devices Meeting, San Francisco, CA.

Jespers, P. G. (2010). *The gm/ID methodology, a sizing tool for low-voltage analog CMOS circuits.* Springer. doi:10.1007/978-0-387-47101-3

Jhon, H.-S., Jung, H., Koo, M., Song, I., & Shin, H. (2009). 0.7 V supply highly linear subthreshold low-noise amplifier design for 2-4GHz wireless sensor network applications. *Microwave and Optical Technology Letters, 51*(5). doi:10.1002/mop.24333

Jiang, M. Hanzo, L. (2007). Multiuser MIMO-OFDM for next-generation wireless systems. *Proceedings of the IEEE,* July 2007.

Jiménez-Pacheco, A., Fernández-Herrero, A., & Casajús-Quirós, J. (2008). Design and implementation of a hardware module for MIMO decoding in a 4G wireless receiver. *VLSI Design, 2008,* 312614. doi:10.1155/2008/312614

Johnson, R. A. (1983). *Mechanical filters in electronics.* New York, NY: Wiley.

Jung, Y.-J., Jeong, H., Song, E., Lee, J., Lee, S.-W., & Seo, D. ... Kim, W. (2003, September). *A dual-mode direct-conversion CMOS transceiver for Bluetooth and 802.11b.* Paper presented at the IEEE European Solid-State Circuits Conference, Lisbon, Portugal.

Juntti, M., Vehkapera, M., Leinonen, J., Zexian, V., Tujkovic, D., Tsumura, S., & Hara, S. (2005, February). MIMO MC-CDMA communications for future cellular systems. *IEEE Communications Magazine.*

Kaiser, S., et al. (2004). 4G MC-CDMA multi antenna system on chip for radio enhancements (4MORE). *Proceedings of the 13th IST Mobile and Wireless Communications Summit,* June 2004.

Kang, I. M., Jung, S.-J., Choi, T.-H., Jung, J.-H., Chung, C., & Kim, H.-S. (2009). RF model of BEOL vertical natural capacitor (VNCAP) fabricated by 45-nm RF CMOS technology and its verification. *IEEE Electron Device Letters, 30*(5), 538–540. doi:10.1109/LED.2009.2015781

Kang, K., & Kim, T. (2009, January). Improved error control for real-time video broadcasting over CDMA2000 networks. *IEEE Transactions on Vehicular Technology, 58*(1), 188–197. doi:10.1109/TVT.2008.926077

Kar-Roy, A., Chun, H., Racanelli, M., Compton, C. A., Kempf, P., & Jolly, G. ... Yin, A. (1999, May). *High density metal insulator metal capacitors using PECVD nitride for mixed signal and RF circuits.* Paper presented at the IEEE International Interconnect Technology Conference, San Francisco, CA.

Karvonen, S. (2006). *Charge-domain sampling of high-frequency signals with embedded filtering.* Unpublished doctoral dissertation, University of Oulu, Finland.

Karvonen, S., Riley, T. A. D., Kurtti, S., & Kostamovaara, J. (2006). A quadrature charge-domain sampler with embedded FIR and IIR filtering functions. *IEEE Journal of Solid-state Circuits, 41*(2), 507–515. doi:10.1109/JSSC.2005.857357

Kawakubo, T., Nagano, T., Nishigaki, M., Abe, K., & Itaya, K. (2006). RF-MEMS tunable capacitor with 3V operation using folded beam piezoelectric bimorph actuator. *IEEE Journal of Microelectromechanical Systems, 15*(6), 1759–1765. doi:10.1109/JMEMS.2006.885985

Kenny, T. P., Riley, T. A. D., Filiol, N. M., & Copeland, M. A. (1999). Design and realization of a digital ΔΣ modulator for fractional-n frequency synthesis. *IEEE Transactions on Vehicular Technology, 2*(48), 510–521. doi:10.1109/25.752575

Kester, W. (2003). *Mixed-signal and DSP design techniques.* Burlington, MA: Newnes.

Ketterl, T., Weller, T., & Fries, D. (2001 August). A micromachined tunable CPW resonator. *IEEE International Microwave Symposium,* (vol. 1, pp. 345-348). Phoenix, AZ.

Kim, C. S., Park, P., Park, J.-W., Hwang, N., & Yu, H. K. (2001, May). *Deep trench guard technology to suppress coupling between inductors in silicon RF ICs.* Paper presented at the IEEE MTT-S International Microwave Symposium, Phoenix, AZ.

Kim, J., Plouchart, J.-O., Zamdmer, N., Sherony, M., Lu, L.-H., & Tan, Y. ... Wagner, L. (2003, June). *3-dimensional vertical parallel plate capacitors in an SOI CMOS technology for integrated RF circuits.* Paper presented at the IEEE Symposium on VLSI Circuits, Honolulu, HI.

Kim, T.-S., & Kim, B.-S. (2008, June). *Linearization of differential CMOS Low Noise Amplifier using cross-coupled post distortion canceller.* Paper presented at the meeting of IEEE Radio Frequency Integrated Circuits Symposium, Atlanta, CA.

Kim, B., Ko, J. S., & Lee, K. (2000). A new linearization technique for MOSFET RF amplifier using multiple gated transistors. *IEEE Microwave Guided Wave Letters, 9,* 371–373.

Kim, D., Kim, J., Plouchart, J.-O., Cho, C., Trzcinski, R., Kumar, M., & Norris, C. (2007). Symmetric vertical parallel plate capacitors for on-chip RF circuits in 65-nm SOI technology. *IEEE Electron Device Letters, 28*(7), 616–618. doi:10.1109/LED.2007.899464

Kim, K., & O. K. (1997). Characteristics of an integrated spiral inductor with an underlying n-well. *IEEE Transactions on Electron Devices, 44*(9), 1565–1567. doi:10.1109/16.622620

Kim, N., Aparin, V., Barnett, K., & Persico, C. (2006). A cellular-band CDMA 0.25um CMOS LNA linearized using post-distortion. *IEEE Journal of Solid-state Circuits, 41*(7), 1530–1534. doi:10.1109/JSSC.2006.873909

Kirschning, M., Jansen, R. H., & Koster, N. H. L. (*1983*). Measurement and computer-aided modeling of microstrip discontinuities by an improved resonator method. *IEEE Transactions on Microwave Theory and Techniques Symposium Digest,* (pp. 495-497).

Kirschning, M., & Jansen, R. H. (1982). Accurate model for effective dielectric constant of microstrip with validity up to millimetre-wave frequencies. *Electronics Letters, 18*(6), 272–273. doi:10.1049/el:19820186

Kirschning, M., Jansen, R. H., & Koster, N. H. L. (1981). Accurate model for open-end effect of microstrip lines. *Electronics Letters, 17*(3), 123–125. doi:10.1049/el:19810088

Kobayashi, M. (1983, November). Frequency dependent characteristics of microstrips on ansiotropic substrates. *IEEE Transactions on Microwave Theory and Techniques, 30*, 89–92.

Kobayashi, M. (1990, August). A dispersion formula satisfying recent requirements in microstrip CAD. *IEEE Transactions on Microwave Theory and Techniques, 36*, 1246–1370. doi:10.1109/22.3665

Koutsoyannopoulos, Y. K., & Papananos, Y. (2000). Systematic analysis and modeling of integrated inductors and transformers in RF IC design. *IEEE Transactions on Circuits and Systems-II: Analog and Digital Signal Processing, 47*(8).

Koutsoyannopoulos, Y. K., & Papananos, Y. (2000). Systematic analysis and modeling of integrated inductors and transformers in RF IC design. *IEEE Transactions on Circuits and Systems-II: Analog and Digital Signal Processing, 47*(8), 699–713. doi:10.1109/82.861403

Krueger, S., & Solzbacher, F. (2003). Applications in intelligent automobiles. *MSTNews - International Newsletter on Microsystems and MEMS,* (pp. 6-10).

Krueger, S., Müller-Fiedler, R., Finkbeiner, S., & Trah, H.-P. (2005, March). Microsystems for automotive industry. *MSTNews - International Newsletter on Microsystems and MEMS,* (pp. 8-10).

Kuang, L., Ni, Z., Lu, J., & Zheng, J. (2005, March). A time-frequency decision-feedback loop for carrier frequency offset tracking in OFDM systems. *IEEE Transactions on Wireless Communications, 4*(2).

Kuhn, W. B., & Ibrahim, N. M. (2001). Analysis of current crowding effects in multiturn spiral inductors. *IEEE Transactions on Microwave Theory and Techniques, 49*(1), 31–38. doi:10.1109/22.899959

Kundert, K. S. (2001). *Modeling and simulation of jitter in phase-locked loops.* San Jose, CA: Cadence Design Systems. Hinz, M., Konenkamp, I., & Horneber, E. H. (2000). *Behavioral modeling and simulation of phase-locked loops for RF front ends.* IEEE Midwest Symposium on Circuits and Systems.

Lackey, R. J., & Upmal, D. W. (1995). Speakeasy: The military software radio. *IEEE Communications Magazine, 33*(5), 56–61. doi:10.1109/35.392998

Lakdawala, H., & Fedder, G. K. (2004). Temperature stabilization of CMOS capacitive accelerometers. *Journal of Micromechanics and Microengineering, 14.*

Lakin, K. M. (2005). Thin film resonator technology. *IEEE Transactions on Ultrasonics, Ferroelectrics, and Frequency Control, 52*(5), 707–716. doi:10.1109/TUFFC.2005.1503959

Lavasani, H. M., Wanling, P., Harrington, B., Abdolvand, R., & Ayazi, F. (2011). A 76 dB Ohm 1.7 GHz 0.18 um CMOS tunable TIA using broadband current pre-amplifier for high frequency lateral MEMS oscillators. *IEEE Journal of Solid-state Circuits, 46*(1), 224–235. doi:10.1109/JSSC.2010.2085890

Le Nir, V., Hélard, M., & Le Gouable, R. (2003). *Space-time block coding applied to turbo coded MC-CDMA.* In Vehicular Technology Conference.

Lee, S., & Nguyen, C. T.-C. (2004 April). Mechanically-coupled micromechanical resonator arrays for improved phase noise. *Proceedings of IEEE International Symposium on Frequency Control,* (pp. 144-150).

Lee, S., Demirci, M. U., & Nguyen, C. T.-C. (2001). A 10-MHz micromechanical resonator Pierce reference oscillator for communications. *Digest of Technical Papers, the 11th International Conference on Solid-State Sensors & Actuators* (Transducers'01), (pp. 1094-1097).

Lee, D. W., Hwang, K. P., & Wang, S. X. (2008). Fabrication and analysis of high-performance integrated solenoid inductor with magnetic core. *IEEE Transactions on Magnetics, 44*(11), 4089–4095. doi:10.1109/TMAG.2008.2003398

Lee, D.-U., Gaffar, A. A., Cheung, R. C. C., Mencer, O., Luk, W., & Constantinides, G. A. (2006). Accuracy-guaranteed bit-width optimization. *IEEE Transactions on Computer-Aided Design of Integrated Circuits and Systems, 25*(10), 1990–1999. doi:10.1109/TCAD.2006.873887

Lee, H. C., Park, J. H., & Park, Y. H. (2007). Development of shunt type Ohmic RF MEMS switches actuated by piezoelectric cantilever. *Sensors and Actuators. A, Physical, 136*(1), 282–290. doi:10.1016/j.sna.2006.10.050

Lee, H., & Mohammadi, S. (2007). A subthreshold low phase noise CMOS LC VCO for ultra low power applications. *IEEE Microwave and Wireless Component Letters, 17*(11), 796–799. doi:10.1109/LMWC.2007.908057

Leeson, D. (1966). A simple model of feedback oscillator noise spectrum. *Proceedings of the IEEE, 54*, 329–330. doi:10.1109/PROC.1966.4682

Lee, T. H. (1998). *The design of CMOS radio-frequency integrated circuits*. Cambridge University Press.

Lee, T. H. (1998). The design of narrowband CMOS low-noise amplifiers. In *The design of CMOS radiofrequency integrated circuits* (pp. 272–306). Cambridge University Press.

Leon, G., & Heffernan, D. (2001, October). Vehicles without wires. *Computing & Control Engineering Journal, 12*(5), 205–211. doi:10.1049/cce:20010501

Li, H., Yu, D., & Chen, H. (2003, September). New approach to multihop - Cellular based multihop network. In *Proceedings of IEEE International Symposium on Personal Indoor and Mobile Radio Communications* (PIMRC'03), Beijing, China, (vol. 2, pp. 1629–1633).

Li, J., & Talty, T. (2006, October). Channel characterization for ultra-wideband intra-vehicle sensor networks. In *Proceedings IEEE Military Communications Conference*, Washington DC, (pp. 1-4).

Li, S. S., Lin, Y. W., Ren, Z., & Nguyen, C. T.-C. (2007 June). An MSI micromechanical differential disk-array filter. *International Conference on Transducers, Solid State Sensors, Actuators and Microsystems*, (pp. 307 –311). Lyon.

Li, S. S., Lin, Y. W., Xie, Y., Ren, Z., & Nguyen, C. T.-C. (2005 March). Small percent bandwidth design of a 431-MHz notch-coupled micromechanical hollow-disk ring mixer-filter. *Proceedings of the IEEE International Ultrasonics Symposium*, (pp. 1295-1298).

Lin, C. C., Hsu, H. M., Chen, Y. H., Shih, T., Jang, S. M., Yu, C. H., & Liang, M. S. (2001, June). *A full Cu damascene metallization process for sub-0.18 /spl mu/m RF CMOS SoC high Q inductor and MIM capacitor application at 2.4 GHz and 5.3 GHz*. Paper presented at the IEEE International Interconnect Technology Conference, San Francisco, CA.

Lin, T. H., Sanchez, H., Rofougaran, R., & Kaiser, W. J. (1998). *Micropower CMOS RF components for distributed wireless sensors*. Paper presented at the IEEE Radio Frequency Integrated Circuits (RFIC) Symposium.

Ling, F., Song, J., Kamgaing, T., Yang, Y., Blood, W., Petras, M., et al. (2002). *Systematic analysis of inductors on silicon using EM simulations*. Electronic Components and Technology Conference.

Lin, M., Wang, H., Li, Y., & Chen, H. (2006). A novel IP3 boosting technique using feedforward distortion cancellation method for 5 GHz CMOS LNA. *Analog Integrated Circuits and Signal Processing, 46*, 293–296. doi:10.1007/s10470-006-2134-3

Lin, Y. D., Hsu, Y. C., Oyang, K. W., Tsai, T. C., & Yang, D. S. (2000, December). Multihop wireless IEEE 802.11 LANs: A prototype implementation. *Journal of Communications and Networks, 2*(4).

Lin, Y. W., Lee, S., Li, S. S., Xie, Y., Ren, Z., & Nguyen, C. T. C. (2004). Series-resonant VHF micromechanical resonator reference oscillators. *IEEE Journal of Solid-state Circuits, 39*(12), 2477–2491. doi:10.1109/JSSC.2004.837086

Liu, R., Lin, C.-Y., Harris, E., Merchant, S., Downey, S. W., & Weber, G. ... Gregor, R. (2000, June). *Single mask metal-insulator-metal (MIM) capacitor with copper damascene metallization for sub-0.18 μm mixed mode signal and system-on-a-chip (SoC) applications.* Paper presented at the IEEE International Interconnect Technology Conference, San Francisco, CA.

Liu, J.-Q., Fang, H.-B., Xu, Z.-Y., Mao, X.-H., Shen, X.-C., & Chen, D. (2008). A MEMS-based piezoelectric power generator array for vibration energy harvesting. *Microelectronics Journal*, *39*(5), 802–806. doi:10.1016/j.mejo.2007.12.017

Liu, Y., Hoshyar, R., Yang, X., & Tafazolli, R. (2006, November). Integrated radio resource allocation for multihop cellular networks with fixed relay stations. *IEEE Journal on Selected Areas in Communications*, *24*(11), 2137–2146. doi:10.1109/JSAC.2006.881603

Long, J. R. (2000). Monolithic transformers for silicon RF IC design. *IEEE Journal of Solid-state Circuits*, *35*(9), 1368–1382. doi:10.1109/4.868049

Long, J. R., & Copeland, M. A. (1997). The modeling, characterization, and design of monolithic inductors for silicon RF ICs. *IEEE Journal of Solid-state Circuits*, *32*(3), 257–369. doi:10.1109/4.557634

López, J. (2004). *Evaluación de los efectos de cuantificación en las estructuras de filtros digitales mediante técnicas de simulación basadas en extensiones de intervalos.* Ph.D. thesis, Universidad Politécnica de Madrid, Spain.

López, J. A., Caffarena, G., Carreras, C., & Nieto-Taladriz, O. (2004). Analysis of limit cycles by means of affine arithmetic computer-aided tests. In *European Signal Processing Conference* (pp. 991–994).

López, J. A., Caffarena, G., Carreras, C., & Nieto-Taladriz, O. (2008). Fast and accurate computation of the round-off noise of linear time-invariant systems. *IET Circuits. Devices and Systems*, *2*(4), 393–408. doi:10.1049/iet-cds:20070198

López, J. A., Carreras, C., & Nieto-Taladriz, O. (2007). Improved interval-based characterization of fixed-point LTI systems with feedback loops. *IEEE Transactions on Computer-Aided Design of Integrated Circuits and Systems*, *26*(11), 1923–1933. doi:10.1109/TCAD.2007.896306

Lopez-Villegas, J. M., Samitier, J., Cane, C., & Losantos, P. (1998). Improvement of the quality factor of RF integrated inductors by layout optimization. *Radio Frequency Integrated Circuits (RFIC) Symposium,* (pp. 169-172).

López-Villegas, J. M., Samitier, J., Cané, C., Losantos, P., & Bausells, J. (2000). Improvement of the quality factor of RF integrated inductors by layout optimization. *IEEE Transactions on Microwave Theory and Techniques*, *48*(1). doi:10.1109/22.817474

Lutz, R. D., Hahm, Y., Weisshaar, A., Tripathi, V. K., Wu, H., & Kanaglekar, N. (1999, June). *Modeling and analysis of multilevel spiral inductors for RF ICs.* Paper presented at the IEEE MTT-S International Microwave Symposium, Anaheim, CA.

Mackensen, E., Kuntz, W., & Müller, C. L. (2005). Enhancing the lifetime of autonomous microsystems in wireless sensor actuator networks. In *Proceedings of the XIX Eurosensors,* Barcelona, Spain.

Mahmoudi, P., Ghavifekr, H. B., & Najafiaghdam, E. (2010). A combined thermo-electrostatic MEMS-based switch with low actuation voltage. *Sensors & Transducers*, *115*(4), 61–70.

Mahnkopf, R., Allers, K.-H., Armacost, M., Augustin, A., Barth, J., & Brase, G. ... Chen, B. (1999, December). *System on a chip technology for 0.18-μm digital, mixed signal and eDRAM applications.* Paper presented at the IEEE International Electron Devices Meeting, San Francisco, CA.

Mak, S.-P. U., & Martins, R. P. (2007). Transceiver architecture selection: Review, state-of-the-art survey and case study. *IEEE Circuits and Systems Magazine*, *7*(2), 6–24. doi:10.1109/MCAS.2007.4299439

Manghisoni, M., Ratti, L., Re, V., Speziali, V., & Traversi, G. (2006). Noise characterization of 130nm and 90nm CMOS technologies for analog front-end electronics. *IEEE Nuclear Science Symposium Conference,* (pp. 214–218).

Manku, T. (1999). Microwave CMOS-device physics and design. *IEEE Journal of Solid-state Circuits*, *34*(3), 277–285. doi:10.1109/4.748178

Manoj, B. S., & Murthy, C. S. R. (2002, June). *A high-performance wireless local loop architecture utilizing directional multi-hop relaying*. Department of Computer Science and Engineering, Indian Institute of Technology, Madras, India, Technical Report.

Manoj, B. S., Ananthapadmanabha, R., & Murthy, C. S. R. (2002, March). Multi-hop cellular networks: The architecture and routing protocol for best-effort and real-time communication. In *Proceedings of Inter Research Institute Student Seminar in Computer Science*. Bangalore, India: IRISS.

Marques, A., Steyaert, M., and Sansen, W. (1998). Theory of PLL fractional-N frequency synthesizers. *Journal Wireless Networks - Special Issue VLSI in Wireless Networks, 1*(4), 79–85.

Matmat, M., Coccetti, F., Marty, A., Plana, R., Escriba, C., Fourniols, J. Y., & Esteve, D. (2009). Capacitive RF MEMS analytical predictive reliability and lifetime characterization. *Microelectronics and Reliability, 49*(9-11), 1304–1308. doi:10.1016/j.microrel.2009.06.049

Melly, T., Porret, A.-S., Enz, C., & Vittoz, E. (2001). An ultralow power UHF transceiver integrated in a standard digital CMOS process: Transmitter. *IEEE Journal of Solid-state Circuits, 36*(3), 467–472. doi:10.1109/4.910485

Menard, D., & Sentieys, O. (2002). A methodology for evaluating the precision of fixed-point systems. In *IEEE International Conference on Acoustic, Speech, and Signal Processing* (pp. 3152–3155).

Menard, D., Rocher, R., Scalart, P., & Sentieys, O. (2004). SQNR determination in non-linear and non-recursive fixed-point systems. In *European Signal Processing Conference* (pp. 1349–1352).

Mendes, P. M., Correia, J. H., Bartek, M., & Burghartz, J. N. (2002). Analysis of chip-size antennas on lossy substrates for short-range wireless Microsystems. In *Proceedings SAFE 2002*, (pp. 51-54). Veldhoven, The Netherlands, November 27-28.

Mendes, P. M., Polyakov, A., Bartek, M., Burghartz, J. N., & Correia, J. H. (2006, January). Integrated chip-size antennas for wireless microsystems: Fabrication and design considerations. *Journal Sensors and Actuators A, 125*, 217–222. doi:10.1016/j.sna.2005.07.016

Meyer, N. M. N. R. G. (1992). Start-up and frequency stability in high frequency oscillation. *IEEE Journal of Solid-State Circuit, 27*, 810–820. doi:10.1109/4.133172

Milanovic, V., Gaitan, M., Bowen, E. D., Tea, N. H., & Zaghloul, M. E. (1997). *Design and fabrication of micromachined passive microwave filtering elements in CMOS technology*. Paper presented at the IEEE Solid State Sensors and Actuators.

Milet-Lewis, N., Monnerie, G., Fakhfakh, A., et al. (2001). *A VHDL-AMS library of RF blocks models*. IEEE International Workshop on Behavioral Modeling and Simulation.

Mitola, J. (1995). The software radio architecture. *IEEE Communications Magazine, 33*(5), 26–38. doi:10.1109/35.393001

Miyashita, K., Nakayama, T., Oishi, A., Hasumi, R., Owada, M., & Aota, S. … Kakumu, M. (2001, June). *A high performance 100 nm generation SOC technology (CMOS IV) for high density embedded memory and mixed signal LSIs*. Paper presented at the IEEE Symposium on VLSI Technology, Kyoto, Japan.

Moeneclae, M., Pollet, M., & Van Bladel, T. (1995, February-April). Ber sensitivity of OFDM systems to carrier frequency offset and Wiener phase noise. *IEEE Transactions on Communications, 45*(2-5), 191–193.

Mohan, S. S., Hershenson, M., Boyd, S. P., & Lee, T. H. (1999). Simple accurate expressions for planar spiral inductances. *IEEE Journal of Solid-state Circuits, 34*(10), 1419–1424. doi:10.1109/4.792620

Moose, P. (1994, October). A technique for orthogonal frequency division multiplexing frequency offset correction. *IEEE Transactions on Communications, 42*, 2908–2914. doi:10.1109/26.328961

Morelli, P., Jay Kuo, C.-C., & Pun, M.-O. (2007, July). Synchronization techniques for orthogonal frequency division multiple access (OFDMA): A tutorial review. *Proceedings of the IEEE, 95*(7). doi:10.1109/JPROC.2007.897979

Moridi, S., & Sri, H. (1985, June). Analysis of four decision feedback carrier recovery loops in the presence of inter-symbol interference. *IEEE Transactions on Communications, 33*, 543–550. doi:10.1109/TCOM.1985.1096331

Mounir, A., Mostafa, A., & Fikry, M. (2003). *Automatic behavioural model calibration for efficient PLL system verification*. Design, Automation and Test in Europe Conference and Exhibition.

Muer, B. D., & Steyaert, M. (2008). *CMOS fractional-N frequency synthesizers*. Dordrecht, The Netherlands: Kluwer Academic Publishers.

Muhammad, K., Leipold, D., Staszewski, B., Ho, Y.-C., Hung, C.-M., & Maggio, K. ... Friedman, O. (2004, February). *A discrete-time Bluetooth receiver in a 0.13µm digital CMOS process*. Paper presented at the IEEE International Solid-State Circuits Conference, San Francisco, CA.

Muhammad, K., Staszewski, R. B., & Leipold, D. (2005). Digital RF processing: Toward low-cost reconfigurable radios. *IEEE Communications Magazine, 43*(8), 105–113. doi:10.1109/MCOM.2005.1497564

Murthy, C. S. R., & Manoj, B. S. (2004). *Ad hoc wireless networks: Architectures and protocols*. Prentice Hall.

Musah, T. (2005). Mos varactors in weak inversion for 0.5 v analog filters. *National Conference on Undergraduate Research*, (pp. 1-8).

Nabki, F., Allidina, K., Ahmad, F., Cicek, P. V., & El-Gamal, M. N. (2009). A highly integrated 1.8 GHz frequency synthesizer based on a MEMS resonator. *IEEE Journal of Solid-state Circuits, 44*(8), 2154–2168. doi:10.1109/JSSC.2009.2022914

Nelson, R., & Kleinrock, L. (1985, September). Spatial TDMA: A collision free multihop channel access protocol. *IEEE Transactions on Communications, 33*(9), 934–944. doi:10.1109/TCOM.1985.1096405

Ng, C. H., Chew, K. W., Li, J. X., Tjoa, T. T., Goh, L. N., & Chu, S. F. (2002, December). *Characterization and comparison of two metal-insulator-metal capacitor schemes in 0.13 µm copper dual damascene metallization process for mixed-mode and RF applications*. Paper presented at the IEEE International Electron Devices Meeting, San Francisco, CA.

Nguyen, C. T.-C. (1995). Micromechanical resonators for oscillators and filters. *Proceeding of IEEE Ultrasonics Symposium*, (vol. 1, pp. 489-499).

Nguyen, C. T.-C. (2000). Micromechanical circuits for communication transceivers (invited). *Proceedings Bipolar/BiCMOS Circuits and Technology Meeting* (BCTM), (pp. 142-149).

Nguyen, H. C., de Carvalho, E., & Prasad, R. (2008, September). A generalized carrier frequency offset estimator for uplink OFDMA. *IEEE 19th International Symposium on Personal, Indoor and Mobile Radio Communications*, (pp. 1-5).

Nguyen, C. T. C. (2007). MEMS technology for timing and frequency control. *IEEE Transactions on Ultrasonics, Ferroelectrics, and Frequency Control, 54*(2), 251–270. doi:10.1109/TUFFC.2007.240

Nguyen, C. T.-C. (1999). Frequency selective MEMS for miniaturized low power communication devices. *IEEE Transactions on Microwave Theory and Techniques, 47*(8), 1486–1503. doi:10.1109/22.780400

Nguyen, C. T.-C. (2002). *MEMS for wireless communications. Technical Report*. University of Michigan.

Nguyen, C. T.-C. (2005). Vibrating RF MEMS overview: Applications to wireless communications. *Proceedings of the Society for Photo-Instrumentation Engineers, 5715*, 11–25.

Nguyen, C. T.-C. (2007). MEMS technology for timing and frequency control. *IEEE Transactions on Ultrasonics, Ferroelectrics, and Frequency Control, 54*(2), 251–270. doi:10.1109/TUFFC.2007.240

Nguyen, C. T.-C., & Howe, R. T. (1999). An integrated CMOS micromechanical resonator high-Q oscillator. *IEEE Journal of Solid-state Circuits, 34*(4), 440–455. doi:10.1109/4.753677

Nguyen, C. T.-C., Katehi, L. P. B., & Rebeiz, G. M. (1998). Micromachined devices for wireless communications. *Proceedings of the IEEE, 86*(8), 1756–1768. doi:10.1109/5.704281

Nickel, N. H., & Terukov, E. (2005). *Zinc oxide - A material for micro and optoelectronic applications*. New York, NY: Springer. doi:10.1007/1-4020-3475-X

Niknejad, A. (2000). *Analysis of Si inductors and transformers for IC's (ASITIC)*. Retrieved from http://rfic.eecs.berkeley.edu/ niknejad/asitic.html

Niknejad, A. M., & Meyer, R. G. (1998). Analysis, design, and optimization of spiral inductors and transformers for Si RF IC's. *IEEE Journal of Solid-state Circuits, 33*(10). doi:10.1109/4.720393

Niknejad, A., & Meyer, R. (1998). Analysis, design, and optimization of spiral inductors and transformers for Si RF ICs. *IEEE Journal of Solid-state Circuits, 33*(10), 1470–1481. doi:10.1109/4.720393

Niu, W., Li, J., Liu, S., & Talty, T. (2008, November). Intra vehicle ultra wideband communication testbed. In *Proceedings of IEEE Globecom, 2008*, 1–5.

Niu, W., Li, J., & Talty, T. (2009). Ultra-wideband channel modeling for intravehicle environment. *EURASIP Journal on Wireless Communications and Networking, 2009*. doi:10.1155/2009/806209

Nordin, A. N. (2008). *Design, implementation and characterization of temperature compensated SAW resonators in CMOS technology for RF oscillators*. Washington, DC: George Washington University.

Nordin, A. N., & Zaghloul, M. E. (2007). Modeling and fabrication of CMOS surface acoustic wave resonators. *IEEE Transactions on Microwave Theory and Techniques, 55*(5), 992–1001. doi:10.1109/TMTT.2007.895408

O, K. (1998). Estimation methods for quality factors of inductors fabricated in silicon integrate circuit process technologies. *IEEE Journal of Solid-State Circuits, 33*(8), 1249–1252.

Okada, K., Yoshihara, Y., Sugawara, H., & Masu, K. (2005). *A dynamic reconfigurable RF circuit architecture*.

Okoniewski, M., & McFeetors, G. (2006). *Radio frequency microelectromechanical systems components*. Paper presented at the International Conference on Microwaves, Radar & Wireless Communications.

Oliveira, L. B., Fernandes, J. R., Filanovsky, I. M., Verhoeven, C. J., & Silva, M. M. (2008). *Analysis and design of quadrature oscillators*. Berlin, Germany: Springer. doi:10.1007/978-1-4020-8516-1

Ong, A. O., & Tay, F. E. H. (2007). Motion characterizations of lateral micromachined sensor based on stroboscopic measurements. *IEEE Sensors Journal, 7*(2), 163–171. doi:10.1109/JSEN.2006.886871

Oppenheim, A. V., & Schafer, R. W. (1987). *Discrete-time signal processing*. Prentice-Hall.

Oppenheim, A. V., & Weinstein, C. J. (1972). Effects of finite register length in digital filtering and the fast Fourier transform. *Proceedings of the IEEE, 60*(8), 957–976. doi:10.1109/PROC.1972.8820

Otis, B. P. (2005). *Ultra low power wireless technologies for sensor networks*. Berkeley: University of California.

Otis, B. P., & Rabaey, J. M. (2003). A 300-/spl mu/W 1.9-GHz CMOS oscillator utilizing micromachined resonators. *IEEE Journal of Solid-state Circuits, 38*(7), 1271–1274. doi:10.1109/JSSC.2003.813219

Pahlavan, K., Krishnamurthy, P., Hatami, A., Yliantila, M., Makela, J., Pichna, R., & Vallström, J. (2000). Handoff in hybrid mobile data networks. *IEEE Personal Communications, 7*(2), 34–47. doi:10.1109/98.839330

Pakdast, H. (2008). Development and characterization of high frequency bulk mode resonators. *DTU Nanotech, June*.

Pamarti, S., Jansson, L., & Galton, I. (2004). A wideband 2.4-GHz delta-sigma fractional-N PLL with 1-Mb/s in-loop modulation. *IEEE Journal of Solid-state Circuits, 1*(39), 49–62. doi:10.1109/JSSC.2003.820858

Park, J. Y., Yee, Y. J., Nam, H. J., & Bu, J. U. (2001 August). Micromachined RF MEMS tunable capacitors using piezoelectric actuator. IEEE International Microwave Symposium, (vol. 3, pp. 2111-2114). Phoenix, AZ.

Park, D., Jeong, Y., Lee, J.-B., & Jung, S. (2008). Chip-level integration of RF MEMS on-chip inductors using UV-LIGA technique. *Microsystem Technologies, 14*(9), 1429–1438. doi:10.1007/s00542-007-0532-9

Paulraj, A. J., Gore, D. A., Nabar, R. U., & Bolcskei, H. (2004). An overview of MIMO communications – A key to gigabit wireless. *Proceedings of the IEEE*, (February): 2004.

Pérez Serna, E., & Herrera Guardado, A. (2006). *VCO CMOS de Bajo ruido a 10 GHz en Tecnología de SiGe de 0.4 µm. Simposium Nacional de la Unión Científica Internacional de Radio* (pp. 1304–1306). URSI.

Perrott, M. H. (2002). Fast and accurate behavioral simulation of fractional-N frequency synthesizers and other PLL/DLL circuits. *Proceedings of the 39th Design Automation Conference.*

Perrott, M. H., Tewksbury, T. L., & Sodini, C. G. (1997). A 27-mW CMOS fractional-N synthesizer using digital compensation for 2.5-Mb/s GFSK modulation. *IEEE Journal of Solid-state Circuits, 12*(32), 2048–2060. doi:10.1109/4.643663

Perrott, M. H., Trott, M. D., & Sodini, C. G. (2002). A modeling approach for Σ-Δ fractional-n frequency synthesizers allowing straightforward noise analysis. *IEEE Journal of Solid-state Circuits, 8*(37), 1028–1038. doi:10.1109/JSSC.2002.800925

Peterson, G., Ashenden, P. G., & Teegarden, D. A. (2002). *The system designer's guide to VHDL-AMS: Analog, mixed-signal, and mixed-technology modeling.* Morgan Kaufmann Publishers.

Piazza, G., Stephanou, P. J., & Pisano, A. P. (2006). Piezoelectric aluminum nitride vibrating contour-mode MEMS resonators. *IEEE Journal of Microelectro-mechanical Systems, 15*(6), 1406–1418. doi:10.1109/JMEMS.2006.886012

Piazza, G., Stephanou, P. J., & Pisano, A. P. (2007). Single chip multiple frequency AlN MEMS filters based on contour mode piezoelectric resonators. *IEEE Journal of Microelectromechanical Systems, 16*(2), 319–328. doi:10.1109/JMEMS.2006.889503

Pinel, S., Cros, F., Nuttinck, S., Yoon, S.-W., Allen, M. G., & Laskar, J. (2003 June). Very high-Q inductors using RF-MEMS technology for system-on-package wireless communication integrated module. *IEEE International Microwave Symposium,* (vol. 3, pp. 1497-1500).

Porret, A.-S., Melly, T., Python, D., Enz, C., & Vittoz, E. (2001). An ultralow -power UHF transceiver integrated in a standard digital CMOS process: Architecture and receiver. *IEEE Journal of Solid-state Circuits, 36*(3), 452–464. doi:10.1109/4.910484

Pourkamali, S., & Ayazi, F. (2005). Electrically coupled MEMS bandpass filters: Part I: With coupling element. *Sensors and Actuators. A, Physical, 122*(2), 307–316. doi:10.1016/j.sna.2005.03.038

Pourkamali, S., & Ayazi, F. (2005). Electrically coupled MEMS bandpass filters: Part II. Without coupling element. *Sensors and Actuators. A, Physical, 122*(2), 317–325. doi:10.1016/j.sna.2005.03.039

Pourkamali, S., Hashimura, A., Abdolvand, R., Ho, G. K., Erbil, A., & Ayazi, F. (2003). High-Q single crystal silicon HARPSS capacitive beam resonators with self-aligned sub-100-nm transduction gaps. *IEEE Journal Micro-electromechanical System, 12*(4), 487–496. doi:10.1109/JMEMS.2003.811726

Pun, M., Morelli, M., & Kuo, C. (2006, April). Maximum-likelihood synchronization and channel estimation for OFDMA uplink transmissions. *IEEE Transactions on Communications, 54*(4), 726–736. doi:10.1109/TCOMM.2006.873093

Pun, M.-O., Morelli, M., & Jay Kuo, C.-C. (2007, February). Iterative detection and frequency synchronization for FDMA uplink transmissions. *IEEE Transactions on Wireless Communications, 6*(2). doi:10.1109/TWC.2007.05368

Qiuting, H., Orsatti, P., & Piazza, F. (1999). GSM transceiver front-end circuits in 0.25-μm CMOS. *Solid-State Circuits. IEEE Journal of, 34*(3), 292–303.

Rabiner, L. R. (1973). Approximate design relationships for low-pass FIR digital filters. *IEEE Transactions on Audio and Electroacoustics, 21*(5), 456–460. doi:10.1109/TAU.1973.1162510

Rai, S., & Otis, B. (2007, 11-15 Feb. 2007). *A 1V 600&mu W 2.1GHz quadrature VCO using BAW resonators.* Paper presented at the Solid-State Circuits Conference, 2007. ISSCC 2007. Digest of Technical Papers. IEEE International.

Ramos, J., Mercha, A., Jeamsaksiri, W., Linten, D., Jenei, S., & Rooyackers, R. ... Decoutere, S. (2004). 90nm RF CMOS technology for low-power 900MHz applications. *Proceedings of 34th European Solid-State Device Research conference, ESSDERC* (pp. 329-332).

Razavi, B. (1997). Design considerations for direct-conversion receivers. *IEEE Transaction on Circuits and Systems II: Analog and Digital Signal Processing, 44*(6), 428–435. doi:10.1109/82.592569

Razavi, B. (1998). *RF microelectronics*. USA: Prentice Hall.

Razavi, B. (2006). A 60-GHz CMOS receiver front-end. *IEEE Journal of Solid-state Circuits*, *41*(1), 17–22. doi:10.1109/JSSC.2005.858626

Razavi, B., & Behzad, R. (1998). *RF microelectronics*. Upper Saddle River, NJ: Prentice Hall.

Rebeiz, G. M. (2003). *RF MEMS, theory, design and technology*. NJ: John Wiley & Sons. doi:10.1002/0471225282

Rebeiz, G. M. (2003). *RF MEMS: Theory, design, and technology*. John Wiley and Sons. doi:10.1002/0471225282

Reed, J. H. (2002). *Software radio: A modern approach to radio engineering*. Upper Saddle River, NJ: Prentice Hall.

Reinke, J., Fedder, G. K., & Mukherjee, T. (2010). CMOS-MEMS variable capacitors using electrothermal actuation. *Journal of Microelectromechanical Systems*, *19*(5), 1105–1115. doi:10.1109/JMEMS.2010.2067197

Riley, T. A. D., Copeland, M. A., & Kwasniewski, T. A. (1993). Delta–sigma modulation in fractional-N frequency synthesis. *IEEE Journal of Solid-state Circuits*, *5*(28), 553–559. doi:10.1109/4.229400

Riley, T. A. D., Filiol, N. M., Du, Q., & Kostamovvra, J. (2003). Techniques for in-band phase noise reduction in $\Sigma\Delta$ synthesizers. *IEEE Transactions on Circuits and Systems II-Analog and Digital Signal Processing*, *50*(11), 794–803. doi:10.1109/TCSII.2003.819132

Roberts, D., Johnstone, W., Sanchez, H., Mandhana, O., Spilo, D., & Hayden, J. … White, B.E. (2005, December). *Application of on-chip MIM decoupling capacitor for 90nm SOI microprocessor*. Paper presented at the IEEE International Electron Devices Meeting, San Francisco, CA.

Rofougaran, A., Chang, J. Y.-C., Rofougaran, M., & Abidi, A. A. (1996). A 1 GHz CMOS RF front-end IC for a direct-conversion wireless receiver. *IEEE Journal of Solid-state Circuits*, *31*(7), 880–889. doi:10.1109/4.508199

Rosa, E. B. (1906). Calculation of the self-inductance of single-layer coils. *Bulletin of the Bureau of Standards*, *2*(2), 161–187.

Ruther, P., Bartholomeyczik, J., Buhmann, A., Trautmann, A., Steffen, K., & Paul, O. (2005). Microelectromechanical HF resonators fabricated using a novel SOI-based low-temperature process. *IEEE Sensors Journal*, *5*(5), 1112–1119. doi:10.1109/JSEN.2005.851009

Ryynänen, J., Kivekäs, K., Jussila, J., Pärssinen, A., & Halonen, K. (2000, May). *A dual band RF front-end for WCDMA and GSM applications*. Paper presented at the IEEE Custom Integrated Circuits Conference, Orlando, FL.

Ryynänen, J., Kivekäs, K., Jussila, J., Sumanen, L., Pärssinen, A., & Halonen, K. (2003). A single-chip multimode receiver for GSM900, DCS1800, PC1900, and WCDMA. *IEEE Journal of Solid-state Circuits*, *38*(4), 594–602. doi:10.1109/JSSC.2003.809511

Salkintzis, A. K., Fors, C., & Pazhyannur, R. (2002). WLAN-GPRS integration for next-generation mobile data networks. *IEEE Wireless Communications*, *9*(5), 112–124. doi:10.1109/MWC.2002.1043861

Samaribba, O. (1995, October). *Multihop packet radio systems in rough terrain*. Department of S3, Radio Communication Systems, Stockholm, Sweden, Tech. Lic, Thesis SE 10044.

Samavati, H., Hajimiri, A., Shahani, A. R., Nasserbakht, G. N., & Lee, T. H. (1998). Fractal capacitors. *IEEE Journal of Solid-state Circuits*, *33*(12), 2035–2041. doi:10.1109/4.735545

Sanchez, H., Mandhana, O. P., Johnstone, B., Roberts, D., Siegel, J., & Melnick, B. … White, B. (2007, June). *Technology and design cooperation: High-K MIM capacitors for microprocessor, IO, and clocking*. Paper presented at the IEEE International Interconnect Technology Conference, San Francisco, CA.

Sanduleanu, M. A. T., Vidojkovic, M., Vidojkovic, V., Roermund, A. H. M. v., & Tasic, A. (2008). Receiver front-end circuits for future generations of wireless communications. *IEEE Transactions on Circuits and Systems II*, *55*(4), 299–303. doi:10.1109/TCSII.2008.919566

Santos, H. J. d. l. (2004). *Introduction to microelectromechanical microwave systems*.

Schiml, T., Biesemans, S., Brase, G., Burrell, L., Cowley, A., & Chen, K. C. ... Leung, P. (2001, June). *A 0.13 μm CMOS platform with Cu/low-k interconnects for system on chip applications.* Paper presented at the IEEE Symposium on VLSI Technology, Kyoto, Japan.

Schmidl, T., & Cox, D. (1997, December). Robust frequency and timing synchronization for OFDM. *IEEE Transactions on Communications, 45,* 1613–1621. doi:10.1109/26.650240

Scholten, A., Tiemeijer, L., van Langevelde, R., Havens, R., Zegers-van Duijnhoven, A., de Kort, R., & Klaassen, D. (2004). Compact modelling of noise for RF CMOS circuit design. *IEE Proceedings. Circuits, Devices and Systems, 151*(2). doi:10.1049/ip-cds:20040373

Schoof, A., Stadtler, T., & ter Hasborg, J. L. (2003, May). Simulation and measurements of the propagation of Bluetooth signals in automobiles. In *Proceedings IEEE International Symposium on Electromagnetic Compatibility,* (pp. 1297-1300).

Scuderi, A., Biondi, T., Ragonese, E., & Palmisano, G. (2004). A lumped scalable model for silicon integrated spiral inductors. *IEEE Transactions on Circuits and Systems-I, 51*(6), 1203–1209. doi:10.1109/TCSI.2004.829301

Sekar, V., Manoj, B. S., & Murthy, C. S. R. (2003, May). *Routing for a single interface MCN architecture and pricing schemes for data traffic in multi-hop cellular networks.* In *Proceedings of IEEE International Conference on Communications* (ICC'03), Alaska, USA, (vol. 2, pp. 969–973).

Shalaby, M., Abdelmoneum, M., & Saitou, M. A. K. (2009). Design of spring coupling for high- Q high-frequency MEMS filters for wireless applications. *IEEE Transactions on Industrial Electronics, 56*(4), 1022–1030. doi:10.1109/TIE.2009.2014671

Shameli, A., & Heydari, P. (2006). *A novel power optimization technique for ultra-low power RF ICs.* International Symposium on Low Power Electronics and Design, ISLPED.

Sheng-Lyang, J., Chih-Chieh, S., Cheng-Chen, L., & Miin-Horng, J. (2010). A 0.18um CMOS quadrature VCO using the quadruple push-push technique. *IEEE Microwave and Wireless Components Letters, 20*(6), 343–345. doi:10.1109/LMWC.2010.2047525

Shi, B. (2001). *Challenges in RF analog integrated circuits.* Paper presented at the IEEE 4th International Conference on ASIC.

Shi, C., & Brodersen, R. W. (2004). A perturbation theory on statistical quantization effects in fixed-point DSP with nonstationary inputs. In *IEEE International Symposium on Circuits and Systems,* vol. 3, (pp. 373–376).

Shi, J., Xiong, Y., Kang, K., Nan, L., & Lin, F. (2009). RF noise of 65-nm MOSFETs in the weak-to-moderate-inversion region. *IEEE Electron Device Letters, 30*(2), 185–188. doi:10.1109/LED.2008.2010464

Silveira, F., Flandre, D., & Jespers, P. G. A. (1996). A gm/ID based methodology for the design of CMOS analog circuits and its applications to the synthesis of a silicon-on-insulator micropower OTA. *IEEE Journal of Solid-state Circuits, 31*(9), 1314–1319. doi:10.1109/4.535416

Snook, S. (2008, October). A touching display. *Automotive Design, 12*(9), 20–24.

Sobhrinho, J., & Krishnakumar, A. (1999, August). Quality-of-service in ad hoc carrier sense multiple access wireless networks. *IEEE Journal on Selected Areas in Communications, 17*(8), 1353–1368. doi:10.1109/49.779919

Speth, M., Fechtel, S., Fock, G., & Meyr, H. (2001, April). Optimum receiver design for OFDM-based broadband transmission part II: A case study. *IEEE Transactions on Communications, 49*(4). doi:10.1109/26.917759

Staszewski, R. B. (2002). *Digital deep-submicron CMOS frequency synthesis for RF wireless applications.* Ph.D. thesis, The University of Texas at Dallas, USA.

Stephanou, P. J., Piazza, G., White, C. D., Wijesundara, M. B. J., & Pisano, A. P. (2007). Piezoelectric aluminum nitride MEMS annular dual contour mode filter. *Sensors and Actuators. A, Physical, 134*(1), 152–160. doi:10.1016/j.sna.2006.04.032

Steyaert, M., Borremans, M., Janssens, J., de Muer, B., Itoh, I., Craninckx, J., et al. (1998, 5-7 February). *A single-chip CMOS transceiver for DCS-1800 wireless communications.* Paper presented at the Solid-State Circuits Conference, 1998, Digest of Technical Papers. 1998 IEEE International.

Steyaert, M. S. J., De Muer, B., Leroux, P., Borremans, M., & Mertens, K. (2002). Low-voltage low-power CMOS-RF transceiver design. *IEEE Transactions on Microwave Theory and Techniques, 50*(1), 281–287. doi:10.1109/22.981281

Stolfi, J., & Figueiredo, L. H. (1997). Self-validated numerical methods and applications. In *Brazilian Mathematics Colloquium Monograph*. IMPA.

Stuber, G. L., Barry, J. R., McLaughlin, S. W., Li, Y., Ingram, M. A., & Pratt, T. G. (2004). Broadband MIMO-OFDM wireless communications. *Proceedings of the IEEE*, (February): 2004.

Su, D. K., Loinaz, M. J., Masui, S., & Wooley, B. A. (1993). Experimental results and modeling techniques for substrate noise in mixed-signal integrated circuits. *IEEE Journal of Solid-state Circuits, 28*(4), 420–430. doi:10.1109/4.210024

Sun, Y.-R. (2006). *Generalized bandpass sampling receivers for software defined radio*. Unpublished doctoral dissertation, Royal Institute of Technology (KTH), Sweden.

Sung, W., & Kum, K. (1995). Simulation-based word-length optimization method for fixed-point digital signal processing systems. *IEEE Transactions on Signal Processing, 43*(12), 3087–3090. doi:10.1109/78.476465

Sun, P., & Zhang, L. (2009, July). Low complexity pilot aided frequency synchronization for OFDMA uplink transmission. *IEEE Transactions on Wireless Communications, 8*(7), 3758–3769. doi:10.1109/TWC.2009.081005

Sun, Y.-R., & Signell, S. (2005). Effects of noise and jitter in bandpass sampling. *Journal of Analog Integrated Circuits and Signal Processing, 42*(1), 85–97. doi:10.1023/B:ALOG.0000042331.21974.85

Talwalkar, N. A., Yue, C. P., & Wong, S. S. (2005). Analysis and synthesis of on-chip spiral inductors. *IEEE Transactions on Electron Devices, 52*(2), 176–182. doi:10.1109/TED.2004.842535

Tanguay, L.-F., & Sawan, M. (2009). An ultra-low power ISM-band integer-N frequency synthesizer dedicated to implantable medical microsystems. *Analog Integrated Circuits and Signal Processing, 58*, 205–214. doi:10.1007/s10470-007-9123-z

Tang, W. C., Nguyen, T. C. H., Judy, M. W., & Howe, R. T. (1990). Electrostatic comb drive of lateral polysilicon resonators. *Sensors and Actuators. A, Physical, 21*(1-3), 328–331. doi:10.1016/0924-4247(90)85065-C

Tan, L. K., & Samueli, H. (1995). A 200 MHz quadrature digital synthezier/mixer in 0.8μm CMOS. *IEEE Journal of Solid-state Circuits, 3*(30), 193–200.

Tasic, A., Lim, S. T., Serdijn, W. A., & Long, J. R. (2007). Design of adaptive multimode RF front-end circuits. *IEEE Journal of Solid-state Circuits, 42*(2), 313–322. doi:10.1109/JSSC.2006.889387

Tasić, A., Serdijn, W. A., & Long, J. R. (2005). Design of multi-standard adaptive voltage controlled oscillators. *IEEE Transactions on Microwave Theory and Techniques, 53*(2), 556–563. doi:10.1109/TMTT.2004.840648

Tea, N. H., Milanovic, V., Zincke, C. A., Suehle, J. S., Gaitan, M., & Zaghloul, M. E. (1997). Hybrid postprocessing etching for CMOS-compatible MEMS. *Journal of Microelectromechanical Systems, 6*(4), 363–372. doi:10.1109/84.650134

Teva, J., Abadal, G., Uranga, A., Verd, J., Torres, F., Lopez, J. L., et al. (2008). *From VHF to UHF CMOS-MEMS monolithically integrated resonators*.

Thielicke, E., & Obermeier, E. (2003). A Fast switching surface micromachined electrostatic relay. *The 12th International Conference on Solid State Sensors, Actuators and Microsystems*, (pp. 899-902).

Third Generation Partnership Project. (2004). *3GPP system to wireless local area network (WLAN) interworking*. System description TS 23.234, v6.0.0, 3GPP2 Technical Specifications.

Thomas, M., Farcy, A., Deloffre, E., Gros-Jean, M., Perrot, C., & Benoit, D. … Torres, J. (2007, June). *Impact of TaN/Ta copper barrier on full PEALD TiN/Ta2O5/TiN 3D damascene MIM capacitor performance*. Paper presented at the IEEE International Interconnect Technology Conference, San Francisco, CA.

Thomas, M., Farcy, A., Perrot, C., Deloffre, E., Gros-Jean, M., & Benoit, D. ... Torres, J. (2007, June). *Reliable 3D damascene MIM architecture embedded into Cu interconnect for a Ta$_2$O$_5$ capacitor record density of 17 fF/ μm^2*. Paper presented at the IEEE Symposium on VLSI Technology, Kyoto, Japan.

Tiebout, M. (2001). Low-power low-phase-noise differentially tuned quadrature VCO design in standard CMOS. *IEEE Journal of Solid-state Circuits, 7*(36), 1018–1024. doi:10.1109/4.933456

Tonguz, O. K., & Ferrari, G. (2006). *Ad hoc wireless networks: A communication-theoretic perspective*. John Wiley and Sons, Ltd.doi:10.1002/0470091126

Toole, B., Plett, C., & Cloutier, M. (2004). RF circuit implications of moderate inversion, enhanced linear region in MOSFETs. *IEEE Transactions on Circuits and Systems. I, Fundamental Theory and Applications, 51*(2), 319–328. doi:10.1109/TCSI.2003.822400

Torri, T., Azuma, S., & Matsuzaki, Y. (1988, May). Multidisplay system. *IEEE Transactions on Industrial Electronics, 35*(2), 201–207. doi:10.1109/41.192650

Tsai, H. M. Tonguz, O. K., Saraydar, C., Talty, T., Ames, M., & Macdonald, A. (2007, December). ZigBee based intra car wireless sensor networks: a case study. *IEEE Wireless Communications*, (pp. 67-71).

Tsai, H. M., Viriyasitavat, W., Tonguz, O. K., Saraydar, C., Talty, T., & Macdonald, A. (2007, June). Feasibility of in car wireless sensor networks: a statistical evaluation. In *Proceedings of 4th Annual IEEE Communications Society Conference on Sensor, Mesh and Ad Hoc Communications and Networks* (SECON'07), (pp. 101-111).

Tsang, T. K. K., & El-Gamal, M. N. (2003). *A high figure of merit and area-efficient low-voltage (0.7-1V) 12-GHz CMOS VCO*. IEEE Radio Frequency Integrated Circuits Symposium.

Tse, D., & Viswanath, P. (2005). *Fundamentals of wireless communication*. Cambridge University Press.

Tseng, S. H., Hung, Y. J., Juang, Y. Z., & Lu, M. S.-C. (2007). A 5.8-GHz VCO with CMOS-compatible MEMS inductors. *Sensors and Actuators. A, Physical, 139*(1-2), 187–193. doi:10.1016/j.sna.2006.12.014

Tsividis, Y. (2000). *Operation and modelling of the MOS transistor* (2nd ed.). Oxford University Press.

Tsividis, Y., Suyama, K., & Vavelidis, K. (1995). A simple reconciliation MOSFET model valid in all region. *Electronics Letters, 31*, 506–508. doi:10.1049/el:19950256

Tsukahara, T., & Ishikawa, M. (1997, February). *A 2 GHz 60 dB dynamic-range Si logarithmic/limiting amplifier with low-phase deviations*. Paper presented at the IEEE International Solid-State Circuits Conference, San Francisco, CA.

Tsung-Hsien, L., Kaiser, W. J., & Pottie, G. J. (2004). Integrated low-power communication system design for wireless sensor networks. *IEEE Communications Magazine, 42*(12), 142–150. doi:10.1109/MCOM.2004.1367566

Tu, H.-L., Chen, I.-S., Yeh, P.-C., & Ciuou, H.-K. (2006). High performance spiral inductor on deep-trench-mesh silicon substrate. *IEEE Microwave and Wireless Components Letters, 16*(12), 654–656. doi:10.1109/LMWC.2006.885608

Tzuen-Hsi, H., & Jay-Jen, H. (2008). 5-GHz Low phase-noise CMOS VCO integrated with a micromachined switchable differential inductor. *IEEE Microwave and Wireless Components Letters, 18*(5), 338–340. doi:10.1109/LMWC.2008.922125

UMC. (2001). *0.18μm 1P6M logic process interconnect capacitance model*. UMC Spec. No. G-04-LOGIC18-1P6M-INTERCAP, Ver 1.7, Phase 1, August 2001.

van Der Tang, J., Kasperkovitz, D., & van Roermund, A. H. M. (2003). *High-frequency oscillator design for integrated transceivers*. Kluwer Academic Publishers.

Van der Ziel, A. (1986). *Noise in solid state devices and circuits*. New York, NY: Wiley.

van Huylenbroeck, S., Decoutere, S., Venegas, R., Jenei, S., & Winderickx, G. (2009). Investigation of PECVD dielectrics for nondispersive metal-insulator-metal capacitors. *IEEE Electron Device Letters, 23*(4), 191–193. doi:10.1109/55.992835

Van Nee, R., & Prasad, R. (1995, February-April). OFDM for wireless multimedia communications. *IEEE Transactions on Communications, 45*(2-5), 191–193.

Van Nee, R., & Prasad, R. (2000). *OFDM for wireless multimedia communications*. Artech House.

Vanhelmont, F., Philippe, P., Jansman, A. B. M., Milsom, R. F., Ruigrok, J. J. M., & Oruk, A. (2006, 2-6 October). *4D-3 A 2 GHz reference oscillator incorporating a temperature compensated BAW resonator.* Paper presented at the Ultrasonics Symposium, 2006. IEEE.

Varadan, V. K., Vinoy, K. J., & Jose, K. A. (2002). *RF MEMS and their applications*. England: John Wiley & Sons. doi:10.1002/0470856602

Vaughan, R. G., Scott, N. L., & White, D. R. (1991). The theory of bandpass sampling. *IEEE Transactions on Signal Processing, 39*(9), 1973–1984. doi:10.1109/78.134430

Vellekoop, M. J., Nieuwkoop, E., Haartsan, J. C., & Venema, A. (1987). *A monolithic SAW physical-electronic system for sensors.* Paper presented at the IEEE Ultrasonics Symposium.

Vishwanathan, H., & Mukherjee, S. (2005, September). Performance of cellular networks with relays and centralized scheduling. *IEEE Transactions on Wireless Communications, 4*, 2318–2328. doi:10.1109/TWC.2005.853820

Visser, J. H., Vellekoop, M. J., Venema, A., Drift, E. d., Rek, P. J. M., & Nederhof, A. J. (1989). *Surface acoustic wave filter in ZnO-SiO2-Si layered structures.* Paper presented at the IEEE Ultrasonics Symposium.

Vittoz, E. A., Degrauwe, M. G. R., & Bitz, S. (1988). High-performance crystal oscillator circuits: Theory and application. *IEEE Journal of Solid-state Circuits, 23*(3), 774–783. doi:10.1109/4.318

Wadell, B. C. (1991). *Transmission line design handbook*. Boston, MA: Artech House.

Wang, J. Butler, J. E., Hsu, D. S. Y., &Nguyen, T.-C. (2002 August). CVD polycrystalline diamond high-Q micromechanical resonators. *The 5th IEEE International Conference on Micro Electro Mechanical Systems*, (pp. 657 – 660). Las Vegas, NV.

Wang, J., Butler, J. E., Feygelson, T., & Nguyen, C. T. C. (2004). *1.51-GHz nanocrystalline diamond micromechanical disk resonator with material-mismatched isolating support.* Paper presented at the Micro-Electro-Mechanical Systems.

Wang, K., Bannon, F. D., III, Clark, J. R., & Nguyen, C. T.-C. (1997). Q-enhancement of microelectromechanical filters via low-velocity spring coupling. *Proceedings of IEEE Ultrasonics Symposium,* (vol. 1, pp. 323-327).

Wang, L., Cui, Z., Hong, J. S., McErlean E. P., Greed, R. B., & Voyce, D. C. (2006). Fabrication of high power RF MEMS switches. *Microelectronics Engineering, 83*(4-9), 1418-1420.

Wang, J., Ren, Z., & Nguyen, C. T.-C. (2004). 1.156-GHz self-aligned vibrating micromechanical disk resonator. *IEEE Transactions on Ultrasonics, Ferroelectrics, and Frequency Control, 51*(12), 1607–1628. doi:10.1109/TUFFC.2004.1386679

Wang, K., & Nguyen, C. T.-C. (1999). High order medium frequency micromechanical electronic filters. *IEEE Journal Microelectromechanical System, 8*(4), 534–556. doi:10.1109/84.809070

Wang, K., Wong, A. C., & Nguyen, C. T.-C. (2000). VHF free-free beam high q micromechanical resonators. *IEEE Journal Microelectromechanical System, 9*(3), 347–360. doi:10.1109/84.870061

Weaver, D. (1956). A third method of generation and detection of single sideband signals. *Proceedings of the IRE, 44*(12), 1703–1705. doi:10.1109/JRPROC.1956.275061

Weon, D. H., Jeon, J. H., & Mohammadi, S. (2007). High-Q micromachined three-dimensional integrated inductors for high-frequency applications. *Journal of Vacuum Science & Technology B Microelectronics and Nanometer Structures, 25*(1), 264–270. doi:10.1116/1.2433984

Werth, T. D., Schmits, C., & Heinen, S. (2009, June). *Active feedback interference cancellation in RF receiver front-ends.* Paper presented at the meeting of IEEE Radio Frequency Integrated Circuits Symposium, Boston, MA.

Wheeler, A. H. (1942, September). Formulas for the skin effect. *Proceedings of IRE, 30*, 412–424. doi:10.1109/JRPROC.1942.232015

Wheeler, H. A. (1942). Formulas for skin effect. [IRE]. *Proceedings of the Institute of Radio Engineers, 30*(9), 412–424.

Wong, A. C., & Nguyen, C. T.-C. (2004). Micromechanical mixer-filters ("mixlers"). *IEEE Journal of Microelectromechanical Systems, 13*(1), 100–112. doi:10.1109/JMEMS.2003.823218

Wu, S.-Y., Chou, C. W., Lin, C. Y., Chiang, M. C., Yang, C. K., & Liu, M. Y. … Liang, M. S. (2007, December). *A 32nm CMOS Low power SoC platform technology for foundry applications with functional high density SRAM.* Paper presented at the IEEE International Electron Devices Meeting, San Francisco, CA.

Wu, X., Chan, S. H. G., & Mukherjee, B. (2000, September). MADF: A novel approach to add an ad hoc overlay on a fixed cellular infrastructure. In *Proceedings of IEEE Wireless Communications and Networking Conference* (WCNC'00), Chicago, USA, (pp. 549–554).

Wu, C. H., & Irwin, J. D. (1998, February). Multimedia and multimedia communication: A tutorial. *IEEE Transactions on Industrial Electronics, 45*(1), 4–14. doi:10.1109/41.661299

Wu, C. H., Tang, C. C., & Liu, S. I. (2003). Analysis of on-chip spiral inductors using the distributed capacitance model. *IEEE Journal of Solid-state Circuits, 38*(6), 1040–1044. doi:10.1109/JSSC.2003.811965

Wu, H., Qao, C., De, S., & Tonguz, O. (2001, October). Integrated cellular and ad hoc relaying systems. *IEEE Journal on Selected Areas in Communications, 19*(10), 2105–2115. doi:10.1109/49.957326

Xie, Y., Li, S. S., Lin, Y. W., Ren, Z., & Nguyen, C. T. C. (2008). 1.52-GHz micromechanical extensional wine-glass mode ring resonators. *IEEE Transactions on Ultrasonics, Ferroelectrics, and Frequency Control, 55*(4), 890–907. doi:10.1109/TUFFC.2008.725

Xu, G., & Yuan, J. (2000, August). *Comparison of charge sampling and voltage sampling.* Paper presented at the IEEE Midwest Symposium on Circuits and Systems, Lansing, MI.

Xue, C., Yaou, F., Cheng, B., & Wang, Q. (2006). Effect of the silicon substrate structure on chip spiral inductor. *Chinese Journal of Semiconductors, 27*(11), 1955–1960.

Yamashita, E., Atshi, K., & Hirachata, T. (1981, June). Microstrip dispersion in a wide frequency range. *IEEE Transactions on Microwave Theory and Techniques, 29,* 610–611. doi:10.1109/TMTT.1981.1130403

Yang, L., Wakayama, C., & Shi, R. C. (2005). Noise aware behavioral modeling of the $\Sigma\Delta$ fractional-n frequency synthesizer. *Proceedings of the Great Lakes Symposium on VLSI.*

Yao, J. J., Park, S., & Natale, D. (1998). High tuning ratio MEMS-based tunable capacitors for RF communications applications. *Solid State Sensors and Actuators Workshop,* (pp. 124-127).

Yim, S.-M., & Chen, T., & O, K. (2002). The effects of a ground shield on the characteristics and performance of spiral inductors. *IEEE Journal of Solid-state Circuits, 37*(2), 237–244. doi:10.1109/4.982430

Yong, Z., Zhou, Z. M., Cao, Y., Gao, X. Y., & Ding, W. (2008). Fabrication and performance of Fe-based magnetic thin film inductor for high-frequency application. *Journal of Magnetism and Magnetic Materials, 320*(20), 963–966. doi:10.1016/j.jmmm.2008.04.136

Yoon, J. B., Han, C. H., Yoon, E., & Kim, C. K. (1999 January). Monolithic integration of 3-D electroplated microstructures with unlimited number of levels using planarization with a sacrificial metallic mold (PSMM). *IEEE International Conference on MEMS,* (pp. 624-629). Orlando, FL.

Yoshida, H., Suzuki, H., Kinoshita, Y., Fujii, H., & Yamazaki, T. (1998, December). *An RF BiCMOS process using high f_{SR} spiral inductor with premetal deep trenches and a dual recessed bipolar collector sink.* Paper presented at the IEEE International Electron Devices Meeting, San Francisco, CA.

Yoshihara, Y., Sugawara, H., Ito, H., Okada, K., & Masu, K. (2004). *Reconfigurable RF circuit design for multiband wireless chip.*

Young, D. J., & Boser, B. E. (1996). A micromachined variable capacitor for monolithic low-noise VCOs. *Technical Digest, IEEE Solid-state Sensor and Actuator Workshop,* (pp. 86-89).

You, Y. H., Lee, K.-T., & Kang, S.-J. (2008, August). Pilot-aided frequency offset tracking scheme for OFDM-based DVB-T. *IEEE Transactions on Consumer Electronics*, *46*, 438–441.

Yücek, T., & Arslan, H. (2007, October). Carrier frequency offset compensation with successive cancellation in uplink OFDMA systems. *IEEE Transactions on Wireless Communications*, *6*, 3546–3551. doi:10.1109/TWC.2007.060273

Yue, C. P., Ryu, C., Lau, J., Lee, T. H., & Wong, S. S. (1996, December). *A physical model for planar spiral inductors on silicon*. Paper presented at the IEEE International Electron Devices Meeting, San Francisco, CA.

Yue, C. P., & Wong, S. S. (1998). On-chip spiral inductors with patterned ground shields for Si-based RF ICs. *IEEE Journal of Solid-state Circuits*, *33*(5), 743–752. doi:10.1109/4.668989

Yue, C. P., & Wong, S. S. (2000). Physical modeling of spiral inductors on silicon. *IEEE Transactions on Electron Devices*, *47*(3), 560–568. doi:10.1109/16.824729

Zamdmer, N., Kim, J., Trzcinski, R., Plouchart, J.-O., Narasimha, S., Khare, M., et al. (2004, June). *A 243-GHz F_t and 208-GHz F_{max} 90-nm SOI CMOS SoC technology with low-power millimeter-wave digital and RF circuit capability*. Paper presented at the IEEE Symposium on VLSI Technology, Kyoto, Japan.

Zander, J. (1991, October). Jamming in slotted ALOHA multihop packet radio networks. *IEEE Transactions on Communications*, *39*.

Zargari, M., Su, D. K., Yue, C. P., Rabii, S., Weber, D., & Kaczynski, B. J. (2002). A 5-GHz CMOS transceiver for IEEE 802.11a wireless LAN systems. *IEEE Journal of Solid-state Circuits*, *37*, 1688–1694. doi:10.1109/JSSC.2002.804353

Zelinski, S. (2001). Design of vertical-lateral thermal actuators for MEMS. *Sensors and Actuators. A, Physical*, *90*, 38–48.

Zemlinanov, A., & Veciana, G. (2005, March). Capacity of ad hoc wireless networks with infrastructure support. *IEEE Journal on Selected Areas in Communications*, *23*(3), 657–667. doi:10.1109/JSAC.2004.842536

Zeng, X. N., & Ghrayeb, A. (2009, May). Joint CFO and channel estimation for OFDMA uplink: An application of the variable projection method. *IEEE Transactions on Wireless Communications*, *8*(5). doi:10.1109/TWC.2009.081100

Zhang, S., Su, W., & Zaghloul, M. E. (2008). *Low noise multi-band voltage controlled oscillator using MEMS technology*.

Zhou, W. (2009). *Integration of MEMS resonators within CMOS technology*. Cornell.

Zolfaghari, A., Chan, A., & Razavi, B. (2001). Stacked inductors and transformers in CMOS technology. *IEEE Journal of Solid-state Circuits*, *36*(4), 620–628. doi:10.1109/4.913740

Zou, Q., Lee, D., Bi, F., Ruby, R., Small, M., Ortiz, S., et al. *High coupling coefficient temperature compensated FBAR resonator for oscillator application with wide pulling range*.

Zou, J., Liu, C., & Ainé, J. E. S. (2001). Development of a wide-tuning-range two-parallel-plate tunable capacitor for integrated wireless communication systems. *International Journal of RF and Microwave Computer-Aided Engineering*, *11*(5), 322–329. doi:10.1002/mmce.1040

Zuo, C., Van der Spiegel, J., & Piazza, G. (2010). 1.05-GHz CMOS oscillator based on lateral-field-excited piezoelectric AlN contour-mode MEMS resonators. *Chengjie Zuo*, 15.

Zuo, C., Sinha, N., Van der Spiegel, J., & Piazza, G. (2010). Multifrequency Pierce oscillators based on piezoelectric AlN contour-mode MEMS technology. *Journal of Microelectromechanical Systems*, *19*(3), 570–580. doi:10.1109/JMEMS.2010.2045879

Zurcher, P., Alluri, P., Chu, P., Duvallet, A., Happ, C., Henderson, R., et al. (2000, December). *Integration of thin film MIM capacitors and resistors into copper metallization based RF-CMOS and Bi-CMOS technologies*. Paper presented at the IEEE International Electron Devices Meeting, San Francisco, CA.

About the Contributors

Gianluca Cornetta obtained his MSc Degree from Politecnico di Torino (Italy) in 1995 and his PhD from Universidad Politécnica de Cataluña (Spain) in 2001, both in Electronic Engineering. In 2003 he joined Universidad CEU-San Pablo in Madrid (Spain), where he is presently an Associate Professor. Prior to joining Universidad CEU-San Pablo, he was a Lecturer in the Departement of Electronic Engineering of Universidad Politécnica de Cataluña (Spain), a Digital Designer at Infineon Technologies Gmbh (Germany), and an ICT Consultant at Tecsidel SA (Spain) in the field of real-time embedded systems. In 2004 he founded the Department of Electronic System Engineering and Telecommunications, which he chaired until February 2008. He is also a research fellow at the Vrije Universiteit Brussel and an invited Professor at the Institut Superieur d'Electronique de Paris (ISEP) where he teaches Wireless System Design in the Advances in Communication Environment (ACE) Master. His current research interests include RF circuit design for wireless sensor networks with special emphasis on IEEE 802.15.4 (ZigBee), digital communication circuits, software radio, and distributed real-time embedded systems.

David J. Santos obtained his MSc and PhD Degrees both from Universidad de Vigo, Spain (in 1991 and 1995 respectively). From 1995 to 2005 he has been a Professor at Universidad de Vigo and a visiting scholar to University of Rochester (USA) and University of Essex (UK). Since 2005 he is an Associate Professor at Universidad CEU-San Pablo in Madrid (Spain) where he also chairs the Division of Engineering of the Escuela Politécnica Superior. His research interests include: quantum information processing, quantum optics, optical communications, communication circuits, and applied mathematics problems related with process modelling, optimisation, and data mining.

José Manuel Vázquez obtained his MSc and PhD Degrees both from Universidad Politécnica of Madrid. He has over thirty years experience in the IT sector, designing and developing a variety of innovative projects for market-leading companies. During his career he has played different roles and positions of responsibility in various areas of business for which he worked such as production, sales, marketing, communication, and R&D. He is currently a Lecturer at University CEU-San Pablo in Madrid and managing partner of a consultancy company focused on the implementation of change management and BPR for new companies in the digital economy. It has also been evaluating research projects of the European Union and has served on various national and international committees related to marketing and regulation in the field of IT.

* * *

Masoud Baghelani was born in Baghelan, Ilam, Iran, in 1984. He received the B.S. degree from Chamran University (Jondi Shapoor), Ahvaz, Iran, in 2005, and M.S. degree from Sahand University of Technology, Tabriz, Iran, in 2009, both in electronic engineering. He currently is PhD student in Communication systems in Sahand University of Technology. His current research interests focus on high-Q RF MEMS resonators and filters for wireless communication systems and microelectronic RF design.

Gabriel Caffarena is currently a Profesor Colaborador Doctor at the Department of Engineering of Information and Telecommunication Systems at Universidad CEU San Pablo. He obtained an MSc in Electronics in 1998 (University of Málaga) and the PhD degree in 2008 (Technical University of Madrid - UPM, Best Thesis Award). He has worked as a Computer Programmer University at College London (1998-2000) and as a Network Support Engineer at Imperial College (2000-2001). He has been a visiting researcher to IMEC (2002) and Imperial College London (2004). He has been an Assistant Professor at the Electronic Engineering Dept. of UPM (2005-2009). His research is focused on hardware design automation and hardware acceleration. He has authored over 25 conference papers and 11 major journal publications. He was Guest Editor of the *Special Issue on Quantization of VLSI DSP Systems, Journal on Advances in Signal Processing*, 2011. He served as Programme Committee member in several international conferences (ERSA'07-11, ReConFig'08-11, IEEE/IFIP VLSI-SOC'10, SPL'11, GLVLSI'11). He is a Member of IEEE and EURASIP.

João Paulo Carmo was born in 1970 at Maia, Portugal. He graduated in 1993 and received his MSc degree in 2002, both in Electrical Engineering from the University of Porto, Porto, Portugal. In 2007, he obtained the PhD degree in Industrial Electronics from the University of Minho, Guimarães, Portugal. Since 2008, he is Assistant Professor in the University of Minho. He is involved in the research on RF applications and wireless microsystems.

Carlos Carreras received the Engineering Degree in 1986 from the Universidad Politécnica de Madrid (U.P.M.) and the MS degree in 1989 from the University of Texas at Austin. He obtained his PhD degree in Electrical Engineering in 1993 also from U.P.M. From 1987 to 1991 he worked Honeywell Bull and Schlumberger Well Services. Since 1991, he is with the Electrical Engineering Department (E.T.S.I.T.) at the U.P.M., where he currently is an Associate Professor. He has actively participated in a number of national and international research projects. His current research interests are in the areas of architecture and electronic design of high-performance computing systems, CAD for system design, synthesis and modeling, hardware-software co-design, and noise and power estimation techniques.

Bogdan Ciubotaru is an IRCSET Postdoctoral research fellow with the Performance Engineering Laboratory, School of Electronic Engineering, Dublin City University (DCU), Ireland. He was awarded the B.Eng. and MSc degrees in System Engineering from the Computer Science Department, "Politehnica" University of Timisoara, Romania in 2004 and 2005, respectively. He was an IRCSET-Microsoft post graduate student in DCU and obtained his Ph.D. degree from DCU in March 2011 for his research in quality-oriented mobility management for multimedia applications. His research interests include wireless mobile networks, multimedia streaming over wireless access networks, as well as wireless sensor networks and embedded systems. He is member of IEEE and Research Institute for Networks and Communications Engineering (RINCE) Ireland and has won a best-paper award from *IEEE Transactions on Broadcasting* for his outstanding publication in the year 2010.

José Higino Correia graduated in Physical Engineering from University of Coimbra, Portugal in 1990. He obtained in 1999 a PhD degree at the Laboratory for Electronic Instrumentation, Delft University of Technology, The Netherlands, working in the field of microsystems for optical spectral analysis. Presently, he is a Full Professor in Department of Industrial Electronics, University of Minho, Portugal. He was the General-Chairman of Eurosensors 2003, Guimarães, Portugal. His professional interests are in micromachining and microfabrication technology for mixed-mode systems, solid-state integrated sensors, microactuators, and microsystems.

Afshin Ebrahimi is an Assistant Professor of Electrical Engineering at Sahand University of Technology, Tabriz, Iran. He obtained the B.S. and M.S. degrees in Communication and Electronics Engineering from the Tabriz University and Tarbiat Modares University in 1999 and 2001, respectively. He received his PhD degree in 2005 from the Tarbiat Modares University, where he worked on the use of holistic shape of subwords for printed Farsi text recognition and retrieval. His research interests are neural networks, document image analysis, handwriting recognition, and image retrieval.

Rafaella Fiorelli received her BSc and MSc degrees in Electrical Engineering from the Universidad de la República, Uruguay, in 2002 and 2005, respectively. Currently, she is working towards the doctoral degree in Electrical Engineering in the University of Seville, Spain. From 2003 until 2009 she worked both in the Uruguayan electronic and microelectronic industry, being part of several projects, and in the Uruguayan academy. From 2009 she has been with the Instituto de Microelectronica de Sevilla (IMSE-CNM), Spain, with a MAE-AECIC Spanish government grant. Her main interests and expertise include the implementation of design methodologies of low power RF blocks as LNAs, VCOs, or PA, as well as designing BIST test in RF.

Habib Badri Ghavifekr received the BS degree from Tabriz University, Iran, and continued his study in Germany and received the MS degree (Diploma Engineer) from Technical University of Berlin, in 1995 both in Electrical Engineering. Immediately after that, he joined the Institute for Microperipheric at the Technical University of Berlin (nowadays BeCAP: Berliner Center for Advanced Packaging) as a scientific assistant and in 1998 the Fraunhofer Institute for Reliability and Microintegration (FhG-IZM) as a research assistant. In 2003 he received his PhD in Electrical Engineering from Technical University of Berlin. Since 2005 he is an Assistant Professor at Sahand University of Technology, Tabriz, Iran. His research interests are microsystem technologies, microelectronic packaging, MEMS, and electronic measurement systems for industrial applications.

Javier González-Bayón was born in Santander, Spain, in 1979. He received the Telecommunications Engineer from the Universidad de Cantabria in 2004. He obtained his PhD degree in Electronic Engineering in 2011 in the Dept. of Electronic Engineering at the Universidad Politécnica de Madrid. He has actively participated in a number of national and international research projects. His main research interest include signal processing focusing in frequency synchronization in multi-standard OFDM and multi-user OFDMA systems and its implementation in reconfigurable devices as Field Programmable Gate Arrays (FPGAs).

Amparo Herrera finished her M.S in Electronic (University of Cantabria in 1987. In 1990 she joined the Electronic Department of the University of Cantabria, for doing the PhD Thesis work on MMIC (Monolithic Microwave Integrated Circuit) design. In 1991 she joined Philips Microwave Limeill in Paris France (Now OMMIC) with different collaboration agreement with the University to design several High Efficiency Power Amplifiers. In 2000 she started the collaboration with Alcatel Space (now Thales Alenia Space) for the design and development of several MMIC functions that substitute the correspondent hybrid circuits on TTC transponder equipment fabricated by Thales. This project finished with the onboard commercial equipment. From the OMMIC collaboration, other contacts were born in France; the collaboration with the ACCO Semiconductor Inc companyis a very interesting collaboration based on the study of electromagnetic influences and modelling on SOP and/or SOC configuration for applying directly on the mass-market communication products.

Angel Fernández Herrero received the MS degree in Telecom Engineering (ETSIT) from the Universidad Politécnica de Madrid (UPM) in 1994. Since 1999 he is working as an Assistant Lecturer within the Department of Electronic Engineering at the ETSIT-UPM. He has actively participated in a number of national and international research projects, with experience in digital signal processing for voice, audio, video, and communications, and implementations for both processors and FPGAs. His current research interests include the VLSI real-time implementation of complex digital signal processing systems; wireless, wideband and multi-antenna communications; system integration considering data acquisition and analog impairments; and, more recently, nonlinear system identification.

Alberto Jiménez got his MSc. and MPhil. degrees in Telecommunications Engineering from Polytechnic University of Madrid (UPM) in 2003 and 2005, respectively. Between 2003 and 2006 he worked as research assistant at the Group of Signal Processing Applications at UPM, participating on several European projects on the fields on OFDM MIMO systems and multi-user detection. Between 2006 and 2008 he worked on radiation hard optoelectronics at the European Organization for Nuclear Research (CERN, Geneva). Since 2009 he works at the Laboratory for Mobile Communications at École Polytéchnique Fédéral de Lausanne (EPFL), researching on signal processing for digital video broadcasting and robotics applications, as well as teaching on software-defined radio.

Juan A. López received the Ingeniero de Telecomunicación degree from the Universidad de Málaga in 1997, and the Doctor Ingeniero de Telecomunicación degree from the Universidad Politécnica de Madrid (UPM) in 2004. Since November 1997, he has been with the Departamento de Ingeniería Electrónica, UPM, where he is currently an Associate Professor. He has been a member of more than 30 R&D projects about the development of CAD tools and the implementation of very high-speed digital signal and image processing systems in different applications. His research interests include interval methods, design automation, and hardware implementation of DSP systems, with particular emphasis on the fixed-point properties of the DSP system structures, quantization, and fast evaluation of the finite word-length effects. He has authored or co-authored more than 30 papers in specialized journals and major congresses of these areas.

Aya Mabrouki received her Master's and PhD degrees in Microelectronics in 2007 and 2010, respectively, both from the University of Bordeaux, France. Her research interests include the study of body bias effect on CMOS LNA design at 2.4 GHz under low power constraint. She is also working on Ultra Wide Band reconfigurable LNA design. She has published more than 10 communications in international and national conferences and journal (RFIT, ICECS, NEWCAS, PRIME, and JOLPE). In 2009, she received the IEEE NEWCAS Best Student Paper Award, in Toulouse, France.

Gabriel-Miro Muntean has established a strong track record in the areas of quality-oriented and performance-aware adaptive multimedia streaming and data communications in heterogeneous wireless environments. Dr. Muntean is the co-Director of a 10-person strong research laboratory since 2003, which has a state-of-the-art facility in the DCU Engineering building and is well equipped for multimedia delivery research. Dr. Muntean has successfully supervised three PhD and three Master's by research students, and is currently supervising seven postgraduate researchers and one postdoctoral researcher. Dr. Muntean has been principal investigators on two EI, one SFI, and five IRCSET grants, and collaborator on another two. In addition, he has been leading Samsung and Microsoft funded research projects. Dr. Muntean has authored one book, edited two, and has published five book chapters, 25 journal, and over 60 conference papers. Dr. Muntean has been awarded four Best Paper Awards and is an Associate Editor for *IEEE Transactions on Broadcasting*.

Anis Nurashikin Nordin received her B. Eng. degree in Computer and Information Engineering from International Islamic University Malaysia (IIUM), Kuala Lumpur, Malaysia in 1999 and her MS degree in Computer Engineering from the George Washington University (GWU), Washington D.C. in 2002. She received the CISCO System Award as the best student for the B. Eng. in Computer Information Engineering in 1999. Her academic career began at IIUM, where she joined as an Assistant Lecturer in the Electrical and Computer Engineering (ECE) department in September 1999. From June 2000 till 2008, she pursued her MSc and DSc degrees at GWU where she was a Teaching Assistant specializing in VLSI CAD tools. Her doctoral dissertation was on CMOS-compatible Surface Acoustic Wave Resonators. Currently, she is an Assistant Professor at IIUM. Her main research interests and publications are in the area of Analog VLSI, RF MEMS, RF-CMOS, SAW resonators, and oscillators in particular. She is also interested in a wide range of RF/Analog VLSI circuits, especially in integration of RF MEMS devices with circuits and their applications in wireless communications.

Ahmed El Oualkadi received PhD degree (with honors) in Electrical Engineering from the University of Poitiers, France, in 2004. From 2000 to 2004, he worked, in collaboration with EADS-TELECOM, on various European projects (CORMORAN & MULTIMODULES) that concern the nonlinear analysis & RF circuit design of switched- capacitor filters for radio-communication systems. In 2005, he joined the Université Catholique de Louvain, Microelectronics Laboratory, Louvain-la-Neuve, Belgium, where he worked on the analog and mixed design of low power high temperature circuits and systems, in SOI technology, for wireless communication. During this period, he participated in several European and regional projects (EUREKA, A 109 Witness, MEDEA+, CROTALE...) in the areas of wireless communication and sensor networking. Currently, he is an Assistant Professor in the Abdelmalek Essaadi University, National School of Applied Sciences of Tangier, Morocco. His main research interest is the analog IC, mixed-signal, and RFIC design for wireless communication, embedded system applications, and Information Technology. He is author/co-author of more than 40 publications and communications in recognized journals and international conferences. He is a member of EuMA and IEEE. He is also a member of the scientific and technical committee of WCECS and WASET, and a member of the editorial board of both the *Journal of Multimedia Processing and Technologies* (JMPT) and the *Journal of Recent Patents on Electrical Engineering*, edited by Bentham Science Publishers.

Eduardo J. Peralías received the PhD degree from the University of Seville, (Spain) in 1999. Since 2001, he has been with the Instituto de Microelectrónica de Sevilla (IMSE-CNM-CSIC), where he is currently a Tenured Scientist. His main research interests have been in the areas of Mixed Design with emphasis on analog-to-digital converters, test and design for testability of analog and mixed-signal circuits, and statistical behavioral modeling. Currently, he is involved in projects of RF CMOS integrated circuit designs for telecommunications and the development of magnetic and piezoresistive nanosensors.

Francisco Javier Casajús Quirós received the MEng and PhD in Telecommunication Engineering from the Universidad Politécnica de Madrid (Technical University of Madrid), Spain, in 1982 and 1988, respectively. He has been an Associate Professor in that university since 1989. His main research interests are in digital signal processing applied to wideband wireless communications and multimedia. His current research work includes the theory of multi-input multi-output systems as applied to multichannel audio signal processing and wireless communications. In those fields, he has authored and co-authored more than 120 publications in journals and conference proceedings.

Fernando Silveira received the Electrical Engineering degree from Universidad de la República, Uruguay in 1990 and the MSc and PhD degree in Microelectronics from Université Catholique de Louvain, Belgium in 1995 and 2002, respectively. He is currently Professor at the Electrical Engineering Department of the School of Engineering of Universidad de la República, Uruguay. His research interests are in design of ultra low-power analog and RF integrated circuits and systems, in particular with biomedical application. In this field, he is co-author of one book and many technical articles. He has had multiple industrial activities with CCC medical devices and NanoWattICs, including leading the design of an ASIC for implantable pacemakers and designing analog circuit modules for implantable devices for various companies worldwide.

Thierry Taris received his Master's and PhD degrees in the 2000 and 2003, respectively, both from the University of Bordeaux. Since 2004 he has been an Associate Professor at the University of Bordeaux I in the integrated circuit design team (EC²) of IMS laboratory. His research activities concern the design of integrated RF front end on Bipolar and CMOS technologies for standards like, UMTS, WLAN, hiperLAN, WiFi, WiMAX, UWB, 60GHz WPAN, and 80GHz RADAR (from 2 up to 80 GHz). During these years, he has published more than 60 communications in international journals (JSSC, Trans. MTT, IEICE), conferences (SBCCI, ESSCIRC, BCTM, DCIS, ICECS, AMPC, RFIC, NWCAS), invited papers, and workshops (ICECS'06, and ICM'05). He is owner of 4 French/US patents and one Best Paper Award in IEEE AMPC'02 conference in Kyoto, Japan.

Hrishikesh Venkataraman is a senior researcher and Enterprise Ireland Principal Investigator with Performance Engineering Laboratory at Dublin City University, Ireland. He obtained his PhD from Jacobs University Bremen, Germany in 2007 for his research on wireless cellular networks. He obtained his Master's degree from Indian Institute of Technology (IIT) Kanpur, India in 2004 and did his Master's thesis from Vodafone Chair for Mobile Communications, Technical University Dresden, Germany in 2003-04 under the Indo-German DAAD Fellowship. His research interest includes mobile multimedia, wireless communications, and energy in wireless. Dr. Venkataraman has published more than 30 papers in journals, international conferences and book chapters and has won a best paper award in an international conference in Berkeley, USA in October 2009. Currently, Dr. Venkataraman is an Executive Editor of *European Transactions on Telecommunications* and *International Journal of Communications Networks and Systems* (IJCNS). In addition, he is a founding member of UKRI chapter of IEEE Vehicular Technology Society.

Index